PATERNALISM TO PARTNERSHIP

Paternalism to Partnership

The Administration of Indian Affairs, 1786–2021

David H. DeJong

UNIVERSITY OF NEBRASKA PRESS

© 2022 by the Board of Regents
of the University of Nebraska

All rights reserved

Library of Congress Cataloging-in-Publication Data
Names: DeJong, David H., author.
Title: Paternalism to partnership: the administration of
Indian affairs, 1786–2021 / David H. DeJong.
Other titles: Administration of Indian affairs, 1786–2021
Description: Lincoln: University of Nebraska Press, [2022] |
Includes bibliographical references and index.
Identifiers: LCCN 2022005547
ISBN 9781496230584 (hardback)
ISBN 9781496230768 (epub)
ISBN 9781496230775 (pdf)
Subjects: LCSH: United States. Office of Indian Affairs—Biography. |
United States. Bureau of Indian Affairs—Biography. | Indians, Treatment
of—United States. | Indians of North America—Government relations. |
BISAC: SOCIAL SCIENCE / Ethnic Studies / American / Native
American Studies | POLITICAL SCIENCE / History & Theory
Classification: LCC E93 .D3459 2022 | DDC 323.1197—dc23/eng/20220611
LC record available at https://lccn.loc.gov/2022005547

S|H **The Sustainable History Monograph Pilot**
M|P Opening up the Past, Publishing for the Future

This book is published as part of the Sustainable History Monograph Pilot. With the generous support of the Andrew W. Mellon Foundation, the Pilot uses cutting-edge publishing technology to produce open access digital editions of high-quality, peer-reviewed monographs from leading university presses. Free digital editions can be downloaded from: Books at JSTOR, EBSCO, Hathi Trust, Internet Archive, OAPEN, Project MUSE, and many other open repositories.

While the digital edition is free to download, read, and share, the book is under copyright and covered by the following Creative Commons License: BY-NC-ND 4.0. Please consult www.creativecommons.org if you have questions about your rights to reuse the material in this book.

When you cite the book, please include the following URL for its Digital Object Identifier (DOI): https://doi.org/10.5250/9781496230584

> We are eager to learn more about how you discovered this title and how you are using it. We hope you will spend a few minutes answering a couple of questions at this URL:
> **https://www.longleafservices.org/shmp-survey/**

More information about the Sustainable History Monograph Pilot can be found at https://www.longleafservices.org.

CONTENTS

List of Tables xiii

Preface xv

INTRODUCTION
The Administration of Indian Affairs 1

CHAPTER 1
John Harris, Superintendent of the Indian Trading Houses 22

CHAPTER 2
William Irvine, Superintendent of the Indian Trading Houses 24

CHAPTER 3
George W. Ingels, Superintendent of the Indian Trading Houses 26

CHAPTER 4
William Davy, Superintendent of the Indian Trading Houses 28

CHAPTER 5
John Shee, Superintendent of Indian Trade 30

CHAPTER 6
John M. Mason, Superintendent of Indian Trade 33

CHAPTER 7
Thomas L. McKenney, Superintendent of Indian Trade, Chief Clerk 40

CHAPTER 8
William Clark, Superintendent of Indian Affairs 46

CHAPTER 9
Samuel S. Hamilton, Chief Clerk 48

CHAPTER 10
Elbert Herring, Chief Clerk, Commissioner of Indian Affairs 51

CHAPTER 11
Carey Allen Harris, Commissioner of Indian Affairs 56

CHAPTER 12
Thomas Hartley Crawford, Commissioner of Indian Affairs 62

CHAPTER 13
William Medill, Commissioner of Indian Affairs 69

CHAPTER 14
Orlando Brown, Commissioner of Indian Affairs 76

CHAPTER 15
Luke Lea, Commissioner of Indian Affairs 80

CHAPTER 16
George W. Manypenny, Commissioner of Indian Affairs 86

CHAPTER 17
James W. Denver, Commissioner of Indian Affairs 95

CHAPTER 18
Charles E. Mix, Commissioner of Indian Affairs 100

CHAPTER 19
Alfred B. Greenwood, Commissioner of Indian Affairs 106

CHAPTER 20
William P. Dole, Commissioner of Indian Affairs 113

CHAPTER 21
Dennis N. Cooley, Commissioner of Indian Affairs 121

CHAPTER 22
Lewis V. Bogy, Commissioner of Indian Affairs 127

CHAPTER 23
Nathaniel G. Taylor, Commissioner of Indian Affairs 130

CHAPTER 24
Ely S. Parker, Commissioner of Indian Affairs 139

CHAPTER 25
Francis A. Walker, Commissioner of Indian Affairs 146

CHAPTER 26
Edward P. Smith, Commissioner of Indian Affairs 154

CHAPTER 27
John Quincy Smith, Commissioner of Indian Affairs 163

CHAPTER 28
Ezra A. Hayt, Commissioner of Indian Affairs 170

CHAPTER 29
Rowland E. Trowbridge, Commissioner of Indian Affairs 178

CHAPTER 30
Hiram Price, Commissioner of Indian Affairs 182

CHAPTER 31
John DeWitt Clinton Atkins, Commissioner of Indian Affairs 190

CHAPTER 32
John H. Oberly, Commissioner of Indian Affairs 200

CHAPTER 33
Thomas Jefferson Morgan, Commissioner of Indian Affairs 205

CHAPTER 34
Daniel M. Browning, Commissioner of Indian Affairs 217

CHAPTER 35
William A. Jones, Commissioner of Indian Affairs 222

CHAPTER 36
Francis E. Leupp, Commissioner of Indian Affairs 231

CHAPTER 37
Robert G. Valentine, Commissioner of Indian Affairs 240

CHAPTER 38
Cato Sells, Commissioner of Indian Affairs 246

CHAPTER 39
Charles Henry Burke, Commissioner of Indian Affairs 254

CHAPTER 40
Charles James Rhoads, Commissioner of Indian Affairs 263

CHAPTER 41
John Collier, Commissioner of Indian Affairs 273

CHAPTER 42
William A. Brophy, Commissioner of Indian Affairs 283

CHAPTER 43
John R. Nichols, Commissioner of Indian Affairs 290

CHAPTER 44
Dillon S. Myer, Commissioner of Indian Affairs 295

CHAPTER 45
Glenn L. Emmons, Commissioner of Indian Affairs 302

CHAPTER 46
Philleo Nash, Commissioner of Indian Affairs 311

CHAPTER 47
Robert L. Bennett, Commissioner of Indian Affairs 320

CHAPTER 48
Louis Rook Bruce, Commissioner of Indian Affairs 328

CHAPTER 49
Marvin L. Franklin, Assistant to the Secretary for Indian Affairs 335

CHAPTER 50
Morris Thompson, Commissioner of Indian Affairs 339

CHAPTER 51
Ben Reifel, Commissioner of Indian Affairs 344

CHAPTER 52
Forrest J. Gerard, Assistant Secretary for Indian Affairs 346

CHAPTER 53
William E. Hallett, Commissioner of Indian Affairs 353

CHAPTER 54
Thomas W. Fredericks, Assistant Secretary for Indian Affairs 357

CHAPTER 55
Kenneth L. Smith, Assistant Secretary for Indian Affairs 363

CHAPTER 56
Ross O. Swimmer, Assistant Secretary for Indian Affairs 367

CHAPTER 57
Eddie F. Brown, Assistant Secretary for Indian Affairs 375

CHAPTER 58
Ada E. Deer, Assistant Secretary for Indian Affairs 382

CHAPTER 59
Kevin Gover, Assistant Secretary for Indian Affairs 387

CHAPTER 60
Neil A. McCaleb, Assistant Secretary for Indian Affairs 394

CHAPTER 61
David W. Anderson, Assistant Secretary for Indian Affairs 399

CHAPTER 62
Carl J. Artman, Assistant Secretary for Indian Affairs 403

CHAPTER 63
Larry J. Echo Hawk, Assistant Secretary for Indian Affairs 407

CHAPTER 64
Kevin K. Washburn, Assistant Secretary for Indian Affairs 413

CHAPTER 65
Tara MacLean Sweeney, Assistant Secretary for Indian Affairs 418

CONCLUSION 422

Notes 427

Bibliography 463

Index 475

Also by David H. DeJong 486

TABLES

1. First Commissioners under the Continental Congress xviii

2. Superintendents of Indian Affairs, 1786–1796 xviii

3. Superintendents of Indian Trading Houses, 1796–1805 xix

4. Superintendents of the Office of Indian Trade, 1806–1824 xix

5. Chief Clerks, 1824–1831 xix

6. Commissioners of Indian Affairs, 1832–1981 xx

7. Assistant Secretaries for Indian Affairs, 1977–Present xxii

8. Indian Office Authority over Tribal Nations, 1887–1934 17

PREFACE

In 2020, I published *The Commissioners of Indian Affairs: The United States Indian Service and the Making of Federal Indian Policy, 1824–2020*. My purpose was to identify the policy emphasis of each commissioner of Indian affairs and assistant secretary for Indian affairs. To do this, I read each of the annual reports of the commissioner of Indian affairs between 1824 and 1964. It took three years to complete this task, and in so doing I identified excerpts describing the personal philosophy of each of the commissioners. I marked these passages and, after completing my policy analysis, later returned to these excerpts describing the commissioners' viewpoints.

While *The Commissioners of Indian Affairs* focused on policy implementation, the present reference resource provides a biographical sketch of each head of Indian affairs between 1796 and 2021, while also excerpting statements describing their political philosophy, no small feat given the length of most of the annual reports of the commissioners of Indian affairs. While somewhat subjective, I searched for passages that best explained or discussed the philosophy of each head of the Indian Office or modern Bureau of Indian Affairs.

Beginning in July 1775, the Continental Congress appointed the first thirteen commissioners to represent the individual colonies in dealing with the tribes. While some of these commissioners served throughout the Continental Congress period, most served short periods. These initial commissioners are shown in table 1.

Under the Articles of Confederation, and continuing with the US Constitution, Congress appointed superintendents of Indian affairs to manage the federal–Indian relationship. These superintendents, subject to the authority of the War Department, are listed in table 2. There were two superintendents, one for a Northern and one for a Southern department. The superintendents were phased out in 1796 when Congress established an Office of Indian Trade.

In 1796, Congress established an Office of Indian Trade within the War Department, appointing a superintendent to oversee the office. The superintendent was subject to the authority of the secretary of war and was responsible for administering the federal trading houses. These "factories" were operated by the United

States in an attempt to control Indian trade in the post–Revolutionary War years. There were no longer multiple departments but a single superintendent responsible for trade. These men were War Department employees, and all had charge of the military store in Philadelphia. There were four superintendents, as shown in table 3.

The superintendents of Indian trade were the first federal administrators of Indian affairs. In 1806, Congress reorganized the Office of Indian Trade, expanding its authority. Between the abolition of the trading houses, in May 1822, and the administrative organization of the Bureau of Indian Affairs by Secretary of War John Calhoun, in March 1824, there was no single individual charged exclusively with administering Indian affairs, although during the interim President James Monroe appointed—with the advice and consent of the Senate—Indian agent William Clark as superintendent of the St. Louis Superintendency. For the next twenty-two months, Clark had as much authority as anyone in administering Indian affairs. The superintendents of the Office of Indian Trade are listed in table 4.

When Calhoun administratively organized the Bureau of Indian Affairs in 1824, he appointed a chief clerk to be responsible for the office, delegating to this clerk authority to oversee Indian affairs. Just three men served in the role, the longest serving of whom was Thomas L. McKenney. These chief clerks are listed in table 5.

When Congress statutorily established the Indian Office in 1832, it also provided for a commissioner of Indian affairs who was charged with the responsibility of implementing and managing all policy as directed by Congress. Between 1832 and 1981, the commissioner of Indian affairs administered the Indian Office and executed federal–Indian policy. The commissioners of Indian affairs are listed in table 6.

When President Carter established the position of assistant secretary of the interior for Indian affairs in 1977, the administration of Indian affairs was elevated to its highest level within the federal government. Unlike the commissioners of Indian affairs, the assistant secretary was in a position to influence and determine policy. The assistant secretary is also charged with fostering tribal self-determination and self-governance. The thirteen assistant secretaries are listed in table 7.

Each superintendent, chief clerk, commissioner, and assistant secretary intellectually or politically influenced the braids of federal policy, some supportive of tribal nations and others acting more deleteriously. What is apparent in analyzing the writings of the administrators of Indian affairs is that US domination of the tribes moved from limited federal authority (1786 to 1819) to considerable authority. In the first decades of the nineteenth century, a series of federal legislative enactments, such as the trade and intercourse acts, civilization act, Indian removal act, and establishment of the Department of the Interior (1849), all furthered federal management of Indian affairs.

In the mid-to late nineteenth century federal authority was furthered by the unilateral ending of treaty making and passage of the Major Crimes Act and the General Allotment Act, with the former undermining tribal criminal authority and the latter privatizing Indian lands. The capstone was the judicial pronouncement in *Lone Wolf v. Hitchcock* that established federal plenary authority over tribal nations. The philosophies of the commissioners of Indian affairs of the period reflect this broader political reality.

For most of the first half of the twentieth century there was a general stasis in political philosophy, notwithstanding the Indian New Deal. In the postwar years, even in the midst of the termination policies of the 1950s and 1960s, the seeds of self-determination were sewn, rooting in the 1970s and expanding throughout the latter twentieth century. Self-governance blossomed in the mid-1990s, and today the exercise of tribal self-government is stronger than at any point in more than 150 years.

The Indian Office, as an executive agency under the authority of the secretary of war (1789 to 1849) or the secretary of the interior (1849 to present), was ultimately directed by the president of the United States. The superintendents, chief clerks, commissioners, and assistant secretaries largely administered policy, although once it was determined by the Congress and the president, the Indian Office was left to implement the details, with the commissioners given a level of discretion in administering policy. Unlike the commissioner, the assistant secretary has exercised far more authority in shaping policy.

Since 1786, the Indian Office has been directed by five superintendents of Indian affairs (1786–1796), eight superintendents of Indian trade, excluding ex officio superintendents (1796–1824), three chief clerks (1824–1832), forty-three commissioners of Indian affairs (1832–1981), and thirteen assistant secretaries (1977–2021). There were forty-two different commissioners of Indian affairs (James Denver served two nonconsecutive terms), all of whom have been men: six American Indians and thirty-six non-Indians. As for the assistant secretary for Indian affairs, there have been eleven men and two women, all of whom have been American Indian or Alaska Native.

TABLE 1. First Commissioners under the Continental Congress

Name	State	Begin Date	Department
Philip Schuyler	New York	July 12, 1775	Northern
Joseph Hawley	Massachusetts	July 12, 1775	Northern
Timothy Edwards[1]	Massachusetts	November 25, 1775	Northern
Turbutt Francis	Pennsylvania	July 12, 1775	Northern
Oliver Walcott	Connecticut	July 12, 1775	Northern
Volkert P. Douw	New York	July 12, 1775	Northern
Edward Wilkerson	South Carolina	July 12, 1775	Southern
George Galphin	Georgia	July 12, 1775	Southern
Robert Rae	Georgia	July 12, 1775	Southern
John Walker	Virginia	July 12, 1775	Southern
Willie Jones	North Carolina	July 12, 1775	Southern
Benjamin Franklin	Pennsylvania	July 12, 1775	Middle
Patrick Henry	Virginia	July 12, 1775	Middle
Thomas Walker[2]	Virginia	September 15, 1775	Middle
James Wilson	Pennsylvania	July 12, 1775	Middle

1. Replaced Hawley.
2. Replaced Henry.

TABLE 2. Superintendents of Indian Affairs, 1786–1796

Name	State	Begin Date	End Date	Department
Richard Butler	Pennsylvania	August 14, 1786	November 4, 1791	Northern
Arthur St. Clair	Pennsylvania	November 4, 1791	1796	Northern
James White	North Carolina	October 6, 1786	February 1788	Southern
Richard Winn	South Carolina	March 31, 1788	March 3, 1791	Southern
William Blount	North Carolina	September 20, 1790	March 30, 1796	Southern

TABLE 3. Superintendents of Indian Trading Houses, 1796–1805

Name	State	Begin Date	End Date
John Harris	Pennsylvania	November 1796	May 10, 1801
William Irvine	Pennsylvania	May 11, 1801	July 29, 1804
George Ingels	Pennsylvania	July 30, 1804	March 26, 1805
William Davy	Pennsylvania	March 27, 1805	April 21, 1806

TABLE 4. Superintendents of the Office of Indian Trade, 1806–1824

Name	State	Begin Date	End Date
John Shee	Pennsylvania	July 8, 1806	October 3, 1807
John Mason	Virginia	October 4, 1807	April 12, 1816
Thomas L. McKenney	Maryland	April 12, 1816	May 6, 1822
William Clark[1]	Missouri	May 28, 1822	September 1, 1838
James Miller[2]	Arkansas	March 3, 1819	June 1823
Lewis Cass[2]	Michigan	October 29, 1813	August 1, 1831
William P. Duvall[2]	Florida	April 17, 1822	April 4, 1834

1. May 1822 to March 1824 as head of the Office of Indian Trade.
2. Ex officio superintendents.

TABLE 5. Chief Clerks, 1824–1831

Name	State	Begin Date	End Date
Thomas L. McKenney	Maryland	March 12, 1824	August 16, 1830
Samuel S. Hamilton	Maryland	September 30, 1830	August 31, 1831
Elbert Herring	New York	August 12, 1831	July 10, 1832

TABLE 6. Commissioners of Indian Affairs, 1832–1981

Name	State	Begin Date	End Date
1. Elbert Herring	New York	July 10, 1832	July 2, 1836
2. Carey Allen Harris	Tennessee	July 4, 1836	October 19, 1838
3. Thomas Crawford	Pennsylvania	October 22, 1838	October 29, 1845
4. William Medill	Ohio	October 29, 1845	June 30, 1849
5. Orlando Brown	Kentucky	June 30, 1849	July 1, 1850
6. Luke Lea	Mississippi	July 1, 1850	March 24, 1853
7. George Manypenny	Ohio	March 28, 1853	March 31, 1857
8. James W. Denver	California	April 17, 1857	December 2, 1857
9. Charles E. Mix	Connecticut	June 4, 1858	November 1, 1858
10. James W. Denver	California	November 9, 1858	March 12, 1859
11. Alfred B. Greenwood	Arkansas	May 4, 1859	April 16, 1861
12. William P. Dole	Vermont	March 12, 1861	July 6, 1865
13. Dennis N. Cooley	Iowa	July 9, 1865	November 1, 1866
14. Lewis V. Bogy*	Missouri	November 1, 1866	March 4, 1867
15. Nathaniel G. Taylor	Tennessee	March 29, 1867	April 23, 1869
16. Eli S. Parker	Seneca Tribe	April 23, 1869	July 24, 1871
Henry R. Clum#		July 24, 1871	November 20, 1871
17. Francis A. Walker	Massachusetts	November 21, 1871	December 26, 1872
18. Edward P. Smith	Connecticut	March 17, 1873	December 11, 1875
19. John Q. Smith	Ohio	December 11, 1875	September 27, 1877
20. Ezra A. Hayt	New York	September 20, 1877	January 29, 1880
21. Roland E. Trowbridge	Michigan	March 2, 1880	March 19, 1881
Henry R. Clum#		March 19, 1881	April 14, 1881
22. Hiram Price	Iowa	May 6, 1881	March 21, 1885
23. John D. C. Atkins	Tennessee	March 21, 1885	June 14, 1888
24. John H. Oberly	Illinois	October 10, 1888	June 30, 1889
25. Thomas J. Morgan	Indiana	July 1, 1889	March 1, 1893
26. Daniel M. Browning	Illinois	April 18, 1893	May 3, 1897

27. William A. Jones	Wisconsin	May 3, 1897	January 1, 1905
28. Francis E. Leupp	New York	January 1, 1905	June 18, 1909
29. Robert G. Valentine	Massachusetts	June 19, 1909	September 10, 1912
Frederick H. Abbott#		September 10, 1912	June 4, 1913
30. Cato Sells	Iowa	June 4, 1913	March 29, 1921
31. Charles H. Burke	South Dakota	May 7, 1921	March 9, 1929
32. Charles J. Rhoads	Pennsylvania	July 1, 1929	April 20, 1933
33. John Collier	Georgia	April 21, 1933	March 5, 1945
34. William A. Brophy	New Mexico	March 6, 1945	June 3, 1948
William R. Zimmermann#		June 3, 1948	March 10, 1949
35. John R. Nichols*	New York	April 1949	May 4, 1950
36. Dillon S. Myer	Ohio	May 5, 1950	March 19, 1953
W. Barton Greenwood#		March 20, 1953	July 28, 1953
37. Glenn L. Emmons	New Mexico	August 10, 1953	January 7, 1961
John O. Crow#	Cherokee	January 7, 1961	July 31, 1961
38. Philleo Nash	Wisconsin	September 26, 1961	March 15, 1966
39. Robert L. Bennett	Oneida	April 27, 1966	May 31, 1969
40. Louis R. Bruce	Oglala Sioux	August 8, 1969	January 20, 1973
Marvin L. Franklin**	Iowa	February 7, 1973	December 4, 1974
41. Morris Thompson	Athabascan	December 4, 1973	November 3, 1976
42. Benjamin Reifel*	Rosebud Sioux	December 7, 1976	January 28, 1977
Raymond Butler#		January 28, 1977	September 19, 1977
43. William E. Hallett	Red Lake Chippewa	December 14, 1979	January 20, 1981

* Not confirmed by the Senate
# Acting commissioner of Indian affairs.
** Assistant to the secretary.

TABLE 7. Assistant Secretaries for Indian Affairs, 1977–Present

Name	State	Begin Date	End Date
1. Forrest Gerard	Blackfeet	September 19, 1977	January 19, 1980
2. Thomas Fredericks	Mandan–Hidatsa	June 18, 1980	January 20, 1981
3. Kenneth L. Smith	Wasco	April 28, 1981	December 7, 1984
4. Ross O. Swimmer	Cherokee	December 4, 1985	January 29, 1989
William Ragsdale[#]	Cherokee	January 29, 1989	June 20, 1989
5. Eddie Frank Brown	Yaqui	June 21, 1989	July 15, 1993
6. Ada E. Deer	Menominee	July 16, 1993	November 9, 1997
7. Kevin Gover	Pawnee	November 12, 1997	January 3, 2001
James H. McDivitt[#]		January 20, 2001	July 3, 2001
8. Neal A. McCaleb	Chickasaw	July 4, 2001	December 31, 2002
Aurene M. Martin[#]	Bad River Chippewa	January 6, 2003	February 2, 2004
9. David A. Anderson	Lac Court Oreille Chip.	February 2, 2004	February 12, 2005
Jim Cason[#]		February 12, 2005	March 5, 2007
10. Carl J. Artman	Oneida	March 8, 2007	May 23, 2008
George T. Skibone[#]	Osage	May 23, 2008	January 20, 2009
11. Larry J. Echo Hawk	Pawnee	May 22, 2009	April 27, 2012
Donald Laverdure[#]	Crow	April 27, 2012	October 9, 2012
12. Kevin K. Washburn	Chickasaw	October 9, 2012	January 1, 2016
Lawrence S. Roberts[#]	Oneida	January 1, 2016	January 20, 2017
Michael S. Black[#]	Oglala Sioux	January 20, 2017	June 27, 2018
13. Tara Maclean Sweeney	Inupiat	June 28, 2018	January 20, 2021

[#] Acting assistant secretary.

Introduction

The Administration of Indian Affairs

WHEN THE DELEGATES TO the constitutional convention met in Philadelphia to amend the Articles of Confederation in 1787, they initially gave little attention to Indian affairs. When the delegates determined to draft an entirely new constitution, there was no mention of how to interact with tribal nations, let alone who was to be responsible for the political relationship with the tribes. James Madison, recognizing this oversight, explained on June 19, 1787, that "transactions with the Indians appertain to Cong."¹ Two months later, Madison proposed that Congress should have the authority "to regulate affairs with the Indians," both within and outside the territorial limits of the United States.

The Committee of Detail, to which the language was referred, reduced this broad grant of authority by adding a phrase to the proposed commerce clause power of Congress to "regulate commerce with foreign nations, and among the several States," by adding "and with the Indian tribes within the limits of any State, not subject to the laws thereof."² On September 4, the Committee of Eleven reported to the full body with a recommendation to amend the commerce clause by simply adding "and with the Indian tribes." The amendment was unanimously approved and became part of the new Constitution of the United States.³

In addition to the treaty-making and national defense powers of Congress, the commerce clause served as the primary basis for federal authority to regulate trade and intercourse with tribal nations. A half-century later, Chief Justice John Marshall used these constitutional authorities to assert a federal right to regulate "our intercourse with the Indians."⁴ Congress, Marshall added, considered tribal nations "as within the jurisdictional limits of the United States" and, therefore, subject to the same "restraints which are imposed on our citizens."

Colonial Antecedents

Throughout the colonial period, the administration of Indian affairs was largely controlled by the colonies, at times by the assemblies, and at times by commissioners appointed by the legislatures or the chief executives. In New England, a superintendent of Indian affairs administered tribal relations, with Daniel Gookin of Massachusetts appointed as the first superintendent in 1656, serving until his death on March 19, 1687.[5] After the outbreak of King Philip's War in 1675, New England colonies asserted veto power over the superintendent. In the postwar years, most work of the superintendent was related to the propagation of the Gospel and the maintenance of peace.[6] In 1687, Gookin was succeeded by Thomas Prentice who served until 1709, when the position was eliminated.[7] Overall, trade in New England was managed by colonial governments, which established trading houses with the tribes in 1694 to facilitate diplomacy.[8]

In New York, control of Indian affairs was in the hands of the governor, with local magistrates executing policy until 1696, when the assembly established a board of four commissioners of Indian affairs (Peter Schuyler, Dirck Wessels, Domine Godfrey Dellias, and Evert Banker) to engage with tribes. Located on the Hudson River, Albany dominated the management of Indian trade throughout the colonial period.[9] In 1746, Governor George Clinton, dissatisfied with the commissioners, granted trader William Johnson control of Indian affairs, a position Johnson retained until he resigned in 1751. Five years later, General Edward Braddock commissioned Johnson a colonel of the Iroquois, and a year later the Crown established two Indian departments, with Johnson named superintendent of the Northern Department.

In Pennsylvania, the colonial assembly appointed commissioners to interact with tribal nations, with some of the more prominent leaders engaged in managing Indian affairs, including Benjamin Franklin, Conrad Weiser, George Croghan, Richard Peter, George Thomas, and Andrew Montour. But the colony never fully succeeded in regulating Indian affairs, and not until 1758 did the assembly enact an Indian trade act that, among other objectives, banned liquor and established a monopoly on the Indian fur trade. The seat of trade was Philadelphia.[10]

In the South, Virginia, Maryland, and North Carolina did not establish government agencies to deal with the tribes, instead appointing commissioners as the situation demanded. In South Carolina and Georgia, however, Indian affairs were formalized to facilitate trade and amity with the powerful Cherokee, Choctaw, Chickasaw, and Catawba nations and to secure land. In 1707, the assembly in South Carolina set up a board of nine commissioners to issue licenses, prohibit the sale and importation of liquor among the Indians, and engage in trade. By 1719, the number of commissioners was reduced to three, and they were allowed to engage in trade even while they licensed other traders. Then, in 1724, the assembly reduced the number of commissioners to one. These commissioners included James Moore (1724), George Chicken (1724–1727), James Herbert (1727–1733), Tobias Fitch (1733), William Drake (1734–1739), Childermas Craft (1739–1747), and William Pinckney (1747–1761), with each under the authority of the governor.[11]

When Parliament took control of Indian affairs in 1755, South Carolina continued to exercise authority over the tribes, although between 1764 and 1767 the Crown gradually assumed control and placed South Carolina under the Southern superintendent of Indian affairs. In Georgia, the legislature governed Indian affairs, appointing commissioners to oversee trade and issue licenses. By 1754, control passed to the governor, and by the end of the French and Indian War, in 1763, the Crown asserted control of Indian affairs, with the governor retaining authority to appoint commissioners and agents as he deemed necessary.[12]

In 1753, the Crown entertained a plan to centralize Indian affairs, and within two years, it mandated control, establishing two Indian departments, each governed by a superintendent. In the North, the influential William Johnson was appointed superintendent, while in the South Edmund Atkins received the appointment. Both men reported to the Crown rather than the governors, colonial assemblies, or military. Their duties centered primarily on handling England's political intercourse with tribal nations; protecting Indians from unscrupulous traders, speculators, and settlers; negotiating territorial boundaries; and working to establish Indian allies. Oversight of Indian trade remained in colonial hands, notwithstanding an attempt by the superintendents to bring trade under their control.[13]

The Potomac and Ohio Rivers generally divided the Northern and Southern departments. In the North, Johnson (1755–1774) controlled Indian affairs until his death on July 11, 1774, when he was succeeded by his nephew Guy Johnson (1774–1783). In large measure because of Johnson's influence, the Northern Department was the more prestigious of the two departments. In the South, Atkins—a Charleston Indian trader—served as superintendent between 1756 and October 8, 1761, when he died.[14] He was replaced by the more able John Stuart, who served from 1762 to 1779. While the colonial governors largely controlled Indian affairs under Atkins, Stuart centralized tribal matters under his direction.

On July 10, 1764, the Board of Trade proposed a "Plan for the Future Management of Indian Affairs" designed to enhance the authority of the superintendents by confining Indian trade to licensed traders stationed at British military posts. Such a plan would have taken control of trade away from the colonial governments, eliciting strong objections. The board further proposed to repeal colonial Indian laws and grant this authority to the superintendents. When Parliament repealed the Stamp Act in 1766, the source of revenue that might have supported the plan disappeared and the proposal withered. Notwithstanding, Johnson and Stuart attempted to implement the plan anyway.[15] By 1767, the colonies proposed reducing the authority of the superintendents by restoring colonial control over Indian trade. The following year Parliament agreed to deregulate Indian trade, granting colonial governments greater control.

When the war for American independence began, the Northern Department gradually shifted to Canada, although Johnson actively engaged maintenance of British alliances with the Iroquois, with the Mohawk inflicting heavy losses on colonial New York. While the Mohawk, Onondaga, Seneca, and Cayuga supported the British, the Tuscarora and Oneida allied with the Americans, fracturing the confederacy.[16] As for the Southern Department, Stuart remained superintendent until 1779, when the department was divided into a Western and Eastern Division. John Graham (1779–1781) and Alexander Cameron (1782–1783) served as superintendents of the Western Division while Colonel Thomas Brown (1779–1783) superintended the Eastern Division.[17]

The Continental Congress and Commissioners of Indian Affairs

Early on the Continental Congress recognized the necessity of maintaining the friendship, or at least the neutrality, of tribal nations, no small task given that the Indian administrative structure of England endeared the tribes to British traders. Under the Continental Congress, the thirteen colonies appointed their own commissioners to negotiate with the tribes, although once war began it became increasingly clear Indian affairs could not be handled by such disparate approaches. On July 12, 1775, the Continental Congress adopted a resolution stating "that the securing and preserving the friendship of the Indian nations appears to be a subject of the utmost moment of these colonies."[18]

To ensure amity and "to strengthen and confirm the friendly disposition" of the tribes, Congress agreed to establish three Indian departments and to periodically appoint commissioners to superintend tribal relations on behalf of the colonies. The three departments included a Northern Department (Iroquois and tribes to the north and east), a Southern Department (Cherokee Nation and tribes to the south), and a Middle Department (tribes in between). Each would be governed by a series of "Indian commissioners" empowered to act on behalf of the colonies.

In theory, each colony was to be represented, although in practice that was not the case. The Southern Department was to be governed by five commissioners while the Northern and Middle departments were each to be administered by three commissioners. The commissioners were to "have the power to treat with the Indians in their respective departments, in the name, and on behalf of the united Colonies." The men were empowered to secure the services of "gentlemen of influence among the Indians" to assist them and to appoint agents to represent the colonies.[19] As importantly, the commissioners were empowered to seize and hold in custody any superintendent, agent, or "any other person" representing the Crown who was "stirring up or inciting the Indians."

A day after adoption of the resolution of friendship, Congress appointed the initial commissioners to represent the departments, agreeing to an additional commissioner for the Northern Department. Congress then elected General Philip Schuyler (New York), Major Joseph Hawley (Massachusetts), Turbutt Francis (Pennsylvania), and Oliver Wolcott (Connecticut) as Northern Department commissioners. Congress then added Volkert P. Douw (New York) as the fifth commissioner for the department, and when Hawley resigned in November, Timothy Edwards (Massachusetts) replaced him. For the Middle Department, Congress elected Benjamin Franklin (Pennsylvania), Patrick Henry (Virginia), and James Wilson (Pennsylvania), although Henry was replaced by Thomas Walker (Virginia) on September 15, 1775, after he resigned his commission. The Southern Department was represented by Edward Wilkerson (South Carolina), George Galphin (Georgia), Robert Rae (Georgia), John Walker (Virginia), and Willie Jones (North Carolina), with the former three commissioners appointed by the Whig-controlled South Carolina Council of Safety and the latter two elected by Congress.[20]

The commissioners of Indian affairs differed considerably from the commissioner of Indian affairs appointed by the president after 1832. Under the Continental Congress, the commissioners were plural (thirteen) and represented sectional, regional, and state interests. They were also more interested in maintaining amity with the tribes than administering congressional policy. In the Southern Department, for instance, North Carolina, South Carolina, and Georgia demanded greater autonomy and control of Indian affairs at the local level. Moreover, the commissioners under the Continental Congress did not administer Indian affairs but were commissioned "to treat with the Indians and secure their Friendship and Neutrality" during the revolution.[21] Furthermore, the commissioners did not devote their full time to their roles as they either served in the military or were members of Congress, statesmen, or seasoned Indian traders.

All were experienced in Indian affairs, with some, such as Benjamin Franklin, deeply respectful and appreciative of the cultural and political strengths of the tribal nations.

Articles of Confederation and Superintendents of Indian Affairs

The Continental Congress adopted the Articles of Confederation on November 15, 1777, with the Articles becoming effective on ratification by the states on March 1, 1781. Under the Articles, Indian affairs became more nationalized, although the states retained certain rights in their relationship with tribal nations, including continuing to execute treaties with the tribes. According to the authority granted to the national government in Article IX, the United States had the "sole and exclusive right and power of regulating the trade and managing all affairs with the Indians not members of any of the States." In order to appease southern interests, Congress agreed it would not infringe on or violate "the legislative right of any State" to manage Indian affairs.[22]

Congress attempted in 1784 and again in 1785 to enact an ordinance to strengthen and unify federal authority over Indian affairs within the several states. The Carolinas and Georgia were hotbeds of resistance to federal involvement, and the South in general was less than receptive to federal control. Consequently, both the 1784 and 1785 ordinances failed to gain approval by Congress. Not until 1786 were conditions mature for an ordinance. Frontier relations were at a critical stage, state treaties with tribal nations were wantonly violated, and hostilities were increasing.

In June, Congress directed a committee to draft an ordinance "for the compleat arrangement and government of the Indian Department." The committee recommended the department be divided into three districts, each headed by a superintendent responsible for overseeing "the political conduct of the Nations over whom they are placed." The superintendents were to encourage tribes "to act as much independent[ly] of each other as possible" so as to facilitate federal control. They were also responsible for licensing traders and ensuring justice on the frontier.[23]

On July 24, Congress amended the proposed ordinance by adding a proviso that precluded the departments from infringing on the "legislative right of any State, within its own limits." States could be involved in licensing traders and responding to threatened hostilities, but if a proposed federal action interfered with the legislative authority of any state, the superintendent was to act in conjunction with local authorities.[24] On August 7, the ordinance was approved with the consent of all of the southern states. The approved ordinance established two—not three—departments: a Northern and a Southern department, with each directed by a superintendent of Indian affairs who was given the responsibility for implementing a policy of amity and trade.[25] Congress continued to periodically appoint special commissioners to negotiate treaties of cession with the tribes.

While the ordinance was the result of compromise, it reasserted federal authority over Indian affairs. It also reinstituted the role of superintendents in lieu of commissioners of Indian affairs. This was a reflection of the success the British Crown had in its administrative model of superintendents during the later colonial era when it developed strong commercial and political relationships with the tribes. The two superintendents each held office for two years or until Congress elected to remove them. They were required to live within their department so as to "attend to the execution of such regulations, as Congress shall from time to time, establish." They were placed under the direction and control of the War Department. They were further authorized to appoint two agents to reside in the frontier communities, and they were granted the power to issue licenses to trade, but only to US citizens.

The Continental Congress elected Richard Butler of Pennsylvania as the first superintendent of Indian affairs on August 14, 1786.[26] Born in Dublin, Ireland, in 1743, Butler immigrated to America at the age of five. After serving in the military, he became an officer in the Continental Army during the revolution. In 1784, he was appointed by Congress as a commissioner of Indian affairs before Congress elected him as the first superintendent for the Northern Department, a position he retained until he was killed at the Battle of the Wabash on November 4, 1791. On October 6, 1786, the Continental Congress also elected James White of North Carolina to serve as the first superintendent of Indian affairs for the Southern Department. Born on June 16, 1749, to a wealthy Philadelphia merchant family, White was a physician, lawyer, and politician before becoming a North Carolina delegate to the Continental Congress.[27] Between 1793 and 1797, he served as a delegate to the US Congress for the Southwest Territory. When Tennessee was admitted to the Union in 1796, White settled there before joining the invasion of Spanish Florida in the late 1790s. He eventually settled in Louisiana where he died in October 1809.[28] White served as superintendent until February 1788, when Congress elected Richard Winn of South Carolina as superintendent on February 29, 1788.[29] Winn served until March 3, 1791, when he took his seat as a representative from South Carolina. William Blount (territorial governor of Tennessee) served as ex officio superintendent until March 30, 1796.

The Continental Congress again asserted federal authority in the Northwest Ordinance of 1787 by declaring: "The utmost good faith shall always be observed towards the Indians [and] their lands and property shall never be taken from them without their consent."[30] Nonetheless, Georgia and North Carolina (and New York, Massachusetts, and South Carolina) continued to negotiate treaties with the tribes within their state boundaries.[31] By the fall of 1787, even as the constitutional convention was winding down in Philadelphia, a congressional committee asserted federal authority over Indian affairs, going so far as to condemn the actions of Georgia and North Carolina for their continued usurpation of and encroachment on tribal lands, further inflaming hostilities with the tribes. This "avaricious disposition," the committee warned, was the "source of difficulties," especially with the Creek and Cherokee nations.[32]

As importantly, the committee elaborated, the federal government had the power to control Indian affairs—and this authority was "indivisible." Either states had this authority or the federal government did; there could be no sharing of it. If the federal government was not supreme in governing Indian affairs, then the ordinances of Congress were "useless," "absurd in theory as well as in practice," and "a mere nullity."[33]

Constitutional Indian Administration

The Continental Congress had reason to tread carefully on the assertion of federal dominance over Indian affairs. This was in response to both tribal nations who might resist further federal control as well as the thirteen independent states that confederated together but were distrustful of a strong central government. The lack of meaningful discussion on Indian affairs at the constitutional convention, then, is perhaps unsurprising given the fragile nature of dissent between federalists and antifederalists. In the end, when the commerce clause was amended to include "and with the Indian tribes," this simple phrase enabled the United States to construct an edifice that in time was reflected in federal plenary authority over tribal nations.

The relationship between the United States and the Indian tribes was initially commercial, with the War Department occupying a central role in implementing and overseeing policy and the secretary of war directly overseeing the management of Indian affairs. As the nation moved west into the Ohio Valley and into the southern frontier, encroachment increased and the commercial relationship competed with one based on military confrontation. The United States quickly realized that its "military might was an indispensable ingredient of the policy it passed."³⁴ While treaties and trade encouraged amity, land encroachment, arson, theft, assault, and murder ensured a prominent role for the military.

The US Army eventually dominated the relationship with tribal nations, with military actions occurring all along the frontier. When Congress approved a series of trade and intercourse acts beginning in 1790, it was the War Department that enforced provisions related to trade and sought to control outrages committed on both sides of the frontier, with the 1796 act specifically authorizing the military to enforce trader violations.³⁵ While the trade and intercourse bill of 1790 proposed the appointment of a military officer as superintendent of Indian affairs, the House of Representatives opposed the bill as "blend[ing] civil and military characters" and infringing on the president's power to appoint men with "the ... proper character."³⁶ The Non-Intercourse Act, meanwhile, was renewed every three years until it was made permanent in 1802.

In 1796, Congress sought to further promote amity along the frontier by authorizing federal trading houses, or "factories," to conduct trade with the tribes. Influenced by George Washington who believed trade carried "on Government Acct." would best adhere tribal nations "strongly to our interests," Congress in 1794 reported on a proposal it believed would "produce [a] laudable and benevolent effect" on tribal nations, including diplomacy by eliminating the profit motive that often undermined peace. The following year, Congress agreed to test the concept by appropriating $50,000 to procure trade goods to stock government trading houses operating under the direction of the president.³⁷ The initial factories were located along the southern frontier to encourage peace with the Cherokee (Tellico) and Creek (Colerain) nations. The 1796 act granted the president broad discretionary authority over the trading houses and, by extension, over tribal nations. President Washington delegated this authority to Secretary of War Timothy Pickering, a tradition that continued in succeeding administrations.

The trading houses were enough of a success that Congress authorized expanding them along the frontier. President Jefferson encouraged, and Congress authorized, further expansion in 1802 and 1805, with reorganizations and administrative adjustments common.³⁸ Successive secretaries of war defined the limits between civilian and military affairs, no small task given both were under the War Department. In 1801, for instance, Secretary Henry Dearborn outlined a division of responsibilities for civilian factors and military officers, delegating to Revolutionary War officer William Irvine, superintendent of military stores, oversight of daily administration of the Indian trading houses.³⁹ Notwithstanding such "factories," private operators were permitted to trade with tribes under regulations enforced by the secretary of war, with a purveyor of public supplies procuring trade items for the factories and disposing of the goods received in exchange.

In November 1796, Secretary of War James McHenry appointed John Harris of Philadelphia as keeper of military stores and the first superintendent of Indian trade. In this role, Harris received trade goods from the frontier factories and disposed of them at public auctions. In May 1801 Dearborn assigned responsibility for Indian trade to Irvine.[40] When Irvine died in 1804, Dearborn appointed George Ingels to assume Irvine's duties. Less than a year later, Dearborn reorganized the Indian trade office and replaced Ingels with the Philadelphia merchant William Davy.

When the House Committee on Commerce and Manufacturing questioned Dearborn's authority to appoint Davy, it called for greater oversight of Indian trade. On April 21, 1806, Congress reorganized the trading houses and established the Office of Indian Trade, separating military and civilian affairs.[41] While still within the War Department, the new office was headed by a superintendent who was bonded, prohibited from engaging in Indian trade, and required to hold six public fur and pelt auctions annually—with no more than two in any one state. The office consisted of a superintendent, chief clerk, bookkeeper, copy clerk, transportation clerk, and janitor.

With Davy's resignation, Dearborn placed Colonel John Shee in the position, with Shee becoming the first superintendent of Indian trade operating under authority of law. He immediately assumed all of the duties of Davy. For the first time there was a single point of responsibility to oversee Indian affairs, with the Office of Indian Trade at the center of the government's objective of pastoralizing the tribes by providing them with items of domestic comfort. Shee referred to his department as the Office of the Superintendent of Indian Trade, although by 1808 it was simply known as the Office of Indian Trade.[42]

Shee organized the Office of Indian Trade in his hometown of Philadelphia, where the military store was housed and the center of Indian trade had resided since before the 1795 act establishing trading houses. The 1806 act, however, directed that the office be relocated to the District of Columbia. Shee, having little interest in the superintendency, refused to move to the nation's new capital, and in October 1807, Dearborn replaced him by appointing John Mason as superintendent. Mason relocated the office to Georgetown in the District of Columbia and remained superintendent for eight and a half years before Secretary of War William H. Crawford appointed Thomas L. McKenney to replace him on April 12, 1816.

Under McKenney, the Office of Indian Trade grew to be responsible not only for trade and the stocking of the government trading houses but also for purchasing and transporting annuities and other goods provided to the tribes under treaty provisions and for encouraging missionary activities among the tribes. Upon his appointment as superintendent, McKenney—recognizing that the factory system was failing—advocated for expanding the office to include the education and "civilization" of the Indians, serving as the driving force behind the 1819 civilization act.[43] The act empowered the federal government for the first time to involve itself in the domestic affairs of tribal nations, no small transformation of the office and opening the door for expansion of federal authority.

The Indian trading houses were a source of contention with private traders and merchants who viewed them as antithetical to American free enterprise. Due to demands from private traders and merchants who decried the government trading houses, Congress closed the factory system in 1822, eliminating the Office of Indian Trade as well.[44] To close government accounts, President James Monroe assigned George Graham to liquidate the Office of Indian Trade, with former Secretary of War and then-current Secretary of the Treasury William H. Crawford overseeing the closure.[45]

Secretary of War John C. Calhoun, who five times between 1818 and 1824 advocated for Congress to establish a more stable office of Indian affairs, turned over all management of Indian affairs to McKenney. When Congress closed the trading houses, Calhoun was convinced the closures would lead to more—not less—work and would require more staff and additional administration.

To fill this gap, Congress, on the same day it abolished the trading houses, amended the 1802 trade and intercourse act to establish a new superintendent of Indian affairs to be organized in St. Louis. The law required the superintendents to be installed with the advice and consent of the Senate. With William Clark already established as superintendent in St. Louis since 1808, Calhoun recommended to President Monroe that he nominate Clark to serve in the new role as superintendent of Indian affairs, with charge over all of the western tribes and agencies. The Senate consented, and on May 28, 1822, Calhoun directed Clark "to make it a part of [his] duty" to exercise management of tribal affairs along the Missouri and Mississippi rivers.[46] Clark served as superintendent in St. Louis until his death on September 1, 1838. Concurrently, three territorial governors served as ex officio superintendents of Indian affairs, including William Cass (Michigan Territory), James Miller (Arkansas Territory), and William Duvall (Florida Territory). These ex officio superintendents, directed by the secretary of war and responsible for Indian affairs within their territory, continued until their positions were abolished by act of Congress in 1834.⁴⁷

On March 12, 1824, Calhoun administratively established a "Bureau of Indian Affairs" within the War Department, appointing McKenney to a vacant chief clerkship and directing him to take charge over all Indian affairs.⁴⁸ As chief clerk, McKenney supervised the expenditure of funds appropriated on behalf of the tribes, executed treaties, managed the provision of Indian schools, regulated trade, and distributed annuities. But he did not have statutory authority to act.⁴⁹ In 1826, John Cocke (Democrat, Tennessee), chairman of the House Committee on Indian Affairs, learned of Calhoun's bureau. In a letter to the former secretary of war, Cocke explained that the bureau was transacting "the affairs of the Government with the several Indian tribes" but he could find no statutory authorization for the office. He pointedly inquired of the secretary "when, and by what law, the said Bureau is authorized," even as he drafted a bill to create a "Home Department."⁵⁰

Calhoun, recognizing the essential nature of government obligations to the tribes and a need to regulate affairs as spelled out in the Non-Intercourse Act, had acted without congressional authorization. McKenney lamented this absence of law, writing in 1828 that Congress should enact "a simple law, connecting the responsibility of this branch of the public service with the Congress."⁵¹ To support the effort, Secretary of War Peter Porter called on two men with considerable experience in Indian Country: Lewis Cass and William Clark. Cass and Clark had controlled Indian policy for nearly two decades, and both men now traveled to Washington, DC, to assist McKenney in drafting proposals for consideration by Congress. Their report was submitted on February 9, 1829, although Congress failed to act on their proposals before adjourning.⁵²

Notwithstanding a lack of statutory authority, McKenney provided stability and expertise in the Indian Office, expanding its role between 1824 and 1830. In this he was aided by the civilization act that authorized the president "to employ capable persons of good moral character, to instruct [the Indians] in the mode of agriculture suited to their situation; and for teaching their children in reading, writing, and arithmetic, and perform other duties as may be enjoined, according to such instructions and rules the President may give and prescribe."⁵³ Such broad language enabled McKenney to increase the scope of the Indian Office. He now asserted—with assistance from Congress—a far greater role in Indian affairs, one that opened the door to domination of the tribes. The Indian Office became the central clearinghouse for all matters pertaining to tribal affairs, including the regulation of trade and intercourse and the enforcement of integrative measures.

Cass and Clark, meanwhile, continued to draft proposals for elevating the Indian Office, and on March 29, 1830, they released a report and introduced a bill into Congress advancing the concept of a "Home Department" for Indian affairs.⁵⁴ Two years later, Congress partially granted McKenney's desire when it authorized the secretary of war to replace the chief clerk with a commissioner of Indian affairs and empower him to have "direction and management" of all Indian affairs.⁵⁵ A commissioner was now lawfully established, being appointed by the president with the advice and consent of the Senate.

The initial decade of the Indian Office was saddled with challenges, as military personnel and Indian Office employees were both subject to the secretary of war. In fact, the War Department's military and Indian affairs goals were often antithetical. The Northwest Ordinance, for instance, required the military to engage tribal nations as the Old Northwest was settled, but the Indian Office was responsible for checking the settlement of the territory and protecting tribal people and property. Moreover, military personnel refused to accept orders from civilians, with competing goals becoming more complicated and pronounced as the nineteenth century unfolded.⁵⁶

By August 1831, Cass had become secretary of war and lobbied for a complete reorganization of the Indian Office. On June 30, 1834, in response to Cass's request, Congress not only statutorily created a Bureau of Indian Affairs and expanded the authority of the commissioner of Indian affairs, but it also for the first time defined Indian Country as those lands for which the Indian title had not yet been extinguished. By then McKenney was gone, having been replaced by Elbert Herring. By the late 1830s, Carey Allen Harris further refined the Indian Office by implementing a series of regulations governing the accounting of tribal annuities, administration of superintendencies, acquisition of treaty goods, use of interpreters and treaty negotiations, and licensing of traders and issuance of passports in Indian Country.⁵⁷ By the 1840s, the Indian Office executed policy as directed by Congress and the president and as influenced by the commissioner of Indian affairs. While the commissioners during the initial decades of the Indian Office exerted limited influence, theirs was a specialized field requiring a level of competency not seen in the commissioners of the postbellum years.

As midcentury approached, the US Supreme Court issued an opinion that generated little attention at the time. In a case that dealt with the matter of jurisdiction and whether the federal–Indian relationship was racially based or politically based, the Court issued a straightforward yet significant ruling. In 1844, William Rogers murdered his brother-in-law Jacob Nicholson. The men were ethnically non-Indians married to Cherokee women, with both men recognized as Cherokee citizens by the Cherokee Nation. The Court assumed jurisdiction, holding that the defendant was a "white m[a]n" who could not legally disassociate himself from the United States absent congressional authorization.[58]

Writing the majority opinion, Chief Justice Roger B. Taney held that the political affiliation of Rogers did not change the fact that he was not Cherokee. In prior cases the federal courts had ambiguously used "race" to refer to Indians as a group with a common biological heritage and a common political identity. In holding divergent political and biological definitions, the Court now redefined "Indian" and used the occasion to subject tribal nations to increased federal authority. In so doing, the Court referenced the 1834 Non-Intercourse Act that declared "so much of the laws of the United States as provided for punishment of crimes committed within any place within the sole and exclusive jurisdiction of the United States, shall be in force in Indian Country." Crimes "committed by one Indian against the person or property of another Indian," however, remained exempt from federal jurisdiction.

In peeling back the layers of jurisdiction, the Court merged the status of Indian Country as federal land with the subjection of American Indians to federal authority, adding to the theoretical framework of federal plenary power that subjected tribal nations to broad federal authority. Taney specifically argued that the United States adopted the principle that tribal nations were not "regarded as the owners of the territories they respectively occupied" but were in fact subject to the authority of the United States.[59] The further legal underpinning of federal administrative control had been constructed with Congress poised to transform the federal–Indian relationship.

Establishing the Department of the Interior

Since the founding of the United States, Indian affairs had been a military matter. By the late 1840s, with emigration of the eastern tribes largely completed, Treasury Secretary Robert Walker encouraged Congress to consider anew the establishment of a cabinet-level department, building on the concept espoused by Lewis Cass and William Clark, as well as John Cocke, two decades earlier. "The duties now performed by the Commissioner of Indian Affairs are most numerous and important," Walker reasoned, "and must be vastly increased." As importantly, Walker added, there had been "interesting progress of so many of the tribes in Christianity, knowledge, and civilization."[60] These duties were not war-related but appertained to peace and what the federal government now perceived as domestic relations with the tribes.

Walker suggested the General Land Office (Treasury), Patent Office (State), Pension Office (War), and Indian Office (War) more logistically fit within a new "interior department." With the addition of new western territories in the 1840s, the duties of the General Land Office would overwhelm the Treasury Department, while the duties of the commissioner of Indian affairs would greatly increase to accommodate the political relationship with the western tribes. Indian affairs, Walker argued, were no longer related "to war, but to peace, and to our domestic relations with these tribes."[61]

The secretary proposed a bill that was introduced in the House by Samuel F. Vinton (Whig, Ohio) on February 12, 1849.[62] The bill was quickly approved in the House but became bogged down in the Senate where John Calhoun (Democrat, South Carolina) expressed concern with an interior department that would increase federal authority over domestic affairs, which, in his opinion, were better left to the states. Moreover, Indian affairs, the elder statesman added, "are so intimately connected with the War Department" that they ought not to be separated from that department. Despite Calhoun's caution, the Senate voted 31 to 25 in favor of the bill.[63] President James Polk signed it into law on March 3, 1849.[64]

With Indian affairs now considered an insular matter, American expansion west accelerated, leading to further encroachment into Indian Country and creating a new dilemma. How should the United States deal with tribes now sequestered within or adjacent to the several states? The answer to this question had tangible political implications. Part of the challenge was that the Indian Office still operated according to the regulations of the 1830s. "However well adapted to the condition of things in 1834," Commissioner Orlando Brown wrote in 1849, "it is incompatible with the present state of affairs."[65] Increased treaty transactions, a significant increase in the number of tribes with whom the United States had to deal, and a glaring shortage of personnel and administrative officers to handle matters in the West encouraged wide-scale, uncoordinated, discretionary action.

Congress initiated a series of modifications to Indian Office authorizations beginning on February 27, 1851, when it reorganized the department by eliminating all superintendencies east of the Rocky Mountains and creating three new ones. Each of the administrative units was governed by a superintendent appointed by the president with the advice and consent of the Senate.[66] Superintendencies within territories were governed by territorial governors who served as ex officio superintendents. Eleven Indian agents replaced twenty-three agents and subagents in the West, with four assigned to the New Mexico Territory and one to the Utah Territory. Trade and intercourse regulations were extended over all of the tribes in the West. A Central Superintendency replaced the St. Louis

Superintendency and governed border tribes in Kansas and Nebraska, while a Southern Superintendency replaced the Western Superintendency for Indian Territory and the Osage in southern Kansas. A Northern Superintendency oversaw tribes in the Great Lakes region. Notwithstanding administrative changes, Commissioner George Manypenny lamented in 1856 that in just four years the functions of the Indian Office had swelled "to an extent almost incredible," despite staffing remaining unchanged.⁶⁷

By 1850, a reservation policy governed Indian affairs, both to prevent the extermination of the border tribes and to further reduce the tribal estate. As the population of the West increased, and with the depletion of game and natural resources, there were no new territories into which the tribes could be settled. A new generation of reformers, reeling from a devastating national Civil War, sought to salve the national honor after a series of Indian wars and massacres in the 1860s by deploying a new policy of assimilation and land severalty. The policy coincided with the advent of the Industrial Age and remained in effect for more than half a century, focusing on the rapid incorporation of the Indians into the nation's social and political fabric.

The structure and purpose of the Indian Office changed little in the late nineteenth and early twentieth centuries, other than to grow to 5,500 employees.⁶⁸ Policy remained assimilative, and the bureau's administrative framework was buttressed by several Supreme Court rulings, the most significant of which was *Lone Wolf v. Hitchcock*. According to the 1867 Treaty of Medicine Lodge Creek, the Kiowa, Comanche, and Apache agreed to reside on a reservation in Indian Territory but with the stipulation that there be no further land cessions absent the consent of at least three-quarters of all adult men. In 1892, the Jerome Commission negotiated an agreement with the tribes for land severalty and the sale of all "surplus" lands. But the agreement did not meet the three-quarter consent requirement of the 1867 treaty. When Congress ratified the agreement, Kiowa Chief Lone Wolf filed suit.⁶⁹

The US Supreme Court upheld ratification based on the Court's view that Congress had plenary power. This authority, Justice Edward White wrote for the majority, "has been exercised by Congress from the beginning, and the power has always been deemed a political one." The United States was completely within its right to change the nature of Indian property from one form (land) to another (money).⁷⁰ And since the matter was deemed by the Court to be political, it refused to overturn the decision of Congress. The ruling not only expanded the authority under which the Indian Office operated, but it also opened the door to near complete control of tribal people and property by the Indian Office.

TABLE 8. Indian Office Authority over Tribal Nations, 1887–1934

* Implement land severalty
* Issue fee patents and determine certificates of competency
* Supervise tribal real estate, including determining heirship, leasing, and rights-of-way
* Manage Indian funds (tribal and individual)
* Provide educational services
* Provide medical services
* Support industrial development, including irrigation
* Promote home economics, including the use of field matrons
* Provide police services
* Enforce prohibition and engage in liquor suppression
* License and control Indian trade and traders
* Supervise and approve of attorney contracts

SOURCE: Schmeckebier, *The Office of Indian Affairs*, 393–394.

Between the 1880s and the 1920s, the Indian Office hastened on with land severalty, opening scores of reservations to homesteading. Moreover, the Indian Office determined the criteria for demonstrating Indian competency for fee patents, leading to rapid alienation of land. Congress also authorized the department to sell millions of acres of inherited lands and lands held by those the Indian Office deemed incompetent. Every commissioner of Indian affairs of the era worked to divest tribes of their land via severalty and sought the complete abolition of tribal life, including reservations and tribal governments. Having near absolute control over American Indians and their property, the commissioners of Indian affairs engaged in myriad activities pointing to the end of Indian affairs. The most significant of these authorities are listed in table 8.

By the 1920s, a generation of secular reformers advocated moving away from the policies of assimilation that, by the early 1930s, had despoiled tribal nations of nearly ninety million acres. The policy changes ushered in an era of cultural pluralism gilded with a thinly veiled acculturative underlining that manifested itself in legislative enactments such as the Indian Reorganization Act, Johnson–O'Malley Act, Pueblo Lands Act, Indian Arts and Craft Act, and others that promoted or at least did not oppose tribalism. Departmental administrative orders closed numerous boarding schools and promoted on-reservation day schools that doubled as community centers. Taken as a whole, however, the Indian Office remained unchanged in that a commissioner still headed the office and implemented congressional policy without any tribal input and the department was still tacitly committed to the abolition of tribal nations.

The cultural pluralism of the 1930s and early 1940s was short lived, as in the postwar years a wave of nationalism and conservatism swept the nation and renewed the efforts to assimilate American Indians. The same Indian Office that promoted pluralism in the 1930s enforced a termination policy in the 1950s that was as harsh as it was ill conceived. By the time termination ended in the 1960s, the United States had severed its political relationship with scores of tribes and tribal groups, leading to an unprecedented level of cynicism and distrust in Indian Country.

The rise of tribal activism in the 1960s facilitated substantive change in the 1970s, including a proposal to elevate Indian affairs to the highest levels in the federal government. American Indians and tribal organizations, such as the National Congress of American Indians and the National Tribal Chairmen's Association, influenced policies to restore tribalism and expand tribal sovereignty, while at the same time facilitate economic and social advancement. As importantly, tribal nations demanded not only a voice in determining their own future but also that a Native American administer Indian affairs while supporting and implementing a policy of self-determination. While Ely Parker (Seneca) served as the first American Indian commissioner of Indian affairs (1869–1871), it would be nearly a century before Robert Bennett (Oneida) became the second Native American commissioner. After 1966, all commissioners of Indian affairs were American Indians.

By 1970, the time was right for change. In July, President Nixon, to the surprise of many in Indian Country, delivered a message to Congress outlining a policy of self-determination. Among his nine proposals, Nixon called on Congress to establish an assistant secretary of the interior for Indian affairs. It was time to elevate "Indian affairs to their proper role" within the federal system, Nixon explained.[71] While the president was committed to elevating the role of the commissioner of Indian affairs within the federal bureaucracy, Congress did not act. In the meantime, the American Indian Policy Review Commission reported "a notable absence of managerial and organizational capacity" within the bureau, and in its final report a year later recommended Indian affairs be elevated to a cabinet-level position.[72]

The election of Jimmy Carter as president brought about the change by administrative act. In February 1977, the president announced plans to elevate the commissioner of Indian affairs to an assistant secretary for Indian affairs level. On July 12, 1977, Carter nominated Forrest Gerard (Blackfeet) as the first assistant secretary for Indian affairs, using as his authority a federal reorganization plan from 1950 that authorized the Department of the Interior to add an additional assistant secretary.[73] With the assistant secretary for Indian affairs in place, Interior Secretary Cecil Andrus revoked all authorities of the commissioner of Indian affairs.[74]

The assistant secretary initially replaced the commissioner of Indian affairs, with Andrus appointing an eleven-member task force to make recommendations for how the Bureau of Indian Affairs should be structured after undergoing its most significant reorganization since 1832. In March 1978, the task force recommended the assistant secretary administer the department with three deputy assistant secretaries, one to oversee finance, one for operations, and one for planning.[75] Gerard, however, revised the recommendations by eliminating the deputy assistant secretaries and reinstituting the commissioner of Indian affairs, who he then directed to manage the day-to-day administration of the bureau. He appointed Martin E. Seneca Jr. (Seneca) as acting deputy commissioner, and on September 28, 1979, at Gerard's request, President Carter nominated William E. Hallett (Red Lake Chippewa) as commissioner of Indian affairs.[76] Hallett was the last commissioner of Indian affairs.

Gerard was instrumental in ensuring the assistant secretary was more than just an administrator. A former legislative staffer for Senator Henry Jackson (Democrat, Washington), Gerard laid the groundwork in the 1960s and early 1970s to foster self-determination. When he resigned from Jackson's staff in November 1976, President Carter asked him to serve as the first assistant secretary. He accepted the nomination with the understanding that the elevated position would "not be absorbed in the day-to-day operations of the BIA" but would, rather, engage with "overall policy, fighting within the Interior Department, dealing with the [Office of Management and Budget], the Congress, and major contacts outside of the department."[77] Gerard ensured that the assistant secretary focused on setting policy, not administering day-to-day activities as an elevated commissioner of Indian affairs.

Today, the assistant secretary plays an increasingly important role within the federal system. The commissioner of Indian affairs, for instance, did not participate in policy-level discussions within the Department of the Interior administrative structure and did not set policy, reporting instead to an assistant secretary. The assistant secretary for Indian affairs, however, is positioned at a level within the department to not only influence policy but also to set it. And while a cabinet-level secretarial position was not established, Indian affairs were elevated to their highest level ever within the federal system.

The administration of Indian affairs is also far more complex than it was prior to 1977. While not perfect, it is also far more responsive to tribal nations than ever before. Indian administration today includes the Office of the Assistant Secretary for Indian Affairs, which directly manages the Office of the Special Trustee for American Indians, Office of Federal Acknowledgment, Office of Indian Gaming, and the Office of Self-Governance. It also provides oversight to the Bureau of Indian Affairs and the Bureau of Indian Education. It is the assistant secretary's duty to strengthen the government-to-government relationships with tribal nations, advance policies of self-determination, and protect Indian trust assets while also developing policy in consultation with tribal nations and organizations, governmental agencies, the executive office, and Congress.

After Hallett's tenure as commissioner of Indian affairs ended in January 1981, the head of the Bureau of Indian Affairs was referred to as a deputy commissioner until 2003 when the modern nomenclature "director" was adopted. The director of the Bureau of Indian Affairs is responsible for implementing policy and managing the day-to-day operations of the central office and the twelve regional offices. Since 2003 there have been eight directors of the Bureau of Indian Affairs: Terrance Virden (White Earth Chippewa), 2003–2004; Brian Pogue (Cherokee Nation), 2004–2005; William Patrick Ragsdale (Cherokee Nation), 2005–2007; Jerald L. Gidmer (Sault St. Marie Chippewa), 2007–2010; Michael Black (Oglala Sioux), 2010–2016; Weldon "Bruce" Loudermilk (Ft. Peck Sioux), 2016–2017; Bryan Price (Cherokee Nation), 2017–2018; and Darryl LaCount (Turtle Mountain Chippewa), 2018–2021.

Equal to and in line with the Bureau of Indian Affairs (BIA) is the Bureau of Indian Education (BIE), the latest addition to Indian affairs. The BIE reflects the increased attention Indian Country places on education. Established on August 29, 2006, the office is led by a director who is charged with managing and administering all Indian education activities, including providing oversight to BIA and tribal contract schools. The Bureau of Indian Education also administers special education programs in BIA and contract schools, oversees elementary and secondary education, and serves similarly to a state department of education when interacting with the US Department of Education. Since its creation, the BIE has been led by seven directors: Thomas Dowd (Hopi), 2006–2007; Keven Skenandore (Oneida/Oglala Sioux), acting 2007–2010; Bart Stevens

(San Carlos Apache), acting 2010; Keith Moore (Rosebud Sioux), 2010–2012; Brian Drapeaux (Yankton Sioux), acting 2012–2013; Charles Roessel (Navajo), 2013–2016; and Tony Dearman (Cherokee Nation), 2016–2021.

Designation of the Indian Office

The commissioner of Indian affairs historically has directed the Bureau of Indian Affairs, but the departmental heads have included other titles, including superintendent of Indian trade, superintendent of Indian affairs, chief clerk, and, after 1977, the assistant secretary for Indian affairs. Just as the title for the head of Indian affairs has changed over the past two and a half centuries, the name of the office has also been modified. Initially referred to as the Office of Indian Trade, by 1808 the department was simply known as the Indian Office. When John Calhoun administratively created a Bureau of Indian Affairs in 1824, Chief Clerk Thomas McKenney continued to use Indian Office or Office of Indian Affairs, the nomenclature used throughout most of the nineteenth century.

Until 1909, congressional appropriations were made for the "Indian Department," although beginning in 1910 Congress made appropriations for the Bureau of Indian Affairs. Because of the criticism of the bureau in the 1920s, Interior Secretary Ray Lyman Wilbur mandated the use of Indian Service in 1929. It was not until June 1947, when a Senate Committee on Expenditures in the Executive Department defined and established a hierarchical nomenclature for all federal agencies, that the term Bureau of Indian Affairs was permanently applied. In descending order, the Senate recommended the following: department, bureau, division, branch, section, and unit.[78] On September 17, 1947, Interior Secretary Julius Krug directed all Department of the Interior agencies to begin using the new naming conventions. No longer would the term Indian Office or Indian Service be employed.[79]

CHAPTER I

John Harris

Superintendent of the Indian Trading Houses
(November 11, 1796–May 11, 1801)

JOHN HARRIS was the first federal employee to serve as superintendent of the Indian trading houses and, therefore, was the first person assigned the responsibilities of overseeing Indian trade. While the record is unclear, it appears that Harris is related to John Harris Sr. (and his son John Jr.), an Englishman who received a grant of land from William Penn and became an early Pennsylvanian who received a colonial license to engage in Indian trade in 1705. The John Harris who became superintendent of the Indian trading houses was born on April 1, 1753, in Pennsylvania.[1]

After service in the Revolutionary War, Harris remained in the US Army as military storekeeper. He apparently expected to be relieved in 1792 when he informed Superintendent of Military Stores Samuel Hodgdon that the business of the department "remains still with me" as no one had yet come "to relieve [me] ... and take charge of the stores."[2] While not specifically assigned to oversee Indian trade, as early as July 1793, Harris was taking receipt of and maintaining various items related to Indian trade goods.[3]

In 1795, in an effort to counter the British trade influence in the Ohio Valley, Congress appropriated $50,000 to encourage a "liberal trade with the Indians," entrusting to the president the responsibility for such goods. The establishment of the government-run trading houses (factories) sought to promote amity with the tribes while also setting fair standards to govern both government and private traders. The central office for the trading houses was in Philadelphia, the then-current seat of the federal government. The fulcrum of Indian trade remained in Philadelphia until 1807, when Congress mandated that the Office of Indian Trade be located in the new capital city of Washington, DC.

Goods for Indian trade were purchased in Philadelphia before being sent to the western and southern frontiers. Between passage of the act in the winter of

1795 and the fall of 1796, no single person was solely responsible for Indian trade. On November 11, 1796, Secretary of War James McHenry, "in conformity with the pleasure of the President," appointed Harris as "Storekeeper of all articles appertaining to the department of war" in and around Philadelphia, including "receiv[ing] all goods from the Indian trading houses."[4] In his role as military storekeeper, Harris assumed the additional responsibility of superintendent of Indian trade, reporting to the secretary of war and accounting for all goods and funds received in conjunction with the trade. McHenry drafted detailed instructions as to how Harris was to account for and distribute such trade goods. No goods were to be sent to the trading houses, for instance, unless directed by the secretary of war and countersigned by the superintendent of military stores.[5]

As military storekeeper, Harris oversaw the receipt and distribution of military goods for the War Department, and as superintendent of Indian trade he received goods and money from the frontier trading houses and then disposed of the furs and pelts at scheduled auctions in various eastern cities. Harris quickly became involved in distributing not only trade goods but also Indian annuities promised by federal treaties to the tribes.[6]

The election of Thomas Jefferson as president in November 1800 and the prevailing spoils system of political patronage ensured a change in leadership. After his inauguration in March 1801, Jefferson named Henry Dearborn as secretary of war, and on May 11, Dearborn replaced Harris and appointed William Irvine, superintendent of military stores, as superintendent of the Indian trading houses. Harris, meanwhile, retained his position as military storekeeper in Philadelphia. He died on December 25, 1838, at the age of eighty-five.

CHAPTER 2

William Irvine

Superintendent of the Indian Trading Houses
(May 11, 1801–July 29, 1804)

WILLIAM IRVINE, the second superintendent of the Indian trading houses, was a prominent Pennsylvanian who was involved in medicine, politics, and trade. A Scots-Irishman born in County Fermanagh, Ulster, Ireland, on November 3, 1741, Irvine pursed classical studies and graduated from Trinity College before studying medicine in Dublin. After serving as a surgeon aboard a British man-of-war during the Seven Years' War, he immigrated to the United States, settling in Carlisle, Pennsylvania, in 1763, where he proceeded to open a medical practice. In 1772, he married Ann Callender, daughter of the wealthy businessman Robert Callender, who found success in commerce and land speculation stemming from conflicts with tribal nations in western Pennsylvania and the Ohio Country.

As American tensions with Great Britain escalated in the early 1770s, Irvine aligned himself with the colonials, serving as a delegate to the Pennsylvania Revolution Committee and later as colonel of the Sixth Pennsylvania Regiment during the Revolutionary War. He saw military action at the Battle of Three Rivers during the Continental Army's ill-fated invasion of Canada, where Irvine was captured and spent months in a military prison. In May 1778, he was part of a prisoner exchange and resumed his role in the colonial war effort.[1] By 1779, he had been promoted to brigadier general and corresponded regularly with George Washington regarding military strategy. By 1781 he was in command of Fort Pitt, where he sought to maintain the peace with tribal nations, especially after the March 8, 1782, massacre of peaceful Lenni Lenape at the Moravian settlement of Gnadenhutten. When Irvine refused to defend local settlers from Indian attacks, he was branded as pro-Indian, a socially dangerous label that imperiled his well-being.

In 1785, when the Pennsylvania legislature set aside 600,000 acres in the western part of the state as bonuses for Revolutionary War veterans, it appointed

Irvine to both survey the land and also dispense of it.² Two years later, he served as a member of the Second Continental Congress before being elected to the US House of Representatives in 1792.³ When the Whiskey Rebellion erupted in western Pennsylvania over a federal excise tax in 1794, Irvine, while sympathetic to the cause of the farmers, commanded Pennsylvania troops in enforcing federal law and quelling the rebellion. Three years later he put down the Fries Rebellion that resulted from federal taxes on houses, slaves, and other property in order to raise revenue for a potential war with France.

In 1792, Irvine moved to Philadelphia where, in 1801, President Jefferson appointed him superintendent of military stores. In this role he was responsible for coordinating the acquisition and distribution of food stores, clothing, and other supplies for the military. On May 11, Secretary Dearborn assigned Irvine the additional responsibilities of superintendent of the Indian trading houses. In this role, Irvine acted with a fair degree of autonomy, receiving and disposing of trade goods at the government trading houses and annually providing Dearborn with estimated trade goods required for the upcoming year.⁴ "The principle [purpose] of the trade," he explained, was "to furnish the Indians with goods at . . . moderate prices [in order] to manifest the Liberality & Friendship of the U.S. and thus by the ties of Interest and gratitude secure their attachments, and lay the foundation of a lasting peace."⁵ Irvine remained superintendent of military stores and superintendent of the Indian trading houses for three years until his death on July 29, 1804. He was sixty-three years of age.

CHAPTER 3

George W. Ingels

Superintendent of the Indian Trading Houses
(July 29, 1804–March 26, 1805)

GEORGE W. INGELS served as the third superintendent of the Indian trading houses. Born in 1746, Ingels was a well-known carpenter and deacon at a Baptist church in Philadelphia. When the American Revolution began, Ingels joined the war, engaging in the battles of Trenton and Princeton, before becoming commissary for the Continental Army's military stores located in Lancaster, Pennsylvania. After the Treaty of Ghent brought the war to an end, Ingels returned to Philadelphia, and in 1787, he was appointed as the Pennsylvania inspector and measurer of lumber, then an important position that supplied the military. When Pennsylvania approved of the new federal Constitution in 1787, it was Ingels who carried the "Carpenter's Company" banner and marched at the head of 450 architects and carpenters in support of the Constitution.[1] In the 1790s he joined the new Democratic–Republican Party and gained election to the Pennsylvania State House of Representatives, where in the fall of 1800 he cast his presidential electoral vote for Thomas Jefferson.

In 1801, prominent Philadelphia Democratic–Republicans Robert Patterson (professor at the University of Pennsylvania) and Andrew Ellicott (astronomer, mathematician, and land surveyor who mentored Meriwether Lewis as he and William Clark prepared for the Corps of Discovery) recommended President Jefferson consider Ingels for the position of superintendent of military stores for the United States. Ingels, the Democratic–Republicans informed Jefferson, was "a suitable person" for the office having served in a similar position during the revolution. Despite the recommendation, Jefferson appointed William Irvine to the position.[2] A year later, Patterson encouraged Jefferson to appoint Ingels to the vacant military storekeeper position at the Schuylkill Arsenal; Ingels received the appointment in April 1802.[3]

When Irvine unexpectedly died, Dearborn appointed Ingels as superintendent of military stores and as superintendent of the Indian trading houses until the president could appoint a replacement. In October 1804, Ingels petitioned Jefferson asking the president to appoint him as head of military stores and Indian trade, a request the president did not grant.[4]

While Ingels was appointed to Irvine's position of superintendent of the Indian trading houses, he remained in his position as military storekeeper. When Dearborn reorganized the Office of Indian Trade in the winter of 1805, he assigned responsibility for overseeing Indian trade to William Davy, a Philadelphia merchant. Ingels remained in Philadelphia as military storekeeper through the conclusion of the War of 1812. George W. Ingels died in 1827 at the age of eighty-one.

CHAPTER 4

William Davy

Superintendent of the Indian Trading Houses
(March 26, 1805–April 21, 1806)

WILLIAM DAVY was the last superintendent of the Indian trading houses before Congress reorganized the Office of Indian Trade on April 21, 1806. Davy was born in Fordton in the parish of Crediton, Devon, England, in 1757.[1] A man of means, Davy, "out of curiosity about America," left England with his family and servants in June 1794, arriving in Philadelphia on August 15. By December, he was corresponding with George Washington regarding his views on American commerce and agriculture, describing for the president that wool could be "advantageously manufactured in America" with minimal labor.[2] Within six months, Davy had established a mercantile in Philadelphia, quickly becoming a successful merchant with a residence in Germantown.

Davy befriended Secretary of State Timothy Pickering in 1797. When the United States entered into an undeclared naval war with Barbary Coast pirates, Davy, in March 1800, outfitted the privateer *Alexander*, commanded by his son, John. President John Adams then commissioned Davy to seize any and all French vessels found in American waters. His privateering proved lucrative, netting $34,600 from a single vessel in 1806.[3]

By 1804, Davy was so well connected that he was being invited to presidential events, including those with President Jefferson. He was elected to the Society of the Sons of St. George at Philadelphia, established to advise and assist Englishmen in need. When Dearborn reorganized the Indian trading houses, he selected Davy as its new superintendent. In this role, Davy segregated his duties related to military stores from those of Indian trade, believing such separation promoted efficiency and enabled him to better manage both offices.

When the House Committee on Commerce and Manufacturing questioned Dearborn's authority to appoint Davy as superintendent, the secretary responded that his authority was implied in the act establishing the trading houses. The committee called for greater oversight of the system, having received numerous complaints from private hatters in Boston, Baltimore, New York, and Philadelphia that Davy was depriving them of the raw materials needed to support their industry by selling furs and pelts at limited auctions in Philadelphia and closing the lucrative Detroit factory. Then, on April 21, 1806, Congress approved a reorganization of the trading houses and formally established the Office of Indian Trade, further separating military and civilian affairs.[4] The new office would be headed by a superintendent who was bonded, prohibited from engaging in Indian trade, and required to hold six public fur and pelt auctions annually—with no more than two in any one state.

Upon passage of the act, Davy resigned as superintendent, with Dearborn appointing Colonel John Shee to the position. Davy, meanwhile, continued his mercantile business. When the War of 1812 began, he was authorized by Congress as a US Marshal in Philadelphia to root out reports "of alien enemies" and act in conformity with State Department directives. In 1817, Davy accepted an appointment as American consul to England, where he remained until his death on September 11, 1827, at the age of seventy.[5]

CHAPTER 5

John Shee

Superintendent of Indian Trade (July 8, 1806–October 1807)

THE FIRST STATUTORY SUPERINTENDENT of Indian trade was John Shee, an Irish-born son of a wealthy family that immigrated to Philadelphia shortly after his birth in 1740. His father, heir to a large estate in Ireland, including the Ardanogroh Castle in County Westmeath in which John was born, established the shipping firm Walter Shee and Sons in Philadelphia. John, his brother Bertles, and their father were among the first to sign the nonimportation agreement drawn up in Philadelphia in 1765 to protest British revenue laws and taxes and boycott the importation of British goods.[1]

On July 3, 1776, Shee—on the recommendation of the Continental Congress—was elected commander of the Third Pennsylvania Battalion of Continentals. During the summer of 1776, the "Shees," as the Third Pennsylvania became known, found action in the Battle of New York, engaging in multiple battles over the next three years. On September 25, 1779, General Shee resigned his command to return to his family in Philadelphia, where he became a physician sometime prior to 1790. After the Revolutionary War, he resumed his business ventures and served as city treasurer between 1790 and 1802. Between 1802 and 1805, he served as flour inspector for the port of Philadelphia.

In November 1796, the War Department designated John Harris keeper of the military store in Philadelphia where he received funds and trade goods from the recently established federal factories or trading posts along the frontier and in Indian Country, and then disposed of such goods received in trade. On May 11, 1801, William Irvine, superintendent of military stores, assumed oversight of the factories. When Irvine died on July 29, 1804, George Ingels, military storekeeper in Philadelphia, assumed responsibility for both superintendent of military supplies and agent for Indian factories. Secretary of War Henry Dearborn appointed William Davy as principal agent for Indian factories on March 26, 1805. Davy was now responsible for both purchasing trade goods for the factories and dispensing of the goods—largely furs—received from the factory trade with the interior tribes. Davy assumed the duty of superintendent of military stores and purveyor of public supplies for the government factories.

The superintendent of Indian trade was established by Congress on April 21, 1806, after private hatters and furriers complained that the existing system of exchange under Davy was depriving them of the necessary raw goods for their trade. Davy, having closed the Detroit factory, organized auctions and sales in Philadelphia where he sold most of the goods received in trade from the Indians to foreign markets. In December 1805, forty-six Philadelphia hatters, as well as scores of others from Baltimore, New York, and Boston, asked Congress to intervene by demanding an accounting into and explanation of Davy's activities and the authorities under which he operated.[2]

Dearborn admitted that he had created Davy's office under the "implied authority" of the 1796 legislation establishing the factory system.[3] Davy defended himself by arguing that he had held multiple auctions but domestic hatters could only purchase a fraction of the furs the factory system procured. The House Committee on Commerce and Manufactures, however, agreed with the petitioners and elected to overhaul factory system oversight. In the process, Congress created an Office of Indian Trade to be managed by a superintendent of Indian trade. The office required the superintendent to not only take an oath and post bond, but also prohibited him from engaging in any private trade or exporting furs for his own profit. By statute, the superintendent was required to hold at least six public auctions each year, with no more than two in any one state.[4]

With passage of the act, Davy resigned, resuming his career as a merchant. On July 8, 1806, Dearborn appointed Shee as superintendent, making him responsible for supervising the increasing number of Indian agents, superintendents, and other personnel.[5] Housed within the War Department, the superintendent was the first full-time position in the federal service devoted to tribal affairs, reporting directly to the president. Shee, however, had little interest in the position, and when asked to relocate the Office of Indian Trade to Georgetown, he refused. He remained as superintendent only until President Jefferson offered him a more lucrative position.[6]

In October 1807, Jefferson offered Shee the position of collector of customs for Philadelphia. A more prestigious position than superintendent of Indian trade, Shee served as customs collector for less than a year. With the appointment of John Mason as the new superintendent, the Office of Indian Trade moved to Georgetown in the District of Columbia, where it remained for fifteen years before the factory system was terminated in 1822.[7]

Shee made no impact on Indian affairs other than in his role as a partner in the Illinois and Wabash Land Company that claimed to have purchased land by private deed in the Illinois Country from the Kaskaskia and Illinois tribes in 1773 and 1775.[8] This land was later ceded by the tribes to the United States by treaty in 1803. That year, and again in 1804, Shee petitioned Congress as the "last sole survivor" of the Illinois and Wabash Land Company to negotiate for control of the land. In 1804, Shee offered to "surrender and convey to the United States" the land in question on the condition that Congress reconvey to the company "one-fourth part of the said land," a proposition that the House of Representatives rejected since the company was not authorized to contract with the tribes for the lands.[9] Shee died in Philadelphia on August 5, 1808.

CHAPTER 6

John M. Mason

Superintendent of Indian Trade (October 1807–April 1, 1816)

JOHN M. MASON was born on April 4, 1766, in Mattawoman, Charles County, Maryland, to a politically prominent and wealthy family. His father, George Mason IV, was one of fifty-five delegates to the 1787 Constitutional Convention in Philadelphia, although he did not sign the Constitution due to concerns over the extent of federal authority. Mason was the fourth of five sons and the seventh of eight children born to George and Ann (Eilbeck) Mason. He spent his childhood at Gunston Hall enjoying all of the comforts and amenities of plantation life. Privately tutored until 1783, Mason then attended Stafford County Academy. He completed his education in 1786 studying mathematics, history, and natural and moral philosophy, after which he served a two-year apprenticeship to learn the art of mercantile trade at the home of the Quaker businessman William Hartshorne in Alexandria, Virginia.[1]

After his training with Hartshorne, Mason and two friends established the trading house of Fenwick, Mason and Company. While James and Joseph Fenwick remained in Maryland, Mason managed the business from Bordeaux, France. An ambitious and politically well-connected man, Mason sought an appointment to the US Consulate in Bordeaux only to see his friend Joseph Fenwick receive the appointment. Mason then closed the Bordeaux office and returned to the United States in 1791, and the following year he opened an office of Fenwick, Mason and Company in Georgetown, an action that was influenced both by the impending revolution in France and declining tobacco profits. By 1798, with the business thriving, Mason became president of the Bank of Columbia.

Friends with Presidents Thomas Jefferson, James Madison, and James Monroe, Mason and his wife, Anna Maria Murray, were active socialites, hosting numerous events at their home on Mason's Island (present-day Theodore Roosevelt Island). When Congress authorized the creation of a militia in 1802 for Washington, DC, President Jefferson appointed Mason as brigadier general, a post he retained until 1811, when he resigned due to conflicts with his duties as superintendent of Indian trade.[2] He continued to expand his business ventures to include shipping flour and trading wheat, as well as speculating in land that increased his wealth. He also invested in the Potowmack Canal Company in the 1790s, serving on the board of directors for thirty years.

Mason had high political ambitions. In October 1807, after Superintendent John Shee refused to move the Office of Indian Trade from Philadelphia to Georgetown in the District of Columbia, President Jefferson appointed Mason as the second superintendent of Indian trade at an annual salary of $2,000.[3] As superintendent, Mason swore an oath to avoid any direct or indirect interest in Indian "trade, commerce, or barter," a matter that was complicated by his interests in the Potowmack Canal Company, which sought to expand its frontier trade with Indians and non-Indians alike.[4] Such trade was in competition with federal trading houses in Indian Country that bought and sold trade goods with the interior tribes, with such factories also designed to protect Indians from unscrupulous traders.

In a letter to Secretary of War William Harris Crawford, Mason expressed concerns that the federal trading houses diminished "Indian proceeds" and reduced the "esteem and fidelity" so necessary in the federal–Indian relationship. Moreover, such factories required the Indians to travel a "considerable distance" to trade, unlike British traders who brought their trade goods to the Indian villages. British traders, Mason explained, created competition for tribal loyalties, with such competition demanding that each trader "do the best business" possible or risk losing the trade. The United States should do the same, Mason argued, or it would risk losing the riches of the interior of the continent, including the immense wealth of the Missouri River basin.

Mason served eight and a half years as superintendent, greatly improving the factories, requiring each factor to submit quarterly accounts and inventories for his review. He asked Congress to remove the 1806 auction rule since it prevented the office from selling to the best market. Entertaining members of Congress regularly, Mason persuaded Congress to increase factor spending from $10,000 to $40,000 and to repeal the auction rule limitation.[5] By 1809, Mason was empowered by Secretary of War William Eustis to appoint factors without War Department approval, helping solidify Office of Indian Trade autonomy.[6] By 1810, Congress had granted most of the reforms Mason requested, including granting him complete approval over the sale of fur pelts. And with the prodigious treaty-making efforts of President Jefferson, Mason's Office of Indian Trade became responsible for the distribution of Indian annuities, further increasing its authority.

Mason remained superintendent until April 1, 1816, when he resigned to attend to personal business.⁷ The following year he became president of the Potowmack Canal Company, but he also began to suffer a series of financial setbacks, including the loss of most of his land along the Potomac River in present-day Arlington, Virginia, including Analostan Island. He lived his final days in Clermont, Virginia, where he died on March 19, 1849.⁸

Factories Diminish Indian Trade
The new method of conducting the Indian trade, for several years past, is the cause of a considerable diminution in the fur trade of the Missouri and Illinois Territories. The Government of the United States thought that, by establishing a system of factories, they would supply all the tribes of Indians, to their satisfaction, with all kinds of goods necessary for their consumption, at such low prices that by these means they would get all the furs and pelts of the Indians, and at the same time would also get their confidence, esteem, and fidelity. But, unhappily, this generous system has had a contrary effect. The diminution of the Indian proceeds, on the one part, and the diminution also of esteem and fidelity in almost all the tribes of Indians towards us in the late war, prove incontestably that the system of factories is not at all proper to conciliate the esteem of the Indians, and less so to obtain in the fur trade a preference over the strangers.

This kind of trade and the trade among whites are entirely different, and to consider them analogous would be erring considerably. It requires on the part of the trader a complete knowledge of the Indian customs, characters, habits, way of living, hunting, & c., to form his plans to trade with them, without which one will always err and fall from errors to errors.

The factories, such as they are now established, are trading-houses fixed at certain points under the protection of a fort, and more or less distant from the Indian villages. Though living at a considerable distance from those houses, Indians are obliged to go to them to trade. They get in exchange for their furs goods at a reasonable price, (however, the difference with strangers is only in powder, rifles, calicoes, saddles, wampum, and a few other articles.)

These factories never sell on credit, whereas, for many years past, Indians have been accustomed to buy in that way, as well from the traders of these two Territories as from the British. The credits are actually indispensable, because the hunting grounds being further than they formerly were, and Indians being obliged to go more than 300 miles from their villages to hunt, if they have not a sufficient quantity of furs to buy their winter goods, they miss their hunt, because it is too hard for them, once on the hunting spot, to return in winter to the factories, through snow and frost, to trade for whatever they want to continue their hunt; and what stops them the most is, the fear of leaving their families alone, exposed to war parties from the other tribes that are constantly going about in the winter season; and themselves, in going to the factories, are exposed to fall into the hands of their enemies: this having already been the case.

The great advantages that the British traders have obtained over the factories on the Mississippi are very well known; but to give an idea of them, I will suppose four British traders going to trade with a certain tribe of Indians; these four traders will certainly be in competition one against the other, and every one of them will try to do the best business; to do which they will carry with them what the Indians love the best in every way, and open their stores in the village of that tribe. Does [a tribe] start to hunt, they follow it by water from 150 to 200 miles, until the place where it stops to go in the interior of the lands. There the traders build houses, and a part of the Indians ther [sic] cabins or lodges. Each Indian hunter buys on credit, sometimes to the amount of $200, according to his reputation. Each trader does his best to sell on credit to those hunters, because it is a custom with the Indians that a family who has obtained goods on credit sells all its furs to the man who has advanced those goods. When the Indian hunters have left the river shore and are on their hunting ground, soon after, the traders try their best to get the furs of those Indians that have not bought on credit; to do that, they send in every direction, to the places fixed upon by the Indian to hunt, men with fancy goods. These men or engagés carry those goods on their shoulders through frost and snow, and do whatever is in their power to trade for the furs of those Indians that have not bought on credit from their employers or bourgeois, (it is what the Indian traders call running a *deouine*). I have gone through this long detail about the British traders, to show all the pains and means they make use of to obtain from the Indians their furs, and that, <u>if we want to go into competition with them, we must do the same; for to be stable on a certain fixed point is giving positively to the strangers</u> all kind of advantages in this kind of trade.

A New Means of Trade?
In the event of the abolition of the factories, the first inquiry that naturally presents itself is, what is to be substituted in place of them? Upon this

subject, I must, in the first place, refer to a publication in the *Ohio Navigator*, which was written by me in 1805, and published in 1811, folio 268, and was the result of fifteen years' observation and experience by myself. In that publication it will be seen that the Missouri only gave annually at that time an amount of $77,971. The same produce would fetch now at least one-third more, on account of the difference in prices; add to this sum the proceeds of the following rivers, St. Peter's, Red, Crow's Wing, and a great many more of the Mississippi that are not comprehended in the observations of 1805, then the sale of furs and peltries could be safely estimated annually (independent of the proceeds of all the trade with the Indian tribes of the Missouri above the Mahas and Poncas) at $150,000 at least.

To obtain all these furs, Government ought to establish at St. Louis a store, with a capital of about $100,000, which ought to be augmented according to the augmentation of the trade. That store ought to be furnished with all kinds of goods suited to the Indian trade, well assorted in quality and quantity, and the articles in proportion to the sum. These goods ought to be selected on the notes of a man who understands perfectly well the Indian trade, and who should also know exactly what suits every nation in particular.

That store, so established, could equip (without exclusive privilege) for the present about twenty-five or thirty traders for the Missouri, Mississippi, and all the rivers that empty in these two. But to enable these traders so equipped to enter into competition with the British traders, Government ought, as much as possible, to sell these goods at a very moderate advance, and take their furs and peltries at a reasonable price. By these means Government would employ its capital to the advantage of its citizens, to the annoyance of British traders, and I am bold to say it is the only means to destroy the British trade; besides which, our two Territories would be greatly benefited thereby.

Twenty-five or thirty traders would employ about two hundred men. The necessary expenses of shipping, and some other expenses, would produce the circulation of a trading medium in the country. Add to these the advantage of forming *voyageurs* fit for those sorts of voyages, which, by the bye, will certainly be of great consequence.

In the above notes I have not mentioned the Indian tribes which live above the Mahas and Poncas; these are the Sioux, divided in several tribes and under different names, the Arickaras, Mandans, Gros Ventres (Big Bellies,) Pieds Noirs (Black Feet,) and a great many others who are little known that inhabit the forks of the Missouri; and particularly those of the left side, which are very near the trading-houses of the Northwest Company of Canada: as to those of the right fork, on which there is a fall, known only since the voyage of Captains M. Lewis and William Clark.... The trade with these tribes cannot be made with any advantage but by a company well organized, and which could dispose annually of about $50,000 in goods, of which sum the company could not expect any good returns before the expiration of three years, that time being necessary to go to and examine the country, build forts on the places which would be thought convenient, make friends, and open the trade with those different tribes. I dare give here my decided opinion, which is founded on premises that I believe just, that a company well conducted, which should have the Indian trade (not exclusively) from Cedar island, above the Poncas, to all the forks of the Missouri, could bring down annually, (once well established,) from that extent of country, a considerable sum in furs and pelts, which could be estimated at more than $200,000. This sum will appear exaggerated, but I found my opinion on the returns of the Northwest Company of Canada, which, though not well known, on account of the profound silence they have kept on this subject, have been thought, through the observations of knowing men, to be at least £200,000 sterling; and this sum is principally got by the trade carried on with those tribes of Indians that reside in the neighborhood of the branches on the left side of the Missouri. To arrive at those trading places, that company incurs very great expenses, which are occasioned by the difficulty of the roads, being obliged to carry those goods in very small bark canoes; and when there is no water, those goods are carried on men's shoulders. The greatest difficulty for them, and which occasions a very great expense, is the carriage of their provisions to the different forts they have on that part of the northwest. The proposed company would have a decided advantage over that of the Northwest, because it would be able to carry its goods wherever it would fix its forts, in large barges, which would save considerable time and expense, as well for sending up their goods and food as for bringing down their produce. It might yet establish easily a fort near the village of the Mandans, or any other place which might be thought proper, and there plant corn, potatoes, &c., which would diminish greatly the expenses of transportation, and even make whiskey, this liquor being indispensable in this kind of trade. With these advantages, added to many others, the proposed company must annoy and even destroy the Northwest Company; but whoever undertakes this trade may be sure that the Northwest Company will do anything in its power, and even sacrifice large sums of money, to prevent that establishment. But if the agents of the proposed company that would be at the head of the business in the neighborhood of the Northwest Company, should act prudently, and have engagès that know well the trade, all the efforts of the Northwest Company would amount to nothing.

The mountains that are on the west side of the Missouri Territory offer riches more considerable than those of all the rest that have been mentioned, and the more advantageous, as there would be no competition on the part of any strangers. That country, covered by a great many Indian tribes, such as Laytanes, Rapahauts, Toquibacoux, and many others, wish and ask constantly to open a trade with us. But, unhappily, we have not yet capitalists and men of enterprise in these Territories; but we may hope that some will come, when this country will be known, and when people will appreciate its great resources in riches that are immense, which time and the enterprise of our citizens cannot fail to develop.⁹

CHAPTER 7

Thomas L. McKenney

*Superintendent of Indian Trade (April 12, 1816–May 6, 1822),
Chief Clerk (March 12, 1824–August 16, 1830)*

THOMAS LORAINE MCKENNEY was born on March 21, 1785, to a prominent eastern Maryland family. At the age of twenty-seven, the socially and politically ambitious McKenney enlisted in the US Army and served in the War of 1812. At the conclusion of the war, McKenney operated a dry goods business with his brother-in-law, while at the same time seeking a position in the federal bureaucracy. With John Mason's resignation as superintendent of Indian trade in April 1816, McKenney petitioned President James Madison for the job, with the president appointing him to the position on April 12, 1816. For six years McKenney administered the government trading houses (factories) along the frontier. Between 1816 and 1822, when Congress discontinued the trading houses, McKenney expanded the role of the superintendent of Indian trade into a clearinghouse for all Indian affairs, not just trade. Secretary of War John C. Calhoun not only supported his administration of Indian affairs and allowed McKenney to expand the office, including petitioning Congress to enact the Civilization Act of 1819, but he also advanced the establishment of a superintendent of Indian affairs.[1] Calhoun recognized that in the post–War of 1812 years there was more work than he could handle alone.[2]

When Congress terminated the trading houses on May 6, 1822, McKenney found himself out of work.[3] Calhoun, who repeatedly advocated for Congress to establish an Indian Office within the War Department, was elected vice president in November 1824, but not before he created a Bureau of Indian Affairs within the department. When a position opened up within the department, Calhoun administratively created a Bureau of Indian Affairs on March 11 and, a day later, appointed McKenney as head of the Indian Office with the title chief clerk.[4] In this capacity, McKenney unsuccessfully advocated for statutory authority for the department, cognizant of the fact that he had no authority outside of that given to him by Calhoun.

While President John Quincy Adams considered a "Home Department" for Indian affairs, Congress did not act on it. In 1829, however, a bill was submitted to Congress to codify the regulations of the Indian Office in its relationship with tribal nations, but it also failed to gain passage. Not until 1832 did Congress act to create a commissioner of Indian affairs.[5] By then, McKenney—who opposed Andrew Jackson's presidential campaign—was no longer in the Indian Office, having been notified by President Jackson on August 16, 1830, that his services were no longer required. McKenney left office on August 31, 1830.

McKenney advocated for a statutory basis of the Indian Office and supported the emigration of the tribes. Regarding the latter, he sought to delineate lands in the West for the emigrating tribes—outside the influences of the frontier element that so often had a deleterious effect on the Indians. To enforce emigration, he supported utilizing contractors rather than government agents, believing that contractors could execute emigration at a cost one-third lower than federal agents, in large measure because market forces would encourage efficiency. Perhaps more importantly, McKenney also recognized that missionaries and Indian agents often had differing views on emigration, with the former opposing it as a disrupting influence on the Christianization process (i.e., Samuel Worcester and the Cherokee Nation), while the latter, even though they were inclined to support emigration, were often socially connected to the missionaries, complicating emigration.

When Peter Buell Porter replaced James Barbour as secretary of war in May 1828, he found Indian affairs "perplexing." In an 1828 report, he added to the discussion of emigration by rhetorically inquiring what justice and humanity demanded of the United States with respect to the Indians. In response he argued American Indians needed to be protected and afforded basic security—especially those choosing to remain in the East. For those emigrating, they needed well-defined lands beyond the Mississippi River and a strategic plan of emigration. Part of this philosophical debate was the question: What were the rights of the Indians with regard to the land? Were they the rightful owners or mere tenants?[6] Porter concluded the latter, and he advocated for a policy of paternalism (guardianship) that ultimately included land severalty.

McKenney was a strong advocate for civilization, believing education was the key to elevating the Indians. But he also believed that Indians and white people could not live together—at least not until the former were civilized and the latter controlled their negative frontier attitudes. Consequently, McKenney supported

President Jackson's plan for removing the tribes to the western territories beyond the Mississippi River where they could be protected from encroachment and other deleterious influences. While seen as the father of the Indian Office and having "left a rich legacy," McKenney died in obscurity and poverty on February 20, 1859.[7]

Need for an Indian Department
A simple law, connecting the responsibilities of this branch of the public service with the Congress, and upon precisely the same basis as rests the other branches of the Department of War, followed by a well digested system of regulations for the better government of the diversified subjects which have to be acted on, would insure to the public, and the Indians, and the agents attached to the service, all that could be desired in the relations that exist between them. Without [a statutory basis for the Indian Office] things must, from necessity, continue in the future as they have been in the past, since no intelligence, however enlightened, nor industry, however untiring, nor experience, however universal, can remedy the evils complained of.

Justice and Humanity
I forbear also to remark . . . upon measures of general policy in regard to our Indians. The subject is growing in interest every day, and is surpassed only by the extreme delicacy of their situation, and of our relations with them. I refer especially to those whose territory is embraced by the limits of States. Every feeling of sympathy for their lot should be kept alive and fostered, and no measures taken that could compromit [sic] the humanity and justice of the nation. . . . But the question occurs. *What are humanity and justice, in reference to this unfortunate race?* Are these found to lie in a policy that would leave them to linger out a wretched and degraded existence, within districts of country already surrounded, and pressed upon by a population whose anxiety and efforts to get rid of them are not less restless and persevering than is that law of nature immutable, which has decreed that, under such circumstances, if continued in, *they must perish?* Or does it not rather consist in withdrawing them from this certain destruction, and placing them, though even at this late hour, in a situation, where, by the adoption of a suitable system for their security, preservation, and improvement, and at no matter what cost, they may be saved and blest. . . ? That something must be done, and done soon, to save these people, if saved at all, it requires

no very deep research into the history of the past, or knowledge of their present condition, embracing especially their relation to the States, to see.[8]

Surely when States, in the exercise of their sovereignty, are extending their laws over a people whose chiefs admit (I refer to the Cherokees) that such a measure would "*seal their destruction*," and when every circumstance appears to have combined to render the great body of our Indians within the limits of States unhappy, and to impoverish and destroy them, something ought to be done for their relief. Justice demands it, and Humanity pleads for these people....

Emigration of the Tribes
A new difficulty has arisen in regard to the Cherokees and between them and the State of Georgia. It relates to boundary.... No report has been received from Gen. Coffee, who was appointed to collect and report all the facts touching the controversy. The Cherokees, however, have furnished the Department, through the Agent, with the grounds upon which they rest their claim to the boundary for which they contend.

In reference to emigration, and to the means necessary for its accomplishment, I beg leave respectfully to add, that, in lieu of the usual mode of *estimating*, for all the different branches of expenditure, upon the basis of numbers, for rations, transportations, &c. &c., which can never be done with certainty, (it not being possible to know beforehand how many will go,) a sum be appropriated and made applicable to emigration *generally*, and to compensation for improvements, and placed at the disposal of the Executive; and for this object I recommend the sum of $300,000 dollars [sic]. It is my opinion, also, that a great saving might be effected by changing the agencies for emigration from the local agents to contractors. I have seen nothing to induce a belief that the Agents employed among the Cherokees and Creeks have not been zealous; but it does appear to me that a saving of more than one-third of the cost of each emigrant could be realized upon contract. The Agents might be well employed, and usefully and abundantly, in co-operating, and especially in seeing that all the terms of the contracts in which the comfort, and health, &c., of the emigrants were concerned, were faithfully executed.

But it does appear to me as indispensable, that, as a first step in any great movement of the sort, the country on which it is proposed to place these people at rest, and forever, should be clearly defined, and nothing left un-provided for by the Government, that concerns either their security, preservation, or improvement. Nor should the emigrants be sent off to settle where and how they might list; but the whole business should, I respectfully submit, be conducted upon one regular and systematic plan; and what may be done in reference to the whole of it ought to be done with a view to their solid and lasting welfare.⁹

A Duty of Paternalism and Guardianship
At the commencement of our present Government, these tribes, with few inconsiderable exceptions, occupied a country in the interior, far beyond the range of our population, and our relations with them, were the simple ones which exist between remote and independent nations, or they were rather the relations of war; and most of our intercourse with them was carried on through the officers of the Army, stationed along our frontier posts; and it was, probably, to the posture in which we then stood in regard to them, that the War Department was first indebted for the Superintendency of Indian Affairs. Since that period, our white population, in its rapid and irresistible progress to the west, has been sweeping past and around them; until now, a large proportion of these tribes are actually embosomed within the organized and settled parts of our States and Territories. . . .

While some of our citizens, who are the advocates of primitive and imprescriptible rights in their broadest extent, contend that these tribes are independent nations, and have the sole and exclusive right to the property and government of the territories they occupy, others consider them as mere tenants at will, subject, like the buffalo of the prairies, to be hunted from their country whenever it may suit our interest of convenience to take possession of it. These views of their rights and disabilities are equally extravagant and unjust: but the misfortune is that the intermediate line has never been draw by the Government. Nothing can be more clear to one who has marked the progress of population and improvement, and is conversant with the principles of human action, than that these Indians will not be permitted to hold the reservations on which they live within the States, by their present tenure, for any considerable period. If, indeed, they were not disturbed in their possessions by us, it would be impossible for them long to subsist, as they have heretofore done, by the chase, as their game is already so much diminished, as to render it frequently necessary to furnish them with provisions, in order to save them from starvation. In their present destitute and deplorable condition, and which is constantly growing more helpless, it would seem to be not only the right, but the duty of the Government, to take them under its paternal care; and to exercise, over their persons and property, the salutary rights and duties of guardianship....

If the project of colonization be a wise one, and of this, I believe, no one entertains a doubt, why not shape all our laws and treaties to the attainment of that object, and impart to them an efficiency that will be sure to effect it? Let such of the emigrating Indians as choose it continue, as heretofore, to devote themselves to the chase, in a country where their toils will be amply rewarded. Let those who are willing to cultivate the arts of civilization be formed into a colony, consisting of distinct tribes and communities, but placed contiguous to each other and connected by general laws, which shall reach the whole. Let the lands be apportioned among families and individuals in severalty, to be held by the same tenures by which we hold ours, with perhaps some temporary and wholesome restraints on the power [of] alienation....

In regard to such Indians as shall still remain within the States, and refuse to emigrate, let an arrangement be made with the proper authorities of the respective States in which they are situated, for partitioning out of them, in severalty, as much of their respective reservations as shall be amply sufficient for agricultural purposes. Set apart a tract, proportioned in size to the numbers of Indians, to remain in common, as a refuge and provision for such as may be improvidence, waste their private property; and subject them all to the municipal laws of the State in which they reside.[10]

CHAPTER 8

William Clark

Superintendent of Indian Affairs (May 28, 1822–March 12, 1824)

WILLIAM CLARK, of Lewis and Clark fame, was born on August 1, 1770, in Caroline County, Virginia, the ninth of ten children born to the Virginia planters John and Ann Rogers Clark. While Clark did not receive a formal education, he was tutored at home and was considered well read. While five older brothers—including George Rogers Clark—served during the American Revolution, Clark, being too young, did not. With the end of the war, the Clark family moved west near present-day Louisville, Kentucky.[1]

At the age of eighteen, Clark joined a volunteer force of local militia engaging tribal nations who were defending their homelands, including the Shawnee and Wea. In 1790, General Arthur St. Clair commissioned Clark as a captain in the Indiana militia. His military career continued until 1796, when poor health forced his return to the family plantation near Louisville. In 1803, his good friend Meriweather Lewis tapped Clark as his partner for the Corps of Discovery. Lewis and Clark spent the next three years exploring the upper Louisiana territory and the Pacific Northwest via the Missouri and Columbia Rivers and their tributaries, gaining a vast knowledge of both the physical and cultural landscape of the region.[2]

As a result of this vast knowledge of the West and Clark's understanding of the tribes in the Missouri River basin, President Thomas Jefferson appointed Clark brigadier general of the Louisiana militia and an Indian agent overseeing trading houses, including the one in St. Louis. With the administration of President James Madison, Clark was appointed the first territorial governor of Missouri, being reappointed to three consecutive terms until Missouri gained statehood in 1821. As territorial governor, Clark served as ex officio superintendent of Indian affairs where he was universally respected by the Indians and known as a capable administrator.[3] In a run for governor of the state of Missouri in 1820, Clark lost to his friend Alexander McNair.

When Congress abolished the Indian trading houses in May 1822, it also repealed the role of the superintendent of Indian trade based in Washington, DC, leaving a void in the administration of Indian affairs. To fill the gap in administration, Congress, on the same day it abolished the trading houses, authorized a new position of superintendent of Indian affairs, with President James Monroe then nominating, and the Senate confirming, Clark as superintendent of Indian affairs for the St. Louis Superintendency. Three territorial governors—William Cass from the Michigan Territory, James Miller from the Arkansas Territory, and William Duvall of the Florida Territory—were made ex officio superintendents, with the governors continuing in their roles until their positions were abolished by act of Congress.[4] In receiving his commission as superintendent, Clark was directed by Secretary of War John Calhoun to exercise "control over the Indian agencies on the Mississippi and Missouri."[5]

Clark remained superintendent of Indian affairs until his death, although he only exercised sole discretion while reporting to Calhoun between May 28, 1822, and March 11, 1824, when the Bureau of Indian Affairs was informally established within the War Department. When Calhoun administratively organized a Bureau of Indian Affairs on March 11 and appointed Thomas McKenney as chief clerk, Clark's role became subservient and he reported to McKenney.

As superintendent, Clark issued licenses to Indian traders, administered justice along the frontier, negotiated treaties, and engaged in diplomacy with the tribes west of the Mississippi River, including those recently removed from the East. He also enforced President Andrew Jackson's policy of Indian removal, calling it "his duty."[6] Over his career as Indian agent and superintendent, Clark negotiated or was part of thirty-seven ratified Indian treaties.[7] He remained superintendent until his death in St. Louis on September 1, 1838, at the age of sixty-eight.

CHAPTER 9

Samuel S. Hamilton

Chief Clerk (September 30, 1830–August 31, 1831)

A CAREER WAR DEPARTMENT BUREAUCRAT, Samuel S. Hamilton was born in the 1780s in Maryland. He joined the War Department immediately after the War of 1812 and was assigned to the Indian Office in 1824 as one of two clerks assisting Thomas McKenney. Between 1824 and 1830, he oversaw all incoming correspondence from the Indian agencies and superintendencies. When President Jackson relieved McKenney of his role as chief clerk, Hamilton sought the position, with Jackson appointing him as McKenney's successor on September 30, 1830.

Hamilton served less than one year as chief clerk and had limited influence on Indian policy. He drafted just one annual report (1830), in which he recommended Congress appropriate funds for all Indian annuity payments in a single appropriation bill rather than in separate bills as was then the case. The funds would then be delegated to the Indian Office for distribution to the Indians. He also encouraged Congress to update the Non-Intercourse Act to better handle depredation claims against the tribes.

Secretary of War John Eaton largely ignored Hamilton's recommendations, and most of the authority for Indian affairs remained in the secretary's office. Consequently, Hamilton largely implemented the decisions of Eaton rather than making his own. When Eaton resigned in August 1831, Jackson replaced him as secretary with Lewis Cass, who in turn relieved Hamilton of his services as chief clerk. His last day in office was August 31, 1831, with Cass's new appointee, Elbert Herring, assuming office two weeks prior on August 12. Hamilton then resumed his former position as clerk within the Indian Office before he unexpectedly died in 1832.[1]

Hamilton served at the time of implementing the Indian Removal Act, an act Andrew Jackson demanded and secured from Congress in May 1830.[2] As chief clerk, Hamilton had limited influence on policy, with many in the federal bureaucracy viewing him as more of a caretaker than a leader. His only report touched on emigration of the tribes, annuity adjustments, and depredation reform. His only significant contribution to the Indian Office came in his role as clerk in 1826 when he compiled a list of Indian treaties, laws, and regulations relative to Indian affairs, an action directed by Secretary of War Calhoun.³

Annuities
The first act providing for Indians annuities, and which is still in force, was passed in 1796.⁴ Other acts for the same object have been since passed, from time to time, as they were required by new treaties, which are limited or permanent, according to the treaty stipulations for which they are intended to provide.⁵ A part of the provisions of some of them, though not directly repealed, has been superseded by treaties or acts of more recent date; hence it is difficult (except for persons who are familiar with these changes) to distinguish the provisions that are still in force from those that are not. There are now twenty-one acts under which Indians annuities are drawn, and they require as many accounts to be opened and kept on the books of the Treasury. If the same system be continued, every new treaty that stipulates for an annuity will necessarily increase the number of acts for that object, and, of course, the number of accounts. I, therefore, respectfully submit, whether it be not desirable to change the system, and adopt one which is more simple, and will require less time and labor to execute it. This, I humbly apprehend, may be attained by repealing all the existing acts of appropriation for annuities, and embodying the whole in one act, to be passed annually, on a statement to be laid before Congress at the commencement of every session, showing the annuities due, and to be provided for, in the ensuing year. This would keep Congress annually informed of the state of the Indian annuities, and the actual amount required from year to year to pay them. The appropriation might be made in one sum, equal to the whole amount of annuities due for the year to be provided for, or for the specific sums due, for such year, to each nation or tribe. In either case, it would never require more than one account to be opened on the books of the Treasury. . . .

Need for Updating the 1802 Non-Intercourse Act
The act to regulate trade and intercourse with the Indian tribes, and to preserve peace on the frontiers, passed in 1802, is the principal one that governs all our relations with the Indian tribes.⁶ Since this act was passed,

many treaties have been concluded, which, with other causes, growing out of the increase of our population, and the consequent extension of our settlements, have contributed to produce changes in our Indian relations, which, it would seem, required corresponding changes in the laws governing them. It is believed that the line defined by the act of 1802 as the Indian boundary, and to which its provisions were intended particularly to apply, has long since ceased to be so. It is, therefore, respectfully submitted whether the public interest does not, also, require such a modification of the act of 1802 as would better adapt its provisions to the present state of our Indian relations. A judicious modification of this act, and others connected with it, (embracing some specific provision for the adjustment of the claims for depredations, &c., which are provided for by the 4th and 14th sections) would, no doubt, greatly facilitate and open the way for other improvements in the administration of the affairs of the Indian Department, of which the claims for depredations just mentioned form no unimportant or inconsiderable part.[7]

CHAPTER 10

Elbert Herring

*Chief Clerk (August 12, 1831–July 9, 1832),
Commissioner of Indian Affairs (July 10, 1832–July 2, 1836)*

ELBERT HERRING became the first person to hold the title of commissioner of Indian affairs after Congress statutorily established the position in July 1832. Born in Stratford, Connecticut, on July 8, 1777, Herring graduated from Princeton College in 1795 before becoming a New York attorney and judge. A close friend of New York Governor DeWitt Clinton and Secretary of War Lewis Cass, Herring was politically well connected. Cass, a loyal supporter of President Jackson's emigration policy, requested the president appoint Herring as chief clerk of the Indian Office. He took office on August 12, 1831, and became a strong advocate for the emigration of the tribes, believing removal outside of the states and beyond the menacing corruption of ruthless frontiersmen was the only way to prevent the ultimate destruction of the Indians. In his words, emigration would elevate the "savage" to the "social" and with it knowledge of agriculture, private property, and Christianity.

The challenges of emigration of the tribes overwhelmed the Indian Office, leading Jackson to introduce legislation calling for a commissioner of Indian affairs with a central office serving as a statutory clearinghouse for all matters Indian. The commissioner of Indian affairs was born in the midst of an emigration policy thought to be the means of saving the Indians from destruction. Despite Herring's shortcomings as an administrator, Jackson and the Senate accepted Cass's recommendation to appoint Herring as the first commissioner of Indian affairs. He assumed office on July 10, 1832.

The Indian Office negotiated scores of treaties during Herring's term in office, often employing bribery and interfering in tribal political affairs to gain the desired outcome. Herring rationalized this meddling as promoting Indian welfare by encouraging emigration. As a result, emigration of the tribes was viewed through the lens of promoting civilization. Emigration consumed the Indian Office, and with the eastern states emptied of tribal nations, Cass urged Congress to enact two laws in 1834 to reflect the new realities. A revised Non-Intercourse Act reflected new treaty boundaries and tribal obligations, including licensure of traders, while a reorganization of the Indian Office updated administrative lines of communication through the creation of a superintendent of Indian affairs based in St. Louis to oversee all western tribal affairs outside of any state or territory.[1]

Herring argued education was the key to advancing the Indians to the social state. He was an ardent supporter of the Choctaw Academy and its focus on the mechanical arts, believing such an institution could send its graduates to Indian schools west of the Mississippi River to encourage civilization among the western tribes. Such schools could also encourage family members to leave tribal life for civilized life.

Herring stressed the fundamentals of policy, opining emigration and education were essential to the survival of the Indians. The humane policy of the government was to educate the Indians in civilization, Christianity, and morals. In short, the Indians were to be assimilated. Schools of mechanical arts would train the Indians in agricultural and mechanical trades. To his credit, Herring recognized that not all Indians should engage in agriculture; they needed to be exposed to all of the trades. Only then, Herring supposed, would the Indian stand as a man equal to his white brother.

Emigration was even more fundamental to the social elevation of the Indians. Herring argued that absent emigration, the Indians would rapidly become extinct. Only government "magnanimity" could save the Indians, and this could only be done by removal to the West. To ensure success, Herring advocated a policy of order and organization in process and delineation of Indian lands in execution. While each tribe would have its own land base, all tribes would be adjacent to each other. Since there was no guarantee federal protection would prevent extinction of the Indians, Herring argued for education that engaged the "physical exertion" and "intellectual exercise" of the Indians. In so doing, the social would supersede the savage.

Herring was never fully supported by President Jackson, and after Cass's departure as secretary of war, the president relieved Herring as commissioner on July 2, 1836, transferring him to a position as paymaster within the War Department. Late in 1836, Herring returned to New York where he resumed his legal career. He died in New York City on February 20, 1876, at the age of ninety-eight.[2]

Emigration as the Only Humane Policy

Many Indian youths, who have . . . received the benefits of tuition, have already returned to their respective tribes, carrying with them the rudiments of learning, the elements of morals, and the precepts of religion, all apparently calculated to subdue the habits, and soften the feelings of their kindred, and to prepare the way for the gradual introduction of civilization and Christianity. That such will be the result of the intellectual and moral cultivation of a portion of the young of their respective tribes, on the life and character of the Indians in their confederacies, cannot be predicted with certainty . . . .

The humane policy, exemplified in the system adopted by the Government with respect to the Indian tribes residing within the limits of the United States, which is now in operation, is progressively developing its good effects; and, it is confidently trusted, will at no distant day, be crowned with complete success. Gradually diminishing in numbers and deteriorating in condition; incapable of coping with the superior intelligence of the white man, ready to fall into the vices, but unapt to appropriate the benefits of the social state; the increasing tide of white population threatened soon to engulf them, and finally to cause their total extinction. The progress is slow but sure; the cause is inherent in the nature of things; tribes numerous and powerful have disappeared from among us in a ratio of decrease, ominous to the existence of those that still remain, unless counteracted by the substitution of some principle sufficiently potent to check the tendencies to decay and dissolution. This salutary principle exists in the system of removal; of change of residence; of settlement in territories exclusively their own, and under the protection of the United States; connected with the benign influences of education and instruction in agriculture and the several mechanic arts, whereby social is distinguished from savage life.[3]

Kindred benefits may be calculated on in the institution of the comprehensive scheme, adopted by the Government for the removal of the Indian tribes to territories in the west . . . . Contiguity of white settlements had invariably tended to depreciate the Indian character. The evil was always without counterbalance of possible good, either present or in reversion, and was always accompanied by a demonstration of decreasing population. It was evident, that they must either be left to the fate that was gradually threatening their entire extinction, or that the Government, by some magnanimous act of interposition, should rescue them from approaching destruction, and devise a plan for their preservation and security. From such benign considerations arose the generous policy of transferring their residence, and congregating their tribes, in domains suited to their condition, and set apart for their use. In the consummation of this grand and sacred object rests the sole chance of averting Indian annihilation. Founded in pure and disinterested motives, may it meet the approval of heaven, by the complete attainment of its beneficent ends. . . .

The public lands west of the Mississippi, yet unappropriated, far exceed, in quantity, what the comfort and welfare of the unprovided tribes may be possibly supposed to require. A sufficient territory will therefore be assigned to each individual tribe; and definite boundaries between the domains of the different tribes will be permanently established, to prevent dispute, and guard against collision on this head. . . .[4]

The Social for the Savage
On the whole, it may be a matter of serious doubt whether, even with the fostering care and assured protection of the United States, the preservation and perpetuity of the Indian race are at all attainable, under the form of government and rude civil regulations subsisting among them. These were perhaps well enough suited to their condition, when hunting was their only employment, and war gave birth to their strongest excitements. The unrestrained authority of their chiefs, and the irresponsible exercise of power, are of the simplest elements of despotic rule; while the absence of the *meum* ["what is mine"] and *tuum* ["what is thine"] in the general community of possessions, which is the grand conservative principle of the social state, is a perpetual operating cause of the *vis inertiae* of savage life. The stimulus of physical exertion and intellectual exercise, contained in this powerful principle, of which the Indian is almost entirely void, may not unjustly be considered the parent of all improvements, not merely in the arts, but in the profitable direction of labor among civilized nations. Among them it is the source of plenty; with the Indians, the absence of it is the cause of want, and consequently of decrease of numbers. Nor can proper notions of the social system be successfully inculcated, nor its benefits be rightly appreciated, so as to overcome the habits and prejudices incident to savage birth, and consequent associations of maturer years, except by the institution of separate and secure rights in the relations of property and person. It is therefore suggested, whether the formation of a code of laws on this basis, to be submitted for their adoption, together with certain modifications of the existing political system among them, may not be of very salutary effect,

especially as co-operating with the influences derivable from the education of their youth, and the introduction of the doctrines of the Christian religion; all centering in one grand object—the substitution of the social for the savage state.[5]

Education
In a former report, [education] was adverted to, and arguments that spontaneously presented themselves were then introduced in support of the views there taken in relation to the subject of Indian instruction in the mechanical arts, as a material part of the system of education. These, in fact, must become, if not the first, the principal step in the ladder that leads from the aboriginal to the civilized state. However agricultural may be the prevailing disposition or pursuit of any mixed community, nothing is more clear than the position that all cannot be agriculturists. Diversity of inclination, physical adaptation, and especially the positive requirements in society for the productions of mechanical skill and labor, set at nought so illusive an opinion. Employments must be found in a wholesome condition of society, suited to different tastes and capacities. But fitness for employment presupposes instruction and acquaintance with the several branches in which it is exercised, by us denominated trades. Apprenticeship only can produce able workmen; and it is believed that the mechanic arts can be the more readily grafted on the Indian stock through the means of mechanical instruction as a part of the system of education patronised by the Government.

These suggestions are offered under a firm persuasion of the capability of the Indian to take his station, through the ameliorating process of letters and the arts, by the side of the civilized man. And surely all will admit that there is a well-founded claim on our sympathies in behalf of the Indian race, when it is considered that our territories were once the hunting grounds of their forefathers, and that our cities occupy the former sites of their wigwams and villages. Humble instruments in the hands of Providence, let us lend our aid to the red man's helplessness, and assist him to ascend where civilization spreads its wide expanse, creative of new impulses, and affording a more genial home to his affections, a richer harvest for his exertions, and a brighter atmosphere for his intellectual vision.[6]

CHAPTER 11

Carey Allen Harris

Commissioner of Indian Affairs (July 4, 1836–October 19, 1838)

CAREY ALLEN HARRIS was born on September 23, 1806, in Williamson County, Tennessee, and at the age of eighteen, he joined his future father-in-law at the *Nashville Republican*, a publication to which President Andrew Jackson subscribed. In 1827, the state of Tennessee licensed Harris as an attorney and he began practicing law, with the goal of relocating to Washington, DC, and joining the federal bureaucracy. After moving to the nation's capital, Secretary of War Lewis Cass employed Harris as a clerk within the War Department. Harris quickly impressed Cass with his work, and the secretary rewarded the young Tennessean with a chief clerk position. Such was Cass's trust in Harris that when Cass was out of the office, Harris served as acting secretary of war. By the mid-1830s, Harris was part of President Jackson's inner circle, and on July 4, 1836, the president appointed Harris as commissioner of Indian affairs.

As commissioner, Harris executed the removal policy and strengthened federal control over the emigrant tribes. With the election of Martin Van Buren as president in the fall of 1836, the president-elect retained Harris as commissioner to ensure the continuity in the execution of the emigration policy. Harris, however, was surrounded by rumors over his alleged involvement in speculating in Creek land allotments in Alabama. Jackson, aware of the allegations, but lacking proof of wrongdoing, stood by his commissioner.

As commissioner, Harris reasoned the course of federal–Indian relations pointed to three principal goals. These in turn dictated his actions and management of the Indian Office. These goals included the emigration of all the tribes from the East to lands west of the Mississippi River and southwest of the Missouri River; the establishment of territorial government for the emigrant tribes, including federal control and oversight of tribal governments; and civilization of the Indians via education in the mechanical arts and agriculture.[1]

Harris was a model supporter of the emigration of the tribes, opining it was the only way to save the Indians from complete and utter destruction. He advocated removal of the Cherokee from Georgia, Tennessee, and North Carolina; the Creek from Alabama; the Chickasaw from Mississippi; and the Seminole from Florida. Speed and economy trumped the well-being of the Indians, with Harris believing the use of threats, fraud, and cajoling were a necessary means to an end. As for the northern tribes, Harris sought the emigration of the Iroquois from New York and the smaller tribes from Ohio, Illinois, and Indiana.

As emigrated tribes settled in the West, Harris believed federal control and supervision was essential, with the commissioner arguing that the federal government should establish civil and legal codes for the tribes. The United States should oversee tribal governments until such time as the tribes could govern themselves. Such oversight, Harris argued, would also assuage the apprehension of the smaller tribes to emigrate since they feared oppression by the more powerful and larger tribes. Harris postulated one means of removing the apprehension of the smaller tribes was to establish federal military posts in the trans-Mississippi Indian territory.

Harris advocated for federal control notwithstanding the pledge President Jackson had made in an address to Congress regarding the Indian Removal Act to respect the right of tribal self-government and tribal control over their lands in the West. By the late 1830s, the president's pledge to respect the rights of the tribes to remain free of outside interference and to exercise sovereignty over their lands faded. As to what the federal–tribal relationship might look like, Harris referred to the 1778 Delaware Tribe's treaty with the United States, whereby the latter offered the former the headship of an Indian confederacy and representation in the US Congress.[2]

The commissioner also promoted the civilization of the emigrant tribes by seeking to plant schools throughout Indian Country in the West, with missionaries instructing the Indians in the mechanical arts, agriculture, and "intellectual education." Such an approach would not only civilize the Indians but would also discreetly serve as a form of social control as they adjusted to new ways. Such common schools in the Indian Country, Harris added, would reduce apprehension related to education and promote tribal affinity for schools. Bringing tribal leaders to Washington, DC, and other eastern seaboard cities was one means of impressing them with the military and industrial capacity of the United States.

By the fall of 1838, President Van Buren had evidence of Harris's involvement in land speculation and requested his resignation effective October 19.[3] Harris then moved to Little Rock, Arkansas, where he died of tuberculosis on June 17, 1842, at the age of thirty-five.

Emigration
The general result (of the emigration of the tribes) is, that within the last eight years, 93,401,637 acres of land have been ceded by the Indians, for which the United States have stipulated to give them $26,982,068 dollars (sic) and 32,381,000 acres of land, valued at $40,476,250 dollars (sic), making the whole consideration $67,458,318 dollars (sic).

The obvious reflection . . . is the <u>increased liberality and kindness of the United States in its intercourse with the aboriginal people</u>. . . . An examination of the earlier treaties will show how little proportion the sums paid bore to the quantity and value of the land acquired. Ten, twenty, or thirty cents per acre were seldom exceeded. The average sum . . . is seventy-two cents per acre. In the late treaties with the <u>Chickasaws</u> and some other tribes, the provisions have been even munificent, the United States having given to them <u>the whole net proceeds of their lands</u>.[4]

The increased extent and diversified character of the operations under the direction of this office . . . embrace negotiations with the tribes east of the Mississippi, for the extinguishment of their titles: with those of the western prairie, for the establishment of friendly relations between them and the United States; and with the indigenous and emigrated tribes beyond the Mississippi and Missouri rivers, for the adjustment of difficulties and the preservation of peace. . . .[5]

Federal Oversight
President Jackson suggested "the propriety of setting apart an ample district west of the Mississippi, and without the limits of any State or Territory now formed, to be guaranteed to the Indian tribes, as long as they shall occupy it; each tribe having a distinct control over the portion designated for its use." "There," he observed, "they may be secured in the enjoyment of governments of their own choice, subject to no other control from the United States, than such as may be necessary to preserve peace on the frontier and between the several tribes. . . ."[6] "[N]o better plan can be thought of, than that the United States shall put in operation such a system of Indian protection and government, west of the Mississippi, as that a confidence may be reposed that they are indeed our fostered children, and the Government not only so disposed to consider, but practically to

evince their good feelings towards them. At present an objection arises with the weaker tribes. They are indisposed to emigrate, from an apprehension that powerful and stronger neighbors may oppress them, and that no surer protection can be obtained from the United States in the west, than is possessed already where they reside. To remove such apprehensions will be of importance.

I beg leave to suggest for your consideration, if an Indian territory, without the range of western States and Territories, might not be advantageously created; and to give efficiency and to inspire confidence, military posts, under some able and discreet officer of the army, to be designated at some central and convenient point. Intrusions from the whites might thus be restrained, and the Indians maintained in quiet with each other. Laws for their general government and to preserve peace amongst the tribes, to be the act of the United States, with a right to the Indians in council to make their own municipal regulations."[7]

[T]he south bank of the Missouri and the Platte rivers as the northern boundary of the proposed territory . . . [is] estimated [to] contain an area of 132,295,680 acres. [A proposed bill in Congress] pledged the faith of the country to the Indians for its perpetual possession; it gave to each of the tribes the right to maintain a government for the regulation of its own internal concerns; it provided for the appointment by the President, with the concurrence of the Senate, of a governor and secretary; it directed that a council should be assembled by the governor, or the chiefs of the various tribes, to which should be submitted a proposition, to assent "to such of the provisions of this act, as require the co-operation of the authorities of the respective tribes;" and that the contemplated confederation should not take effect until the Choctaw, Creek, and Cherokee tribes gave their assent thereto.

According to its provisions, a general council of the tribes joining the confederacy, elected by the tribes, or selected by the chiefs, as the governor might determine, was to be held annually, whose duty it should be to make all necessary regulations respecting the intercourse among the various tribes; to preserve peace; to put a stop to hostilities; to settle any questions of dispute respecting boundaries; to arrest and punish all Indians who may commit offences within the district of one tribe, and who may flee to another, and generally, to take such measures as may be necessary. . . .

A [second] bill was introduced, "to provide for the security and protection of the emigrant and other Indians west of the State of Missouri and of the Territory of Arkansas." This bill reserved the lands, described in the preceding one, for the use of the various tribes who have or may have a right to the same. It was to be called "the Indian Territory," and to be secured to the tribes forever. A superintendent of Indian affairs and a secretary were to be appointed by the President, with the advice and consent of the Senate. Each tribe might establish such government and laws for the regulation of its internal concerns, as it thought proper. Any three or more tribes might form a confederation with each other, for the purpose of regulating the intercourse and preserving peace among such tribes, and of defending themselves from the aggressions of other tribes.

It provided further, that the Choctaw, Creek, and Cherokee tribes should be invited by the superintendent to unite in a general council to form such confederation; and that any other of the tribes might become parties to it. After its formation a general council should be held annually, the members to be chosen in the manner that might be pointed out in the articles of confederation; The powers of this council were [internal], with the important exceptions, that it was not authorized itself to raise a force to support the government, nor could the troops of the United States be employed to give effect to its regulations and laws. Only in the event of "an aggression having been or being about to be committed by a foreign tribe, or by one of the tribes in said territory on a tribe therein," might the superintendent call upon the other tribes or the troops of the United States for military aid. . . .

It is worthy of remark, that the proposition, to admit a delegate from the Indians to a seat in the national council, was first made to them by the United States, during the war of the revolution. In the 6th article of the treaty with the Delawares, of September 17, 1778, "it is further agreed on between the contracting parties, (should it for the future be found conducive for the mutual interest of both parties,) to invite any other tribes, who have been friends to the interest of the United States, to join the present confederation, and to form a State, whereof the Delaware nation shall be the head, and have a representation in Congress."

Education

The communications that have been received upon this subject show the existence of a strong desire among the tribes, generally, for the education of their children. The Chippewas and Ottawas in the Northwest desired that a very liberal provision should be made for this object in the last treaty concluded with them. The United nation of Chippewas, Ottowas, and Potawatomies, who are emigrating from Illinois, have preferred an earnest request, that the interest of seventy thousand dollars, appropriated for education under the treaty with them of September 26th, 1833, may be applied to the support of schools in the country to which they are removing. Even more ample means were set apart for this purpose, in the treaty with the Cherokees of December 29, 1835. The schools among the Choctaws are favorite institutions with them.... The Shawnees and Delawares have been improved by the labors of the instructors, who for many years have lived with them.... The Civilization Fund is distributed, principally, with a view to the improvement of those Indians residing upon the remote frontier, and those for whom no provision has been made by treaty. The sums allowed have been expended under the direction of the various societies, by whom teachers have been employed.

In all these establishments, instruction in mechanical arts and in agriculture is combined with intellectual cultivation. There is an increasing disposition among the Indians to have [schools] located in their own country, where they become objects of common feeling and interest, and the ties of family and kindred are not separated or weakened.[8]

It is believed that the visits of the several tribes to [Washington, DC] and to others upon the seaboard, has had, and will have a most salutary effect. So far as a correct judgment can now be formed, they will return to their kindred with just ideas of the strength and resources of the country, and of the friendly dispositions of our people towards them, and impressed with the conviction of the propriety of remaining at peace with us and with each other....[9]

CHAPTER 12

Thomas Hartley Crawford

Commissioner of Indian Affairs (October 22, 1838–October 29, 1845)

THOMAS HARTLEY CRAWFORD was born on November 14, 1786, to an upper-class family in Chambersburg, Pennsylvania. After graduating from Princeton College in 1804, he studied law for three years before passing the bar and setting up a law practice in Chambersburg. He was elected as a Jacksonian Democrat to the Twenty-First and Twenty-Second Congresses (1829–1833) before serving in the Pennsylvania State House for one term (1833–1834). In 1836, President Jackson appointed him to a commission investigating allegations of land fraud on Creek allotments in Alabama, with the commission's report issued in 1838 culminating in the resignation of Commissioner Carey Allen Harris.[1]

With the removal of Harris, on October 22, 1838, President Martin Van Buren appointed Crawford as commissioner of Indian affairs, a position in which he remained for seven years. Crawford served four presidents: Van Buren, William Henry Harrison, John Tyler, and James K. Polk. President Polk (Whig) asked for and received his resignation on October 29, 1845. During his tenure in office, Crawford focused on expediting emigration of the tribes, promoting peaceful Indian–white relationships by attempting to correct trade discrepancies and abuses, and accelerating civilization through coeducation. He worked closely with Secretary of War Joel Poinsett to improve communications, especially between the central office and the field agencies, and he advocated for creating field inspectors and increasing the remuneration of Indian Office staff, proposals that Congress rejected.[2]

Congress and the administration supported Crawford's efforts to expedite emigration of the tribes, with the Indian Office negotiating thirteen treaties during Crawford's tenure as commissioner.[3] Crawford concluded there were but three options for the Indians. They could integrate with the white population, an option he thought individual Indians might accept but not whole tribes; they could emigrate to British Canada, although he did not support such a move since he believed the Indians would be driven back by cold weather to the United States; or they could move west with their kindred tribes or be placed on small reservations and taught the morals and values of white Americans and enjoy the protection of the United States.

Crawford was also concerned about the continued abuses the Indians received at the hands of traders and whiskey peddlers, both of which kept the Indians in debt and poverty by taking advantage of their willingness to purchase goods at almost any cost. While not advocating for the return of the federal factory system that Congress terminated in 1822, Crawford proposed stocking each Indian agency with "necessities" that could be sold to the Indians at cost and paid for by their annuities. This would promote amity between Indians and whites, and in time, the former would come to view "the Government as their best friend."

Finally, to accelerate civilization, Crawford emphasized coeducation. The means by which to accomplish civilization of the Indians was not only to replace tribal customs and cultures with American values and mores, but also by educating girls to be future wives and mothers who would cradle the emerging civilization among the Indians by lifting their husbands and children into morality and thrift. Without effecting change among females, the instruction of Indian boys would be like a "rope of sand." To this end, Crawford advocated for local manual labor schools, each with a farm or "plantation" attached to demonstrate yeoman farming and industrious housewifery and home care. The best and brightest graduates of the Indian schools could then be sent to off-reservation institutions for advanced learning and then return to the reservations as teachers.

Six months after the election of President James Polk, the president requested the resignation of Crawford. He then appointed Crawford as judge of the criminal court of the District of Columbia, where he served until 1861, when the court was reorganized. Crawford died in Washington, DC, on January 27, 1863, at the age of seventy-seven.[4]

Emigration Is Their Destiny
One of three destinies awaits [the] Indians. First, they may become . . . incorporated into the mass of our population, and partake of all our privileges. I wish I could think so. An Indian of more than ordinary cleverness may occasionally fix himself among us, or even a very small body of partially civilized Indians, and live and die there, respectable and respected; and even these are exceptions to the general rule. But, that a mass of wild and savage men should, in a body, attach themselves to a civilized

community, and the mass, being decomposed quietly flow off in different channels into and through the social superiority around them, is what has never happened when both bodies were free, and ever will happen. There are too many sources of disagreement—too much in each that would grate upon the habits and feelings of the other.

If I be correct in the opinion, that with rare exceptions, this is not to be expected, there remains for them removal alone; and the neighborhood of the British possessions, with the presents annually distributed there by authority, makes that quarter alluring in spite of the inhospitality of the climate, and the rigors of a winter that will freeze up their energies and efforts, if not their life-blood. We should take all possible pains to save them from adopting this alternative. We feel it incumbent on us to save them if we can: at least we are able to stay their downward course. If they should fix themselves permanently in Canada, it cannot be for good; for they would forfeit their interest in the annuities and other benefactions due from the United States. If (as is most probable) they should be driven by tempests and snows into our territories again, it would be with wasted means, more corrupted morals, and enervated bodies. Politically, it does not strike me as deserving of the consideration and weight usually given to it, whether they shall go or remain on our soil.

The most beneficial course remains. The Indians, when they must leave their present homes, which they have or shall have ceded away, must remove among their kindred tribes north and west of them, or to a country to be provided at the public expense. They will not be permitted to sit down in or among other tribes; and the aversion to it has been fixed by the fact, that those who have [lately] sold their lands, and who would wish to throw themselves on the liberality of their kinsmen or kindred tribes, have refused (and rightly) to allow any to participate in the consideration of their grants, who did not live on, and had not an interest in, the land conveyed. The expectation of relief to them from that quarter cannot . . . be indulged.

The only expedient—the wisest, the best, the most practicable and practical of all—now presents itself: to purchase whatever land may be necessary, in addition to what we now possess, to enable us to secure to the beneficiaries . . . a home and a country free from the apprehension of disturbance and annoyance, from the means of indulging a most degrading appetite, and far removed from the temptations of bad and sordid men; a region hemmed in by the laws of the United States, and guarded by virtuous agents, where abstinence from vice, and the practice of good morals, should find fit abodes in comfortable dwellings and cleared farms, and be nourished and fostered by all the associations of the hearthstone.[5]

Trade and Annuity Abuses
The love of change, which is so striking a characteristic of civilized man, except in the highest stages of refinement and wealth, is not known to the character of the Indian, whose natural indolence and pride, and a long course of unbroken traditionary customs, bind him to his original cast. A tree is scarcely more tenacious of the earth than a savage man of his habits; hence the great difficulty of meliorating his condition.

The experience necessarily given me by the discharge of official duty . . . exhibits so conclusively the unmixed recklessness with which Indians buy whatever is placed before them, with a total disregard of the adaptation of the thing bought to their real wants or means of payment, of the amount they purchase, or its price. . . . I refer not to naked frauds, but to actual sales of goods, in many instances of good quality, but frequently wholly unfit for Indian use, and as unsuitable often from the quantity purchased and enormity of the price as from the nature of the articles themselves. If downright dishonesty is practised by the seller, his license may be revoked, and he dismissed from the country; but when he sells sound goods, according to the course of the trade, extravagant though the prices may be, and the articles useless to the buyer, the case seems to be without remedy short of a modification of the system, which in any form to which it can be shaped must be defective, for it is radically so. Its evils spring out of the cupidity of the American citizen, and the general imbecility his customer. Let the trader be never so honest, the Indian cannot resist the temptation of purchasing to a shockingly extravagant extent; and the merchant, fearing the decline of his business if he does not gratify improvident fancy or whim, extends his credits. The debts thus made swallow up the next annuity, leaving the Indian still in debt, and a new account follows. Sometimes the enormous amounts thus run up are lost, or at best the creditors await a cession of land by the Indians to the United States.[6]

The factory system, or the plan formerly pursued, I would not reestablish if I could; but its principle is valuable. . . . I would make a small establishment of goods, suitable to Indian wants, according to their location, at each agency. I would not allow these goods to be sold to anyone except Indians entitled to a participation in the cash annuities, and I would limit the purchases to their proportion of the annuity; so that the

Government would, instead of paying money to be laid out in whiskey and beads, or applied to the payment of goods at two prices bought from others, meet the Indians to settle their accounts, and satisfy them that they had received, in articles of comfort or necessity, the annuity due them for the year, at cost, including transportation. The Indians would be immensely benefited; and the expense would not be greater than that of the money payments now almost uselessly made them. . . . The accounts would be annually settled as quickly as the money payments are made, for each party would recollect every purchase. The agents would have the weight and consideration they ought to have with the Indians; while the latter would feel that the Government was their best friend, would be taught to look to it alone for aid in any emergence, and manifest their attachment to it under all circumstances. It cannot be doubted that this is the secret of the great attachment of the Indians to the British Government. Their donations, as well as dues, are received directly from the officers of the Queen, with much parade and ostentation; and the head of the Government is studiously represented as the fountain of all benefaction. This, it is true, would not be desirable under our form of government; nor could it be done, where all the branches of the administration together represent the sovereignty which rests in the people; but they, or some of their chiefs, have penetration enough to see that the large sum of money paid them annually by us are swept away by their own improvidence and the cupidity of others—o en without any essential benefit, sometimes to their positive injury. To do them good—to give them what they want at what it costs—to deal with them justly and kindly too—to address their understandings through their necessities, and by supplying comforts, cannot fail to conciliate them.[7]

Manual Labor and Co-Education
The principal lever by which the Indians are to be li ed out of the mire of folly and vice in which they are sunk is education. The learning of the already civilized and cultivated man is not what they want now. It could not be advantageously ingra ed on so rude a stock. In the present state of their social existence, all they could be taught, or would learn, is to read and write, with a very limited knowledge of figures. There are exceptions, but in the general the remark is true, and perhaps more is not desirable or would be useful. As they advance, a more liberal culture of their minds may be effected. . . . To attempt too much at once is to insure failure. You must lay the foundations broadly and deeply, but gradually, if you would succeed. To

teach a savage man to read, while he continues a savage in all else, is to throw seed on a rock. In this particular there has been a general error. If you would win an Indian from the waywardness and idleness and vice of his life, you must improve his morals, as well as his mind, and that not merely by precept, but by teaching him how to farm, how to work in the mechanic arts, and how to labor profitably; so that, by enabling him to find his comfort in changed pursuits, he will fall into those habits which are in keeping with the useful application of such education as may be given him....

Manual labor schools are what the Indian condition calls for.... [We have a plan] ... for establishing a large central school for the education of the Western Indians. Into [this] scheme enter a farm, and shops for teaching the different mechanic arts.... [It] may not be improper to state that the funds which have been set apart for education purposes belong to the several tribes, without whose consent the Government could not devote them to a general school.... But whatever reform may be deemed advisable in the direction and economy of the separate schools, it appears to me that if the proposed central school shall be established, they should be kept up, too. They may, perhaps, be more numerous than is necessary or advantageous; they may be too expensively conducted, or more scholars ought to be taught for the money expended, or they may be badly located; but each, or all, of these objections may be obviated, and the schools improved. For such minor institutions, would not the central school be able to furnish teachers? [A] certain number of young Indians of capacity should yearly leave the central school qualified to be instructors, who shall make compensation for their own education by teaching as long as might be thought a suitable return? After such a plan had been in operation three or four years there would be an annual supply.[8]

One great mistake has, I think, been made. In every instance that is now recollected, more boys are educated than girls, and the preparatory arrangements seem to contemplate it. Upon what principle of human action is this inequality founded? All experience and observation throughout the world argue against it. Unless the Indian female character is raised, and her relative position changed, such education as you can give the males will be a rope of sand, which, separating at every turn, will bind them to no amelioration. Necessity may force the culture of a little ground, or the keeping of a few cattle, but the savage nature will break out at every temptation. If the women are made good and industrious housewives, and taught what befits their condition, their husbands and sons will find comfortable homes and social enjoyments, which, in any state of society, are essential to morality and thrift. I would therefore advise that the larger proportion of pupils should be female. The effect may not be, and, I presume, will not be suddenly perceived, but they will acquire influence and weight, and must form, in a good degree, there as elsewhere the characters of their children. Without this ever busy and ever affectionate auxiliary there can be no radical success. Failure, substantially, so far, has marked the kind and beneficent agency of the Government and of good men and benevolent societies—if the manual labor system and a liberal extension of female instruction shall also prove unavailing after years of trial, then, but not until then, the hope of the philanthropist may be abandoned. . . .[9]

CHAPTER 13

William Medill

Commissioner of Indian Affairs (October 28, 1845–June 30, 1849)

WILLIAM MEDILL was born in February 1802 in New Castle County, Delaware, to Irish emigrants William and Isabella Medill. After graduating from Newark Academy in 1825, Medill studied law, and in 1830, he was admitted to the bar in Delaware before moving to Lancaster, Ohio, where he was admitted to the Ohio bar two years later. He entered Democratic politics in Ohio, and in 1835, he was elected to the state legislature, where he served two years as speaker of the House. In the fall of 1838, he was elected as a Van Buren Democrat to the US House of Representatives for two terms in the Twenty-sixth and Twenty-seventh Congresses; he failed to win reelection in 1843.[1]

With the election of James Polk as president in 1844, Van Buren supporters advocated the president-elect to appoint Medill to a prominent position within the federal bureaucracy; Polk appointed Medill as second assistant postmaster. When the commissioner position became available with the resignation of Thomas Crawford in the fall of 1845, Polk appointed Medill as head of the Indian Office. He took office on October 28, despite having no experience in Indian affairs.

Medill faced several challenges as commissioner, including reducing government spending; promoting civilization; reforming Indian trade; and dealing with the impacts of a rapid western advance of Americans into and across Indian Country. To address the first challenge, Medill consolidated Indian agencies and subagencies, which in turn freed up funds that he argued could be used to better remunerate—and attract—Indian Office employees. To promote civilization, he advocated for manual labor schools in Indian Country, and using civilization act funding, he encouraged the hiring of missionaries to educate Indians. He also proposed abandoning all Indian schools in the East, believing the focus of civilization should be in the West where the tribes were concentrated.

Reforming Indian trade and dealing with the rapid expansion of the United States proved to be more challenging. As for the former, Medill opposed paying cash annuities to traders for Indian debt, arguing they intentionally kept Indians in indebtedness, leading to debauchery, disease, and shortened lives. In 1847, he advocated updating the Non-Intercourse Act to include imprisonment for anyone selling alcohol to Indians and, at the discretion of the Indian Office, making lawful the paying of annuities to family heads. Medill also proposed indemnifying the government of all individual Indian debt to traders and prohibiting the use of tribal annuities for such debt since it was individual not corporate. This was a proposition traders vehemently opposed as interfering with their profits. Ensuring that annuity funds went to heads of families would also fulfill congressional intent. In the end, Congress agreed with imprisonment for those selling alcohol to the Indians and with the Indian Office having the discretion to distribute annuity payments to heads of family but no more.[2] Medill's efforts to curb trader abuses, however, failed when Interior Secretary Thomas Ewing overturned his annuity plans and agreed to pay funds directly to the traders.

It was in the area of western expansion that Medill had his greatest impact. With the emigration of tribes largely completed, non-Indians believed the legal conundrum of sovereign tribes within the borders of sovereign states was settled. Then, in rapid succession, the United States secured its interests in the Oregon Country, annexed Texas, and concluded the Mexican War by acquiring the Southwest. This unleashed a flurry of emigrants across the Plains through the heart of the recently established Indian Country. The issue now was how to maintain order on the frontier, address the complaints of the Indians over lost and destroyed resources along the western trails, and protect the settlers heading west.

With no civil government yet established in the western territories to implement federal policy, Medill had no authority to appoint Indian agents or implement policy until Congress amended the Non-Intercourse Act. To address the matter, Medill suggested a modification to Indian Country by proposing to establish two large "colonies" (or reservations) for the Indians, one in the north and one in the south. Border tribes in the middle would be relocated again to clear a path for the emigrants heading west. The colonies would theoretically protect the Indians from lawless white people, facilitate the teaching of agriculture and the mechanical arts, and enable the establishment of manual labor schools. Medill was sowing the seeds of the reservation policy.

Before such a policy could be implemented, Congress created the Department of the Interior on March 3, 1849, and moved the Indian Office into the new executive department. In November 1848, Zachary Taylor (Whig) was elected president and forthwith appointed Ewing as the first secretary of the interior. Ewing strongly supported the traders, and in April 1849, he issued policy allowing annuities to be paid directly to traders to cover Indian debt. When Taylor offered Orlando Brown the position of commissioner, Medill's days were numbered and he left office on June 30, 1849. He returned to Ohio where he resumed his involvement in state politics, gaining election as lieutenant governor (1852–1853) and then governor (1853–1855), before losing to Salmon P. Chase in the 1855 governor's race. Between 1857 and 1861 he served as the first comptroller of the United States (under President James Buchanan), retiring due to poor health in 1861. He died in Lancaster, Ohio, on September 2, 1865, at the age of sixty-three.[3]

Manual Labor Schools
A portion of these [manual labor school] funds has heretofore been applied to the education of boys at literary institutions in the various States, and even to the preparation of some of them for the practice of the learned professions; and although important advantages have thereby resulted in the diffusion of information among the different tribes, yet it is believed that the money can now be more beneficially expended at the homes and in the midst of the Indian people. The prejudices of the red man will be thus more easily overcome, and the benefits extended alike to both sexes of the tribe.

In manual labor schools knowledge of letters will go hand in hand with the acquirement of a practical use of the tools of the artisan and the implements of the farmer. Those which have already been established in the Indian country afford abundant evidence of the advantages of the system, and its superiority over any other plan of education for the Indians which has yet been tried or suggested. To induce the untutored savage to enter upon any new course of conduct, or to adopt any plan of operation, or of subsistence, different from that to which he has always been accustomed, you must convince his senses that some beneficial result is certainly to follow. He must experience the advantages, in order to appreciate them. Let him merely look on and observe the white man laboring in his fields and maturing his crops, and he learns comparatively nothing but place in his hands the plough, the axe, and the hoe, and teach him to use them; let him see the product of his labor in the abundant yield of the necessaries and comforts of life; and then, and not till then, can you exemplify to him the difference between the civilized and the savage state. Let him sit down amidst his family and his people during the inclemency of winter, surrounded by the fruits of his labor, raised at a more congenial season, and he will soon be able to appreciate the difference between the hard and precarious life of a hunter and that of an agriculturalist.[4]

Time and experience are essential to the development and correct application of all systems of instruction. The practice so long pursued of selecting a few boys from the different tribes, and placing them at our colleges and high schools, has failed to produce the beneficial results anticipated; while the great mass of the tribe at home were suffered to remain in ignorance. It has, therefore, been nearly abandoned, and will be entirely discontinued as soon as existing arrangements will justify a withdrawal of the boys who are now at such institutions, and all the means and resources at the disposal of the Department applied to the establishment and maintenance of manual labor and other schools in the Indian country. The advantages will in this way be extended to both sexes, and be more generally diffused among the great body of the tribe.[5]

Displacement from the Land Is Not Unusual
While, to all, the fate of the red man has, thus far, been alike unsatisfactory and painful, it has, with many, been a source of much misrepresentation and unjust national reproach. Apathy, barbarism, and heathenism must give way to energy, civilization, and Christianity; and so the Indian of this continent has been displaced by the European; but this has been attended with much less of oppression and injustice than has generally been represented, and believed. If, in the rapid spread of our population and sway, with their advantages and blessings to ourselves and to others, injury has been inflicted upon the barbarous and heathen people we have displaced, are we as a nation alone to be held up to reproach for such a result? Where, in the contest of civilization with barbarism, since the commencement of time, has it been less the case than with us; and where have there been more general and persevering efforts, according to our means and opportunities, than those made by us, to extend to the conquered all the superior resources and advantages enjoyed by the conquerors? Of the magnitude and extent of those efforts but little comparatively is generally known.[6]

Diminishing Annuities
[The treaty with the Chippewa, Ottawa, and Pottawatomie] embraces an entirely new principle, by which, after a certain period, should there be any decrease in the number of the tribe, their annuities are to diminish

in proportion so that their general interests and resources will remain the same in proportion to numbers, instead of increasing with any decrease of the tribe. The operation of this principle will, it is believed, be salutary. The practice has been to stipulate a fixed sum for the annuities of the different tribes with which treaties have been made, so that in case of a decline in numbers the general and individual interests of those remaining are proportionately increased. The greater the resources of a tribe the greater the hope and chance of gain by whiskey sellers and other interested and avaricious persons; and hence the inducement to such persons to encourage dissipation and debauchery among the Indians, calculated to engender disease, and to shorten and destroy life, when the resources of the survivors would be thereby augmented, and their chances of gain increased. Hence, also, the liability of those of a tribe not addicted to such self-destructive habits, feeling less interest in, and making less exertion for, the welfare of their more unfortunate brethren, by whose deaths they would be benefited....

I have become satisfied that there is no evil so great to which a tribe can be subjected as the possession of resources, not the fruit of their own industry and frugality, in the form of large and extravagant annuities. They lead to indolence and to other habits, which not only prevent their moral and social improvement, but tend eventually to their corruption and diminution, if not extermination. When misapplied or withheld for their own benefit by the chiefs, into whose hands they are by law made payable, as is more or less liable to be the case, dissatisfaction, and even strife and bloodshed may be the result. When duly paid over to all those entitled, the Indian, who is naturally improvident and has little regard for money when it comes into his possession, after supplying his temporary wants, has the means of living for a time, independent of industry or exertion, in idleness and profligacy, until the indisposition to labor or the habit of intemperance becomes so strong, that he degenerates into a wretched outcast, and eventually parts even with his actual necessaries in order still longer to avoid exertion for a subsistence or to obtain the means of further indulgence in drink; thus reducing himself to a state of the greatest want and suffering. It would be far better for every tribe if the means at their own disposal, which are not derived from their own industry, were sufficient only to satisfy such actual necessities and wants as they could not provide for by their own exertions; so that they would have no surplus to tempt them into idle and dissipated habits, or to make them victims to be preyed upon by depraved and avaricious whites.[7]

CHAPTER 13

Colonizing the Indians

It may be said that we have commenced the establishment of two colonies for the Indian tribes that we have been compelled to remove; one north, on the head waters of the Mississippi, and the other south, on the western borders of Missouri and Arkansas, the southern limit of which is the Red river. The northern colony is intended to embrace the Chippewa's of Lake Superior and the Upper Mississippi, the Winnebagoes, the Menomonies, such of the Sioux, if any, as may choose to remain in the region, and all other northern Indians east of the Mississippi (except those in ... New York) who have yet to be removed west of that river.

The southern boundary of this colony will be the Watab river [in Minnesota], which is the southern limit of the country of the Winnebagoes, who have removed there from Iowa within the last year. The Menomonies, now residing near Green Bay in Wisconsin, are to be located above and adjoining the Winnebagoes, a treaty having recently been concluded with them to that effect. Above these, our northern boundary line, and westward to the Red river of the north, the country is owned by the Chippewas, many of whom now live there, though they still own a large tract east of the Mississippi, computed at 10,743,000 acres.... But with reference to the civilization and welfare of these people, it would be a wise and even necessary measure, to purchase all the lands they own east of the Mississippi, and concentrate them altogether upon those that would still remain to them west of that river....

If the Kanzas river were made the northern boundary of the southern colony there would be ample space of unoccupied territory below it for all the Indians above it that should be included in this colony. But the Delawares, Pottawatomies, and possibly the Kickapoos, who, or nearly all of whom, are just above that river, it would not probably be necessary to disturb. Above these, and on or adjacent to the frontier, are the band of Sacs and Foxes [of the Missouri], the Iowas, the Ottoes and Missourias, the Omahas, the Poncas, and the Pawnees....

The other tribes [Ponca, Omaha, Iowa, and Sac and Fox] can gradually be removed down to the southern colony, as the convenience of our emigrants and the pressure of our white population may require; which may be the case at no distant day, as the greater portion of the lands they occupy are eligibly located on and near the Missouri river, and from that circumstance, and their superior quality, said to be very desirable. Indeed, it would be a measure of great humanity to purchase out and remove the Omahas and the Ottoes and Missourias at an early period, particularly the former, who are a very interesting people, being mild and tractable in disposition, and much attached to the whites. Were they in a better position, they might, with proper measures, be easily civilized, and be made the instruments of imparting civilization to others. Their proper position would be with the Osages or Kanzas, as they speak nearly if not quite the same language, and are probably of the same primary stock. They are the original owners of the soil, and receive no annuities from the United States; and they are circumscribed in their hunting expeditions by the Sioux and Pawnees, they are liable at times to destitution and great suffering. The Sioux also not unfrequently attack and murder them in their own country, so that their situation is truly an unfortunate one. Their country is estimated to contain from five to six millions of acres of valuable land, which could be obtained at this time at a very moderate price. . . . Reasons of a similar kind exist for buying out and removing at an early period, the Ottoes and Missourias, whose affinities of character and language are said to be with the Iowas. The lands claimed by them are estimated to embrace from two to three millions of acres. These two measures consummated, the Pawnees all removed north of the Platte, and the Sioux of the Missouri restrained from coming south of that river, there would be a wide and safe passage for our Oregon emigrants; and for such of those to California as may prefer to take that route, which I am informed will probably be the case with many.[8]

CHAPTER 14

Orlando Brown

Commissioner of Indian Affairs (June 30, 1849–July 1, 1850)

ORLANDO BROWN was born on September 26, 1801, to a distinguished Kentucky family, with his father John Brown serving as Kentucky's first representative to the US Congress. Brown graduated from Princeton University in 1820 and then studied law at Transylvania University in Lexington. By 1833, he was the editor of the *Frankfort Commonwealth*, where he defended the Union, opposed nullification, and rejected Southern views regarding states' rights. He soon became an ally of John Crittenden, the Whig statesman from Kentucky. In 1848, Crittenden appointed Brown Kentucky's secretary of state.

The election of Zachary Taylor (Whig) as president in 1848 renewed hope that Kentucky would secure its share of political spoil. In June 1849, President Taylor appointed Brown commissioner of Indian affairs, and he took office on June 30. Brown was reluctant to accept the position, doing so not because of any pecuniary reward but a desire "to serve the country." While intending—and expected—to send patronage back to Kentucky, Brown was stymied by Interior Secretary Thomas Ewing, who not only controlled the spoil but also determined policy for the department. Brown quickly realized he had little political influence and even less opportunity to bring home patronage.

Brown's role as commissioner was largely one of executing policy. He agreed that manual labor schools were part of the "moral and social revolution" occurring in Indian Country. He also believed that the United States had a moral duty to assist the Indians in achieving civilization since it was the American people who had displaced the Indians from the land and now enjoyed the fruits thereof.

The western migration of settlers to California and Oregon in the late 1840s created difficulties with the border and Plains tribes, with the latter complaining of the invasion of their land and the destruction of its resources. Ewing proposed a treaty with the Plains tribes in 1849 and directed Brown to make the diplomatic arrangements. In his only annual report, Brown recommended all of the border tribes be placed on reservations far from the trails heading west. He also requested independent superintendencies for the newly acquired western territories in order to interact with and control the tribes. Congress refused funds for both the treaty and additional superintendencies, with sectional politics over governance of the western territories dividing the nation. Moreover, Democrats refused to give Whigs any advantage in establishing territorial governments in the West until such sectional differences (i.e., the question of slavery in the new territories and popular sovereignty) were resolved.

Ewing continued to control the Indian Office, and because of his support for Indian traders in the payment of annuities, Congress investigated his actions and relationship with the traders. Brown was guilty by association, and lost what little influence he had. On May 22, 1850, he offered his resignation, effective July 1. He returned to Kentucky and largely refrained from politics. He was considered "one of the most learned men" to serve as commissioner of Indian affairs, but he was also one of the least successful. He died on July 26, 1867.[1]

Reduce Indian Lands by Creating Reservations
The great destruction of the buffalo by the emigrants has caused much dissatisfaction among [the tribes], as it has more or less interfered with their success in the chase, and, if continued, must, at no late day, so far diminish this chief resource of their subsistence and trade, as not only to entail upon them great suffering, but it will bring different tribes into competition in their hunting expeditions, and lead to bloody collisions and exterminating wars between them, in which some of our border Indians will become more or less involved, and the peace and security of our frontier may thus be seriously disturbed. It is also much to be feared, that the unfavorable feelings engendered by the circumstances named may, at an early period, break out into open hostilities on the part of the Indians, which would be attended with serious consequences to our emigrants, or compel the Government, at an enormous expense, to afford them protection by the employment of a large military force on both routes. Under these circumstances, it has been deemed expedient and advisable to take measures to bring about a proper understanding with the Indians, which will secure their good will, prevent collisions and strife among them, by obligating each tribe to remain as much as possible within their respective districts of country, and providing that, where disputes or difficulties occur, they shall be submitted to the Government and the Indians abide by its decision. Instructions have

accordingly been given to hold a treaty with the different tribes, making provisions for the accomplishment of these objects, and stipulating that, for the unrestricted rights of way through their country, for their good conduct towards our emigrants, and for the destruction of game unavoidably committed by them, they shall be allowed a reasonable compensation annually; to consist principally of presents of goods, stock, and agricultural implements, with assistance to instruct and aid them in cultivating the soil, and in other kindred pursuits, so that they may thus be enabled to sustain themselves when the buffalo and other game shall have so far disappeared as no longer to furnish them with an adequate means of subsistence.[2]

The situation of some of the smaller border tribes . . . requires the attention of the Government. Most, if not all of them, possess an extent of country, which, however desirable originally, with reference to their maintaining themselves by the chase, now that the game has become scarce, is not only of no use, but a positive disadvantage to them; as it has a tendency to keep them from concentrating and applying themselves with any regular or systematic effort to agriculture and other industrial pursuits. They are also thus thrown into detached and isolated positions, which renders them more liable to be attacked and plundered, as is too frequently the case, by larger and stronger tribes; and from which they would be safe if brought nearer together, so that they could aid and sustain one another, and protection could be more conveniently and promptly extended to them by the Government. Another good result of their being more concentrated would be, that the good example and more prosperous state of those more advanced in civilization, would exert a powerful influence upon those less so, and stimulate them to exert themselves to produce a like change in their condition and circumstances; while at the same time, it would enable the Government, without any enlargement in the scale of operations, or any increase of expenditure, to extend to a great number the benefits of its policy and measures for their civilization and improvement....

A prominent feature of this course of policy should be . . . that the smaller tribes scattered along the frontier, above the Delawares and Kickapoos, embracing the Sacs and Foxes of the Missouri, the Iowas, the Ottoes and Missourias, the Poncas, and, if possible, the Pawnees, should be moved down among the tribes of our southern colony, where suitable situations may be found for them, in connection with other Indians of kindred stock. Such an arrangement, in connection with the change which must inevitably take place in the position of the Sioux, would . . . open a wide sweep of country between our northern and southern Indian colonies, for the expansion and egress of our white population westward, and thus save our colonized tribes from being injuriously pressed upon, if not eventually overrun and exterminated.³

The measures to which we are principally indebted for the great and favorable change that has taken place, are the concentration of the Indians within smaller districts of country, where the game soon becomes scarce, and they are compelled to abandon the pursuit of the chase, and to resort to agriculture and other civilized pursuits, and the introduction of manual labor schools among them, for the education of their children in letters, agriculture, the mechanic arts, and domestic economy. . . . As has heretofore been strongly done, I would, therefore, urgently recommend the increase of that sum [$10,000 for the civilization of the Indians] to at least fifty thousand dollars; as an act of liberality and humanity towards a helpless and destitute people, whom we have displaced, and whose former possessions we enjoy; and who unless the fostering care of the Government be extended to them, must continue to decline and soon disappear, leaving us as a legacy, a constant source of regret, if not self-reproach, in our having done too little to avert their melancholy fate.⁴

CHAPTER 15

Luke Lea

Commissioner of Indian Affairs (July 1, 1850–March 24, 1853)

Luke Lea was the sixth commissioner of Indian affairs. He was born on November 16, 1810, in Grainger County, Tennessee. After studying law, Lea and his brother Pryor opened a law office in Jackson, Mississippi, in 1836, and soon thereafter he entered Mississippi politics. He served one term in the Mississippi state legislature, and in 1849 he ran—and lost—as the Whig candidate for governor. Lea was a staunch supporter of Zachary Taylor's bid for the presidency, and after his defeat in the governor's race, he asked Taylor for a federal appointment, with the president offering him the position commissioner of Indian affairs. He accepted and took office on July 1, 1850, despite not having any prior experience in Indian affairs.

Just eight days into his federal service, President Taylor died and was succeeded by Vice President Millard Fillmore, who then appointed Alexander H. H. Stuart to replace Thomas Ewing as secretary of the interior. Unlike Ewing, who directed Indian affairs, Stuart left Lea to run the Indian Office as he saw fit. Lea did not implement any radical changes in policy, but he did oversee the initiation of the reservation policy and resolved to assimilate the Indians as their only hope of survival.

Lea believed Native Americans were just as capable as non-Indians and that they could take their place in the nation as productive citizens. In the interim, he had to deal with Indian wars in Texas and New Mexico, threats of extermination of the border tribes, and the near annihilation of the California Indians at the hands of gold seekers. Consequently, Lea was under pressure to open the central Plains for American expansion west. While he favored assimilation, dealing with national expansion across the Great Plains became Lea's top priority.

In his first annual report, Lea outlined his plans for dealing with tribal affairs. He proposed extending Indian Office jurisdiction over Texas, New Mexico, and California. The only way to establish control over the tribes was through civil government and federal agents assigned to each. It was also time to negotiate treaties with the tribes to open a path across the central Plains. Establishing rights-of-way and compensating the tribes for lost resources (and initiating assimilation) through cattle and other goods were the first steps to establishing peace on the Plains. The border tribes had to be placed on reservations, engage in agriculture, and assimilate—or face certain extermination. Finally, Lea advocated for a national plan of establishing reservations for all the Indians.

Lea assumed office at a time of sectional strife that was temporarily appeased when Congress enacted into law a series of bills collectively referred to as the Compromise of 1850. With passage of the acts, popular sovereignty governed the expansion of slavery in the western territories, Texas surrendered her claims to New Mexico, California was admitted as a free state, the slave trade was abolished in Washington, DC, and a strict Fugitive Slave Law governed runaways.[1] Congress authorized territorial governors in Utah and New Mexico to serve as ex officio superintendents of Indian affairs, and Lea secured three Indian agents in California. In 1851, Congress authorized a reorganization of the Indian Office and established a Northern, Central, and Southern Superintendency east of the Rocky Mountains. The Southern Superintendency covered the tribes that immigrated to Indian Territory; the Central replaced the St. Louis Superintendency and engulfed most of the border tribes and tribes east of the Rocky Mountains; and the Northern included tribes in Wisconsin and Michigan.[2] Four agents were assigned to the New Mexico Territory and one to the Utah Territory.

Congress also authorized $100,000 for the long-awaited diplomacy with the Plains tribes, with the goal of executing treaties and establishing reservations for each of the tribes. The treaty of Fort Laramie was held on September 17, 1851, with the tribes agreeing to a right-of-way through the central Plains. Lea also advocated emigration of the border tribes further to the Southwest (into what became Indian Territory). He argued civilization had failed and emigration was essential lest the tribes be exterminated. In addition, despite the fact that border tribes owned most of the Nebraska Territory, there was pressure to organize that territory. Moreover, railroad interests identified routes across the central Plains. Congress, however, did not appropriate funds, and this secondary emigration would have to wait until the mid-1850s.

Annuity distribution remained a substantive policy matter, with Lea favoring the traders, leading to a continuation of Indian abuses. In Lea's mind, these abuses were part of the system and there was little that could be done to ameliorate it. With the election of Democrat Franklin Pierce as president in November 1852, Lea's days were numbered. He resigned on March 24, 1853, after Pierce's supporters advocated for one of their own in the Indian Office. Lea returned to Mississippi and largely avoided politics. He died at the age of eighty-seven on May 14, 1898.[3]

Need for Reservation Policy
In the application of this policy to our wilder tribes, it is indispensably necessary that they be placed in positions where they can be controlled, and finally compelled, by stern necessity, to resort to agricultural labor or starve. Considering, as the untutored Indian does, that labor is a degradation, and that there is nothing worthy of his ambition but prowess in war, success in the chase, and eloquence in council, it is only under such circumstances that his haughty pride can be subdued, and his wild energies trained to the more ennobling pursuits of civilized life. There should be assigned to each tribe, for a permanent home, a country adapted to agriculture, of limited extent and well-defined boundaries, within which all, with occasional exceptions, should be compelled constantly to remain until such time as their general improvement and good conduct may supersede the necessity of such restrictions. In the meantime, the government should cause them to be supplied with stock, agricultural implements, and useful materials for clothing; encourage and assist them in the erection of comfortable dwellings, and secure to them the means and facilities of education, intellectual, moral, and religious. The application of their own funds to such purposes would be far better for them than the present system of paying their annuities in money, which does substantial good to but few, while to the great majority it only furnishes the means and incentive to vicious and depraving indulgence, terminating in destitution and misery, and too frequently in premature death.[4]

I find a measure of policy strongly urged with reference to the tribes located on the borders of our western States. . . . It is, by a partial change in their relative positions, to throw open a wide extent of country for the spread of our population westward, so as to save them from being swept away from the mighty and advancing current of civilization, which has already engulphed a large portion of this helpless race. To a large majority of those that have been removed there from the States, we are under obligations of the highest character, enjoined alike by contract and conscience, to secure to them their present homes and possessions forever; and, ere it be too late, we should make all the arrangements necessary and proper to a faithful discharge of this solemn duty. . . .

That the border tribes in question are in danger of ultimate extinction... must be evident to every well informed and reflecting mind; and it is equally clear that the adoption of the policy recommended is the only practicable means of averting the melancholy fate with which they are threatened. If they remain as they are, many years will not elapse before they will be overrun and exterminated; or, uprooted and broken-spirited, be driven forth towards the setting sun to perish amidst savage enemies on the plains, or the sterile and inhospitable regions of the Rocky Mountains. Such a catastrophe would be an abiding reproach to our government and people, especially when it is considered that these Indians, if properly established, protected, and cherished, may at no distant time become intelligent, moral, and Christian communities fully understanding, and appreciating the principles and blessings of our free institutions, and entitled to equal participation in the rights, privileges, and immunities of American citizens.[5]

Treaties
It is much to be regretted that no appropriation was made at the last session of Congress for negotiating treaties with the wild tribes of the great western prairies. These Indians have long held undisputed possession of this extensive region, and regarding it as their own, they consider themselves entitled to compensation, not only for the right of way through their territory, but for the great and injurious destruction of game, grass, and timber, committed by our troops and emigrants. They have hitherto been kept quiet and peaceable by reiterated promises that the government would act generously towards them, and considerations of economy, justice, and humanity, require that these promises should be promptly fulfilled. They would doubtless be contented with a very moderate remuneration, which should be made in goods, stock animals, agricultural implements, and other useful articles.

As a further measure for securing the friendship and good conduct of these Indians, it is earnestly recommended that a delegation of their principal and most influential men be brought in for the purpose of visiting some of our larger cities and more densely populated portions of country. These delegates would thus be impressed with an idea of the great superiority of our strength, which, being imparted to their people, would have a powerful and most salutary influence upon them.[6]

The want of uniformity in our Indian treaties is a source of much confusion and embarrassment. They have been made from time to time to meet the emergency of particular occasions, and without reference to system or general principles. They, however, constitute an important part of the supreme law of the land, and there are peculiar reasons why they should be carried faithfully into effect. But this it is extremely difficult to do, in consequence of their discordant and multifarious provisions. The whole code ... is a singular compound of crude and cumbrous matter, prolific of vexatious questions, and incapable of harmonious adjustment. There are no doubt many of the tribes with whom new treaties could easily be concluded, superseding those previously made, and simplifying, to a most desirable extent, all our relations with them....

If a large number of existing treaties were swept away, and others substituted in their stead, containing only a few plain, necessary, and assimilated provisions, serving as models for future treaties, and all looking mainly to the concentration of the several tribes; to their permanent domiciliation within fixed and narrow limits; to the establishment of efficient laws for the protection of their persons and property; and to a more judicious administration of the means provided for their support and improvement, the day would not be distant when the whole subject of our Indian affairs would assume a far more consistent and systematic form, presenting to the eye of the philanthropist and Christian a spectacle no longer cheerless and dispiriting, but redolent of consolation, encouragement, and hope.[7]

Prejudices Hold Back the Indians
The history of the Indian furnishes abundant proof that he possesses all the elements essential to his elevation; all the powers, instincts, and sympathies which appertain to his white brother; and which only need the proper development and direction to enable him to tread with equal step and dignity the walks of civilized life. He is intellectual, proud, brave, generous; and in his devotion to his family, his country, and the graves of his fathers, it is clearly shown that the kind affections, and the impulses of patriotism, animate his heart. That his inferiority is a necessity of his nature, is neither taught by philosophy, nor attested by experience. Prejudice against him, originating in error of opinion on this subject, has doubtless been a formidable obstacle in the way of his improvement; while on the other hand, it is equally certain that his progress has been retarded by ill-conceived and misdirected efforts to hasten his advance. It is even questionable whether the immense amounts paid to them in the way of annuities have not been, and are not now, all things considered, a curse to them rather than a blessing.

Certain it is, there has not at all times been the most wise and beneficial application of their funds. To arouse the spirit of enterprise in the Indian, and bring him to realize the necessity of reliance upon himself, in some industrial pursuit, for his support and comfort, is, generally, if not universally, the initiative step to his civilization, which he is often prevented from taking by the debasing influence of the annuity system. But the system is fastened upon us, and its attendant evils must be endured.[8]

Civilization
When civilization and barbarism are brought in such relation that they cannot coexist together, it is right that the superiority of the former should be asserted and the latter compelled to give way. It is, therefore, no matter of regret or reproach that so large a portion of our territory has been wrested from its aboriginal inhabitants and made the happy abodes of an enlightened and Christian people. That the means employed to effect this grand result have not always been just, or that the conquest has been attended by a vast amount of human suffering, cannot be denied. Of the Indian's wrongs there is, indeed, no earthly record. But it will not be forgotten, by those who have a correct understanding of this subject, that much of the injury of which the red man and his friends complain has been the inevitable consequence of his own perverse and vicious nature. In the long and varied conflict between the white man and the red—civilization and barbarism—the former has often been compelled to recede, and be destroyed, or to advance and destroy. The history of the contest, however, bears witness to the fact that the victor has, in general, manifested a generous desire, not only to spare the vanquished, but to improve his condition. It would be a difficult task to count the enormous sums of money that have been expended by the government and by philanthropic individuals in their manifold efforts to reclaim and civilize the Indians within our limits; and who can fail to remember, with reverence and regret, "the noble army of martyrs" who have sacrificed themselves in this holy cause? The results, it is true, have not been commensurate with the means employed; but enough has been achieved to attest the practicability of the Indian's redemption, and to stimulate to further and persevering exertions to accomplish the work.[9]

CHAPTER 16

George W. Manypenny

Commissioner of Indian Affairs (March 31, 1853–March 30, 1857)

GEORGE WASHINGTON MANYPENNY was born in Uniontown, Pennsylvania, in 1808. After moving to Ohio as a young man and working on the National Road, he acquired the *St. Clairsville Gazette* and developed it into a prominent newspaper. In 1838, he relocated to Zanesville, Ohio, and a year later began a ten-year stint as chairman of the Democratic Association; by 1842 he was admitted to the Ohio bar and practiced law. In 1850, the politically connected Manypenny was elected to Ohio's Board of Public Works, and three years later he sought the Democratic nomination for governor, losing the bid to former Commissioner of Indian Affairs William Medill.

With the election of Democrat Franklin Pierce as president, the politically influential Ohio congressional delegation recommended Manypenny for the post of first assistant postmaster general; Pierce instead appointed him commissioner of Indian affairs on March 28, 1853. He took office two days later on March 31, and despite no experience in Indian affairs, he served exactly four years.

Manypenny was known for his role in the second emigration of the border tribes. He was part of forty-three ratified and twenty-three unratified treaties that opened more than 174 million acres of land for settlement.[1] Gaining the consent of the border tribes west of Missouri and Iowa to emigrate south became his primary focus.[2] After Congress appropriated funds for treaties with the border tribes on April 27, 1853, Manypenny notified Interior Secretary Robert McClelland of his intent to head west and begin negotiations. In August, McClelland authorized the commissioner to treaty with any tribe willing to do so. Manypenny began with a two-month reconnaissance tour of the border tribes before returning to Washington, DC, lamenting the conditions of the tribes and their lack of agrarian progress.

In his first annual report, Manypenny recommended several policy changes that were influenced by long-time Indian Office Chief Clerk Charles E. Mix. The

Non-Intercourse Act had to be revised, Manypenny pointed out, if the Indians were to be controlled, civilized, and taught to farm. Without government support it would be unlikely that the Indians would take up farming. In his opinion, annuities were an obstacle to civilization and encouraged indolence. Instead, Manypenny opined that future treaties include money to purchase farm implements, goods, and stock, and that a portion of the funds be used for education. In the interim, he allowed annuity funds to go directly to traders to pay individual Indian debt, an action that continued to penalize Native Americans who were not in debt but forfeited a portion (or all) of their annuities, nonetheless. To correct trade deficiencies, Manypenny supported revising the licensing of traders.

The first of the second wave of emigration treaties was executed by Manypenny with the Ottoe and Missouria tribes on March 15, 1854. It became the model of Manypenny's treaties and authorized the president to cause the allotment in severalty of tribal lands. The border state (and other) treaties also provided for the relinquishment of annuities from earlier treaties and stipulated end dates. Manypenny also was active in the Pacific Northwest, executing seventeen treaties with the tribes in Washington and Oregon, where settlers were calling for extermination.

While he originally favored large annuity payments for a short term, Manypenny later favored semiannual disbursements that he believed would nudge the Indians into agrarian economies. With emigration and land severalty creating new reservations, Manypenny established thirteen new Indian agencies and nine subagencies to administer tribal affairs. By the mid-1850s, he argued against any further emigration, explaining that the United States had a duty to protect the remaining tribal lands—especially land allotments.

With the election of James Buchanan as president in November 1856, Manypenny's days were numbered. He submitted his resignation on March 11, 1857, and left office on March 30. He returned to Ohio where he remained active in local, state, and national politics. In 1876, President Grant appointed him to the Sioux Commission to negotiate treaties of cession in the Dakota Territory, and in 1880 President Hayes appointed him to the Ute Commission to secure cessions from the Ute Tribe in Colorado. Manypenny died in Bowie, Maryland, on July 15, 1892, at the age of ninety-four.[3]

Treaties

By a provision contained in an act of Congress . . . the President was authorized to enter into negotiations with the Indian tribes west of the States of Missouri and Iowa, for the purpose of procuring their assent to the settlement of our citizens upon the lands claimed by them, and of extinguishing their title, in whole or in part, to those lands.⁴ The Commissioner of Indian Affairs was designated by the President as the officer of the Indian department to conduct the necessary negotiations, and that duty was undertaken by him at the earliest period consistent with his other official engagements.... While thus engaged, he visited the Omahas, Ottoes and Missourias, Ioways, Sacs and Foxes of Missouri, Kickapoos, Delawares, Shawnees, Wyandotts, Pottawatomies, Sacs and Foxes of the Mississippi, Chippewas of Swan creek and Black river, Ottowas of Roche de Boeuf and Blanchard's fork, Weas and Piankeshaws, Kaskaskias and Peorias and Miamies. These embrace all the tribes located immediately west of Missouri and Iowa, except the bands of Quapaws, Senecas and Shawnees, and Senecas, who have small tracts adjacent to the southwest corner of the State of Missouri, and who, for want of time, the commissioner was unable to visit. The same cause operated to prevent his seeing the Pawnees, Kanzas, and Osage Indians, with whom, although their lands are not contiguous to the boundaries of either of these States, it is desirable that treaties also be made, should a civil government be established and the country opened for settlement.

The commissioner held councils with every tribe whom he visited, and disclosed to them the object of his journey to their country. He found the Indian mind in an unfavorable condition to receive and calmly consider his message. For some time previous to his arrival in the Indian country, individuals from the States had been exploring portions of it, with the intention . . . of attempting to make locations and settlements. The discussion of the subject, and the exploration of the country by citizens of the States, alarmed and excited the Indians. Some of them were proposing a grand council, at which it was designed to light up the old Indian fires, and confederate for defence against the white people, who they believed were coming in force to drive them from their country, and to occupy it without their consent and without consideration. Under such circumstances it was very difficult to quiet the Indians, or divest their minds of an impression that the commissioner's visit was not in some way or other intended to aid the whites in a forcible occupation of the country. As he progressed in his journey, and conferred with the tribes, the difficulty was gradually removed.⁵

[Between 1853 and 1856] fifty-two treaties with various Indian tribes have been entered into. These treaties may, with but few exceptions of a specific character, be separated into three classes: first, treaties of peace and friendship; second, treaties of acquisition, with a view of colonizing the Indians on reservations; and third, treaties of acquisition, and providing for the permanent settlement of the individuals of the tribes, at once or in the future, on separate tracts of lands or homesteads, and for the gradual abolition of the tribal character. The quantity of land acquired by these treaties, either by the extinguishment of the original Indian titles, or by the re-acquisition of lands granted to Indian tribes by former treaties, is about one hundred and seventy-four millions of acres. Thirty-two of these treaties have been ratified, and twenty are now before the Senate for its consideration and action. In no former equal period of our history have so many treaties been made, or such vast accessions of land been obtained.[6]

Emigration Policy Must Be Abandoned

The wonderful growth of our distant possessions, and the rapid expansion of our population in every direction, will render it necessary, at no distant day, to restrict the limits of all the Indian tribes upon our frontiers, and cause them to be settled in fixed and permanent localities, thereafter not to be disturbed. The policy of removing Indian tribes from time to time, as the settlements approach their habitations and hunting-grounds, must be abandoned. The emigrants and settlers were formerly content to remain in the rear, and thrust the Indians before them into the wilderness; but now the white population overleaps the reservations and homes of the Indians, and is beginning to inhabit the valleys and the mountains beyond; hence removal must cease, and the policy abandoned. Injury will not necessarily result to the Indian race from a change. By the operations of the former system, some tribes have become extinct; and the reduced numbers and enfeebled and demoralized condition of many of those who now rest upon the frontier, furnish unmistakable evidence of the effect of the system upon them. It is believed that by the proposed change, advantages will also result to the white population, while the heavy drafts heretofore made on the national treasury for removing Indian tribes will be saved.[7]

It is impossible to avoid the conclusion that in a few years, in a very few, the railroads of the east, from New Orleans to the extreme west end of Lake Superior, will be extended westwardly up towards the Rocky mountains, at least as far as good lands can be found, and that roads from the Pacific coast will be built as far east as good lands extend; and that in both cases an active population will keep up with the advance of the railroads—a population that will open farms, erect workshops, and build villages and cities.

When that times arrives, and it is at our very doors—ten years, if our country is favored with peace and prosperity, will witness the most of it—where will be the habitation and what the condition of the rapidly wasting Indian tribes of the plains, the prairies, and of our new States and Territories?

As sure as these great physical changes are impending, so sure will these poor denizens of the forest be blotted out of existence, and their dust be trampled under the foot of rapidly advancing civilization, unless our great nation shall generously determine that the necessary provision shall at once be made, and appropriate steps be taken to designate suitable tracts or reservations of land, in proper localities, for permanent homes for, and provide the means to colonize, them thereon. Such reservations should be selected with great care, and when determined upon and designated, the assurances by which they are guaranteed to the Indians should be irrevocable, and of such a character as to effectually protect them from encroachments of every kind.[8]

Reservations
With but few exceptions, the Indians were opposed to selling any part of their lands, as announced in their replies to the speeches of the commissioner. Finally, however, many tribes expressed their willingness to sell, but on the condition that they could retain tribal reservations on their present tracts of land. This policy was deemed objectionable, and not to be adopted if it could be avoided . . . with the hope that the Indians . . . might see that their permanent interests required an entire transfer of all their lands and their removal to a new home. Some tribes declined to dispose of any portion; and all, with the exception of the Wyandotts and Ottowas, who expressed an opinion on the subject of an organization of a civil government in that territory, were opposed to the measure. They have, with but few exceptions, a very crude and unintelligible idea of the "white man's laws," deeming them engines of tyranny and oppression, and they dread as well as fear them. Before the commissioner left the country quite a change was perceptible among the Indians; and it is believed that, with but few exceptions, the tribes will next spring enter into treaties and dispose of large portions of their country, and some of them will sell the whole of their land. The idea of retaining reservations, which seemed to be generally entertained, is not deemed to be consistent with their true interests,

and every good influence ought to be exercised to enlighten them on the subject. If they dispose of their lands, no reservations should, if it can be avoided, be granted or allowed. There are some Indians in various tribes who are occupying farms, comfortably situated, and who are in such an advanced state of civilization, that if they desired to remain, the privilege might well, and ought perhaps to be granted, and their farms in each case reserved for their homes. Such Indians would be qualified to enjoy the privileges of citizenship. But to make reservations for an entire tribe on the tract which it now owns, would, it is believed, be injurious to the future peace, prosperity, and advancement of these people.[9]

In the recent negotiations for their lands the Indians dwelt upon the former pledges and promises made to them, and were averse generally to the surrender of any portion of their country. They said that they were to have the land "as long as grass grew or water run," and they feared the result if they should consent to yield any part of their possessions. When they did consent to sell, it was only on the condition that each tribe should retain a portion of their tract as a permanent home. All were unitedly and firmly opposed to another removal.

The residence of the tribes who have recently ceded their lands should, therefore, be considered (subject in a few cases to a contraction of limits) as permanently fixed. Already the white population is occupying the lands between and adjacent to the Indian reservations, and even going west of and beyond them; and at no distant day all the country immediately to the west of the reserves which is worth occupying will have been taken up. And then the current of population, until within a few years flowing only from the east, now comes sweeping like an avalanche from the Pacific coast, almost overwhelming the indigenous Indians in its approaches. It is therefore, in my judgment, clear, beyond doubt or question, that the emigrated tribes in Kansas Territory are permanently there—there to be thoroughly civilized, and to become a constituent portion of the population, or there to be destroyed and exterminated.... With reservations dotting the eastern portion of the Territory, there they stand, the representatives and remnants of tribes once as powerful and dreaded as they are now weak and dispirited. By alternate persuasion and force, some of these tribes have been removed, step by step, from mountain to valley, and from river to plain, until they have been pushed half-way across the continent. They can go no further; on the ground they now occupy the crisis must be met, and their future determined.[10]

In regard to the Indians . . . within our newly-acquired and remote possessions [Southwest and Texas], there is, in my judgment, but one plan by which they can be saved from dire calamities, if not entire extermination, and that is, to colonize them in suitable locations, limited in extent, and distant as possible from the white settlements, and to teach and aid them to devote themselves to the cultivation of the soil and the raising of stock. This plan would be attended with considerable cost in the outset, as will any other that can be suggested for their safety and permanent welfare; but the expenses would diminish from year to year, and in the end it would, I am confident, be the most economical that can be devised. Thus far we have adopted no particular or systematic course of policy in regard to any of these Indians except those in California. They have been left to roam over immense districts of country, frequently coming into hostile collision with our citizens. . . .[11]

The policy of fixed habitations I regard as settled by the government, and it will soon be confirmed by an inevitable necessity; and it should be understood at once that those Indians who have had reservations set apart and assigned them, as well as those who may hereafter by treaty have, are not to be interfered with in the peaceable possession and undisturbed enjoyment of their land; that no trespasses will be permitted upon their territory or their rights; that the assurances and guarantees of their treaty grants are as sacred and binding as the covenants in the settler's patent; and that the government will not only discountenance all attempts to trespass on their lands and oust them from their homes, but in all cases where necessary will exert its strong arm to vindicate its faith with, and sustain them in, their rights. Let combinations, whether formed to obtain the Indian's land or to make profit by jobs and contracts in his removal, or other causes, be resisted; and let it be understood that the Indian's home is settled, fixed, and permanent, and the settler and the Indian will, it is believed, soon experience the good effects that will result to both. The former will then regard the latter as his neighbor and friend, and will treat him with the consideration due to this relation. And the Indian will look upon his habitation as permanent and his reservation as his home, and will cease to regard the white man with that restless doubt and distrust which has been so disastrous to his comfort and peace and so fatal to his civilization and improvement.[12]

Annuities
The results of long and ample experience conclusively prove that the money-annuity system has done as much, if not more, to cripple and thwart

the efforts of the government to domesticate and civilize our Indian tribes, than any other of the many serious obstacles with which we have had to contend. As a principle, applicable with but occasional exceptions so long as an Indian remains in expectation of money from the government, it is next to impossible to induce him to take the first step towards civilization, which step is to settle himself in a fixed habitation and commence the cultivation of the soil. However inadequate the pittance he may be entitled to receive, he continues to look forward to it in the vague expectation of its sufficiency; and lives on from year to year an idle and dependent being, and dies miserably as he had lived. Whatever may be the extent of consideration allowed for lands hereafter ceded to the government by an undomesticated tribe, it should consist chiefly of goods, subsistence, agriculture implements, and assistance, stock animals, and the means of mental, moral, and industrial education and training. Let this principle be adopted with all the tribes, wherever located, to whom we have not set the pernicious precedent of payments in money, and thus freed from the injurious effects of money annuities, they will present a more favorable field for the efforts of the philanthropist and Christian.[13]

Amending Non-Intercourse Act
Occasions frequently arise in our intercourse with the Indians requiring the employment of force, although the whites may be, and often are, the aggressors. The Indian Bureau would be relieved from embarrassment, and rendered more efficient, if, in such cases, the department had the direct control of the means necessary to execute its own orders. A force better adapted to the Indian service than any now employed, could, it is believed, be readily organized. But careful attention and kind and humane treatment will, generally, have more influence upon the savage than bayonets and gunpowder.[14]

The existing laws for the protection of the persons and property of the Indian wards of the government are sadly defective. New and more stringent statues are required. The relation which the federal government sustains towards the Indians, and the duties and obligations flowing from it, cannot be faithfully met and discharged without ample legal provisions, and the necessary power and means to enforce them. The rage for speculation and the wonderful desire to obtain choice lands, which seems to possess so many of those who go into our new territories, causes them to lose sight of and entirely overlook the rights of the aboriginal inhabitants.

The most dishonorable expedients have, in many cases, been made use of to dispossess the Indian; demoralizing means employed to obtain his property; and, for the want of adequate laws, the department is now often perplexed and embarrassed, because of inability to afford prompt relief and apply the remedy in cases obviously requiring them.[15]

CHAPTER 17

James W. Denver

Commissioner of Indian Affairs (April 17, 1857–December 2, 1857, and November 8, 1858–March 31, 1859)

JAMES WILLIAM DENVER was born in Winchester, Virginia, on October 23, 1817. In 1830, he and his family moved to Wilmington, Ohio, where he attended public schools. After graduating from high school, Denver taught school in Missouri for a year before graduating from the Cincinnati School of Law in 1844. After being admitted to the Ohio bar, he practiced law in Xenia, where he also published *The Thomas Jefferson* newspaper. In 1845, after relocating to Platte City, Missouri, he joined the American war in Mexico, where he served as captain of the Twelfth Regiment, US Infantry.

In 1850, after the Mexican War, Denver moved to California and was elected to the state senate the following year. A year later, he was appointed California's secretary of state before being elected to the Thirty-fourth Congress of the United States (1855–1857); he did not run for reelection in 1856.[1] As a representative, Denver—like most members of Congress—focused on two primary issues: the transcontinental railroad and slavery in the western territories—Kansas in particular. In Congress, he served as chairman of the Telegraph and Railroad committees and sat on the committee concerned with the question of slavery in the Kansas Territory.

Newly elected President James Buchanan appointed Denver commissioner of Indian affairs on April 8, 1857, and he took office nine days later. He resigned as commissioner on December 2, 1857, to become secretary of the Kansas Territory before being appointed governor of the territory. President Buchanan specifically appointed Denver to the Kansas positions to bring a level of tranquility as the matter of slavery was turning the territory into "Bloody Kansas." During his administration, the Colorado Territory was carved out of the Kansas Territory with the new capital of the former named in his honor.

Denver was reappointed commissioner of Indian affairs on November 8, 1858, and served until he submitted his resignation on March 12, 1859, with his last

95

day in office being March 31. In between his two terms, an influential chief clerk named Charles E. Mix served as commissioner. Denver's tenure as commissioner of Indian affairs was too brief to admit of any significant policy change, and much of what he did was influenced by Mix.

Denver's political philosophy with regards to Indian affairs was laid out in his only annual report in 1857, and it applied primarily to the border tribes. He believed each tribe was entitled to a unique but small reservation that was to be allotted in severalty although still owned by the tribe. Giving too much land to the tribes would create conflict, Denver reasoned, and would foster extermination of the Indians. Reflecting Mix's views on the matter, Denver believed paying annuities to the Indians led to dependence and indolence. Consequently, he argued any annuities should be used for homes, farm buildings and equipment, and other basic supplies.

Beyond that, Denver favored manual labor schools and a prohibition of non-Indians in Indian Country except government employees. A reflection of his view that Indians were a hindrance to settlement, Denver encouraged tribes to sell as much land as possible so it could be opened to settlement by non-Indians. As an example, he pointed to the Winnebago Tribe, which he believed had far too much land. While never charged with duplicity, Denver and his family speculated heavily in Indian allotments, owning land across the West.

After resigning as commissioner, Denver returned to California, where he failed in his reelection bid to Congress. He was commissioned a brigadier general in the Union Army on August 14, 1861, serving until March 5, 1863, when he resigned. After returning to Ohio, he unsuccessfully ran for Congress again in 1870. He was a delegate to the Democratic National Convention in 1876, 1880, and 1884. He died in Washington, DC, on August 9, 1892, and was buried in Sugar Grove Cemetery in Wilmington, Ohio. His last years were spent in Washington, DC, where he successfully represented several Indian tribes in their claims against the United States.[2]

Reservations Too Large
There have been two great and radical mistakes in our system of Indian policy—the assignment of an entirely too large body of land in common to the different tribes which have been relocated, and the payment of large money annuities for the cessions made by them; the first tending directly to prevent the Indians from acquiring settled habits and an idea of personal property and rights, which lie at the very foundation of all civilization; the second causing and fostering a feeling of dependence and habits of idleness,

so fatally adverse to anything like physical and moral improvement. With regard to the Indians in Nebraska and Kansas especially, it is all important that these mistakes shall not be perpetuated or repeated. They are in a critical position. They have been saved as long as possible from the contact and pressure of [the] white population, which has generally heretofore been regarded as fatal to the Indian. They are now becoming rapidly surrounded by such a population, full of enterprise and energy, and by which all the surplus lands, as far west as any of the border tribes reside, will necessarily soon be required for settlement. There is no place left where it is practicable to place these tribes separate and apart by themselves. Their destiny must be determined and worked out where they are. There they must advance and improve, and become fitted to take an active part in the ennobling struggles of civilization; or, remaining ignorant, imbecile and helpless, and acquiring only the fatal vices of civilized life, they must sink and perish, like thousands of their race before them. A solemn duty rests upon the government to do all in its power to save them from the latter fate, and there is no time to be lost in adopting all necessary measures to preserve, elevate and advance them.

Agricultural and Domestic Education
With large reservations of fertile and desirable land, entirely disproportioned to their wants for occupancy and support, it will be impossible, when surrounded by a dense white population, to protect them from constant disturbance, intrusion and spoliation by those on whom the obligations of law and justice rest but lightly; while their large annuities will subject them to the wiles and machinations of the inhuman trafficker in ardent spirits, the unprincipled gambler, and the greedy and avaricious trader and speculator. Their reservations should be restricted so as to contain only sufficient land to afford them a comfortable support by actual cultivation, and should be properly divided and assigned to them, with the obligation to remain upon and cultivate the same. The title should remain in the tribe, with the power reserved to the government, when any of them become sufficiently intelligent, sober and industrious, to grant them patents for the lands so assigned to them, but leasable or alienable only to members of the tribe, until they become so far advanced as to be fitted for the enjoyment of all the rights and privileges of citizens of the United States. Their annuities should be taken and used for the erection of comfortable residences and requisite out-buildings, and otherwise in gradually improving their farms.

Manual labor schools should be established, where they could learn how to conduct properly their agricultural pursuits, and especially where the boys could be educated as farmers, and the girls in housewifery and the dairy; and where also there could be imparted to both the rudiments of a plain and useful education. Mechanics' shops should also be established where necessary, and where as many of the boys as possible should be placed and trained to a knowledge of the mechanic arts suited to the condition and wants of their people. It is, if possible, more important that the Indian should be taught to till the soil, and to labor in the mechanical shops, than to have even a common school education.

The adult Indians should be encouraged to cultivate the lands assigned to them, each to have the exclusive control, under the tribal right of his own possessions, and of the products of his own labor; and to encourage them to part with their children willingly to be instructed at the manual labor schools and in the mechanical shops, the surplus productions of the one or profits of the other should be divided among the parents of the children who aided to produce them. All these arrangements should be under the exclusive control of the department, as well as the annuities, so far as they can be withdrawn from that of the tribe, and applied to accomplish the objects mentioned.[3]

Selling Tribal Lands and the End of Annuities
The settlement of the questions arising under various treaties in which reservations have been granted in severalty to Indians in Kansas and Nebraska presents many difficulties which I know of no way of overcoming, except by Congress authorizing the department to sell the lands and to control the proceeds thereof in such manner as to render them effective for the assistance and benefit of the reserves.[4]

While on the subject of payments to Indians, I beg leave to call attention to the evil effects of *per capita* payments, which system has been in force for some years. The great body of the Indians can be managed only through the chiefs. The *per capita* system breaks down the latter, reduces them to the level of the common Indians, and destroys all their influence. It thus disorganizes and leaves them without a domestic government; lessens their respect for authority, and blunts their perceptions of the necessity and advantages of any proper and effective system of governmental organization; turning them backward, instead of leading them forward, in the scale of advancement. With the diminished control and influence of the chiefs, there is increased lawlessness on the part of the members; and hence the greater number of outrages on the persons and property of other Indians and our citizens. Nor is the *per capita* payment system of any protection or advantage to the individual Indians. His share of the annuity is known beforehand, and it is an easy matter to induce him in advance to gamble it off, or pledge it for whiskey or articles of no material use to him, and at or after the payment to take or collect the amount from him. The distribution of the money should be left to the chiefs, so far at least as to enable them to punish the lawless and unruly by withholding it from them, and giving it to the more orderly and meritorious. They should be allowed to report on the conduct of the individuals of the tribe, being as far as possible held responsible therefor, and the agents to pay the money according to a graduated scale, having reference to the industrious habits and good conduct of individuals as he should find to be just, reserving to him the right to inquire into the action of the chiefs whenever complaint shall be made, and to change or modify such action whenever he may discover that they have dealt unjustly with any member of their tribe.[5]

CHAPTER 18

Charles E. Mix

Commissioner of Indian Affairs (June 14, 1858–November 8, 1858)

CHARLES ELI MIX was born in New Haven, Connecticut, on February 4, 1810. At the age of eighteen he moved to Washington, DC, and by his early twenties, he had become a waterfront merchant. When his business failed in the Panic of 1837, he sought government employment. The following year, he joined the Indian Office as clerk. He remained clerk until 1850, when he rose to the position of chief clerk, where he remained nearly twenty years. He was widely known for his integrity and efficiency.

As chief clerk, Mix supervised staff, prepared correspondence, drafted treaties—including the April 19, 1858, Yankton Sioux Treaty—met tribal leaders, and engaged in daily correspondence with field staff scattered throughout Indian Country. In his role as chief clerk, Mix was second only to the commissioner of Indian affairs. Such was his ability that he influenced Indian policy for nearly twenty years (the late 1840s to 1868, when he retired). He was most well known for drafting the 1850 Office Copy of the Laws, Regulations, Etc., of the Indian Bureau, a set of regulations that touched all aspects of implementing and governing Indian affairs and was provided to every field and central office agent, staff, and bureaucrat.[1]

Mix signed the 1858 annual report and, in an acting capacity, the 1867 annual report of the Indian Office, although his hand was in nearly every report between the late 1840s and 1868. When President Buchanan appointed Denver secretary and then governor of the Kansas Territory, Mix became commissioner. He assumed office on June 14, 1858, and he resigned November 8, 1858, preferring to work behind the scenes. While he had definite policy thoughts, Mix administered the policies handed down by Congress and the president.

Mix's philosophy governed two significant policies. He supported the reservation policy, believing each tribe was entitled to a small reservation that would aid it in transitioning to an agrarian culture. The continued emigration of the tribes had to stop, as it was interfering with the civilization process. Only stability, good land, severalty, and isolation from unscrupulous white people would facilitate civilization. He was also ardent in his views that assimilation was the only path forward for American Indians. Not surprisingly, Mix believed large annuities promoted "indolence."

After more than thirty years with the Indian Office, Mix retired in 1869, remaining in Washington, DC. He died in Georgetown on January 15, 1878, just weeks short of his sixty-eighth birthday. Charles Mix County (South Dakota) was named for Mix when it was organized on May 8, 1862.[2] Mix's tenure as commissioner of Indian affairs was the shortest of any commissioner until Benjamin Reifel's fifty-four days in the winter of 1976–1977.

Land Acquisitions via Treaty

The whole number of ratified treaties with Indians entered into since the adoption of the federal Constitution is three hundred and ninety-three, nearly all of which contain provisions that are still in force, and the proper execution of which occupies a large portion of the time and attention of this office from year to year. Most of them were treaties of cession, by which large bodies of land were acquired from the tribes with which they were made, for occupation and settlement by our white population. It is estimated that the quantity of land thus acquired is about 581,163,188 acres, and that the entire cost thereof, including the expense of fulfilling all the stipulations of the treaties, will be $49,816,344. From a considerable portion of these lands the general government derived no pecuniary advantage, as on the extinguishment of the Indian usufruct title they became the property of the States within whose boundaries they were situated. From what has up to this time been sold of the others, it is estimated that there has been received into the federal treasury an amount which exceeds the entire cost of the acquisition of the whole and the expense of surveying and selling those disposed of by at least one hundred millions of dollars. The amount applicable for fulfilling treaty stipulations with the various tribes and for other objects connected with our Indian policy, during the present fiscal year, was $4,852,407.34; of which sum $204,662.89 was derived from investments of trust funds in stocks of various States and the United States. The whole amount of trust funds held on Indian account is $10,590,649.62, of which $3,502,241.82 has been invested in that manner; the remainder, viz: $7,088,407.80 being retained in the Treasury, and the interest thereon annually appropriated by Congress. As by this latter arrangement the government every twenty years pays an amount equal to that of the principal so retained, it is worthy of consideration whether it will not be expedient and advisable, when the national treasury shall be in a condition to admit of it, also to invest that amount in like manner with the other Indian trust funds.³

Three Fatal Flaws in Federal Policy
From the commencement of the settlement of this country, the principle has been recognised and acted on, that the Indian tribes possessed the occupant or usufruct right to the lands they occupied, and that they were entitled to the peaceful enjoyment of that right until they were fairly and justly divested of it. Hence the numerous treaties with the various tribes, by which, for a stipulated consideration, their lands have, from time to time, been acquired, as our population increased.

Experience has demonstrated that at least three serious, and, to the Indians, fatal errors have, from the beginning, marked our policy towards them, viz: their removal from place to place as our population advanced; the assignment to them of too great an extent of country, to be held in common; and the allowance of large sums of money, as annuities, for the lands ceded by them. These errors, far more than the want of capacity on the part of the Indian, have been the cause of the very limited success of our constant efforts to domesticate and civilize him. By their frequent changes of position and the possession of large bodies of land in common, they have been kept in an unsettled condition and prevented from acquiring a knowledge of separate and individual property, while their large annuities, upon which they have relied for a support, have not only tended to foster habits of indolence and profligacy, but constantly made them the victims of the lawless and inhuman sharper and speculator. The very material and marked difference between the northern Indians and those of the principal southern tribes, may be accounted for by the simple fact that the latter were permitted, for long periods, to remain undisturbed in their original locations; where, surrounded by, or in close proximity with a white population, they, to a considerable extent, acquired settled habits and a knowledge of and taste for civilized occupations and pursuits. Our present policy . . . is entirely the reverse of that heretofore pursued in the three particulars mentioned. It is to permanently locate the different tribes on reservations embracing only sufficient land for their actual occupancy; to divide this among them in severalty, and require them to live upon and cultivate the tracts assigned to them; and in lieu of money annuities, to furnish them with stock animals, agricultural implements, mechanic-shops, tools and materials, and manual labor schools for the industrial and mental education of their youth. Most of the older treaties, however, provide for annuities in money, and the department has, therefore, no authority to commute them even in cases where the Indians may desire, or could be influenced to agree to such a change. In view of this fact, and the better to enable the department to carry out its present and really more benevolent policy, I would respectfully recommend and urge that a law be enacted by Congress, empowering and requiring the department, in all cases where money annuities are provided for by existing treaties, and the assent of the Indians can be obtained, to commute them for objects and purposes of a beneficial character.

The principle of recognizing and respecting the usufruct right of the Indians to the lands occupied by them has not been so strictly adhered to in the case of the tribes in the Territories of Oregon and Washington. When a territorial government was first provided for Oregon, which then embraced the present Territory of Washington, strong inducements were held out to our people to emigrate and settle there, without the usual arrangements being made, in advance, for the extinguishment of the title of the Indians who occupied and claimed the lands. Intruded upon, ousted of their homes and possessions without any compensation, and deprived, in most cases, of their accustomed means of support, without any arrangement having been made to enable them to establish and maintain themselves in other locations, it is not a matter of surprise that they have committed many depredations upon our citizens, and been exasperated to frequent acts of hostility.[4]

Small Reservations
The policy of concentrating the Indians on small reservations of land, and of sustaining them there for a limited period, until they can be induced to make the necessary exertions to support themselves, was commenced in 1853, with those in California. It is, in fact, the only course compatible with the obligations of justice and humanity, left to be pursued in regard to all those with which our advancing settlements render new and permanent arrangements necessary. We have no longer distant and extensive sections of country which we can assign them, abounding in game, from which they could derive a ready and comfortable support; a resource which

has, in a great measure, failed them where they are, and in consequence of which they must, at times, be subjected to the pangs of hunger, if not actual starvation, or obtain a subsistence by depredations upon our frontier settlements. If it were practicable to prevent such depredations, the alternative to providing for the Indians in the manner indicated, would be to leave them to starve; but as it is impossible, in consequence of the very great extent of our frontier, and our limited military force, to adequately guard against such occurrences, the only alternative, in fact, to making such provision for them, is to exterminate them.

The operations thus far, in carrying out the reservation system, can properly be regarded as only experimental. Time and experience were required to develop any defects connected with it, and to demonstrate the proper remedies therefor. From a careful examination of the subject, and the best information in the possession of the department in regard to it, I am satisfied that serious errors have been committed; that a much larger amount has been expended than was necessary, and with but limited and insufficient results.⁵

No more reservations should be established than are absolutely necessary for such Indians as have been, or it may be necessary to displace, in consequence of the extension of our settlements, and whose resources have thereby been cut off or so diminished that they cannot sustain themselves in their accustomed manner. Great care should be taken in the selection of the reservations, so as to isolate the Indians for a time from contact and interference from the whites. They should embrace good lands, which will well repay the efforts to cultivate them. No white persons should be suffered to go upon the reservations, and after the first year the lands should be divided and assigned to the Indians in severalty, every one being required to remain on his own tract and to cultivate it, no persons being employed for them except the requisite mechanics to keep their tools and implements in repair, and such as may be necessary, for a time, to teach them how to conduct their agricultural operations and to take care of their stock. They should also have the advantage of well conducted manual labor schools for the education of their youth in letters, habits of industry, and a knowledge of agriculture and the simpler mechanic arts. By the adoption of this course, it is believed that the colonies can very soon be made to sustain themselves, or so nearly so that the government will be subjected to but a comparatively trifling annual expense on account of them. But it is essential to the success of the system that there should be a sufficient military force in the vicinity of the reservations to prevent the intrusion of improper persons upon them, to afford protection to the agents, and to aid in controlling the Indians and keeping them within the limits assigned to them.[6]

CHAPTER 19

Alfred B. Greenwood

Commissioner of Indian Affairs (May 4, 1859–April 13, 1861)

ALFRED BURTON GREENWOOD was born on July 11, 1811, in Franklin County, Georgia, the eldest of five children of Hugh B. and Elizabeth Ingram Greenwood. He earned a degree from the University of Georgia before studying law and being admitted to the bar in Monroe, Georgia, in 1832. After a brief stent with the Indian Office as a commissary agent for Cherokee emigration, he resigned and moved to Bentonville, Arkansas, in 1838 and opened up a law practice. Four years later, he was elected to the state legislature for two terms before being appointed by the legislature as the state prosecuting attorney for ten Arkansas counties. By 1850, he was an Arkansas circuit judge, and two years later, he was elected as a Southern Democrat to the Thirty-second through the Thirty-fourth Congresses, where he defended the South and supported the Kansas–Nebraska Act and popular sovereignty. During his final term in Congress, he chaired the House Committee on Indian Affairs.[1]

Greenwood did not seek reelection to Congress in 1858 and retired in January 1859, although as a supporter of President James Buchanan, he was in line for political patronage. When James Denver resigned as commissioner of Indian affairs in March 1859, Buchanan appointed Greenwood to the position on April 27; he assumed office on May 4, 1859, as acting commissioner, and was sworn in as commissioner on January 10, 1860. He led the Indian Office during a time of sectional strife, with the Civil War looming on the horizon. To a Congress preoccupied with potential war, Indian affairs were of secondary importance.

As commissioner, Greenwood did not propose any new policies, and, as with nearly all commissioners of his time, he was influenced by the political philosophy of Chief Clerk Charles Mix. Greenwood opined that the Non-Intercourse Act of 1834, which still governed Indian affairs in 1859, was out of date, underscoring the lack of importance Congress placed on the matter. He argued that it was "defective" to try to administer policies that were no longer applicable or relevant due to shifts in Indian policy and the conditions of the tribes, noting the act was approved by Congress before the United States incorporated the western tribes.

Greenwood started his tenure with a trip to the border tribes in Kansas and Nebraska, returning to Washington, DC, with new treaties of cession and allotment with the Chippewa–Munsee tribes, the Kaw Tribe (200,000 acres), and the Sac and Fox of the Mississippi (300,000 acres).[2] As for reservations, Greenwood supported concentrating the Indians on small tracts of land—but was adamant that the United States had an obligation to provide for the needs of the tribes, including protecting their reservation boundaries. He also proposed inserting severalty provisions into all new treaties to facilitate further land reduction. The need for a settled reservation policy in California was critical, as Indians were being indentured by local citizens and demoralized by loss of their land and resources. Above all, Greenwood sought a "uniform" policy applied to all tribal nations, a philosophy that governed Indian affairs until the 1920s.

To his credit, Greenwood was the first commissioner to note the difficulty of applying policy to treaty tribes and nontreaty tribes, believing the former had rights to their land while the latter were subject to the whims of Congress. This was further convoluted by the distinction between treaty tribes with permanent annuities and those without annuities. The former were further subdivided into communal landholding tribes and tribes with allotted reservations. Each of these distinctions complicated matters and had to be considered in any policy application. In his view, private property was indispensable to the advancement of the Indians, and it was axiomatic that land severalty was the basis of all policy. He also advanced the view of segregating Indians from non-Indians until such a time when the former were able to compete with the latter. In principle, Greenwood was committed to Indian autonomy, believing that Indians were as capable as non-Indians in succeeding. Permanence of land ownership in severalty was central to all policy considerations.

While he supported the Union, Greenwood had Southern sympathies, including proslavery views that left him vulnerable to criticism. When Free-Soilers preempted Cherokee lands, Greenwood supported expelling them, finding himself castigated in the process. When he opposed antislavery missionaries among the Cherokee, believing they exerted undue political influence, he was further marginalized.

With the election of Republican Abraham Lincoln as president in 1860, Greenwood's opponents grew increasingly vocal. As the Southern states seceded from the union, Greenwood's friend and fellow Southerner, Secretary of the Interior Jacob Thompson, resigned, with Buchanan offering the cabinet position to Greenwood, who declined. Greenwood remained in office until Lincoln was sworn in. With the imminent secession of Arkansas (May 6, 1861), Greenwood resigned effective April 13, 1861. He was then elected to the Confederate Congress, serving until 1865. With the end of the Civil War, he returned to Bentonville to practice law. Greenwood died in Bentonville at the age of seventy-eight on October 4, 1889.³

Need for Defined Reservation Boundaries

The policy heretofore adopted of removing the Indians from time to time, as the necessities of our frontier population demanded a cession of their territory, the usual consideration for which was a large money annuity to be divided among them per capita had a deleterious effect upon their morals, and confirmed them in their loving, idle habits. This policy we are now compelled by the necessity of the case to change. At present, the policy of the government is to gather the Indians [within the border states] upon small tribal reservations, within the well-defined exterior boundaries of which small tracts of land are assigned, in severalty, to the individual members of the tribe, with all the rights incident to an estate in fee-simple, except the power of alienation. . . . Wherever separate farms have been assigned within the limits of a tribal reservation to individual Indians, and the owners have entered into possession, a new life is apparent, comparative plenty is found on every hand, contentment reigns at every fireside, and peace and order have succeeded to turbulence and strife.

This is now adopted as the fixed policy of the government, and, sanctioned by Congress, has been the leading idea in all the treaties recently negotiated with the Indians. It is, however, only by slow degrees that so radical a change can be effected—a whole nation will not move at once. But the superior advantages and comforts enjoyed by those who labor over those who hunt, operating as a constant stimulus to the former to persevere, and to the latter to follow their example, will, it is hoped, eventually induce the great mass of the Indians to cooperate cheerfully in the general introduction of this system. As an additional means to this end, the superintendents and agents have been instructed to use every exertion to persuade the Indians to consent that the large money annuities they now receive, and which ha.ve hereto-for proved the fruitful source of drunkenness, insubordination, and vice, shall be applied to the purchase of stock and agricultural implements, the opening of farms, building houses, and other useful purposes.[4]

California and Need for a Reservation Policy

I regret extremely to have to report the existence of an entirely unsatisfactory condition . . . in California, and that the Indian reservation policy, as it has there been pursued, has almost wholly failed to accomplish the beneficent purposes for which it was inaugurated. It is difficult to trace this failure to the true cause which has prevented its success; perhaps it may justly be attributable to several, not the least of which is the fact that the reservations are within the limits of a sovereign State, and neither the Government nor California recognizes any right in the Indians of that State to one foot of land within her borders. An unnecessary number of reservations and separate farms have been established; the locations of many of them have proved to be unsuitable, and have not been sufficiently isolated; too many persons have been employed to aid and work for the Indians, instead of their being thrown more upon their own resources and required to labor for themselves. . . . At the outset it was confidently expected that, in the course of a year or two, the expenses would diminish, and in the meantime, the Indians would be taught to labor and to support themselves by their own exertions. This expectation has not been realized.

It is evident, however, that some change in the policy for California must take place; indeed . . . almost any change would be better than the present system as administered. . . . All the reservations, except Klamath, are in a dilapidated condition, and in a short time will go entirely to waste unless immediate steps are taken to prevent it. Under these circumstances, and being desirous to initiate a policy for California which will secure our own citizens from annoyance, and, at the same time, save the Indians from the speedy extinction with which they are threatened, I feel constrained to recommend the repeal of all laws authorizing the appointment of superintendents, agents, and sub-agents for California, and the abandonment of the present, and the substitution of a somewhat different plan of operation. This office has attempted to correct the errors in the administration of the system adopted for California without success. In the first place, the State should be divided into two districts, and an agent appointed for each, with a supervisor to lead and direct the Indians in their labors, with only such laborers and mechanics, at first, as may be necessary to keep the tools and implements in repair. It should be the duty of the agent for each district to keep a vigilant watch over the subordinate employees in his district, and from time to time keep the department regularly and fully advised of the condition and progress of the reservations within his district. The agents should give the Indians in their respective districts to understand that they are not to be fed and clothed at government expense; but that they must supply all their wants by means of their own labor.[5]

Treaty v. Non-Treaty Tribes
In reviewing the results of the policy pursued by the government of the United States towards the Indian tribes within their limits, it should be borne in mind that, while the same general relation exists between the United States and all the tribes, that relation has been modified in respect to many of them by treaty stipulations and acts of Congress, and as these modifications vary in each case, and often in essential particulars, the subject becomes complicated, and the difficulty of subjecting the Indians to a uniform policy greatly increased. With the wild tribes in the heart of the continent, in Arizona, and in California, constituting, possibly, the majority, we have no treaties whatever. With respect to policy, then, it is obvious that the Indians must be divided into two classes—those with whom we have treaties, and those with whom we have not. In the case of the former we are clearly bound to be guided by treaty stipulations; in the case of the latter the government is free to pursue such a policy as circumstances may render expedient, subordinate, of course, to those general principles which have been declared in the statutes and sanctioned by the Supreme Court.

Again, the treaty or annuity Indians may be arranged in two divisions. With one we have treaties of amity, and we pay them annuities, either in money, goods, or provisions, or perhaps all three, for a longer or shorter period, but without recognizing their title to any particular tract of country. We not only pay annuities to the other, but we recognize their title to particular tracts of country, described by metes and bounds; and guaranty them undisturbed possession of the same forever. This latter class, again, must be subdivided into those who hold their lands in common, whether in fee, or by the usual Indian title, and those whose lands are held in severalty by the individual members of the tribe. There is yet a further distinction to be made between those cases where the several reservations are in a compact body, surrounded by a well-defined exterior boundary, constituting them a tribal reservation, over which the intercourse laws can be enforced, and those in which the individual reservations are scattered among the white settlements, and subjected to the operation of the laws of the State or Territory in which they are situated.

Our intercourse with those tribes with whom we have no treaties, except those in California, Utah, and New Mexico, who are under the control of agents, is limited to impressing upon them the necessity of maintaining friendly relations with the whites and assuring them that acts of violence and rapine will be sure to draw upon them severe chastisement. This intercourse is had mainly through the medium of officers of the Army, stationed on the remote frontier, or engaged in exploring and surveying expeditions.

Need for Private Property among the Indians
Of those Indians, to whom reservations are secured by treaty, it is to be observed that those who hold their lands in common, and those who hold in severalty, but whose reservations are scattered about among the white settlements, have made, and are making little or no progress. There are of course exceptions, but they are few in number, and result from fortuitous circumstances. Experience has satisfied me that the two conditions are indispensable to the success of any policy, looking beyond the mere immediate and temporary relief of the Indians. If it is designed to effect a radical change in their habits, and modes of life, and establish for them a permanent civilization, the ideas of separate, or rather private property, and isolation, must form the basis alike of our diplomacy and our legislation.

Private property in the soil and its products stimulates industry by guarantying the undisturbed enjoyment of its fruits, and isolation is an effectual protection against the competition, the cunning, and the corrupting influences of the white man. This is not mere theory, it has the sanction of successful application in practice; and notable examples may be cited—those of the Winnebagoes and Sisseton and Wahpeton Sioux, reclaimed in an incredibly short time by this policy, from the idleness, drunkenness, and degradation for which they were conspicuous.[6]

Indian Autonomy
As early as the year 1849 it was contended by the office of Indian affairs that the capability of the Indian (for self-government) was no longer a problem; that although, with some tribes, all efforts for their civilization had proved unavailing, yet, with others, the fostering care of the government

accomplished the main design of substituting the pursuits of civilized for those of savage life, and impressed their minds with elevated modes of thought which gave them a proper appreciation of moral responsibility; and the future to them was promising....

[H]istory furnishe[s] abundant proof that the Indian possesses all the elements essential to his elevation to all the powers and sympathies which appertain to his white brother, and which only need proper development to enable him to tread with equal step and dignity the walks of civilized life. But the direction to be taken for that development was a question which had never received a satisfactory answer. The magnitude of the subject and the difficulties connected with it seemed to have bewildered the minds of those who had attempted its investigation; and then, perhaps, for the first time, the idea was entertained that any plan of civilization would be defective if it did not provide in some efficient manner for concentration and domestication.

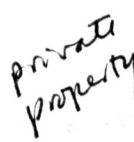
private property

It has become the policy to locate a tribe within such limits as would not at first, or too suddenly, change the modes and manners of hunter life for purely agricultural, yet, at the same time, compel the members to labor in part for subsistence; and, as they become habituated to labor, gradually to restrict their possessions and finally to divide their reservations in severalty, giving to them distinct and separate farms, and securing to them the comforts of life from the results of their own industry.[7]

CHAPTER 20

William P. Dole

Commissioner of Indian Affairs (March 12, 1861–July 11, 1865)

WILLIAM PALMER DOLE was born on December 3, 1811, in Danville, Vermont, to Enoch and Harriet Dexter Dole. As a young child, he and his farming family moved west to Ohio before settling in Terre Haute, Indiana, in 1821. In Indiana, Dole worked miscellaneous jobs, including navigating flatboats down the Mississippi River to New Orleans. By his early twenties, he was involved in local politics and had passed the bar in Indiana. In 1838, he was elected as a Whig to the Indiana state legislature; six years later he gained election to the state senate.

As the railroads extended west, Dole relocated his dry goods business to Paris, Illinois, where, in 1860, he was elected as a delegate to the Republican National Convention, helping elect Abraham Lincoln as president. Lincoln in turn appointed Caleb Smith from Indiana as secretary of the interior and Dole as commissioner of Indian affairs. Dole was formally nominated on March 8, 1861, and was confirmed by the Senate four days later. He assumed office on April 13.

Once in the Indian Office, Dole expressed strong views regarding the necessity of executing treaties with all of the tribes and was heavily influenced by Charles Mix's reservation policy. In fact, Dole followed Mix's manual on the rules and regulations of the Indian Office in executing his duties. While supportive of the assimilation policy, Dole modified and extended the policy by arguing that the proceeds from the sale of tribal land should go into a permanent trust fund for education.

After the Mexican War concluded with the Mexican cession, Congress shifted away from treaties in the Southwest, arguing that Spain had already extinguished aboriginal title and that Mexico never recognized it. Moreover, Congress was convinced that the Indians squandered annuity funds, and of what remained, they were cheated by traders. Dole, however, opined that it was essential for the United States to negotiate treaties with all tribal nations. In fact, he argued that all tribes should be brought under treaty relations in order to provide tribes with legal definition of their land. While Dole negotiated or oversaw the negotiation of fifty-three treaties—with nearly all describing the land reserved by the tribe—the Senate ratified just twenty of them and inserted disclaimers on any recognition of aboriginal land title.

Dole also facilitated the policy of concentrating tribal nations on three large reservations that were isolated from non-Indian communities. He also worked to further encourage the border tribes to relocate to Indian Territory, and he disliked the fact that some forty religious denominations operated tribal schools, calling them a "nuisance." Indian schools needed families and faculty who knew how to teach and model behaviors for Indian children to emulate, Dole reasoned. This social engineering could accomplish more for the Indians than scattered religious schools staffed with untrained personnel.

Dole headed the Indian Office at a critical time when there was heated debate as to who should be responsible for Indian affairs. The Methodist preacher John Beeson, the Episcopal priest Henry B. Whipple, and Army General John Pope all assailed the Indian Office for its inability to control the smuggling of liquor into Indian Country, to allot in severalty reservation lands, to train Indians as farmers, and to distribute annuities in a timely manner. The solution was to place the Indian Office back into the War Department, where it resided prior to 1849. Dole devoted a good portion of his 1864 annual report refuting the War Department's claim to jurisdiction, arguing that military oversight and the forcible relocation of the Navajo and Mescalero Apache to Bosque Redondo, New Mexico, demonstrated the failure of the department to handle Indian affairs.

The failure of Bosque Redondo temporarily convinced Congress that military control was not the answer. The Sand Creek Massacre of Southern Cheyenne men, women, and children in November 1864, and the ensuing report that was published the following year, encouraged Congress to seek the removal of all those who were in any manner associated with the attack. President Lincoln's assassination on April 15, 1865, and the ascension of Vice President Andrew Johnson to the presidency left Dole vulnerable, and he submitted his resignation on July 6, 1865; he left office five days later.

After retiring, Dole remained in Washington, DC, serving as an attorney supportive of American Indians and prosecuting tribal claims against the United States. He died in the capital city at the age of seventy-eight on October 3, 1889.[1]

Need for Settled Policy

From a glance at the history of our relations with the Indians, it will appear that we have been governed by the course of events, rather than by the adoption of a well-settled policy. The early settlers of the country everywhere met with a kind reception from the Indians, but as the settlements increased in numbers and extended their borders, it soon became manifest to the Indians that their hunting grounds were being invaded and their limits gradually restricted. Their feelings of hospitality were in time changed to sentiments of bitterest hostility, and that dark page of our national history, containing a recital of our numerous Indian wars, and the peculiarly bloody and barbarous scenes attending them, has been the result. As our borders have been extended, and civilization with its attendant blessings has taken possession of the once unbroken wilderness home of the Indians, treaties have been negotiated with them from time to time, and uniformly, and in almost innumerable instances, they have been recognized as a separate and distinct people, possessing in a restricted sense the peculiarities and characteristics of distinct nations. These treaties, with but few exceptions, have defined by natural metes and bounds the portion of the public domain which, from the time of their negotiation, were, by their terms, to be regarded as the separate and exclusive homes of the respective tribes with which they were negotiated; and it would form a not uninstructed subject of inquiry to investigate and define the various portions of the States, now exclusively occupied by our own people, which at times have been set apart under the sanction of solemn treaties for the exclusive use of the Indians; and if in connexion with this inquiry the actual causes which have led to the removal of the different tribes from the districts thus formally dedicated to their use were investigated, it is greatly to be feared that, in a majority of instances, the result would not be highly creditable to our national reputation for honor and integrity....[2]

Need for Treaties

The policy of negotiating treaties with Indian tribes has recently attracted a large share of public attention, and it may not, therefore, be considered inappropriate to again allude to the subject.... Indeed, it seems to have been taken for granted by all who have engaged in the discussion of this question, that the [Indians] are to be regarded and treated as a separate and distinct people; and this being the case, it follows that, whatever may be the policy adopted, they cannot be permitted to roam at will throughout those portions of the country which are occupied by our own people. It is, then, a necessity that there should be a common understanding between the two races as to the extent and boundaries of the districts to be inhabited by the Indians, the laws by which they are to be governed, and the reciprocal duties and obligations resting upon each race....

There are two methods by which this mutual understanding may be had. First, by availing ourselves of our overwhelming numerical, physical, and intellectual superiority, we may set apart a country for the use of the Indians, prescribe the laws by which they shall be governed, and the rules to be observed in the intercourse of the two races, and compel a conformity on the part of the Indians; or, secondly we may, as has been the almost universal practice of the government, after resorting to military force only as far as may be necessary in order to induce the Indians to consent to negotiate, bring about this understanding through the instrumentality of treaties to which they are parties, and as such have yielded their assent. Fortunately, the immense disparity in the relative power and resources of the two races enables us to pursue either of these methods, and it is therefore incumbent upon us to adopt that course which, judged by past experience, is best calculated to produce the desired results, viz: the security of our frontier settlements, and the ultimate reclamation and civilization, and consequently the permanent welfare, of the Indians. By the one course, it is contemplated that the independence of the Indians shall be entirely ignored, and that they shall be reduced to absolute subjection; by the other, that they shall not be altogether deprived of their sense of nationality and independence as a people. By the one course, the most savage and vindictive traits of their national character will be fostered and perpetuated; by the other, they will be gradually led to a more hopeful view of their situation, and to regard us as friends, seeking their elevation as a race. By the one course, they will ever regard us as merciless despots and tyrants, who have deprived them of their homes and liberties; by the other, while they are effectually taught their utter inability to cope with us as belligerents, they will gradually learn to appreciate the advantages of civilization and its attendant blessings. To my mind, the advantages of the latter over the former policy seem so apparent that I can hardly realize that the former is seriously advocated.[3]

Lands in the Mexican Cession

The Mexican government, formerly in possession of [the Southwest], differed widely from ours in its policy and views in relation to the rights of the Indians in the soil. That government regarded itself the absolute and unqualified owner of the soil, and held that the Indian had no usufructuary or other rights therein which it was in any manner bound to respect. Hence it negotiated no treaties with the Indians for the extinction of their title to land, and in pushing forward new settlements made no provision for their welfare or future homes. It has been claimed that inasmuch as Mexico asserted and exercised this absolute and unqualified right of ownership in its soil, we, in acquiring from that nation the Territory in question, succeeded to its rights in the soil, and are therefore under no obligation to treat with Indians occupying the same for the extinguishment of their title. If this position is correct, it would seem to follow that the policy long pursued by government in negotiating treaties with Indians, and thus extinguishing their titles to land within our border, has been radically wrong; for as the Indians occupied the territory of both nations prior to the advent of the European races upon this continent, it seems clear that they held lands in the territory of Mexico and the United States by precisely the same tenure....

[There is] but one course ... left, and that is the concentration of the Indians upon ample reservations suitable for their permanent and happy homes, and to be sacredly held for that purpose. To effect this desirable object two methods are suggested; the one is to set apart from the public domain ample and suitable reservations, and by liberal appropriations provide a fund whereby the Indians may be located thereon, and enabled to commence their new mode of life under favorable circumstances; the other is to acknowledge that they hold the public domain by the same tenure that Indians held in other Territories, negotiate treaties with them for the extinguishment of their title, and thus provide a fund for the purpose above mentioned. That the latter method is preferable I have no doubt, for the reason that whichever may be adopted will be attended with the same expense; while the latter, by a treaty, to which the Indians are themselves parties, forever silences all claims they may have to that part of the public domain not reserved by them, for which they will feel that they have received a fair equivalent. Besides, they will not feel, as would be the case if the former method is adopted, that they have been removed by irresistible power from the lands over which they and their ancestors once held absolute dominion, and that to make room for the white man they are robbed of their hunting grounds, crowded upon scanty reservations, and compelled to subsist upon his bounty.[4]

Recognizing Aboriginal Title

The condition of the Indians in California is one of peculiar hardship, and I know of no people who have more righteous claims upon the justice and liberality of the American people. Owing to the discovery of its mines, the fertility of its soil, and the salubrity of its climate, that State within a few years past became the recipient of a tide of emigration, almost unexampled in history. Down to the time of the commencement of this emigration nature supplied all the wants of the Indians in profusion. They lived in the midst of the greatest abundance, and were free, contented, and happy. The emigration began, and every part of the State was overrun, as it were, in a day. All, or nearly so, of the fertile valleys were seized; the mountain gulches and ravines were filled with miners; and without the slightest recognition of the Indians' rights, they were dispossessed of their homes, their hunting grounds, their fisheries and to a great extent, of the production of the earth. From a position of independence, they were at once reduced to the most abject dependence. With no one of the many tribes of the State is there an existing treaty. Despoiled by irresistible force of the land of their fathers; with no country on earth to which they can migrate; in the midst of a people with whom they cannot assimilate, they have no recognized claims upon the government, and are almost compelled to become vagabonds—to steal or to starve. They are not even unmolested upon the scanty reservations we set apart for their use. Upon one pretext or another, even these are invaded by the whites, and it is literally true that there is no place where the Indian can experience that feeling of security which is the effect of just and wholesome laws, or where he can plant with any assurance that he shall reap the fruits of his labor. The great error in our relations with the California Indians consists ... in our refusal to recognize their usufructuary right in the soil, and treat with them for its extinguishment; thereby providing for them means of subsistence. ...[5]

Border Tribes

A fruitful source of difficulty, and one which detracts very much from the success of our Indian policy, is found in the fact that most of the reservations within this [Central] superintendency are surrounded by white settlements; and it has heretofore been found impossible to prevent the pernicious effects arising from the intercourse of vicious whites with the Indians. To remedy this, it has been suggested that the various tribes should be removed to the Indian country immediately south of Kansas. This suggestion is heartily approved by the whites and by many of the Indians, and, under favorable circumstances, I should have no hesitation in recommending its adoption. It cannot be doubted that most, if not all, of the tribes of the Indian country have, in a greater or less degree, compromised their rights under existing treaties, and upon the restoration of our authority their treaty relations will require readjustment, not only to provide for the punishment of those who have aided the rebellion, but also to secure the rights of those who have remained loyal. This will present a favorable opportunity for providing homes for such of the tribes and portions of tribes of the central superintendency as may desire to emigrate to that country. I do not wish to be misunderstood upon this point either as to the action which should be had in relation to the tribes of the central or those of the southern superintendency. Those of the central superintendency who desire to remain there should be permitted to do so, without molestation in any form whatever. Most, if not all, of them hold their lands by the most indisputable of titles and by the most solemn forms, and upon every proper occasion have received the plighted faith of our people that they shall remain forever unmolested in their possession. For these possessions they have surrendered rights elsewhere, which we have always acknowledged to have been justly theirs, and a full and fair equivalent for all they have received. Any action therefore on our part which does not leave them perfectly free to elect whether they will remain where they now are or seek new homes, and that does not secure to them ample remuneration for their present possessions, and the quiet and peaceable possession of their new homes, in the event that they shall elect to emigrate, will be a wanton and disgraceful breach of national faith, and all the more so because of their undoubted loyalty and their physical inability to resist any policy we may seek to force upon them.[6]

Managing Indian Affairs

The plan of concentrating Indians and confining them to reservations may now be regarded as the fixed policy of the government. The theory of this policy is doubtless correct; but I am satisfied that very grave errors have been committed in carrying it into effect. Prominent, and perhaps the chief among these, is the establishment of numerous small reservations within a given territory.... It is apparent that the establishing of numerous small reservations in every part of a territory, and locating upon each a tribe or band of Indians, only serves to increase their exposure to the evils to which I have alluded. I believe that the most efficient remedy for these evils will be found in concentrating the various tribes within suitable territories set apart for their exclusive use, and the enactment of such laws as will effectually prevent all whites settling among them, excepting only such soldiers and officers as may be actually required in order to preserve peace among the Indians, enforce the necessary police regulations, instruct the young, and render the necessary aid to the adults while acquiring a knowledge of the arts of civilized life. I am aware that it will require time, patience, and persevering effort to thus concentrate all the Indians within our borders, and to perfect the details of a system for their management, education, and control; but I am fully persuaded that in the end it will be found much more economical than our present system, be more simple in its operations, and in its results will be of inestimable value to the Indians.

I have frequently urged the propriety of the system of allotting land to Indians, to be held by them in severalty, in the strongest terms of commendation, and in this regard my experience and observation have not in the least changed my opinion. Indeed, it seems to me perfectly manifest that a policy designed to civilize and reclaim the Indians within our borders, and induce them to adopt the customs of civilization, must of necessity embrace, as one of its most prominent features, the ideas of self-reliance and individual effort, and, as an encouragement of those ideas, the acquisition and ownership of property in severalty. It is equally apparent from the antecedents and the present surroundings of the Indians that their first efforts for the attainment of civilization should be directed towards the acquisition of a knowledge and practice of the simple arts of husbandry and pastoral life. From these two propositions it is easy to arrive at the conclusion that the theory of allotments of land to be held by the Indians in severalty is correct. The error into which I think we have fallen, in the practice of this theory, has been in making a general allotment to all the individuals of a band or tribe who could be induced to make a selection without regard to the disposition of the allottee to occupy the land allotted him, his previous good conduct, or his ability to cultivate or derive any benefit therefrom. This practice should be abandoned, and in its stead, we should make the allotment of a tract of land to the Indian a special mark of the favor and approbation of his "Great Father," on account of his good conduct, his industry, and his disposition to abandon the ancient customs of his tribe, and engage in the more rational pursuits of civilization.[7]

CHAPTER 21

Dennis N. Cooley

Commissioner of Indian Affairs (July 9, 1865–November 1, 1866)

DENNIS NELSON COOLEY was born on November 7, 1825, in Lisbon, New Hampshire, the son of a farmer and one of eight children. When he was two years of age, his father died, with his maternal grandfather, Timothy Taylor, becoming his teacher, mentor, and friend. While attending Newberry Academy in Vermont in 1843, he earned a teaching certificate and began his career as an educator. In 1847, he moved to Wisconsin and went into business with his future father-in-law. Three years later, he moved to Iowa, where he studied law, passing the Iowa bar in 1854 and setting up a law practice in Dubuque. By the 1860s, he was secretary of the National Republican Congressional Campaign Committee and a supporter of Abraham Lincoln.

With the resignation of William Dole as commissioner on July 6, 1865, and the earlier departure of Interior Secretary John P. Usher in March, President Andrew Johnson appointed Senator James Harlan (Republican, Iowa) secretary of the interior, with his nomination confirmed in May. Harlan had predetermined views of Indian affairs and sought a complete overhaul of the Indian Office. He sought someone to lead Indian affairs who he could trust and who would take orders; experience in Indian matters was not a prerequisite. Harlan found such a man in his close personal friend, Dennis Cooley, a fellow Iowan. Within four days of Dole's resignation, Johnson—at Harlan's request—nominated Cooley as commissioner of Indian affairs.

In the mid-1860s, Indian policy was directed by four men: Harlan (who held radical views on Indian affairs); Secretary of War Edwin Stanton; Army General John Pope; and President Johnson. Cooley entered office just months after the Sand Creek Massacre in eastern Colorado and a series of Indian wars in the West. It was the massacre of Southern Cheyenne and Arapaho men, women, and children in November 1864 that awakened the nation—and Congress—to the necessity of acting lest the Indians be exterminated.

Cooley's policy focus was largely dictated by Harlan, and included dispossessing the Indians of their land as quickly as possible. Starting in Indian Territory, Cooley—pushed by Harlan—sought to establish civil government. In part because of Pope's influence, Cooley supported the use of military force to quell any tribal resistance. Harlan and Stanton agreed that the War Department would exercise authority over hostile tribes, while the Indian Office would assert jurisdiction over the peaceful tribes. Harlan forbade any Indian Office employee from publishing any information on Indian affairs.

To his credit, Cooley sought peace with the tribes and advocated improved administration, cognizant that the Minnesota Sioux War erupted in part due to poor Indian Office management. He also advocated the prevention of state taxation over allotted border state reservations, with the Supreme Court issuing a favorable ruling on the matter in 1866.[1] He also supported utilizing religious leaders to oversee Indian agencies, a precursor to President Grant's peace policy.

In the immediate postbellum months, Cooley met with the border tribes and tribal nations in Indian Territory. From the former, he sought their concurrence to emigrate to Indian Territory, while from the latter he sought their assent to cede land for such emigrating tribes. Cooley met with twelve tribes at Fort Smith, Arkansas, in September 1865, but managed only a treaty of amity, which the Senate rejected since it did not include any provisions for civil government.[2] By late fall 1866, he managed to negotiate (and the Senate ratified) twenty-two treaties, including individual agreements with each of the Five Tribes (Reconstruction treaties and additional cessions), nine Sioux bands (amity), and the Osage, who agreed to sell their land in Kansas and emigrate to Indian Territory.

The Senate did not confirm Cooley's appointment until April 23, 1866. Four months later, on August 31, Harlan, an opponent of Radical Reconstruction, resigned and was replaced by Orville H. Browning, a friend of Cooley's and Harlan's political opponent. Cooley remained commissioner until October 1, 1866, when he submitted his resignation, effective November 1. In his final annual report, he addressed the treaties he negotiated, arguing peace could be maintained only by treaty arrangements. Before leaving office, he also enforced the reduced reservation policy, and he opened the door for Indian Territory to become the home of as many tribal nations as the United States could induce to relocate to the territory in the coming decades. Despite the influence of Stanton and Pope, Cooley and Harlan resisted a takeover of the Indian Office by the War Department.

Upon leaving the Indian Office, Cooley remained in Washington, DC, practicing law until 1870. He then purchased the controlling interests in the First

National Bank of Dubuque, Iowa, where he served as president for the next twenty-one years. In 1874, he was elected to the Iowa State Senate (1875–1878) and continued to be active in business and legal interests. He died in New York at the age of sixty-seven on November 13, 1892.[3]

Difficulties of the Indian Office
It does not seem a great risk to attend to the business of directing the management of about three hundred thousand Indians; but when it is considered that these Indians are scattered over a continent, and divided into more than two hundred tribes, in [the] charge of fourteen superintendents and some seventy agents, whose frequent reports and quarterly accounts are to be examined and adjusted; that no general rules can be adopted for the guidance of those officers, for the reason that the people under their charge are so different in habits, customs, manners, and organization, varying from the civilized and educated Cherokee and Choctaw to the miserable lizard-eaters of Arizona; and that this office is called upon to protect the Indian, whether under treaty stipulations or roaming at will over his wild hunting-grounds, from abuse by unscrupulous whites, while at the same time it must be conceded every reasonable privilege to the spirit of enterprise and adventure which is pouring its hardy population into the western country; when these things are considered, the task assigned to this bureau will not seem so light as it is sometimes thought.[4]

Military vs. Civilian Control
The policy of the total destruction of the Indians has been openly advocated by gentlemen of high position, intelligence, and personal character; but no enlightened nation can adopt or sanction it without a forfeiture of its self-respect and the respect of the civilized nations of the earth. Financial considerations forbid the inauguration of such a policy. The attempted destruction of three hundred thousand of these people, accustomed to a nomadic life, subsisting upon the spontaneous productions of the earth, and familiar with the fastnesses of the mountains and the swamps of the plains, would involve an appalling sacrifice of the lives of our soldiers and frontier settlers, and the expenditure of untold treasure. It is estimated that the maintenance of each regiment of troops engaged against the Indians of the plains costs the government two million dollars per annum. All the military operations of last summer have not occasioned the immediate destruction of more than a few hundred Indian warriors. Such a

policy is manifestly as impractical as it is in violation of every dictate of humanity and Christian duty. It is therefore recommended that stringent legislation be adopted for the punishment of violations of the rights of persons and property of members of Indian tribes who are at peace with the government.

Sufficient appropriations should be made to supply the pressing wants of these wards of the government, resulting from the encroaching settlements springing up in every organized Territory. The occupation of their hunting grounds and fisheries by agriculturalists, and even of their mountain fastnesses by miners, has necessarily deprived the Indians of their accustomed means of support, and reduced them to extreme want. If the deficiency so occasioned should not be supplied, it is not expected that a savage people can be restrained from seeking, by violence, redress of what they conceive to be a grievous wrong.[5]

Need for Treaties
Believing that peace can best be maintained with our Indian tribes, after the whites begin to encroach upon their ancient hunting grounds, by treaty arrangements, liberal and just in their provisions, and faithfully carried into execution by the government and its agents, this staff urges the continuance of the policy which has met with such gratifying success during the present and last year; and the condition of the Indians of Kansas presses first upon the attention. Intermingled as the Kansas reservations are with the public lands, and surrounded in most cases by white settlers who too often act upon the principle that an Indian has no rights that a white man is bound to respect, they are injured and annoyed in many ways. Their stock are stolen, their fences broken down, their timber destroyed, their young men plied with whiskey, and their women debauched, so that while the less civilized are kept in a worse than savage state, having the crime of civilization forced upon them, those further advanced, and disposed to honest industry, are discouraged beyond endurance. In nearly every tribe the majority desire to remove southward to the Indian country, and the sale of their Kansas reservations and improvements will furnish the means of purchasing and establishing them in new homes. I see no other alternative than to provide for their removal as soon as practicable. Whatever may be the issue of the suit in the Supreme Court in relation to the questions of taxation and citizenship, we shall know with whom we are to treat among the tribes which have taken land in

severalty, or taken preliminary steps towards citizenship; and as to the other tribes, no obstacle exists to immediate action.⁶

Treaties are imperatively necessary with some of the Indians in Idaho, and measures should be taken at an early day to effect the necessary arrangements; and a proposition is under consideration for bringing upon the Flathead reservation in Montana, which is amply large, or upon a new reservation in northern Idaho, various kindred bands in that locality and the eastern part of Washington Territory. It has not been the policy of the government to make treaties with the tribes inhabiting the region ceded by Mexico, although it has been done in some cases; but it may be found advisable to do so in the case of the sundry tribes in New Mexico, whom it is desirable to place on reservations....⁷

Amending the Non-Intercourse Act
Among other subjects... I refer to that of the necessity of providing some effectual code of laws for the arrest, conviction and punishment of crimes committed by whites against Indians, or by Indians against whites, or by Indians against each other, upon reservations, or in regions chiefly inhabited by Indians. The intercourse laws, passed over thirty years since, and apparently sufficient at that time, before the tide of emigration had begun to set strongly towards the frontier, and while none but occasional hunters or trappers interfered with the occupancy of the country by the Indians, are insufficient now, when the white population west of the Mississippi begins to number its millions. It is much to be hoped that Congress will at its next session take this subject into careful consideration, and provide a plain, comprehensive code, by which the superintendents and agents may dispense justice within their jurisdiction, and the infliction of appropriate penalties may be rendered certain, whether the offender be red or white. Retaliation is the law of the Indians; and if, in his early approaches to civilization, he is compelled to abandon that law, he looks for a substitute in the white man's law. In too many cases, indeed almost universally, where a white offender against the rights or life of an Indian is brought into our courts through the efforts of the agent, he is sure of acquittal; but reverse the case, and the Indian almost surely suffers....

We have laws which provide for the arrest of whites trespassing upon Indian reservations, but no provision is made for retaining them in custody, or on proper bail to be tried. So for offences of Indians upon their own people; they may be sent to the nearest military post to be confined, and may be, at the will of the officer in command, released the next day. So we have a law against the settlement of whites upon Indian reservations, and a provision that they may be ejected by the superintendent or agent, but no provision is made for the expense of a posse of whites, while the use of an Indian posse is but the beginning of war upon a small scale, to increase according to circumstances....[8]

Schools
Special efforts have been made for the improvement of our Indian schools.... Particularly has this been the case as to the schools in Kansas and Nebraska, the most accessible of all; but the more distant agencies have not been forgotten.... An earnest endeavor has been made to awaken or revive the interest of officers and teachers in the work of educating the children of the Indians, as the only means of saving any considerable portion of the race from the life and death of heathen. That the labor of reclaiming the American Indian is more difficult than that relating to any other race, is the universal testimony of those who have devoted themselves most earnestly to it; and the reasons for this state of things do not alone inhere in the nature of the Indians, but arise to a great extent from the character of the whites with whom they are brought into contact upon the frontier, who are too often unprincipled and reckless, devoid of shame, looking upon an Indian as a fair object of plunder, and disgrace of their race and color. It is only to be wondered at that so much good has been accomplished, and there are many cases of great encouragement to the sincere philanthropist and Christian.[9]

CHAPTER 22

Lewis V. Bogy

Commissioner of Indian Affairs (November 1, 1866–March 29, 1867)

Lewis Vital Bogy was born on April 9, 1813, to Joseph and Marie Beauvais Bogy in Sainte Genevieve, Missouri Territory. Bogy's father was politically connected, having served as the secretary to Intendent Juan Ventura Morales during the period of Spanish control of Louisiana. After the United States purchased Louisiana from France in 1803, Bogy's father remained involved in local political and economic matters in Missouri.[1]

A product of the frontier, Bogy was in frail health much of his childhood, but that did not stop him from earning a law degree from Transylvania University in Lexington, Kentucky, in 1835. The following year, he moved to St. Louis to practice law, while at the same time he clerked in a mercantile and taught school. He also began investing in land, eventually amassing a fortune in real estate in eastern Missouri. When he married Pelagie Pratte, the daughter of General Bernard Pratte and from a prominent St. Louis family, Bogy gained access to the St. Louis elite.

In 1838, at the age of twenty-five, Bogy was elected to the St. Louis board of aldermen, and two years later, he was elected as a Whig to the Missouri State House of Representatives; he failed to gain reelection in 1849 and then ran for the US Senate the following year, losing to Thomas Hart Benton. Bogy was reelected to the state legislature in 1854. During his term in the state legislature, Bogy became a strong supporter of states' rights Senator David R. Atchison (Democrat, Missouri) and the Confederacy. In 1862, Bogy again attempted to gain election to Congress, losing to Representative Francis Preston Blair Jr., a supporter of Abraham Lincoln.[2]

After the Civil War, Bogy took a leadership role in opposing the Missouri Radical Republicans, and in 1866, he defended President Johnson's veto of a Freedman's bill. By the mid-1860s, Bogy had positioned himself for a federal appointment. When Johnson appointed anti-Radical Republican Orville H. Browning of Ohio as secretary of the interior, Bogy saw his opportunity. Browning was connected to the Indian trader Thomas Ewing of Ohio, who in turn was associated with the Indian contractors William Bent and Charles Bogy, Lewis's brother. When Browning began searching for a new commissioner of Indian affairs, he sought someone who was "flexible" politically and supportive of frontier expansion. Connected to Browning through his brother, Bogy was the choice for the position. On October 8, 1866, Browning appointed Bogy commissioner of Indian affairs, and he took office on November 1.

Browning and Bogy supported Indian traders in annuity distributions and in particular backed one of the most powerful traders—Thomas Ewing. Bogy agreed with the policy of concentrating the Indians on smaller reservations. The December 21, 1866, Fetterman Massacre near Ft. Phil Kearney added to the list of Bogy's challenges. While he saw the propriety of negotiating treaties with the tribes and urged Browning to remind the War Department that its role was to support the Indian Office, not supplant it, Congress was not convinced. When he asked Congress for a $50,000 appropriation to negotiate treaties with the border tribes calling for their emigration to Indian Territory, the House refused. Bogy was disappointed, believing that if Congress was going to give the War Department control of Indian affairs then it might as well do away with the Indian Office.

While President Johnson supported Bogy's nomination as commissioner, Congress did not, in part because of the continuing power struggle between the War Department and Interior Department over who would control Indian affairs. Concurrently, Senator James R. Doolittle (Democrat, Wisconsin) released a special Senate investigation on the conditions of the Indian tribes and the interactions of the civil and military branches. Indian hostility, the Doolittle report concluded, was the result of the aggression of "lawless white men."[3] As Congress considered the report, the news arrived of the massacre of Fetterman and his troops at the hands of Sioux warriors and the attack by General Winfield Scott Hancock on the Cheyenne and Lakota villages in early 1867.

By March 1867, the House was investigating Bogy's award of Indian contracts to firms in which his brother had connections. On March 12, the Senate considered—and refused—to confirm Bogy as commissioner. Browning immediately appointed Bogy as a special agent to oversee the purchasing of goods and merchandise and the contracting of freight to deliver such goods to fulfill treaty obligations.[4] The appointment was unacceptable to the Senate Judiciary Committee, which in quick fashion confirmed Nathaniel G. Taylor as commissioner on March 29, 1867. Bogy, meanwhile, remained special agent for two months before he conceded and resigned in June.

In 1870, Bogy ran for Congress as a liberal Republican from Missouri but lost. He was then elected to the St. Louis city council and served as president of the St. Louis Iron Mountain Railway in 1872. That same fall he ran for and was elected as a Democrat to the US Senate, where he served until he died on September 20, 1877, at the age of sixty-four.[5] Bogy did not draft an annual report.

CHAPTER 23

Nathaniel G. Taylor

Commissioner of Indian Affairs (March 29, 1867–April 25, 1869)

NATHANIEL GREEN TAYLOR was born on December 29, 1819, in Happy Valley, Carter County, Tennessee, to James P. Taylor, a prominent attorney and Tennessee attorney general, and Emmeline Haynes Taylor, sister of Confederate Senator Landon C. Haynes. After studying at Washington College in Tennessee, Taylor graduated from Princeton University in 1840, and that same year he passed the bar in Tennessee. Intending to practice law, Taylor instead became a Methodist–Episcopalian priest after the sudden death of his sister. Having inherited his father's substantial farm, he was also a gentleman farmer in Tennessee.

In 1849, Taylor unsuccessfully ran as a Whig (against Andrew Johnson) for the First Congressional District of Tennessee. Four years later he lost to Brookins Campbell, although when Campbell died in December 1853, Taylor was elected to fulfill the term; he failed to win reelection in 1854. In 1860, he joined the National Constitutional Union Party and increased in popularity. He opposed secession and in the postbellum years raised funds to rebuild eastern Tennessee towns devastated by the Union and Confederate armies. When Tennessee was readmitted to the Union in December 1865, Taylor gained election to Congress as a moderate Republican, taking office on July 24, 1866, serving until the end of his term on March 3, 1867.[1]

Taylor became commissioner of Indian affairs in the midst of the turmoil surrounding Lewis Bogy. When it was apparent the Senate would not confirm Bogy, President Johnson appointed his fellow Tennessean to the position, one for which he neither had interest nor was prepared. As a moderate, Taylor fit the political need of the Johnson administration; he was confirmed by the Senate on March 29, 1867. Secretary Orville Browning, however, did not support Taylor, favoring Bogy or, when it became apparent Bogy would not be confirmed, General Henry H. Sibley. In Browning's opinion, Taylor was unqualified for the position, and in an effort to minimize his influence, Browning appointed Bogy as special agent—with a higher salary than Taylor's—to oversee the purchase and transportation of treaty goods to the tribes.

Above all, Taylor sought peace on the Plains and strongly opposed any War Department involvement in Indian affairs. After General Winfield Scott Hancock burned a Cheyenne village on the Pawnee Fork in western Kansas, the Plains tribes were restive, with Taylor complaining that the Army had spent millions of dollars on the war with the Cheyenne and that it was costing the government $1 million for every Indian killed.[2] A man of amity, Taylor began formulating a peace policy and advocating for the creation of a peace commission.

A peace commission, Taylor argued, would meet and negotiate treaties of friendship with the Plains tribes. In fact, he believed treaty violations were the main cause of warfare, and when the tribes retaliated, their lands were further invaded and hostilities increased. Taylor went to Congress seeking authority to negotiate such treaties, with a bill introduced on July 16, 1867, and approved by Congress four days later. Congress expressed a clear intent that the treaties were to open a path to the Pacific Ocean for the transcontinental railroad, and should they fail to establish peace, the US Army was authorized to "suppress" all hostilities.[3]

Taylor also supported policy creating three large reservations into which all tribes would be relocated. While not a novel idea, Taylor gave form to the policy by recommending one reservation north of Nebraska and west of the Missouri River (Dakota Territory) for tribes east of the Rocky Mountains. He advocated for a second territory south of Kansas and west of Arkansas (Indian Territory) for the tribes south of the Platte River. A third reservation was to be established west of the Rocky Mountains in an undetermined location for the tribes in the Southwest.

Congress authorized, and Taylor convened, the peace commission in the summer of 1867, with Taylor appointed as chairman. Members included Senator John Brooks Henderson (Republican, Missouri); Samuel Tappan, Indian rights advocate and former military officer; John Sanborn, former attorney general and chairman of the Senate Committee on Indian Affairs; General William Tecumseh Sherman; General Alfred Terry; and General William S. Harney. The commission negotiated a series of treaties in 1867, including the Treaty of Medicine Lodge Creek (Kansas) with the Kiowa, Comanche, and Apache, and with the Southern Cheyenne and Arapaho. The following year, the commission negotiated treaties of peace with the Sioux and Arapaho, the Crow, and the Northern Cheyenne and Arapaho at Ft. Laramie (Wyoming Territory). The treaties, however, did little to establish peace, as Sherman, Terry, and Harney were not fully vested in the policy, and by the fall of 1868 the Indian wars resumed, culminating in the 1876 invasion of the Black Hills by the US Army.

As commissioner of Indian affairs and chairman of the peace commission, Taylor advocated for keeping the Indian Office in the Interior Department—and out of the War Department. In a January 1868 report prepared by Taylor, the commission agreed with his views on the Interior Department's control. By the fall of 1868, the commission recommended the United States cease making treaties with tribal nations and no longer politically treat with them as foreign nations. With the War Department controlling "belligerent" tribes by forcing them back to their reservations, it assumed authority over Indian affairs by default. Taylor's peace plan unraveled before it was fully deployed.

With charges of impeachment brought against Andrew Johnson in March 1868, most matters of policy came to a halt. Browning, who gave tacit support to the peace commission, opened the door for military control as hostilities in the West renewed. When General William T. Sherman created two military districts—and Congress approved the War Department budget—that generally paralleled the two reservations Taylor proposed, the Plains tribes were all but placed under military control. General George A. Custer's November 1868 attack on Southern Cheyenne Chief Black Kettle's village on the Washita River shattered the peace.

Taylor continued to advocate that peace was "worthy of the highest consideration." But the damage was done. He left office on April 25, 1869, after the election of General Ulysses S. Grant as president. In some ways Taylor was vindicated when President Grant adopted a peace policy of his own, borrowing from Taylor the concentration of the tribes on large reservations, educating Indians in Western ways, providing a Christian civilization, and advocating land severalty. After leaving office, Taylor retired to Tennessee and continued preaching, farming, and lawyering. In January 1880, he sought a second time to gain appointment as commissioner of Indian affairs, failing when President Rutherford B. Hayes nominated Roland Trowbridge as head of the Indian Office. Taylor died on April 1, 1887, in Happy Valley, Tennessee.[4]

Opposition to Military Control
Shall the bureau be transferred to the War Department; or shall it remain under the direction of the Secretary of the Interior; or shall it be erected into an independent department, upon an equal footing in all respects with the other departments, as recommended, unanimously, by the peace commission in their report to the President of 7th January [1867]. I shall endeavor to present some reasons against the transfer.

1. *That prompt, efficient, and successful management and direction of our Indian affairs is too large, onerous, and important a burden to be added to the existing duties of the Secretary of War.* There is a limit to human capacity and endurance, and when either is taxed beyond that limit, it must fail in the performance of its functions, and the result must be disappointment, and most probably disaster, to the service.

    The business of the War Department, in all its varied and complex ramifications, is sufficient already, if properly transacted, to employ all the faculties of the most accomplished head, even with all the aids he may summon to his assistance; and there are few men living, if any, who can give the requisite attention to its demands, and at the same time discharge properly and with requisite promptness the delicate, important, and numerous duties the care of Indian affairs super-add....

2. *The "transfer" ... will create a necessity for maintaining a large standing army in the field.* The safety of the country in peace is not to be sought in a magnificent array of bayonets; but in the virtue, intelligence, industry, and patriotism of the citizens. With the restoration of all the States to their peaceful relations to the federal government, and the return of their population to industrial avocations and prosperity, if peace is maintained, as at the present, with all foreign powers, our military establishment should soon be reduced to a peace footing, its material returned to industrial and producing employments, and the people, to the extent of many millions of dollars, annually relieved of taxes now expended in the support and pay of the army....

3. *Our true policy towards the Indian tribes is peace, and the proposed transfer is tantamount ... to perpetual war.* Everybody knows that the presence of troops, with the avowed purpose of regulating affairs by force, arouses feelings of hostility and begets sentiments of resistance and war even in the most civilized and peaceful communities. How much more intense and bitter are the feelings of hostility engendered in the bosoms of barbarians and semi-civilized Indians by the presence of soldiers, who they know are sent to force them into subjection and keep them so. To their ears the sounds of the camp and the boom of the morning and evening gun are the infallible signs of oppression and war; and the very sight of armed and uniformed soldiers in their haunts and hunting grounds provokes and inflames the profoundest feelings of hostility and hate....

4. *Military management of Indian affairs has been tried for seventeen years and has proved a failure, and must ... in the very nature of things, always*

prove a failure. Soldiers are educated and trained in the science of war and in the arts of arms. Civilians are taught in the sciences and arts of peaceful civilization. In lifting up races from the degradation of savage barbarism and leading them into the sunlight of a higher life, in unveiling to their benighted vision the benefits of civilization and the blessings of a peaceful Christianity, I cannot for the life of me perceive the propriety or the efficacy of employing the military instead of the civil departments, unless it is intended to adopt the Mohammedan motto, and proclaim to these people "Death or the Koran...."

5. *It is inhuman and unchristian ... leaving the question of economy out of view, to destroy a whole race by such demoralization and disease as military government is sure to entail upon our tribes.* I know no exception to the rule that the presence of military posts in the Indian country is speedily subversive of even the sternest ideas of Indian domestic morale. Female chastity, the abandonment of which in some tribes is punished with death, yields to bribery or fear; marital rights are generally disregarded, and shameless concubinage, with its disgusting concomitants, spreads its pestiferous stench through camp and lodge. The most loathsome, lingering, and fatal diseases, which reach many generations in their ruinous effects, are spread broadcast, and the seeds of moral and physical death are planted among the miserable creatures....

6. *The conduct of Indian affairs is ... incompatible with the nature and objects of the military department.* The policy of our government has always been to secure and maintain peaceful and friendly relations with all the Indian tribes and to advance their interests, by offering them inducements to abandon nomadic habits and the chase, and to learn to adopt the habits and methods of civilized life. To carry this benevolent and humane policy into practical effect, we have stipulated to settle them upon ample reserves of good land, adapted to pastoral and agricultural pursuits; to subsist them as long as requisite; to supply them with all necessary stock and implements, and teachers to instruct them in letters, in the arts of civilization, and in our holy religion. But all these things pertain properly, as all will admit, to civil affairs, not military....

7. *The transfer to the War Office will be offensive to the Indians, and in the same proportion injurious to the whites.* Let it be remembered that the demoralization resulting from the presence of military posts is not confined to the Indian, but reacts, with accumulated power, upon the soldier. The nature and objects of the War Department, as indicated by its

very name, WAR, are essentially military, while the nature of our relations with the Indians ought to be, and the objects aimed at in their conduct are, essentially civil....

8. *In the report... of the peace commission, after full examination of the whole question, the commission unanimously recommended that the Indians affairs should be placed, not in the War Office, but upon the footing of an independent department or bureau.* It is but natural they should desire [the transfer]. It is the history of power to seek more power, and the dispensation of patronage is power. Besides, it is but natural that gentlemen educated to arms, and of the army, should desire to see the aggrandizement of the army.

9. *The methods of military management are utterly irreconcilable with the relation of guardian and ward.* The self-assumed guardianship of our government over these unlettered children of the wilderness, carries with it all the obligations that grow out of that relation. These can neither be shaken off nor disregarded without national crime as well as disgrace. Guardianship is a most sacred and responsible trust, and as a nation we must answer to the God of nations for its faithful administration....

10. *The transfer will... entail upon the treasury a large increase of annual expenditure.* It is clearly demonstrable that the war policy in conducting our Indians affairs is infinitely more expensive than the peace policy; and if the transfer is made, as a matter of course the former will prevail. If so, it seems to me, our legislators would do well to investigate the question of comparative cost. It will not surprise me if an examination will show that in the last 40 years the war policy and management of Indian affairs have cost the nation little if any less than $500,000,000 and also that the civil management or peace policy has cost less than $60,000,000, including annuities, presents, payments for immense bodies of land, and everything else....

11. *The presence in peaceful times of a large military establishment in a republic always endangers the supremacy of civil authority and the liberties of the people.* History is so replete with striking illustrations of the truth of this proposition that argument to sustain it would be simply attempting to prove an axiom. I therefore close the argument by merely announcing it.

This brings me to the question, *whether the bureau ought not to be erected into an independent department?* I reach the conclusion... that the only wise and proper answer to the question is that Congress ought

How to Civilize the Indians?

How can our Indian tribes be civilized?—Assuming that the government has a right, and that it is its duty to solve the Indian question definitely and decisively, it becomes necessary that it determine at once the best and speediest method of its solution, and then, armed with right, to act in the interest of both races.

If might makes right, we are the strong and they the weak; and we would do no wrong to proceed by the cheapest and nearest route to the desired end, and could, therefore, justify ourselves in ignoring the natural as well as the conventional rights of the Indians, if they stand in the way, and, as their lawful masters, assign them their status and their tasks, or put them out of their own way and ours by extermination with the sword, starvation, or by any other method.

If, however, they have rights as well as we, then clearly it is our duty as well as sound policy to so solve the question of their future relations to us and each other, as to secure their rights and promote their highest interest, in the simplest, easiest, and most economical way possible. But to assume they have no rights is to deny the fundamental principles of Christianity, as well as to contradict the whole theory upon which the government has uniformly acted towards them; we are therefore bound to respect their rights, and, if possible, make our interests harmonize with them. This brings us to the consideration of the question:

How can the Indian problem be solved so as best to protect and secure the rights of the Indians, and at the same time promote the highest interests of both races?—This question has long trembled in the hearts of philanthropists, and perplexed the brains of statesmen. It is one that forces itself at this moment upon Congress and the country, for an immediate practical answer.

The time for speculation and delay has passed; action must be had, and that promptly. History and experience have laid the key to its solution in our hands, at the proper moment, and all we need to do is to use it, and we at once reach the desired answer. It so happens that under the silent and seemingly slow operation of efficient causes, certain tribes of our Indians have already emerged from a state of pagan barbarism, and are today clothed in the garments of civilization, and sitting under the vine and fig tree of an intelligent scriptural Christianity. Within the present century their blanketed fathers struggled in deadly conflict with our pioneer ancestors in the lovely valleys of Georgia, Alabama, and Mississippi; among the mountain gorges and along the banks of the beautiful streams of western North Carolina and East Tennessee, and in the everglades of Florida....

Within the memory of living men, their tomahawks reflected the light of the burning cabins of white settlers on the Nolachucky and French Broad, the Hiawassee and the Tennessee rivers and their tributaries; their scalping-knives dripped with the blood of our border settlers, and their defiant battle-yells woke the echoes among the green savannahs and vine-tangled forests of the south.

But behold the contrast which greets the world to-day! The blanket and the bow are discarded; the spear is broken, and the hatchet and war-club lie buried; the skin lodge and primitive tepe have given place to the cottage and the mansion; the buckskin robe, the paint and beads have vanished, and are now replaced with the tasteful fabrics of civilization. Medicine lodges and their orgies, and heathen offerings, are mingling with the dust of a forgotten idolatry. School houses abound, and the feet of many thousand little Indian children—children intelligent and thirsting after knowledge—are seen every day entering these vestibules of science; while churches dedicated to the Christian's God, and vocal with His praise from the lips of redeemed thousands, reflect from their domes and spires the earliest rays and latest beams of that sun whose daily light now blesses [the] ... nations so recently heathen savages.[6]

What Is the Duty of the United States?
What, then, is our duty as the guardian of all the Indians under our jurisdiction? To outlaw, to pursue, to hunt down like wolves, and slay? Must we drive and exterminate them as if void of reason, and without souls? Surely, no. It is beyond question our most solemn duty is to protect and care for, to elevate and civilize them. We have taken their heritage and it is a grand magnificent heritage. Now is it too much that we carve for them liberal reservations out of their own lands and guarantee them homes forever? Is it too much that we supply them with agricultural implements, mechanical tools, domestic animals, instructors in the useful arts, teachers, physicians, and Christian missionaries? If we find them fierce, hostile and revengeful; if they are cruel, and if they sometimes turn upon us and burn, pillage, and desolate our frontiers, and perpetrate atrocities that sicken the soul and paralyze us with horror, let us remember that two hundred and fifty

years of injustice, oppression and wrong, heaped upon them by our race with cold, calculating and relentless perseverance, have filled them with the passion of revenge, and made them desperate.

It remains for us, if we would not hold their lands with their blighting curse, and the curse of a just God, who holds nations to a strict accountability upon it, to do justice, and more than justice, to the remnant; to hide our past injustice under the mantle of present and future mercy, and to blot out their remembrance of wrongs and oppressions by deeds of God-like love and benevolence.

That they can be elevated and enlightened to the proud stature of civilized manhood is demonstrated. We know the process by which this result is accomplished. Our duty is plain; let us enter upon its discharge without delay; end the war policy; create a new department of Indian affairs; give it a competent head; clothe him with adequate powers for the performance of all his duties, define those duties clearly, and hold him to a strict accountability.[7]

CHAPTER 24

Ely S. Parker

Commissioner of Indian Affairs (April 26, 1869–July 24, 1871)

ELY SAMUEL PARKER was born in 1828 into the Wolf Clan of the Seneca Nation to William Parker (Seneca Chief) and Elizabeth Parker, a descendant of the Seneca prophet Handsome Lake and a grandniece of the sachem Red Jacket.[1] His Seneca name was Hasanoanda, or "Leading Man," and he was born and raised on the Tonawanda Seneca Reservation near Buffalo, New York. At the age of twelve, he gained election as clerk of the Seneca Tribal Council before becoming a leading man among the Seneca. Parker was the first American Indian commissioner of Indian affairs, while at the same time serving as a hereditary grand sachem of the Iroquois Confederacy.

Parker was a learned man who protected Seneca land rights and protested the Ogden Land Company's preemption of Tonawanda and Buffalo Creek Seneca reservation land. With the support of the Quakers, Parker argued and demonstrated that the 1838 Buffalo Creek treaty granting Ogden preemption rights was obtained through fraud and deceit. In defending his people, he took his case all the way to a sympathetic President James Polk, eventually helping negotiate an 1857 federal treaty restoring about half of the Tonawanda Reservation by purchase from the Ogden Land Company.[2] In 1851, at the age of twenty-three, Parker was named Donehogawa, or "Open Door," after becoming a sachem in the Iroquois Confederacy.

A graduate of Yates and Cayuga academies, Parker studied law for three years but was denied the bar in New York because he was not a US citizen. He then entered the Rensselaer Polytechnic Institute and studied civil engineering, eventually working on canals in New York and Virginia, lighthouses in Michigan, and a marine hospital and customs house in Galena, Illinois, where he befriended merchant Ulysses S. Grant, beginning a lifelong friendship.

During the Civil War, Parker served as aide-de-camp for General Grant, eventually penning the surrender papers for Robert E. Lee's signature at Appomattox

Court House in April 1865. After the war he was promoted to a brevet rank of brigadier general, even though as an American Indian he was still denied US citizenship. He remained with Grant as general-in-chief, and in the fall of 1865, he was sent to Indian Territory to negotiate with the tribes that had aligned with the Confederacy, signing 1866 reconstruction treaties with the Choctaw and Chickasaw, as well as the Seminole. He also served as an investigator in the Fetterman Massacre of 1866, touring the Upper Missouri River reservations in the process.³

In January 1867, at General Grant's request, Parker drafted a plan "for the establishment of a permanent and perpetual peace" with the Indians. In it, Parker opined that Indian affairs be returned to the War Department and that Indian agencies be placed under Army officers since he believed they were more honest and forceful than civilian agents. This would eliminate the corrupting influences of Indian traders and the "Indian rings" that took advantage of the tribes. He also recommended guaranteed territories for tribes and a plan for their eventual territorial organization. He advocated for a board of inspectors to monitor Indian Office expenditures and agency funds until such time that Indian affairs returned to the auspices of the War Department. This was essential, Parker noted, and would ensure government goods and supplies pledged to the tribes were actually delivered. Finally, he recommended an Indian commission be established to visit with all tribes to promote peace, with the commission to be made up of trustworthy nonIndians and reputable and educated Indians.⁴

By 1868, Parker modified his thinking on who should serve as heads of the Indian agencies. Having experienced the good will of the Quakers in defending Seneca land claims, Parker believed that the "Friends" were worthy of service as Indian agents. When Grant was elected president in November 1868, and after he was sworn into office in March 1869, he nominated Parker as commissioner of Indian affairs on April 13, 1869. Parker, the president stated, understood the intricacies of Indian policy better than most having experienced it firsthand. On April 16, the Senate confirmed Parker by a 36–12 vote, and on April 26, he resigned his commission in the US Army and became the sixteenth commissioner of Indian affairs.

Parker grasped how policy was influenced by treaties, budgets, politics (both sectional and national), social realities, and tribal acceptance. He did not accept the status quo that Indian agents should be recipients of patronage, and in 1869 he convinced the War Department to detail sixty-eight "surplus" officers to the Indian Office. In addition, with Grant's support, he appointed eighteen Quakers as Indian agents, stating in his first annual report that the agents were a success.

Congress, concerned over the loss of patronage, disagreed and in 1870 prohibited military officers from serving in civilian posts.[5] Grant then filled all vacant agent and superintendent positions with men recommended by the various religious denominations.

Following up on Parker's recommendation for a board of oversight, Grant established a Board of Indian Commissioners in 1869 to help ensure success in Indian affairs. When Congress granted the board more authority than Grant desired, the president and Parker sent a policy directive to the board limiting its authority over policy matters, leading to the resignation of Chairman Herbert Welsh, a prominent Philadelphia philanthropist. A year later, Congress attempted to clarify the board's authority, granting it jurisdiction to supervise "all expenditures of money appropriated for the benefit of Indians in the United States, and to inspect all goods purchased for said Indians."[6] Parker continued to argue that the board's dominion was limited to annuity goods, not rations and other material.

Parker clearly favored military control of Indian affairs, especially if Indians were off their reservations, a position that was complicated by the fact that some tribes, such as the Sioux, had reserved by treaty the right to hunt off-reservation. He also advocated ending the "fictitious practice" of negotiating treaties with tribal nations, although he advocated enforcement of existing treaties. Congress agreed in 1871, unilaterally ending treaty making, although it did so more due to political infighting between the House and Senate over control of the process than Parker's admonition.

Like most commissioners, Parker found himself in political difficulty when, in 1871, Welsh accused him of defrauding the government in procuring Indian rations and in the bidding of Indian trade goods. While he was exonerated of the charges, Parker lamented the fact that "it was no longer a pleasure to discharge patriotic duties." In June 1871 he submitted his resignation, leaving office on July 24. Parker's final days were as an obscure, disabled pensioner with a low-level position with the New York City Police Department. He died on August 30, 1895.[7]

A New Policy

With a view to more efficiency in the management of affairs of the respective superintendencies and agencies, the Executive has inaugurated a change of policy whereby a different class of men from those heretofore selected have been appointed to duty as superintendents and agents. There was doubtless just ground for it, as great and frequent complaints have been made for years past, of either the dishonesty or inefficiency of many of these officers. Members of the Society of Friends, recommended by the society, now hold these positions in the Northern Superintendency, embracing all Indians in Nebraska; and in the Central, embracing tribes residing in Kansas, together with the Kiowas, Comanches, and other tribes in the Indian country. The other superintendencies and agencies, excepting that of Oregon and two agencies there, are filled by army officers, detailed for such duty. The experiment has not been sufficiently tested to enable me to say definitely that it is a success, for but a short time has elapsed since these Friends and officers entered upon duty; but so far as I can learn the plan works advantageously, and will probably prove a positive benefit to the service, and the indications are that the interests of the government and the Indians will be subserved by an honest and faithful discharge of duty, fully answering the expectations entertained by those who regard the measure as wise and proper.

I am pleased to have it to remark that there is now a perfect understanding between the officers of this department and those of the military, with respect to their relative duties and responsibilities in reference to Indian affairs. In this matter, with the approbation of the President . . . a circular letter was addressed by this office . . . to all superintendents and agents defining the policy of the government in its treatment of the Indians, as comprehended in these general terms, viz: that they should be secured [in] their legal rights; located, when practicable, upon reservations; assisted in agricultural pursuits and the arts of civilized life; and that Indians who should fail or refuse to come in and locate in permanent abodes provided for them, would be subject wholly to the control and supervision of military authorities, to be treated as friendly or hostile as circumstances might justify. The War Department concurring, issued orders upon the subject for the information and guidance of the proper military officers and the result has been harmony of action between the two departments, no conflict of opinion having arisen as to the duty, power and responsibility of either.[8]

End Treaty-Making

Arrangements now, as heretofore, will doubtless be required with tribes desiring to be settled upon reservations for the relinquishment of their rights to the lands claimed by them and for assistance in sustaining themselves in a new position, but I am of the opinion that they should not be of a treaty nature. It has become a matter of serious import whether the treaty system in use ought longer to be continued. In my judgment it should not.

A treaty involves the idea of a compact between two or more sovereign powers, each possessing sufficient authority and force to compel a compliance with the obligations incurred. The Indian tribes of the United States are not sovereign nations, capable of making treaties, as none of them have an organized government of such inherent strength as would secure a faithful obedience of its people in the observance of compacts of this character. They are held to be the wards of the government, and the only title the law concedes to them to the lands they occupy or claim is a mere possessory one. But, because treaties have been made with them, generally for the extinguishment of their supposed absolute title to land inhabited by them, or over which they roam, they have become falsely impressed with the notion of national independence. It is time that this idea should be dispelled, and the government cease the cruel farce of thus dealing with its helpless and ignorant wards. Many good men, looking at this matter only from a Christian point of view, will perhaps say that the poor Indian has been greatly wronged and ill-treated; that this whole country was once his, of which he been despoiled, and that he has been driven from place to place until he has hardly left to him a spot where to lay his head. This indeed may be philanthropic and humane, but the stern letter of the law admits of no such conclusion, and great injury has been done by the government in deluding this people into the belief of their being independent sovereignties, while they were at the same time recognized only as its dependents and wards. As civilization advances and their possessions of land are required for settlement, such legislation should be granted to them as a wise, liberal, and just government ought to extend to subjects holding their dependent relation. In regard to treaties now in force, justice and humanity require that they be promptly and faithfully executed, so that the Indians may not have cause of complaint, or reason to violate their obligations by acts of violence and robbery.⁹

Utilization of Missionaries as Indian Agents
The presidential plan of inaugurating a greater degree of honesty in our intercourse with the Indians, by the appointment of "Friends" to some of the superintendencies and agencies, has proven such a success that, when Congress, at its last session, prohibited the employment of army officers in any civil capacity, thereby practically relieving those who were detailed for duty as Indian superintendents and agents, the President at once determined still further to carry out the principle by inviting other religious

denominations of the country to engage in the great work of civilizing the Indians. By his direction a correspondence was opened with different missionary associations explaining to them the purpose and desire of the Government, to combine with the material progress of the Indian race, means for their moral and intellectual improvement, and, if they concurred in the plan, asking them to designate the names of such persons, possessing good Christian characters, as would be willing to accept the position and discharge the duties of Indian agents, and who would, at the same time, lend their personal and official influence to such educational and missionary or religious enterprises as the societies might undertake. The plan is obviously a wise and humane one. Under a political management for a long series of years, and the expenditure of large sums of money annually, the Indians made but little progress toward that healthy Christian civilization in which are embraced the elements of material wealth and intellectual and moral development. Indeed, it has seemed to the humanitarian, that the more the Indian was brought into contact with modern civilization the more degraded he became, learning only its vices and adopting none of its virtues. Not, therefore, as a dernier resort to save a dying race, but from the highest moral conviction of Christian humanity, the President wisely determined to invoke the cooperation of the entire religious element of the country, to help, by their labors and counsels, to bring about and produce the greatest amount of good from the expenditure of the munificent annual appropriation of money by Congress, for the civilization and Christianization of the Indian race. Most of the religious organizations promptly responded, heartily indorsing the proposition and agreeing to assist in its execution. Men of their designation have been appointed agents, some of whom have gone out to their respective agencies, while others are preparing to do so. The prayers of all good Christians will go with them that they may succeed in the great work for which they have been specially chosen; and I earnestly hope that the country generally will approve the course adopted, and give it all the support necessary.[10]

Consolidation of All Tribes in Indian Territory
The Indians under the jurisdiction of the United States are now located on reservations of land amounting in the aggregate to 228,473 square miles, or 137,846,971 acres. Deducting from this statement the Indian Territory south of Kansas, and there remains a population of 172,000 occupying reservations of land amounting to 96,155,785 acres; being a per capita of

558 acres. . . . The Indian Territory, so called, lying west of Missouri and Arkansas, and south of Kansas, contains 44,154,240 acres of land, and a population of about 60,000. Westward to the 96° of west latitude the soil is of the very best quality, well watered and timbered, capable of producing the largest returns to the labors of the farmer. West of the 96°, and lying between that and the valley of the Arkansas River, the country is mountainous, and offers fewer inducements to the settler. The mountains are known to contain very rich deposits of coal, and are supposed to contain other valuable minerals. In the valley of the Arkansas River the soil is of excellent quality for a width of ten miles, while to the west of that valley the entire country, although not so desirable for location as that in the eastern portion of the Territory, is well adapted to the wants of the farmer. The present population of the Territory is but one person to every 630 acres. Could the entire Indian population of the country, excluding Alaska and those scattered among the States . . . be located in the Indian Territory, there would be 180 acres of land, per capita, for the entire number, showing that there is an ample area of land to afford them all comfortable homes. . . . [S]uch a disposition of the now scattered tribes would release from Indian occupancy 93,692,731 acres of land, and throw it open to white settlement and cultivation.[11]

CHAPTER 25

Francis A. Walker

Commissioner of Indian Affairs (November 27, 1871–January 1, 1873)

FRANCIS AMASA WALKER was born in Boston, Massachusetts, on July 2, 1840, to Amasa and Hanna (Ambrose) Walker. His father, a prominent and well-respected economist and state politician, was both a friend of and a neighbor to Oliver Wendell Holmes. Walker learned at an early age that change comes incrementally, a philosophy that guided his work throughout his life. After beginning formal education at the age of seven and studying Latin and the classics, he graduated from college preparatory school and entered Amherst College at age fifteen, graduating with a law degree in 1860 and joining a Worcester law firm.

In July 1861, Walker joined the Fifteenth Massachusetts Infantry, eventually being promoted to a brevet brigadier general. He was wounded at the Battle of Chancellorsville in 1863 and the following year was captured during the Richmond–Petersburg campaign and sent to the infamous Libbey Prison. After the war, Walker taught Latin, Greek, and mathematics at Williston Seminary in Massachusetts before becoming editor of the *Springfield Republican,* where he opined on Reconstruction politics and railroad deregulation. He was firmly of the conviction that Indian reformers who did not consider evolutionary forces and the frailty of humanity would never succeed in effecting change.

Walker became commissioner of Indian affairs by accident. A brilliant statistician, he was appointed chief of the Bureau of Statistics in 1869 and superintendent of the 1870 Census, winning acclaim for the first scientific statistical atlas of the census. Congress, however, failed to approve of legislation authorizing Walker to control the census process outside of political interests.[1] Rather than lose him to private service, Interior Secretary Columbus Delano encouraged Grant to appoint Walker as commissioner of Indian affairs, even though the New York Times offered him $8,000 per annum to join its editorial staff. While he began his tenure at the Indian Office on November 27, 1871, he was not formally appointed until December 16. At thirty-one years of age, Walker is the youngest commissioner to date; he continued to serve as chief of the Census Bureau without remuneration.

Walker assumed the mantle of Indian Office leadership at a time when the peace policy was struggling to root. Ely Parker had abruptly resigned, and the eastern press demanded a commissioner who would be sympathetic, but fair to the Indians. The press supported Walker's nomination, believing his honesty, economy, and integrity would go far in ending the corrupt Indian ring that plagued the Indian Office. Walker also proved acceptable to western frontiersmen because he was willing, if necessary, to use military force to establish peace. Former Interior Secretary Jacob Cox—who nominated Walker as superintendent of the census in 1869—believed Walker's primary role as commissioner was to balance the concerns of frontier influences with those of the eastern philanthropists.

Commissioner Walker thought it a matter of economy to bring tribal leaders to Washington, DC, and other eastern cities to impress upon them the industrial and military strength of the nation rather than battling them on the Plains. In his short tenure he supported the reservation policy, believing it was essential for tribes to remain self-sufficient lest they become "festering sores" on the public corpus. The public was tired of tribal appeals, Walker argued, as he administered policy focusing on the inevitability of assimilation. Nonetheless, he believed the United States had an obligation to treat tribes fairly and to compensate them for land and resources taken and then provide them with legal protections until such time as they could be absorbed into the body politic.

Walker was firm in implementing policy, recognizing that it worked only if the Indians were protected. To this end, he paid attorneys to defend tribes and he opposed the opening of the Black Hills to exploration, calling it "most dishonorable." Walker penned but one annual report and, in the end, had limited impact on policy.

The start of the Modoc War in November 1872 hastened Walker's departure. He resigned on December 26, 1872, and left office on January 1, 1873, to accept a faculty position at Yale University. In 1874, he published The Indian Question, in which he criticized the corruption and graft of the Indian Office. In 1879, he accepted the position of superintendent of the 1880 Census after James A. Garfield (Republican, Ohio) spearheaded passage of a law enabling Walker to train census takers in a manner that would support a scientific analysis of census data. The 1880 Census earned Walker praise as the best census to date and acclamation as the premier statistician of his time. In 1881, after the election of Garfield as president, the president was poised to nominate Walker as secretary of the interior. Walker instead accepted an offer to become president of Massachusetts Institute of Technology. The author of numerous texts on economics, Walker later served as president of the American Statistical Association (1882–1897), the American Economics Association (1885–1892), and vice president of the National Academy of Sciences (1891–1897). Walker remained president of MIT for fifteen years. He died on January 5, 1897, at the age of fifty-six.[2]

What Is the Indian Policy of the United States?

The Indian policy, so called, of the Government, is a policy, and it is not a policy, or rather it consists of two policies, entirely distinct, seeming, indeed, to be mutually inconsistent and to reflect each upon the other: the one regulating the treatment of the tribes which are potentially hostile, that is, whose hostility is only repressed just so long as, and so far as, they are supported in idleness by the Government; the other regulating the treatment of those tribes which, from traditional friendship, from numerical weakness, or by the force of their location, are either indisposed toward, or incapable of, resistance to the demands of the Government. The treatment of the feeble Poncas and of the friendly Arrickarees, Mandans, and Gros Ventres of the north is an example of the latter; while the treatment of their insolent and semi-hostile neighbors, the Sioux, furnishes an example of the former. In the same way at the south, the treatment of the well-intentioned Papagoes of Arizona contrasts just as strongly with the dealings of the Government by their traditional enemies, the treacherous and vindictive Apaches. This want of completeness and consistency in the treatment of the Indian tribes by the Government has been made the occasion of much ridicule and partisan abuse; and it is indeed calculated to provoke criticism and to afford scope for satire; but it is none-the-less compatible with the highest expediency of the situation. It is, of course, hopelessly illogical that the expenditures of the Government should be proportioned not to the good but to the ill-deserved of the several tribes; that large bodies of Indians should be supported in entire indolence by the bounty of the Government simply because they are audacious and insolent, while well-disposed Indians are only assisted to self-maintenance, since it is known they will not fight. It is hardly less than absurd, on the first view of it, that delegations from tribes that have frequently defied our authority and fought our troops, and have never yielded more than a partial and grudging obedience to the most reasonable requirements of the

Government, should be entertained at the national capital, feasted, and loaded with presents....

The mistake of those who oppose the present Indian policy is not in erroneously applying to the course of the Government the standard they have taken, but in taking an altogether false standard for the purpose. It is not a whit more unreasonable that the Government should do much for hostile Indians and little for friendly Indians than it is that a private citizen should, to save his life, surrender all the contents of his purse to a highwayman; while on another occasion, to a distressed and deserving applicant for charity, he would measure his contribution by his means and disposition at the time. There is precisely the same justification for the course of the Government in feeding saucy and mischievous Indians to repletion, while permitting more tractable and peaceful tribes to gather a bare subsistence by hard work, or what to an Indian is hard work. It is not, of course, to be understood that the Government of the United States is at the mercy of Indians; but thousands of its citizens are, even thousands of families. Their exposed situation on the extreme verge of settlement affords a sufficient justification to the Government for buying off the hostility of the savages, excited and exasperated as they are, and most naturally so, by the invasion of their hunting-grounds and the threatened extinction of game. It would require one hundred thousand troops at least to form a cordon behind which our settlements could advance with the extent of range, the unrestrained choice of location, the security of feeling, and the freedom of movement which have characterized the growth of the past three or four years. Indeed, the presence of no military force could give that confidence to pioneer enterprise which the general cessation of Indian hostilities has engendered. Men of an adventurous cast will live and work behind a line of troops with, it is possible, some exhilaration of feeling on that account; but, as a rule, men will not place women and children in situations of even possible peril, nor will they put money into permanent improvements under such circumstances. Especially has the absence of Indian hostilities been of the highest value, within the last few years, in directing and determining to the extreme frontier the immigrants arriving in such vast numbers on our shores. Americans habituated to the contemplation of this species of danger as one of the features of pioneer life, will scarcely comprehend the reluctance with which men accustomed to the absolute security of person and property in the settled countries of Europe expose themselves and their families to perils of this kind.[3]

The Use of the Military

The system now pursued in dealing with the roving tribes dangerous to our frontier population and obstructing our industrial progress, is entirely consistent with, and, indeed, requires the occasional use of the military arm, in restraining or chastising refractory individuals and bands. Such a use of the military constitutes no abandonment of the "peace policy," and involves no disparagement of it. It was not to be expected—it was not in the nature of things—that the entire body of wild Indians should submit to be restrained in their Ishmaelitish proclivities without a struggle on the part of the more audacious to maintain their traditional freedom. In the first announcement made of the reservation system, it was expressly declared that the Indians should be made as comfortable on, and as uncomfortable off, their reservations as it was in the power of the Government to make them; that such of them as went right should be protected and fed, and such as went wrong should be harassed and scourged without intermission.

It was not anticipated that the first proclamation of this policy to the tribes concerned would effect the entire cessation of existing evils; but it was believed that persistence in the course marked out would steadily reduce the number of the refractory, both by the losses sustained in actual conflict and by the desertion of individuals as they should become weary of a profitless and hopeless struggle, until, in the near result, the system adopted should apply without exception to all the then roving and hostile tribes. Such a use of the strong arm of the Government is not war, but discipline. Yet it would seem impossible for many persons to apprehend any distinction between a state of general Indian war, and the occasional use of the regular military force of the country in enforcing the reservation individuals or bands. Such persons appear to think that the smallest degree of Indian hostilities is equivalent to the largest degree of such hostilities, or at least to hold that if we are to have any Indian troubles whatever—if everything in the conduct of Indian affairs is not to be as clam and serene as a summer day—we might just as well have all the Indians of the continent on our hands at once. Upon the other side, many persons zealously and painfully intent on securing justice to the aborigines of the country, bewail the slightest use of the military in carrying out the reservation system and repressing depredations, as in effect a making of war upon the Indians and a resort to the bloody methods of the past. . . .

It will be sufficient, perhaps, to mark the distinction, to say that a general Indian war could not be carried on with the present military force of the

United States, or anything like it. Regiments would be needed where now are only companies, and long lines of posts would have to be established for the protection of regions which, under the safeguard of the feeding system, are not left wholly uncovered. On the other hand, by the reservation system and the feeding system combined, the occasions for collision are so reduced by lessening the points of contact, and the number of Indians available for hostile expeditions involving exposure, hardship, and danger is so diminished through the appeal made to their indolence and self-indulgence, that the Army in its present force is able to deal effectively with the few marauding bands which refuse to accept the terms of the Government.[4]

Submission Is the Only Hope of the Indians
No one certainly will rejoice more heartily than the present Commissioner when the Indians of this country cease to be in a position to dictate, in any form or degree, to the Government; when, in fact, the last hostile tribe becomes reduced to the condition of suppliants for charity. This is, indeed, the only hope of salvation for the aborigines of the continent. If they stand up against the progress of civilization and industry, they must be relentlessly crushed. The westward course of population is neither to be denied nor delayed for the sake of all the Indians that ever called this country their home. They must yield or perish; and there is something that savors of providential mercy in the rapidity with which their fate advances upon them, leaving them scarcely the chance to resist before they shall be surrounded and disarmed. It is not feebly and futilely to attempt to stay this tide, whose depth and strength can hardly be measured, but to snatch the remnants of the Indian race from destruction from before it, that the friends of humanity should exert themselves in this juncture, and lose no time. And it is because the present system allows the freest extension of settlement and industry possible under the circumstances, while affording space and time for humane endeavors to rescue the Indian tribes from a position altogether barbarous and incompatible with civilization and social progress, that this system must be approved by all enlightened citizens.

Whenever the time shall come that the roving tribes are reduced to a condition of complete dependence and submission, the plan to be adopted in dealing with them must be substantially that which is now being pursued in the case of the more tractable and friendly Indians.... This is the true permanent Indian policy of the Government.[5]

The assistance due to the Indians from the Government in the discharge of those obligations which have been adverted to should not much longer be irrespective of their own efforts. Just so soon as these tribes cease to be formidable, they should be brought distinctly to the realization of the law that if they would eat they must also work. Nor should it be left to their own choices how miserably they will live, in order that they may escape work as much as possible. The Government should extend over them a rigid reformatory discipline, to save them from falling hopelessly into the condition of pauperism and petty crime. Merely to disarm the savages, and to surround them by forces which it is hopeless in them to resist, without exercising over them for a series of years a system of paternal control, requiring them to learn and practice the arts of industry at least until one generation has been fairly started on a course of self-improvement, is to make it pretty much a matter of certainty that by far the larger part of the now roving Indians will become simply vagabonds in the midst of civilization, forming little camps here and there over the face of the Western States, which will be festering sores on the communities near which they are located; the men resorting for a living to basket-making and hog-stealing; the women to fortune-telling and harlotry. No one who looks about him and observes the numbers of our own race who, despite our strong constitutional disposition to labor, the general example of industry, the possession of all the arts and appliances which diminish effort while they multiply results, and the large rewards offered in the constitution of modern society for success in industrial effort, yet sink to the most abject condition from indolence or from vice, can greatly doubt that, unless prompt and vigorous measures are taken by the Government, something like what has been described is to be the fate of the now roving Indians, when they shall be surrounded and disarmed by the extension of our settlements, and deprived of their traditional means of subsistence through the extinction of game. Unused to manual labor, and physically disqualified for it by the habits of the chase, unprovided with tools and implements, without forethought and without self-control, singularly susceptible to evil influences, with strong animal appetites and no intellectual tastes or aspirations to hold those appetites in check, it would be to assume more than would be taken for granted of any white race under the same conditions, to expect that the wild Indians will become industrious and frugal except through a severe course of industrial instruction and exercise, under restraint. The reservation system affords the place for thus dealing with tribes and bands, without the access of influences inimical to peace and virtue. It is only necessary that Federal laws, judiciously framed to meet all the facts of the case, and enacted in season, before the Indians begin to scatter, shall place all the members of this race under a strict reformatory control by the agents of the Government. Especially is it essential that the right of the Government to keep Indians upon the reservations assigned to them, and to arrest and return them whenever they wander away, should be placed beyond dispute.[6]

CHAPTER 26

Edward P. Smith

Commissioner of Indian Affairs (March 17, 1873–December 11, 1875)

EDWARD PARMELEE SMITH was born on June 3, 1827, in South Britain, Connecticut, to Noah and Laura (Parmelee) Smith. While his father died when he was three years of age, Smith went on to graduate from Hanover School and Theological Academy. He then transferred to Dartmouth College before graduating from Yale University. After teaching school for three years, he matriculated at Yale Theological Seminary in 1852. The following year he transferred to Union Theological Seminary before graduating from Andover Theological Seminary in 1854. The following year, he earned his doctor of divinity degree from Andover and was ordained in the Pepperell (Massachusetts) Congregational Church, where he spent the next eight years pastoring.[1]

In 1863, Smith took a leave of absence from his pastorate to serve as field secretary for the United States Christian Association, ministering to Union soldiers during the Civil War. By April 1864, he was appointed a field agent for the Army of the Potomac; after resigning his pastorate, he remained with the Army for two years before joining the American Missionary Association based in New York City to help establish schools for Southern freedmen. That same year, Smith, Erastus M. Cravath, and John Ogden founded Fisk College (later Fisk University) in Nashville.

When President Grant initiated his peace policy and solicited mission organizations to nominate Indian agents and superintendents, Interior Secretary Columbus Delano requested the American Missionary Association (AMA) nominate men as Indian agents in Minnesota and Wisconsin. On February 18, 1871, the AMA nominated Smith as agent for the Chippewa (Minnesota) Agency, where he proposed sending the Pembina Band to Turtle Mountain in the Dakota Territory or to the White Earth Agency in Minnesota. He also advocated for harvesting timber from the reservations in order to provide income for the Indians. In a sign of the respect granted to him, Commissioner of Indian Affairs Francis Walker sent Smith with Brigadier General Oliver Otis Howard on a peace commission to the Apaches in Arizona.

With the resignation of Walker, President Grant nominated Smith as commissioner of Indian affairs on March 12, 1873. Supported by Delano, Smith was confirmed by the Senate on March 17. He remained an ardent supporter of nominating missionaries as Indian agents, noting in his 1874 annual report that such men were "harmonious" in their relationships with the Indians and "conscientious" in their duties.[2]

Smith had strong opinions on policy, beginning with his view that the United States need not treat tribes as sovereigns and should not, therefore, feel bound to the "literal terms" of treaties. The United States should, instead, emphasize the wardship of the Indians and extend federal jurisdiction over all Indian criminal acts. He opposed cash annuities and tribal ownership of land while supporting land severalty on the reservations before opening them to homesteading. Smith subscribed to military force when Indians remained off their reservations, specifically recommending the stationing of federal troops at each of the Sioux agencies to enforce policy.[3]

As did all commissioners, Smith supported the policy of civilization, although he argued that without a definitive plan and clear objectives, any such policy was a waste of money. While the United States may have met the letter of the law in negotiating treaties with tribal nations and providing goods and services in exchange for land, the government did not, Smith stated, meet the spirit of the treaties, which he believed mandated civilizing the Indians. American Indians, he explained, had a "large moral claim upon the United States" that included the exchange of goods and services and created a debt against the American people of civilizing the Indians. This final obligation was to begin with teaching the Indians to labor for their own food.

Tribes on the northern Plains occupied much of Smith's energy in his last year in office, especially the Sioux and Northern Cheyenne who left their reservations with impunity. On December 6, 1875, Smith directed the agents to notify Sitting Bull to return to the reservation before January 31, 1876, or face military consequences. But Smith was not around to see the consequences, as he resigned on December 11, 1875, three months after Delano left office. Smith was then elected president of Howard University, a black college founded by the American Missionary Association. Before assuming office, he traveled to Gambia and Sierra Leone, Africa, where he became ill while visiting the island of Sheroro (near Accra). He died on July 27, 1876, and was buried in Africa.

The Fiction in Indian Relations

A radical hindrance is in the anomalous relation of many of the Indian tribes to the Government, which requires them to be treated as sovereign powers and wards at one and the same time. The comparative weakness of the whites made it expedient, in our early history, to deal with the wild Indian tribes as with powers capable of self-protection and fulfilling treaty obligations, and so a kind of fiction and absurdity has come into all our Indian relations. We have in theory over sixty-five independent nations within our borders, with whom we have entered into treaty relations as being sovereign peoples; and at the same time the white agent is sent to control and supervise these foreign powers, and care for them as wards of the Government. This double condition of sovereignty and wardship involves increasing difficulties and absurdities, as the traditional chieftain, losing his hold upon his tribe, ceases to be distinguished for anything except for the lion's share of goods and moneys which the Government endeavors to send, through him, to his nominal subjects, and as the necessities of the Indians, pressed on every side by civilization, require more help and greater discrimination in the manner of distributing the tribal funds. So far, and as rapidly as possible, all recognition of Indians in any other relation than strictly as subjects of the Government should cease....

The Evils of Cash Annuities

The second hindrance, growing directly out of the first, is found in the form in which the benefactions of the Government reach the Indian. In treaties heretofore made with many of the tribes, large sums are stipulated to be paid in cash annuities. Facts show that ordinarily the Indians who have received the most money in this form are in the most unfavorable condition for civilization. The bounty of the Government has pauperized them, and in some cases has tended to brutalize more than to civilize. There are instances where for many years tribes have been receiving from $300 to $500 cash annually to each family of four or five persons, and in all such cases the Indians have made no use of the soil which they possess, and are annually reduced to extreme want within a short time after receiving annuities. These Indians would probably have been far better off to have had only their lands, out of which they might have dug a living, if compelled by hunger, than to have received this bounty in a form that tends to perpetuate idleness and poverty. I recommend that hereafter the appropriations to fulfill these promises for annuities of cash in hand be made for the same amounts, to be expended, in each case, under the direction of the Secretary of the Interior, for purposes of civilization of the tribe, reserving to the discretion of the Secretary the power to pay cash annuities whenever, in his judgment, it is found expedient.

If the objection should be made that this is a violation of a treaty stipulation, the answer is, that the Government is bound to consider the best interests to its wards. And if, in previous years, wrong methods have been adopted, or if the present condition and exigencies require a different method of dealing with the Indians in order to secure their improvement and greatest good, then both justice and humanity require that the change be made.

The Need for Individual Property Rights
The third hindrance is found in the want of individual property rights among Indians. A fundamental difference between barbarians and a civilized people is the difference between a herd and an individual. All barbarous customs tend to destroy individuality. Where everything is held in common, thrift and enterprise have no stimulus of reward, and thus individual progress is rendered very improbable, if not impossible. The starting point of individualism for an Indian is the personal possession of his portion of the reservation. Give him a house within a tract of land, whose corner stakes are plainly recognized by himself and his neighbors, and let whatever can be produced out of this landed estate be considered property in his own name, and the first principle of industry and thrift is recognized. In order to reach this first step, the survey and allotment in severalty of the lands belonging to the Indians must be provided for by congressional legislation.

Law among the Indians
The fourth hindrance is the absence of law for Indians. The first condition of civilization is protection of life and property through the administration of law. As the Indians are taken out of their wild life, they leave behind them the force attaching to the distinctive tribal condition. The chiefs inevitably lose their power over Indians in proportion as the latter come in contact with the Government or with white settlers, until their government becomes, in most cases, a mere form, without power of coercion and restraint. Their authority is founded only on "the consent of the governed," and only as they pander to the whims or vices of the young men of the tribe

can they gain such consent. As a police restraint upon lawlessness, they are of no avail, being themselves subject to the control of the worst element in the tribe. An Indian murdering another Indian is accountable only to the law of retaliation. The State authorities do not concern themselves in punishing the murders among Indians, even when such murder is committed under the shadow of their criminal courts.

I submit... whether it is not necessary that crimes among Indians shall be defined by United States law, and made punishable before United States courts, or whether it may not be practicable to invest magisterial powers in agents and superintendents, by which they may summon a jury among the Indians or other persons residing at the agencies by authority of law, before whom any serious offense against law and order may be tried. Such a court would be the beginning of administration of justice, out of the workings of which would gradually grow a code of laws, which would cover these cases arising in the Indian country, and come to be enforced by a police among themselves....[4]

The Indian Territory
No marked change has appeared in the condition of the five civilized tribes in the Indian Territory. They number 55,000, and occupy a country containing 62,000 square miles, or more than one square mile to a person. No statistical reports having been received concerning them since 1872, the Office has no means of making a comparative statement of their condition, but there is abundant evidence that socially they are in a transition state. They feel the pressure of the white man on every side, and, among the full-bloods especially, there is a growing apprehension that before long the barriers will give way, their country be overrun, and themselves dispossessed. To the more intelligent among them, and especially the mixed-bloods, who are able to see that close contact with the civilization of the whites will help forward rather than retard their own civilization and prosperity, this outlook is not so full of apprehension. Indeed, it is probable that if the question were left to this class among the Indians, with primary reference not only to their own interests, but to the common welfare, they would regard the settlement of families of respectable whites in such numbers as to fairly populate the country as a contribution to the prosperous condition of the Indians, rather than otherwise; provided that before the pressure and competition of white neighbors is permitted, the Indians themselves should have first come into individual ownership of a

homestead, without power to alienate the title, and with a fair acquaintance by experience of its value as a home. In other words, this people are now at the point in civilization where the next lesson can be given, not in councils or in continued isolation, but in the living example of a neighbor, who, by his skill and industry in cultivating the same soil from which they procure a scanty and precarious livelihood, comes rapidly into comfort and wealth. The time has not by any means arrived for throwing this country open to settlement, but the fact is before them, and should now be embraced in their plans for the future, that it is not possible for them and would by no means be well for them, if it were possible, by perpetuating their Indian nationalities, to live always outside the pale of United States citizenship, and that no Indian country can exist perpetually within the boundaries of this Republic without becoming in all essential particulars a part of the United States: and they should at once begin to shape their affairs with reference to this fact, by taking their lands in severalty, and by using all possible means of giving their children such education as will prepare them for contact and competition with white men.

Government for Indian Territory
In order, however, to render such preparatory steps possible by the Indians, a long-neglected duty of providing adequate means for protection of life and property and punishment of crime among 71,000 people who are practically without law or means of justice should at once be undertaken by the United States.

Further effort has been made by leading men among these different tribes in the Indian Territory to procure the establishment of a consolidated government of Indians by Indians; but it has not succeeded, and this large population becomes more and more helpless under the increasing lawlessness among themselves and the alarming intrusion of outlawed white men.

The nearest United States court for this whole Territory is that of the western district of Arkansas at Fort Smith. The expense of making arrests by marshals, and securing the attendance of witnesses over the great distances of the Indian Territory, makes the court practically of little avail for protection or punishment. Meanwhile the country continues to afford an asylum for refugees from justice from the States and to invite the immigration of the very worst class of men that infest an Indian border. The need of this Territory today is a government of the simplest form possible;

and, in my judgement, a government similar to that provided for "the territory of the United States northwest of the river Ohio," preliminary to the organization of a general assembly, would, I think, be the best adapted for the Indian Territory at present, both on account of its simplicity and of its economy....

The anomalous state of social and political affairs in this Territory renders some such form of government as above set forth much better adapted to the circumstances and necessities of the case than an elective and representative government could possibly be for several years. Of the seventy-one thousand, all but seven thousand have attained to such a degree of civilization as to be capable of appreciating and profiting by a government of this character, and the remainder being the wilder and wholly uneducated tribes could be readily brought to feel its force in restraint and education. On the other hand, an elective government for these people would bring together representatives from thirty-five different tribes, and any legislation or any discussion to be made intelligible must be translated into as many different tongues. But a more serious, and I think more fatal, objection would be found in the sectional and tribal jealousies, which have their strength in proportion to the ignorance of a people, and among these thirty-five tribes would render most, if not all, the enactments of such a representative body practically of no avail to govern its people or enforce its laws.[5]

Civilization

The question of Indian civilization is deeper and broader than is to be found in the inquiry and answer as to whether an Indian can be civilized. The question in that form has been long since answered, and the only form remaining, which is of practical interest to the American people, relates to the methods which are essential to any extended and successful effort for that end. I believe that the present unsatisfactory condition in which Indians of this country are still found, notwithstanding the large and increasing outlays of money which the Government has been making for a half-century, is due to the fact that by far the largest portion of the expenditures have been made with no practical reference to the question of civilization. An annuity in money or blankets, or bacon and beef, may have a tendency to draw the Indians within the reach of the Government, and prepare them for the beginning of a work of civilization, and also to render them disinclined to take up arms and go upon the war path. But with any tribe a few years of this treatment is sufficient for the purpose, and after this end has been gained, a continuation of the feeding and clothing, without a reference to further improvement on the part of the Indians, is simply a waste of expenditure. This has been the case with a large portion of the money spent upon Indians during the last fifty years. It is true that the letter of treaties may have been complied with by such expenditures, and thus the credit of the nation saved in form. But the spirit of the treaties, which uniformly looked toward the civilization of the Indians, has been disregarded, in that no reasonable methods have been devised and adopted for promoting civilization. This is manifest from the fact that the question has not been raised as to whether an Indian should be subjected to a system of enforced industry, and no plan has been devised looking toward his elevation, by bringing to bear upon him the ordinary motives of industry, which are found in the responsibilities that attach to self-support and individual manhood.

This negligence or long continued disregard of the main question relative to Indians has largely resulted from the theory adopted from the beginning as to the political status of Indians. They have been treated as if capable of acting for themselves in the capacity of a nation, whereas all history shows no record of a tribe, within our republic, able to assume and continue the character and relations of a sovereign people. There may have been a reason in the weakness of the early colonies, and far superior numbers of their Indian foes, for recognizing this condition of Indian sovereignty. But that has long since passed away, and there is no longer any occasion for recognizing the tribes who remain with us as foreigners. Their own interests, more strongly even than those of the Government, require that they should be recognized and treated for what they are, an ignorant and helpless people, who have a large moral claim upon the United States—a debt which cannot be discharged by gifts of blankets and bacon, or any routine official care for their protection or relief. These are trifles compared with the one boon—civilization—which every consideration of humanity requires that we should give them. We have taken from them the possibility of living in their way, and are bound in return to give them the possibility of living in our way—an obligation we do not begin to discharge when we merely attempt to supply their wants for food and clothing. They need to be taught to take care of themselves. If any demonstration of the feasibility of this teaching is required, there are very few Indian agents now in the service who cannot, each out of his own experience and observation, furnish facts remarkably conclusive on this subject. An Indian is subject to like passions with the rest of us. So long as he can be subsisted by rations or by the chase, he will not labor; so long as he declines to labor, he cannot take the first step in civilization. The call to labor must come to him, not through memorials or treaties, councils or presents, but through his necessities.[6] He must be driven to toil by cold and the pangs of hunger. Then, when he has taken this first step toward self-support, his wants, which at the beginning were registered only in his stomach, take on multiplied forms, and urge to increased industry. Naturally, when a man begins to toil for that which he receives, he begins to learn the value of personal-property rights, and thus takes the first step in separating from his tribe, and toward individual manhood....[7]

CHAPTER 27

John Quincy Smith

Commissioner of Indian Affairs
(December 11, 1875–September 27, 1877)

JOHN QUINCY SMITH was born on November 5, 1824, near Waynesville, Ohio, to Thomas Edward Smith and Mary Kennedy Whitehill. While his early education was limited due to working on his family's farm, Smith attended but did not graduate from Miami University. In 1852, he married Lydia Emeline Evans and moved to Clinton County, Ohio. In 1859, he was elected to the Ohio State Senate where he roomed with future President James A. Garfield and became friends with John Sherman and Ulysses S. Grant. In 1861, Smith gained election to the Ohio State House of Representatives, serving two years (1862–1863). He was later elected to the Ohio Board of Equalization and was reelected to the state senate in 1871.[1]

In the fall of 1872, the politically ambitious Smith was elected to the US Congress, where he served two years before losing reelection to John S. Savage in 1874. With the resignation of Edward Smith as commissioner of Indian affairs in December 1875, Senator John Sherman (Republican, Ohio) recommended to President Grant that he nominate Smith as commissioner of Indian affairs. The Senate confirmed Smith on December 11, 1875, and he took office immediately, serving near the end of the president's peace policy.[2]

Smith did not propose any new policy as commissioner. He did, however, argue that the United States never had a coherent and intelligent policy toward tribal nations, adding that it might be too late to adopt such a policy since tribes had lost so much land, making it impossible to live as they once had. This "utter destruction" of Indian civilization was inevitable, Smith supposed, leading him to accept as fact that policy should work toward civilizing and assimilating the Indians before they died as "miserable and degraded" human beings.[3]

While he penned only one annual report, Smith was committed to the consolidation of the tribes and the opening of reservations to settlement. He proposed allotting in severalty the best land to Indians and then making it inalienable for twenty years—and then alienable only to other Indians. While the latter concept was a novel and progressive idea, it did not gain political traction. Smith also advocated for US law and federal court jurisdiction over the Indians and granting them American citizenship as soon as they were ready. American Indians were then to be treated as any other American.

Smith proposed relocating the Sioux and all tribal nations from Kansas, Nebraska, Colorado, Arizona, New Mexico, Nevada, Wyoming, Montana, and the Dakota Territory to Indian Territory; all the tribes from Minnesota and Wisconsin to the White Earth Reservation in northern Minnesota; and all tribes from the Pacific Northwest to the Yakima Reservation. If the Indians "did well," Smith reasoned, they would be left where they were to adjust to modern America. If they did not cooperate, military force would be used, an option Smith was not afraid to employ to enforce policy, as demonstrated by the Battle of the Little Bighorn and the forced removal of the Ponca. While supportive of the military to enforce policy, Smith did not support the transfer of the Indian Office to the War Department, and he opposed utilizing Army officers as Indian agents, preferring civilian missionaries. The former congressman believed friendship rather than military force would win over the Indians. In early 1876, Smith argued that the Indian wars were over and that peace would prevail. The June 25, 1876, Battle of the Little Bighorn proved otherwise. In 1877, when Congress enacted legislation permitting—but not mandating—the removal of the Ponca to Indian Territory, Indian affairs became more complicated.[4]

Smith implemented strict controls on Indian Office purchases, with the Board of Indian Commissioners carefully observing all expenditures. In the end, as was the case for many commissioners, Smith was charged with incompetence in managing the Indian Office, which led the Board of Indian Commissioners to investigate his actions. Ezra Hayt, chairman of the board, was especially critical of Smith, who resigned before the board issued its finding; he left office on September 27, 1877.

Just months later, President Rutherford B. Hayes appointed Smith as United States counsel general in Montreal, where he remained until 1882. With the election of Grover Cleveland as president in 1884, and the Democratic Party's views on tariff reform, Smith chose to join the Democratic Party. By then he had left public life and retired to his farm near Waynesville, Ohio. He died at the age of seventy-seven on December 30, 1901.

An Incoherent Policy

In order to form any wise opinion as to the best method of dealing hereafter with our Indians, a clear conception of their actual condition, and of our present relations with them, is necessary. From the first settlement of the country by white men until a comparatively recent period, the Indians have been constantly driven westward from the Atlantic. A zigzag, ever-varying line, more or less definitely marked, extending from Canada to the Gulf of Mexico, and always slowly moving west has been known as the "frontier" or "border." Along this border has been an almost incessant struggle, the Indians to retain and the whites to get possession; the war being broken by periods of occasional and temporary peace, which usually followed treaties whereby the Indians agreed to surrender large tracts of their lands. This peace would continue until the lands surrendered had been occupied by whites, when the pressure of emigration would again break over the border, and the Indian, by force or treaty, be compelled to surrender another portion of his cherished hunting-grounds.

So long as the illimitable West offered to the Indian fresh hunting grounds, he was unwilling to exchange his wild freedom and indolent existence for the restraints and toil of the rude and imperfect civilization to which it was possible for him in only one life-time to attain. If any tribe of Indians in this country had made the effort to abandon their savage mode of life and undertake self-support by labor, it is at least doubtful whether for many years the change would not have rendered them more miserable and retched. Their lack of means, or knowledge, and of previous training would in all probability, have made such an attempt a conspicuous failure. If individual Indians had succeeded in acquiring property, they would probably have been swindled out of it by unscrupulous white men. The natural and the easiest course was to remove west and continue to hunt....

No new hunting grounds remain, and the civilization or the utter destruction of the Indians is inevitable. The next twenty-five years are to determine the fate of a race. If they cannot be taught, and taught very soon, to accept the necessities of their situation and begin in earnest to provide for their own wants by labor in civilized pursuits, they are destined to speedy extinction....

[T]he road out of barbarism is a long and difficult one. Even in enlightened Europe there are millions of people whose ancestors a few generations ago were as ignorant and poor and degraded as our most advanced Indian tribes now are. Civilization is a vague, indefinite, comparative term. Our children's grandchildren may look upon our civilization as very rude and imperfect. It is not my wish to give any rose-colored view of the present condition of our Indians. Many of them are as miserable and degraded as men can be; but it cannot be denied that others are making reasonably satisfactory progress.

In considering whether modifications of existing methods may not be desirable, I have arrived at the conviction that the welfare and progress of the Indians require the adoption of three principles of policy: First: Concentration of all Indians on a few reservations; Second: Allotment to them of lands in severalty; Third: Extension over them of United States law and the jurisdiction of United States courts.

Consolidation of Reservations

The reservations upon which . . . the Indians should be consolidated, are the Indian Territory, the White Earth reservation in Northern Minnesota, and a reservation in the southern part of Washington Territory, probably the Yakama reservation. If it should be found impracticable to remove the Indians of Colorado, Utah, New Mexico, and Arizona, to the Indian Territory, they might be concentrated on some suitable reservation either in Colorado or Arizona.

I am well aware that it will take a long time, much patient effort, and considerable expense, to effect this proposed consolidation; but after consulting with many gentlemen thoroughly acquainted with Indian questions and Indian character, I am satisfied that the undertaking can be accomplished. If legislation were secured giving the President authority to remove any tribe or band, or any portion of a tribe or band, whenever in his judgment it was practicable, to any one of the reservations named, and if Congress would appropriate, from year to year, a sum sufficient to enable him to take advantage of every favorable opportunity to make such removals, I am confident that a few years' trial would conclusively demonstrate the entire feasibility of the plan. I believe that all the Indians in Kansas, Nebraska, and Dakota, and a part at least of those in Wyoming and Montana, could be induced to remove to the Indian Territory. There is also ground for the belief that the Colorado, Arizona, New Mexico Indians, and a part if not all of those in Nevada, could also be taken to that Territory. . . .

That the Indian sentiment is opposed to such removal is true. Difficulties were experienced in bringing to the Territory its present inhabitants from east of the Mississippi; but the obstacles were overcome, and experience shows that there the race can thrive. With a fair degree of persistence, the removal thither of other Indians can also be secured. The Pawnees have recently gone there and seem content with their new home. The Poncas, and even the Red Cloud and Spotted Tail Sioux, give evidence that they are ready for the change; and if Congress will make a liberal appropriation to effect the removal of these Sioux, it is quite likely that within a year or two, other bands now on the Missouri River may also be induced to remove. If the Sioux are given a suitable reservation in that Territory for a permanent home, and are aided by the Government for a few years in their efforts at agriculture and stock-raising, I know of no reason why they may not, in one generation, become as far advanced as are the Cherokees and Choctaws now.

It is to be regretted that all the Indians in the United States cannot be removed to the Indian Territory; but it is doubtful whether, at least for many years, it will be best to attempt to remove Indians thither from the region of the great lakes or from the Pacific coast. I would therefore suggest that, for the tribes of Wisconsin and Minnesota, and the wandering Pembinas in Dakota, the White Earth reservation is best adapted as a permanent home. Containing thirty-six townships of well-watered timber and wheat lands, it offers far better agricultural facilities than do other reservations in those States, and is in about the same latitude with them.

My information in regard to the proper reservation for the Indians on the Pacific Coast is less definite, and I have suggested the Yakama reservation, mainly because it is well known that the Indians there . . . have made remarkable progress. . . . By the concentration of Indians on a few reservations, it is obvious that much of the difficulty now surrounding the Indian question will vanish. Many agencies now conducted at large expense could be abolished. The aggregate boundary-lines between the reservations and country occupied by white people would be greatly reduced, and the danger of violence, bloodshed, and mutual wrong materially lessened. The sale of liquors and arms could be more effectually prevented; bad white men could more easily be kept out of the Indian country; necessary supplies could be more cheaply furnished; a far smaller military force would be required to keep the peace; and generally, the Indians, being more compact, could be more efficiently aided and controlled by the officers of the Government. Moreover, large bodies of land would be thrown open to settlement, proceeds of whose sale would be ample to defray all expense of the removals.

Allotment in Severalty

It is doubtful whether any high degree of civilization is possible without individual ownership of land. The records of the past and the experience of the present testify that the soil should be made secure to the individual by all the guarantees which law can devise, and that nothing less will induce men to put forth their best exertions. No general law exists which provide that Indians shall select allotments in severalty, and it seems to me a matter of great moment that provision should be made not only permitting, but requiring, the head of each Indian family, to accept the allotment of a reasonable amount of land, to be the property of himself and his lawful heirs, in lieu of any interest in any common tribal possession. Such allotments should be inalienable for at least twenty, perhaps fifty years, and if situated in a permanent Indian reservation, should be transferable only among Indians.

I am not unaware that this proposition will meet with strenuous opposition from the Indians themselves. Like the whites, they have ambitious men, who will resist to the utmost of their power any change tending to reduce the authority which they have acquired by personal effort or by inheritance; but it is essential that these men and their claims have pushed aside and that each individual should feel that his home is his own; that he owes no allegiance to any great man or to any faction; that he has a direct personal interest in the soil on which he lives, and that that interest will be faithfully protected for him and for his children by the Government.

Law for Indians

My predecessors have frequently called attention to the startling fact that we have within our midst 275,000 people, the least intelligent portion of our population, for whom we provide no law, either for their protection or for the punishment of crime committed among themselves. Civilization even among white men could not long exist without the guarantees which law alone affords; yet our Indians are remitted by a great civilized government to the control, if control it can be called, of the rude regulations of petty, ignorant tribes. Year after year we expend millions of dollars for these people in the faint hope that, without law, we can civilize them. That hope has been, to a great degree, a long disappointment; and year after year we repeat the folly of the past. That the benevolent efforts and purposes of the Government have proved so largely fruitless, is, in my judgment, due more to its failure to make these people amenable to our laws than to any other cause, or to all other causes combined.

I believe it to be the duty of Congress at once to extend over Indian reservations the jurisdiction of United States courts, and to declare that each Indian in the United States shall occupy the same relation to law that a white man does. An Indian should be given to understand that no ancient custom, no tribal regulation, will shield him from just punishment for crime; and also that he will be effectually protected, by the authority and power of the Government, in his life, liberty, property, and character, as certainly as if he were a white man. There can be no doubt of the power of Congress to do this. . . . I regard this suggestion as by far the most important which I have to make in this report.[5]

CHAPTER 28

Ezra A. Hayt

Commissioner of Indian Affairs (September 20, 1877–January 29, 1880)

EZRA AYRES HAYT was born on February 23, 1823, near Patterson, New York, and by the age of twenty-one, he was a successful dry goods businessman, making a good fortune before retiring in 1868. While he was brought up in the Presbyterian Church, Hayt identified with the Reformed Church of America. In 1868, he became president of the International Trust Company of New Jersey while remaining active in church affairs. Six year later, thanks to President Grant's peace policy, the Reformed Church nominated Hayt for a position on the Board of Indian Commissioners; he served six years on the board before resigning in protest when the board was made subordinate to the authority of Interior Secretary Carl Schurz.[1]

While serving on the board, Hayt oversaw the purchasing of goods for the Indian Office, ensuring that tribes received the goods they had been promised. In 1876, when Commissioner John Quincy Smith purchased flour to be sent to Indian Territory, the Indian Office shipped the flour before it was inspected for quality and quantity, precipitating a dispute between the board and the commissioner. Hayt accused Smith of refusing to cooperate in the investigation, with Smith's chief clerk, Samuel A. Galpin, charging Hayt with making derogatory remarks toward the commissioner, escalating the tension. On January 12, 1877, President Grant demanded and received Hayt's resignation, and he left the Board of Indian Commissioners on January 20.[2]

In the meantime, Rutherford B. Hayes was elected president in November 1876 and sworn into office the following March. Hayes immediately nominated Carl Schurz as his secretary of the interior, much to the chagrin of Republicans who recognized Schurz was a bitter enemy of Grant.[3] Schurz forced Smith to resign, intending to nominate the philanthropist Herbert Welsh of Philadelphia as commissioner. When Welsh declined, Schurz instead nominated Hayt, a man who vigorously investigated and resisted the infamous Indian rings. Hayt agreed to accept the position if Schurz would seek to increase the annual remuneration from $3,500 to $5,000 and do all he could to prevent the transfer of the Indian Office to the War Department. Schurz agreed and appointed Hayt as commissioner on September 17, 1877; he took office three days later. The Senate, divided over Hayt's fitness for office, did not confirm the commissioner until December 12, notwithstanding numerous newspapers supporting Schurz and Hayt.[4]

Hayt's tenure was tempestuous, as he dealt with the residual effects of the Sioux War of 1876, the remnants of the 1873 Modoc War, the Nez Perce/Chief Joseph ordeal in 1877, the Bannack outbreak of 1878, Ponca removal, the flight of the Northern Cheyenne from Indian Territory in 1878, and the Ute outbreak of 1879. These matters consumed much of Hayt's time as commissioner, which was largely filled with responding to exigencies with expediency, rather than well-thought-out policies.

Schurz exercised a strong hand in Indian affairs, seeking wide-ranging reforms, including keeping the Indian Office out of the War Department. As for Hayt, he largely continued the policies of his predecessors, including advocating for an Indian police force, a code of law for Indian Country, allotment in severalty, education, missionary work, Indian labor in exchange for rations, and consolidation of the tribes on smaller reservations. But Hayt also advanced the idea of establishing different classifications for Indian agents, depending on agency size among others, and he recommended Congress authorize a solicitor for Indian affairs.[5]

The commissioner primarily focused on consolidation of agencies and land severalty. For the former he proposed a plan whereby thirty-six reservations could be consolidated into nine, reducing the tribal land base for these tribes from 21,922,507 acres to 4,239,052. In his first annual report he acknowledged it was unwise to relocate northern tribes to Indian Territory due to health and logistical concerns. But this did not stop him from favoring the removal of all tribes from Arizona and New Mexico to Indian Territory, a proposition that Congress rejected in 1878.[6] As for severalty, Hayt proposed allotting land but opposed unrestricted fee patents since they would encourage alienation of land. And despite having been a Reformed Church appointee to the Indian Office, Hayt opposed filling Indian agent vacancies with churchmen. He supported Frank Armstrong's (Hampton Institute) and Richard H. Pratt's (Carlisle Indian School) experiment in Indian education, opening the door for government-sponsored schools for Indians.

Hayt made two major policy decisions that cast doubt on his tenure. The first was the flight of the Northern Cheyenne from Indian Territory back to the northern Plains. In September 1878, chiefs Dull Knife and Little Wolf headed north with 353 Northern Cheyenne, in part due to promised goods and supplies not arriving in Indian Territory in a timely fashion. Hayt shouldered the blame on the matter that garnered widespread media attention. When the White River Utes killed agent Nathan Meeker in 1879 after annuities were unpaid and food and supplies did not arrive, Hayt's response was to remove the Utes to Indian Territory, with the press lambasting his callous comments.

When Hayt's former chief clerk, William Leeds, testified that Hayt spent much of his time on his private business interests, Hayt's days were numbered. In 1879, irregularities among the San Carlos Apache led to an investigation that uncovered evidence that Hayt's son, Edward Knapp Hayt, was surreptitiously seeking to sever a portion of the reservation so he could purchase a mine then located on tribal lands.[7]

The Board of Indian Commissioners, on which Hayt once served for six years, no longer supported him. On January 29, 1880, Schurz was forced to ask for—and received—Hayt's resignation. Hayt then disappeared from public life and returned to New York, losing much of his wealth during the 1893 depression. Ezra Hayt died on January 13, 1902, discredited and with a tarnished reputation.

An Indian Police Force

The preservation of order is as necessary to the promotion of civilization as is the enactment of wise laws. Both are essential to the peace and happiness of any people. As a means of preserving order upon an Indian reservation, Indian police have been found to be of prime importance. I have recommended an additional outlay of money to enable the government to extend the usefulness of a police system now in its infancy with us. In Canada, the entire body of Indians are kept in order by such force. In this country, as far as it has been tried, it works admirably. I would recommend that the force be composed of Indians, properly officered and drilled by white men, and where capable Indians can be found, that they be promoted to command, as reward for faithful service. The Army has used Indians for scouts with great success, and wherever employed the Indian has been found faithful to the trust confided to him. I would also recommend that the police force be supplied with a uniform . . . with the addition of a few brass buttons by way of distinction. The employment of such a force, properly officered and handled, would, in great measure, relieve the Army from doing police duty on Indian reservations. I am thoroughly satisfied that the saving in life and property by the employment of such a force would be very large, and that it would materially aid in placing the entire Indian population of the country on the road to civilization.

Education and Civilization

There is little hope of the civilization of the older wild Indian, and the only practical question is how to control and govern him, so that his savage instincts shall be kept from violent outbreaks. There is, however, much encouragement to work for the gradual elevation of the partially civilized adult Indians, and especially of the youths of both sexes; and considerable progress has been made, notwithstanding the difficulties which a humane treatment of the Indians has had to encounter. These difficulties may be stated as partially growing out of the dishonesty of Indian agents, traders, and contractors, by which Indians have been deprived of their just dues, and sometimes of the necessaries of life. Another and serious drawback is to be found in the encroachment of greedy white men, who surround them and continually plot to deprive them of their possessions. Unfortunately, Indians judge all white men by these specimens, with which they are only too familiar. Notwithstanding all the disadvantages, there is ... a perceptible progress, which, under more favorable circumstances, might be greatly accelerated.

Undoubtedly our chief hope is in the education of the young, and just here our best and most persistent efforts should be made. The Indian youths in the various schools show surprising progress in penmanship and drawing, and can be taught the ordinary branches of a common-school education as readily as white children, except, perhaps, arithmetic. Such being the case, every effort should be made to take advantage of the aptitudes they have exhibited, and to bring Indian children into schools. I would advise the establishment of a rule making it compulsory upon all Indian children between the ages of six and fourteen years to attend schools, and requiring English alone to be spoken and taught therein; and it is decidedly preferable that as many of them as possible should be placed in boarding schools, which possess more advantages in every way than day schools, for the reason that the exposure of children who attend only day schools to the demoralization and degradation of an Indian home neutralizes the efforts of the school teacher, especially those efforts which are directed to advancement in morality and civilization. Forty children can be boarded and instructed at an expense of one hundred and twenty-five dollars each per annum, the cost being slightly reduced in schools containing a larger number of pupils.

I recommend that provision be made to give a higher education, in some of our normal schools at the East, to Indian youths sufficiently advanced to enable them to enter such schools, in order that the bureau may be supplied with educated interpreters to take the place of the incompetent men who now perform the service with discredit to themselves and detriment to the Indians.

In order to carry out the policy... I have recommended an appropriation of fifty thousand dollars, as a special fund, for the establishment and support of additional schools wherever, in the judgement of the Secretary of the Interior, they may be most needed. In addition to the ordinary schools, I particularly recommend the establishment of industrial schools, in which those over fourteen years of age may be taught the various trades and thus be qualified to become self-supporting.[8]

Rethinking Relocation

Experience has demonstrated the impolicy of sending northern Indians to the Indian Territory. To go no farther back then the date of the Pawnee removal, it will be seen that the effect of a radical change of climate is disastrous, as this tribe alone, in the first two years, lost by death over 800 out of its number of 2,376. The northern Cheyennes have suffered severely, and the Poncas who were recently removed from contact with the unfriendly Sioux, and arrived there in July last, have already lost 36 by death, which, by an ordinary computation, would be the death rate for the entire tribe for a period of four years.

In this connection, I recommend the removal of all the Indians in Colorado and Arizona to the Indian Territory. In Colorado, gold and silver mines are scattered over a wide extent of territory, and are to be found in every conceivable direction, running into Indian reservations. Of course, miners will follow the various leads and prospect new ones without regard to the barriers set up by an Indian reservation. Hence the sojourn of Indians in this State will be sure to lead to strife, contention, and war, besides entailing an enormous expense to feed and provide for them. Again, there is no hope of civilizing these Indians while they reside in Colorado, as all the arable land in the State is required for its white settlers. A mining population needs in its immediate vicinity abundant facilities for agriculture to feed it. The question of feeding the white population of the State is one of paramount importance, and will certainly force itself on the attention of the government.

What is true of Colorado is to a certain extent true of Arizona also; but in addition, thereto, it must be considered that the expense of transporting annuities and supplies is enormous. The government has been paying eight and ten cents per pound for the transportation of flour and other necessaries to feed the Indians, and the total cost of maintaining the Indian tribes of Arizona for the past three years has been $1,084,000. While the Indians are kept there this expenditure will go on, perhaps indefinitely increasing, without any corresponding improvement in their welfare or civilization.[9]

Consolidation as a Means of Economy
During the last session of Congress, at the verbal request of the House Committee on Indian Affairs, a bill was drawn in this office and sent to the committee, providing for the removal and consolidation of certain Indians in the States of Oregon, Colorado, Iowa, Kansas, Nebraska, Wisconsin, and Minnesota, and the Territories of Washington and Dakota.

The objects sought to be attained by the bill were as follows: First, the reduction of the number of agencies, and consequently a large annual reduction of the expense attending the civilization of the Indians and the management of their affairs. Second, the consolidation of the Indians upon reservations where they might be best protected in their personal and property rights. Third, the sale of the lands vacated by the consolidation, and the use of a portion of the funds arising therefrom in the removal and settlement of the Indians, now residing on the reservations to be vacated, on the reservations where the consolidation is to be effected, the balance of the money to be funded for their use, the interest thereon to be expended in lieu of direct appropriations for the benefit of all the Indians on the reservation as created by the bill....

[I]t may be said that the various tribes and bands of Indians embraced in the bill now occupy thirty-six reservations, containing 21,922,507 acres of land, under charge of twenty agents and the necessary attendant corps of teachers and other employees. Upon the reduction proposed in the bill they will occupy nine reservations, containing 4,239,052 acres, under the charge of nine agents, all of whom are now provided for by law. A reduction of twenty-five reservations and eleven agencies will thus be effected. There will be restored to the public domain 17,642,455 acres of land, and an annual saving in agency expenses to the amount of $120,000 will be effected, after making a liberal allowance for an increase of teachers, farmers, &c., at the several consolidated agencies.

Since the presentation of the bill to the committee a more particular investigation of the subject has convinced me that further consolidations of like character are not only possible, but expedient and advisable. There is a vast area of land in the Indian Territory not yet occupied. Into this should, and may, be gathered the major portion of the Indians of New Mexico, Colorado, and Arizona. The Klamath Indians of Oregon can, with material advantage to themselves and the government, be removed to the Yakama Reservation, in Washington Territory, to which reservation the Bannocks and Malheur Indians will also be immediately sent. This policy should also be pursued with the Indians of Western Dakota, Montana, Idaho, and other sections; the paramount object being to locate them on good agricultural lands to which permanent title can be given, and to sustain and aid them thereon until they become self-supporting.

A Policy of Self-Support
Among the most radical defects of the policy formerly pursued with the Indians has been the frequent changes in their location which have been made, and the fact that the method of distributing the annuities which they have received under various treaties has, in general, encouraged them in idleness and dependence on the government, whereas they should have been used in locating them in permanent homes and in educating them in agricultural and other civilized pursuits. But a small proportion of the lands now occupied by the Indians is utilized for any purpose. They are, in the main, dependent upon the charity of Congress for the little aid that is given to assist them in agricultural pursuits, and in many cases the meager amount given, however honestly expended, is wasted on account of its insufficiency to accomplish the desired ends. In my judgment, permanent homes, sufficient aid to enable them to build houses, cultivate the soil, and to subsist them until they have harvested their first crops, will wean them entirely from their old methods of life, and in the course of a few years enable them to become entirely self-supporting.[10]

It is no longer a question whether Indians will work. They are steadily asking for opportunities to do so, and the Indians who today are willing and anxious to engage in civilized labor are largely in the majority. There is an almost universal call for lands in severalty, and it is remarkable that this request should come from nearly every tribe except the five civilized tribes in the Indian Territory. There is also a growing desire among Indians to live in houses, and more houses have been built, and are now in course of erection, than have been put up during any previous year. The demand for agricultural implements and appliances, and for wagons and harness for farming and freighting purposes is constantly increasing, and an unusual readiness to wear citizens' clothing is also manifest.

The loss of the buffalo, which is looked upon by Indians as disastrous, has really been to them a blessing in disguise. They now see clearly that they must get their living out of the soil by their own labor, and a few years' perseverance in the beneficial policy now pursued will render three-fourths of our Indians self-supporting. Already very many tribes have a surplus of products for sale.

A Patent for Land

The more intelligent and best disposed Indians are now earnestly asking for a title in severalty to their lands as a preliminary to supporting themselves from the products of the soil. The number of persons who can be employed in stock raising is small, since comparatively little labor is required and a few men can herd and take care of a thousand head of cattle; but the cultivation of the soil will give employment to the whole Indian race. The only sure way to make Indians tillers of the soil, under the best conditions to promote their welfare, is to give each head of a family one hundred and sixty acres of land, and to each unmarried adult eighty acres, and to issue patents for the same, making the allotments inalienable and free from taxation for twenty-five years.[11]

CHAPTER 29

Rowland E. Trowbridge

Commissioner of Indian Affairs (March 15, 1880–March 19, 1881)

ROWLAND EBENEZER TROWBRIDGE was born to Stephen and Elizabeth Trowbridge on June 18, 1821, in Horseheads, Chemung County, New York. Just months after his birth, Trowbridge's father, a politically active and deeply religious man, moved his family to Oakland County, Michigan, where he served as a Presbyterian elder and was elected as a state senator. Trowbridge graduated from Kenyon College in Gambier, Ohio, in 1841, where he became good friends with Rutherford B. Hayes. Upon graduation, Trowbridge returned to Michigan and engaged in farming with his father, although he soon entered politics as a Whig. After the birth of the Republican Party, he became a strong supporter of Abraham Lincoln. He was elected to the Michigan State Senate in 1856, serving four years in the statehouse.[1]

In the fall of 1860, Trowbridge was elected as a Republican to the US Congress, taking office on March 3, 1861. Although he failed to gain reelection in the midterm election of 1862, he regained his seat in 1864, serving an additional two terms in Congress with his college friend Rutherford B. Hayes (Republican, Ohio). During his final term in the House, he served as chairman of the Committee on Agriculture. When he lost reelection in 1868, he returned to Michigan and resumed farming.[2]

The election of Hayes as president in the fall of 1876 opened a new opportunity for Trowbridge. Hayes appointed Carl Schurz secretary of the interior to root out corruption in the Indian Office. When Ezra Hayt became the object of corruption charges, the president turned to his trusted friend, Rowland Trowbridge, to serve as commissioner of Indian affairs. While the Board of Indian Commissioners recommended General Eliphalet Whittlesey, Hayes stuck with his college friend. At the president's request, Schurz nominated Trowbridge as commissioner on February 20; the Senate confirmed him seven days later, and he assumed office on March 15, 1880.

Trowbridge never penned an annual report, with the 1880 report signed by E. M. Marble, acting commissioner, due to Trowbridge's continued illness. Nonetheless, the 1880 report included Trowbridge's views, and while he did not identify any new policy, he supported church-nominated Indian agents and superintendents, and he advocated for a policy of assigning a single religious denomination to each agency, a policy Protestants supported and Catholics despised. Interior Secretary Schurz reversed this policy and opened the reservations to all denominations.

As commissioner, Trowbridge advocated strict social controls, including institutionalizing marriages between Indians and prohibiting polygamy, employing Indian police to enforce such policies. He supported government boarding and day schools (boasting that some seven thousand children were enrolled in such schools by 1880), and he supported the Hampton Institute and Carlisle Indian School industrial models. For the latter, he favored not only agricultural education but also animal husbandry, with the Indian Office assigning 10,283 cattle to Indians to encourage ranching. He also initiated land severalty on the Crow and Fort Hall (Shoshone and Bannock) reservations by employing provisions from agreements executed in the spring of 1880.[3] Perhaps his greatest contribution was the level of honesty he brought to the Indian Office.

But Trowbridge was ill during much of his tenure as commissioner, limiting his effectiveness. Schurz assumed control over all Indian inspectors and was active in setting and advocating policy. Due to poor health, Trowbridge was absent from office nearly half of the time he served. In November 1880, he offered to resign due to ill health, but Schurz convinced him to stay. He resigned on March 19, 1881. He died thirty-two days later on April 20 in Birmingham, Michigan, at the age of fifty-nine.

Industrial Education
In June last, in fulfillment of a promise made when their children were surrendered to Lieutenant [Henry] Pratt, a "school committee" of chiefs and headmen, representing nine Missouri River agencies, visited Carlisle and Hampton. They were highly pleased with the comforts their children enjoyed and the care bestowed upon them, and proud of the manifest improvement which they had made....

Of the eighteen Florida prisoners, with whom the experiment at Hampton was first inaugurated, thirteen have returned to their homes in the Indian Territory, partly to make room for younger pupils and partly because they had become sufficiently advanced to render valuable service at their respective agencies. Of these, eleven were transferred from Hampton to Carlisle, where they remained for a time to form a nucleus for the new school, and where, Lieutenant Pratt reports, they rendered him most valuable assistance in the care and management of the new scholars who came directly from the camps.

Home sickness and several deaths have occurred among the pupils at Carlisle and Hampton. When the first company of scholars was selected for the latter school, it was impossible to secure as thorough an examination of the children and to insist as strenuously upon the requirement of perfect health as was desirable, and in almost every instance the deaths have resulted from diseases contracted before the pupils left their homes. The most careful physical examination is now made of every applicant for admission to the Hampton and Carlisle schools, and only those who are certified to by a physician as being absolutely healthy are accepted. . . .

But the number who can be educated in Eastern schools is and always must be a small fraction of the Indian youth who are entitled to receive an education at the hands of the government, and the necessity for agency schools is not done away with, but increases yearly. The expense of educating Indians away from their homes will preclude the possibility of more than a limited number ever receiving the advantages which those schools afford. The largest results for the expenditure made will, therefore, be obtained by selecting from the agency schools the best material to be found therein; at the same time the hope of being thus chosen to receive such special training, as a recognition of merit, will operate upon the pupils attending agency schools as a powerful stimulus to earnest and persistent study and work.

Indian Police

The duties performed by the police are as varied as they are important. In the Indian Territory they have done effective work in arresting or turning back unauthorized intruders, in removing squatters' stakes, and in driving out cattle, horse, and timber thieves, and other outlaws who infest the country. . . . In Dakota, surveying parties have required no other escort than that furnished by detachments of police from the different agencies. In Arizona, the San Carlos police for six years past have rendered invaluable service as scouts; and, in general, at all agencies Indian policemen act as guards at annuity payments; render assistance and preserve order during ration issues; protect agency buildings and property; return truant pupils to school; search for and return lost or stolen property, whether belonging to Indians or white men; prevent depredations on timber, and the introduction of whiskey on the reservation; bring whiskey sellers to trial; make arrests for disorderly conduct, drunkenness, wife-beating, theft, and other offenses; serve as couriers and messengers; keep the agent informed as to births and deaths in the tribe, and notify him promptly as to the coming on the reserve of any strangers, white or Indian. Vigilant and observant by nature, and familiar with every foot-path on the reservation, no arrivals or departures, or clandestine councils can escape their notice, and <u>with a well-disciplined police force an agent can keep himself informed as to every noteworthy occurrence taking place within the entire limit of his jurisdiction.</u>[4]

Issuance of Wagons

Up to a very recent period, but few wagons were furnished for the Indian Service, and then generally only for the use of the agents and their employees at the headquarters of the agencies, to enable them to perform the necessary work of hauling fuel for agency buildings and fodder for the government stock. Within the past five years it has been found advisable to furnish the Indians with wagons for farming purposes, and for freighting their own supplies. . . . Nearly three thousand wagons with the necessary harness therefor, have been furnished the Indians since 1875, and the flattering prospects of the future, evidenced by the manifest interest of the Indians in farming pursuits, make it almost certain that still larger quantities will be needed by them in the next two years.[5]

CHAPTER 30

Hiram Price

Commissioner of Indian Affairs (May 6, 1881–March 26, 1885)

HIRAM PRICE was born on January 10, 1814, in Washington County, Pennsylvania, where he attended local public schools. As an adult he labored on his family's farm, worked as a bookkeeper at a commission house, and was a small business owner. At the age of thirty, he moved to Davenport, Iowa, and engaged in the mercantile business, before becoming a tax collector, treasurer, and recorder in Scott County, Iowa. In 1859, he became president of the Iowa National Bank, where he remained until 1866. Price enjoyed several decades of prominence and prosperity before the Methodist layman was elected to Congress as a Republican in 1862. He served in the House for the Thirty-eighth through the Fortieth Congresses but declined to run in 1868. He was later elected to the Forty-fifth and Forty-sixth Congresses and was an ardent supporter of Grant's peace policy.[1]

In Congress, Price served with his friend James A. Garfield (Republican, Ohio) for all five of his terms in the House. In 1880, Garfield was elected president of the United States, and although Price was an outspoken critic of Indian affairs, he chose not to run for reelection and retired to Iowa. Less than two months later, Interior Secretary Samuel J. Kirkland—a fellow Iowan—invited Price to serve as commissioner of Indian affairs, well aware that Price held the same political views as the president.[2]

As importantly, Garfield and Kirkland wanted a man who could quiet the fervor resulting from Helen Hunt Jackson's book *A Century of Dishonor*, which lamented the failure of Indian policy. Jackson's denunciation of policy fed the critics of Indian affairs and created no small commotion throughout the country, especially in the politically active philanthropic communities, much to the chagrin of Garfield. Desiring to fill the position as rapidly as possible, Kirkland temporarily appointed Price chief clerk on April 14, 1881, until the Senate confirmed him on May 6.[3]

Price's first annual report was issued just months after Garfield was assassinated, and in it the commissioner argued there was need for a "thorough and radical change" in policy. It was impossible to assimilate the Indians without first making them self-supporting, Price explained, but federal policy did just the opposite by providing the Indians with annuities and tools. In short, the commissioner proposed changes that could be summed up in three words: work, land, and law. Price argued rations should be withheld unless Indians agreed to work for food. This was the only way to make them "self-supporting," Price added, since the alternative resulted in vagabondage. On September 27, 1882, Price issued a circular to all agents notifying them to withhold rations from those unwilling to work, and he encouraged Congress to reduce appropriations to only those guaranteed by treaty.[4]

The commissioner also was a proponent of land severalty—with a "perfect and permanent" title—arguing it alone would solve the age-old Indian question. Land ownership would teach individualism, responsibility, industry, frugality, and the accumulation of property. But since there was no general allotment act—Price favored such legislation—the commissioner was limited to allotting reservations under treaty provisions. For instance, some treaties authorized severalty, but most did not; some authorized fee patents, while others provided simple allotment certificates. None authorized alienation. Nonetheless, using applicable law, Price allotted in severalty the Minnesota–Wisconsin Chippewa reservations, several bands of Pottawatomie, the Sisseton–Wahpeton Sioux, and numerous tribes in the Pacific Northwest.

To promote law and order, Price argued for state jurisdiction over Indian tribes. As territories were admitted to statehood, Price argued, Congress should grant the states complete civil and criminal jurisdiction over the Indians within their borders—unless a treaty or federal statute preempted such jurisdiction. Moreover, in his plan to solve the Indian problem, he sought from Congress money to survey reservations and clearly define tribal lands. He also requested funds to prosecute those who sold liquor to the Indians, and he sought authority to arrest those selling guns to the Indians.

Price found reform more difficult than he expected, as the Indian Office was highly institutionalized. Moreover, when Chester A. Arthur became president after Garfield's assassination, the new president replaced Kirkland with former Senator Henry Teller, an ardent supporter of severalty. Teller retained Price who, in 1882, sought to develop a legal code covering all criminal acts in Indian Country, arguing that existing codes dating to the 1834 Non-Intercourse Act were obsolete. In December of that year, Teller directed Price to proceed with

CHAPTER 30

creating a list of rules that would facilitate the abolition of Indian rites and customs that were, in his opinion, "injurious to the Indians." On April 10, 1883, Teller approved of Price's plan to create courts of Indian offenses across Indian Country to punish those who engaged in tribal dances or polygamy, purchased wives, followed medicine men, etc.

Price increased the number of Indian police to enforce the codes. After the federal district court for the Dakota Territory ruled in favor of Crow Dog (who had murdered Spotted Tail within the confines of the Great Sioux Reservation and had been punished by the customs of the Brule Sioux), in the 1883 *Ex Parte Crow Dog* decision, Price worked with Congress to enact into law the Major Crimes Act of 1885, mandating federal jurisdiction over seven criminal acts involving Indians.[5]

Price stressed harmonious relations with all religious organizations, and during his tenure the Indian Rights Association and the Lake Mohonk Conference were established as tribal support groups, presumably to protect Indian rights. By March 1884, Price was ready to retire, only to be dissuaded by Teller. The commissioner retired on March 26, 1885, at the age of seventy-one. He died in Washington, DC, on May 30, 1901, at the age of eighty-seven.

Need a Radical Change in Policy
In the outset, I desire to urge with earnestness the absolute necessity for a thorough and radical change of the Indian policy.... It is claimed and admitted by all that the great object of the government is to civilize the Indians and render them such assistance in kind and degree as will make them self-supporting, and yet I think no one will deny that one part of our policy is calculated to produce the very opposite result. It must be apparent to the most casual observer that the system of gathering the Indians in bands or tribes on reservations and carrying to them victuals and clothes, thus relieving them of the necessity of labor, never will and never can civilize them. Labor is an essential element in producing civilization. If white men were treated as we treat the Indians the result would certainly be a race of worthless vagabonds. The greatest kindness the government can bestow upon the Indian is to teach him to labor for his own support, thus developing his true manhood, and, as a consequence, making him self-relying and self-supporting.[6]

Among the things needed to secure success and efficiency in solving what is called the Indian problem are: First: *An appropriation to survey the out boundaries of Indian reservations*, so that both Indians and white men may know where they have rights and where they have none. This will save not only much trouble and expense, but also many lives of both white men and Indians.... Second: *A law for the punishment of persons who furnish arms or ammunition to Indians.* No such law now exists. Third: *More liberal appropriations for Indian police.*... [V]ery little reflection will satisfy any one that the present pay is no just compensation for the services of a man and horse. Our Indian police are an absolute necessity, and have in almost every instance rendered very valuable service, and ought to have more encouragement and support. The pay of these police as now fixed by law is $5 per month for privates and $8 per month for officers, a compensation entirely inadequate to their proper support, especially as many of them have families, which at non-ration agencies are not entitled to rations. As it is the duty of an agent to be careful in making his selections for the force, good men are secured only with the greatest difficulty.... I must, therefore, take this opportunity of repeating the recommendation... "that commissioned officers be paid $15 per month, sergeants, $10 per month, and privates $8 per month."[7] I am still, however, of the opinion... that "a much more satisfactory arrangement would be to invest the Commissioner of Indian Affairs with discretionary power as to pay of Indian police, the service at some agencies being of vastly more importance than at others...." Fourth: *An appropriation of money sufficient to defray the expense of detecting and prosecuting persons who furnish intoxicating liquor to Indians....* . [Liquor] has been productive of more disease, crime, and loss of life, than all other causes combined....[8]

Land Severalty
No question which enters into the present and future welfare and permanent advancement of the Indians is of so much importance as the question of allotment to them of lands in severalty, with a perfect and permanent title.... Much has been said in Congress, in the public press of the country, in public meetings, and otherwise, and various plans suggested with reference in solving the "Indian question," but no definite and practical solution of the question has been reached. In my judgment, the first step to be taken in this direction is the enactment of a law providing for the allotment of land in severalty....

The system of allotment now in force under the various treaties and acts of Congress is crude and imperfect, with no provisions for a title which affords sufficient protection to the Indians. In some of the treaties which authorize the allotment of land in severalty, provision is made for the issuance of patents, with restricted power of alienation, (with the consent of the President or the Secretary of the Interior). In others, allotments are authorized with no provision for the issuance of patent, but simply authorizing the issuance of a certificate of allotment, which carries with it no title at all. This system of allotment, so far as carried into effect, has been fraught with much success and encouraging improvement. The fact, however, that the Indians are not guaranteed a title affording them perfect security from molestation, and the fear that their lands may be taken from them, has created apprehension in the minds of many, and has been a bar to progress in this direction. The allotment system tends to break up tribal relations. It has the effect of creating individuality, responsibility, and a desire to accumulate property. It teaches the Indians habits of industry and frugality, and stimulates them to look forward to a better and more useful life, and, in the end, it will relieve the government of large annual appropriations. . . .⁹

Missionary Work
One very important auxiliary in transforming men from savage to civilized life is the influence brought to bear upon them through the labors of Christian men and women as educators and missionaries. This I think has been forcibly illustrated and clearly demonstrated among the different Indian tribes by the missionary labors of the various religious societies in the last few years. Civilization is a plant of exceeding slow growth, unless supplemented by Christian teaching and influences. I am decidedly of the opinion that a liberal encouragement by the government to all religious denominations to extend their educational and missionary operations among the Indians would be of immense benefit. I find that during the year there has been expended in cash by the different religious societies for regular educational and missionary purposes among the Indians the sum of $216,680, and doubtless much more which was not reported through the regular channels. This is just so much money saved to the government, which is an item of some importance, but insignificant in comparison with the healthy influences created by the men and women who have gone among the Indians. . . .

This kind of teaching will educate them to be sober, industrious, self-reliant, and to respect the rights of others; and my deliberate opinion is, that it is not only the interest but the duty of the government to aid and encourage these efforts in the most liberal manner. No money spent for the civilization of the Indian will return a better dividend than that spent in this way.... If we expect to stop sun dances, snake worship, and other debasing forms of superstition and idolatry among Indians, we must teach them some better way....[10]

Need for Law
[A]ttention has been invited to the urgent necessity for the enactment of some suitable code of laws for Indian reservations. Indians in the Indian country are not punishable for crimes or offenses committed against the persons or property of each other. Such offenses are generally left to the penalties of tribal usage, involving personal vengeance or pecuniary satisfaction, or the offenders are subjected to a few weeks or months arbitrary confinement in an agency guardhouse or military fort. The Indian is not a citizen of the United States. He cannot sue or be sued under the judiciary act of 1789, and only gets into Federal courts as a civil litigant, in occasional instances, by favor of special law, and in many of the States and Territories he has no standing at all in court.

The evils resulting from this state of affairs are forcibly described by Bishop Hare [who] says: "Civilization has loosened, in some places broken, the bonds which regulate and hold together Indian society in its wild state, and has failed to give the people law and officers of justice in their place. This evil still continues unabated. Women are brutally beaten and outraged; men are murdered in cold blood; the Indians who are friendly to schools and churches are intimidated and preyed upon by the evil-disposed; children are molested on their way to school, and schools are dispersed by bands of vagabonds; but there is no redress. This accursed condition of things is an outrage upon the One Lawgiver. It is a disgrace to our land. It should make every man who sits in the national halls of legislation blush. And, wish well to the Indians as we may, and do for them what we will, the efforts of civil agents, teachers, and missionaries are like the struggles of drowning men weighted with lead, as long as by the absence of law Indian society is left without a base...."

It has occurred to me that, pending the long delay in the enactment of a general law on the subject, a considerable body of Indians might soon be brought within jurisdiction of courts in another way. In Dakota and New Mexico are nearly 60,000 Indians. If, when those Territories become States, it shall be provided that the respective State courts shall have jurisdiction over Indian reservations within the boundaries of those States, the condition of the Indians residing therein will be vastly improved. And I would particularly recommend that hereafter, whenever a State is admitted into the Union, the act of admission shall contain a provision giving to Indians within its limits all the rights, privileges, and immunities enjoyed by the citizens thereof, and subjecting them to like penalties, liabilities, restrictions, &c., except in cases specially otherwise provided for by treaty or act in Congress.[11]

Industrial Education
The principle educational advance of the year has been the starting of the three new training schools ... at Genoa, Nebr., Chilocco, Ind. Ter., and Lawrence, Kans.... The latter is only just under way, and has now 125 out of the 340 pupils which it will accommodate. The Chilocco and Genoa schools have made a good record with their 319 pupils. They have the advantage of both Carlisle and Forest Grove in possessing sufficient land, and are giving special attention to stock-raising and farming. The Chilocco boys have a herd of 425 cattle, and the Genoa boys have cultivated faithfully 202 acres and raised 6,000 bushels of corn, 2,000 bushels of oats, and 1,200 bushels of vegetables. The nearness of the schools to Indian reservations greatly reduces cost of transportation, but at the same time it suggests to the pupils a prompt remedy for homesickness and restiveness under restraint. Both schools have been annoyed by runaways, but it is hoped that serious embarrassment from this quarter need not be anticipated. Several of the employees of these schools are Carlisle and Hampton graduates. If Congress had not modified its appropriation and removed the restriction which limited the amount to be expended in support of these schools to $200 per pupil, including traveling expenses, they could not have been carried on. To require that the first expense of an industrial school shall not exceed the lowest sum at which it has been found possible to continue a school already established is unjust and unreasonable....

The other three training schools, at Carlisle, Forest Grove, and Hampton, have had an uneventful, useful year.... Of the special work which is undertaken at Carlisle called "planting out," the superintendent [has] "placed out on farms and in families during the year, for longer or shorter periods, 44 girls and 173 boys, and have arranged for keeping out about 110 the ensuing winter to attend the public schools where they are located, or to receive private instruction in the families. This is by far the most important feature of our work...."

I established a regulation that all who went out from the school should do so entirely at the expense of their patrons, and should receive pay according to their ability. The results have been most satisfactory. The absence from the school has been in nearly every case a clear saving to the Government of their support during such period of absence, and many of the boys and girls, besides supplying themselves with clothing, have earned and saved considerable sums of money, which I find has a most excellent influence....

"Two years of school training and discipline are necessary to fit a new pupil for this outing. The rapid progress in English speaking, the skill in hand and head work, the independence in thought and action pupils so placed gain, all prove that this method of preparing and dispersing Indian youth is an invaluable means of giving them the courage and capacity for civilized self-support. An Indian boy placed in a family and remote from his home (and it is better distant from the school), surrounded on all sides by hardworking, industrious people, feels at once a stronger desire to do something for himself than he can be made to feel under any collective system, or in the best Indian training-school that can be established. His self-respect asserts itself; he goes to work, behaves himself, and tries in every way to compete with those about him."[12]

CHAPTER 31

John DeWitt Clinton Atkins

Commissioner of Indian Affairs (March 21, 1885–June 14, 1888)

JOHN DEWITT CLINTON ATKINS was born to John and Sarah (Manly) Atkins on June 4, 1825, near Manley's Chapel, Henry County, Tennessee. After attending private school in Paris, Tennessee, Atkins graduated from East Tennessee University in 1846, studying law. While he was admitted to the Tennessee bar, he never practiced law, choosing instead to engage in agricultural activities and participate in local and national politics.

In 1848, Atkins was elected to the Tennessee House of Representatives for a single term (1849–1850) before gaining election to the state senate in 1854. Two years later, he was elected to the US House of Representatives from Tennessee's Ninth district before losing reelection in the fall of 1858. With the advent of the Civil War, Atkins joined the Confederacy and served as lieutenant colonel of the Fifth Tennessee Regiment. In 1861, he was a delegate to the Provisional Confederate Congress before being elected to the First Confederate Congress in November; he was reelected to the Second Confederate Congress in 1863. With the end of the Civil War, he returned to Tennessee and resumed farming.[1]

In the fall of 1872, Atkins was elected to the US House of Representatives as a Democrat, serving in five consecutive Congresses. He declined to run for reelection in 1882 and returned to Tennessee to engage in agricultural activities. With the election of Grover Cleveland as president in 1884, the reform-minded former governor of New York sought someone who shared his civil service reform convictions and who would work to improve the United States' relationship with tribal nations. Interior Secretary Lucius Q. C. Lamar of Tennessee and First Assistant Secretary Henry L. Muldrow of Mississippi (and a friend of Lamar) shared a special interest in Indian affairs. Cleveland then nominated Atkins as commissioner of Indian affairs, with the Senate confirming him on March 21, 1885.[2]

In his first annual report, Atkins outlined his goals, proposed changes, and problem areas. His primary goal remained civilization of the Indians through Jeffersonian agrarianism, arguing that those who were ignorant of agriculture "were also ignorant of almost everything else." The policy of concentrating the tribes in Indian Territory (or in a few select areas in the West) was preferred, Atkins argued, as it would hasten civilization and save the United States management expenses in maintaining agencies in Indian Country. It would also reduce the military presence to "convenient" locations near Indian Territory. To ensure tribal lands were beneficially used, Atkins supported legislation authorizing the leasing of Indian land.

Atkins ardently supported a proposed General Allotment Act, although he cautioned there would be challenges with severalty if it were implemented improperly. For instance, Atkins argued it was imperative that Indians receive the best land in order to farm, with the size of the allotment dependent on local conditions. Poor land or too little land (or even too much land) might impede the Jeffersonian goal. To protect the land, he advocated a minimum twenty-five-year federal trust period, and he supported opening allotted reservations to homesteading, arguing the money from the sale of surplus land could be used for civilizing functions such as education. Implemented correctly, Atkins believed most Indians would be farming within five years of taking an allotment.

The commissioner was a strong supporter of forcing the Five Civilized Tribes to integrate into the United States, believing they had no legal right to remain separate governments. If the United States forced the Five Tribes to amalgamate with the surrounding non-Indian population, Atkins reasoned, it could also force the sale of surplus tribal land by forcing the Five Tribes to take homesteads (allotments in severalty) and organize a territorial government. There would be no better example to the rest of Indian Country than the Five Civilized Tribes capitulating. This, Atkins suggested, the tribes should "cordially" do "in a spirit of friendly gratitude for what has been done for them" by the federal government.

The commissioner also supported industrial education at boarding schools. While such schools focused on teaching youth in the mechanical arts and agriculture, Atkins envisioned on-reservation day schools teaching the basics of reading, writing, and arithmetic, as well as general agriculture. It was under Atkins's watch that the Indian Office ordered all Indian schools to teach English only and forbade the use of tribal languages at schools, government or private. While he was not opposed to mission schools, Atkins did not mix religious denominations on the reservations, and he emphasized federal control of Indian education.

As for civil service reform, Atkins was a disappointment. Although he focused on improving the professionalism of the Indian Office—largely via John Oberly's appointment as superintendent of Indian schools—he did little to curb nepotism. Both Atkins and his assistant commissioner, Alexander Upshaw, were spoilsmen, proving a disappointment to Cleveland. Atkins also focused on the legal rights of Indians in each of his three annual reports, seeking the permanent establishment of courts of Indian offenses on all reservations and empowering Indian agents with authority to remove criminals from the reservations. And while he agreed with the Major Crimes Act granting the federal government jurisdiction over major crimes in Indian Country, he advocated for amending the act since it required local residents in territories with reservations to pay for the criminal prosecution of Indians while states with reservations were exempt from paying for such prosecutions. Congress disregarded his request as it assumed the great pulverizer—the General Allotment Act—would eliminate the conflict in short order.

Atkins elected to resign on June 14, 1888, in part due to Cleveland's disappointment in his civil service reform and in part because he intended to run for the US Senate. When he failed to secure the nomination for the US Senate seat from Tennessee, he returned to Tennessee where he resumed farming. He retired to Paris, Tennessee, in 1898. He died two days shy of his eighty-third birthday on June 2, 1908, having failed to accomplish the primary reform President Cleveland sought: civil service reform.

Agriculture Is Civilization

It requires no seer to foretell or foresee the civilization of the Indian race as a result naturally deducible from a knowledge and practice upon their part of the art of agriculture; for the history of agriculture among all people and in all countries intimately connects it with the highest intellectual and moral development of man. Historians, philosophers, and statesmen freely admit that civilization as naturally follows the improved arts of agriculture as vegetation follows the genial sunshine and the shower and that those races who are in ignorance of agriculture are also ignorant of almost everything else. The Indian constitutes no exception to this political maxim.... This brings me directly to the consideration of the practical policy which I believe should be adopted by Congress and the Government in the management of the Indians. It should be industriously and gravely impressed upon them that they must abandon their tribal relations and take lands in severalty, as the corner stone of their complete success in agriculture, which means self-support, personal independence, and material thrift. The Government should, however, in order to protect them, retain the right to their lands in trust for twenty-five years or longer, but issue trust patents at once to such Indians as have taken individual holdings. When the Indians have taken their lands in severalty in sufficient quantities (and the number of acres in each holding may and should vary in different localities according to fertility, productiveness, climatic, and other advantages), then having due regard to the immediate and early future needs of the Indians, the remaining lands of their reservations should be purchased by the Government and opened to homestead entry [and the] money paid by the Government for their lands should be held in trust in 5 per cent bonds.... This is all the Indians need to place them beyond the oppression and greed of white men.[3]

Policy of Concentration
Many theories have been advanced by as many theorists as to what policy it is proper to pursue with the Indian.... The friends of the Indians have differed among themselves as to the best mode of promoting their true welfare, one view being to concentrate them upon the Indian Territory, which ... was set apart for the use and occupancy of the Cherokees, Creeks, Seminoles, Choctaws, Chickasaws, and other tribes; a portion of which has by subsequent treaties been ceded to the United States for the purpose of locating friendly Indians and freedmen thereon, and upon another portion of which the Government is, by treaty stipulations, permitted to settle friendly Indians....

The Indian Territory has an area of about 64,222 square miles, or about 41,102,280 acres.... The advantages of this country for the location, advancement, and civilization of the Indian is strikingly illustrated by the progress of the five civilized tribes. These tribes will compare favorably in wealth and prosperity with almost any agricultural or pastoral community of the same number of persons in any of the States or Territories, and rank fairly in education, intelligence, and progress. Each tribe has an organized government, divided into three branches, the legislative, executive, and judicial. They publish newspapers, carry on manufacturing and merchandising; they have their churches and ministers of the Gospel; they have their courts and judges, and lawyers, and stock-raisers, and farmers, and mechanics; they have their schools, seminaries, and other institutions of learning, built and supported by the tribal funds of the Indians, without other aid from the General Government, and in fact there is nothing in any civilized and enlightened community which they do not have.

Now, there is land enough in the Indian Territory, if all the Indians in the United States, excepting those in Alaska, were removed there, to give to each person—man, woman, and child—160 acres. There are ... 79,380 Indians in the Indian Territory, and if the lands there were equally divided among them each person would have about 500 acres....

I have referred thus particularly to the advantages of this Territory, in order that the argument of those advocating the "concentration" policy may be fairly understood. On the other hand, the opponents of this plan advocate the idea of the general diffusion of the Indian tribes over as large a space as practicable, with the view of bringing the Indians more directly in contact with a higher type of civilization, so that they can, as they allege, be the more easily absorbed or assimilated and become the more easily citizenized. They also urge that the Indians have strong local attachments to the homes of their ancestors and to the haunts of their childhood; that their consent to sell their ancestral homes and move to a strange land among strangers, although of their own race, could not be obtained, and that hence it is idle to expect that they will voluntarily concentrate in the Indian Territory....

But a stronger and more potent objection to concentration in the Indian Territory exists than any yet given, and that is the fierce and uncompromising opposition which this proposition meets in the almost unanimous sentiment of the white citizens of the four great States of Missouri, Kansas, Texas, and Arkansas, which surround this Territory. Such an array of political power and influence, speaking as one man, is entitled to respect and grave consideration. In a country like ours, where public opinion crystalizes into law, where it makes presidents, and Congress, and courts, and commands armies, it cannot safely be disregarded. And although the representatives of the other States of the Union might believe that the concentration of the savage Indian tribes of this country in the Indian Territory would be best for the Indians and greatly relieve the treasury of the United States, as it would, nevertheless, I would not advise such a step, even if it should be agreeable to the Indians not scattered over a vast area of country, against the earnest protestations of the people of the four great States referred to....

[I]f all the Indian tribes were concentrated upon the soil of the Indian Territory, it is reasonable to suppose that the United States Army, of which detachments are now stationed at numerous posts all over the country, near the Indian reservations, for the purpose of protecting white settlers and preserving the peace, would no longer be needed at these remote posts, and could be more conveniently massed near the Territory, where it could prevent any disturbances between the Indians in the Indian Territory and the people of adjacent States. Therefore, so far as the peace of the country is concerned, and so far as the army is potent to preserve it, there would be less danger to be apprehended were the entire Indian population settled within the Indian Territory than there is at this time, when only a small portion of the army can be stationed near it. Moreover, any apprehension of danger on the part of white citizens of those States seems less reasonable and well founded, when we take into consideration the additional safeguard afforded for the protection of their communities by the extension, in almost every direction, of railroads and telegraphic lines.

And yet it is said that this sentiment of opposition exists universally among the good people of these four States against the settlement of any more Indians of the wild tribes in that Territory, and some say, of any more Indians at all, friendly or unfriendly, civilized or semi-civilized, or savage. Of course, with the vast unimproved acreage of valuable and fertile lands within the borders of each of those four States, it cannot be that the lands of the Indian Territory have tempted any of their citizens. Still the prejudice exists so strongly as to satisfy me that for Congress to adopt legislation looking toward obtaining the consent of the scattered Indian tribes to give up their present localities and remove to the Indian Territory would be impolitic and would disturb the political and social tranquility of a very large, respectable, and powerful section of the country....

Assuming, however, that I have correctly divined the almost unanimous wish of the States mentioned, and that Congress would feel disposed to respect their wishes, then the further question of purchasing from the Indians all of the lands of the Indian Territory, and of other Indian reservations, which the Indians do not need now, or will not need in the early future, and of opening them to homestead settlement, presents itself for consideration. After allotting to each head of a family and to each child whatever quantity of land Congress, in its wisdom and humane guardianship of this helpless race, shall consider and determine as just and necessary, the purchase of the balance of their lands at a fair price would seem to be wise and expedient, as the proceeds of the sale would subserve a far more valuable end in contributing to their education and material advancement in agriculture and the mechanical arts . . . than would be subserved by permitting the lands to remain permanently in idle and unproductive waste.

It might be that a prudent economy and a wise administrative policy in dealing with the Indians would suggest another view which is, to remove, with the exception of those who have taken lands in severalty and who desire to continue to remain on their respective allotments, all of the Indians in the States of Minnesota, Wisconsin, and Michigan, to the Red Lake and White Earth Reservations; those in Montana, Idaho, Wyoming, and Dakota, to the Flathead and Great Sioux Reservations, and those in Nevada, Upper California, Oregon, and Washington Territory, to the Yakama Reservation, or some suitable one in that vicinity, selected for that purpose; while the southwestern Indians might be advantageously concentrated upon one or two existing reservations in that locality. Of course, this policy could only be adopted by first obtaining the consent of the Indians already on the reservations upon which concentration is suggested, and the consent of those whom it is suggested to remove, all of which would be dependent upon action by Congress.

The money received from the sale of the lands thrown open to settlement under this policy would make the Indians thus consolidated wealthy, and if properly invested the income therefrom would be ample to start them in agricultural and pastoral pursuits, leaving a fund sufficient for educational purposes and the care of the old and infirm. This plan would not only be advantageous to the Indians, but likewise to the Government. The concentration of the various Indians upon suitable and convenient reservations would relieve the Government of a large annual expense in its management of the Indians. It would result in the doing away with a number of agencies, and necessarily dispense with the services of an equal number of agents and many other employees, and save the incidental expenses connected with such agencies.[4]

Leasing Indian Land
Recurring to the general subject of leasing Indian lands . . . the Attorney General . . . rendered his opinion that under existing statutes of the United States . . . the several Indian nations or tribes, regardless of the character of the title by which they hold their lands, whether the same be a fee simple or a right of occupancy only, are precluded by the force and effect of the statute from either alienating or leasing any part of their several reservations,

or imparting any interest or claim in or to the same, without the consent of the Government of the United States, and that a lease of land for grazing purposes is as clearly within the statutes as a lease for any other or for general purposes, the duration of the term being immaterial.

[In] the absence of any treaty or statutory provisions to that effect, neither the President, Secretary of the Interior, nor any other officer of the Government has power to make, authorize, or approve any leases of lands held by Indian tribes.... Indian tribes cannot lease their reservations without the authority of some law of the United States. I cannot too strongly impress upon the Department the importance of any early disposition of this much vexed question. The leasing system should either be legalized, with proper restrictions, or it should be abolished altogether.[5]

Need to Force the Integration of the Five Civilized Tribes as an Example
It is reasonable that the Indian Bureau and the country should look to the five civilized tribes of the Indian Territory about whom so much has been said by orators and statesmen, and of whom so much is expected by the friends of the Indian, to set freely and promptly such an example as shall advance the civilization of their savage brethren of other tribes. The influence of their example upon the semi-civilized and savage tribes makes the study of their condition and methods a matter not only of great interest but also of first importance.

The treaties of 1866, and other treaties also, guarantee to the five civilized tribes the possession of their lands; but, without the moral and physical power which is represented by the Army of the United States, what are these treaties worth as a protection against the rapacious greed of the homeless people of the States who seek homesteads within the borders of the Indian Territory? If the protecting power of this Government were withdrawn for thirty days, where would the treaties be, and the laws of the Indians and the Indians themselves? The history of Payne and Couch[6] and their followers, and the determined effort of both Republican and Democratic administrations to resist their unlawful claims and demands, is too recent not to be still fresh in the memory of these Indians. It is not reasonable to expect that the Government will never tire of menacing its own people with its own Army. Therefore it becomes vastly important that these five civilized tribes, who have among them men competent to be Representatives and Senators in Congress, governors of States, and judges on the bench, should cordially, and in a spirit of friendly gratitude for what has been done for them, co-operate with the Government in bringing about such a change of affairs in their midst as will bring peace and quiet to their borders, settle existing agitations as to their rights and interests, and dispose of disquieting questions which will surely grow out of the present alarming condition of things in . . . Indian Territory. . . .

It is alleged that Congress has no power, in view of the treaties with those Indians, to do away with their present form of government and institute in its stead a Territorial government similar to those now existing in the eight organized Territories. While I greatly prefer that these people should voluntarily change their form of government, yet it is perfectly plain to my mind that the treaties never contemplated the un-American and absurd idea of a separate nationality in our midst, with power as they may choose to organize a government of their own, or not to organize any government nor allow one to be organized, for the one proposition contains the other. These Indians have no right to obstruct civilization and commerce and set up an exclusive claim to self-government, establishing a government within a government, and then expect and claim that the United States shall protect them from all harm, while insisting that it shall not be the ultimate judge as to what is best to be done for them in a political point of view. I repeat, to maintain any such view is to acknowledge a foreign sovereignty, with the right of eminent domain, upon American soil—a theory utterly repugnant to the spirit and genius of our laws, and wholly unwarranted by the Constitution.

Congress and the Executive of the United States are the supreme guardians of these mere wards, and can administer their affairs as any other guardian can. Of course, it must be done in a just and enlightened way. It must be done in a spirit of protection and not of oppression and robbery. Congress can sell their surplus lands and distribute the proceeds equally among the owners for the purposes of civilization and the education of their children, and the protection of the infirm, and the establishment of the poor upon homesteads with stock and implements of husbandry. Congress cannot consistently or justly or honestly take their lands from them and give or sell them to others except as above referred to, and for those objects alone.[7]

General Allotment Act
There is danger that the advocates of land in severalty will expect from the measure too immediate and pronounced success. Character, habits, and

antecedents cannot be changed by an enactment. The distance between barbarism and civilization is too long to be passed over speedily. Idleness, improvidence, ignorance, and superstition cannot by law be transformed into industry, thrift, intelligence, and Christianity. Thus, the real work yet remains to be done and can be accomplished only by persistent personal effort. In fact, the allotment act instead of being the consummation of the labors of missionaries, philanthropists, and Government agents, is rather an introduction and invitation to effort on their part, which by the fact of this new legislation may be hopeful and should be energetic. Moreover, with this new policy will arise new perplexities to be solved and new obstacles to be overcome which will tax the wisdom, patience, and courage of all interested in and working for Indian advancement.... Under this act it will be noticed that whenever a tribe of Indians or any member of a tribe accepts lands in severalty the allottee at once, *ipso facto*, becomes a citizen of the United States, endowed with all the civil and political privileges and subject to all the responsibilities and duties of any other citizen of the Republic....[8]

CHAPTER 32

John H. Oberly

Commissioner of Indian Affairs (October 10, 1888–June 30, 1889)

John H. Oberly was born in December 1837 in Cincinnati, Ohio. By the age of thirty he had launched and edited the *Cairo Bulletin* and later edited the *Wayne County Democrat*. In 1880, Oberly was elected to the Illinois House of Representatives, and by 1884, he was the executive chairman of the Illinois Democratic Party. That same year he traveled to Albany, New York, on assignment for the *Chicago Tribune*, where he caught the eye of the reform-minded governor of New York, Grover Cleveland.[1]

Like Cleveland, Oberly was committed to civil service reform in the federal government. While Cleveland nominated John D. C. Atkins as commissioner of Indian affairs, Atkins asked Oberly to serve as superintendent of Indian schools, where he recognized the failure of the schools. "It may be said, unwelcome as it must be to the many people interested in the subject of Indian education that the day-school education of Indian children has, so far, brought forth but little good fruit."[2] This was due in part to political patronage, which favored jobs over the education of children.

When Atkins resigned, as many predicted he would, to run for the Senate, Cleveland nominated Oberly as commissioner of Indian affairs in September 1888. Supported by the Indian Rights Association and its chairman, Herbert Welsh—in part because Welsh opposed Atkins's assistant commissioner, Alexander B. Upshaw (a fellow Tennessean like Atkins) who was a supporter of patronage, and in part because Welsh was civil service minded—Oberly was confirmed by the Senate and took office on October 10. He was one of Cleveland's three civil service commissioners, seeking to implement government-wide civil service reform.

Oberly was the first commissioner since Thomas McKenney to enter office with experience in Indian affairs. While committed to the policy of assimilation, Oberly also sought to reform abuses in Indian Country, in the appointment and removal of Indian school employees in particular. As superintendent, he garnered the wrath of Indian agents who coveted autonomy and control over patronage in administering Indian agencies and schools. Oberly was committed to making Indian schools more than just schools in name.³

On June 29, 1888, Congress gave then-Indian School Superintendent Oberly near complete authority over Indian schools.⁴ He now appointed and dismissed teachers at the scattered schools across Indian Country, removing them from political spoil. In addition, he was authorized to improve the schools through rules and regulations governing student activities, curriculum, and facilities. As commissioner, he standardized regulations, conducted school inspections, implemented reforms, and initiated standardized curriculum intending to use boarding schools to socially reengineer Indian children. He hoped that civil reform in the schools would extend to reform throughout the Indian Service.

Oberly was progressive in his views that American Indians had rights the government was obliged to respect. For instance, in the late 1880s, Wild West shows were widely popular, with most reformers opposed to Indian participation on the grounds that such shows were regressive and showcased "barbarism." Oberly, however, did not believe he had the authority to forbid—and that the Indians had never given up the right to participate in—such shows. At the same time, he believed he was within his authority to force "civilization" on the Indians.⁵

With President Cleveland's loss to Republican Benjamin Harrison in the 1888 election, Oberly's efforts appeared to be at an end. While Welsh tried to persuade the incoming president to retain Oberly in the name of continuing civil service reform, neither Harrison nor influential Senator Henry Dawes (Republican, Massachusetts) was willing to support him. Nonetheless, scores of newspaper editors from across the country backed him, with Welsh fearing that Upshaw, whom he described as "subservient to the spoils system," would be nominated as commissioner by the president-elect.⁶

Oberly's tenure was short, at just over eight months, and he penned only one annual report. With no support from the incoming administration, Oberly submitted his resignation on June 6, 1889, effective June 30. He never again entered the fray of politics, returning to his journalistic career in New Hampshire. John Oberly died at the age of sixty-two on April 15, 1899, having had minimal impact on policy, although he was part of the vanguard that initiated civil service reform throughout the federal government.

Need for Merit System
To obtain suitable employees, particularly at remote places where attractive surroundings are wanting and discomforts abound, is the first, the greatest,

and an abiding difficulty of the Indian service.... The clerk of an agency or of a school should be a man of strict business integrity, a rapid and accurate accountant, with good general clerical acquirements; and the clerk of an agency should have sufficient executive ability to enable him to perform, in the absence of the agent, the duties of that position also. The physician of an agency or of a school should have a thorough medical education and should bring to his work, to even a larger degree than usual, the skill and self-denial which characterize his profession. These qualifications are essential because of the ignorance and helplessness of those to whom he must minister, and the need that he should win them from the superstitious, barbarous, and destroying practices of the "medicine man" to faith in the scientific treatment of the white man.

The farmer and the additional farmer should have not only practical knowledge of husbandry in general but they should also be familiar with the particular kind of farming that the locality of the reservation to which they are to be assigned requires; and in addition to a practical and particular knowledge, these employees should also have the ability to impart their knowledge to others, to induce the Indians to become interested in farm work, and to compel the indolent to share in the labors willingly undertaken by the industrious.

The blacksmith should have a good, practical knowledge of his special trade, with enough acquaintance with ironworking in general and with sufficient native ingenuity to enable him, when circumstances require, to do fair work in various allied lines of handicraft even without a complete outfit of tools. The same holds true of the carpenter, the miller, the sawyer, and other mechanics....

It is thus . . . that there are inherent difficulties in the way of securing competent employees. . . ; and when to these are added the demands of political partisans that agency and school positions shall be used as rewards of labor for a party or for a party leader, these difficulties become insuperable, and because of them merit is too frequently compelled to stand aside while demerit crowds into the small as well as into the more important places. And this is the system under which the Indian service has been for many years supplied with employees. Wherefore it has become apparent to all candid persons who take any interest in the administration of Indian affairs that all the places in the Indian branch of the civil service should be filled by persons selected not only with reference to their ability to discharge, and their adaptability to, the duties of such places, but absolutely without reference to their partisan affiliations or to the effect their employment would have upon [anyone's] personal or partisan interests.⁷

Educational Philosophy
Anyone who thoughtfully considers the subject of Indian education must conclude that industrial training should be the principal feature in every Indian school; and by "industrial training" is not meant the mere teaching of the trades and arts. The Indian child must be taught many things many which come to the white child, because of environment, without the school-master's aid. From the day of its birth the child of civilized parents is constantly in contact with civilized modes of life—of action, thought, speech, dress—and is surrounded by a thousand beneficent influences that never operate upon the child of savage parentage, who, in his birth-hour, is encompassed by a degrading atmosphere of superstition and of barbarism. Out from the conditions of his birth he must be led in his early years into the environments of civilized domestic life. And he must be thus led by the school teacher. But under the present school system, with its large boarding-school buildings crowded with pupils, and its many-bedded dormitories and great dining rooms, the Indian child cannot receive an adequate idea of civilized home life. At the schools conducted in large buildings, matrons, cooks, seamstresses, laundresses, and other employees, who should teach the girl pupils the difficult art of the housekeeper, are too busily occupied in keeping up their respective departments of work to devote the time necessary for the painstaking training of awkward or ignorant girls in the skillful performance of the numberless duties which appertain to civilized housekeeping and home-making; and of just this sort of instruction these pupils stand more in need than they do of literary attainments. For a large boarding school, it would therefore be better to have a main building, which should contain only the recitation rooms, with perhaps quarters for the superintendent and literary teachers, and to have other buildings which should each accommodate a small number of children. Each of these buildings could be made the home of the children domiciled therein, and in this home the girls could be taught by actual practice, how to cook, to wash, to make and mend clothes, to sweep, to make beds—in short, could be instructed in all things that are taught to white girls in the homes of civilized communities; and boys, while thus enabled to enjoy the advantages of home life, could be taught farming and trades suitable to their various localities. Gardens attached to these homes

could be cultivated by both boys and girls. The effect of such an industrial school system would be to build up a community, a little village, in which the children would become acquainted with and would actually practice the customs and habits, the arts and the trades, which, at least in part, distinguish civilized life from barbarism.[8]

Need the Egotism of American Citizenship
[O]n the war-path and in the chase [the Indian] cannot exalt himself by bravery and endurance, and he should not be permitted to live any longer in idleness and debauchery. He should be brought under the operations of the law, "In the sweat of thy face shalt thou eat bread till thou return unto the ground." He should be educated to labor. He does not need the learning of "William and Mary," but he does need the virtue of industry and the ability of the skillful hand. He should, therefore, be taught how to work, and all the schools that are opened for his children should be schools in which they will be instructed in the use of agricultural implements, the carpenter's saw and plane, the stonemason's trowel, the tailor's needle, and the shoemaker's awl. And the Indian should be taught not only how to work, but also that it is his duty to work; for the degrading communism of the tribal reservation system gives to the individual no incentive to labor, but puts a premium upon idleness and makes it fashionable. . . . And he must be imbued with the exalting egotism of American civilization, so that he will say "I" instead of "We," and "This is mine," instead of "This is ours." But if he will not learn. . . ? Then the Guardian must act for the Ward, and do for him the good service he protests shall not be done—the good service that he denounces as a bad service. The Government must then, in duty to the public, compel the Indian to come out of his isolation into the civilized way that he does not desire to enter—into citizenship—into assimilation with the masses of the Republic. . . .[9]

CHAPTER 33

Thomas Jefferson Morgan

Commissioner of Indian Affairs (July 1, 1889–March 3, 1893)

THOMAS JEFFERSON MORGAN was born in Franklin, Indiana, on August 17, 1839. He graduated from Franklin College in 1861 and immediately enlisted in the Union Army as a first lieutenant in the Seventieth Indiana Volunteer Infantry commanded by Benjamin Harrison. Two years later, Morgan organized the Fourteenth US Colored Infantry and was promoted to colonel and later was brevetted as major general. After the war, Morgan enlisted in the Rochester Theological Seminary, and by 1869, he was ordained a Baptist preacher. After several years as a pastor, the education-minded Morgan became the principal of the Nebraska State Normal School in Peru, and two years later, he moved to the Baptist Union Theological Seminary in Chicago, where he remained for seven years before transitioning to the State Normal School at Potsdam, New York, for two years. In 1883 he became principal of the State Normal School in Providence, Rhode Island.[1]

In the fall of 1888, Morgan's former military commander Benjamin Harrison was elected president of the United States, with Morgan seeking the position of US commissioner of education. Instead, on June 10, 1889, Harrison nominated Morgan as commissioner of Indian affairs; he took office on July 1, 1889, but was not confirmed by the Senate until the following February, facing stiff opposition from Catholics who feared he would drive them from the field of Indian education.

Morgan's arrival as commissioner came at a critical juncture after two decades of reform with the United States seeking to resolve the so-called Indian problem. Reform efforts focused on detribalization, mandating the English language in schools, and making Indians amendable to federal and state law. The culmination of these efforts was the General Allotment Act, a legislative enactment Morgan expected would transform Indians into hard-working, independent American citizens. He accepted these reforms with a "few simple, well defined and strongly cherished convictions." These included abolition of the "anomalous" reservation system and the enforcement of "individuality." "This civilization may not be the best possible," Morgan wrote in 1889, "but it is the best the Indians can get. They cannot escape it, and must either conform to it or be crushed by it."[2]

Allotment in severalty was the "essential element" of federal policy, and this was the only way Morgan, colored by the myopias of his day, saw to transform wards of the government into citizens. Since Indians were not using their land, Morgan rationalized, it was better for them to be paid by the United States for the land so that they could use the money to further their civilization and develop their allotments. Morgan calculated there were 116 million acres in Indian Country for 250,483 Indians, excluding Indian Territory. Allotting 160 acres per capita would utilize 30 million acres, and after excluding 20 million acres owned by the Five Civilized Tribes, there would be 66 million acres that could be sold. At $1 per acre this would net the Indians $66 million, ample funds to transition into the modern world.[3]

Morgan was above all an educator, and he was intent on establishing a universal, federally controlled, compulsory Indian education system that would lead the Indians to accept their responsibilities under severalty and citizenship. In 1889, he provided a detailed proposal of this educational system to the Lake Mohonk Conference, and in December of that year, he submitted a "Supplemental Report on Indian Education" to the secretary of the interior. Two years later, he penned *Studies in Pedagogy*, a scholarly look at public schools in the United States, with a primary goal of creating universal Americanism based on a single language—English—and the concept of a national race that would be model citizens.[4] As commissioner of Indian affairs, Morgan intended to bring American Indians into this plan, believing education was the only means of "convert[ing] them into American citizens" and enabling them to "successfully compete with white men."

The Indian school system Morgan envisioned included three types of schools: common schools on reservations, agency boarding schools, and national industrial schools. A universal course of study patterned after public schools included standardized textbooks and teaching methods. It was to be nonpartisan and nonsectarian. Industrial education was the center of curriculum, but it also included cultural literacy; all schools receiving federal funds would be restricted to English only. Coeducation was essential to Morgan's plan, as it was the means of lifting women out of servile roles.

The nonsectarian nature of the schools raised the dander of the Bureau of Catholic Missions, which at the time received the largest share of federal Indian education funds. This disparity accelerated when Protestant schools dropped their contracts when government-administered schools favored Protestant teachings in the classroom. But it was not only Catholics who opposed Morgan's plan. Many American Indians refused to send their children to schools, viewing them as destructive of tribal cultures. Morgan's response was that "We must either fight the Indians, feed them, or else educate them. To fight them is cruel, to feed them is wasteful, while to educate them is humane, economic, and Christian."[5]

Morgan introduced new rules for the Courts of Indian Offenses, prohibiting dances, polygamy, and shaman. A new ordinance charged individuals with a misdemeanor if they refused to adopt "habits of industry or to engage in civilized pursuits." He also opposed Indian participation in Wild West shows, and he fired inebriated employees. With these additions to the legislative enactments of Congress, Morgan believed everything was in place to civilize the Indians and all the Indian Office had to do was administer the programs. The Indian Office, Morgan believed, was on the threshold of becoming an administrative agency.

President Harrison failed to gain reelection in 1892, losing to the man he replaced in March 1889—Grover Cleveland. Morgan submitted his resignation on January 10, 1893, effective March 3. He left office and remained committed to universal education. While he was criticized in office as focusing too heavily on education—and opposing Catholic schools—he was, in fact, hesitant to terminate Catholics from the Indian Service, facing the criticisms of Protestant reformers in turn. Morgan died a month short of his sixty-third birthday on July 13, 1902.

Morgan's Convictions
Unexpectedly called to this responsible position, I entered upon the discharge of its duties with simple, well defined and strongly-cherished convictions:

First. The anomalous position heretofore occupied by the Indians in this country cannot much longer be maintained. The reservation system belongs to a "vanishing state of things" and must soon cease to exist.

Second. The logic of events demands the absorption of the Indians into our national life, not as Indians, but as American citizens.

Third. As soon as a wise conservatism will warrant it, the relations of the Indians to the Government must rest solely upon the full recognition of their individuality. Each Indian must be treated as a man, be allowed a man's rights and privileges, and be held to the performance of a man's obligations. Each Indian is entitled to his proper share of the inherited wealth of the tribe, and to the protection of the courts in his "life, liberty, and pursuit of happiness." He is not entitled to be supported in idleness.

Fourth. The Indians must conform to "the white man's ways," peaceably if they will, forcibly if they must. They must adjust themselves to their environment, and conform their mode of living substantially to our civilization. This civilization may not be the best possible, but it is the best the Indians can get. They cannot escape it, and must either conform to it or be crushed by it.

Fifth. The paramount duty of the hour is to prepare the rising generation of Indians for the new order of things thus forced upon them. A comprehensive system of education modeled after the American public-school system, but adapted to the special exigencies of the Indian youth, embracing all persons of school age, compulsory in its demand and uniformly administered, should be developed as rapidly as possible.

Sixth. The tribal relations should be broken up, socialism destroyed and the family and the autonomy of the individual substituted. The allotment of lands in severalty, the establishment of local courts and police, the development of a personal sense of independence, and the universal adoption of the English language are means to this end.

Seventh. In the administration of Indian affairs there is need and opportunity for the exercise of the same qualities demanded in another great administration—integrity, justice, patience, and good sense. Dishonesty, injustice, favoritism, and incompetency have no place here anymore than elsewhere in the Government.

Eighth. The chief thing to be considered in the administration of this office is the character of the men and women employed to carry out the designs of the Government. The best system may be perverted to bad ends by incompetent or dishonest persons employed to carry it into execution, while a very bad system may yield good results if wisely and honestly administered.[6]

A Settled Indian Policy
A variety of causes have of late conspired to stimulate public interest in the subject of Indian administration, and to provoke a very widespread discussion of the so-called Indian problem.... I think ... there is coming to be a very general consensus of opinion as to the essential elements that should enter into the settled policy of the Government in all its dealings with these people, and I venture to suggest the most important of them here....

(1) Comprehensiveness. The Indians, while alike as belonging to one common race and as sustaining to the United States Government the general relation of wards, differ among themselves very widely in language, manners, customs, religion, and environment. They represent a great number of distinct phases of human development.... Any theory which ignores these essential facts and attempts to deal with them *en masse* must, of necessity, be radically and fatally defective....

(2) Definiteness of aim. There has hitherto been more or less confusion in the public mind as to precisely what the Government is aiming to accomplish, and so long as this uncertainty exists there can be no considerable progress toward determining the best measures to be adopted. If it were the purpose of the Government to exterminate the Indians by violence, or to leave them to shift for themselves ... this purpose would necessarily determine legislation and administration. If the object were to simply guard them as prisoners of war, feeding and supporting them in idleness ... this purpose should be clearly avowed and should have its weight in determining everything pertinent to Indian matters. If, however, the purpose is to incorporate the Indians into the national life as independent citizens ... not as American Indians but Americans, or rather as men enjoying all the privileges and sharing the burdens of American citizenship, then this purpose should be not only clearly and definitely stated, but should be dominant in all matters of legislation and administration....

(3) Clearness of Outline. In the process of elevating a rude and barbarous people to the plane of civilization there is involved a combination of many forces—heredity, tradition, soil, climate, food supply, and the needs of surrounding civilization. There are also involved the great forces of legislation, administration, and institutions—such as industrial schools and missionary agencies—and a failure to comprehend the legitimate work of each of these great factors leads inevitably to gross errors in judgment....

(4) Adaption of means to ends. If the Indians are expected to thrive by agriculture they should not be thrust aside onto sterile plains or into the mountains, but should be allowed to occupy such portions of the country as are adapted to agricultural pursuits.... A little timely help would, in many cases, be sufficient to put them upon the road to self-support and independence.... If we expect the rising generation to become intelligent, we should see to it that they have ample opportunities for education. If we desire that they should be industrious we should encourage among

them all forms of handicraft. If we wish them to become self-reliant, we should throw them upon their own responsibility and exact of them strict obedience to law. If we expect them to be just, we should set them an example. It is as true in our dealings with them as it is in the natural world that "Whatsoever a man soweth that shall he also reap."

(5) Justice. The charge most frequently brought against the American people in reference to their dealings with the Indians is that of injustice. This charge is sometimes flippantly made, and oftentimes rests upon no historical basis, and yet it is unfortunately true that the impression widely prevails in the popular mind and is deeply rooted in the mind of the Indians that treaties have been broken and that the Government has failed in numerous instances to perform its most solemn obligations. . . . But justice is two-sided. It demands as well as concedes. While it is desirable that we should pay the Indian to the last dollar all that is due them, we should expect of them the fulfillment of their obligations. They should be held to a strict accountability for their deliberate actions, and where, without provocation, they go upon the warpath, commit outrages, destroy property, or otherwise disturb the peace, they should be punished. . . .

(6) Firmness. Thousands of them are yet in a stage of childhood; they are living in the twilight of civilization, weak, ignorant, superstitious, and as little prepared to take care of themselves as so many infants. It is therefore unwise . . . to defer wholly to their wishes with reference to what is clearly for their good. The allotment of land, the restriction of the power of alienation, the compulsory education of their children, the destruction of the tribal organization, the bestowment of citizenship, the repression of heathenish and hurtful practices, the suppression of outbreaks, and punishment for lawlessness are among the things which belong unmistakably to the prerogatives of the National Government. . . . If, after this reasonable preparation, they are unable or unwilling to sustain themselves, they must go to the wall. It will be survival of the fittest. It is rightly claimed that thus far they have not had an equal chance with the rest of us, by reason of their isolation, and the present effort of the Government in the establishment of costly Indian schools is for the purpose of removing this inequality and bringing the Indian children into competitive relations with other children. Justice demands this, but it asks no more.

(7) Humanity. It should be borne in mind, however, that this peculiar people are our brethren, made of the same blood, and as such have claims upon us. This vast country which is now the scene and the support of our

greatness once belonged to them. Step by step they have been driven back from the hills and beautiful valleys of New England, the fertile fields of Ohio, the prairies of the West, until today, for the most part, they are gathered together on reservations poorly suited for agricultural purposes, and where the conditions of life are the hardest. . . . As a people they are poor and weak and well-nigh helpless. The vast and resistless tide of European emigration and the overflow of our aggressive population have despoiled them of their hunting grounds, robbed them of their richest fields, restricted them in their freedom, destroyed thousands of them in battle, and inflicted upon them great suffering. . . .

(8) Radicalness. "Whatever is worth doing is worth doing well." The course of the Government has not always been self-consistent. Legislation has been tentative and administration fitful. Many things have been attempted, but few have been accomplished. Now that there is coming to be a pretty well-organized national policy, it should be carried into execution with as much vigor as is practical, to the end that the results anticipated from it may be reached as speedily as possible. If the policy of allotting lands is conceded to be wise, then it should be applied at an early day to all alike wherever the circumstances will warrant. If we have settled upon the breaking up of the tribal relations, the extinguishment of the Indian titles to surplus lands, and the restoration of the unneeded surplus to the public domain, let it be done thoroughly. If reservations have proven to be inadequate for the purposes for which they were designed, have shown themselves a hindrance to the progress of the Indian as well as an obstruction in the pathway of civilization, let the reservations, as speedily as wisdom dictates, be utterly destroyed and entirely swept away.

(9) Stability. Having determined upon a policy, we should regard it as permanent until its work is accomplished. Whatever laws are to be passed should be framed with reference to the perfecting and not the essential modification of the plan. All acts of administration should be with reference to its success. . . . The day of experiment should be ended. Consistency in legislation, uniformity in administration, permanence of the tenure of office based upon intelligent comprehension of the work to be done, and competence and fidelity in the discharge of duty would very materially hasten the successful accomplishment of the wise ends of the Government.

(10) Time. The great forces now at work; land in severalty with its accompanying dissolution of the tribal relation and breaking up of the

reservation; the destruction of the agency system; citizenship, and all that belongs thereto of manhood, independence, privilege, and duty; education, which seeks to bring the young Indians into right relationships with the age in which they live, and to put into their hands the tools by which they may gain for themselves food and clothing and build for themselves homes, will, if allowed to continue undisturbed a reasonable length of time, accomplish their beneficent ends. They should be fostered, strengthened, maintained, and allowed to operate....

How long it will take for the work to be completed depends partly upon the wisdom of Congress when making necessary laws, partly upon the wisdom of the Executive in making appointments and giving direction to Indian affairs, partly upon the fidelity and intelligence of agents and others chosen to superintend the work, partly upon the vigor and efficiency of the schools and those employed to teach industries, partly upon the zeal of Christian churches and humanitarians, and partly upon the spirit of those of our people who find themselves in face-to-face relationships with Indian families and individuals, on the reservations and elsewhere.... I will venture to say that it is possible, before the close of the present century, to carry this matter so far towards its final consummation as to put it beyond the range of anxiety....[7]

Patenting Indian Land

This might seem like a somewhat rapid reduction of the landed estate of the Indians, but when it is considered that for the most part the land relinquished was not being used for any purpose whatever, that scarcely any of it was in cultivation, that the Indians did not need it and would not be likely to need it at any future time, and that they were ... reasonably well paid for it, the matter assumes quite a different aspect. The sooner the tribal relations are broken up and the reservation system done away with the better it will be for all concerned. If there were no other reason for this change, the fact that individual ownership of property is the universal custom among the civilized people of this country would be a sufficient reason for urging the handful of Indians to adopt it.

As a general rule, I would not advise the purchase of the surplus lands until the Indians have been located upon and are absolutely secured in their individual holdings. Give them their patents and see that they are fairly started in the paths of civilization, with their children in school, and then it will be time enough to negotiate with them for the sale of the surplus....

Their lands are becoming more valuable every year, so that they can lose nothing, in a pecuniary sense, by withholding the sale of so much as they may have to dispose of until after this has been done....

Leaving out the five civilized tribes and the Alaska Indians, it would take about 30,000,000 acres of land to give to every Indian in the United States—man, woman, and child—160 acres each. There would still remain, in round numbers, 66,000,000 acres of Indian land, (exclusive of the reservations of the five civilized tribes), which, at $1 per acre, probably a fair average, would yield $66,000,000, the annual interest on which, at five percent, would be $3,300,000—a sum sufficient to pay the entire cost of educating all the Indian children in the United States. At the end of a few years, the principal sum might properly be distributed per capita among the rightful owners to assist them in improving their homes, when they could be left like other citizens to care for themselves.[8]

Status and Rights of Mixed Bloods
When Indian reservations were remote from white settlements and practically valueless for the purposes of those engaged in civilized pursuits, questions concerning the rights of persons of mixed blood to tribal benefits were rarely presented, and were deemed of little moment. But since the steady march of civilization has brought the red man into close contact with the dominant race, and the real value of tribal lands has consequently increased, and since the Government has inaugurated the system of allotment to Indians of lands in severalty, many persons claiming to be mixed bloods have urged this bureau to enroll them as members of Indians tribes....

Some of the applicants for tribal rights have but the slightest trace, if any, of Indian blood; and in some instances, they have lived among and affiliated exclusively with white people. Indeed, applications have been made to this office for participation in tribal benefits by United States citizens whose sole title thereto rested upon their claim of having aboriginal blood in their veins by descent from Powhatan, through Pocahontas....

Attorney General Cushing . . . held that half-breed Indians were to be treated as Indians in all respects, so long as they retained their tribal relations. . . .[9] He concluded that the incapacity of race attached to an Indian, as such, may and must be susceptible of being determined, by intermarriage with persons of the dominant race, but declined to lay down a rule as to the period or stage of descent at which this occurs.

It was subsequently decided, in the case of *Ex Parte Reynolds*[10] . . . that whether an individual of partial Indian descent is independent of jurisdiction of our courts as an Indian or is amenable to it as a subject of the national or State government, is to be determined (if the question depends on race, not on residence) not upon the quantum of Indian blood, but upon the condition of his father, under the rule of civil law *partus sequitur patrem*, which governs in this class of cases. . . .[11]

Nearly all questions which might arise, under the principles to be deduced from the above opinion and decision, as to the loss of tribal right by residing away from the tribe and assuming United States citizenship, are set at rest by the general allotment act. Section 4 . . . authorizes allotments upon the public domain to Indians not residing upon a reservation or for whose tribe no reservation has been provided; and section 6 declares that every Indian to whom allotment shall have been made who has voluntarily taken up his residence separate and apart from any tribe in the United States and adopted the habits of civilized life, is a citizen of the United States and entitled to all rights, etc., as such citizen, without in any manner impairing or otherwise affecting his right to tribal or other property.

But the question still remains, where the point as to residence is not involved, as to the extent to which the principles laid down in the case of Reynolds should be applied to the applications for tribal relations of persons of mixed blood. Should the rule that nationality or citizenship follows the father's condition be construed to determine property rights in Indian tribes, or should it be confined only to questions of citizenship and nationality to which it in turn applies?

The Indians living in tribal relations have been declared by the courts to be "distinct political communities" and "domestic dependent nations;" also to be "under the pupilage of the Government." The peculiarity of their status, as thus defined, appears still more anomalous when we consider the fact that each Indian is entitled to and will obtain his individual estate by division of the tribal property, and is thus virtually in the attitude of a tenant, in common with his brethren of the domain of his tribe. The political status and nationality of the Indian tribes is thus interwoven with the property rights of the Indians individually. . . .

After careful consideration of the question, I incline to the opinion that the rule laid down in the *Reynolds* case should not be held conclusive as against the application of mixed bloods for tribal benefits where the claimants in other respects clearly prove their rights thereto. There is no doubt that there is a stage at which, by the admixture of white blood and non-affiliation with the Indian tribes, persons would be debarred from participating in tribal benefits....[12]

From Guardianship to Citizenship
The Government has now full care of the estates of the Indian tribes as represented by their land and by their trust funds upon which interest is annually paid to them and for their benefit, and, to a limited extent, it has control over and care of the persons of the Indians themselves. It is in these respects that our relations to the Indian tribes and to the Indians themselves have been said to resemble those of a guardian to his ward.... When the Indians shall have become citizens of the United States this paternal control will ease. They will no longer be subject in any respect to restraint by this office but will have the right to go where they please and when they please....

At the same time, with the exception that their lands received under allotment laws will be exempt from taxation for a period of twenty-five years, and possibly longer, they will be subject to the burdens borne by other citizens, and must manage their own affairs.

Except in a very few cases when members of a particular tribe have had peculiar advantages over others, in acquiring the habits and customs of our civilization and a knowledge of the laws of our commerce, the Indian naturalized into the United States, under recent laws provided for the purpose, will find himself in a most precarious and dangerous situation. Unaccustomed to the recognition in him of any rights as an individual, and accustomed as he is to regard himself only as an integral part of the unit represented by his tribe, subject to the control and protection of the United States, he will find himself suddenly released from his wardship and ushered upon the threshold of a new life, with new privileges and new responsibilities, the gravity of which his untutored mind is possibly incapable of comprehending. In this new career he will be alone, and alone he must solve the problems of his life. Whether he will be able to successfully conduct his own affairs, cope with his more intelligent and more active white neighbor, and make himself a good citizen, is a problem for the future to solve.[13]

So far as I now see, the only methods that have presented themselves for consideration in competition with the one adopted by the Government are [to] continue the present reservation system and the exercise of guardianship over these people in the future as in the past for an indefinite period to come ... [or] by one act of law the Indians should be made citizens of the United States, thrown upon their own resources, and relieved of the guardianship of the Government. . . .[14]

CHAPTER 34

Daniel M. Browning

Commissioner of Indian Affairs (April 13, 1893–May 3, 1897)

DANIEL M. BROWNING was born in Benton, Illinois, in 1846. After graduating from law school, Browning served as a county and circuit court judge in Illinois for over two decades. When Grover Cleveland was elected to a second nonconsecutive term as president in November 1892, Vice President Elect Adlai Stevenson of Illinois recommended Browning as commissioner of the General Land Office.[1] The president, meanwhile, considered a number of men to serve as commissioner of Indian affairs before settling on Browning, who was passed over as land commissioner. Browning had no interest in or prior knowledge of Indian affairs.[2]

When he assumed office on April 13, 1893, Browning served under Interior Secretary Hoke Smith, who took great interest in Indian affairs. Federal policy toward Native Americans, however, was well established by 1893, and Browning brought little to the office, with his primary intent seemingly to offer patronage to his political friends in Illinois. With all Indian school positions now under civil service, however, and with President Cleveland appointing Army officers as Indian agents, there were few positions of patronage for Browning to fill.

Browning followed the well-established policy of assimilation and severalty but was dominated in office by Assistant Commissioner Frank Armstrong, who was both a veteran Indian Office employee and well versed in Indian affairs. With Congress controlling the purse, there was little for Browning to do. As commissioner, he had a simple philosophy that governed his actions: place Indians on allotments and inform them that the government would not provide for them and they should become self-supporting and citizens of the United States and the state in which they lived. To succeed, the Indians would have to take advantage of the opportunities the government afforded them and make use of their own labor for self-support. Not surprisingly, Browning opposed leasing of allotted lands, which he argued was counter to the goal of land severalty.³

Browning's educational policy was equally simple: provide a practical education since Indian children were not capable of competing with non-Indian children. While Congress enacted legislation requiring parental consent for children to be sent to distant off-reservation schools, Browning did not agree. While he supported the policy, he was not averse to withholding rations from parents who did not agree with him. In an 1896 letter to Captain W. H. Clapp, the Indian agent at Pine Ridge, Browning argued parents had no right to designate which school their children attended. In fact, he ordered government schools filled first and permitted the Indian Office to "steal" children from sectarian schools, if necessary, to fill government schools. "Browning's Rule" remained in effect until 1902.

Browning also believed that Indian children for whom the government had a continuing responsibility should be educated in government schools, not mission or sectarian schools.⁴ That the majority of government funding for sectarian schools aided the Bureau of Catholic Missions was no small consideration in the school debate, especially since government schools were dominated by Protestant thinking and educators.

The only significant policy resulting from Browning's tenure was a departmental ruling that addressed the issue of Indian women marrying non-Indian men and the legal status of their children. In line with the philosophy of the day, the Indian Office ruled such women became US citizens upon marriage to non-Indian men, with their children also citizens. Such children were no longer to have any right or interest in the tribal estate.⁵ A second matter Browning weighed in on was utilization of Indian allotments. While he was opposed to leasing allotments as counter to the intent of severalty, he acknowledged that exceptions for "age or disability" were legitimate. He recognized that not all allotments were tillable—although they might be good ranching lands—and that many were too small to enable the allottee to make a living.

While commissioners prior and subsequent to Browning opposed Indian participation in Wild West shows, Browning did not. Browning remained in office for the duration of the Cleveland administration and resigned from office on May 3, 1897, two months after the inauguration of President William McKinley. By the time he left office, President Cleveland had brought nearly all Indian Office positions under civil service reform. Upon retirement from government work, Browning moved to St. Louis and practiced law. He died at the age of fifty-seven on January 13, 1903.

A Philosophical Framework

The main effort now is, and for many years must be, to put the Indian upon his allotment, get him to support himself there, protect him from encroachment and injustice, and educate and train his children in books and industries. As a first step, so far as treaty obligations do not interfere by requiring the payment of moneys and issuance of rations or annuities, the Indians are given to understand that the Government will not feed and clothe them while they remain in idleness. Such funds as are available for the purpose are devoted to starting Indians in homes. If an Indian will go upon an allotment and work to improve it, the Government assists him in building a house, gives him a team, agricultural implements, wire for fencing, and grain for seeding, and the supervision and counsel of a practical farmer to aid him in the cultivation of his crops.[6]

The policy of the Government ... (is) to lead the Indian into habits of self-support and to fit him for citizenship. The consensus of opinion ... seems to be that these much-desired ends can better be accomplished through allotment of land in severalty than in any other way. An allotment in severalty, however, is but an opportunity of which the Indian must take advantage. If he has no desire to better his condition at the cost of personal exertion and through the means thus opened up to him and cannot be made to appreciate the benefits conferred on him, but little good will have been accomplished by the allotment. The object is to make him feel a personal interest in a particular piece of land; to have him learn by its cultivation with the labor of his own hands how to gain a better subsistence than he has previously enjoyed, and at the same time acquire the arts of civilization and learn the means of self-support thereby.

But to permit the indiscriminate leasing of allotted lands would defeat the purpose for which allotments are made; so, the law provides that the allottee will not be permitted to lease his lands until he shall have made it appear to the Secretary of the Interior that "by reasons of age or disability" he cannot personally and with benefit to himself, occupy or improve his allotment. There are cases, however, where "by reason of age or other disability" the allottee should be permitted to lease his lands, and to meet these exceptional cases the provision authorizing the leasing of allotted lands was enacted.[7]

Educational Philosophy

Any system ... which overlooks that method of industrial instruction by which the great masses of our people, who do not intend to enter the professions, are to be benefited must be condemned as unwise. Few Indians, in the brief time which has elapsed since their race emerged from barbarism, have sufficient natural aptitude and acquirements to compete successfully with the white race in those professions which are the outgrowth of higher collegiate training. Therefore . . . our Indian youth should receive a vigorous practical education to fit them for the average walks of life.[8]

An effort is also being made to define the localities from which the respective non-reservation schools, both Government and contract, may draw their pupils, the object being twofold: First, so far as practicable, it will keep the young people within the climate and latitude to which they are accustomed. This will, of course, favorably affect the health question. . . . Second, it will modify, if not wholly break up, a practice, which has gradually grown until it has become pernicious, of having many different schools searching for pupils on the same reservation [leading to] rivalry and competition in obtaining Indian pupils. This leads to the making of promises to parents and pupils and holding out of inducements which are very difficult of fulfillment afterward, and very disappointing to the Indians when not strictly fulfilled according to their understanding of the arrangements made. Such a course also fosters in the Indian an idea, which he is too ready to cherish, that he confers rather than receives a favor giving up his child to be educated free of any expense to himself.[9]

The course . . . relative to obtaining pupils for non-reservation schools only with the voluntary consent of their parents or near relatives has been strictly adhered to. . . .[10] The effect of this policy, which is well understood among all the Indians, has been only salutary, and the result which was anticipated, viz, that it would ultimately increase the attendance at non-reservation schools. . . . Of course, upon reservations the knowledge on the part of the Indians that rations can be withheld quickens the interest of ignorant or careless parents in school attendance.[11]

Children of Indian Women Married to U.S. Citizens

A very important decision was made by the Department May 8, 1894, relative to the rights of children of Indian women the offspring of marriages between said Indian women and citizens of the United States entered into since the act of August 9, 1888. . . .[12]

Prior to this act, an Indian woman entering into marriage with a citizen of the United States did not become a citizen, for the reason that the act of February 10, 1855, under which women of a different nationality became citizens of the United States by marriage to a citizen of this country, provided only for the admission to citizenship of such women as might "be lawfully naturalized under the general naturalization laws of the United States."[13] An Indian woman could not be naturalized under the laws of the United States.... Therefore, the children of Indian women married to citizens of the United States prior to August 9, 1888, have been regarded and treated as Indians and as members of the tribe to which their mother belonged, so far as their rights of property were concerned.

In a report of March 21, 1894,.... this office [was asked] whether the children of an Indian woman married to a citizen of the United States since the act of August 9, 1888, would be entitled to a share in the per capita payment.... [I] indorsed the position taken on the subject by my predecessor... which was that in marrying a citizen of the United States... an Indian woman by such marriage separates herself from her tribe and becomes identified with the people of the United States, and her children are citizens of the United States in all respects, and in no respect can be deemed members of the tribe to which the mother belonged prior to her marriage. They would, therefore have no right to share in the property of the tribe except such as they might take by representation of the mother on her death.[14]

CHAPTER 35

William A. Jones

Commissioner of Indian Affairs (May 3, 1897–January 1, 1905)

WILLIAM ATKINSON JONES was born on September 17, 1844, in Pembrokeshire, Wales, with his family immigrating to Mineral Point, Wisconsin, in 1851. After graduating from Platteville Normal School in 1872, Jones began a career as a teacher before gaining election as a county superintendent of schools in 1875. In 1881, he transitioned into banking at the First National Bank of Mineral Point. Three years later, the politically ambitious Jones was elected mayor of Mineral Point, and in 1894 he was elected as the Iowa County representative to the Wisconsin State House, where he became connected with the political hierarchy of the Republican Party.[1]

With the election of William McKinley as president in 1896, Jones sought an appointment in the federal government. John Spooner, an influential Wisconsin politician and supporter of McKinley, assisted Jones in gaining nomination as commissioner of Indian affairs and guided him through the Senate confirmation process. Jones was confirmed on May 3, 1897, and took office immediately; he served nearly eight years.

Jones followed the same policy blueprint as did all commissioners over the previous fifteen years, writing extensive philosophical statements on how policy should be implemented. A master administrator, Jones worked with the leading reform groups of his day, including the Board of Indian Commissioners, Indian Rights Association, and the Lake Mohonk Conference to emphasize a policy centered on Indian self-support through assimilation.

Since he followed the established political paradigm on Indian affairs, Jones argued reservations and everything associated with them were an evil that needed to be mitigated as quickly as possible. Reservations were to be subdivided through land severalty so that Indians could become self-supporting. Excess lands could be sold to white farmers "who needed" such lands. In accordance with late nineteenth-century policy, all Indians were to become farmers, ranchers, or laborers, with Jones instructing government school teachers to ingrain into each child that when he left school he would need to "practice what he has been taught or starve."[2] He advocated for compulsory education, believing it was especially needed in Indian Country. He also directed the Indian Office to place students in boarding schools and to fill such institutions to their capacity.[3] Parents had no right to impede the education of their children.

Jones implemented regulations requiring Indians to follow certain habits deemed to be civilized. These included marriage licenses, shearing long hair before entering government schools, and no participation in the Wild West shows. While Indians were both wards of the state and political sovereigns, Jones treated them as wards that had no right to interfere with the federal plan for their future. He eliminated rations (except for those physically unable to work) believing they were detrimental to self-support. He further authorized agents to find employment on-or off-reservation for all Indians.[4] Similarly, he worked to commute annuities and sought to distribute the common property in severalty. His message was clear: work or go hungry.[5]

Jones opposed payments from timber, cattle, and agricultural leases, viewing them as undermining individual responsibility and encouraging tribalism and dependency. His solution was to expedite the allotment process while limiting the leasing of land. As land was allotted in severalty, Indians were to be on their own. If they wished to sell their interest in the tribal estate, Jones did not object, although he issued regulations in 1902 requiring such sales to be under the watch of the Indian Office.[6] In line with this emphasis on individualism and self-support, Jones railed against an educational system that gave Indian youth an education (and medical care, food, recreational facilities, athletics, etc.) at no cost to them. This "poverty to affluence" policy of education exacerbated the problem, he stated, and only when Indians were thrown to their own resources and reservations were abolished could they be assimilated.

To his credit, Jones was among the first to recognize that many allotments in the West required irrigation in order to be productive, arguing it would be cruel to place an individual on an allotment without access to water. His was also the first administration to recognize the need for good health care for the Indians, as an allotment was of little value to an individual who was too ill to make the land productive. For these and others reasons, Jones came to recognize by the end of his tenure as commissioner that severalty was not the sole answer to the Indian problem. By then poor health plagued him, and he resigned effective January 1, 1905. He returned to Mineral Point with his family and died at the age of sixty-eight on September 17, 1912.

Education

To educate the Indian in the ways of civilized life . . . is to preserve him from extinction, not as an Indian, but as a human being. As a separate entity he cannot exist encysted, as it were, in the body of this great nation. The pressure for land must diminish his reservations to areas within which he can utilize the acres allotted to him, so that the balance may become homes for white farmers who require them. To educate the Indian is to prepare him for the abolishment of tribal relations, to take his land in severalty, and in the sweat of his brow and by the toil of his hands to carve out, as his white brother has done, a home for himself and family.[7]

The disposition and hereditary instinct of the old and conservative Indian cannot be changed, but it is the duty of the Government to train the next generation of these people so that they may become stronger mentally, morally, and physically. Therefore, it is for this purpose that the young Indian child is taken from its home to the boarding school, where the moral influences of white civilization and culture may be thrown around it and love of the civilized home instilled in its heart, in the hope that it will bear fruit in future generations. This is the policy which induces the Government to take these children during the formative period of their lives, in order that a character may be molded which will make each boy and girl a home builder and a homemaker upon those principles underlying our own civilization, prosperity, and happiness. It is a firmly fixed policy, which it is believed that succeeding generations must approve, and it is a condition which must be brought about regardless of the wishes of those parents who are unfortunately so blind as not to see the advantages accruing to their race.

Many old Indians look upon governmental school work as hostile to them and the taking away of their children as hostages; others view it as a special mark of favor that their little ones should be permitted to attend school and they demand a payment for the favor. These conflicting arguments must be combatted and the opposition overcome.[8]

Wards of the Government

The trend of public and legal thought is away from the traditional idea that the Indian is both a ward and a sovereign to the practical everyday fact that he is simply a ward of the Government; that he is in his tutelage, and requires the tender care and corrective authority which should always be lodged in the hands of a guardian. . . . [T]he old Indian [should not be] permitted to stand in the pathway of his child's entrance into that [Anglo-Saxon] civilization—to obstruct by ignorance and hereditary impulses the material welfare and prosperity of his offspring and hinder the Government in its efforts to prepare the younger generation of Indians for their incorporation into our complex political organization.... [N]o parent ... has a moral or legal right to stand in the way of his child's advancement in life; no nation has a similar right to permit a portion of its embryo citizens to grow up in ignorance and possible vice....[9]

This policy, by force of circumstances, is based upon the well-known inferiority of the great mass of Indians in religion, intelligence, morals, and home life. Their theory and practice of existence has been antagonistic to that of the more fortunate whites, who have behind them long ages of slow and successful progress and struggle for supremacy. Originally kind-hearted, contact with the European strangers who landed on the shores of his country, and were themselves just emerging from the superstitions of the Dark Ages, did not tend to impress him with any very great love for those who introduced themselves for purposes of their own aggrandizement; nor has the attitude of his conquerors for many years since given him a different conception of them. Naturally filled with a love of his country and its vast hunting ground, he has seen them gradually slipping from his grasp and becoming the abiding place of those whom he at first welcomed to his shores. But, notwithstanding all these years of appropriation and oppression, earnest men and women have held faith in the justice of the Indians' right to existence, a home, and final absorption into the body politic of their country....

The hope of the Indian race lies in taking the child at the tender age of four or five years, before the trend of his mind has become fixed in ancient molds or bent by the whims of his parents, and guiding it into the proper channel. Children who have been thus early placed under the influences of the schools show a percentage of success equal to, or greater than, that which attends the public schools of any of the great cities of the world which draw their material from the slums. A greater percentage of the latter sink back into the degradation of their parents and revert to the life from which they were taken than do the Indian boys and girls who have received proper training in Indian schools. The educated child of the average Indian reservation has no severer or harder lot when he returns to his old home than does his white brother of the city slums. It is sometimes stated in the public prints, and by those who should be better informed, that the present method of educating the Indian is a failure, because, in many instances, the pupils, after receiving the advantages of a Government school and living for years in its moral associations, return home, take up the blanket and relapse into the manners and customs of their parents. This may sometimes be true, but, on the other hand, vast numbers of white children who have attended the public schools and been surrounded with the refining influences of Christian churches and happy homes, take up a life of vice and degradation. But no one will honestly contend that, because such is the fact, the State should abandon its splendid system of schools or fail to give the children a good common school education....[10]

Obstacle #1 to Self-Support: The Ration System
To confine a people upon reservations where the natural conditions are such that agriculture is more or less a failure and all other means of making a livelihood limited and uncertain, it follows inevitably that they must be fed wholly or in part from outside sources or drop out of existence. This is the situation of some of the Indian tribes today. It was not always so. Originally and until a comparatively recent period the red man was self-supporting. Leading somewhat of a nomadic life, he roamed with unrestricted freedom over the country in pursuit of game, which was plentiful, or located upon those spots fitted by nature to make his primitive agriculture productive. All this is changed. The advent of the white man was the beginning of the end. From east to west, from one place to another ... the Indian has been "movin' on" until he can go no further. Surrounded by whites, located upon unproductive reservations often in a rigorous climate, he awaits the destiny which under existing conditions he is powerless to avert....[11]

Notwithstanding all this, it is the consensus of opinion of those who from observation and experience are qualified to speak intelligently on the subject that the gratuitous issue of rations, except to the old and helpless, is detrimental to the Indian. It encourages idleness and destroys labor; it promotes beggary and suppresses independence; it perpetuates pauperism and stifles industry; it is an effectual barrier to the progress of the Indian towards civilization. Yet, objectionable as it is, the system must continue as long as the present reservation system continues. Until the Indians are placed in a position where the way is open before them to support themselves, they must be assisted. A civilized nation will not permit them to starve....[12]

Obstacle #2: Annuities
The ultimate disposition of the Indian trust funds is a subject for the most serious consideration. In some cases, they are small and in others very large. With respect to the former they can, as a rule, be paid out to the Indians with little, if any, evil consequences. With respect to the latter their proper disposition is more difficult. It is admitted that great wealth is a source of weakness to any Indian tribe and productive of much evil. How to apply it so as to avoid evil consequences and produce only beneficial results is a problem which, though having occupied the earnest attention of the best and wisest friends of the Indians seems so far not to have been satisfactorily solved. [T]he best means of remedying the evils . . . are . . . provid[ing] for the gradual extinction of these funds. This is to be done by setting aside a sufficient sum to maintain the reservation schools as they now exist for a definite period of years—say twenty-one—and then dividing the balance per capita and paying to each member of the tribe. . . . As a corollary to this, divid[ing] the land belonging to the tribe per capita, if applied, the immediate result would almost invariably be to relegate the Indians affected, or many of them, to a state of poverty. The remote result might be . . . that finding their substance gone and themselves in actual want they would realize that they must work or starve, and so from necessity, if not from choice, put forth some effort in their own behalf. The result would be that in time they would become industrious, prosperous members of the community.[13]

Obstacle #3: Leasing of Allotments
It is more difficult to create than to destroy, and it is easier to point out an evil than to afford a remedy; but it is believed that in the allotment system wisely adapted lies the true solution of the Indian problem. . . . The true idea of allotment is to have the Indian select, or to select for him, what may be called his homestead, land upon which by ordinary industry he can make a living either by tilling the soil or in pastoral pursuits. The essentials for success are water and fuel, but above all the former. . . . To put him upon an allotment without water and tell him to make his living is mere mockery. His allotment having been selected he should be required to occupy it and work it himself. In this he must have aid and instruction. If he has no capital to begin on, it must be given him; a house must be built; a supply of water must be assured and the necessaries of life furnished. . . . To better assist them the allottees should be divided into small communities each to

be put in charge of persons who by precept and example would teach them how to work and how to live.

This is the theory. The practice is very different. The Indian is allotted and then allowed to turn over his land to the whites and go on his aimless way. This pernicious practice is the direct growth of vicious legislation.[14] The amended rules governing the leasing of allotted lands [must] provide that each able-bodied adult male Indian not engaged in some occupation by which he is gaining a livelihood for himself and family will be required to reserve not less than 40 acres of cultivable land from his own allotment for occupancy and cultivation by himself, which shall always be exempt from leasing....[15]

Obstacle #4: A Free Education
Further observation and reflection leads to the unwelcome conviction that another obstacle may be added to these already named, and that is education.... [T]he present Indian educational system, taken as a whole, is not calculated to produce the results so earnestly claimed for it and so hopefully anticipated when it was begun.... The pupils are gathered from the cabin, the wickiup, and the tepee. Partly by cajolery and partly by threats; partly by bribery and partly by fraud; partly by persuasion and partly by force, they are induced to leave their homes and their kindred to enter these schools and take upon themselves the outward semblance of civilized life. They are chosen not on account of any particular merit of their own, not by reason of mental fitness, but solely because they have Indian blood in their veins. Without regard to their worldly condition; without any previous training; without any preparation whatever, they are transported to the schools—sometimes thousands of miles away—without the slightest expense or trouble to themselves or their people.

The Indian youth finds himself at once, as if by magic, translated from a state of poverty to one of affluence. He is well fed and clothed and lodged. Books and all the accessories of learning are given him and teachers provided to instruct him. He is educated in the industrial arts on the one hand, and not only in the rudiments but in the liberal arts on the other.... Matrons wait on him while he is well and physicians and nurses attend him when he is sick. A steam laundry does his washing and the latest modern appliances do his cooking. A library affords him relaxation for his leisure hours, athletic sports and the gymnasium furnish him exercise and recreation, while music entertains him in the evening. He has hot and cold baths, and steam heat and electric light, and all the modern conveniences. All of the necessities of life are given him and many of the luxuries. All of this without money and without price, or the contribution of a single effort of his own or of his people. His wants are all supplied almost for the wish. The child of the wigwam becomes a modern Aladdin, who has only to rub the Government lamp to gratify his desires. . . .

What, then, shall be done? And this inquiry brings into prominence at once the whole Indian question. . . . In the last thirty-three years over $240,000,000 have been spent upon an Indian population not exceeding 180,000, enough, if equitably divided, to build each one a house suitable to his condition and furnish it throughout; to fence his land and build him a barn; to buy him a wagon and team and harness; to furnish him plows and the other implements necessary to cultivate the ground, and to give him something . . . to embellish and beautify his home. . . .

What is his condition today? He is still on his reservation; he is still being fed; his children are still being educated and money is being paid him; he is dependent upon the government for existence; mechanics wait on him and farmers still aid him; he is little, if any, nearer the goal of independence than he was thirty years ago, and if the present policy is continued, he will get little, if any, nearer in thirty years to come. . . .

The Solution: Throw the Indian on His Own Resources
It is easy to point out difficulties, but it is not so easy to overcome them. Nevertheless, an attempt will now be made to indicate a policy which, if steadfastly adhered to, will not only relieve the Government of an enormous burden . . . [but] will practically settle the entire Indian question within the space usually allotted to a generation. Certainly, it is time to make a move toward terminating the guardianship which has so long been exercised over the Indians and putting them upon equal footing with the white man so far as their relations with the Government are concerned. . . .

It . . . must be remembered that there is a vital difference between white and Indian education. When a white youth goes away to school or college his moral character and habits are already formed and well-defined. In his home, at his mother's knee, from his earliest moments he has imbibed those elements of civilization which, developing as he grows up distinguish him from the savage. He goes to school not to acquire a moral character, but to prepare himself for some business or profession by which he can make his way in life.

With the Indian youth it is quite different. Born a savage and raised in an atmosphere of superstition and ignorance, he lacks at the outset those advantages which are in inherited by his white brother and enjoyed from the cradle. His moral character has yet to be formed. If he is to rise from his low estate the germs of a nobler existence must be implanted in him and cultivated. He must be taught to lay aside his savage customs like a garment and take upon himself the habits of civilized life....

What, then, is the function of the state? Briefly this: To see that the Indian has the opportunity for self-support and that he is afforded the same protection of his person and property as is given to others. That being done, he should be thrown entirely upon his own resources to become a useful member of the community in which he lives, or not, according as he exerts himself or fails to make an effort. He should be located where the conditions are such that by the exercise of ordinary industry and prudence he can support himself and family. He must be made to realize that in the sweat of his face he shall eat his bread. He must be brought to recognize the dignity of labor and the importance of building and maintaining a home. He must understand that the more useful he is there the more useful he will be to society. It is there he must find the incentive to work, and from it must come the uplifting of his race....[16]

CHAPTER 36

Francis E. Leupp

Commissioner of Indian Affairs (January 1, 1905–June 18, 1909)

FRANCIS ELLINGTON LEUPP was born in New York City in 1849, graduating from Columbia Law School in 1872. A journalist by interest, Leupp owned the *Syracuse Herald* and in 1885 corresponded for the *Washington Evening Post*. As an editor, Leupp supported President Cleveland's civil service reform, although he was a good friend of Theodore Roosevelt as well. Leupp developed an early interest in Indian affairs, and in 1895 he joined the Indian Rights Association where he took on the notorious rings that plagued Indian agencies. A year later, Interior Secretary Hoke Smith appointed Leupp to the Board of Indian Commissioners, where he opposed the educational methods and philosophy of Richard Henry Pratt at Carlisle Indian School, believing the focus of education should be local, not in distant cities where youth were forced into the outing system.[1]

With the election of William McKinley as president in 1896, Leupp hoped the president would select Roosevelt as secretary of the interior or as commissioner of Indian affairs. When McKinley nominated William Jones as commissioner, Leupp opposed him as weak on policy. When McKinley appointed Cornelius Bliss as secretary, Leupp's days as a member of the conservative Board of Indian Commissioners were numbered, as he did not agree with the focus of the secretary. When Bliss asked for his resignation, Leupp obliged.

By 1897 Leupp traveled west to Indian Territory, Arizona, New Mexico, and Montana defending Native Americans. A year later he resigned from the Indian Rights Association to focus on journalism, writing very little on Indian affairs. In November 1904, now President Roosevelt nominated Leupp as commissioner of Indian affairs, and he took office on January 1, 1905.

As commissioner, Leupp largely followed the prevailing policy although he adopted a number of philosophical changes. He did not believe American Indians could ever become white men—not because they were inherently unfit but because they had a right to be Native American. While he acknowledged that older Indians would always remain as they were, he believed the focus of policy should be on children and the utilization of day schools, not distant boarding facilities. Utilizing the former would aid older Indians in understanding and learning to appreciate modern civilization.

Leupp also emphasized off-reservation employment as a means of enabling Indians to engage in self-help. When trachoma threatened Indian Country, Leupp secured congressional appropriations to deal with the epidemic. In the summer of 1905, he visited the Uintah Ute to stave off the opening of their reservation to homesteading. And while he recommended the president oppose the use of tribal funds for sectarian schools, he ultimately adopted a funding formula that deducted from tribal funds the expenditures by the government, with the remainder of the funds to be available on a pro rata basis for sectarian schools. When Roosevelt rejected the formula, more tribal funds were available for sectarian schools, a position the US Supreme Court adopted in the 1908 *Quick Bear v. Leupp* decision.²

Leupp supported land severalty, and in accordance with the Burke Act of 1906, he granted fee patents to Indians deemed competent, although the land remained in trust for twenty-five years. By 1907, the Indian Rights Association criticized Leupp for land sales he approved on the Rosebud Sioux Reservation. When he proposed legislation mandating fee patents to any parents refusing to send their children to school, Indian reform groups turned against him. With the election of William H. Taft as president in 1908, new reformers demanded a change. Leupp resigned effective June 18, 1909, after naming his own replacement, Robert G. Valentine, his personal secretary. Despite his often harsh and autocratic nature, Leupp had a secular outlook reflected in his tolerance for tribal religious beliefs and practices that set him apart. He had a genuine sympathy for Indian rights, and he encouraged arts and crafts as a form of economic development. Leupp died on November 19, 1918, in New York.

Outlines of an Indian Policy
The commonest mistake made by his white well-wishers in dealing with the Indian is the assumption that he is simply a white man with a red skin. The next commonest is the assumption that because he is a non-Caucasian he is to be classed indiscriminately with other non-Caucasians, like the negro, for instance. The truth is that the Indian has as distinct an individuality as any type of man who ever lived and he will never be judged aright till we learn to measure him by his own standards, as we whites

would wish to be measured if some more powerful race were to usurp dominion over us.

Suppose, a few centuries ago, an absolutely alien people like the Chinese had invaded our shores and driven the white colonists before them to districts more and more isolated, destroyed the industries on which they had always subsisted, and crowned all by disarming them and penning them on various tracts of land where they could be fed and clothed and cared for at no cost to themselves, to what condition would the white Americans of today have been reduced? In spite of their vigorous ancestry, they would surely have lapsed into barbarism and become pauperized. No race on earth could overcome, with forces evolved from within themselves, the effect of such treatment. That our red brethren have not been wholly ruined by it is the best proof we could ask of the sturdy traits of character inherent in them. But though not ruined, they have suffered serious deterioration, and the chief problem now before us is to prevent its going any further. . . .

First, little can be done to change the Indian who has already passed middle life. By virtue of that very quality of steadfastness which we admire in him when well applied, he is likely to remain an Indian of the old school to the last. With the younger adults we can do something here and there, where we find one who is not too conservative; but our main hope lies with the youthful generation, who are still measurably plastic.

The picture which rises in the minds of most Eastern white persons when they read petitions in which Indians pathetically describe themselves as "ignorant" and "poor," is that of a group of red men hungry for knowledge and eager for a chance to work and earn their living like white men. In actual life and in his natural state, however, the Indian is suspicious of the white race—we can hardly blame him for that—and wants nothing to do with us; he clings to the ways of his ancestors, insisting that they are better than ours; and he resents every effort of the Government either to educate his children or to show him how he can turn an honest dollar for himself by other means than his grandfathers used—or an appropriation from the Treasury. That is the plain truth of the situation, strive as we may to gloss it with poetic fancies or hide it under statistical reports of progress. . . . It is a great mistake to try, as many good persons of bad judgment have tried, to start the little ones in the path of civilization by snapping all the ties of affection between them and their parents, and teaching them to despise the aged and non-progressive members of their families. The sensible as well as the humane plan is to nourish their love of father and mother and home—a wholesome instinct which nature planted in them for a wise end—and then to utilize this affection as a means of reaching, through them, the hearts of the elders....

The foundation of everything must be the development of character. Learning is a secondary consideration. When we get to that, our duty is to adapt it to the Indian's immediate and practical needs.... Most of these [children] will try to draw a living out of the soil; a less—though, let us hope, an ever increasing—part will enter the general labor market as lumber men, ditchers, miners, railroad hands, or what not. Now, if anyone can show me what advantage will come to this large body of manual workers from being able to reel off the names of the mountains in Asia, or extract the cube root of 123456789, I shall be deeply grateful. To my notion, the ordinary Indian boy is better equipped for his life struggle on a frontier ranch when he can read the simple English of the local newspaper, can write a short letter which is intelligible though maybe ill-spelled, and knows enough of figures to discover whether the storekeeper is cheating him. Beyond these scholastic acquirements his time could be put to its best use by <u>learning how to repair a broken harness, how to straighten a sprung tire on his wagon wheel, how to fasten a loose horseshoe without breaking the hoof,</u> and how to do the hundred other bits of handy tinkering which are so necessary to the farmer who lives 30 miles from a town. The girl who has learned only the rudiments of reading, writing and ciphering, but knows also how to make and mend her clothing, to wash and iron, and to cook her husband's dinner will be worth vastly more as mistress of a log cabin than one who has given years of study to the ornamental branches alone.

[margin note: vocational training]

Moreover, as fast as an Indian of either mixed or full blood is capable of taking care of himself, it is our duty to set him upon his feet and <u>sever forever the ties which bind him either to his tribe, in the communal sense, or to the Government.</u> This principle must become operative in respect to <u>both land and money.</u> We must end the un-American absurdity of keeping one class of our people in the condition of so many undivided portions of a common lump. Each Indian must be recognized as an individual and so treated, just as each white man is....

I should seek to make of the Indian an independent laborer as distinguished from one for whom the Government is continually straining itself to find something to do. He can penetrate a humbug, even a benevolent humbug, as promptly as the next man; and when he sees the

Government inventing purely fictitious needs to be supplied and making excuses of one kind and another to create a means of employment for him, he despises the whole thing as a fraud, like the white man whom some philanthropist hires to carry a pile of bricks from one side of the road to the other and then back again....

Th[is] process of general readjustment must be gradual, but it should be carried forward as fast as it can be with presumptive security for the Indian's little possessions; and I should not let its educative value be obscured for a moment. The leading strings which have tied the Indian to the Treasury ever since he began to own anything of value have been a curse to him. They have kept him an economic nursling long past the time when he ought to have been able to take a few steps alone....

I should not feel satisfied to leave [the subject] without trying to meet a few conventional objections which I know from experience are sure to be raised. "Would you," one critic will ask, "tie the Indian down in his schooling to 'the three R's' and then turn him loose to compete with the white youth who have had so much larger scholastic opportunity?" I answer that I am discussing the Government's obligations rather than the Indian's. I would give the young Indian all the chance for intellectual training that the young Caucasian enjoys; he has it already between governmental aid and private benevolence, and in a population teeming with benevolent men and women of means no young Indian with the talent to deserve and the ambition to ask for the best there is in American education is likely to be refused. All that I have asserted is what anybody familiar with the field can see for himself—that the mass of Indian children, like the corresponding mass of white children, are not prepared for conveyance beyond the elementary studies. They are not in a condition to absorb and assimilate, or to utilize effectively, the higher learning of the books, and it is unwise to promote an unpractical at the expense of an obviously practical system of teaching.... I insist that it is foolish to force upon an Indian those studies which have no relation to his environment and which he cannot turn to account, as long as there is so much of a simpler sort which he is capable of learning and which he actually must know in order to make his way in the world.

A second critic will doubtless air his fears as to what will become of the Indian's land and money under this "wide-open" policy. To such an one I would respond: "What is to become of the land or money that you are going to leave to your children, or I to mine? Will they be any better able to take care of it for having been always kept without experience in handling property of any kind?" Swindlers will unquestionably lay snares for the weakest and most ignorant Indians, just as they do for the corresponding class of whites. We are guarding the Indian temporarily against his own follies in land transactions by holding his allotment in trust for him for twenty years or more unless he sooner satisfies us of his business capacity. Something of the same sort will be done with respect to the principal of his money. In spite of all our care, however, after we have taken our hands off, he may fall a victim to sharp practices; but the man never lived—red, white or any other color—who did not learn a more valuable lesson from one hard blow than from twenty warnings.

A great deal has been said and written about the "racial tendency" of the Indian to squander whatever comes into his hands. This is no more "racial" than his tendency to eat and drink to excess or to prefer pleasure to work: it is simply the assertion of a primitive instinct common to all mankind in the lower stages of social development. What we call thrift is nothing but the forecasting sense which recognizes the probability of a tomorrow; the idea of a tomorrow is the boundary between barbarism and civilization, and the only way in which the Indian can be carried across that line is by letting him learn from experience that the stomach filled today will go empty tomorrow unless something of today's surplus is saved overnight to meet tomorrow's deficit....

A further charge will be hurled against my programme—that it is premature.... One day must come to the Indian the great change from his present status to that of the rest of our population, for anomalies in the social system are as odious as abnormalities in nature. Either our generation or a later must remove the Indian from his perch of adventitious superiority to the common relations of citizenship and reduce him to the same level with other Americans....

Improvement Not Transformation
I have spoken of the mistake of assuming that the Indian is only a Caucasian with a red skin. A twin error into which many good people fall in their efforts to educate the Indian is taking it for granted that their first duty is to make him over into something else. If nature has set a different physical stamp upon different races of men, it is fair to assume that the variation of types extends below the surface and is manifested in mental and moral traits as well.... Scarcely less plain is the line—not the line of civilization and convention, but the line of nature—between the Indian and the white man. What

good end shall we serve by trying to blot out these distinctions? How is either party to benefit by the obliterations? When we have done our best artificially to turn the Indian into a white man, we have simply made a nondescript of him. Looking among our own companions in life, whom do we more sincerely respect—the person who has made the most of what nature gave him, or the person who is always trying to be something other than he is?

Now, how are we to apply this philosophy to the case of the Indian? Are we to let him alone? By no means. We do not let the soil in our gardens alone because we cannot turn clay into sand: we simply sow melon seed in the one and plant plum trees in the other. It does not follow that we must metamorphose whatever we wish to improve. Our aim should be to get out of everything the best it is capable of producing, and in improving the product it is no part of our duty to destroy the source. What would be thought of a horticulturist who should uproot a tree which offers a first-rate sturdy stock simply because its natural fruit is not of the highest excellence? A graft here and there will correct this shortcoming, while the strength of the parent trunk will make the improved product all the finer, besides insuring a longer period of bearing. We see this analogy well carried out in the case of an aboriginal race which possesses vigorous traits of character at the start. Nothing is gained by trying to undo nature's work and do it over, but grand results are possible if we simply turn her forces into the best channels.[3]

A Wasteful School System
I entered office . . . to enlarge the system of day school instruction as opposed to the increase of the boarding schools and among the boarding schools the preference of those on the reservations to those at a distance. Briefly stated, it pivots on the question whether we are to carry civilization to the Indian or carry the Indian to civilization, and the former seems to me infinitely the wiser plan. To plant our schools among the Indians means to bring the oldest members of the race within the sphere of influence of which every school is a center. This certainly must be the basis of any practical effort to uplift a whole people. . . .

Though the day school system is the ideal mechanism for the uplifting of the Indians, we cannot yet wholly dispense with boarding schools, because so many tribes still continue the nomadic or seminomadic habits which would require the continual moving of the day schools from place to place in order to keep near a sufficient number of families for their support. . . .

But boarding schools . . . are an anomaly in our American scheme of popular instruction. They furnish gratuitously not only tuition—the prime object of their existence—but food, clothing, and permanent shelter during the whole period of a pupil's attendance. In plain English, they are simply educational almshouses, with the unfortunate feature, from the point of view of our ostensible purpose of cultivating a spirit of independence in the Indians, that the charitable phase is obtrusively pushed forward as an attraction instead of wearing the stamp which makes the almshouse wholesomely repugnant to Caucasian sentiment. This tends steadily to foster in the Indian an ignoble willingness to accept unearned privileges; nay, more, from learning to accept them he presently comes, by a perfectly natural evolutionary process, to demand them as rights. . . .

Was ever a worse wrong perpetrated upon a weaker by a stronger race? If so, history has failed to record it. . . . [Some] have overlooked entirely the vastly greater moral damage wrought upon the same victim under the guise of a benevolent desire to civilize him at long range. As if self-reliance was not at the very foundation of our own civilization! The evils of war, of graft, big and little, of business frauds and all other forms of bad faith are capable of remedy in the same monetary terms in which we measure and remedy evils among our own race; but what compensation can we offer him for undermining his character, and doing it by a method so insidious and unfair?

Unhappily our generation cannot go back and make over from the start the conditions which have come down to us by inheritance. We can, however, do the next best thing, and avoid extending or perpetuating the errors for which we are not responsible, and we can improve every available opportunity for reducing their burden. Just as we have undertaken to free the Indian from the shackles which the reservation system has imposed upon his manhood, so we should recognize it as a duty to free him from the un-American and pauperizing influences which still invest his path to civilization through the schools. The rudiment of an education, such as can be given his children in the little day school, should remain within their reach, just as they are within the reach of the white children who must be neighbors and competitors of the Indian children in their joint struggle for a livelihood. Indeed, this being a reciprocal obligation—the right of the child, red or white, to enough instruction to enable him to hold his own as a citizen, and the right of the Government to demand that every person who handles a ballot shall have his intelligence trained to the point that reading, writing, and simple ciphering will train it—I believe in compelling the Indian parent, whether he wishes to or not, to give his offspring this advantage....

This proposed obliteration of the exclusively Indian character of schools can be accomplished by throwing them open to pupils of all races alike. But the maintenance of institutions of the higher learning, looking to no special end for the national profit, does not seem to me a legitimate function of the United States Government. I should therefore do one of two things with each school: Either (1) open it to youth of all races as a training school for Government servants of some particular class—as, for instance, for the enlisted men of the Army or for the observers' corps of the Weather Bureau—or (2) sell or give it to the State or the county where it stands....[4]

CHAPTER 37

Robert G. Valentine

Commissioner of Indian Affairs (June 29, 1909–September 10, 1912)

ROBERT GROSVENOR VALENTINE was born on November 29, 1872, in West Newton, Massachusetts. After graduating from Harvard University, he taught English literature at Massachusetts Institute of Technology (MIT) before moving to New York City where he went to work for the National City Bank and the Union Pacific Railroad. Valentine returned to MIT in 1901 and during summer recesses engaged in settlement house work before poor health led him into semiretirement. Upon moving to Washington, DC, he met Francis Leupp at a civil service reform meeting. When President Roosevelt appointed Leupp commissioner of Indian affairs in 1905, Leupp asked Valentine to serve as his personal secretary.[1]

During Leupp's tenure, Valentine became superintendent of Indian schools and then assistant commissioner. When Leupp left office, he recommended Valentine as his replacement. President Taft then appointed Valentine as commissioner of Indian affairs on June 19, 1909, much to the chagrin of the Indian reformers, including Samuel Brosius of the Indian Rights Association.[2]

As commissioner, Valentine supported land severalty, something he coined as "the business aspect" of preparing American Indians for citizenship. In other words, Valentine was convinced, as many before him, that severalty was the primary means of transforming Indians into self-supporting, independent citizens. Allotment was simply a business proposition intended to instruct American Indians on how to use their land for personal, beneficial use, which to Valentine meant an agricultural use. With the West rapidly being settled, the commissioner argued, the Indians either had to learn to use their land productively or be overrun by those who would.

For Valentine, the work of the Indian Service was educational, with 300,000 "students" having the whole of the indoors and outdoors as their classroom.[3] The "teachers" of this school were the five thousand Indian Service employees, with Valentine the "principal teacher." Cultivation of crops was the essential component of this educational philosophy, making it essential that all Indian Service resources were utilized to promote farming. While he favored allotment in severalty, Valentine was cautious of issuing fee patents unless circumstances warranted it.

Land was integral to the education of the Indians in other ways as well. Only through land severalty could the "abolition of the old tribal relations" occur, Valentine mused, and the "treatment of every Indian as an individual" materialize.[4] But Valentine also lamented the alienation of land, which he was quick to point out "thwart[ed] the policy" of the government to develop self-supporting yeoman farmers. Social engineering remained front and center to the government's efforts to assimilate Native Americans.

Valentine was also forced to deal with the continued declining health status of the Indians, with the extent of tuberculosis and trachoma revealed in 1912 after the US Public Health Service, at the request of President Taft, conducted a health survey of Indian Country. As for the overall status of Indian health care, Valentine directed the Indian Service to not just care for and cure the sick but to also "increase the vitality of the Indian race" by establishing "a new standard of physical stamina for future generations."[5]

To encourage self-reliance, Valentine worked to commute permanent annuities tribes had based on treaty provisions that the commissioner believed were a "great bar" to Indian progress by keeping them in "a condition of dependence." To this end, a series of agreements in 1910 commuted the permanent annuities of the Wisconsin and Kansas bands of Pottawatomie and the Oklahoma and Iowa bands of Sac and Fox.

Valentine continued the industrial education of his predecessors but adapted the education of teenage Indian girls to include "domestic service cottages," in which a small group of girls lived together under the watchful eye and tutelage of an experienced teacher who taught the young women to perform all household duties, including preparation of meals.[6] "As the Indians learn to substitute *our* economic necessities and wants for their own older necessities and wants which the progress of time has lost to them," Valentine wrote in 1911, "they are proving not at all the lazy and unwashed beings that many people have thought [them to be], but [are instead] diligent and efficient laborers in our national economy."[7]

By 1911, Valentine's health gave out, along with his optimism as a Progressive reformer. The remainder of his tenure was spent defending policies and decisions. On September 10, 1912, he submitted his resignation and left office to work for the Progressive Party in New England. Robert G. Valentine died of a heart attack on November 14, 1916. He was forty-four years old.

Method of Assimilation

The Indian Service is primarily educational. It is a great outdoor-indoor school, with the emphasis on the outdoor. The students in the school are 300,000 individuals, ranging in age from babes at the breast to the old men and women of the tribes, and with a range of characteristics which is indicated by no one fact perhaps better than that these 300,000 individuals speak about 250 fairly district dialects. The plant which composes the physical properties of this school consist of an area of land twice the size of the State of New York, or larger than the State of Missouri, scattered through 26 States, in areas ranging from a few hundred acres to some as large as the smaller States of the Union. The funds to carry on and to be cared for in connection with this plant amount to approximately $85,000,000, of which $62,000,000 belong to the tribes; $13,000,000 belong to individual Indians; and approximately $10,000,000 are contributed by appropriations annually. The value of the physical plant, including lands, buildings, reclamation works, and forests is hundreds of millions. The teachers in this school, of which the commissioner is the principal teacher, form a force of 5,000 employees, covering all the grades and classes of work which go to make a human being a useful citizen of the United States. Whether in the schoolroom or on the irrigation ditch, whether in leasing part of an allotment or in the issuance of a patent in fee or in the use of individual or tribal funds, the one test to be brought to the business aspect of the case is: Will doing this and the way of doing it educate the child or the woman or the man for citizenship?[8]

Farming

The Indian Service realizes that instruction in farming is an essential basic part of its present educational policy and is, therefore, making use of every possible resource in order to promote farming among the Indians. Farmers are employed on reservations to teach Indians how to farm according to the most improved modern methods. Experimental farms have been established in different sections to discover the best crops for the Indians of the district, to improve the quality of the seed, and raise the standard of the product. The cooperation of the Department of Agriculture and the agricultural colleges and experiment stations of the various States has been solicited, and valuable assistance and advice have been procured from those sources in finding what class of cereals, plants, fruits, berries, and other industries carried on by farmers were best adapted to the various Indian reservations. Instruction in agriculture is receiving new emphasis in the schools. The Indians are being encouraged to hold agricultural fairs where their stock and produce are exhibited. The standard of Indian live stock is being raised by cooperation with the Bureau of Animal Industry.[9]

Th[is] policy for the economic and social emancipation of the Indians from the protection of the Government requires that they, like other Americans, should found their prosperity and development upon the basic industry of the utilization of land. The Indians' capital is very largely land, and their environment and every natural circumstance make it peculiarly necessary that the great majority of them should become farmers and stock raisers. In parts of the country, especially in the Southwest, some tribes were agricultural when Europeans first penetrated to their villages, and today every family in many of these tribes cultivates at least a garden. Once established intelligently on the soil and independent, the Indians may well develop talents for purely mechanical arts and commerce—but that is a matter for the future.[10]

Land
The essential feature of the Government's great educational program for the Indians is the abolition of the old tribal relations and the treatment of every Indian as an individual. The basis of this individualization is the breaking up of tribal lands into allotments to the individuals of the tribe. Until their lands are allotted, the Government is merely marking time in dealing with any group of Indians.[11]

There is ordinarily so little legitimate reason for the Indians alienating their lands, and the disposal of their farms so effectively thwarts the policy of the Government in developing self-support, that I am opposed to granting patents in fee unless circumstances clearly show that a title in fee will be of undoubted advantage to the applicant. A substantial class under this exception to the general rule is comprised, of course, of those who are making a living in other industries, or are honestly trying to do so. Not all Indians can or should become farmers; it is, however, the best chance of the majority.

It is noticeable that industrious Indians who actually cultivate their lands seldom apply for patents in fee. Consequently, as the great majority of applicants belong to the class which inclines most toward shiftlessness, it is not surprising to find that in the past the greater number of successful applicants have made such haste to sell their land that they have gotten considerably less money than they would have received from sales through the superintendents. In a period of idleness, they have squandered the entire proceeds, and in a short time have had neither land nor a substitute for any part of it, but in fact have been morally and industriously the worse for ever possessing land. In the face of existing evidences of carelessness and incompetence any liberal policy of giving patents in fee would be utterly at cross-purposes with the other efforts of the Government to encourage industry, thrift and independence.[12]

Leasing as a Policy Failure

[I]n the last 10 years Indian Office affairs have taken on a magnitude, a breadth, and a detail which are significant or a real attempt to master the Indian problem by preparing the Indians to leave their status of wardship, at last to lose their anomalous character as a people set apart and to join their white neighbors in the body of American citizenship.

For 15 years after the general allotment act was passed its benefits fell short of its promise, for the essential purpose of the statute was perverted, since under the act of February 28, 1891, Indians who had received allotments were able to take the line of least resistance by leasing their lands to white farmers and by continuing to live quite after their former fashion.[13] Thus it happens that present policies are comparatively recent developments—the policies which center upon individual Indians and individual Indian families, seeking to give each Indian the health and the knowledge of health which will enable him to associate and to compete with his fellow Americans, to place each Indian upon a piece of land of his own where he can by his own efforts support himself and his family, or to give him an equivalent opportunity in industry or trade, and to lead him to conserve and utilize his property as means to these ends rather than to have it as an unappreciated heritage, through the loss of which only moral and industrial debasement and eventually pauperism are to be derived.[14]

Health and Well-Being

The Government no longer looks upon its duty to the Indians as merely involving an honest accounting for its trusteeship of Indian lands and funds. It considers the trusteeship of this property as the means of bringing the

Indian to a position of self-reliance and independence where he may be able to accept the opportunities and responsibilities of American citizenship.

In all questions relating to the management of Indian properties the problem of the Indian Office under the direction of the Department is to find that method or combination of methods which is not only transparently just and honorable, but which is at the same time educative and capable of inspiring the Indian to greater personal effort. Important progress is being made in this direction. A case in point is the commutation of annuities. The perpetual annuities provided for in the treaties of various groups of Indians have been a great bar to the Indians' progress. These annuities have tended to keep the Indian in a condition of dependence, as they assured him of an income without labor or effort.[15]

The Indian Service in its health work is not aiming merely to more effectively care for and cure those that are sick. The reduction of the death rate is not its primary interest. It is working rather to increase the vitality of the Indian race and to establish for it a new standard of physical well-being. The work is being scientifically developed along lines which have already been successfully tried out by modern preventive medicine. The principal features of this work as it is now organized are: 1) An intensive attack upon the two diseases that most seriously menace the health of the Indians—trachoma and tuberculosis; 2) preventive work on a large scale, by means of popular education along health lines and more effective sanitary inspection; 3) increased attention to the physical welfare of the children in the schools, so that the physical stamina of the coming generation may be conserved and increased.[16]

CHAPTER 38

Cato Sells

Commissioner of Indian Affairs (June 2, 1913–March 29, 1921)

CATO SELLS was born on October 6, 1859, in Vinton, Iowa, and after graduating from Cornell College and passing the Iowa bar, he became city attorney and then mayor of La Porte City, Iowa. With Grover Cleveland's election to the presidency in 1892, the thirty-three-year-old Sells became US district attorney. In 1907, the Progressive Democrat moved to Texas and established the Texas State Bank and Trust Company while at the same time entering the arena of politics, supporting Woodrow Wilson's presidential candidacy in 1912. Wilson then appointed Sells commissioner of Indian affairs effective June 2, 1913.[1]

Sells entered his duties as commissioner as so many before him: without any knowledge of or experience in Indian affairs. In his first annual report, he laid the groundwork of his administration: "It is my fixed purpose to bring about the speedy individualizing of the Indians."[2] To accomplish this, Sells labored to allot land in severalty, worked to dissolve tribal affairs as rapidly as possible, and emphasized industrial education. In the process, the Progressive prohibitionist set out to eliminate alcohol in Indian Country, with the US Supreme Court abetting his efforts by authorizing the Indian Service to enforce liquor restrictions for both citizen and noncitizen Indians.[3]

During his tenure as commissioner, Sells dealt with the wide-scale corruption and rapid loss of land and resources after the recent allotment and dissolution of the Five Tribes in Oklahoma. Sells called out the corrupt county probate system that despoiled the Cherokee, Choctaw, Chickasaw, Creek, and Seminole nations, labeling the network of judges and attorneys a mix of corrupt guardians and "insolvent bondsmen."[4] While he removed 2,500 county-appointed guardians, this success was short lived when Congress ordered the Indian Service to cease representing minors in probate matters in 1918, with the Oklahoma state legislature repealing all probate reforms adopted in 1914, leading to further fraud and land loss among the Indians.[5]

Sells encouraged self-support among the Indians by stock-raising and agricultural production, emphasizing the importance of tribal landowners farming or grazing the land rather than leasing it to non-Indian producers. Recognizing that the General Allotment Act did not provide capital to assist Indian landowners in improving the land or procuring farm equipment, seed, and tools necessary to make productive use of the land, the commissioner asked Congress to expand the reimbursable loan program, using tribal moneys as collateral. Congress obliged by increasing the funds available, most of which were used to improve the quality of stock animals among the Plains tribes.

While the stock program was initially successful, the advent of American involvement in World War I in 1917 and a severe drought in 1919 led the Indian Service to encourage tribal ranchers to sell their herds. The deadly winter of 1920–1921 further decimated Plains cattlemen. The same was true of tribal growers who lacked water and machinery to irrigate and cultivate the land. When these growers did not expand their agricultural production as rapidly as Sells desired, the commissioner took "aggressive steps" to lease tribal land under "liberal terms."[6] While tribal growers cultivated 676,691 acres in 1917, the Indian Service approved 21,624 agricultural leases totaling 2,458,749 acres.[7]

The central policy of Sells's administration was his "Declaration of Policy." While Sells extended the first expiring trust patents by ten years in 1913, he was under pressure to issue fee patents and release from federal supervision most Indians, even while reformers demanded the extension of federal supervision to protect the land and resources of those not yet ready for emancipation. Not questioned were the eventual emancipation of all American Indians and the liquidation of the federal–Indian relationship.

In his effort at compromise, Sells issued his "Declaration of Policy." For those deemed "competent," Sells issued fee patents and ended federal guardianship, emancipating this class of Indians from federal supervision. This, Sells argued, would enable the Indian Service to give "closer attention" to the incompetent so that they might eventually be freed of federal oversight. All healthy adult Indians with less than 50 percent Indian blood and who were Indian school graduates demonstrating competency, were to be emancipated from federal control upon reaching the age of twenty-one. Those with greater than 50 percent Indian blood were deemed incompetent and remained under federal guardianship. The old and feeble deemed incompetent were allowed to sell their land and given unrestricted control over their money held in trust by the United States. Those owning inherited lands were encouraged to sell it, with the proceeds to be used to develop their homestead.

Sells also called for the liquidation of all tribal funds on a per capita basis. The Indian Service also refused any Indian child of parents deemed capable of "pay[ing] for their education" admittance at Indian Service schools.⁸ So doing, Sells opined, would give Indians "self-respect" and encourage "independence" while at the same time "reduce appropriations by the Government." The net result was the "beginning of the end of the Indian problem."

Sells issued 17,376 fee patents between 1917 and 1920, nearly double the number of the previous ten years. He pledged he would "not be outdone by anyone who would hasten Indian progress by the extension of freedom and obligation."⁹ In 1919, he ended the competency commissions by empowering local agency superintendents to identify which Indians were competent and which were not. By the time he left office, 504,661 acres of "non-competent" land and 498,398 acres of inherited land had been alienated, excluding the Five Tribes.

By 1920, Sells faced harsh criticism for being too liberal in emancipating Indians from federal supervision. With the election of Republican Warren G. Harding as president in 1920, Sells resigned effective March 29, 1921. He returned to Texas where he died in 1948 at the age of eighty-nine.

A Charge to Indian Youth

In our labors with these primitive people, we are too prone to become impatient. There is a disposition to expect a revolution rather than an evolution such as has come about in 2,000 years of the white man's civilization. It is unfair, it is unjust, to expect more rapid progress from the Indian than is shown in the development of the white race. If I were called upon to indicate the one important word in our relations with the Red Man, it would be patience....

The responsibility resting upon the Indian youth of today is greater than has ever fallen upon the young men and women of any race in the history of the world. Your success or failure will largely determine the future of the Red Man of America. The eyes of the Caucasian race are upon you. If you demonstrate your capacity to take on the education offered in Indian schools; if you utilize the equipment thus acquired and affirm your capacity for advancement and self-support; if you rise to the occasion and give living evidence of the progress of your people, the expenditures in your behalf will have been justified; then you and your friends who are earnestly undertaking to work out a future for you and perpetuate your race will be equipped with armor to make a successful defense of your people and their property; insure the permanent establishment of your schools; and all that goes to justify the denial that the Indian is a "vanishing race." If you do not measure up to your opportunities, you fail at your peril. Whether you are able to meet these demands depends upon you. If you fail there are those who will use it as an argument in support of their aggressions upon your people and their property and thus endanger the possibility of the next generation having similar opportunities. I have faith in you and believe you will make good.

Speaking now more generally, I repudiate the suggestion that the Indian is a "vanishing race." He should march side by side with white men during all the years to come. It is our chief duty to protect the Indian's health and to save him from premature death. Before we educate him, before we conserve his property, we should save his life. If he is to be perpetuated, we must care for the children. We must stop the tendency of the Indian to diminish in number and restore a condition that will insure his increase. Every Indian hospital bed not necessarily occupied with those suffering from diseases or injury should be available for the mother in childbirth. It is of first importance that we begin by reestablishing the health and constitution of Indian children. Education and protection of property are highly important, but everything is secondary to the basic condition which makes for the perpetuation of the race. . . . I firmly believe that if the industrial progress of the last 2 years is continued for 10 years our Indians will be practically self-supporting, with correspondingly reduced congressional appropriations.[10]

Ensuring the Well-Being of the Indians
It is our chief duty to protect the Indian's health and to save him from premature death. Before we educate him, before we conserve his property, we should save his life. If he is to be perpetuated, we must care for the children. We must stop the tendency of the Indian to diminish in number, and restore a condition that will insure his increase. Every Indian hospital bed not necessarily occupied with those suffering from disease or injury should be available for the mother in childbirth. It is of first importance that we begin by reestablishing the health and constitution of Indian children. Education and protection of property are highly important, but everything is secondary to the basic condition which makes for the perpetuation of the race.

That thought has deepened its hold upon my convictions. We must guarantee to the Indian the first of inalienable rights—the right to live. No race was ever created for utter extinction. The chief concern of all ethics and all science and all philosophies is life. The Indian has demonstrated his humanity and his capacity for intellectual and moral progress amid conditions not always propitious and I am eager to participate with all the favoring forces that contribute to his racial triumph, believing as I do that when he comes to himself as a factor in the modern world his achievements will enrich and brighten the civilization of his native land.

I should like to get the feeling I have upon this question into the conscience and aspirations of every Indian Service employee until there shall prevail a sort of righteous passion to see that every Indian child has a fair chance to live. There is something fundamental here: We cannot solve the Indian problem without Indians. We cannot educate their children unless they are kept alive. All our Indian schools, reservations, individual allotments, and accumulated incomes tend pathetically toward a wasted altruism if maintained and conserved for a withering, decadent people. If we have an Indian policy worthy of the name, its goal must be an enduring and sturdy race, true to the noblest of its original instincts and virtues and loyally sympathetic with our social and national life; a body of efficient citizens blending their unique poise and powers with the keen and sleepless vigor of the white man....

I shall expect each superintendent to acquaint himself with the home conditions of every Indian family on the reservation and to adopt practical and effective means for quick and certain improvement. Superintendents must organize such a system of cooperative information through their employees as will enable them to do this, exercising, of course, great care and discretion in gathering the requisite information....

The crux of the matter is this: We must, if possible, get rid of the intolerable conditions that infest some of the Indian homes on the reservation, creating an atmosphere of death instead of life. It will be the duty of the field matron to learn of conditions existing in Indian homes and of cases requiring medical attention and report them to the superintendent. It will be her duty to see that the prospective mother knows what equipment is necessary for the proper care of her new-born babe, and the importance of the provision which the husband shall make for the health and comfort of the mother and child should be early and urgently impressed upon him.[11]

Declaration of Policy
During the past four years the efforts of the administration of Indian affairs have been largely concentrated on the following fundamental

activities—the betterment of health conditions of Indians, the suppression of the liquor traffic among them, the improvement of their industrial conditions, the further development of vocational training in their schools, and the protection of the Indians' property. Rapid progress has been made along all these lines, and the work thus reorganized and revitalized will go on with increased energy. With these activities and accomplishments well under way, we are now ready to take the next step in our administrative program.

The time has come for discontinuing guardianship of all competent Indians and giving even closer attention to the incompetent that they may more speedily achieve competency. Broadly speaking, a policy of greater liberalism will henceforth prevail in Indian administration to the end that every Indian, as soon as he has been determined to be as competent to transact his own business as the average white man, shall be given full control of his property and have all his lands and moneys turned over to him, after which he will no longer be a ward of the Government. Pursuant to this policy, the following rules shall be observed:

Patents in fee.—To all able-bodied adult Indians of less than one-half Indian blood, there will be given as far as may be under the law full and complete control of all their property. Patents in fee shall be issued to all adult Indians of one-half or more Indian blood who may, after careful investigation, be found competent, provided, that where deemed advisable patents in fee shall be withheld for not to exceed 40 acres as a home. Indian students, when they are 21 years of age, or over, who complete the full course of instruction in the Government schools, receive diplomas and have demonstrated competency will be so declared.

Sale of lands.—A liberal ruling will be adopted in the matter of passing upon applications for the sale of inherited Indian lands where the applicants retain other lands and the proceeds are to be used to improve the homesteads or for other equally good purposes. A more liberal ruling than has hitherto prevailed will hereafter be followed with regard to the applications of non-competent Indians for the sale of their lands where they are old and feeble and need the proceeds for their support.

Certificates of competency.—The rules which are made to apply in the granting of patents in fee and the sale of lands will be equally applicable in the matter of issuing certificates of competency.

Individual Indian moneys.—Indians will be given unrestricted control of all their individual Indian moneys upon issuance of patents in fee or certificates of competency. Strict limitations will not be placed upon the use of funds of the old, the indigent, and the invalid.

Pro rata shares—trust funds.—As speedily as possible their pro rata shares in tribal trust or other funds shall be paid to all Indians who have been declared competent, unless the legal status of such funds prevents. Where practicable the pro rata shares of incompetent Indians will be withdrawn from the Treasury and placed in banks to their individual credit.

Elimination of ineligible pupils from the Government Indian schools.— In many of our boarding schools Indian children are being educated at Government expense whose parents are amply able to pay for their education and have public school facilities at or near their homes. Such children shall not thereafter be enrolled in Government Indian schools supported by gratuity appropriations, except in payment of actual per capita cost and transportation.

These rules are hereby made effective, and all Indian Bureau administrative officers at Washington and in the field will be governed accordingly.

This is a new and far-reaching declaration of policy. It means the dawn of a new era in Indian administration. It means that the competent Indian will no longer be treated as half ward and half citizen. It means reduced appropriations by the Government and more self-respect and independence for the Indian. It means the ultimate absorption of the Indian race into the body politic of the Nation. It means, in short, the beginning of the end of the Indian problem.[12]

The cardinal principle of this declaration revolves around this central thought—that an Indian who is as competent as an ordinary white man to transact the ordinary affairs of life should be given untrammeled control of his property and assured his personal rights in every particular so that he may have the opportunity of working out his own destiny. The practical application of this principle will relieve from the guardianship of the Government a very large number of Indians who are qualified to mingle on a plane of business equality with the white people. It will also begin the reduction of expenditures, and afford a better opportunity for closer attention to those who will need our protecting care for some years longer....

This new declaration of policy is calculated to release practically all Indians who have one-half or more white blood, although there will be exceptions in the case of those who are manifestly incompetent. It will also give like freedom from guardianship to those having more than one-half

Indian blood when, after careful investigation, it is determined that they are capable of handling their own affairs. This latter class, however, will be much more limited since only about 40 per cent of the Indians of the country speak the English language and the large majority of this latter class still greatly needs the protecting arm of the Government.

As an additional safeguard for those Indians of half or less white blood, a homestead commensurate with the value of the property to be patented may be retained by the allottee and made inalienable except by the approval of the Secretary of the Interior. In other cases of manifest incompetency, the trust period on their land will be extended whenever it is deemed beneficial and in the interest of the Indians themselves.[13]

It is not intended to declare every graduating student competent to handle his own affairs, but to select those who are 21 years of age and who by their conduct through the years of instruction have profited by wise discipline and shown that they possess the qualities of scholarship and character that fit them for responsibility and competition. To these graduates you will have the happy privilege on the day you hand them diplomas to give them also this declaration of their independence. It should be to them the Magna Charta of their freedom from the restraints not imposed upon other citizens of our country, and in thus granting it I know you will fully represent me with yourself in the hope that no recipient will ever strive for less than the most honorable and loyal fulfillment of American citizenship.[14]

CHAPTER 39

Charles Henry Burke

Commissioner of Indian Affairs (May 7, 1921–June 30, 1929)

CHARLES HENRY BURKE was born in Batavia, New York, on April 1, 1861, before moving to the Dakota Territory in 1882, where he homesteaded in Beadle County. At the age of twenty-seven he was admitted to the Dakota bar and moved to Pierre where he established a real estate investment company. After serving two terms in the South Dakota state legislature, Burke ran for the US House of Representatives from South Dakota in 1898, winning the first of four consecutive terms. In the House he served on the Committee on Indian Affairs and in 1906 authored the Burke Act, which amended the General Allotment Act by extending federal supervision for Indian allottees and delayed US citizenship until the end of the trust period, unless the Indian Service determined an allottee competent to handle his own affairs.¹

While he failed to win reelection to the House in 1906, Burke again was elected to the House in 1908, serving until 1915. He did not run in 1914, having been nominated to run for the open South Dakota US Senate seat, losing to Democrat Edwin S. Johnson. Burke then returned to his real estate business in Pierre. When Warren G. Harding was elected president in 1920, he asked Burke to serve as his commissioner of Indian affairs. Burke was nominated on April 1 and entered office on May 7, 1921.²

Burke served as commissioner of Indian affairs during a time of great controversy, facing criticism from those favoring rapid assimilation and emancipation of the Indians, as well as those advocating for abandonment of the assimilation policy. Moreover, Burke served under Secretary of the Interior Albert B. Fall whose two years as head of the Interior Department were marred by scandals and attempts at personal gain at the expense of tribal nations. With the resignation of Fall in March 1923, Burke sought a middle ground that ultimately appeased neither side in the policy debate.

254

Burke viewed the work of the Indian Service as one of education, and in 1923, he outlined his goals: "Every eligible Indian child in school every day" and "Every Indian School filled to its limit."[3] He enumerated 25,000 children not in school, 18,000 of whom were eligible to attend but were not enrolled due to insufficient schools. Two-thirds of these eligible students were from the Navajo, Hopi, Hualapai, and Papago tribes in Arizona. Burke committed to constructing no new schools except for the Navajo and Papago. "I am not willing to overlook the future to provide schools for these Native Americans," he wrote, and a year later he requested additional resources from Congress for children to attend public schools, except Navajo and Papago children.[4]

When Congress enacted legislation making school attendance compulsory, the Indian Service adopted the truancy laws of the states for its schools.[5] Where distance or conditions made attendance problematic, children were placed in boarding or other schools as designated by the commissioner. To fill government schools and maintain efficiencies, Burke extended day schools to grade six and added grades eleven and twelve to the larger off-reservation boarding schools. "Adoption of such a policy," Burke noted, "constitutes a recognition of the fact that if Indian young people are to compete with those of other nationalities, they must have equal educational opportunities."[6]

Burke also focused on improving medical services, which had been decimated by World War I, the Spanish influenza epidemic, and the draining of Indian Service physicians and nurses. Low salaries—the lowest in the federal government—and long hours contributed to the difficulty of the Indian Service in filling positions, with some of those hired unqualified for the work.[7] When Burke asked the American Red Cross to survey Indian health conditions in 1922, he was disheartened to learn that disease and poor health were more rampant than he initially thought. But whereas he intended to use the report "to seek such provisions as are now lacking to accomplish a higher average of Indian health," when the report was released, he failed to seek additional resources from Congress. In fact, he banished the report from the public record and had chief medical director Robert E. Lee Newberne rebuke the three public health nurses involved in the study out of concern that the report would add to the criticisms of the Indian Service.[8] Two years later, Burke announced that improving health care was his number one priority. "Public health is purchasable" and "under adequately funded health efforts, a decrease in illness and in the death rate can be attained."[9]

Burke revoked Cato Sells's Declaration of Policy in 1921, acknowledging it had resulted in unnecessary loss of land for Indian landowners. In its place, Burke instituted procedures that better protected land, going so far as to ask

Congress to cancel all patents issued since 1917, a matter that Congress agreed to but that did nothing to recover the alienated lands.[10] Burke also presided over the long-cherished hope of citizenship when Congress, in 1924, approved of the Indian Citizenship Act, which granted US citizenship to all American Indians, whether competent or incompetent, allotted or unallotted. But he also worked to prohibit Indian ceremonies and dances, viewing both as superstitious and backward. While he could not impose Christianity on the Indians, he did support missionary work, which exposed him to additional criticism. When he attempted to force compulsory school attendance and limit religious absences from school in the New Mexico pueblos of Taos, Jemez, and Zia, and when he sought to assert federal control over Indian probate in Oklahoma, Burke unleashed a storm of opposition that eventually forced him to resign from office. After the Brooking's Institute issued its report—the Meriam Report—in 1928, and after John Collier encouraged the Senate to conduct its own investigation of Indian affairs, Burke's days were numbered. On March 9, 1929, Burke submitted his resignation, leaving office on June 30, 1929. Charles Burke died at the age of eighty-three on April 7, 1944, in Washington, DC.

Indian Competency

The general course of treaties, agreements, and legislation has been in line with the purpose of reserving definite areas of land as tribal estates and of allotting therefrom as rapidly as possible freeholds in severalty, with the aim of inducing by this transfer of tribal to individual holdings a departure from old communal traits and customs to self-dependent conditions and to a democratic conception of the civilization with which the Indian must be assimilated if he is to survive.

In the process of allotting lands to the Indians, and the sale of such surplus as they do not need, many reservations have acquired a mixed population of both Indians and whites which has hastened local self-government, public schools, and other social, civic, and industrial benefits to the backward race.

Various reservations indicate this evolution, and some are now practically merged with white settlements and show but little racial divergence in the prevailing customs and activities. There are, it is true, a few exceptions to this transforming process, as in some semiarid portions of the Southwest where tribal relations must largely continue until existing physical conditions have been changed. The Navajo country is the most conspicuous of these exceptions and for some time to come will call for exceptional consideration, particularly as regards education, health, and such industrial advancement as the physical character of the country will permit. But the general out-work of the reservation system, with certain curable defects, is in the right direction.

As is well known, the law provides for issuing to the Indian a trust patent upon the land allotted to him, which exempts it from taxation and restricts him from its sale or encumbrance until he is declared competent to manage his business affairs, when he may, upon application, receive a patent in fee and be free to handle or dispose of his land the same as any white citizen.

It is doubtful if a satisfactory method has been found for determining the competency upon which to base a termination of the trust title. Applications for patents in fee have too often been adroitly supported by influences which sought to hasten the taxable status of the property or to accomplish a purchase at much less than its fair value, or from some other motive foreign to the Indian's ability to protect his property rights.

Notwithstanding the sincere efforts of officials and competency commissions to reach a safe conclusion as to the ability of an Indian to manage prudently his business and landed interests, experience shows that more than two-thirds of the Indians who have received patents in fee have been unable or unwilling to cope with the business acumen coupled with the selfishness and greed of the more competent whites, and in many instances have lost every acre they had. It is also true that many of the applications received for patents in fee are from those least competent to manage their affairs, while the really competent Indians are in large numbers still holding their lands in trust. It is evident to the careful observer that degree of blood should not be a deciding factor to establish competency, as there are numerous instances of full-bloods who are clearly demonstrating their industrial ability by the actual use made of their land and who are shrewdly content with a restrictive title thereto that exempts them from taxation. At the same time the instances are far too frequent where those of one-half or less Indian blood—often young men who have had excellent educational privileges—secure patents in fee, dispose of their land at a sacrifice, put most of the proceeds in an automobile or some other extravagant investment, and in a few months are "down and out," as far as any visible possessions are concerned.

The situation, therefore, suggests the need of some revision of practice as a check upon the machinations of white schemers who covertly aid the issuance of fee patents in order to cheat the holders out of their realty, and as a restraint upon those who are not so lacking in competency as in the disposition to make the right use of it, and also as a stimulant to the thrifty holder of a trust title to accept the entire management of his estate with the full privileges and obligations that follow.

The well-known purposes of the Government are to fit the Indian for self-support and to protect his interests while doing so, and then to expect him to do his best toward independent living. The Government should not be expected to shirk its trust. It should not be made easy for young men to squander their substance and drift into vagrancy, nor for successful landholders to remain under restrictions not justified by their qualifications for citizenship.

It is hoped to find a way through which the competency of an applicant for a patent in fee can be tested by actual accomplishments on his land or in the particular industry in which he may be engaged, such as the maintenance of himself and family, if married, in a fair degree of comfort for a definite period prior to his application, so that not only the ability but the inclination and ambition to exert it will be evidence and constitute a determining element. The same principle also argues that this standard of competency should bar an extension of the trust period to every energetic Indian who is getting ahead year after year, proving himself a capable farmer, stock grower, or a thrifty provider for his family in some vocation, and because of this ability to manage well his affairs should gladly assume the full rights and obligations which the issuance of a patent in fee confers. In all such instances of unquestionable competency consideration might well be given to the matter of determining the individual interests in tribal property and turning over to these progressive Indians their full share of the tribal estate.[11]

Every Eligible Pupil in School

Questions of enrollment and attendance in schools of all kinds—Government, mission, and public—have been considered matters of first importance by all supervisors, and they have urged cooperation on the part of not only Government field officials and employees, but also of public-school authorities in sections of the country where public schools are accessible to the Indians. For various reasons, including insufficient support funds, the attendance had diminished during the war period and the years immediately following. Many schools had not been utilizing their entire capacity, and it seemed that Indians and those responsible for their education needed to be awakened to the prime value of education in the preparation of Indians to take their rightful places as productive citizens. With that end in view a school enrollment campaign week was planned and an urgent appeal issued on August 12, 1921, indicating in detail the course to be taken by all superintendents in fulfilling the slogan, "Every eligible pupil in school," and outlining the cooperation that should be sought from missionary workers, Indian traders, and all service employees, with the definite view of filling all available capacity in Government, mission, and public schools.

The response was prompt and whole-hearted, with the result that very early in the school year practically all schools were filled to utmost capacity and many, particularly the large non-reservation boarding schools, were compelled to turn away hundreds of boys and girls who were eager for education. The school year of 1921–22 has broken all previous records of enrollment and attendance. The total increase in average attendance in schools of all kinds was approximately 3,000, a very large proportion of which was in the Government boarding schools and in the public schools.... There was considerable unused day-school capacity, which may be attributed to several facts: First, economic conditions among Indians in many sections of the country made them desirous of placing as many as possible of their children in school where they could be clothed, fed, and cared for; second, many children who had previously gone to Government day schools enrolled in public schools; third, in a very large number of day school districts there are not enough children to fill the schools to capacity. Especially is this true when the day school course is limited to three grades, and therefore it is proposed to extend the grades in day schools where children are available and can be accommodated for higher work. In this way boarding-school capacity will be released for those who cannot have day school privileges.

A further study of statistics reveals some facts that demand the attention of those who are responsible for Indian education in this country. There are in round numbers 90,000 Indian children between 5 and 18 years of age. Approximately 65,000 of them have been enrolled in school during the school year 1921–22, leaving 25,000 out of school. Of that number, approximately 7,000 are ineligible to attend schools for normal children because of ill health, defective eyesight, early marriage, and other reasons. These unfortunate ones, however, should not be neglected. Eliminating the ineligibles, there are still approximately 18,000 Indian children of school age to be provided for in some way. I desire to call special attention to the

States that have large numbers of Indian children out of school, growing up without an English education and without industrial training of any kind to prepare them for independent living; in other words, following in the footsteps of their parents and soon to become another generation of non-English–speaking people, a dependent group unfitted for American citizenship who, if given equal opportunities with all other nationalities in this country to go to school, will become an economic asset instead of a liability....

[A]n analysis of the [situation] shows that the problem of providing school facilities for these children may not be as difficult as it would seem. The explanation is in the fact that in many of these States, particularly in California, Minnesota, Montana, North Dakota, Oklahoma, South Dakota, and Washington, public schools are available for large numbers of Indian children, and every year the enrollment of Indians in public schools in these States is increasing. Therefore, aside from utilizing to full capacity the Indian schools already in existence in those States, the problem will be largely one of cooperation with the public school authorities in enrolling Indian children.[12]

Although it has never been possible to get an actual and reliable census of the Navajos, it is estimated that there are several thousand Navajo children of school age out of school because of lack of school facilities. The capacity of schools is being increased quite rapidly, but it is very expensive to build boarding schools which are the only type practicable for the Navajos because of the economic conditions among them. Therefore, it will be several years until school facilities will be available for all of the Navajo children; moreover, the sheep industry being the principal source of income of the Navajos, they must have some of their children to help with the sheep during all seasons of the year. Because of these conditions it would be a means of getting all of their children into school at an early date and also of great economy in connection with the building program if the Navajo school plants were kept in operation during the entire year instead of for nine months as at present. Those children who are at home helping with the sheep during the regular school year while the others are in school could attend summer sessions and thus at least get a start in learning English and in elementary education instead of growing up in ignorance. Such a plan would undoubtedly appeal to the Indian parents as they feel, and are justified in the opinion, that they must have the help of some of their children at all seasons of the year in the care of their flocks. If such a policy were adopted practically all of the Navajo children would be given at least a short term in schools without further delay....[13]

Indian Dances
A long-time tendency of the Indians has been to give too much time to dances, powwows, celebrations, and general festive occasions to the interruption of their self-supporting duties, and these meetings have frequently given opportunity for excesses of one kind or another detrimental to their moral and economic welfare. To correct this practice, a letter was widely circulated among the Indians last year urging the need of more serious attention to their home interests, particularly in the planting and harvest seasons and, while granting them the privileges of wholesome amusements and occasional feast days, earnest appeal was made that they shorten somewhat the length of these gatherings and omit from them the use of harmful drugs, intoxicants, gambling, and degrading ceremonials. The main purpose, however, was to draw their attention more closely to the industrial necessity of making their own living; of doing their work well at seasonable times, caring for their crops and livestock; and of awakening in them a home-making interest with higher ideals of family life.[14]

The Struggle for Bureau Employees
The direction of Indian affairs today affects the education, health, morals, and religion of approximately 350,000 people, all of them recently made citizens of the United States. There are 193 Indian tribes, speaking 58 languages; 200 reservations, widely separated in 26 different States and occupying a territory as large as New England and New York combined; 106 superintendents in charge of reservations; 202 Indian schools, with 700 teachers; and 96 hospitals, with 178 physicians and 146 nurses.

The efficiency of an organization depends on the rank and file of its personnel. Supervisors may be competent, but the struggle with untrained, incompetent, or dissatisfied help, especially when far removed from final administrative authority, is discouraging. With a moral stable field force, the officers of the Indian Service could devote more attention to constructive work and less to training new employees and doing the work of the inefficient. Authority could then be decentralized by transferring more of the administrative responsibility from Washington to the field, where it belongs. The Assistant Secretary of the Interior in Washington, having supervision over the Bureau of Indian Affairs, for example, was required to take 18,000 administrative actions on Indian cases last year, in addition to many thousands receiving final action in the Indian Bureau. Much of this work should have been handled in the field offices.

That the situation has not been entirely hopeless is due to a great extent to competent supervision and to the innate missionary spirit of many of the employees. Advancement among the Indians has been accomplished despite the financial handicap, but the missionary spirit largely depended upon to hold underpaid employees in the Indian Service years ago is not now adequate in itself. The greater opportunities for remunerative employment in all lines which have developed during the past decade have made it more difficult each year to find capable young people willing to sacrifice their most productive years to a service that offers a restricted social life and little opportunity for a successful career.

The turnover of physicians in the Indian field service for the fiscal year 1927 was 56 per cent; for nurses, 122 per cent; for teachers, 48 per cent; while the average turnover for all permanent employees in the service was 67 per cent. These figures cannot be ignored. They are a definite expression of the conditions underlying the so-called Indian problem and have their origin in shortage of funds. The constant capitulation between necessities and means brings despair to those engaged in the work, because the necessities of the human element in the Indian Service should dominate.[15]

CHAPTER 40

Charles James Rhoads

Commissioner of Indian Affairs (April 18, 1929–April 20, 1933)

CHARLES JAMES RHOADS was born on October 4, 1871, in Germantown, Pennsylvania, to a devout Quaker family, with his father, James E. Rhoads, among those who persuaded President Grant to appoint as Indian agents men nominated from various church denominations, including the Society of Friends. Rhoads graduated from Haverford College in 1893 before rising to the position of vice president of Girard Trust Company of Philadelphia in 1914. With the establishment of the Federal Reserve System that same year, Rhoads became governor of the Federal Reserve Bank of Philadelphia. With the end of World War I, he resigned to serve as director of the Society of Friends' Office of the American Red Cross, where he met fellow Quaker Herbert Hoover. Rhoads joined the Indian Rights Association in 1898 and served as treasurer until 1927, when he became president.[1]

With the election of Herbert Hoover as president in 1928, Rhoads recommended to the president-elect his friend Joseph Henry Scattergood as commissioner of Indian affairs. Hoover instead selected Rhoads, who agreed to accept the nomination if Hoover would support the implementation of the Brookings Institute's recommendations regarding Indian affairs (Meriam Report). Upon taking office on April 18, 1929, Rhoads named Scattergood his assistant commissioner, with the two men seated at adjoining desks in the Indian Service.[2]

Five months after taking office, Rhoads worked with Matthew K. Sniffen of the Indian Rights Association, Lewis Meriam of the Brookings Institute, and John Collier of the American Indian Defense Association to prepare a series of policy considerations that were sent to Lynn Frazier (Republican, North Dakota), chairman of the Senate Indian investigating subcommittee of the Committee on Indian Affairs. The first policy consideration encouraged Congress to consider changes to reimbursable loans that totaled $25 million by 1929. The second urged Congress to revamp land policy by statutorily empowering tribes to consolidate and control their lands, lest "the Government 100 years from now [finds] itself still charged with this responsibility." A third supported an Indian claims commission to address tribal claims against the United States, "as there can be no liquidation of the Government's guardianship" until Congress addressed this matter. The final recommendation called for an investigation of Indian irrigation projects and their transfer to the US Reclamation Service. Collier, the leading voice of the new reformers, viewed the policy considerations as simply the beginning, urging Rhoads to engage with Congress to translate ideas into law.

Rhoads was influenced both by the Meriam Report and an Indian irrigation report that was conducted by the Reclamation Service and Indian Irrigation Service that illustrated the shortcomings of Indian irrigation policy. The "Preston–Engel Report" pointed to the realization that Indian irrigation projects did not benefit Indian landowners but non-Indian lessees and landowners who acquired Indian land. Compounding matters, the Indian landowner remained liable for the repayment obligation, often having no residual money after the sale. Rhoads found little success in the House Committee on Indian Affairs where Chairman Louis Cramton (Republican, Michigan) refused to consider the bill. When Cramton failed to gain reelection in 1930, the bill passed the Democratic-controlled committee and was approved by the House and Senate in 1932. The Leavitt Act, as it became known, discharged most reimbursable debt.[3] As for transferring Indian irrigation projects to the Reclamation Service, Rhoads had a change of heart in 1930 and instead invested over $5 million in Indian irrigation infrastructure.

As for governance of Indian lands, Rhoads supported policy transforming Indians into "self-supporting and self-respecting" citizens.[4] But rather than ending land severalty, he supported continuation of the policy with adjustments that included establishing tribal corporations in conjunction with the federal trust to protect land. Secretary of the Interior Ray Lyman Wilbur agreed, identifying a goal of putting the Indian Service out of business within twenty-five years. Rhoads, meanwhile, parted ways with Collier, who advocated for ending land severalty and empowering tribal governments to control and develop their remaining lands.

Beyond this Rhoads implemented a number of Meriam Report recommendations, including doubling Indian education expenditures and adding eight hundred education positions while at the same time moving thousands of children out of boarding schools into day and public schools. He also aligned Indian school curricula with that of the state in which the school was located. Preventive medicine was implemented and additional doctors and nurses were hired. Rhoads's goal was to facilitate the day when state and county governments would take over the physical plants and responsibilities for health, education, and social services.

The end of the Rhoads administration proved acrimonious, and with the Democrats gaining control of the House in 1930, the leadership of the Committee on Indian Affairs shifted in favor of Collier's proposals. When Franklin D. Roosevelt was elected president in 1932, the Indian Rights Association encouraged the president-elect to retain Rhoads as commissioner. Roosevelt, however, followed the advice of his secretary of the interior, Harold L. Ickes, who supported Collier. Rhoads left office on April 20, 1933. He died in Pennsylvania at the age of eighty-three on January 2, 1954.

Overall Policy View
In order to have a clear understanding of the American Indian and his relationship to our own existing civilization we must consider the Indian's history, environment (past and present), religion, and the effect these have had on his point of view and development. His conception of property and ownership is not the same as ours; he has little understanding of individual property rights in land, and no background affording him such an understanding. His view of ownership has been limited to personal possessions, but only such as met his traditional needs. The trait of acquisitiveness is undeveloped, and so far as this would constitute an incentive to personal effort the motive for industry fails. His interests have been in doing the things which his forefathers have always done and it is difficult to substitute for him a real interest instead in the activities of the white citizen. While inevitably the Indian must develop such interests as may enable him to become a component part of our organized civilization and be self-sustaining, we should not destroy what is best of his own traditions, arts, crafts, and associations, but encourage their development and survival. In assisting in his development, we must build on his own inherited good traits. These conditions suggest the need for the proper kind of social service for the Indian, a work which has been overlooked in the past in the struggle to protect the property rights of a minority race. Our task is the practical problem of preparation which will enable the Indian through his own acquired resources to become an independent, self-supporting, self-respecting member of the communities which now surround him.[5]

It is not the present policy to try to make farmers or stockmen of all Indians nor to force them into these occupations where all the attendant circumstances do not offer assurance of successful results or of contentment on their part. However, so far as it be found that a large number of adults will depend upon their land for support, we must endeavor to offer them practical assistance and encouragement. . . . This work will continue also with regard to employment of the adult Indian and the affording of all other assistance through the personnel of placement organization which will enable him to successfully engage in work adapted to his wishes and abilities, but which will nevertheless eventually teach him the lesson of self-dependence.[6]

Federal–State Relations

It is assumed by some that the Federal Government is attempting to unload the Indian educational problem upon the States. This is not the fact. The historic Federal obligation in Indian education cannot be denied. What is necessary, however, is a realization that Indian education is in no sense solely a Federal problem, but a State and local problem as well. When Congress in 1924 made all Indians citizens it served notice that Indians could no longer be overlooked in the citizenry of any State. Most of the States do recognize the joint problem and some of them, Minnesota for example, have taken a conspicuously fine attitude toward Indians and Indian education. . . .

At the Milwaukee meeting of the National Council of State Superintendents and Commissioners of Education in December, 1930 . . . representatives of the Office of Indian Affairs put forth the following proposals in the form of "suggested next steps in Federal–State cooperation in Indian education":

1. Furnish to the State education authorities the most recent accurate data we can get as to the location of Indian children of school age in their States.
2. Wherever State and local communities are willing and able to take over the schooling of Indian children, give them every possible encouragement and help.
3. Study carefully each existing boarding-school situation to determine whether the school is one that should be closed soon, continued for some other purpose, or maintained indefinitely.
4. Put our existing Indian schools into a position where they constitute a real part of the educational program of the State, using State courses of study wherever possible as a basis and meeting State requirements in so

far as these are consistent with an education planned to meet the needs of the Indian children.
5. Make better tuition arrangements, using tuition payment in particular as a means for getting a better quality of education for both whites and Indians; better qualified teachers, health follow-up, hot lunch, visiting teacher (school social worker) to work between the school and the home.
6. Develop a more modern type of supervision:
    (a) Supervisors from the Indian Office who seek to help the people in the field, rather than merely to inspect; these supervisors to visit public and private schools where Indian children are as well as Government Indian schools.
    (b) In States where numbers warrant, a State supervisor of Indian education as part of the staff of the department of public instruction, working directly under the State superintendent or commissioner of education.

That the Indians themselves should be consulted regarding these and other plans for education of their children is axiomatic. We welcome signs of initiative on the part of Indians to work themselves free from dependence and take an interest in their own educational affairs. . . .[7]

Reimbursable Loans
Since entering the Indian Office I have become increasingly and gravely impressed with certain conditions growing out of the operation of the general allotment act and various special allotment acts, and likewise growing out of the system of placing reimbursable liens on Indian allotted lands. . . . Indian allotted lands held under Government trust is at present burdened with a lien in excess of $25,000,000. The history of this lien is briefly as follows: the general allotment act provides (sec. 5) that at the expiration of the trust period "The United States will convey the same (allotted land) by patent to said Indian or his heirs . . . in fee, discharged of said trust and free of all charge or encumbrance whatsoever."

The above language has been carried over into the special allotment acts, and the trust patents of the Indians repeat the language of these guaranties. For a long term of years expenditures authorized by Congress for irrigation construction and maintenance on Indian reservations were gratuitous. The act of August 1, 1914, translated these accumulated gratuities into reimbursable obligations. . . .[8] Since 1914 substantially all of the appropriations for irrigation work on Indian lands, allotted lands included, have been reimbursable. In addition, other improvements, including bridges and public highways, have been paid for with appropriations made reimbursable sometimes against allotted land.

Thus, far from being "discharged at the end of the trust period free of all charge or encumbrance whatsoever," as provided in the allotment acts, the Indian allotments are burdened during their trust period with charges sometimes as great, or almost as great, as the present value of the land. Has the imposition of these liens, under the circumstances, been constitutional? The question has never been passed on by the higher courts, but the collection of the liens has proceeded in all those cases where Indian allotted land, burdened with a lien, has been sold. The Government is reimbursed, and the reimbursement is taken out of the sales price of the land. The Indian, not the purchaser of the allotment, pays the reimbursable lien. . . .

The second aspect of the allotment situation appears to be of greater urgency. Under the act of June 25, 1910, it is practically, though not technically, mandatory that Indian allotted land be sold on the death of the allottee.[9] Even in the absence of statutory direction, such sale would be difficult to avoid under the conditions created by the allotment acts. The indefinite partitioning of allotments is not practicable; the Indian heir who may desire to remain on his allotment and cultivate it rarely would be able to buy out those heirs who might desire a liquidation of the heirship estate.

The consequences are mathematically certain: the allotted Indians of the second generation largely become landless. By the time the third generation has arrived, substantially all of the allotted Indian land will have passed into white ownership. What this means is appreciated when it is noted that the Indian allotted land constitutes more than one-half of the whole area of Indian country and much more than half of the surface value of Indian country, and when it is further noted that more than two-thirds of the Indians are now allotted. . . .

I make the very tentative suggestion that part, at least, of the loss of Indian heirship land to the Indians might be averted if there were some means provided whereby the allotted land could revert to the tribal estate. . . . It has been suggested that Indian tribes might be permitted and assisted to form themselves into corporate bodies and that allotments might be turned back into the tribal estate in exchange for shares of stock. Such a method, it would seem, might be practicable for those reservations possessed of large tribal assets, such as timber, oil, minerals, or water power. . . .[10]

The Tribal Estate

We are confronted with the problem of what to do with the indivisible tribal estates of the Indians. There are conditions with which it seems impossible to deal satisfactorily under existing law. . . . Indian wealth totaling hundreds of millions of dollars—possibly a billion dollars—is essentially indivisible. It includes such items as mineral and oil resources, power sites, timber wealth, the large bodies of grazing land, and even farm lands. . . .

At present and under existing law the Government, through the Interior Department, is charged with the direct and highly paternalistic administration of these properties, and unless existing law be changed it may well be that the Government 100 years from now will find itself still charged with this responsibility and still maintaining the paternalistic administration. The properties in question, in order to be conserved or sufficiently developed, ought in many cases to be treated as estates not capable of subdivision. It even seems possible that the only way to salvage some classes of Indian allotted land may prove to be by turning them back into the community estate.

As I have stated, under existing law the Government may find itself administering these vast and varied properties to the end of time. And through all this time the Indians, so far as existing law is concerned, must remain in a state of dependency, being neither forced nor permitted to take on the business responsibilities of American life or to make use of the instrumentalities of modern business.

It is true that under existing law the Interior Department can and does, in a more or less formal way, recognize Indian tribal councils. It might even be possible, through an elaboration of rules and regulations, to vest in such councils a considerable responsibility for the operation of their tribal properties. But such action of the administrative kind would be revocable by any succeeding administration; it would not provide a firm basis for the development of responsibility on the part of the Indians and it would not do away with the underlying condition, которая is that the minutia of tribal affairs rest in the hands of the department and Congress. It is not a hopeful or practicable situation for building up the group self-help of the Indians.[11]

Indian Claims against the United States

[T]he perplexities growing out of the past are . . . greater in number and variety than would be displayed by all possibly successful Court of Claims suits.

There are, for example, the many items of reimbursable indebtedness—tribal indebtedness as well as the indebtedness on allotted lands. There are claims by Indians who never subsisted in treaty relations with the Government; in such status are most of the Indians of the far West and many of the Southwest tribes. My thought on its positive side is as follows: Could not all of these matters be dealt with, and brought to a finality within a limited number of years, if a special Indian claims commission were created? This commission might and probably should be altogether independent of the Interior Department; its members might be named by the President, subject to confirmation by the Senate; it should be adequately budgeted.

This claims commission might be given power to reach final settlements—essentially judicial power—in specified classes of cases where the Indian claim rested on a legal right assertable as such. But the commission should hear all causes, those that are human and moral as well as those that are legal and equitable; and its findings, submitted to Congress, could be the basis of settlement of a gratuitous kind which Congress might authorize...

The mechanism which I suggest might not be practicable; but the conditions which I have referred to are indeed real, vexing, grievous to the department at least, and in many cases, they are matters of heartbreak to Indians and of hopes long postponed, often hopes never to be realized, which yet are operating to create dissension within tribes and to deter Indians from self-help.

The further thought occurs to me. There can be no liquidation of the Government's guardianship over Indians until this inheritance of treaties and alleged broken treaties and governmental laches of the past is absorbed. The process, even with the most expeditious procedure, will require years. With procedure as at present, it might well require 100 years. Hence, any plan contemplating the gradual diminution and the ultimate and final termination of Indian tutelage must concern itself with this aspect of the situation.[12]

Indian Irrigation Policy
Briefly it may be pointed out that during earlier times irrigation, in a small way at least, was started on a number of Indian reservations where conditions were favorable, largely as an industrial aid to the Indians, and in some instances for the purpose of affording temporary employment to the Indians at a daily living wage. Available appropriations and even tribal Indian

funds were used in such work, which under the legislation then prevailing were not "reimbursable." In fact, no thought was had at that time of ever requiring reimbursement from the Indians of the funds so expended....

Subsequent legislation, however, particularly such as that found in the act of August 1, 1914, directing that all funds theretofore or thereafter expended in such work should be reimbursed, came as a distinct surprise to most of the Indians. In particular instances or on particular reservations ... the legislation dealing with such matters carried a positive declaration to the effect that the irrigable lands allotted to the Indians should have a right to so much water as might be necessary for irrigation purposes "without cost to the Indians." Naturally under such conditions the Indians feel that the subsequent repudiation of such a declaration, even by legislation, does not come with very good grace on the part of the Government. In this connection it might also be pointed out that most of our Indian allottees within these irrigation projects hold trust patents declaring that at the expiration of the trust period the allottee or his heirs will then be given fee title, free from any lien, charge, or encumbrance of any nature whatsoever. The subsequent imposition of a lien, therefore, requiring repayment of irrigation charges may very properly raise some question about the validity of a lien so imposed....

Originally most of our Indian projects were purely Indian; that is, only Indians and Indian lands were involved. Gradually due to death of the Indian allottees within such projects, the inherited lands were sold and a good deal of such land has now passed into white ownership, leaving, as we now find them, a good many so-called mixed people, partly Indian and partly white, in so far as ownership of the land is concerned. Also, in practically all of such projects, particularly the older ones, we find the problem of white lessees of valuable irrigable lands, and incidentally complaint from the State authorities in some instances as to the taxability, or rather nontaxability, by the State authorities of such holdings so occupied by white citizens and residents of the States.

Due to a number of causes, such as excessive floods, destruction of works originally installed and rebuilt, in order to save the entire system from total loss, the per acre reimbursable cost on a number of these irrigation projects is now almost equal to or even greater than the value of the land itself, hence we now find ourselves practically in that unfavorable position of virtually holding a lien or mortgage against property in excess of the value of the property itself. As a result of an extensive field investigation, made only a few years ago, it was even suggested that three of these Indian irrigation projects, on which considerable sums have been expended, should be abandoned entirely. In view of the large investment made by the Government in such projects, and as the expenditures so made were primarily for the benefit of the Indians, we have not felt warranted in recommending that these projects be abandoned without further trial or giving them opportunity for further development. . . . It has also been suggested that the operation of Indian irrigation works might be transferred to the Bureau of Reclamation . . . which has a force equipped to handle them under a general irrigation policy in cooperation with the Bureau of Indian Affairs.[13]

CHAPTER 41

John Collier

Commissioner of Indian Affairs (April 21, 1933–January 22, 1945)

JOHN COLLIER was born on May 4, 1884, in Atlanta, Georgia, attending Columbia University and studying psychology at College de France in Paris. In 1907, Collier became the civic secretary of the People's Institute in New York City, which had been founded ten years earlier by Charles Sprague Smith to educate immigrants and workers in New York City on the theory and practice of government and social philosophy. Collier worked as a teacher and social worker the rest of his life, seeking to use community life to overcome poverty and the challenges of integration.[1]

Collier believed the preindustrial culture of immigrants—and later the American Indians—deserved to be preserved as a means of mediating the social ills in urban settings by reinforcing community obligations. In New York City, he promoted this social philosophy by engaging in the community center movement through which public schools became the focus of neighborhood life. A student of cultural pluralism, Collier feared rapid Americanization created social disconnectedness rather than integration.

In 1919, Collier moved to Los Angeles to become director of adult education for the state of California, a position he retained just one year before being forced to resign due to his nonconventional ideas. Mabel Dodge, a friend from New York, then invited Collier to Taos, New Mexico, in the winter of 1920, where he found his "Red Atlantis," discovering the Pueblo people had managed to maintain a communal life despite "immense historical shocks" to their culture.[2] Leaving Taos in the summer of 1921, Collier moved to San Francisco to lecture on sociology at San Francisco State College.

The following year, Collier began his involvement in Indian affairs as an agent for the General Federation of Women's Clubs, gaining national prominence by blocking passage of the Bursum Bill that threatened Pueblo lands in New Mexico. He parlayed this experience into becoming the executive director of the newly formed American Indian Defense Association, established to repeal the General Allotment Act and halt further allotment of Indian land. In this capacity, Collier criticized Charles Burke for continuing the assimilation policies, including banning tribal dances, while at the same time charging the Indian Service with mismanagement for failing to protect tribal assets, resources, and lands. It was largely in response to these charges that Interior Secretary Herbert Work invited the Brookings Institute to undertake an analysis of Indian affairs, resulting in the Meriam Report that sharply rebuked the Indian Service's land, health, education, and assimilation policies. At Collier's request, the Senate initiated its own study (1928–1943) of Indian affairs that exposed widespread poverty, disease, and poor economic conditions.

With the election of Franklin D. Roosevelt in 1932, Collier was appointed commissioner of Indian affairs, taking office on April 21, 1933. He immediately began the Indian New Deal by convincing Congress to approve of the Pueblo Relief Act (1933) to compensate the Pueblo tribes for land lost to squatters. This was followed by the Johnson–O'Malley Act (1934) to authorize federal contracts with state and local governments for educational, health, and social services for tribes, and the Indian Reorganization Act (1934) that ended land severalty and supported tribal self-government. The Indian Arts and Crafts Act (1935) protected and promoted authentic Indian arts and crafts. Collier administratively closed a number of off-reservation boarding schools and constructed scores of day schools that he used to promote his ideology of community life. He also hired Willard Beatty as director of education to implement a progressive education that supported and reinforced rural Indian life while providing training for teachers in cross-cultural education.

To encourage tribal life, Collier invited social scientists to assist him rather than relying on missionaries who once influenced much of the policy in Indian Country. While social scientists aided Collier's "rehabilitation" of Indian Country and his call for self-government, by the end of his tenure Collier was criticized for interjecting his own opinions on tribal leaders. For good measure, Collier convinced President Roosevelt to abolish the conservative Board of Indian Commissioners in 1933, and he improved tribal judicial forums and codified Indian law, a task completed by Felix Cohen in 1943 and published as *The Handbook of Federal–Indian Law*.[3]

By 1940, there was mounting opposition to Collier's reforms, within and without Indian Country. Both the House and Senate committees on Indian affairs attempted to repeal parts of the Indian New Deal, including the Indian Reorganization Act. The fact was there was little more self-government in 1940 than there had been in 1934. When the Indian Service was moved to Chicago during World War II, Collier lost additional influence, and by January 1945, he was ineffective as commissioner. On January 22, 1945, he resigned as commissioner of Indian affairs. Collier continued to advance cultural pluralism and his idea of self-government until his death in Taos on May 8, 1968, at the age of eighty-four.

Changing History

For many decades the Indians were thought of, and they thought of themselves, as a dying race. Numerically they were dying. As battling groups, they had lost their fight. As civilization their day was ended. Then very gradually but unmistakably the Indians' life-tide seemed to turn. The critical change goes back a decade and a half, or longer. Three years ago, the basis of Indian law was altered. Indian law had presumed the cessation of Indians. The changed law presumed their permanence and their increase. The Indian Service, the Indians' mind, the general public's mind, became hopeful of the Indians' future. This future would be realized in terms of numbers increasing, not dwindling; of property-holdings increasing, not continuing to melt away; of cultural values preserved, intensified, and appreciated and sought for by the white world, and no longer treated as being significant only in terms of an outlived or crushed primitive world.

All of these evidences of new birth and new assurance have been forthcoming in the recent years, and never so richly as during the year just closed. The population record alone is an impressive one. Indians are increasing faster than any other group in the United States. Full-blood Indians are increasing at more than one percent a year. This, although the preventable morbidity rate is still excessive.[4]

Restoring Tribalism

Through 50 years of "individualization," coupled with an ever-increasing amount of arbitrary supervision over the affairs of individuals and tribes so long as these individuals and tribes had any assets left, the Indians have been robbed of initiative, their spirit has been broken, their health undermined, and their native pride ground into the dust. The efforts at economic rehabilitation cannot and will not be more than partially successful unless they are accompanied by a determined simultaneous effort to rebuild the shattered morale of a subjugated people that has been taught to believe in its racial inferiority. . . .

Even before the passage of the [Indian Reorganization Act] a great spiritual stirring had become noticeable throughout the Indian country. That awakening of the racial spirit must be sustained, if the rehabilitation of the Indian people is to be successfully carried through. It is necessary to face the fact that pauperization, as the result of a century of spoliation, suppression, and paternalism, has made deep inroads. Of necessity it will take time, patience, and intelligent, sympathetic help to rebuild the Indian character where it has been broken down.

The first step in this rebuilding process must be the reorganization of the tribes.... In the past they managed their own affairs effectively whenever there was no white interference for selfish ends. They can learn to do it again under present conditions with the aid of modern organization methods, once they realize that these organizations will be permanent and will not be subject to the whims of changing administrations. These organizations, both tribal and corporate, will make many initial mistakes; there will be many complaints against shouldering the load of responsibility that accompanies authority. The task of organizing and incorporating the tribes will be difficult and laborious, calling for the maximum amount of skill, tact, firmness, and understanding on the part of the organizers. But the result should be the development of Indian leadership capable of making the Indian tribal organizations and corporations function effectively with the minimum of governmental interference.[5]

Direction of Policy
The Indian Service is confronting certain main problems and is moving on certain main lines of policy [including]:

Indian lands.—The allotment system has enormously cut down the Indian landholdings and has rendered many areas, still owned by Indians, practically unavailable for Indian use. The system must be revised both as a matter of law and of practical effect. Allotted lands must be consolidated into tribal or corporate ownership with individual tenure, and new lands must be acquired for the 90,000 Indians who are landless at the present time. A modern system of financial credit must be instituted to enable the Indians to use their own natural resources. And training in the modern techniques of land use must be supplied Indians. The wastage of Indian lands through erosion must be checked.

Indian education.—The redistribution of educational opportunity for Indians, out of the concentrated boarding school, reaching the few, and into the day school, reaching the many, must be continued and accelerated. The boarding schools which remain must be specialized on lines of occupational need for children of the older groups, or of the need of some Indian children for institutional care. The day schools must be worked out on lines of community service, reaching the adult as well as the child, and influencing the health, the recreation, and the economic welfare of their local areas.

Indians in Indian Service.—The increasing use of Indians in their own official and unofficial service must be pressed without wearying. To this end, adjustments of Civil Service arrangements to Indian need must be sought; but in order that standards may not be lowered, opportunities for professional training must be made genuinely accessible to Indians. With respect to unofficial Indian self-service, a steadily widening tribal and local participation by Indians in the management of their own properties and in the administration of their own services must be pursued.

Reorganization of the Indian Service.—A decentralizing of administrative routine must be progressively attempted. The special functions of Indian Service must be integrated with one another and with Indian life, in terms of local areas and of local groups of Indians. An enlarged responsibility must be vested in the superintendents of reservations and beyond them, or concurrently, in the Indians themselves. This reorganization is in part dependent on the revision of the land allotment system; and in part it is dependent on the steady development of cooperative relations between the Indian Service as a Federal agency . . . and the States, counties, school districts, and other local units of government. . . .[6]

Reorienting Land Policy

It is only recently that we have come fully to realize the magnitude of the disaster which the allotment law of 1887 has wrought upon the Indians. This law, in its origin, was intended to be a civilizing instrument for the Indians. It was reasoned that white civilization was based on the individual property system, and it was naively assumed that the way to make the Indian a responsible citizen was forcibly to give him private property and extinguish his concern in community property. . . .

How, then, shall we reorient Indian land policy? It is clear that the allotment system has not changed the Indians into responsible, self-supporting citizens. Neither has it fitted them to enter into urban industrial pursuits. It has merely deprived vast numbers of them of their land, turned them into paupers, and imposed an ever-growing relief problem on the Government. As a starting point for a rational policy, we can categorically say that the immediate problem is not that of absorbing the Indians into the white population, but first of all of lifting them out of material and spiritual dependency and hopelessness. It is equally clear that the place to begin this process is on the land; for if the Indian cannot pursue the relatively simple and primitive arts of agriculture, grazing, and forestry, there seems little prospect that he can be fitted for the more exacting technology of urban industry. Even if he could be at once so fitted, the industrial depression has taught us that we already have far too many industrial workers. And the agricultural depression has taught us that we have a great surplus of farm land. Through subsistence farming and animal husbandry, the Indian can become self-supporting without competing, on the one hand, with white industrial labor or, on the other hand, the white commercial agriculture.

If these assumptions are sound, the main lines of the new land policy are clear. The allotment system must be reversed. We must reacquire enough of the lost lands or of other lands to provide subsistence for eighty or ninety thousand landless Indians. In the case of forest and range lands, we must reestablish tribal ownership and build up Indian use of these resources instead of allowing the resources to be exploited by whites. Even in the case of agricultural lands, community ownership, with assignment of use to individual Indians, will in many reservations be the best system of ownership. In addition to land, we must provide capital in the way of buildings and other improvements, work, stock, livestock, and farming equipment to help the Indian farmer or livestock grower onto his feet. In the forests we must provide small portable sawmills and logging equipment in order to employ the Indian workers in harvesting their own tree crops. Equipping the land for productive use will require, in short, the provision of credit facilities.

If we can relieve the Indian of the unrealistic and fatal allotment system, if we can provide him with land and the means to work the land, if through group organization and tribal incorporation we can give him a real share in the management of his own affairs, he can develop normally in his own natural environment. The Indian problem as it exists today, including the heaviest and most unproductive administration costs of public service, has largely grown out of the allotment system which has destroyed the economic integrity of the Indian estate and deprived the Indians of normal economic and human activity.[7]

Additional Land as the First Essential in Rebuilding

A problem scarcely less important is that of land utilization and management. It is most graphically illustrated in the case of heirship lands which have become so entangled in a welter of fractionate ownership that Indians and agency officials alike get to the point of throwing up their hands in despair. Meantime, the land lies idle or is leased, usually to non-Indians. Through the machinery for exchange of lands, which the [Indian] Reorganization Act authorizes, an indication is given of how the problem might be solved. It could be solved far more quickly if money were available to purchase lands in such dolorous standing. It can be appreciated, however, how much money would be required when it is considered that approximately 7,000,000 acres are involved. At one reservation, Flathead in Montana, the Indians have taken the initiative in this matter by having a bill introduced in Congress which would permit them to use their own tribal funds for the purchase of lands within the reservation borders. This would allow them to purchase not only heirship lands but lands which have gone into white ownership.[8]

The task of consolidating lands checker boarded through allotment, of salvaging the allotted heirship land, and of restoring to many tribes enough of balanced landholdings to make a permanent subsistence economy possible . . . [is doable]. The procurement of land for Indians is but an incident in the reconstruction of the individual and tribal economy of groups with the most varying backgrounds, situated among the most varying present conditions. Land acquisition, if unconnected with a feasible scheme of economic operation, is of little value to Indians, or of none at all. Indian initiative, and some amount of definite sacrifice by Indians, is quite essential if the land-acquisition program is to be humanly successful. Therefore, the land program of the Indian Service interrelates itself with every other service function and with the whole range of Indian life, and many other functions of the Indian Service are intimately linked with the land acquisition program.[9]

The Need for Funds

The problems which immediately confront newly organized tribes are several, but perhaps the most immediate and most pressing is that of getting funds on which to operate. Tribal funds, which are derived from a cash conversion of tribal capital assets or from income on tribal property, are deposited in the Treasury and cannot be appropriated to tribal use except by Congress or, in some instances, with the approval of the Secretary of the Interior. Therefore, even though tribes may have funds to their credit, under still-existing law they are in the position of incompetent wards with inheritances lying securely in the hands of a guardian. These tribes must find their own sources of revenue. If they are fortunate enough still to own unallotted tribal land, they may cause the rental on the land to be paid into their tribal treasury instead of into the Federal Treasury, as previous law required. Several tribes have already taken steps to bring about this change of procedure, and others will follow. This advantage . . . is accessible only to tribes owning undivided communal land.

As tribes become incorporated and borrow money from the revolving credit fund to establish and develop business or agricultural enterprises, other revenue will come in. Such revenue will also be under tribal rather than governmental control. Another means of securing revenue . . . would be a system of fees for services which the tribal government renders its members and for privileges which it extends to nonmembers. This task of obtaining revenue to cover the costs of tribal government operations is critical, and in its solution will lie the future of successful group activity for many tribes.

New Educational Paradigm
The new pattern of education for the Indians attempts to adjust the school program to the needs of the Indian community, recognizing and preserving significant factors in Indian life and aiding in adjustment to white culture at points where such adjustment appears inevitable. However, it is not enough to declare that a new policy is in order. It must somehow or other be incorporated into the living of a staff which for many years may have been practicing quite the reverse. . . .

The growing emphasis upon day-school attendance of Indian pupils has resulted in an increase of Indian day-school enrollment in Federal schools from 4,532 pupils in 1928 to almost 12,000 during the school year 1936–37. More than half of this increase represents children not previously enrolled in any school. During the same period of time Indian pupils in public schools have increased from 34,163 to 50,328.

The most spectacular development of the new day-school policy has been on the Navajo Reservation. Here there has been an increase of 37 new day schools during the last 2 years, with a resultant increase from 822 pupils in attendance at day schools to an enrollment of 2,147. Because of the tremendous number of Navajo children estimated not in any school at all, there has been no decrease in boarding-school enrollment during this period of time. There are still more than 7,000 Navajos of school age who are not enrolled in any kind of school.

There has been a continuing increase of Indian pupils enrolled in federally operated high schools. Many of these, because of the sparsity of population on some of the larger reservations, are and must continue to be boarding schools. On some of the smaller reservations or in areas where the population is more compact, these high schools are operated on a day basis.

The new Indian Service high schools are developing a program the major objective of which is to produce economically self-sustaining citizens. Recognizing that for many Indians their remaining lands constitute a major asset, these high schools are bending every effort to produce groups of young people who are not only interested in farming or stock raising, but who, through the course of their high-school careers, have engaged in farming under the supervision of the school on a practical self-supporting scale. This type of program has undergone gratifying development at the Chilocco School in Oklahoma on whose 8,000-acre campus the children are operating individual farms of 40 to 80 acres, caring for a substantial beef herd, raising chickens on a commercial scale, and otherwise experiencing the problems involved in making a living on a farm typical of that area....

One of the most serious problems of the Indian Service lies in dealing with races of people, large numbers of whom still speak their native languages and for whom English is a little-used foreign tongue. In many of these groups, as for instance the Navajo, the Pima and the Papago, written records are entirely foreign to the racial experience, and reading, therefore, lacks the functional reality which it occupies in the thinking of the average white child. Furthermore, on the most isolated reservations, Indian young people have no opportunity for contact with ferryboats and steamers, firemen, policemen, postmen, railroad trains and streetcars, and many other objects and people whose activities form the familiar basis of elementary school reading. The problem of teaching these young people to read, to make intelligent use of numbers, and in other ways to accept the basis of American education would be greatly simplified if textbook material existed which was phrased in terms of the Indian child's experiences. During the last year the Education Division has, therefore, accepted as one of its responsibilities the encouragement of the preparation of materials to be used in Indian schools. Some of this material will probably be published by the Government because of its exclusive application to limited areas in the Indian Service. In other cases, the Indian Service will encourage its commercial publication because it would appear to be valuable for use in white schools as well as Indians schools.[10]

CHAPTER 42

William A. Brophy

Commissioner of Indian Affairs (March 6, 1945–June 3, 1948)

WILLIAM A. BROPHY was born in New York City on February 7, 1903, before moving to New Mexico where he graduated from the University of New Mexico. He then earned a law degree from the University of Colorado and returned to Albuquerque where he engaged in private practice before serving as a special attorney for Pueblo land issues between 1934 and 1942, believing protection of tribal rights was fundamentally a federal responsibility.[1] His nomination as commissioner was not without controversy, including concerns from the New Mexico Pueblos stemming in large measure from his wife, Sophie Aberle, whose actions as superintendent of the United Pueblo Agency were at times contrary to the wishes of the Pueblo people.[2] While the All-Pueblo Council supported Brophy, some of the Pueblos were further concerned that Brophy would restore paternalistic policies that might set back tribal affairs. Some members of Congress, including Representative George Schwabe (Republican, Oklahoma), argued it was time for an American Indian to serve as commissioner of Indian affairs.[3]

Between 1943 and 1944, Congress shifted policy away from self-governance. In a set of reports issued at the end of its fifteen-year investigation of Indian affairs, the Senate altered policy away from self-governance to withdrawal of federal trusteeship. With Collier's resignation, the Senate, in February 1945, initiated hearings on the president's nominee, William Brophy, seeking answers to two questions. First, was Brophy, as Collier's choice to head the Indian Service, committed to furthering Collier's policies? And second, would Brophy enforce the policies enumerated by Congress? Brophy publicly agreed to follow the policies set down by Congress, explaining he would implement, not make, policy.[4] On March 6, 1945, Brophy was confirmed as commissioner and took office.

Brophy was not cut from the same cloth as Collier, and while he worked to stem the growing sentiment regarding withdrawal of federal services, he accepted termination as a long-range goal and labored to prepare tribes for when the policy was deployed. In his first annual report he outlined his primary objective: aid the Indians in becoming economically independent.⁵ Indian lands, he noted, "were insufficient in quantity and quality to enable the Indian owners to derive from them a livelihood comparable to that of their rural white neighbors." Poverty was due to land severalty, the alienation of the Indians' best lands, and their lack of "experience, equipment, and capital" necessary to make productive use of their remaining lands. If the goal was for the United States to withdraw as trustee and eliminate federal services, the only means by which tribal nations could provide for themselves was "through the development of [their] resources to maximize productivity."⁶ The execution of this policy had to be accomplished without "throwing an undue burden on States and counties."

More fundamentally, Brophy argued that the United States had an obligation to assist tribal nations in developing their resources, raising their standard of living, improving their health, and preparing for the withdrawal of federal services and responsibility. Developing resources included improving the breed of livestock, increasing irrigated and dry land agriculture, making use of timber resources, and maximizing mineral lands—and all without the tribes simply providing raw goods and seeing others enriched at their expense.

Brophy also believed that it would be an injustice for Congress to simply exercise its plenary authority, and it would be economically disastrous to tribes for Congress to capriciously withdraw services. Aided by Assistant Commissioner William Zimmerman, Brophy outlined a process by which the United States might withdraw as trustee of land and resources, recommending the Indian Service analyze the status of each tribe and determine which were largely integrated, as measured by adoption of "white habits and acceptance of the Indians by the white community." Then the Indian Service would determine the economic condition of the tribes and consider the reasonableness of the Indians making a living off their resources. Moreover, the department would need to consider the willingness of the tribes to accept federal withdrawal; and it was critical to understand the ability and secure the affirmation of the state and local governments to provide such services. It was immaterial if this process was not the most prudent, Brophy explained, since Congress had already resolved to throw the Indians "upon their own resources" and remove restrictions on the land "regardless of their readiness for such a move."⁷

Brophy was progressive in his commitment to addressing social and resource concerns on a tribe-by-tribe basis rather than applying a one-size-fits-all policy that historically governed Indian affairs. This was demonstrated in the consideration by Congress of a Navajo–Hopi rehabilitation bill, "the first time that a plan for a specific Indian area has reached the stage of Congressional consideration." Zimmerman, who took over for Brophy in June 1948 and finalized that year's annual report, explained the bill would "determine whether our national Indian policy in the future is to be based on division of the total problem of human adjustment and resource utilization into parcels of a size that can be measured and dealt with on a time schedule" or whether Congress would continue its one-size-fits-all policies.[8]

It was during Brophy's administration that Congress approved of the Indian Claims Commission Act, which was first advocated by the Brookings Institute in 1928. The act enabled tribes and tribal groups to present claims against the United States in an effort to begin termination of the federal–Indian relationship. In the winter of 1947, Brophy contracted tuberculosis while visiting Alaska Natives, with Zimmerman thereafter assuming much of the day-to-day responsibilities as head of the Indian Service. When Secretary of the Interior William E. Warne outlined a policy of the newly renamed Bureau of Indian Affairs working itself out of business, he used the Zimmerman tribal listing as the basis of withdrawing federal services. A policy of termination had begun. Brophy, meanwhile, resigned on June 3, 1948, returning to New Mexico where he again represented the Pueblos on various resource matters. He remained active in Indian affairs until his death at age fifty-nine on March 24, 1962.

Returning War Veterans
It is expected that the reorganization and the addition of new powers to field officials will be of considerable aid in their efforts to help Indians, Eskimos, and Aleuts faced by postwar difficulties. The new factors which accompanied the war and its termination were having their effects ... but it was still too early to determine whether there were any general war-induced trends which would persist in the future.

A question which presented itself was whether there would be any general drift away from the Indian homelands.... There was the further question as to how many would remain and how many would take advantage of opportunities seen outside the reservations. Early in 1946, many of the reservations reported the belief that the great majority, and in some instances all, would remain. Military service in some cases seemed to have drawn veterans closer to their homes, as was reported at the Navajo Reservation in Arizona, New Mexico, and Utah, even though educational and economic opportunities there were poor. This trend is little different from that of the non-Indian population. The people were returning to their homes.

In various places, it was believed that some Indians would do as they had done in the past, take temporary employment outside when it was offered, but return to their own lands when employment ceased. On the other hand, from the Shawnee Agency in Oklahoma came word that the war seemed to have made Indians there dissatisfied with opportunities for making a living on the reservation so long as they could get outside employment, but this was recognized to be merely an acceleration of a process which had begun prior to the war. A similar condition was reported at the Potawatomi Agency in Kansas where it was felt that participation in the war and in war work had speeded tremendously the process of Indian assimilation into the social, economic, and political life of the United States....

It became clear that Indians of the postwar world were attacking their problems of readjustment according to no fixed pattern. Their approaches to the task were as varied as those of other citizens. For they earn their livelihoods according to the conditions which obtain in their environments. They are farmers, stockmen, fishermen, lumbermen, or workers in other occupations in accordance with the nature of the country in which they live. These and many other occupations are followed by Indians. Some never have lived on a reservation, but have earned their livings in city or town, on farm or ranchland far from reservation, and some even in foreign countries, and have little or no contact with the Indian Service.[9]

Improving Indian Economics

While there have been losses and costly postponements, there have been significant gains also. Owing to servicemen's allotments, to the increased quantity and value of their agricultural products, and to the wages earned by more than 40,000 Indians who have left their reservations to work in various industries, the total income of Indians has been greater than ever before. The acquaintance with a wider world and a higher standard of living acquired by many of the home folk, together with a more alert awareness and increased self-confidence of 25,000 young men and women returning from the armed services, may well prove a powerful stimulus to Indian progress.

A fundamental problem, however, is accentuated by this situation. Even with the most efficient use, Indian resources in some areas are far from sufficient to provide a decent livelihood for all Indians. A portion of the 65,000 who left their homes to fight and work, and who are now returning, can find opportunity on their reservations; but thousands cannot, and thousands of others who remained at home are in the same predicament. Since Indian resources cannot be sufficiently augmented to support the population, which is increasing rapidly, many thousands of Indians must be helped to find economic opportunity and acceptance in the general national economy. So long as thousands of Indians exist below the subsistence level on poverty-stricken reservations, so long as employment opportunities are scarce, Federal expenditures for program services to Indians cannot be appreciably decreased.[10]

Inadequacy of the Indian Land Base
Just as the Indian Service, in partnership with Indian tribal and other organizations, acts to provide ever better health and education facilities, so does it assist the Indians to make the best use of their material resources to produce increasingly better livelihoods, and so does it protect their ownership of them.

Chief of these resources is land. This land belongs to the Indians—to individuals, tribes, bands, and other groups. It is held in trust for them by the Government but it nevertheless is the private property of the Indians.... The Office of Indian Affairs has jurisdiction over [these] land areas amounting roughly to 57 million acres, nearly all of which is held in trust for Indian tribes and individual Indians. Of this, approximately 31 million acres are classified as open grazing land and are valued at about $90,000,000. Another 16 million acres are forest and woodlands worth about $170,000,000, including the standing timber and reproduction and protection value. Approximately 7 million acres are agricultural lands, valued at $100,000,000. Barren and waste lands comprise about 3 million acres. Alaskan lands are not included in those figures, because the process of determining and confirming Indian, Eskimo, and Aleut occupancy rights there has barely begun....

The land available for Indian use is insufficient in quantity and quality to support their entire population. About 7 million acres of the best lands are practically unusable by Indians because their ownership is scattered in small, undivided interests. During the war years no appropriations were made for land acquisition under the authority of the Indian Reorganization Act, and there was insufficient personnel to prosecute successfully the readjustment of the Indian land ownership pattern. Thus, maladjustments multiplied during that period. Return of veterans and war workers to Indian lands complicated the task of providing sufficient land.

Inflated land prices throughout the country have resulted in a flood of applications to this Office for sales of Indian trust lands and patents in fee. Sales and the issuance of patents in fee have been limited to the lowest possible number since the total Indian land base is inadequate for their support on many reservations particularly those where land had been allotted to individuals in the past.[11]

Preparing to Withdraw Federal Services
How the Federal Government may remove itself as trustee over Indian property and how it may discontinue the services which it now provides are questions requiring the most careful examination. With its plenary power in matters affecting the Indians and their property, the Congress could at any moment withhold all appropriations for Indian administration and it could remove all trustee safeguards now in force. Entirely apart from the injustice which such precipitate action would inflict on these first Americans, whose property rights do not derive from any benevolence of the United States, it would prove economically disastrous to reduce the resources available to the Indians.

In testimony before the Senate Civil Service Committee in February 1947, an attempt was made to suggest a fair and equitable basis upon which the Government might measure its responsibility toward a tribe and so determine when it might withdraw as trustee. Four factors were suggested: 1) The degree of assimilation of a tribe, as indicating acceptance by the Indians of white habits and acceptance of the Indians by the white community; 2) economic condition of a tribe, to indicate a reasonable possibility of gaining a livelihood through the use of available resources; 3) willingness of the tribe to dispense with Federal aid and guidance, and 4) willingness and ability of States and [local] communities to provide public services.

The testimony further indicated that, on the suggested basis of judgement, certain tribes and groups were at the point where, at an early date, if not in all cases immediately, Federal supervision could be curtailed or eliminated. For a second list of tribes, a somewhat longer period of adjustment and preparation was indicated. Finally, as to certain tribes and groups, where conditions with respect to all four factors were unfavorable, continued Federal assistance for an indefinite period seemed unavoidable.

Whether these are the proper factors to consider, or whether they are the only factors that need to be considered, is immaterial at the moment. It is certain, however, that only through such a procedure of measuring accomplishments and estimating needs can the Federal Government discharge its responsibility with any degree of satisfaction.[12]

CHAPTER 43

John R. Nichols

Commissioner of Indian Affairs (April 13, 1949–March 23, 1950)

JOHN RALPH NICHOLS was born on September 19, 1898, in New York City and graduated from high school in Palo Alto, California, in 1916. After service in World War I, he earned a degree in agriculture from Oregon State Agricultural College before earning a master's degree in education and a doctorate in educational administration from Stanford University in 1930. Upon earning a second master's degree in international administration from Columbia University, Nichols was appointed advisor on educational reorganization for the supreme commander of the Allied forces in the Pacific in 1946–1947.[1]

When President Truman nominated Nichols to replace William Brophy as commissioner of Indian affairs on March 10, 1949, Nichols was president of New Mexico A&M University in Las Cruces, where he took a one-year leave of absence to serve as Indian commissioner. Just prior to becoming commissioner of Indian affairs Nichols was a member of the Commission on Organization of the Executive Branch (Hoover Commission), where he served on the committee on Indian affairs, a role that shaped his policies as commissioner. As with Brophy before him, Nichols's nomination was met with opposition, both in Congress and throughout Indian Country. Senator William Langer (Republican, North Dakota) of the Committee on Indian Affairs was especially critical, arguing that during Brophy's confirmation hearing three years earlier he had been promised that the next commissioner would "have some Indian blood in him."[2]

Nichols took office on April 13, 1949, despite not having been confirmed by the Senate, and he immediately announced plans for termination. When Assistant Secretary Bill Warne met with the Association of American Indian Affairs, he explained that Indian Country needed less traditional leaders who would follow the government's plan for them. "What we need most is knowledge which will enable us to awaken in our Indian fellow citizens a desire to move away from the past of their fathers to the future we have arranged for every youngster."[3] A month later, Nichols addressed the same forum, explaining that one day tribal designations and treaty rights would be a vestige of the past.

Nichols had served as one of four men to draft the Hoover Commission's report on Indian affairs, concluding that integration was the only policy the federal government could adopt. In his only annual report, he quoted extensively from the Hoover Commission's report, writing: "It is not the intention of the Federal Government to continue in the role of trustee of the Indians' property. The role was not assumed arbitrarily but devolved upon the United States out of historic antecedents."[4] Quoting from Thomas Jefferson a century and a half earlier, Nichols summed up his views: "The ultimate point of rest and happiness for [the Indians] is to let our settlements and theirs meet and blend together, to intermix and become one people."[5]

From Nichols's perspective, the federal trust responsibility evolved out of specific treaty obligations "in which the tribe requested protection for its members and its property." Such a policy, "if pursued without regard to the welfare of the persons protected," he added, would "defeat its purpose." The goal was to develop tribal resources and property to their fullest and then encourage Indians "to accept responsibility for management." This was the vehicle by which the federal government, "within a reasonable time, [may] withdraw entirely from its historic role and turn over its trusteeship to a trained and responsible Indian people."[6]

Nichols suggested an expenditure of $150 million was necessary to fit Indians "into the economic and social structure of the country." A federal investment in resource development was essential if tribal citizens were to make "full use of their soil and water resources on a sustained yield basis." Past expenditures were not based on "any long-term plans for the orderly solving of the problem," Nichols argued, but were "sporadic, discontinuous, and generally insufficient." What was needed to solve the challenge was "men, money, and . . . management," which would facilitate a policy of "complete integration" on a gradual and carefully planned basis of self-sufficiency.[7]

Congress, Nichols surmised, had only recently been apprised of the depth of need, and on December 19, 1947, Congress directed the department to submit recommendations for a long-term program for Navajo and Hopi rehabilitation. This admonition resulted in an appropriation of $88.57 million over ten years to prepare the two tribes for release from federal administration. A similar $24 million plan for the Papago Tribe in southern Arizona was solicited, followed by a series of bills introduced into Congress to rehabilitate the Standing Rock, Sisseton–Wahpeton, Fort Berthold, Chippewa–Cree and Rocky Bois, Devil's

Lake, and Blackfeet reservations. When tribes were ready for emancipation, Nichols encouraged Secretary of the Interior Oscar Chapman to release them from federal supervision.

Nichols believed the United States had only two responsibilities: protecting Indian property and providing services that were not otherwise available by state and local governments. He further believed that in order for Indians to make productive use of their land and resources they had to be educated, with education the fulcrum of any plan for rehabilitation and termination. Consequently, he focused on assisting tribes to develop their resources and become self-sufficient, which in turn would prepare them for termination. This sentiment governed what limited influence Nichols had on federal policy before President Truman, on March 22, 1950, unexpectedly announced that Dillon S. Myer would replace Nichols. A surprised Nichols submitted his resignation a day later and was reassigned as a special assistant to the secretary of the interior to supervise the transfer of Pacific trust possessions from the Navy to the Interior Department, formally leaving the Indian Service on May 4. He died at the age of sixty-nine on May 5, 1968, in New York City.

The Role of Government

It is not the intention of the Federal Government to continue in the role of trustee of the Indians' property. The role was not assumed arbitrarily but devolved upon the United States out of historic antecedents. Colonial law generally guaranteed the Indians protection in their land holdings. The Royal Proclamation of October 7, 1763, was a declaration by the King of England that the several nations or tribes of Indians "who live under our protection, should not be molested or disturbed in the possession of such parts of our dominion and territories as, not having been ceded to, or purchased by us, are reserved to them." The United States incorporated similar policy into its basic law, declaring in the Northwest Ordinance of 1787: "The utmost good faith shall always be observed towards the Indians; their land and property shall never be taken from them without their consent."

The protective role was dictated as a matter of public policy; moreover, it was most often the direct result of a treaty provision between an Indian tribe and the United States, in which the tribe requested protection for its members and property. It is realized, however, that protective guardianship, if pursued without regards to the welfare of the persons protected, can defeat its purpose. Development of the property to full utilization and encouragement of the owner to accept responsibility for management . . .

are the proper goals of Indian administration. They are the means by which the United States may ... withdraw entirely from its historic role and turn over its trusteeship to a trained and responsible Indian people.⁸

Magnitude of the Problem
Since Congress in 1819 first appropriated funds "for introducing among [the Indians] the habits and arts of civilization," it has been the policy of the United States Government to educate the Indian people, to direct them into pursuits by which they might gain a livelihood, and seek to incorporate them into the general population.

While this has been the basic and continuing objective of our Nation, the means of successfully accomplishing it has never been placed in the hands of the responsible administrative branch. It is to be doubted that the executive has ever presented to the legislative branch a complete estimate of what the "cost" of "civilizing" the Indians might entail. Through the years it was assumed in the executive branch and in Congress that the annual requests for funds and for authorities to act in Indian affairs were in fact annual installments and steps leading toward the final liquidation of the problem.

Problems of human adjustment do not solve themselves, not when the people seeking to make the adjustment are hampered by lack of education, poor health, and deficient resources. The expenditures which have been made over the years in behalf of our Indian people were not based on any long-term plan for the orderly solving of the problems they faced. Rather, the record indicates that these expenditures and the physical effort released by them have been sporadic, discontinuous, and generally insufficient.

This record explains why today many Indian children of school age have no schoolrooms and no teachers to provide for their education; why so many Indians are still without any kind of health care; why thousands of Indians are without any means of livelihood, either in the form of productive resources or marketable skills; why irrigable lands owned by Indians lie undeveloped in the arid West; why countless Indian communities are without roads on which to travel to school, to hospital, or to market....

Basically, the Indian "problem" is one that calls for men, money, and imaginative and patient management. There are no panaceas, no "overnight" solutions.... An ultimate substantial reduction in Federal expenditures in the field of Indian affairs is possible [but] no immediate reduction can be made without delaying progress and postponing the time when expenditures can be curtailed substantially.... The length of time before expenditures can be reduced, without building up future costs, will depend largely upon the vigor with which the program is pushed. Vigor will depend on clear and consistent policy, leadership, and financial support.⁹

The Ultimate Goal

The United States has two responsibilities toward the Indian people: to protect their property, and to provide services not otherwise available to them. The Government's protective function was not imposed. It was an obligation assumed in part payment for value received. The "Indian problem" that all of us face—Indians and non-Indians alike—is to develop to the utmost such resources of the Indians as are capable of development, and to provide safeguards to insure the continued right to use so long as the resources are needed. As a coordinate of this program, the Government must intensify its efforts to train Indians, to secure them in good health, and to work toward placing them in communities where they can support themselves, when such support cannot be obtained in the reservation areas. The ultimate purpose of Indian policy is to attain that objective stated by Thomas Jefferson: "The ultimate point of rest and happiness for them is to let our settlements and theirs meet and blend together, to intermix, and become one people."¹⁰

CHAPTER 44

Dillon S. Myer

Commissioner of Indian Affairs (May 5, 1950 – March 19, 1953)

DILLON SEYMOUR MYER was born in Hebron, Ohio, on September 4, 1891. After graduating from Ohio State University with a business administration degree, he earned a master's degree from Columbia University. He began federal service in the US Department of Agriculture in 1934, remaining there until he became director of the War Relocation Authority (WRA) in 1942, overseeing the internment of Japanese–Americans during World War II. When the WRA closed in 1946, Myer served in other federal agencies before President Truman nominated him as commissioner of Indian affairs.[1]

Myer accepted the nomination on the condition that Truman support increased appropriations so that the Bureau of Indian Affairs could prepare Indian Country for the department going "out of business as quickly as possible." He also demanded a free hand in administering the Indian Service.[2] With Truman's support, Myer replaced the upper management of the Indian Bureau, bringing in H. Rex Lee from the WRA to serve as assistant commissioner and replacing well-respected Chief Counsel Theodore Haas with Edwin E. Ferguson, also of the WRA. He then made a clean sweep of key staff positions at both the central and area offices. John Collier and former Interior Secretary Harold Ickes opposed Myer's nomination, with the latter convinced Myer ruthlessly replaced senior bureaucrats who disagreed with his harsh termination mindset.[3]

Myer articulated the goal of the bureau as "the step-by-step transfer" of all federal functions to the Indians themselves or to appropriate local, state, or federal agencies.[4] He supported House Joint Resolution 490 (the Bosone resolution) that would have immediately declared American Indians "free, unrestricted Americans." Myer rapidly transferred students from government schools to public schools and expanded state and local responsibilities for health care. He then negotiated the transfer of civil and criminal jurisdiction over tribal lands to the states, and he prepared for use by Congress a process for how tribes might negotiate with the Indian Service for the liquidation of the federal trust relationship.⁵

Myer acknowledged that any termination proposal resulting in "exploiting Indian groups by the precipitate withdrawal of guarantees protecting property rights, or the termination of Federal services in advance of others being made available, would be disastrous." At the same time, he inaugurated a policy of issuing one-year trust extensions rather than the usual twenty-five-year extensions. He also proposed reestablishing the forced patent system to expedite federal withdrawal. He then began the relocation of young Navajo and Hopi men and women to the Colorado River Indian Reservation or to off-reservation employment centers.⁶

By the midpoint of his tenure as commissioner, Myer declared that nearly every phase of the bureau was focused on termination. Indian schools no longer encouraged pluralism, but assimilation. High schools prepared students to make "the best use of the[ir] resources" and taught them the basic "mechanical and industrial skills necessary to obtain employment away from the reservation." He negotiated new Johnson–O'Malley contracts and initiated an adult education program that provided basic literacy to enable unskilled Navajos to gain employment off-reservation. It was obvious to Myer "that all of the Indians cannot continue to live on livestock operations and that the solution lies in developing livelihoods" away from reservations.

Myer also worked to confer on state and local governments' civil and criminal jurisdiction over Indian Country, thereby eliminating federal law enforcement. He supported measures to establish state jurisdiction, and he negotiated with a number of tribes and states regarding a legislative transfer of civil and criminal jurisdiction, including Minnesota, Wisconsin, Nebraska, California, Oregon, and Washington. While none of the bills was enacted during Myer's tenure, they continued the trajectory of divesting the federal government of its Indian responsibilities. Similar bills were introduced in the first session of the Eighty-Third Congress seeking to confer state jurisdiction over Indian Country, but failed to gain passage. As a first step in assisting "the Indians in becoming accustomed to the laws of the state," the commissioner encouraged tribes to adopt state statutes as tribal ordinances and to contract with county judges and sheriffs to serve as judicial and law enforcement officers.⁸

By early 1952, Myer defined the process by which tribes might sever their federal relationship, recommending legislation terminating the trust relationship for any tribe that believed the bureau was "a handicap to its advancement." If a tribe wished to modify its existing trust relationship in order to enhance control over its own affairs, and if it were willing to discuss the details of a partial termination, Myer agreed to assign staff to work with the tribe. If a tribe desired to assume some federal responsibilities without terminating the trust relationship, Myer agreed to develop the appropriate agreement, viewing it as a first step in the withdrawal process.

In the summer of 1952, Myer prepared a report enumerating which tribes could be immediately terminated and how the Bureau of Indian Affairs could prepare itself for abolition, relying on the Zimmerman plan for implementation. He then sent a letter to all bureau personnel informing them to prepare for withdrawal of services, threatening to terminate the federal–Indian relationship by any means, whether it was full or partial.

Complementing termination was the policy of relocating Indians from reservations to urban centers, a matter Myer envisioned as tripling or quadrupling the effort of the WRA.⁹ The majority of the Indians would need to find their "livelihood off reservation," Myer argued, as the Bureau of Indian Affairs expanded its relocation efforts to the Aberdeen, Billings, Minneapolis, Muskogee, and Portland area offices, as well as Alaska.

The election of Dwight D. Eisenhower brought Myer's tenure to an end, with the president requesting and securing Myer's resignation effective March 19, 1953. His resignation, however, did not slow termination, as Congress remained committed to emancipating all American Indians. Myer continued his federal service until 1964, when he retired. He died on October 21, 1982, in Silver Spring, Maryland, at the age of ninety-one.

Education for off-Reservation Employment

The Federal Indian school ... has become a basic assimilative influence in the lives of the full-blood children. Its job is not alone to teach the three R's in accordance with the public-school pattern. It has a much broader and more important responsibility: To teach the use and understanding of the English language; to present, through the school, experiences in preparing and serving meals, in dressing, and in personal cleanliness; in the care and training of livestock; in the preparation, care, harvest, and preservation of new types of garden and field crops; and in the use and maintenance of new tools, new materials, and new machinery.

All of these disciplines the average non-Indian child simply acquires from living among adults and from performing the everyday chores of the American farm or home. These things are so much a part of the daily cultural experiences of most rural non-Indian children that they are not taught in the public schools, but are acquired in the home. Indian schools devote a considerable portion of their school day to providing such assimilative experiences, in addition to the three R's of the public schools. Tests recently administered in Federal and public schools prove that Indian children in Federal schools, as a result of this type of instruction, are acquiring many of these skills which they would otherwise lack.

In addition, the Federal high schools are offering training in vocations designed to do one or both of two primary things: (1) Prepare the children for the best use of the resources of their Indian lands, i.e., teach them agriculture, stock raising, and similar skills, or (2) train them in the mechanical or industrial skills necessary to obtain employment away from the reservation areas. In view of the fact that large numbers of Indian school children are born in areas where the Indian population has outstripped the resources to the point that these will no longer support the population, it is important that many Indian youngsters find employment elsewhere. Many Federal Indian schools are making real progress in preparing and placing such students in off-reservation employment.[10]

Employment Placement Program
On most Indian reservations the . . . population is increasing much faster than the national rate, industrial development is negligible, and a large portion of the inhabitants face the alternative of remaining wholly or partially unemployed or of leaving home to seek employment. In a study of 16 reservation areas where the problem is considered most serious, it is estimated that resources available within the reservation can support only 46 percent of the reservation population even at a minimum standard of subsistence. To attain a fully adequate standard of living comparable to that of the national average, it is probable that more than half of all Indians would have to seek their livelihood off-reservation.

The objectives of the Bureau placement program are to make known to Indians the opportunities existing for permanent off-reservation work and living, to assist those who are interested in improving their lot to plan for and successfully carry out their movement to places of greater opportunity, to ensure their acceptance in employment, and to facilitate their social adjustment in communities to which they may go. Placement in the limited sense of completion of the hiring process is, by formal agreements entered into during the past year, the function of the United States Employment Service, State employment services and of the Railroad Retirement Board.

Preference is given in recruitment to employment in industries essential to the national defense.

A placement program to facilitate employment of Indians was begun with the Navajo and Hopi tribes early in 1948 and was introduced on a skeletal basis in five additional areas—Aberdeen, Billings, Minneapolis, Muskogee, and Portland—during the early part of 1950, and into Alaska in February 1951.

Except for Navajo–Hopi in the Window Rock Area, the placement staff has consisted of only one or two placement officers in each extensive and diverse geographical area and has served to lay a ground-work and to point to the need for more intensive and well-rounded services rather than to accomplish large numbers of permanent placements. For the Navajo and Hopi, the staff has been adequate to work closely with Indians in the various districts on their reservations and one placement officer has been assigned to each of four cities: Los Angeles, Phoenix, Denver, and Salt Lake City, to assist workers to make adjustment when taking jobs in California, Arizona, Colorado, and Utah.

The placement staff has worked with Indian organizations, Indian leaders, and individual Indians to stimulate interest in employment, educate them regarding working and living conditions off the reservation, and assist them to use established employment agencies. The staff has worked with employers, employer groups, community welfare, civic and religious organizations, and other interested agencies to promote acceptance of Indians as employees and as community residents. The staff has assisted employment agencies and employers to recruit workers, and has secured cooperation of State employment agencies in extending special services to Indians.[11]

Withdrawal of Services
Federal responsibility for administering the affairs of individual Indian tribes... should be terminated as rapidly as the circumstances of each tribe will permit. This should be accomplished by arrangements with the proper public bodies of the political subdivisions to assume responsibility for the services customarily enjoyed by the non-Indian residents of such political subdivisions and by distribution of tribal assets to the tribes as a unit or by division of the tribal assets among the individual members, whichever may appear to be the better plan in each case. In addition, responsibility for trust properties should be transferred to the Indians themselves, either as groups or individuals as soon as feasible.[12]

As part of the general pattern of withdrawal activities, the Bureau took additional steps... to accelerate the transfer of responsibilities for educating Indian children to the regular public school system of the country. In a number of areas, where there are both Indian and non-Indian children to be educated, public schools and Indian Service schools were merged under a plan of pooled resources and joint responsibility for operations. In other areas, where the school-age population is almost exclusively Indian, consultations were held with local school districts or with State educational officials looking to the outright transfer of responsibilities for the operation of Indian Service schools. Plans for transferring 25 Indian Service schools on this basis were developed before the close of the fiscal year and were expected to be consummated [in] 1953. At the close of the year the Bureau had contracts providing for the education of Indian children with 14 State departments of education and 27 local school districts.

Similar activities were carried on looking to the transfer of responsibilities for the protection of Indian health from the Bureau to appropriate State or local agencies. While no transfers of Indian Service hospitals were accomplished during the year, basic authority for such transfers was provided by enactment of Public Law 291 which was approved April 3, 1952.[13] This act also authorized the admittance of non-Indians as patients in Indian Service hospitals in areas where other hospital facilities are not available.

In presenting its appropriation estimates for the fiscal year, the Bureau requested funds to be used specifically for contracting under the Johnson–O'Malley Act with non-Federal hospitals for the care and treatment of tubercular Indians, particularly Navajos. It was hoped that a total of 400 beds in various hospitals throughout the country could be provided... as one important means of relieving the serious tuberculosis problem on the Navajo Reservation. The Bureau also continued its contracting with States under the Johnson–O'Malley Act for provision of public health and preventive medical services to the Indians by the county health departments. At the close of the year the Bureau had 30 contracts of this kind in effect with States, counties, or local health units.

In the field of law enforcement the Bureau conducted numerous negotiations with various tribal groups and with State authorities looking toward a transfer of jurisdictional responsibilities within Indian reservations from the Federal Government to the States. Bureau-sponsored bills were introduced in Congress providing for a transfer of Indian civil and criminal jurisdiction to the States of Minnesota, Wisconsin, Nebraska,

California, Oregon, and Washington. Although none of these bills were enacted, committee hearings were held on several and one (the California transfer bill) was passed by the House of Representatives.[14]

How to Start the Process of Withdrawing Services
Another principle which received considerable emphasis during the year was that the development of a withdrawal program affecting any particular Indian group must be preceded by and based upon a compilation of all the relevant factual data. This includes such things as an inventory of tribal and individual Indian resources, a study of the laws and treaty obligations affecting the group, an appraisal of the status and effectiveness of existing tribal organization, and many others. . . .

Another facet of Bureau policy on withdrawal . . . follow[ed] a visit to the Washington Office of the Bureau by several leading members of the Osage Tribe of Oklahoma. In a letter to the chairman of the Osage Tribal Council the Commissioner of Indian Affairs enunciated three major points which were subsequently reproduced and brought to the attention of other tribes throughout the country. The three points are:

1. If any Indian tribe is convinced the Bureau of Indian Affairs is a handicap to its advancement, I am willing to recommend to the Secretary of the Interior that legislative authority be obtained from the Congress to terminate the Bureau's trusteeship responsibility with respect to that tribe.
2. If any Indian tribe desires modification of the existing trusteeship in order that some part or parts thereof be lifted (such as the control of tribal funds, the leasing of tribal land, as examples), and if the leaders of the tribe will sit down with Bureau officials to discuss the details of such a program of partial termination of trusteeship, we will be glad to assign staff members to work with the group with a view to developing appropriate legislative proposals.
3. If there are tribes desiring to assume themselves some of the responsibilities the Bureau now carries with respect to the furnishing of services, without termination of the trusteeship relationship, we are prepared to work with such tribes in the development of an appropriate agreement providing for the necessary safeguards to the tribe and its members.

This statement constitutes, in effect, a standing offer by the Bureau to work constructively with any tribe which wishes to assume either full control or a greater degree of control over its own affairs.[15]

CHAPTER 45

Glenn L. Emmons

Commissioner of Indian Affairs (August 10, 1953–January 7, 1961)

GLENN LEONIDAS EMMONS was born in Atmore, Alabama, on August 15, 1895. At the age of nine his family moved to Albuquerque, where Emmons later attended the University of New Mexico, leaving his studies after his junior year to serve in World War I. With cessation of war, Emmons returned to Gallup, New Mexico, and began a career in banking.[1]

With the election of Dwight D. Eisenhower as president in 1952, the president-elect nominated fifty-seven-year-old Glenn Emmons, who was intimately familiar with Navajo relocation, a matter that had gained national attention.[2] Emmons was confirmed as commissioner on July 28, 1953, and took office on August 10, just days after the Senate approved House Concurrent Resolution 108 establishing the congressional goal of subjecting American Indians "to the same laws and entitled to the same privileges and responsibilities" as other Americans.[3]

HCR 108 set the tempo for Emmons's seven and a half years in office, declaring the congressional intent to emancipate Native Americans from federal supervision, enumerating as a priority the termination of the federal–Indian trust and government-to-government relationship with all tribes in California, Florida, New York, and Texas, as well as the Flathead, Klamath, Menominee, Pottawatomie, and Turtle Mountain Chippewa. Once the political basis of these tribes was ended, all federal services to them would cease.

Eisenhower continued with the termination and emancipation of tribal people from federal supervision, with Emmons cooperating with a Congress engrossed with integration; Emmons supported a series of termination bills his first year in office. That same fall, the president directed the commissioner to meet with tribes and tribal leaders where he learned firsthand the primary needs of Indian Country were better educational, medical, and economic opportunities.[4]

Emmons consulted with the tribes as part of his tour of Indian Country, and while not included in HCR 108, he added to the termination list the tribes

302

and bands of western Oregon, presenting to Congress a full report at the start of the 1954 legislative session. In addition, he proposed a series of bills to terminate several small bands and rancherias in Nevada and Utah, as well as the mixed-blood Ute from the Uintah–Ouray Reservation. Congress held hearings on each of the termination bills (except the New York Indians), with one—Public Law 399, calling for the termination of the Menominee Tribe—becoming law on June 17, 1954.[5]

Just days after Emmons took office, Congress enacted a series of termination-related bills calculated to end the political distinction of American Indians from the rest of the American citizenry. The most significant was Public Law 83-280, which conferred civil and criminal jurisdiction over delineated tribal lands in California (all), Oregon (except Warm Springs), Nebraska (all), Minnesota (except Red Lake), and Wisconsin (except Menominee).[6] Congress authorized other states to assume jurisdiction by simply amending their constitutions or state statutes; tribal consent was not necessary. The act relieved the Indian Service of law enforcement responsibilities within these reservations, although the federal government coordinated with each state to transition the assumption of jurisdiction. On the same day, Congress approved two other bills, including Public Law 83-277, which repealed federal prohibitions on the sale of alcoholic beverages to Indians outside of Indian Country and legalized the introduction of alcohol in Indian Country by recognizing a local option to determine whether to allow such beverages.[7] Public Law 83-281 repealed the federal restriction on the sale, purchase, or possession of guns by Indians.[8]

Emmons refined the termination process, emphasizing consultation with, but not the consent of, tribal nations. To enforce economy and efficiency, he adopted three procedures, including preparing draft termination bills for departmental consideration; implementing area office and agency consultation with tribes, as well as state and county governments; and drafting legislation for submission to Congress. The purpose was to assist tribes in preparing "for the eventual cutoff of Federal trusteeship."[9]

Although Emmons supported termination, congressional support for it waned after the 1956 election, when Democratic victories changed the composition of congressional committees and as national opposition increased. For the 118 tribes and bands that were terminated, their status fundamentally changed, as the federal trust ended, state jurisdiction and judicial authority began, and federal services were withdrawn. Although some of the acts expressly extinguished tribal sovereignty, all terminated tribes were divested of their self-governing ability, and in some cases the land over which they exercised sovereignty was gone.

In tandem with termination Emmons expanded his priorities, with an adult education program deployed among a number of tribes with the goal of making adults more attractive in the market.[10] With Emmons's support, Congress approved of the Indian Vocational Training Act, which provided funds for adult education but tied such services to relocation, making education an integral part of relocation.[11] He modified bureau policy by selecting for relocation those Native Americans "of good character, in reasonably good health, and show[ing] evidence that they want[ed] to live permanently away from the home area." If they met these requirements, the Indian Service paid one-way travel expenses. The principal purpose of relocation, Emmons argued, was simply "too many people and not enough land."[12] To improve health care, Emmons supported the Indian Health Transfer Act that moved the Division of Indian Health out of the bureau and into the US Public Health Service.[13]

Outside of education and health care, economic development was the staple of Emmons's administration. On April 12, 1956, he sent a memorandum to all tribes and agencies encouraging tribal governments "to work out and adopt programs for their own social and economic betterment."[14] He then met with nearly all of the western tribes in the summer and fall of 1956 to promote economic development, confident a grassroots effort would blossom into stronger tribal economies. With the election of John F. Kennedy as president in November 1960, Emmons elected to resign, submitting his resignation on December 23, remaining in office until January 7, 1961. He returned to Gallup where he resumed his banking career. Glenn L. Emmons died on March 14, 1980, in Canton, Oklahoma.

Too Many People and Not Enough Land

My own personal feeling has always been that our Indian people, taken by and large, are just as capable as any other group in the American population and that all they need is a chance to make a decent livelihood and to realize their inherent possibilities for advancement and personal growth. Ever since the days when [our] ancestors . . . were fighting to establish our national independence, this country has been known as the land of opportunity. Yet the ironic fact is that this kind of opportunity has never been made fully available to our first Americans—the people whose ancestors preceded ours on this continent by probably several thousand years. My number one objective as Commissioner of Indian Affairs is to see that our Indian people get this kind of opportunity so that they can take their rightful place alongside other citizens in the broad pattern of our national life.

If the Indians have the kind of natural abilities which I have been emphasizing, why is it that many of them are mired down in poverty around the reservations? Unfortunately, there is no simple answer to this question but a large part of the answer, I believe, can be summed up in a very short phrase. It is "too many people and not enough land."

Although some of the tribes like the Utes and the Jicarilla Apaches have been getting excellent returns recently from the mineral resources of their lands, most of the tribes are not so fortunate. Even the Navajos, with their recent unusual 33 million dollar bonus income, have to spread these proceeds rather thin in programs that will benefit some 80,000 people and there are many tribal groups throughout the country that have never realized a dollar from mineral leasing on their lands. Taken as a whole, the lands available on Indian reservations and similar areas are not large— something over 50 million acres altogether—and their capacity to provide a decent livelihood for the families dependent on them is highly restricted. On reservation after reservation, we find that the present resources will furnish an adequate living for only a fractional part of the present population. And, on top of this, the Indian population is growing in most places at a faster rate than the general population of the country.

On the Navajo Reservation, for example, the population when I first came to Gallup, New Mexico, in 1919 was estimated to be around 29,000. Today it stands at 80,000; in another five years it will reach the 100,000 mark; and by the year 2000, which is only 43 years away, it could be somewhere in the neighborhood of 350,000. . . .

There, in a nutshell, [is] the problem which we face not only on the Navajo Reservation but on scores of others throughout the Western States. Now what are we trying to do about it? First . . . we are emphasizing the progressive development of the resources available on the reservations—the lands and water, the timber, the grass and the minerals. We want to be sure that these resources are developed to the highest feasible point and that they are producing the maximum income for the Indian people that is consistent with sound principles of conservation. . . .

[R]esource development alone will not provide a total answer to the problem. Even with the fullest development that we can imagine, the resources of the Navajo Reservation will probably never support more than 45,000 people at an acceptable standard of living. Those on the Pine Ridge Sioux Reservation of South Dakota will not support more than about 500 families out of the 1,800 families now living there; those on the

Papago Reservation in Arizona will not support more than about half of the present population. And so it goes.

Then we also have to think about the aptitudes and the inclinations of the Indian people. On many of the reservations the major part of the Indian land is not today being used by Indian farmers and stockmen but is being leased out to non-Indians and is producing a rental income for the Indian owners. Now, of course, there is nothing unusual about this; thousands of non-Indians throughout the country also own agricultural or grazing lands which they lease out to others for operation and production. But the point I want to emphasize is that it's only a minor segment of our population—Indian or non-Indians—which has any real aptitude or interest in making a living directly from the land. Even in rural areas, large numbers of the younger people, both Indian and non-Indian, have no desire to be stockmen or farmers today and would much prefer to be mechanics or accountants or industrial workers. I firmly believe they should have this opportunity.

So it is important to put our resource development work in proper perspective and to supplement it with other types of "economic opportunity" programs. As matters now stand, we have two of these programs actively under way. . . . One of the active programs is what we call "relocation services." Essentially it's a program of guidance and assistance for Indian people—both workers and their families—who want to leave the reservations and establish themselves in metropolitan areas where jobs are more plentiful and easier to find. Under this program we have counselors on the reservations to advise the Indian people who are thinking about a move and inform them realistically about the kinds of adjustments they will have to make. Then on the receiving end—in Los Angeles, San Francisco, San Jose, Denver, Chicago, and St. Louis—we have offices which actively help the new arrivals in finding jobs, locating suitable housing, and getting generally adjusted to their new environment.

Now it is true that about one-fourth of the Indian people who have gone out under this program each year have eventually returned to the reservations because they found big-city life incompatible or for some other reason. But the other three-fourths, comprising about 12,000 Indian people altogether, have made some pretty remarkable adjustments. Nearly all of them are making far more money than they ever did previously; many of them are enjoying comforts and conveniences that they had never known before; and the great majority of them are gradually acquiring a new kind of self-reliance which is a wonderfully heartening thing to see.

But we also recognize that relocation is not the total answer even for the nonagricultural Indians since there are and always will be many thousands of Indian people who are understandably reluctant to leave their home areas and take up life in a city like Los Angeles or Chicago. So the second phase of our "economic opportunity" work is aimed at attracting new industries or manufacturing plants to the vicinity of the reservations. On this we are cooperating closely with the tribal organizations. Although this is a comparatively young program, dating back a little over a year, already some highly encouraging results have been achieved.[15]

A Land Policy

During the 1930's and the early 1940's the Department followed substantially the same policy on land sales that is now being so strenuously urged by the outstanding critics of the present policy. In other words, it strongly discouraged individual Indian landowners from selling their holdings and permitted such sales ordinarily only to other Indian individuals or to tribal groups. During this period hundreds of Indian landowners who wished to convert their land holdings in excess of their needs into cash for various purposes were completely frustrated and tied to lands that may have produced little or no benefit to them. Where sales are permitted with the market limited to Indian purchasers, thousands of acres were sold at prices substantially below the returns that the Indian sellers might have realized if free and unrestricted bidding had been permitted.

During the late 1940's the former policy of restricting the market to Indian purchasers began to break down as Indian landowners demanded to be allowed to sell their holdings for a maximum price. They developed the practice of going directly to Congress for individual legislation that gave them "fee patents" or unrestricted title to their lands. Although the Department in this period generally recommended against the enactment of such bills, a great many of those introduced in each Congressional session were nonetheless enacted. A substantial acreage of individually owned Indian land was removed from Federal trusteeship through this process and undoubtedly the major portion of it was sold to non-Indian purchasers.

The policy which the Department and Bureau have been following . . . since 1955, is based on a full recognition of the individual Indian property rights which are unquestionably involved. In allotting lands to individual Indians on many of the reservations and the public domain under Congressional law during the latter part of the 19th century and down through the 1920's, the Federal Government, in effect, gave these Indian (sic) a deed to the lands allotted. It thus vested in these individual Indians (and their rightful heirs) a valid property right, though under trust, fully equivalent, in the last analysis, to that enjoyed by any other American property owner.

Under the system of free democracy few concepts are more centrally important than respect for individual property rights. . . . At the same time, however, we are also fully aware of our trust responsibilities for tribal property and we recognize that many of the tribal organizations have a legitimate and valid interest in acquiring individual Indian properties that may be offered for sale. The problem, in essence, has been to work out a method for permitting the fullest possible development of sound tribal land acquisition plans without violating the property rights and interests of the individual tribal members.

During the past four years the Department and Bureau have been giving a great deal of intensive study to this problem and we have recently developed a policy which . . . goes a long way toward attainment of the desired objective. The essential elements of this policy are as follows:

1. Wherever a single Indian owner of an allotment asks that his land be sold and, after careful examination of the circumstances in his case, a sale appears to be clearly justified in the light of his long-range best interests, a sale will be authorized.
2. In all such cases the tribal organization will be notified that the particular allotment is being offered for sale. This will give the tribe an opportunity to negotiate a purchase with the owner. If the owner insists on competitive bidding, he will be specifically asked whether he is willing to let the tribal organization meet the high bid that may be offered. The land will then be advertised for sale and sealed bids will be received. If all bids fall substantially below the Bureau's appraisal of the property's value, all will be rejected. If one or more of the bids are acceptable, the tribe will be given the opportunity to buy the land by meeting the high bid provided that the owner has agreed in advance to such an arrangement. If the owner has not agreed and one or more sealed bids exceed the appraisal, the land will be put up for auction with the amount of the highest sealed bid as the floor of the auction bidding. This will give the tribe an additional opportunity to acquire the property in competition with other bidders.

3. In connection with Indian allotments which are in multiple ownership as a result of inheritance, the same general procedure will be followed with a few noteworthy exceptions. Such properties will be sold only if a sale is requested by one of the owners and approved by or on behalf of all the others. If any one of the owners is interested in buying out the others, he will be given first opportunity to purchase the land at the Bureau's appraisal figure unless one or more of the other owners object. A sale may also be made to one of the owners at less than the appraisal if the other owners are agreeable. If more than one of the owners wishes to buy the allotment, all of those interested will submit sealed bids and the property will be sold to the highest bidder. If none of the owners is interested, the property will be offered to the tribal organization at the appraisal price unless one of the owners objects. If there is objection by an owner, then the procedure outlined under Number 2 above, involving sealed bids to be followed by an auction, will be used.

The Department and its Bureau of Indian Affairs recognize that there are difficulties in the present situation which will hinder the tribes from full realization of their land acquisition and development plans even under the policy outlined above. One of these is the difficulty of securing the approval of frequently dozens of owners for sale of multiple-ownership lands as required under existing law. Another is the fact that many, perhaps most, of the tribes do not now have the financial resources needed for a substantial land purchase program.[16]

Slowing Termination

One of the most important developments of the year in Federal administration of Indian affairs was Secretary of the Interior [Fred] Seaton's radio address of September 18, 1958, from Flagstaff, Ariz., clarifying the Department's position on the centrally important question of terminating Federal trust responsibilities for Indian tribal groups.

Referring to the resolution on this subject adopted by Congress in 1953 (H. Con. Res. No. 108), Secretary Seaton called attention to the varying interpretations given to this document over the preceding 5 years and specifically mentioned the impression created by some interpreters that "it is the intention of Congress and the Department of the Interior to abandon Indian groups regardless of their ability to fend for themselves."

In his talk, Secretary Seaton strongly repudiated any such interpretation. "To me," he said, "it would be incredible, even criminal, to send any

Indian tribe out into the mainstream of American life until and unless the educational level of that tribe was one which was equal to the responsibilities which it was shouldering."

At another point, he summarized his position succinctly in the following words: ... "No Indian tribe or group should end its relationship with the Federal Government unless such tribe or group has clearly demonstrated—first, that it understands the plan under which such a program would go forward, and second, that the tribe or group affected concurs in and supports the plan proposed."[17]

[tribal consent required for termination 1958]

CHAPTER 46

Philleo Nash

Commissioner of Indian Affairs (September 26, 1961–March 15, 1966)

PHILLEO NASH was born in Wisconsin Rapids, Wisconsin, on October 25, 1909, to an agricultural family. In 1937, he earned a PhD in anthropology from the University of Chicago and began teaching at the University of Toronto and University of Wisconsin. He then moved to Washington, DC, in 1942 to work in the Office of War Information, and between 1946 and 1952, he served as special assistant to President Truman for Department of the Interior matters before becoming the president's administrative assistant. In 1958, he was elected as a Democratic lieutenant governor of Wisconsin, losing reelection two years later.[1]

With the election of John F. Kennedy as president in 1960, Nash was one of seven men appointed by the president in January 1961 to a task force on Indian affairs, which concluded that economic development was the key to improving conditions in Indian Country. On July 31, Kennedy nominated Nash as commissioner of Indian affairs. A former board member of the Association on American Indian Affairs, Nash had only the tacit support of the Senate Committee on Interior and Insular Affairs. Despite antagonizing the committee with his candor, Nash was confirmed by the Senate and took office on September 26, 1961.[2]

Nash encouraged economic self-sufficiency and industrial development on or near tribal lands, seeking to enhance tourism and recreation. In the process, he shifted the focus of the Bureau of Indian Affairs from custodial care to economic development, walking a fine line between two prevailing theories regarding the role of the bureau. "One held that the reservation system, with attendant trusteeship and the existence of the Bureau of Indian Affairs, with its program of property management and human betterment," restrained American Indians. The other supported the idea that federal "protection of property and the provision of special services" was all that stood between the Indians and "ultimate poverty, destitution and dependency."³ Nash believed the reality was somewhere in the middle.

Nash was convinced life in Indian Country could be improved if the bureau strategically directed economic development and matched it with specific reservation resources. Contrary to popular opinion, Nash declared, poverty was neither a result of any inherent deficiency of Indian Country nor was it the result of tribalism. An escape from poverty required patience, but it also demanded "respect for a way of life that is different from ours." The key was the raising of capital—private and public—constructing a modern transportation system, and creating incentives to attract businesses to Indian Country, no small task since most tribal economies were agrarian-based and the transition to a commercial, industrial, or recreational economy required changes in posture, processes, priorities, and policy.

To encourage development, Nash reorganized the department and established a Division of Economic Development that rested on two pillars. The first was "proper management of land, timber, water, range, livestock, minerals, and other resources," while the second was resource development by which such assets could be employed for maximum productivity. Using an array of War on Poverty programs, including Economic Opportunity Act funding, Nash established Job Corps for employment and training; Youth Corps to encourage at-risk students to remain in school; Head Start for prekindergarten education; and Community Action Programs for adult education, preemployment training, and manpower availability to build capacity for long-term sustainability. To underscore the potential for renewal, Nash visited every tribal and Alaska Native community during his tenure in office.

But resource development in Indian Country would be successful only if Native Americans received an education commensurate with the need. Nash argued that improved educational opportunity was essential to realize the goal of "maximum Indian economic self-sufficiency."⁴ To this end, Nash in 1963 moved the bureau a step closer to its goal of every child in school by constructing thirty-eight new schools accommodating five thousand additional students. He also opened the Institute of American Indian Arts in the old Santa Fe Indian School to encourage and promote fine arts; he also converted Haskell Indian School into Haskell Junior College.

While the Kennedy task force identified inadequate housing as a concern, it was Nash who championed the application of the Public Housing Administration to Indian Country in 1961. As a result, tribal nations for the first time established housing authorities, with eighty in place by 1966. While encouraging economic development and providing a host of social resources, the challenge in Indian Country was securing capital, a need that nearly overwhelmed tribes. As for the relocation policy, Nash argued it solved nothing, as transporting people "from one pocket of poverty to another" simply moved the problem away from the reservations.[5]

By mid-decade, there was a palpable rise in expectation throughout Indian Country. For the first time, federal policy encouraged tribal participation in programs established for their benefit. But Interior Secretary Stewart Udall required more radical change—the "best, boldest and most imaginative thinking"—than the slower, long-term approach adopted by Nash.[6] When Senator Henry Jackson (Democrat, Washington), who advocated for termination of the Colville tribes, which was opposed by Nash, became chairman of the Committee on Interior and Insular Affairs, Nash knew his tenure as commissioner was at an end. "The gains made so far have not yet wiped out all Indian unemployment," he lamented in his final report, "nor raised the average level of Indian income above the poverty line, nor eliminated substandard housing, nor brought equal educational opportunity."[7] He recognized time was a requisite for change, a strategy Udall refused to accept. While reestablishing trust with tribal nations, Nash was forced to resign on March 9, 1966; he left office six days later.

After leaving the bureau, Nash engaged in political consulting in Washington, DC, and directed the Special Needs Program at American University. In 1977, he returned to Wisconsin to oversee his family's farm. He died of renal cell cancer in Marshfield, Wisconsin, on October 12, 1987.

What Is the Root of Poverty?
We place our faith in . . . the development of resources and the development of people. We intend to accelerate and improve education at all levels. We intend to accelerate and improve economic growth on the reservation. We are calling these programs the "New Trail."

Yet, despite this record of national concern for the welfare of Indians, despite the rapid extension of our Indian programs in recent years, what is the situation today? Adult Indians are, on the whole, only half as well educated as other Americans; they live only two-thirds as long; and their annual incomes are somewhere between one-fourth and one-third as large. Unemployment is between six and seven times the national average. . . .

The long-standing poverty on the reservations shows that the problem cannot be solved merely by pouring in more and more public money unaccompanied by other changes. Is [poverty] the fault of the Bureau of Indian Affairs? Since its creation the Bureau has been a favorite whipping boy for those who desire better results but are not necessarily familiar with the problem. The Bureau has also been the target of merited criticism from those who are better informed and just as sincere. We are a public agency and we do our business in the spotlight of public attention. We need and invite public scrutiny. I do not propose to defend the Bureau from our critics....

Strung out along the East Coast of the United States are dozens of small Indian communities and many thousands of Indian individuals who are not Federal service Indians. They are the remnants of the bands and tribes with whom our Colonial ancestors made settlement for lands and forests long before the formation of the Federal Union. Their property is unrestricted; their standing in the law is exactly the same as [other Americans]. On the whole they are poor people with all the social ills that poverty brings with it. But they have never received services from the Bureau of Indian Affairs and their poverty cannot be attributed to it.

Is it, then, the fault of the Indians that they find themselves today at the bottom of the national economic ladder? Have they simply failed to make the most of their potentialities and of the opportunities available to them...?

Some people think the reservation system itself is responsible for Indian poverty. To test this proposition, let us look at Oklahoma. There the reservation concept was never fully developed. Moreover, tribal governments there were stripped of their principal functions with statehood, more than half a century ago. Indians do, in fact, have a fuller participation in community life in Oklahoma than in most states.... But Indian poverty has not been eliminated in Oklahoma.

Closely associated with reservation life in some parts of the country is the Allotment Act of 1887. With the exception of the eastern side of the Navajo Reservation, there are not many allotted lands in the Southwest. Across the Northern Plains, however, the consequences are distressingly evident of what was intended to be a great reform, undertaken toward the end of the last century....

The tragic consequences in the loss of land ownership were with us until the Indian Reorganization Act. The economic aftermath is still with us. The first trust period began to come to an end in 1912. Large scale loss of ownership began immediately. Altogether, before extension of trusteeship by the act of 1934, 90 million acres of land—nearly two-thirds of the Indian estate—passed irretrievable from Indian ownership.

We need to reflect on the lessons of allotment. In retrospect we can see that our forefathers had the cart before the ox.... Experience taught us that people hang onto land only if it has meaning to them. And anthropology tells us that people have land use and ownership patterns because their culture tells them what they have is right, not the other way around.

Allotment cannot be the sole cause of poverty on the reservations. If it were, all the unallotted reservations in the Southwest would be rich. Here we would have no problems of land use and ownership, and plainly this is not true. Finally, there are those who would lay the blame on the Indian Reorganization Act and its philosophy. The philosophy of that act is to protect tribalism; and tribalism, they say, is the evil that lies behind poverty. I cannot accept this.

Tribalism is not an evil; and in any case its elimination or perpetuation should not be the choice of the bureaucrat. It should be for those who choose to live within tribalism to continue it; and for those who choose to live outside of it, to part company with it. Some, but not all, Indians prefer it. We do not solve other problems by compelling people to give up a form of association which they had before they came here. We should respect the freedom of association of Indians under tribal government just as we respect other ways in which people band together for their mutual advancement and comfort.

This is what we call the "Indian Problem." A national conscience; appropriations; a big bureau; and the end result: poverty.

I think there is a way out. It is not a panacea. There is no magic in it. It requires much work and patience and above all, respect for a way of life that is different from ours. The way is the path of economic development ... to increase employment and income, and to raise living standards....

A common characteristic of underdeveloped communities, on reservations and off, at home and abroad, is lack of capital. Without capital, a community must lead a hand-to-mouth existence, and the hand cannot be really productive nor the mouth well fed. To accumulate capital out of precariously low incomes is extraordinarily difficult; that is why poverty-stricken communities and Nations tend to remain poverty-stricken. Some outside force, an economic lift from outside the community, is one way—often the only way—of breaking the year-in-year-out cycle in which poverty breeds poverty.

There are two broad kinds of capital, private and public. One takes the form of factory buildings and equipment, of trucks and bulldozers, of stores and the goods that stock their shelves—all the private capital that makes it possible for business to operate. The other kind—public capital—takes the form of roads, waterworks, and sewerage systems, of schools and hospitals, of fire-fighting equipment, public auditoriums, and the whole apparatus of law and order. These, too, are essential to the operation of business and of the community. Both are capital and the Indian reservations are starved for both kinds....

The New Trail along which we are moving with the Indian people is the sound path of economic development. It is the path the advanced nations of the world have followed to the achievement of high production and high living standards. It is not an easy path, nor can we expect progress along it to be rapid. The main thing is that we have made a beginning.[8]

How to Stimulate an Indian Economy
Much development has been achieved on the reservations during the past 30 years by tribal and individual enterprise with practical help and technical guidance from the Bureau of Indian Affairs.... But it is also clear that the potential of these 53,000,000 acres [in Indian Country] has never come anywhere near fulfillment. The existing land base could be much more profitably utilized if it were worked by its Indian owners instead of being leased, as it is so often, to non-Indian tenants. In addition to that, several hundred thousand acres of additional lands have irrigation potential but have not been brought under ditch. Continuing progress on this front is essential for two reasons: First, to improve the economic well-being of the Indian landowners; but also to safeguard the valuable water rights that go with the land under various laws and court decisions....

One of the most pressing of all Indian land problems is that which follows from the multiple ownership of land which has been passed undivided to heirs of an allottee. There are now more than 10 percent of the total Indian estate [that is] unproductive because of multiple ownership. Generally speaking, there are so many owners that the consent of all of them cannot be obtained to a lease....

One solution [is to] loan the tribes the money so they can buy up the multiple interests. [A]nother solution [is to] permit the tribes to buy the multiple interests on the installment plan. Out of these two ... a composite solution must be found. I pledge my best efforts to work toward a common sense solution of this intensely important problem....

Some tribal groups are favored by nature with rich deposits of oil, gas and other minerals which have recently been discovered [and] are being commercially developed and are producing substantial tribal income. A full program of resource development would provide for the use of the best modern techniques in minerals exploration and development throughout the entire Indian Country.

One of the great potentials for Indian resource development is in the field of recreation. Our national population is growing, and will continue to grow for some decades, at an explosive rate. As the work week shortens, and as the ease of travel increases, the demand on recreation facilities throughout the entire Nation will multiply.... So the recreation industry, which is already big business, will become increasingly bigger business in the immediate future, and its growth will continue for a long time to come.

Think of the potential tourist attractions on many of our Indian reservations: Trout streams, natural lakes, man-made lakes, scenery, history, Indian arts and crafts. Careful planning is essential. It is necessary to maintain high standards because our national parks and our state parks have accustomed people to high quality features. But is seems clear that recreation is a richly promising field for Indian economic development....

As mechanization and automation have moved into farming and ranching the opportunities for seasonal unskilled labor become smaller every year. This hits the Indian worker harder than others. How can we meet this situation? By economic development measures [that] stimulate a wage economy in the reservation areas, using the natural resources and the labor potential that are already there. Management skill and trained workers are an essential ingredient of successful economic development. It is greatly desired that Indian tribes with assets in the form of income, cash or judgment moneys should contribute from their own capital to the fullest extent possible. [We] can bring manufacturing employment to the reservation areas through special inducements, such as plant sites, facilities, and on-the-job training programs. This is industrial development [that] must be accompanied by stable conditions of law and order and the economic and business climate which makes it attractive for manufacturing industries to locate on reservations.

A depressed reservation area can be improved by bringing individual Indians into contact with areas of greater opportunity. This means education in the broad sense; it means vocational training; it means job placement; and for those who wish it, it means relocation....⁹

Goals for Indian Country
Three main goals... provide the orientation of all of our program activities. They are 1) maximum Indian economic self-sufficiency, 2) full participation of Indians in American life, and 3) equal citizenship privileges and responsibilities for Indians. These are not novel goals. They are merely a statement with respect to Indians of what the rest of us seek for ourselves. The question is not whether they are desirable goals. I have yet to hear anyone disagree with them. The question is, "What are the best means by which these ends may be reached?"

There are two philosophies. One holds that the reservation system, with its attendant trusteeship and the existence of the Bureau of Indian Affairs with its programs of property management and human betterment hold back individual Indians from reaching these desirable goals. The other philosophy holds that the protection of property and the provision of special services is all that stands between Indian individuals and ultimate poverty, destitution, and dependency.

The truth, as usual, lies between the two extremes. Our present programs are designed to take into account the realities of Indian life as it is actually lived on and near the reservations, not as the ideologists of either extreme visualize it. The facts are that Indian people themselves place a high value on the Indian trusteeship. In the main they do not wish it to come to an end but regard it as a necessary and desirable relationship which is due them in return for lands ceded and promises made long ago. Individually they chafe under its restrictions; collectively they resist efforts to end it.... As long as reservations exist, the trusteeship continues, and the people live on reservations, it is the duty of the Bureau of Indian Affairs to devise programs and operate them so that these conditions of life will improve.

The goals... described are attainable, not a dream. Life on reservations can be much better; while those who desire to leave the reservations and seek opportunity nearby or in metropolitan centers should be prepared or helped to succeed. The programs [of] the Bureau of Indian Affairs are programs of education and individual betterment both on and off the reservation, looking toward a better life for all.... I welcome an awakening of the national conscience and the spotlight that is focused on the Bureau of Indian Affairs. In the revitalized bureau of today we are determined to bring the reservation communities into the stream of social and economic advance, so that they too may be swept along to a better life and a brighter future.[10]

CHAPTER 47

Robert L. Bennett

Commissioner of Indian Affairs (April 27, 1966–May 31, 1969)

ROBERT LA FOLLETTE BENNETT became the second American Indian to serve as commissioner of Indian affairs and the first since Ely Parker (Seneca) in 1869. Bennett was born on November 16, 1912, on the Oneida Reservation in Wisconsin. He graduated from Haskell Institute with an associate's degree in business administration, and in 1941, he earned a law degree from Southeastern University School of Law in Washington, DC. He began his career with the Indian Service in 1933, remaining with the bureau until 1969 with the exception of a stint in the US Marine Corps during World War II and a brief stay in the Veteran's Administration immediately after the war.[1]

President Lyndon Johnson nominated Bennett to replace Nash in the winter of 1966, with the new commissioner confirmed by the Senate and taking office on April 27, 1966.[2] When Johnson administered the oath of office, he charged Bennett to be "progressive, venturesome, and farsighted." If he did, the president pledged "the full power of the institution of the Presidency of the United States" would support him.[3] Bennett vowed to bring American Indians "to the forefront of the national conscience," stating that the tribal voice had for too long "been like whispers." It was time for this voice to be "raised in one chorus," Bennett added, as the federal–Indian relationship was at a crossroads.[4]

In an address before the National Congress of American Indians, Bennett urged tribal leaders to unify their voice to shape policies, programs, and laws. Tribal nations were in a position to increase their contact and relationship with federal agencies, and the time was at hand for them to once again negotiate as political equals with the United States and for the bureau to reduce "its day-to-day involvement" in their affairs.[5] At the same time, the bureau was under pressure by senators Henry Jackson (Democrat, Washington), Clinton Anderson (Democrat, New Mexico), and Frank Church (Democrat, Idaho) to press a full-fledged termination policy. Indeed, as part of Bennett's confirmation, the

Senate requested a report describing how Bennett would handle the challenges of Indian Country. While the Committee on Interior and Insular Affairs argued that if the bureau had prepared tribes to "go their own way more than a decade ago" they would now be prepared to go alone, Bennett replied that until Congress changed its political relationship with tribes, it had to "meet its responsibilities to [the tribes] of maximum social and economic development."[6]

Bennett was committed to the goal of tribes setting their own priorities, seeking to turn the bureau into a consulting agency, not a federal agency promoting the government's policy for Indian Country. When the Senate Subcommittee on Interior and Insular Affairs inquired as to the policy of the United States with respect to termination, Bennett was forthright: the tribes "will have to help us define [the role]." He covenanted with tribal leaders to foster decision making, accelerate and improve public school opportunities for Indian children, and assist tribes in expanding industrial and recreational/tourism opportunities. Whether Indians settled in urban centers where there were better educational and economic opportunities or remained on their reservations was a personal choice.

In 1968, Bennett announced that he was working to develop tribal capacity to assume "full responsibility for managing their own property and income," and that he was seeking to transfer "management responsibilities from the Federal trustee to Indians and Indian tribes."[7] Paternalism "must be a thing of the past," Bennett stated, as it was time for a policy of self-determination. President Johnson supported Bennett's vision in a March 1968 message to Congress when he called for "a goal that ends the debate about 'termination' ... and stresses self-determination."

Bennett heeded the voice of Indian Country and worked to eliminate the "stifling effects" of federal domination. In an address to the Governors' Interstate Indian Council, he reminded state executive leaders that "civil rights remain theoretical as long as economic exclusion continues."[8] The most significant obstacle to development was keeping tribes "in isolation from, rather than in relationship with ... the total community." If state and local governments corroborated with tribes, Bennett reasoned, state and local economies would also be strengthened. It was no longer practical for federal, state, local, and tribal governments to work in isolation.

The commissioner continued the poverty programs initiated by Nash but faced an Indian citizenry concerned about termination, with tribes continuing to view policies and agencies suspiciously when federal officials discussed turning over management to them. While Bennett was reticent to put out policy statements, believing they would limit what he might accomplish, he instructed his staff to follow his philosophy to its logical conclusion and support tribal needs. One of these changes was Bennett's support for locally controlled schools and the active participation of Indians in "all phases of community life."⁹

Bennett served at a time when Congress granted tribes a partial victory when it enacted the Indian Civil Rights Act on April 11, 1968, which amended Public Law 280 by mandating tribal consent before any state assumed civil or criminal jurisdiction over Indian Country. But while the act extended basic civil rights to all American Indians in Indian Country, it also limited the authority of tribal governments through the extension of the due process and equal protection clauses of the US Constitution to tribal governments.

With the election of Richard M. Nixon as president in 1968, Bennett chose to resign effective May 31, 1969. He left Washington, DC, and moved to Albuquerque where he directed the new American Indian Law Center at the University of New Mexico. He also remained active in the National Congress of American Indians and the National Tribal Chairmen's Association. Robert L. Bennett died at the age of eighty-nine on July 11, 2002.

Freedom of Choice

When I accepted the post of Commissioner of Indian Affairs, I expressed faith and confidence in the Indian people, their abilities and capabilities, and my firm belief that great things can be accomplished if tribal and Federal officials pool their best thinking. One of our first jobs is to demonstrate to tribal leaders that we mean business—that their suggestions, plans, and proposals are urgently needed. Indian intelligence and imagination are needed if we are to surmount the problems that have relegated many reservation dwellers to back row seats in the theater of modern life.

There is a new social and political interest stirring among Indians. [I]t is a positive sign that they are determined to take their place in our society as fully participating Americans—as Indian Americans—without loss of all the values they have so long and vigilantly guarded. And I am certain that in the years ahead the Indian heritage of this country will come to be regarded as a national treasure. It should not be otherwise.¹⁰

Our goal must be a standard of living for humans equal to that of the country as a whole; freedom of choice—an opportunity to remain in their homeland, if they choose, without surrendering their dignity, and an opportunity to move to the towns and cities of America, if they choose, equipped with skills to live in equality and dignity; and participation in the life of modern America, with a full share of economic opportunity and equal justice....

[I have] espoused greater Indian involvement in decision-making and program execution and emphasized the concept that the reality facing young Indian people in Indian areas is: they must learn to live in two worlds so as not to become the victims in either or both. Fifty percent of the Indian population is 17 years of age or under, although 50 percent of the general population of this country is approximately 28 years of age and under. Today's challenge is making Indian youth a positive force for good.

Indian culture of the past did not provide a place for the young person because he went directly from child to man. Wisdom was related to age, and silence among the young was a virtue. But Indian youth of today have been stimulated by education and enriching experiences. They must take their place among the youth of the Nation.[11]

Raising an Indigenous Voice
The war on poverty, and our strivings toward a Great Society, have brought the American Indian people into the forefront of the national conscience. There are organizations, such as the Indian Rights Association, which have for years plugged away in behalf of reservation Indians, but the voices have been like whispers under the din of other issues. The voice of the Indian people themselves has not yet been raised in one chorus, although there are signs that this is happening now.

We are therefore at a crossroads in Federal–Indian relations, and I sense that it may be the last cross-road wherein the choices remain wide and good. Let us, therefore, pool our best judgments in order to arrive at the destination all of us seek: A place in contemporary American history in which the Indian people may take as full a part in the affairs of this country as do other American citizens....

Secretary [Stewart Udall] said: "We cannot make policy and implement it on our own, particularly policy requiring appropriations or new laws. The Congress is our partner. As far as the Indian people themselves are concerned, I think they have been too content at times to make the Bureau a scapegoat. There has been too much timidity. I think that our Indian people must realize that the way to progress in this country is usually that of boldness and taking of risks, not of timidity. Several States and local governments are also responsible. The attitude is 'the Indian people are not our problem; let the Federal Government take care of them.'

I intend to . . . meet with . . . Federal administrators of Indian policy and the Indian people who are directly affected by policy decisions . . . [and] come back with more concrete ideas as to: "What is the Federal policy with respect to termination of Federal trusteeship responsibility for Indian lands?" On this point, I should say that the policy remains the same as it has consistently been over the past five years. But the gray area of what constitutes the proper approach is one which the Indian people themselves will have to help us define.

The second issue . . . involves trusteeship responsibilities, and deals with the multiplying heirship problem. Indian trust lands that are individually rather than tribally owned have, over the years, become fractionated into many non-economic holdings as the result of inheritances. The Bureau of Indian Affairs is bookkeeper. The bookkeeping is highly costly. . . .

A third point demanding attention is the status of Federal education programs for Indian people. What are the routes we might best travel to accelerate public school opportunity for all Indian children? At present, our Federal schools enroll about 50,000—or one-third—of the reservation Indian children. The remainder are in public schools, or, in a few instances, parochial or other schools. Our major school construction programs during the past five years have been in areas which are remote from public schools; and we have been concentrating upon elementary school construction. Is it advisable to attempt more of the 'peripheral dormitory' approach—i.e., establishing dormitories adjacent to public schools so that Indian children from remote areas may attend public schools? This is being done in some cases with respect to teenagers. But what about the little ones?

Another question [is] that of industrial-business development of Indian reservation lands versus an all-out effort to encourage migration outward into the centers of job opportunity. The ultimate answers must be the result of voluntary decisions by the Indian people. By an enlightened program of vocational training and job placement aid—which we have—it has been possible . . . to help . . . Indian people settle successfully in off-reservation communities. There are some Indian areas that offer very little promise in the way of massive commercialization. These are the areas that are removed geographically from the business and industrial centers. Development for tourist recreational purposes remains a good hope, but not necessarily the whole answer. On the other hand, there are some reservation areas that hold tremendous potential for varied economic development. But no matter what approaches may seem best as the result of feasibility studies . . .

there must be a comprehension on the part of the Indian people as to the nature of the national economy and the means they must take to benefit from our continuing economic growth. These fundamental questions—and other questions that arise out of them must become the focus of our attention.

The national conscience has been stirred by the plight of reservation Indians. We no longer need to "sell" Indians to the people of this country. What we need now is to draw the Indian people to the conference tables, together with the best minds in education and finance and community development and government administration. The paternalistic approach is good no longer. It has resulted, in its worst manifestations, in a culture of poverty, and even at best it encourages a dependency approach to life. This is not the way to fulfillment of the American dream. And surely the American dream of the good life, the active life, the life of self-determination, should be the fire to rekindle the hearts of the first Americans.[12]

Modifying the Role of the Bureau of Indian Affairs

The Indian people of this continent have traditionally followed their own instincts and clung to their own convictions through trial and strife. It is for organizations such as [the NCAI], made up of Indians, to foster the Indian spirit of independent thought. There is no need to fall into the pattern of racial agitation in order to attract attention. You already have the attention of this country. There is need, however, for some clear statements of principle, and for some constructive suggestions relating to Federal–Indian relations. . . .

First, there is the fact that the Bureau of Indian Affairs is no longer the one agency in Indian affairs. Congress has passed numerous laws in recent years providing a wide range of programs and services for all citizens, including Indians. These programs are geared to relieving adverse social and economic conditions among the poverty groups in our Nation. Indian people are now in a position where it becomes increasingly necessary to broaden their contacts and relations with other Federal agencies in order to take advantage of the new Federal aids.

The Bureau of Indian Affairs and other active organizations in the Indian field have found themselves in a position where traditional roles have become obsolete and new ones must be created to enable them to serve Indian people most effectively. The Bureau, in the past, has been both protagonist and antagonist in the eyes of Indian tribal groups. Now, with all the other sources of aid available, it should decrease its day-to-day involvement in tribal affairs. It should give way to a new role by tribal governments themselves—a role in which the tribal governments will be the negotiators with Federal aid programs. The Bureau of Indian Affairs, then, could become more of an advisory and coordinating agency.

Recognition must be given to the fact that new authorities are needed in order to broaden opportunities for Indian people to improve their social and economic status. Nothing is more important... than to accomplish a change in the policies and laws that are inhibiting the fullest development of Indian economic opportunity. This can be accomplished without jeopardy to existing protections now enjoyed by Indian people. I consider it my first obligation to the Indian people that such new legislation be formulated.[13]

Civil Rights and Ending Economic Exclusion
Our American society as a whole has assumed new dimensions within the past few years. The place of minority groups has been redefined—or, rather, the inherent rights of citizens, whatever racial minority groups they may represent, have been reinforced. But civil rights remain only theoretical as long as economic exclusion continues. This is frequently the situation in localities where American Indians constitute a significant and socially conspicuous minority.

Life among Indians today is often far more cruel than was the simple and primitive struggle of their ancestors for survival against the forces of nature. They are a people surrounded by a value system they must grope to comprehend because it is a value system that differs basically from their own tradition. Indians are generally oriented to the here-and-now, while the dominant culture is motivated by planning for the future. Beyond the cultural outlooks is also the difference in economic outlook between Indian people accustomed to a consumption economy and a people dependent upon a production economy. Still another factor contributes to the aloofness of Indians, especially the older ones; they still remember the bitter history of the 19th Century and find it incompatible with their experience to regard America's expansion era as glorious.

Alienated because of their cultural background, Indians are further alienated by their economic circumstance, and the alienation is accentuated by the attitude of the dominant cultural group toward people who are both poor and "different." But today's generation of Indians have found their voice, and demand to be heeded. They are expecting to be recognized as a minority group of citizens with all the rights of social and economic choice enjoyed by the majority. They are looking more in the direction of political and social action than ever before, and many are making their way in the once alien circle of State politics. They are looking to play a role in the determination of their own destinies within the States and local communities in which they reside.

[P]art of the trouble lies in the fact that States and local communities have consistently taken the attitude that Indians are a "Federal problem," wholly and exclusively. With the great financial contributions that States are receiving from the Federal Government for schools, roads, health programs, water, housing... it is difficult to understand how community planning can continue to exclude consideration of the needs, as well as the resources, of the Indian segment.

Few States have really encouraged Indians to participate fully in their political life; and many have been indifferent much of the time toward the general welfare of their Indian citizens. I am not suggesting that all of the Federal Government's responsibilities towards Indians should now be shifted to the States. I am intimating that most of the States have done too little too late to aid the cause of Indian development. Some States, worse, have missed what I believe to be the main point—that the economy of every State will be strengthened as the Indians are helped to develop their human and natural resources to the maximum.[14]

CHAPTER 48

Louis Rook Bruce

Commissioner of Indian Affairs (August 8, 1969–January 20, 1973)

WHEN ROBERT BENNETT resigned after the election of Richard M. Nixon as president, tribal leaders expressed concern with the president-elect, as many leaders had fresh in their minds the termination mindset of the previous Republican president, Dwight D. Eisenhower. Tribal leaders "waited for the axe to fall," but in the end they "were pleasantly surprised" with the policies of the Nixon administration.[1] But while the president committed to filling the commissionership with a Native American leader, he discovered most qualified candidates were Democrats. After a seven-month search, the president found his man: Louis Rook Bruce.[2]

Bruce was born on December 30, 1906, on the Onondaga Reservation to a Mohawk father and an Oglala Sioux mother. He attended on-reservation schools before transferring to, and excelling in sports and leadership at, Cazenovia (Methodist) Seminary where he earned a sports scholarship to Syracuse University. In 1930, Bruce earned a degree in business administration and psychology before going to work for the state of New York.[3]

While Bruce was not a well-known tribal leader, he had been involved in various tribal programs in New York and in Washington, DC. He was one of the founders of the National Congress of American Indians where he served as executive secretary, and he organized the first Native American Youth Conference in 1957 and the National Indian Conference on Housing four years later. Throughout his life he owned and operated a dairy farm in upstate New York while also working in a New York City advertising agency and as a community consultant. President Nixon nominated Bruce as commissioner on August 7, and he assumed office on August 8, 1969; three days later the Senate confirmed his nomination, just months before the occupation of Alcatraz Island and the rise of Indian activism.

Bruce surrounded himself with young Native American activists and advocated self-determination and Indian empowerment. Interior Secretary Walter

J. Hickel supported an increased voice for tribes, directing Bruce to restructure the bureau to encourage tribal empowerment. Bruce dismantled some of the bureaucratic restrictions that interfered with self-determination and set out to "assist Indians to develop themselves and their resources to the maximum."[4] In his first policy address to the National Congress of American Indians in October 1969, Bruce pledged to "develop a climate of understanding" that would permit "full development" of the tribes without termination.[5]

Bruce reorganized the bureau, seeking to make it responsive to the needs of Indian Country by supporting tribal decision making. He targeted a redefinition of education (prekindergarten to adulthood), tribal government, community services, and tribal control. He abolished bureaucratic agency superintendents and replaced them with field administrators before eliminating the deputy director and six assistant commissioners in the central office and replacing them with two associate commissioners of his own choosing.

Hickel and Bruce concurred on the direction they sought to bend federal policy, with the former explaining it was "time to stop thinking merely of 'economic development'" while the latter argued that the Great Society was "just not our thing."[6] Now was the time for tribal leaders to define policies that would govern them in the future, Bruce explained, with Indian decision making the only means of improving tribal economies and self-governance. "I want non-Indians to stop telling us what is wrong, what to do, and how it should be done," the commissioner shared with western Oklahoma tribal leaders, as he pledged Indian direction would henceforth be "the standard operating procedure" for the bureau.[7] Restructuring the bureau to support the tribal voice was his priority.[8]

Bruce advised President Nixon to define a new direction in policy, and on July 8, 1970, the president outlined his policy vision in an address to Congress in which he described why "the time has come to break decisively with the past and to create the conditions for a new era in which the Indian future is determined by Indian acts and Indian decisions." Federal policy had oscillated between termination and paternalism, with both equally harmful. It was time for a policy of self-determination "without the threat of eventual termination."

By fall 1970, Bruce deployed his policy priorities, beginning with the transformation of the bureau from a management to a service agency. He reaffirmed the trust status of Indian land, pledged assistance and training for tribes to assume control over federal programs—if they chose—and he incorporated protection of tribal natural resources by establishing an Indian Water Rights Office with representatives from the solicitor's office, the bureau, and the US Geological Survey.

To facilitate tribal capacity, Bruce offered a Tribal Affairs Management Program, with the bureau initiating training in 1972 for tribes to plan and manage their own development programs and administer day-to-day governmental functions. He utilized the Reservation Acceleration Program to enable tribes to negotiate changes in local bureau budgets to support tribal priorities, an early effort to make the Indian Service amenable to local needs. Bruce also worked with the newly established National Tribal Chairmen's Association to solicit input on policy and continued coordinating with the National Congress of American Indians to develop policy.

President Nixon supported Bruce's efforts to increase the tribal voice, but after the November 1969 takeover of Alcatraz Island by members of "Indians of All Tribes," a more militant voice emerged in Indian Country. By the following fall, the president asked for Hickel's resignation, with Rogers C. B. Morton confirmed as the new secretary of the interior in January 1971. Morton was not as supportive as Hickel and forthwith promoted John O. Crow to the reestablished position of deputy director "to tighten [the bureau's] administrative management," and he eliminated the two assistant commissioners Bruce had established.

The action resulted in a power struggle within the Bureau of Indian Affairs, with Bruce supportive of younger activists and Crow supporting the establishment. In October 1972, activists embarked on a national Trail of Broken Treaties, converging on Washington, DC, during the final week of the 1972 presidential campaign. On November 3, the activists occupied and then ransacked the bureau offices in Washington, resulting in complete disorganization of Indian affairs. Bruce personally met with the protestors in an unsuccessful attempt to bring the occupation to a close.

On December 8, President Nixon fired Bruce, who was caught between an evolving policy of self-determination and militant activism. Bruce left office on January 20, 1973. By then, Morton had vested all administrative authority of the bureau in Assistant Secretary of the Interior Richard S. Bodman. After he left office, Bruce established Native American Consultants, Inc. to support and guide tribal organizations to prepare for self-government. He remained in the Washington, DC, area until his death in Arlington, Virginia, on May 24, 1989.

Importance of Tribal Youth Being Engaged in Planning
As Commissioner I want to get Indians fully involved in the decisions affecting their lives; then to get the Bureau of Indian Affairs to be totally responsive to Indian needs; and to develop a climate of understanding

throughout the United States which will permit the full development of Indian people and their communities without the threat of termination....

I want to underscore...that I accepted the appointment of commissioner with the commitment and understanding that this administration was not going to become a termination administration and that I would have the fullest high-level cooperation in my efforts to reorganize the Bureau of Indian Affairs. I have been given these assurances....

Indians have had a unique relationship with the Federal Government since its inception. The core of this relationship has been the trust status of Indian lands. Because of the existence of the trust land status Indian tribes have continued to exist and [have been] provided some degree of continuity for their culture and some identity for their members. I... hold this trust sacred, not just because I am an Indian who has invested much time and effort to protect it, but also because I believe sound government policy dictates this view as derived from federal treaties, public laws, and court opinions. We propose to undertake an extensive study of the federal trust relationship to make it a more flexible instrument for Indian development while fully protecting Indian resources. I will invite Indian people, as well as other experts in Indian law, corporation law, and property law, to assist us in defining the best way to obtain this flexibility....

What I am emphasizing is the fact that a primary role for the Bureau staff will be to improve the conditions of American Indian people by utilizing resources from the public as well as private sectors. Under our administration, the thrust of the Bureau will be to advocate and create improved conditions of Indian life and to activate Indian involvement in all matters affecting their lives. In order to do this, we must have a Bureau of Indian Affairs structure, from headquarters to the agency level, which will support and direct the development of this role....

One of my special interests is Indian youth. They are the largest and fastest growing segment of our Indian population, and our greatest asset for the future of Indian people.... I am forming a special youth advisory committee responsible to my office. As we form our other committees, advisory groups, and task forces, young people will be asked to serve as an important part of these. We will be asking a number of young Indian people to work with us in bringing insights and understanding to their problems.

No one person can hope to achieve the many things I have [outlined]. It will require negotiations and building of relationships and commitments to

Indian people and their future and by the Indian people for our future.... To do all this, the Indian Commissioner must operate as a part of the governmental process bouncing on the tightrope, and yet keeping his feet firm, his eyes sharp, and maintaining the cooperation and support of this entire process and the Indian people.⁹

Controlling the Decision-Making Process
How do we make the trust relationship more responsive and more flexible, so it can meet the human needs of the Indian people? So that it is more effective in developing the maximum productivity from the rich natural resources to be found on Indian land? So that it can eliminate the scars of poverty from Indian communities and the Indian faces?

Indian development in decision-making is the only means by which this can be done and assured. I mean legitimate, formal, recognized grassroots Indian participation. I mean the kind of participation in which all tribal members turnout to vote on issues of concern at the local, regional, and national levels. I mean the kind of participation in which Indians volunteer and have opportunity to render their services on committees in their communities—school boards, recreation and economic planning committees, social service committees, and such other activities as they relate to ... everyday lives.

Meaningful, legitimate, Indian-directed and controlled involvement in these processes is not there—it can't be there—and it won't be there until effective mechanisms for it to work are provided. As it is, Indians have been "used" to legitimize the processes of bureaucracy. I do not intend to fall into this trap. I do not believe that Indian people want to travel down the same old road again. I do not believe they will accept it. And I intend to provide the leadership required to ensure that changes are made in the processes associated with Indian administration and its policies that will ensure productive Indian participation....

We Indians having been demanding the privilege of full involvement, and an opportunity to plan programs for our own destiny and that of our children.... The time has come for that to take place. I want to make it clear that the Bureau of Indian Affairs under my direction has no intention of laying out the decisions for you. I want non-Indians to stop telling us what is wrong, what to do, and how it should be done. We are as capable of deciding issues that affect us as are they—but we the Indian people must take the initiative.

Where are we headed in the immediate future? We are not standing idle. Every stone is being turned to expose that method that can best serve to install legitimate, formalized, recognized, Indian involvement in all activities of the Bureau of Indian Affairs, at all levels on a continuing basis. This requirement carries top priority and no other action will be taken until this is accomplished.... Indian participation and direction in all activities will be standard operating procedure in the Bureau from this day forth....[10]

Full Participation of American Indians in Self-Determination
I have outlined a four-point set of goals that seem to me to be the ones deserving priority effort from this moment forward.... Our goal is that each Indian community be given an opportunity to expand into an economically viable and socially progressive environment—a place that can pridefully be called home, a place that emanates the spirit of modern Indian America.

Our goal is that no Indian shall be relegated to the rank of unemployables because of lack of opportunity for training in occupations that are relevant to these times and relevant to Indian hopes. This means that the land and all its resources will be put to full use as a base for the Indian economy—in the spirit of the old Indian ways, but in the forms that are meaningful for today and the future.

Our goal is that every Indian child shall have the best education, suited to his needs and talents and interests, and that all the signs of the second-rate in teaching methods, curriculum, materials and facilities will be replaced.

Our goal of goals is to provide the base within Government and within the private sector for all Indians to be full participants in the planning and execution of all policies and programs affecting their destinies.[11]

The idea of self-determination—the right of Indians to make their own choice and decision—is ... becoming a reality as Indian people begin to assume the authority to manage their own affairs.... As the BIA is gradually being converted from a management organization to an agency of service, counsel and technical assistance, we are encouraging and assisting tribes in their assumption of program operations. We cannot and do not intend to force this policy on the Indian people. We are allowing them to decide whether they want to take over programs and, if so, how much responsibility they are willing to assume....

The response to this take-over policy has been a somewhat cautious one. Many tribes have waited to see how others responded and how the few tribes that have assumed control fare under the federal–tribal relationship. . . . Today we believe that all people should have the right to determine their own destinies. Unlike past programs which have all been designed to lead to Indian assimilation, the new BIA program directions deal with developing natural and human resources on the reservations, not off.[12]

CHAPTER 49

Marvin L. Franklin

Assistant to the Secretary for Indian Affairs
(February 7, 1973–December 4, 1973)

INTERIOR SECRETARY ROGERS C. B. MORTON did not immediately replace Bruce, instead appointing Marvin Lyle Franklin, a member of the Iowa Tribe, as an assistant to the secretary for Indian affairs, on February 7, 1973.¹ Franklin was born on July 18, 1916, in Ponca City, Oklahoma. He earned a bachelor's degree from Northern Oklahoma College in 1940 before serving as a fighter pilot during World War II. In 1955, he earned a law degree from Oklahoma City University and then was elected to the Iowa Tribal Council before being elected tribal chairman. Beginning in 1947 and continuing until his retirement, he served as an executive of Phillips Petroleum Company.

Morton established a new assistant to the secretary position and assigned to Franklin the responsibility for overseeing all Bureau of Indian Affairs' programs and functions, with a direct line of authority to the secretary's office. To his credit, Franklin did not sit passively, positing that the federal government had "exhausted the limits of existing [Buy Indian Act] authority" to provide tribes with opportunities to achieve self-determination and that now was the time for additional authority.² While he served as head of the Bureau of Indian Affairs for just ten months, Franklin defined grand goals for Indian Country, including establishing a national Indian advisory board.

To take self-government to the next level, the Nixon administration had prepared a series of legislative proposals, including elevating the commissioner of Indian affairs to an assistant secretary of the interior position to increase the visibility of Indian affairs. While not a new concept, the administration proposed a policy of tribes assuming control of bureau programs and enabling federal civil servants to transfer with the programs while retaining their federal benefits. The administration also proposed guarantees for loans to make Indian Country more attractive to private lenders while at the same time raising the ceiling to

$75 million for Indian financing. The president also proposed the creation of an Indian Trust Council to provide independent legal counsel for tribes to better protect natural resources and authorized tribes to enact laws governing trader licenses on reservations and providing penalties for individuals allowing stock animals to trespass on trust or restricted land.

Franklin outlined four objectives to lay the groundwork for the future of Indian affairs, including a constitutional amendment to lay "to rest once and forever the matter of termination." If self-government were to materialize, the assistant to the secretary stated, the United States could not take unilateral action without tribal involvement. Moreover, Franklin proposed a national banking system for Indian Country and an Indian Reservation Renewal Act that would provide $250 million annually for ten years to improve tribal economies. Tribal unity was essential, Franklin added, since the federal courts were engaged in an "insidious encroachment" upon tribal rights each year.³

Franklin also lamented the continued lack of understanding of American Indians on the part of the American public. This failure to understand tribes jeopardized their resources—human and natural—Franklin explained, since half of the Native Americans in the country were either not federally recognized or urbanized and "unjustly separated from [their] base of services." Equal treatment for all Indians, Franklin added, meant that urban and nonfederally recognized tribes should also be eligible for federal services.

When the Senate confirmed Morris Thompson as the forty-first commissioner of Indian affairs, Franklin continued to serve as an assistant to the secretary before returning to Phillips Petroleum. He retired to Oklahoma and died in Oklahoma City on January 1, 2016, just short of his one-hundredth birthday.

The Federal Obligation to Tribal Nations
The federal government assumed an obligation by treaty or agreement to a limited portion of the total Indian population. Many tribal groups are not federally recognized and are not extended the services of the Bureau of Indian Affairs. For the most part, those served by the government are those tribes having a land base in which the government has a trust responsibility. From this responsibility came the obligation for education and eventually a variety of services. . . .

The American Indian has a basket of mixed blessings in his relationship to the Federal Government. On the one hand, he has the resources of government to sustain him and provide him some degree of self-development. On the other hand, he is the victim of our political process. The Bureau of Indian Affairs is his only exclusive agency in government and while we hear a great deal about its omissions as expressed by the Indian community, seldom do we hear of the ill treatment it gets from the many agencies of government as it carries out the role of being an advocate for the Indian in general.

[T]here are four things I deem important to the protection of the American Indian and have laid the groundwork for their future development.

First, an amendment to the United States Constitution that lays to rest once and forever the matter of termination of Federal services by the unilateral action of any branch of government.

Second, a better opportunity for participation in the financial resources of our country. This can be done in three ways: an improved budget process, the use of revenue bond financing for physical improvements, and a national banking system for the Indian community.

Third, a massive Indian Reservation Renewal Act that would provide $250 million each year for ten years to bring not only needed improvements in the reservation properties, but simultaneously eliminate unemployment and within the ten-year period develop a "gross national product" for each reservation area. Today, the Federal dollar merely passes through the reservation without the benefit of being "turned over" to generate a local economy.

Fourth, a complete study of all laws, rules, regulations, codes and manuals that affect the Federal relationship to the American Indian.[4]

The First Steps

The Bureau of Indian Affairs . . . has run programs out of the Washington office and tribal groups have come into Washington for services. We feel it would be a little bit more efficient to have the central office consolidated into a lesser number of people in which it involves itself with policy mainly, and having 12 area offices throughout the United States which are located geographically so that they serve the tribes [by providing] technical and management assistance centers, with the main thrust of the BIA being at the local level through the agencies where the programs are delivered to the Indian people themselves. . . .

Our main goal is to develop this area where the tribal governing body begins to be the responsible agency to the tribal members with the assistance of the Government itself. These governing bodies then would be working with the local areas. We would recommend that each governing body have a member on an advisory board which would work at the area level.

We are also recommending that each of these tribal governing bodies consider the objectives they have for their tribes, setting up . . . authority within the tribe that may be appropriate, or an entity of some nature in which that entity has a relationship to talk to Federal, State, and local governments in order to provide the means of serving their people.

We also recognize that there are many things that can be done . . . [to] assist not only the tribal members but government in determination of policy in the future. So we are recommending that we take a representation from the membership organizations as well as the tribal government and form a <u>national advisory board</u> which can be helpful to the Congress and to the executive branch in establishing policy. . . . The self-determination policy . . . will open the door and permit the Indian to become involved in what is happening within his Indian community, in how his Indian community is involved with his neighboring non-Indian community, then within his state and finally within the United States. . . .[5]

CHAPTER 50

Morris Thompson

Commissioner of Indian Affairs (December 4, 1973–November 3, 1976)

IN THE FALL OF 1973, President Nixon settled on a candidate to lead the Bureau of Indian Affairs. On October 30, 1973, the president nominated for commissioner of Indian affairs thirty-four-year-old Morris Thompson, an Athabascan from Alaska.[1] Thompson was born on September 11, 1939, to a Koyokan Athabaskan mother in Tanana, Alaska. After graduating from Mt. Edgecombe High School, Thompson earned a degree in civil engineering from the University of Alaska. In 1966, he met the Alaskan businessman Walter J. Hickel, who was running for governor. Thompson supported Hickel, and when the latter was elected governor, the twenty-eight-year old Thompson was rewarded by being appointed deputy director of the Alaska Rural Development Agency. When President Nixon selected Hickel as secretary of the interior, Hickel brought Thompson with him, appointing him a special assistant to the secretary for Indian affairs. In 1971, Thompson was the first Native American appointed area director for the Bureau of Indian Affairs in the Alaska area office.[2]

Thompson was active in shaping the Alaska Native Claims Settlement Act of 1971, an act that resolved Alaskan Native claims within the state. He was confirmed as commissioner of Indian affairs by the Senate on November 28, 1973, and sworn into office on December 4, stressing his optimism that the nation was coming to grips with a "new awareness of Indian needs" and that the climate was favorable for "truly meaningful progress." The bureau was not "the total answer" to tribal concerns, Thompson stated, as the federal, state, and local governments had responsibilities as well. Thompson's primary focus was to "overcome the fear of termination" in Indian Country, viewing such concern as a "major barrier in the development of Indian resources, enterprises, and governments."[3] Thompson was the first commissioner of Indian affairs to report directly to the secretary of the interior.

In his first address to tribal leaders, Thompson opined that if all of the president's legislative agenda was enacted into law, tribes would "be further ahead in self-determination than we have been in 150 years."[4] He immediately called tribal leaders from the National Tribal Chairmen's Association and the National Congress of American Indians to Washington, DC, for a two-day conference on the organization of the bureau, its recruitment efforts for management positions, and budgetary goals. He pledged effectiveness and efficiency in bureau operations and called for increased tribal involvement in determining priorities.[5]

Thompson helped convince Congress to enact into law another of the president's priorities with the 1974 passage of the Indian Financing Act, which provided capital to Indian Country on a reimbursable basis to develop and utilize tribal resources, with Title I establishing a $50 million revolving loan fund and Title II including a $20 million loan guaranty and insurance subsidy.[6] But the most significant legislative enactment and the culmination of more than a decade of effort was the Indian Self-Determination and Educational Assistance Act of 1975, an act Thompson viewed as the commencement of a new era in the federal–Indian relationship.[7] The Indian Self-Determination Act was a watershed event in Indian Country, with the United States formalizing its obligation to respect and enhance self-government and its commitment to achieving "maximum" and "meaningful" tribal involvement for all federal programs in order to make them responsive and responsible to Native Americans by establishing a legal framework for contracting such control.

Thompson also unveiled a student bill of rights that guaranteed every child in a bureau or tribal contract school the right to an education free from unreasonable searches, guaranteeing reasonable privacy, with a safe and secure school environment, individual freedom of religion and cultural expression, free speech and expression, the right to peaceably assemble, petition for redress of grievances, and due process. He also clarified that the Department of Health, Education, and Welfare's financial aid package for Indian college students was supplemental to, not in lieu of, other financial aid. As a precursor to a religious freedom bill, Thompson issued protections for tribal members using federally protected bird feathers for ceremonial or cultural reasons.

On November 3, 1976, a day after President Ford's election defeat, Thompson resigned as commissioner, returning to Alaska to become vice president of Alcan Pipeline Company. He had assumed leadership of the bureau at its nadir, leading it out of the 1972 occupation of the Washington, DC, offices and through Wounded Knee and during a time when there were few Republican American Indians willing to serve, taking the department from fostering an idea of self-determination and transitioning it into a policy-supporting, rather than a policymaking, role.

In 1981, Thompson became president of Doyon Limited, an Alaskan Native corporation established under the Alaska Native Claims Settlement Act. When he retired in January 2000, Thompson had transformed the corporation from an operating loss to annual revenues of nearly $78 million. To celebrate his retirement, Thompson and his family vacationed in Mexico. On January 31, 2000, on the return flight, his airplane crashed into the Pacific Ocean off the California coast. Morris Thompson was dead at the age of sixty.

An Outline of a Policy
I am [not] an expert on Indian affairs, [as] there's no one who can make that claim. But I have plans and programs that will help build the future for Indian citizens, and I will need [the] help of [tribal leaders] every step of the way.

The Federal Government's policy today . . . offers self-determination and self-government to Indian people as rapidly as Indians want it and can assume responsibility for it. In other words, tribes have the option of assuming control of their own programs whenever they wish to do so. Furthermore, they will not be cut off from Federal support; they need only demonstrate strong and responsible tribal government and the ability to handle programs on their own. . . .

Federal programs have been transferred to [tribes] so that Indians themselves can shape their direction and manage their operation. This option will continue to be made available. In no cases will the Federal Government abandon its trust relationship with Indian tribes and groups.

Pending in the Congress, in varying stages of progress but not yet law, are 7 pieces of Indian legislation. . . . [I will] push hard for the passage of these bills. If they were all passed next week, we would be further ahead in self-determination than we have been in 150 years. . . .

One of these pieces of legislation is call the Block Grant Program. It would channel an additional $25 million in block grants to tribes for economic development. . . . [T]he single most important step in Indian self-help is economic stability on reservation. Any and all programs that strengthen tribal government, develop tribal resources, improve community facilities and create jobs for Indians will get the full support of the Bureau. Second in our priority list to economic development is education. It is [important] for Indian young people to be properly equipped to compete in today's world.

We are speeding up our education assistance programs and will continue to do so. Much progress has been made in Indian education, particularly in the last ten years. In 1960 only one-fifth of all Indians aged 25 and older had a high school education. Today the figure is better than one-third. Since 1950 the number of American Indians attending college has doubled.

Scholarships for Indians going to college have skyrocketed. In 1973 alone, some 14,000 Indian students are receiving scholarship aid. This is 20 times the score of ten years ago and 5 times the number receiving assistance only 4 years ago. More than 100 of these students are in law school, and another 100 are in other post graduate programs.

In my opinion, that's good—but not good enough. We need better education techniques, better qualified teachers, and more dedication on the part of everyone involved in Indian education. Our goal is quality in elementary schools, in high schools and in college education for Indians.

In land management and land awards—dear to the hearts of many Indians, this administration has a solid record of achievement. In recent years, Native Americans have received increasingly large restorations of land. The Taos Pueblo received 48,000 acres that had been part of Carson National Forest in New Mexico. In May 1972, in the state of Washington, 21,000 acres were restored to the Yakima Nation. Alaska Natives will soon begin to get one-twelfth of the land in their state and a sizeable chunk of cash as well under the provisions of the Alaska Native Claims Settlement Act....

Last month after years of effort on the part of Indian leaders and non-Indian Americans sympathetic to our goals, the American Indian National Bank was chartered and opened for business. This bank is the keystone of financial structure, owned and operated by Indians that will involve banking operations, industrial capital and insurance services to Indians throughout the United States. Although many people assisted in the project, the one man whose patient work over several years was most responsible for making the Indian bank a reality is... Marvin Franklin— my good friend and trusted advisor.

I intend to seek the advice and counsel of tribal leaders, individual Indian citizens, Indian Organizations, and [the National] Tribal Chairmen's Association. No one can do this job alone and there is a tremendous amount of work to be done, but we all know what the goals are....[8]

Indian people, their tribal councils and organizations fully involved in decisions that will directly affect them, and I want to establish better communications between the Bureau of Indian Affairs and the tribes and their members so that Indian groups this Agency serves can realize fully self-determination.

American Indians have the right to expect an effective and efficient Bureau of Indian Affairs. They have the right to expect that the money appropriated by Congress for Indians is spent wisely, and that each dollar directly or indirectly benefits Indians at the local and individual level. Indian people have a right to determine what the Indian priorities will be, and how they are to be met.[9]

CHAPTER 51

Ben Reifel

Commissioner of Indian Affairs (December 7, 1976–January 28, 1977)

WITH THE RESIGNATION OF Morris Thompson after the 1976 election of Georgia Democrat Jimmy Carter as president, President Ford made a lame duck recess appointment by nominating former South Dakota Congressman Ben Reifel to serve as commissioner of Indian affairs. Reifel was born on September 19, 1906, near Parmalee, South Dakota, on the Rosebud Sioux Reservation. He was enrolled in the Rosebud Sioux Tribe and attended school in Todd County before earning a degree from South Dakota State University in 1932, and then earning a master's and doctorate in public administration from Harvard University in 1952. He served in the US Army as a lieutenant colonel in World War II. He then began his career with the Indian Service as a farm agent on the Pine Ridge Reservation before working his way up to a tribal relations officer at Pine Ridge; he was later promoted to the position of superintendent of the Ft. Berthold Agency and later the Pine Ridge Agency.[1]

After a stint in the US Army during World War II, Reifel returned to the Bureau of Indian Affairs, being appointed Aberdeen Area director in 1955, remaining there until 1960. He then was elected as a Republican congressman to South Dakota's first congressional district, which included all of the state east of the Missouri River.[2] He was the only American Indian elected to Congress in the 1960s and considered himself a conservative Republican. In Congress he served on the House Agricultural Committee and later the Committee on Appropriations. He strongly supported Indian education, believing the isolation of Indian students was the primary cause of their limited success. In 1970, Reifel chose not to run for reelection, intending to retire, only to accept an appointment as chairman of the National Capital Planning Commission and to serve as special assistant for Indian programs at the National Park Service.

Reifel served as chairman of the American Indian National Bank from its inception in 1973 until he retired in March 1976. In December, President Ford asked Reifel to accept a lame duck appointment as commissioner of Indian affairs. He was sworn in as commissioner on December 7, 1976.³ At the age of seventy, he was the oldest man to serve as commissioner of Indian affairs, but he had little impact on policy. After Jimmy Carter was inaugurated as president on January 20, 1977, he asked for and received Reifel's resignation effective January 28, 1977. Reifel retired to South Dakota where he served as a trustee for the South Dakota Art Museum. On January 2, 1990, Benjamin Reifel died of cancer at the age of eighty-three in Sioux Falls, South Dakota.

CHAPTER 52

Forrest J. Gerard

Assistant Secretary for Indian Affairs
(September 12, 1977–January 19, 1980)

FORREST JOSEPH GERARD was born on January 15, 1925, on a ranch along the Middle Fork of the Milk River near Browning, Montana, on the Blackfeet Reservation. During the Great Depression the Gerard family moved into Browning so his father could work to support his family. After graduating from Browning High School in 1943, Gerard volunteered for service with the Army Air Corps in World War II, participating in thirty-five B-24 combat missions over Nazi-occupied Europe. After the war, Gerard took advantage of the GI Bill of Rights and became the first in his family to earn a college degree, graduating from the University of Montana in 1949 with a degree in business administration.[1]

Between 1949 and 1953, Gerard worked as a field auditor for the Montana State Department of Public Instruction before spending two years as a field consultant for the Montana Tuberculosis Association and another two years as executive secretary of the Wyoming Tuberculosis and Health Association. In 1957, he began a six-year stint as tribal relations officer for the recently established Indian Health Service, building an "extensive network of contacts" that would later serve him well. After serving as a congressional fellow for both Representative Al Ullman (Democrat, Oregon) and Senator George McGovern (Democrat, South Dakota), Gerard was hired as a legislative officer for the Bureau of Indian Affairs before becoming director of the Office of Indian Affairs within the Department of Health, Education, and Welfare.[2]

In 1971, Gerard made a strategic move when he went to work as a staff assistant for Senator Henry M. Jackson (Democrat, Washington), chairman of the Senate Committee on Interior and Insular Affairs and proponent of termination. Jackson was looking to rebrand his approach to Indian affairs and sought someone who had the confidence of the tribes. Having presidential aspirations, Jackson wanted Gerard to help him implement and coopt President Nixon's

Indian policy. Gerard agreed under the condition that Jackson support self-determination for tribal nations.³

Jackson empowered Gerard to oversee the development of a new policy premised on self-governance, with Gerard providing him with both the experience and a network of tribal relationships needed to consider and implement such a policy change. Gerard then guided Jackson in establishing a self-determination policy based on the principles outlined in the congressional message of President Nixon in 1970.

As a result of Gerard's influence, Jackson introduced—and the Senate approved of—Senate Concurrent Resolution 26 in 1971, halting the termination policy, reversing House Concurrent Resolution 108, and developing a federal commitment to enable tribes to determine their own future. Over the remainder of his career on Capitol Hill, Gerard fostered self-determination, including passage of the Indian Financing Act of 1974 and the Indian Healthcare Improvement Act of 1976, an act Gerard saw as the capstone of his legislative career.⁴ Aided by Gerard, Senator Jackson also initiated legislation to restore 48,000 acres of sacred Blue Lake to Taos Pueblo.

Gerard was a primary architect of the Indian Self-Determination and Educational Assistance Act, which was introduced to the Senate by Jackson in 1973. A revolutionary bill, the act was approved by Congress the following year and was signed into law by President Gerald R. Ford on January 4, 1975.⁵ Met with skepticism and distrust by many tribal leaders, the act launched the era of self-determination for which Gerard was belatedly recognized on the floor of the US Senate in July 2013 for his "dedication, intelligence, and persistence" that transformed the political landscape for tribal nations.⁶

Gerard shared a tribal goal of self-determination and self-governance that blossomed in the 1990s, and he worked to ensure that the tribal voice was heard on all policies affecting them. For this, he was a pioneering voice in Indian Country for tribes to assume control of federal programs and the funds necessary to operate them. In so doing, tribes were now accountable for the programs they operated and at the same time began building institutional capacity. When Congress established the position of assistant secretary for Indian affairs in 1977, tribes made forty recommendations, with President Jimmy Carter nominating Gerard for the position on July 12. The Senate confirmed him on September 12, and he was sworn in as the first assistant secretary of the interior for Indian affairs on October 13, 1977.⁷

The elevation of the commissioner of Indian affairs to an assistant secretary was substantive, as Gerard described in 1977. "Under the new arrangement, the

Assistant Secretary for Indian Affairs will not be absorbed in the day-to-day operations of the BIA," Gerard explained, but would be focused on the "overall policy" of dealing with the Interior Department, the Office of Management and Budget, and Congress.[8] While the commissioner of Indian affairs reported to an assistant secretary, he did not participate in the policy-making process. The assistant secretary, however, reported directly to the secretary of the interior and participated in and helped formulate the course of policy, giving Indian affairs a higher profile than it had ever had. Gerard not only established the role of the new office of Indian affairs, but he was also empowered to promote self-determination at the highest level in the federal government, viewing his role as encouraging self-determination while ensuring the federal government maintained its trust responsibilities.

Gerard encouraged, and President Carter implemented, a water policy that fostered negotiated settlements, a process the assistant secretary called "the rational development and protection of [tribal] water resources."[9] A year later, Gerard reminded tribal leaders that the matter of educating Indian children was now in their hands. "The generation of the 1980s will receive the benefits of the crucial federal–Indian policy changes of the 1970s—just as the legislation of the 1970s resulted from the unfinished agenda for racial and social justice in the 1960s."[10]

Gerard elected to resign on December 3, 1979, leaving office on January 19, 1980, to return to his private lobbying firm where he wanted to "prove that [he] could make it in the private sector." He was temporarily replaced by the Oglala Sioux Sidney L. Mills, who served as acting deputy assistant secretary for Indian affairs. Gerard spent the next thirty years advising tribes and tribal people on how to develop policy and increase their role in the political process. He retired to New Mexico and died in Albuquerque on December 28, 2013. He was eighty-eight years old.

Upholding the Federal Trust Responsibility
I am committed to three basic principles as assistant secretary. First, to strengthen the Bureau's capacity to fulfill its role as trustee; Second, to continue to aid tribal governments as they assume more responsibilities in the era of self-determination; and third, to improve service delivery . . . whether it be direct delivery through federal programs or through self-determination mechanisms at the tribal level.

Let's take the first point: trust responsibility. We are going to stand firm on treaty and other legal rights that Indian tribes have with the United States Government. I am going to take an active rather than a reactive position as to the trust obligation. And in order to accomplish this we are going to strengthen the capabilities of the Bureau to deal with trust responsibilities. This will mean increasing staffing in the area of natural resource specialists within the office of trust responsibilities. And I also will work to get additional staffing in the division of Indian Affairs in the office of the solicitor.

Now to strengthen the Bureau's capability to administer the trust take[s] money. I am willing to make some tough trade-offs in other program areas to accomplish this goal. One of the things I have been looking at . . . has been the travel of the headquarters personnel [and] I must say I am not impressed. . . . [T]here is much work to be done in Washington . . . and if I am going to act as [tribal] advocate in government I can only do it in Washington, not in an airplane. . . . And that goes for the entire headquarters staff in Washington. If they are going to represent [tribal] interests they have to be there to do it. . . .[11]

Th[e] trust relationship places a solemn, legal and moral obligation on the United States to protect valuable Indian lands and natural resources. It also places a responsibility on the federal government to assure that tribal governments are allowed to participate fully in the decisions that affect their reservations. These responsibilities cannot be taken lightly. . . .

In order to carry out these commitments I will . . . advocate for the Indian people, keeping in mind always the trust relationship. For the past 150 years the Bureau of Indian Affairs has been the agency in the federal government charged with carrying out the major portion of the trust responsibility to Indian tribes. Because of this long-standing role the Bureau has often been criticized for its seeming inability to carry out the trust and program responsibilities to the tribes. Although some criticism is surely warranted, the Bureau has not always been able to respond fully to all demands because of inadequate staffing, structure and resources.

Recently there has been an increasing awareness on the part of Congress and the Administration that changes must be made not only in the Bureau but in Indian affairs generally so that the needs of Indian people will be better served. Consequently, I want to see the Bureau moving toward an organization that would develop more comprehensive planning processes in order to achieve both short and long-range goals and objectives.

As a first step in strengthening the administration of Indian affairs . . . Secretary [Cecil] Andrus announced the creation of a new position—Assistant Secretary for Indian Affairs. This change of status provides an unparalleled opportunity for Indians to influence policy at the highest levels of the Department. The Assistant Secretary will participate more in policy formulation in the Office of the Secretary and will be more directly involved with the Office of Management and Budget, and the Congress. Never before in the long history of Federal–Indian relations has the head of the Bureau been so strategically placed within the Executive Branch....

My long-range view of the Bureau of Indian Affairs is one of an organization that will be seen by the Indian tribes as an advocate rather than an adversary; that will serve as a dynamic force in carrying out the unique trust relationship between Indian tribes and the United States Government; and that will fulfill its trustee and programmatic responsibilities to Indians.[12]

Elevating Indian Policy

I am convinced that with the new framework [of assistant secretary] we really have an unparalleled opportunity to deal with Indian policy at a level that has never been reached before in the history of Indian Affairs. In the past the Commissioner did not enjoy this kind of relationship at the policy level. For many years the Commissioners reported to the Secretary through one of the other assistant secretaries, so that there was always that control in between them. In this fashion the Assistant Secretary for Indian Affairs will be on a par with the other decision-makers who have a direct line to the Secretary. There will be a more direct line to the Solicitor.

I [will emphasize] intergovernmental coordination. First of all, I think we have to view that within two contexts: The positive context is in this regard. Prior to the 1960's Indian people and Indian tribes really had about one agency they could look to for services. That was to the Bureau of Indian Affairs, although the Indian Health Service had been moved out [of the Bureau] in 1955. As a result of the Nation's concern for poverty stricken who are depressed, landmark legislation was enacted throughout the 1960's. This created a multitude of new social action programs which became available to citizens in need. Indians, being citizens, qualified for many of those programs....

As I view the mission of the other departments and agencies, it is mostly national. However, the trust responsibility should be viewed as a government-wide responsibility. I think where we run into trouble with the other agencies is that they think more in terms of their national mission. It is difficult for them to focus down and deal with a lot of the unusual characteristics of the Indian field.¹³

By operating as an Assistant Secretary . . .give[s] one an opportunity to deal with his peers in other departments and to begin pointing out some of the specific areas where we might think about coordination. Economic development might be a good example. I find it a little difficult to believe that the Bureau cannot discover the fact that the Economic Development Administration, for example, is building a facility on some reservation that they are expected to help run in a later year. . . .

I would consider to be absolutely crucial would be to develop a strong intergovernmental relations component within the Bureau of Indian Affairs. Specifically, what I . . . have in mind here would be to . . . recruit . . . someone with a legal background—a tough, consumer-minded person. If we are going to play a coordinating role within the Bureau, then I think it is critical that we know more about the statutory base of many of the other programs and services in other departments. . . .

Importance of the Assistant Secretary for Indian Affairs
In the past the Commissioners were responsible for running the Bureau on a day-to-day basis. They were the men who fought the crisis syndrome. There are many of them confronting the organization each day. On the other hand, the key policy [decisions were] made by other people at higher levels. . . . The Assistant Secretary [will] not be involved so much with the day-to-day operations of the Bureau. That would be left to these key deputies and the team of people who share his views, his philosophies, and so on.

The Assistant Secretary, on the other hand, would operate at the departmental level out of the Office of the Secretary. . . . He would be on a par with those other Assistant Secretaries and the Solicitor. I think he would be more involved in formulating policy initiatives. For example, in the area of intergovernmental relations or coordination, it could be developed free of some of those day-to-day pressures. In addition, that person would deal a little more closely, perhaps, than the Commissioners have in the past with the Office of Management and Budget, which is a very critical element in our system of Government. That person would also deal a little more closely with the Congress and most certainly the Indian community. . . .

I think I would be remiss if I did not say that we are perhaps in the most difficult era in Indian affairs that we have faced since the Indian wars.

What I am alluding to here is the fact that many of our legal victories, ranging from fishing rights to the land claims ... have created new kinds of pressures on the Indian field. I think it is more important than ever that we have an organization that is responsive to these demands.... [I]t is going to be very important that we try to get some of these major claims behind us and settled in a negotiated fashion rather than long, acrimonious litigation, or rather to some hard-fought legislative effort. For too long the tribes and their respective members have been on the lower end of the totem pole. I think our real responsibility, now that we do have some policies in place that permit us to turn more of these functions and activities over to the Indians, is to get that kind of structure in place which will allow just that.[14]

CHAPTER 53

William E. Hallett

Commissioner of Indian Affairs (November 16, 1979–January 19, 1981)

WILLIAM EDWARD HALLETT was born on May 18, 1942, on the Red Lake Chippewa Reservation in northern Minnesota. After attending Red Lake public schools, he attended Brigham Young University for two years before graduating from Bemidji State University in 1965 with a degree in business administration and a minor in economics. He went to work in the Chicago Police Department before serving as director of housing for the Red Lake Tribal government. After an eighteen-month stint as director of industrial development for the National Congress of American Indians, Hallett joined the Department of Housing and Urban Development as an advisor, assistant director, and then director of Indian programs. President Carter nominated Hallett to be commissioner of Indian affairs on September 28, 1979.[1]

The Senate confirmed Hallett as the forty-second and last commissioner of Indian affairs on November 16, 1979. He was the first commissioner of Indian affairs to report to the assistant secretary of the interior for Indian affairs. Hallett served just thirteen months as commissioner and consequently had limited impact on policy, although he repeatedly emphasized the importance of the federal–Indian political relationship. He expressed his sentiments that the head of the Bureau of Indian Affairs was responsible for "one of the most supreme challenges" in Indian Country: fulfilment of the federal trust responsibility while at the same time ensuring tribal nations had the appropriate resources to regain self-governance.

Hallett believed tribal nations enjoyed a political recognition unparalleled in the history of the United States. He also recognized that tribal nations had the energy and natural resources to contribute to the country's overall energy independence and at the same time increase their economic well-being. The key was to ensure tribes were prepared for the coming "tidal wave" of economic development.

Hallett's main contribution was in setting goals for the bureau to enhance self-determination. He sought to make sure the federal government provided the resources to enhance tribal self-governance without stifling it. As importantly, he worked to preserve and enhance the federal trust relationship, a relationship, he reminded others, that was politically—not racially—based. Resources and support for the latter might be unilaterally terminated, Hallett explained, while the former was based on treaties, statutes, and court rulings. Self-determination implied independence for tribes to set their own goals while at the same time allowing them the "opportunity to make mistakes." Tribes would need flexibility to bend federal programs to meet their unique needs.

Hallett deployed several policy changes, including an affirmative action plan to recruit, employ, and promote Native American women to mid-and senior-level management positions within the bureau.[2] He also deployed a plan to generate more opportunities for Indian-owned businesses by modifying the definition of an Indian contractor from 100 percent Indian-owned to 51 percent.[3] The election of Republican Ronald Reagan as president in November 1980 signaled that Hallett's tenure was nearing an end. He resigned effective January 19, 1981.

After leaving office Hallett worked as a consultant specializing in Indian economic development before returning to work for the Red Lake Chippewa Tribe in 1990 where he oversaw economic development, including expanding Indian gaming in Minnesota. William E. Hallett was killed in an automobile accident on February 3, 1992, when his automobile slid off a road near Bemidji, Minnesota. He was forty-nine years old.

The Supreme Challenge
The commissionership . . . is one of the supreme challenges in the field of Indian affairs. The responsibilities and the tasks are enormous. This position affects the social, the economic and physical environments of more than 1 million Native Americans, Alaskan Natives, and approximately 500 tribal governments for not only today but for the many years to come. . . .

History has imposed a perspective upon the federal–tribal relationship that places [the commissioner] in a position few administrators in the Bureau of Indian Affairs have ever had to reconcile. The Native American world of this continent has now a recognition factor within the global community unparalleled at any other time in our Nation's [history].

As this country has awakened to the realization that energy resources are not limitless and that this continent does not have an endless supply of life-support materials, the remaining land held in trust for Native Americans and tribal governments has received extraordinary attention. The Bureau of Indian Affairs in its 155-year existence has not ridden such a tidal wave of economic and realty pressures as it is riding now....

Two Primary Responsibilities
The charge of the Commissioner is two-fold. First, is the delivery of resources and services that enhance the social, economic and physical environments of individuals and promote self-sufficiency and self-determination for and by tribal governments.... [R]esources and services... must be delivered in a responsive, efficient and effective manner. The term responsive is interpreted to mean a positive relationship with clients and entails program flexibility to meet geographical or other unique situations. The term efficient means the elimination of those processes, reports or requirements that are neither mandated by law nor serve a meaningful purpose.... The term effective relates to the achievement of the purpose of the program. Too often programs address the problems but not the cause of the problems. The second is the preservation, protection and enhancement of the Federal trust responsibility as it relates to estates of individuals and tribes for not only present but future generations.

The difficulty in carrying out [this] two-fold mission is immediately apparent. To say that the Bureau's only role is to deliver services is to misunderstand completely the basis for the relationship which exists between the United States and the tribes.... The relationship is a political relationship between governments. It is a unique relationship in that it is unlike the relationship which the United States has with foreign countries or with states. It is a relationship with political entities denominated "domestic dependent sovereigns," and its terms are spelled out in a myriad of treaties, statutes, regulations and executive orders....

The commitment of the federal government is that there is not going to be an end to the relationship. Through the Indian Self-Determination Act there was... a commitment to the maintenance of the Federal Government's unique and continuing relationship with and responsibility to the Indian people.... Despite this well-established relationship, questions concerning the status and rights of Indian tribes and the correlative responsibilities of the United States continue to be subjects of real confusion. The fundamental distinction must be understood by both the general public and those who serve in government. Too often American Indians are thought of as simply another racial minority group and their concerns are mistakenly placed in the same category as those of other racial minority populations. The very real threat that these misunderstandings pose today [could result in] an arbitrary termination of assistance to Indian tribes without regard to the Federal–Tribal relationship. . . . [I]f the Congress and the Administration are aware that the unique political relationship between the United States and the Indian tribes is the basis for special programs for Indians, then it will be with different considerations on the part of the decision makers that the special programs are terminated. . . .

Opportunity to Make Mistakes
I espouse the concept of self-determination for and by American Indians, Alaskan Natives, and tribal government. However, I recognize the harsh fact of reality that there is a direct correlation between the level of attainment for self-determination and one's ability to manage human, natural or fiscal resources. Self-determination infers an independence to establish goals and seek their attainment. Further it infers an opportunity to make mistakes, to learn from those mistakes, and involves certain economic and psychic risk. Self-determination can and should be a slow process, particularly when one considers the movement from over 150 years of dependence to independence and from a defensive to a futuristic planning posture. . . .

But tribes will never achieve full self-government until Bureau officials accept that tribes can govern [themselves]. Federal officials must also accept that self-determination . . . is a process and not an event.[4]

CHAPTER 54

Thomas W. Fredericks

Assistant Secretary for Indian Affairs
(November 16, 1979–January 19, 1981)[1]

THOMAS WADE FREDERICKS was born on March 3, 1943, in Elbowoods, North Dakota, on the Fort Berthold (Mandan, Hidatsa, and Arikara) Reservation. He was born into the Prairie Chicken Clan of his Mandan mother Catherine (Medicine Stone) Fredericks; his father was the rancher John Fredericks Sr. Of the nine Fredericks children, eight earned college degrees, with multiple earning advanced degrees, a testimony to Catherine and her belief in the importance of education. While a young boy Fredericks and his family relocated to Twin Buttes after the recently completed Garrison Dam began impounding Missouri River water and inundated the family's ranch. A member of the Three Affiliated Tribes, Fredericks graduated from Killdeer High School, earning a football scholarship to Minot State College where he graduated with a bachelor's degree in 1965. Seven years later he earned a law degree from the University Colorado, Boulder.

Upon graduation, Fredericks taught high school mathematics at Bowbells High School before beginning a three-year stint as an Office of Economic Opportunity administrator for the Standing Rock Sioux Tribe. In 1970, he successfully encouraged the University of Colorado to introduce the first Indian law class in an American university. A year later, Fredericks and Vine Deloria Jr. convinced University of Colorado administrators to allow the recently established Native American Rights Fund (NARF)—then housed in Berkley, California—to relocate to the school. Fredericks went to work as a staff attorney for, and then became chief executive officer of, NARF. In 1973, he was a founding member, and between 1973 and 1976 was the first president of, the National Native American Bar Association.

As staff attorney and CEO of NARF, Fredericks was instrumental in moving Indian law to the foreground of the American legal system, improving the political relationship between tribal governments and the state and federal governments. On July 12, 1977, President Jimmy Carter appointed Fredericks as associate solicitor for Indian affairs, a position he retained until November 16, 1979, when he was named assistant secretary for Indian affairs. These experiences, Fredericks later explained, gave him "a better insight as to the problems facing Indian people from a political as well as a legal standpoint."[2]

President Carter nominated Fredericks to succeed Forrest Gerard as assistant secretary on June 18, 1980. But while Carter had consulted with tribal leaders on the nomination of Gerard, he did not do so with Fredericks's nomination. Consequently, the National Congress of American Indians (NCAI) opposed his nomination due to lack of tribal consultation, expressing frustration with the "indifference" of the Carter administration toward Indian affairs. The NCAI was joined by the All Pueblo Council, among others, in opposing the nomination of Fredericks, with the Senate withholding confirmation.[3] President Carter then appointed Fredericks as deputy assistant secretary, enabling him to serve as acting assistant secretary for the remainder of his administration; Fredericks left office on January 19, 1981. His nomination formally returned to the executive office on January 22, 1981, two days after Ronald Reagan was sworn in as president.

Fredericks was committed to tribal participation in the making of all federal–Indian policy, going so far as to call for policy being developed on a "tribe-by-tribe and reservation-by-reservation" basis and based on land use plans reflecting the unique needs of each tribal nation. Such a policy, he argued, should be tethered to the principles of treaty rights and trust law to ensure the protection of tribal resources. And to ensure meaningful tribal involvement, tribes had to be brought into the discussion early before major policy decisions were already made.

Fredericks departed office as deputy assistant secretary on January 19, 1981. He then founded his own law firm, Fredericks Peebles and Morgan, LLC, in Colorado. By 2017, Fredericks Peebles and Morgan had offices in seven states and the District of Columbia, focusing on tribal natural resources, energy, and environmental law; sovereignty and government; and gaming and economic development. In 2014, he was recognized with the Lawrence R. Baca Lifetime Achievement award for excellence in federal Indian law. In 2017, he received the Spirit of Excellence Award from the American Bar Association.

A Tribe-by-Tribe Approach to Policy

The Assistant Secretary of the Interior for Indian Affairs has responsibilities in three areas. First, implementing policies of the Congress and decisions of the courts; second, recommending changes in Federal Indian-policy and programmatic authorities; and, third, guiding the many programs and services administered by the United States as trustee for the benefit of American Indian and Alaskan Native tribes and individuals....

Indian tribes have been hard hit by the economic conditions and resource demands affecting the Nation as a whole. During this critical time of austerity, it becomes more important that Federal agencies effectively and efficiently administer service delivery systems designed to meet the pressing needs and long-term objectives of the tribes. This approach must be carried out on a tribe-by-tribe and reservation-by-reservation basis with an emphasis on land use plans that fully reflect the unique situation of each tribe. Many tribes have sufficient resources to lessen their dependence upon Federal programs and to make self-determination a reality. This can only be accomplished, however, if the bureaucracy works with the tribal leadership to eliminate barriers which stand in the way of this goal....

Toward this end, quality and excellence must be the order of the day.... Once issues have been fully analyzed and appraised with the Indians involved, it is essential that firm decisions are made quickly with a full understanding of their potential consequence. The Indian community has suffered too long from indecisiveness [in] the decision-making process....

Indian policy is well established ... [with] a strong commitment to the principles of treaty and trust law and to the protection of Indian resource, cultural, and human rights. I am committed to this policy and to programs that lead to reservation development that enhances the tribal economies without disrupting traditional Indian values and without resulting in boom-town/ghost-town cycles. These programs must be designed at the local level and must be implemented as a cross-government effort. Many agencies in many departments have resources and systems well suited to meet tribal demands. Both tribes and agencies should be encouraged to coordinate these programs within the existing policy framework [and] I [will] work with the tribes and States in their efforts to achieve mutual consent agreements leading toward regional economic development and cooperation in the human services area.[4]

Tribes Must Be Involved in Setting Indian Policy
[T]ribes ought to participate [in setting policy] as a fuller partner with the Department in these important issues. When we develop policy, we are affecting the daily lives of the Native Americans.... Policy participation

ought to be at the reservation level where appropriate, or if the policy affects a particular region of the country, we ought to involve that particular region.... If policy is national in scope ... we could participate with ... a cross-section of the reservation communities, a cross-section of the regional representatives, and with the national Indian organizations.

[O]ne of the things that I would like to see a little more of is this. When we are going to initiate a major policy objective, I would like to ... utilize the Federal Register to serve notice, putting in a certain date to comment on a particular policy objective. Then take that notice and mail it to the tribes so that the tribes get an early start and can participate from the beginning of policy and are not reacting to a particular policy.... I want ... meaningful input at the beginning when we are starting to formulate a particular policy.[5]

Status of Tribal Governmental Authority
Recent decisions of the United States Supreme Court with respect to the nature, scope and limitations on the powers of tribal governments have raised almost as many questions as the Court has answered. Moreover, it has made such basic changes in what was commonly accepted as the law in accordance with lower court decisions that we are now in a time of reappraisal and of recharting....

The Court [recently] handed down three landmark decisions—decisions on questions so basic you would have thought they would have been decided long ago. In *Oliphant v. Suquamish Tribe*, the Court held that Indian tribes do not possess criminal jurisdiction to try and to punish non-Indians.[6] In *United States v. Wheeler*, the Court held that prosecutions by a tribe and the United States do not violate the double jeopardy provision of the United States Constitution.[7] And [more recently] the Court decided *Santa Clara Pueblo v. Martinez*, holding that the Indian Civil Rights Act did not waive tribal sovereign immunity and that under the Act habeas corpus is the exclusive remedy in the federal courts.[8]

Each of these decisions ... addressed questions which have been around for a long time. And in only one case, Wheeler, did the Court sustain a commonly accepted view. It held that tribal sovereigns are separate from that of the United States. Each of the other cases breaks new ground....

The Oliphant case ... raised [the question] if the tribes can't keep law and order on their reservations where non-Indian offenders are concerned, who can do so and whose obligation is it? The answer depends ... on whether any jurisdiction has been conferred upon a state by P.L. 83-280 or similar statute. If a state has not been conferred such jurisdiction, the jurisdiction over offenses by non-Indians against Indians is in the federal courts and the obligation to provide protection is that of the United States [via the General Crimes Act and the Assimilative Crimes Act].

An unresolved issue which Oliphant raises is that of jurisdiction over the so-called "victimless" crimes, for example, such crime as drunk-driving, disorderly conduct, reckless driving, and public drunkenness.... The question of which sovereign possesses jurisdiction over crimes between these categories—the victimless crimes—has become an important question. One way to handle the matter, of course, would be to consider the jurisdiction of the United States and the states to be concurrent. However, in all the cases decided under the General Crimes Act, no case has held that the United States and a state share concurrent jurisdiction.

A factor which must be considered in resolving the question of jurisdiction over victimless offenses is the point emphatically made by the Court in Oliphant, which in large measure underlies this decision that Indian tribes are dependent upon the United States for protection and gave up much of their sovereignty in exchange for that protection. The implication is clear that the United States owes the protection.... No statute has changed that obligation if it existed—except P.L. 83-280 and similar statutes....

Martinez involved the validity of a tribal ordinance which denied membership to children of women who married outside the tribe, while allowing membership to children of men who married outside the tribe. Mrs. Martinez challenged the ordinance as being in violation of the equal protection clause of the Indian Civil Rights Act. The Court did not decide the question of equal protection because it held that tribes and their officers may not be sued under the Act in federal court. Though the substantive rights afforded to individuals by the Act may not be indicated in federal courts, those rights are still in effect, and the Court by its decision has expressed confidence in a belief that tribes themselves can fairly administer justice....

A factor the Court felt Congress may have considered in not providing for federal reviews under the Act is that issues likely to arise will frequently depend on questions of tribal tradition and custom which tribal courts are better able to evaluate. The Court issued what seemed to be a Congressional invitation should tribes not adequately protect those rights. It noted that Congress retains authority expressly to authorize civil actions for relief in the event tribes did not apply and enforce the Act. [Therefore,] it is ... incumbent upon the Department to assist tribes in their present efforts to strengthen their councils and courts in their law making and law enforcing functions....[9]

CHAPTER 55

Kenneth L. Smith

Assistant Secretary for Indian Affairs (May 13, 1981–December 7, 1984)

KENNETH LEROY SMITH was born on March 30, 1935, in The Dalles, Oregon. A member of the Wasco Tribe, Smith was raised by his grandparents on Dry Hollow Ranch on the Warm Springs Reservation, learning the value of hard work and self-reliance, two pillars of his political philosophy. He attended bureau boarding schools before graduating from Madras (Oregon) High School, where he was elected junior class president and became a member of the National Honor Society. In 1959 he earned a bachelor's degree in business administration with an emphasis in accounting, becoming just the second Native American to graduate from the University of Oregon.[1]

Upon university graduation, Smith was named the Outstanding Junior Citizen by the Jefferson County (Oregon) Jaycees. Ten years later, the Jaycees named Smith as one of Oregon's five outstanding young men. In 1971, he received the Indian Leadership Award from Commissioner of Indian Affairs Louis R. Bruce, one of many awards Smith earned over the course of his career.[2]

Smith began his professional career in 1959 when he went to work for the Confederated Tribes of the Warm Springs Reservation. He began as an accountant before being named controller, assistant general manager, and then general manager; he also served as a tribal council member between 1965 and 1978. As a result of his leadership abilities, Smith was named to Task Force 7 of the American Indian Policy Review Commission in 1974, focusing on tribal resource development. Four years later President Carter considered Smith as his commissioner of Indian affairs, but Smith declined consideration.[3]

Smith spent twenty-two years managing the Confederated Tribes of Warm Springs, developing cooperative relationships with local, state, and federal agencies. Under his leadership, the Confederated Tribes developed and implemented a plan for economic development, including Kah-Nee-Ta Resort, the Warm Springs Forest Products, and low-head hydrogeneration that led to the Warm

Springs Power Enterprises, the first federally licensed tribal hydrogeneration facility in the United States. He also served on more than a dozen boards, including the board of directors for the Portland branch of the Federal Reserve Bank of San Francisco.

It was this forward thinking that led President Reagan to nominate Smith as the third assistant secretary of the interior for Indian affairs on March 30, 1981.[4] At his confirmation hearing in April, Smith stressed the need for strong tribal governments, with the Senate unanimously confirming him on May 13. As assistant secretary, Smith not only stressed strong tribal leadership but also advocated for tribes to establish stable governments in order to foster an environment of successful economic development in Indian Country.

Smith reminded tribal leaders that they had the "primary responsibility for the social and economic well-being" of tribal citizens and that the federal government would be diminishing its role in local, state, and tribal affairs.[5] He reminded the National Tribal Chairmen's Association that he would not "go back to the old paternalistic band aid approach that cover[ed] the symptoms and does nothing to address the real problems."

Smith influenced the Reagan policy, believing tribes not only had the ability to be self-governing but also had the responsibility to govern from within. As he explained: "tribal government . . . must be the foundation" of progress in Indian Country, with the federal government serving in "an important assistance role." In fact, Smith opined that the federal trust relationship would be stronger as tribes grew stronger and operated independently.

Not surprisingly, Smith was a forceful advocate for encouraging tribes to develop their resources to gain economic independence and engage in genuine self-determination, a position that did not always sit well with tribal nations, many of which viewed Reagan's Indian policy as a form of economic termination.[6] Smith, nonetheless, praised the policy as returning decision-making authority to tribal governments while not abdicating the federal government's trust responsibilities.

Smith remained assistant secretary through Reagan's first term, fulfilling his commitment to the president. He submitted his resignation on November 29, 1984, leaving office December 7. In his resignation letter, Smith explained it was time "to take on new challenges and opportunities."[7] Between 1985 and 1989, he served as a consultant to numerous tribes on economic development. In 1989, and continuing until 1995, he returned to Warm Springs to serve as chief executive officer of the Confederated Tribes, establishing a number of new enterprises, including a cultural center, an early childhood center, Indian Hand Casino, and a shopping plaza. Kenneth L. Smith died at his home on the Warm Springs Reservation on May 13, 2020, at the age of eighty-five.

Empowering Tribes to Engage in Self-Government
The challenge to Indian affairs lies in forming a policy which is commensurate with the restraint that must be exercised to restore stability to [the tribal] economy and which, at the same time, continues the progress that we have seen in the last 10 years....

First, I believe in the strengths of Indian people which have enabled them to endure and survive as a people through adversities and oppressions unparalleled in history.

Second, I believe Indian people have the will and the ability to self-govern and exercise wisely their remaining sovereign powers within the framework of the federal Indian relationship.

Third, I believe that the fulfillment of hopes and aspirations of the Indian people and their tribal governments must come from within, from their own will and determination.

Fourth, I believe Indian people and their tribal governments, not the Federal Government, have the prime responsibility for improvement of their social and economic growth and development.

Fifth, I believe the proper role of the Bureau of Indian Affairs and other Federal agencies with their limited funding, is to encourage and foster an atmosphere that will enable tribal governments to move toward less dependency on the Federal Government as they seek to improve the social and economic conditions of their people.

Sixth, I believe the goal of moving tribes away from dependence on the Federal Government is in complete accord with the existing government-to-government relationship and does not in any manner diminish or alter the Federal trust responsibility.

And seventh, I believe the governmental trust relationship will be stronger and more meaningful when Indian tribal governments are stronger and stable and less dependent on Federal funds for operation of their governmental programs.[8]

A Commitment to Strengthen Tribal Governments
Two years ago ... I stressed ... the need for strengthening tribal governments and lessening the dependence on the Federal government. I said then that I thought any genuine economic development required strong, stable

self-government. And I expressed my faith in the ability of Indian people to meet the challenge of assuming real governmental responsibilities.

I have not changed in my philosophy or beliefs. I know now much more about the difficulties of making changes in and through federal government agencies. I am also more aware of the variety and complexity of problems encountered on Indian reservations. The solutions are not quick and ready. I remain convinced, however, that tribal government, rather than the federal bureaucracy, must be the foundation on which reservation progress and achievement will be built.

To inform tribes that we are serious about using [federal] resources wisely, I have initiated a management by objective plan for resource management and development.... The plans call for an assessment of the [tribes'] economic resources and the development potential which will enable the tribes to plan for future development of their natural resources based on economic modeling. As a result, the needs for this development and management are identified and targeted to coincide with the planned development rather than [on] an ad hoc basis. The federal government has an important assistance role—but it must be auxiliary to that of the tribal government.

The philosophy I talked about two years ago has now been formally adopted and enhanced by President Reagan and established as the basic Indian policy of the United States.... This policy emphasizes [a] commitment to encourage and strengthen tribal government and makes the policy of self-determination a reality. It calls for the removal of obstacles to self-government and the creation of a more favorable environment for development of healthy reservation economies. The policy reiterates that the federal government will continue to fulfill its traditional responsibility for the physical and financial resources held in trust for the tribe and their members....

[Such] a policy statement, of itself, does not effect changes in the day-to-day life on reservations. But it sets a direction and gives impetus to actions that do bring change. Ideas have consequences in that humans usually manage to achieve whatever they can conceive as possible. The President's policy statement is, I believe, a powerful force in the movement toward self-government and self-sufficiency for Indian tribes.[9]

CHAPTER 56

Ross O. Swimmer

Assistant Secretary for Indian Affairs
(December 5, 1985–January 29, 1989)

WITH THE RESIGNATION OF Kenneth Smith, Deputy Assistant Secretary John Fritz served as acting assistant secretary until President Reagan nominated Ross Owen Swimmer, an attorney and principal chief of the Cherokee Nation, as the fourth assistant secretary for Indian affairs on September 26, 1985.[1] Swimmer was born on October 26, 1943, in Oklahoma City, Oklahoma, to a father who was a Cherokee attorney. After graduating from Putman (Connecticut) High School in 1961, he earned a degree in political science from the University of Oklahoma in 1965 and a juris doctorate in 1967. He then became a partner at Hanson, Peterson and Thompkins, an Oklahoma City law firm where he remained for five years. While there Swimmer did pro bono work for the Cherokee Nation Housing Authority, opening the door for Swimmer to become general counsel for the Cherokee Nation.[2]

In 1974, Cherokee Chief William Wayne Keeler announced he would not seek reelection, encouraging Swimmer to run for the office. That fall, the thirty-one-year-old Swimmer was elected principal chief of the Cherokee Nation, beginning a rebuilding of tribal government and Cherokee economic infrastructure. That same year, Swimmer became vice president, and then president, of the First National Bank in Tahlequah. He was elected to four terms as principal chief, leaving office midterm in 1985 when President Reagan nominated him as assistant secretary for Indian affairs. Two years earlier, the president appointed Swimmer cochair of the Presidential Commission on Indian Reservation Economies, providing Swimmer with a deeper insight into the challenges facing Indian Country and further shaping his political philosophy. Swimmer was confirmed by the Senate on December 4, 1985, and took office a day later in the midst of additional federal budget cuts.

Shortly after being sworn in, Swimmer addressed bureau staff by informing them their object was "to work themselves out of a job. [Tribes] don't need the BIA; we need to plan ten years from now [for when] we've worked ourselves out of a job."³ Tribes expressed concern that the president and the new assistant secretary might abolish the bureau, notwithstanding Interior Secretary Donald Hodel's assurances to the contrary. Swimmer informed tribal leaders that if they desired strong and effective governments, they needed to develop robust economies. Tribes could no longer be "islands surrounded by the rest of America," Swimmer explained, and they could no longer rely on automatic federal budget increases. Funds might be available but only to tribes "willing to accept the challenge of economic, political, and social development."⁴

Swimmer believed that fundamental changes were necessary to fulfill the tribal goal of self-determination. Despite myriad commissions seeking to solve the challenges facing Indian Country, the only consensus was the need for economic development and a desire of tribes to set their own goals. The federal government had to "give the tribes the responsibility they seek," the assistant secretary stated in 1987, as he described the perpetual clash between paternalism and self-determination. "One must give way in order for the other to survive." The Bureau of Indian Affairs was expected to "address almost every social and economic ill known to mankind," Swimmer noted, an "overwhelming" task that was complicated by a lack of consensus as to what the priorities should be.⁵

Swimmer supported the president's goal of reducing regulatory restrictions to enable tribes to develop their economies. He encouraged Congress to help identify bureau functions related to trust resource management and then to transfer such functions to other federal agencies better qualified to carry them out. As for nontrust assets, Swimmer advocated Congress authorize self-determination grants through which tribes would receive federal dollars with complete autonomy to determine which programs to fund. If tribes chose not to contract for such services, the bureau would continue to provide them, or tribes could contract for programs and then subcontract them back to the bureau to fulfill.

As the Reagan administration wound down, Swimmer announced his resignation on September 22, 1988. He left office on January 29, 1989, days after George H. W. Bush took office as president. Bush then named William P. Ragsdale of the Cherokee Nation as acting head of the Bureau of Indian Affairs while he began a search for the next assistant secretary. Swimmer, meanwhile, returned to the private sector, being invited by the Citizen Potawatomie Tribe to serve on its board of directors for the First National Bank and Trust Company. He also served as president of the Cherokee Group LLC between 1995 and 2001, encouraging economic development and self-governance in Indian Country.

On November 26, 2001, President George W. Bush appointed Swimmer director of the Office of Indian Trust Transition. Fourteen months later, Bush nominated Swimmer as first special trustee for American Indians, with the Senate confirming his nomination on April 17, 2003. As special trustee, Swimmer viewed his responsibilities as ensuring that "tribal trust funds [were] accounted for, paid out as the tribes' desire[d], and [were] properly managed."[6] Swimmer remained special trustee until January 19, 2009. He then retired from public life to his native Oklahoma.

An Impossible Task

The Bureau of Indian Affairs is a microcosm of activities benefitting Indians that are generally provided for non-Indians by the local, state and federal governments. From education programs to trusteeship of tribal lands, natural resources, and monies, the Bureau's scope is enormous. . . . I have shared the frustration of waiting for months, even years, for the Bureau to respond with a definite answer on a variety of issues. I have observed reorganizations come and go but attitudes that remain the same. I have also observed some very hard working, dedicated servants of the Indian people that have brought tribes into an era of responsibility, self-sufficiency and commitment. . . .

Bureau employees face the challenge of being grant administrators and . . . contract monitors under P.L. 93-638. They seek economic growth through development of Indian natural resources while demanding environmental protection and exclusion of sacred grounds from development. The Bureau spends millions of dollars on education programs, yet seems unable to cope with problems such as literacy rates, substance abuse, dropouts and social development. These are but a few of the conflicts within the Bureau that must be addressed. . . .

Regular consultation with tribal leaders is necessary if we are to accomplish the goals of Congress, the Administration and Tribes. [There is a need] to visit frequently with the elected leadership in Indian Country and the leaders of the national Indian organizations so that issues can be negotiated and resolved in a satisfactory manner. . . .

The Bureau of Indian Affairs should continue encouraging tribes to take more responsibility by contracting programs that are now run by the Bureau. An integral part of any government is the responsibility to raise money and spend it as is needed for the common welfare of its citizens. Much of the money tribes have access to is now spent by the Bureau instead of tribes. We must also realize that some tribes will not move as fast as other tribes toward self-government and we have to be patient. We need to move at the tribe's pace and be aware of the unique circumstances of each tribe. On the other hand ... we should encourage and stimulate movement of tribes toward self-government and self-sufficiency through regulations and incentives that reward the tribes that take on these additional responsibilities.[7]

Need to Involve All Federal Agencies
With the exception of national defense and health care, some form of virtually every other federal, state and local program is found in the Bureau of Indian Affairs: BIA operates schools and colleges, police departments, courts, social services, job training and employment programs. It acts as a bank for deposits, payments, investments and credit programs, and as a trustee of tribal and individual Indian assets. The Bureau oversees forests and fisheries, and irrigation and power systems. It employs experts in mining and minerals, and agriculture and archeology. The Bureau builds houses, dams, roads, schools, and jails. Bureau employees operate programs while preparing to work themselves out of a job by providing training and technical assistance to allow tribal contracting. . . .

The Bureau of Indian Affairs is expected to address almost every social and economic ill known to mankind through approximately 100 discrete programs. The BIA provides services to almost 500 tribes and Alaska Native groups in 30 states from California to Maine. Rather than asking why there are problems in the operation of Indian programs, we should ask how anyone can realistically think that one Bureau could fulfill such expectations.

If a member of Congress requests funds to expedite cadastral surveys in his state, the Committee does not add the money to the Smithsonian budget—it goes to the BLM because they have the expertise. Funds to increase reforestation efforts go to the Forest Service, not the Bureau of Mines. Yet, if these activities were proposed for Indian country, the money would not be added to the Bureau of Land Management or the Forest Service but to the budget of the Bureau of Indian Affairs—not because we have the best surveyors or the best foresters, but simply and solely because it is an Indian project.

We are all responsible for this anomaly: the Administration, the Congress, and the Indian tribes. No one identifies a need in Indian country and then asks which Federal agency is most capable to do the job. If it's not health related, the responsibility is usually given to the Bureau. There are obvious reasons for this. We want to hold someone accountable; we want to be able to readily identify expenditures for Indian programs; and we want to ensure that within the competing demands for Federal services, the voice of the Indian people is heard.... The Bureau is often criticized for not meeting all of its responsibilities but those responsibilities have become truly monumental, and in some cases, conflicting.

Even with all these duties, it might be possible for the Bureau to operate in a manner which meets with the approval of the Administration, the Congress, and the tribes–if everyone could agree on the priorities. What is the most important program of the Bureau—where should we concentrate most resources and energies? What program is second on the list? I would suggest that if you posed that question ... to each tribe and each Member of Congress with an interest in Indian affairs, that you wouldn't get a dozen identical lists. There simply is no agreement on the priorities of the Bureau of Indian Affairs. No agreement among tribes, members of Congress, or even among employees of the Bureau. Without such consensus among those who pass the laws, those who are charged to carry out the laws and those whom the laws are designed to serve, how much of the fault can really be laid on the management of the Bureau...?

We recognize that the Congress is sincere in its desire to help Indian people.... I would agree that the administration of Indian programs has been and continues to be plagued with many problems, program deficiencies and shortcomings. I have tried, and will continue to try, to work with Congress and the Indian tribes to resolve these issues. Having served as a tribal chairman for years, when I came to Washington, I had some ideas on changes that could be made to improve Bureau operations. A number of these ideas ... met with approval of the Secretary and the Administration: placing control of education programs at the local level; combining a number of disparate programs to create a unified job training–job creation effort as an alternative to welfare; standardizing contract support payments, while including a subsidy to stabilize funding to small tribal governments; and, securing competent, professional, private sector assistance to properly manage one and one-half billion dollars in trust funds. Unfortunately, the Bureau apparently did not present a sufficiently compelling case for adoption of these recommendations, as most have met with strong opposition....

Trust Assets

[I am] prepared to make two very basic recommendations which ... will require time and effort, but it is an effort the Department is willing to make if the tribes and the Congress will do the same.... The development of specific recommendations will require coordination with other affected executive branch agencies prior to submission of an Administration proposal.

First, we should specifically identify those federal programs which deal with the management of Indian trust resources, i.e., lands, mineral resources, and trust funds. Trust programs need to be distinguished from other programs which may be necessary and important, and which may meet very real needs, but do not involve the management of trust assets. I would not argue against the need for other programs in addition to those necessary to fulfill trust responsibilities but "need" does not necessarily equate with "trust responsibilities."

We should then determine if there are other agencies of the Federal Government more capable to upgrade and carry out the various program functions involved in the management of trust assets. These programs should not reside solely within the Bureau of Indian Affair[s]—it is a responsibility of the entire Federal Government to ensure that the best available services are provided in connection with the management of Indian lands, resources and trust funds.

The Bureau of Indian Affairs and the Indian Health Service are subject to "Indian preference" in hiring and promotion of employees. I fully subscribe to the intent of Indian preference, and feel that the fact that 83 percent of BIA employees are Indians is proof of our sincere attempts at compliance, but it should be examined in context of changed conditions. Less than one-half of one percent of the population of the United States meets the requirements to be extended Indian preference in Federal hiring. I have been told that of the working-age population, only 47,000 Indians have completed college. The BIA, IHS, national Indian organizations, some Committees of Congress, and hundreds of tribal governments are all competing to obtain the best of a very small workforce. And, of course, not all Indians are interested in working for either the Federal government or tribal governments. Congress has allowed tribal contractors operating programs with Federal funds to waive Indian preference. At a minimum, I think we need to review the categories of employment where we currently have, or are projecting, a shortage and be granted waiver authority at the Federal level.

Autonomy and Self-Governance

The following recommendation concerns the operation of all other programs which have not been specifically identified through the foregoing process. Our recommendation is that there be only one other category in the Bureau's budget—true self-determination is limited to allowing tribes to contract for programs which the Bureau has operated in the past. And the tribes are supposed to run the programs in much the same way as the Bureau had, being held to the same requirements and regulations. If, for instance, a tribe spends education funds on a social services program that cost would most likely be disallowed under an audit and the Bureau would be directed to recoup those funds from the tribe. It doesn't matter that the need is real and the funds were put to good use. It only matters that the expenditure was outside the scope of the contract. This occurs because of the large number of separate programs the Bureau is required to operate, since notwithstanding the rhetoric of self-determination, both the Administration and the Congress want to know exactly how much we are spending on every conceivable activity in Indian country.

A formula should be established as the basis for the distribution of these self-determination funds. Since the Bureau's budget is based largely on historical spending, including tribal-specific increases over a number of years, there is currently a great disparity in funds available to similarly situated tribes. In establishing the formula, [I] suggest that it be based primarily on a per capita distribution, with some adjustment for small tribes and perhaps an adjustment for tribes which have no economic or natural resource base....

With these self-determination funds the tribes would have complete autonomy in determining what programs would be provided. Tribes not wishing to operate the programs directly could contract with the Bureau to operate the programs for them. Thus, rather than having programs which the tribe can contract from the Bureau, the tribes could design their own programs and contract them to the Bureau, or if they chose, to another

Federal or local agency.... Once the statutory responsibilities were defined and staff resources identified to meet these responsibilities the size of the BIA workforce would be a result of specific tribal requests for services. It would be necessary to establish some broad parameters in that the use of the funds would have to be legal; that it comport with certain minimum standards with respect to protection of individual rights and public safety; that programs contracted to the Bureau not include requirements which civil servants are not otherwise allowed to perform; and that sufficient advance notice be given for any new program to be contracted to the Bureau so that appropriate staff could be made available....

I do not underestimate the time and effort that would be involved in reaching a consensus with the tribes and the Congress in identifying those specific activities required to meet the statutory responsibility, or in devising a fair way to distribute the remaining federal resources. Such an undertaking could, however, profoundly affect the way the Bureau of Indian Affairs currently operates and would better enable the Department and the Bureau to carry out their responsibilities once we have all agreed on exactly what those programs should be.

It would also provide much needed changes by making self-determination truly meaningful. Responsibility would properly be placed at the tribal level for the design and oversight of programs that respond to local needs.... A policy statement without a concomitant change in structure and direction to implement the policy has hampered the ability of the Federal government to meet the raised expectations of the Indian people.

True self-determination cannot be limited to programs designed 50 years ago—or even those designed 15 years ago. Those programs and delivery systems represent Washington's view of what is needed or what will work on reservations; and being Bureau-wide programs, they also operate on the assumption that what works on the Navajo Reservation should work on the Mississippi Choctaw Reservation. True self-determination must mean more, and it is time to revisit the concepts of self-determination and self-government—not merely to tinker with the law which maintains a contractual relationship between the Bureau and the tribes within the limitations imposed by pre-established funding levels for specific programs. It is time to give the tribes the responsibility they seek.[8]

CHAPTER 57

Eddie F. Brown

Assistant Secretary for Indian Affairs (June 26, 1989–July 16, 1993)

EDDIE FRANK BROWN was born on December 26, 1945, in Ajo, Arizona, a border town near the Tohono O'odham Nation. The youngest of eight children born to Homer Brown and Julia Leon Valenzuela, Brown is an enrolled member of the Pascua Yaqui Tribe and affiliated with the Tohono O'odham Nation. He earned a bachelor's degree in social science from Brigham Young University (BYU) in 1970 and master's and doctorate degrees in social work from BYU in 1972 and 1975, respectively. After a brief tenure as assistant professor at the University of Utah, Brown in 1975 became assistant professor at Arizona State University's Graduate School of Social Work.

Brown then went to work for the state of Arizona as assistant director for the Department of Economic Security, where he won acclaim for his ability to work with state, tribal, and federal agencies. In 1985, he accepted a position with the Bureau of Indian Affairs in Washington, DC, as the head of the Social Services Division. He then returned to Arizona State University before joining the Arizona Department of Economic Security as its director in 1987. On April 13, 1989, President George H. W. Bush nominated Brown as the fifth assistant secretary for Indian affairs; he was unanimously confirmed on June 21 and took office on June 26.

Brown emphasized education, economic development, trust reform, and self-governance, placing education at the top of his agenda. He initiated background checks and "pledged . . . to hire the best qualified staff to fill Bureau schools," including the position of director of Indian education. To mitigate the "deplorable conditions" at many bureau schools, Brown proposed to move education into a separate Office of Indian Education, a move Congress blocked until Brown appointed a task force to evaluate how the bureau should be structured.[1] Brown also accelerated funding for the $550 million backlog of repairs and maintenance of bureau facilities, although Congress was reticent to appropriate the necessary funds.

To facilitate economic development, Interior Secretary Manuel Lujan formed a Working Group on Indian Water Rights to establish principles to guide settlements, linking agreements with overall national water resource management and conservation. The group facilitated a series of water rights settlements across the West in the 1990s. The driver of federal policy remained economic development, with Brown informing tribal leaders there was "no single magical formula that would solve unemployment and poverty."[2]

By summer 1990, Lujan and Brown announced "a new chapter giving form and substance" to self-government. In a series of agreements with the Quinault Nation, Lummi Tribe, Jamestown Clallam Tribe, Hoopa Valley Tribe, Cherokee Nation, and Mille Lac Band of Chippewa, the bureau established pilot self-governance agreements enabling tribes to gain authority for budgeting and spending bureau funds with annual funding agreements defining the scope of services. For the first time, tribes were afforded latitude to modify federal programs to meet their unique needs.

Brown was a strong proponent of intergovernmental cooperation, recognizing the role of tribal, federal, state, and local governments. But he also believed the government closest to the people was best able to provide for their needs. Change was inevitable, Brown asserted, as self-government was the new norm, with intergovernmental cooperation a key component. All the while the federal trust responsibility had to remain resolute but without stifling tribal responsibility.

Brown urged Congress to expand the policy of entering into annual funding agreements that would enable tribal nations to direct their own affairs while at the same time ensure federal support for tribal governments. In the process, a policy of New Federalism began to take shape. Self-governance through voluntary agreements would enable tribes to assume responsibility for self-government, with federal assets and appropriations transferred to tribes under written compacts. The pilot project proved such a success that on October 25, 1994, Congress amended the Indian Self-Determination Act and authorized tribal self-governance.[3]

Under self-governance, Congress authorized the secretary of the interior to select up to twenty tribes annually to participate, and using annual funding agreements, it enabled tribes to "plan, conduct, consolidate, and administer programs, services, functions, and activities" then operated by the Department of the Interior. Tribes could now assume control over Department of the Interior programs, including the Bureau of Reclamation and the National Park Service. Notwithstanding such latitude, the Tribal Self-Governance Act expressly prohibited the secretary from "waiving, modifying, or diminishing" his trust responsibilities.

Brown was less successful in addressing the long-standing mismanagement of Indian trust funds, which totaled $2 billion, even though the department deployed a strategic plan that included fifty action items.[4] For more than two centuries, the United States had deposited treaty or trust funds into accounts for tribes and individuals, often losing track of or mismanaging them or misidentifying ownership interests for hundreds of thousands of Native Americans. By the 1990s, the problem had become acute, with Brown committing to resolve accounting discrepancies, improve the collection, investment, and distribution of funds, and ameliorate deficiencies and "complexities" in the accounts.

With the election of William J. Clinton as president in November 1992, Brown stayed on as assistant secretary, but only until the president nominated his replacement. He left office on July 16, 1993. For the next three years he served as executive director of the Tohono O'odham Nation's Human Resources Department. He then served eight years as dean/director of the American Indian Studies program at Washington University in St. Louis. Between 2004 and 2010, he was director of Arizona State University's American Indian Studies program where he cofounded (along with Kevin Gover) the American Indian Policy Institute in 2007. Beginning in 2010 he served as professor and executive director of the institute before retiring in 2016 to Tucson, Arizona.

Change Is Possible
It has been stated that there are certain moments in history when change is particularly possible. [W]e ... are living in one of these moments. But unlike the past, the opportunity for change will not be brought about by a single great hero, or heroine, but will be the work of many people, both Indian and non-Indian.... [We must] actively work with tribal officials and members of Indian communities to support the positive efforts of tribal governments. Too often Indian tribes are discussed in terms of overwhelming needs and failures.... However, it is essential to recognize that one of the basic precepts of this administration is that the governments closest to the people are the most responsive to the desires of their citizens. [I]t follows that improvements of tribal communities and economies can most be successful when they are directed and controlled by tribes themselves....

Tribal governments are going through a period of dynamic and exciting change. They are developing more control over their resources. Tribes are engaging in important and successful economic development efforts.

Indian people are making positive choices and are developing programs to address serious needs in their communities. Tribal governments are making improvements in their constitutions that result in more stable government and more effective representation of Indian citizens. It is vitally important for the Federal government to recognize and support the economic, social and governmental initiatives of Indian governments and to improve the government-to-government relationship between the United States and the tribes.⁵

Guiding Principles
I [am] guided by the following principles: First, tribal self-determination. I fully support the policy of tribal self-determination by supporting and further strengthening the effective and meaningful participation by tribal governments in the planning, conduct, and administration of the Bureau of Indian Affairs. . . . Second, government-to-government relationships with Indian tribes. [We must] develop stronger intergovernmental relationships between the Federal Government and tribal governments. The relationships between the tribes and the Bureau [must] be based upon intergovernmental communication, mutual accountability . . . and joint planning for more effective and efficient utilization of Federal staff and institutional resources on Indian lands. And third, trust responsibility. [T]he Department [must] fulfill the Federal Government's trust responsibility at the highest degree of fiduciary standards in securing and protecting the rights of Indian tribes and people. . . .⁶

Recognizing Tribal Successes
In the area of economic development, many tribes are successfully supporting economic ventures on Indian lands. These range from manufacturing industries to grocery stores, retail stores and gas stations. . . . In the area of natural resources management, a number of tribes . . . have developed comprehensive land use and natural resource planning and management systems. . . . In the area of human services, there have been many highly publicized cases of child abuse on Indian lands. What is not so apparent, however, are the responses of Tribal governments to these troubling problems. In Arizona, fifteen of the twenty Tribal governments have enacted mandatory child abuse and neglect reporting laws. A number of tribes have implemented specialized programs for child protective services. The tribes in Arizona have also organized a professional-level child

protective services training academy that is equivalent to the State's child protective... academy....

Another important trend among Tribal governments is the strengthening of tribal constitutions and institutions of government. A number of tribes are changing their constitutions to provide 4-year terms for elected officials, at-large election of the chief elected official and the separation of powers, all of which can contribute to more stable and effective Tribal governments.... Like other governments, tribes have faced the challenges of fulfilling their jurisdictional responsibilities and providing services for their citizens. At the same time, tribes have been developing procedures for resource allocation, designing methods for citizen participation in decision-making, struggling with changes in their constitutions and implementing efficient management systems.

Developing Clear Directions
[We need] cooperative tribal and federal planning processes which will be used to provide administrative direction for the Bureau. Strategic plans could be developed in such critical areas as education and economic development as well as trust responsibilities and natural resources management.... In the process of developing better intergovernmental working relationships with Tribal governments, we need to recognize that we are working within a highly complex and ever-changing environment. All of the tribes have different needs and conditions. We cannot impose policies that will work the same in all cases. We need to be flexible and responsive to individual tribes.[7]

Based on my philosophy and approach to working with tribal governments, there are five areas that [need] considerable emphasis... given the changes in tribal governments and the heightened awareness of human and economic needs on Indian lands....

[E]ducation is a number one priority. In support of its critical importance, I [am] promoting effective schools, strengthening local control and accountability, and providing a special emphasis on literacy and employment. I [will increase] early childhood education, higher education and adult and vocational educational opportunities [by seeking] greater cooperation with the Department of Education and public schools.

Tribes must control and direct economic development on Indian lands. The role of the Department of the Interior is to assist tribes in their economic development efforts and to ensure that trust resources are not alienated or degraded.... Tribal economic development policy... should

be based on the following three goals. First, Federal resources should be redirected towards enabling tribes to effectively initiate, control and direct economic development on Indian lands. Tribes should be encouraged to conduct economic development planning to attract industry, to enter into business ventures and to encourage local entrepreneurs. Recognizing that most tribal economic development opportunities are based upon development of land and natural resources, tribes must be given the support to conduct comprehensive land use and natural resources planning and management.

[Second,] Federal policies should result in tribes making maximum use of tribal financial resources for investment in economic development. Most tribes have independent sources of revenue from trust funds and tribal enterprises. Many tribes use their revenue from trust funds and enterprises to invest in economic development on Indian lands. However, many Tribal governments annually spend considerable amounts of tribal funds to subsidize indirect costs on self-determination contracts. The[se] dollars represent economic opportunities that are lost to Indian communities. Tribal dollars and staff time would be much better spent on economic development projects.

[Third,] the Federal government must support Tribal governments in their efforts to attract private capital for Indian economic development. The Department can assist tribes to provide tax incentives for businesses to locate in Indian communities, to provide tailored training for tribal work forces, and to offer grants, direct loans and guaranteed loans to support start-up costs and working capital for new businesses.

The conditions that are necessary for economic development on Indian lands are the same as those necessary for any other community. These conditions include stable and effective law enforcement, courts, roads, utilities systems, housing, schools and human services. . . . Private investors and industrial developers will not be attracted to Indian communities where tribes cannot afford to provide public safety services and drug free environments. Businesses cannot thrive in conditions of poor roads and substandard housing and schools for their employees. . . . The Department can help tribes develop and maintain strong community infrastructures by stabilizing [these] resources.

The Department . . . must exercise its trust responsibilities for securing and protecting Indian rights and resources to the highest degree of fiduciary standards. . . . It is important to recognize that the Department must work cooperatively with tribes in order to effectively protect Indian lands, environmental values and natural resources....

Too often, reorganization is proposed as a panacea to all Indian affairs problems. The problem with reorganization proposals is that, coming from the top, they attempt to impose the same solution in all BIA areas, regardless of the needs and conditions of the tribes. Instead, I propose cooperative planning for more effective and efficient use of federal resources. This planning will involve Tribal government and BIA field offices on a local and regional basis.[8]

CHAPTER 58

Ada E. Deer

Assistant Secretary for Indian Affairs
(July 16, 1993–November 12, 1997)

ADA ELIZABETH DEER was born on August 7, 1935, on the Menominee Reservation in Wisconsin. The oldest of five children born to Joseph and Constance (Wood) Deer, she grew up in a log cabin on the banks of the Wolf River. Her Philadelphia-born non-Indian mother "was the single greatest influence" on Deer's life, taking her to Menominee tribal council meetings beginning at the age of four. This mentoring shaped Deer's "lifetime commitment to serve."[1] At the age of five, Deer and her family moved to Milwaukee, with her father soon after drafted into the US Army.

After the war, her family moved back to Menominee where Deer attended Bureau of Indian Affairs schools, before graduating from Shawano High School in 1952, where, as a senior, she served on the Governor's Youth Advisory Board of the Wisconsin Commission on Human Rights, further shaping her political philosophy. She then enrolled in the University of Wisconsin–Madison (UWM) as a pre-med student before changing her major to social work and becoming the first Menominee to graduate from UWM in 1957. Four years later she earned a master of social work from Columbia University in New York and later served as a fellow at the John F. Kennedy School of Politics at Harvard University.

In 1958, she began her career as a social worker at the Henry House in Manhattan, New York, and then at the Edward Waite House in Minneapolis, Minnesota, before joining the Bureau of Indian Affairs as a community service coordinator in 1964. Three years later she began a long collegiate career coordinating Indian affairs at the University of Minnesota and later at the University of Wisconsin–Stevens Point. By 1972, Deer had become intimately involved in Menominee restoration, serving as vice president of, and lobbyist for, the Menominee Restoration Committee. In so doing, she helped define a new federal policy: restoration. Upon the political restoration of the Menominee Tribe to federal status in 1973, Deer was elected tribal chairman.²

After a three-year term as chairman, Deer worked as a legislative liaison with the Native American Rights Funds, and in 1977, she became a senior lecturer at UWM, remaining until 1993. In 1978 and again in 1982 she unsuccessfully ran for Wisconsin's secretary of state, and in 1992 she was the Democratic nominee for Wisconsin's second congressional district.³

On May 11, 1993, recently elected President William J. Clinton nominated Deer as the assistant secretary of the interior for Indian affairs—making her the first woman ever to be nominated and confirmed to lead the Bureau of Indian Affairs.⁴ She was highly recommended by scores of tribes and tribal organizations and was unanimously confirmed by the Senate on July 16, 1993, pledging to create a "progressive federal/tribal partnership." She assumed office immediately.

Deer's tenure as assistant secretary was during a time of further federal budget reductions by a Republican-led Congress committed to a "Contract with America." In the fall of 1995, the House Indian appropriations conferees reduced the bureau's central office budget by 26 percent and the area office budgets by 28 percent, affecting the bureau's ability to carry out its trust obligations. That same year, Congress sought to weaken the Indian Child Welfare Act (ICWA) and reduce tribal jurisdiction over adoptions by limiting Indian sovereignty by amending the act to grant non-Indian social service agencies authority to determine whether a biological parent retained sufficient tribal "social, cultural, or political affiliation" to warrant ICWA jurisdiction.⁵ Deer countered that "this basic determination should rest with . . . tribal courts," as to do otherwise would strip tribal judicial forums of their fundamental authority.⁶

When Congress considered subjecting tribes to taxation on gaming and other economic activities in Indian Country, Deer strongly opposed the proposals, explaining that taxation of tribes was not only counter to the Indian Self-Determination Act but also foiled the federal trust responsibility. Moreover, taxation would contradict the intent of Congress in enacting into law the Indian Gaming Regulatory Act, which mandated gaming revenues be used to support economic development, self-sufficiency, and stable tribal governments. The federal government did not tax the several states, Deer explained, and it should not tax tribal governments, which were "struggling to overcome centuries of poverty."⁷

Deer remained an ardent proponent of tribal sovereignty at a time when Congress sought to reduce budgets and erode tribal authority. Her outspoken nature, however, led Interior Secretary Bruce Babbitt to ask for and receive her resignation on January 9, 1997. She agreed to remain in office until the president appointed a successor, leaving on November 12, 1997. Deer then returned to UWM, and in 2000 she became director of the American Indian studies program. She was the recipient of numerous awards, including Woman of the Year by Girls Scouts of American, Wonder Woman Award, Indian Fire Council Achievement Award, and the National Distinguished Achievement Award. In 2019, she was inducted into the National Native American Hall of Fame.[8] Deer retired from the University of Wisconsin in 2007. She lives at Menominee.

Strong and Effective Tribal Sovereignty
My vision for the Bureau of Indian Affairs is to create a progressive federal/tribal partnership. First and foremost, the heart of Indian policy must be strong, effective tribal sovereignty. There is no reason ... to be reluctant to support the permanency of tribal sovereignty any more than [to] be reluctant to support the permanency of Federal or State sovereignty.

There are three kinds of sovereignty recognized in the U.S. Constitution: tribal, State, and Federal. It is our moral obligation to ensure that these rights are supported vigorously. The role of the Federal Government should be to support and to implement tribally-inspired solutions to tribally-defined problems....

If our new partnership is to be effective, Indian policy must be coordinated closely between the Bureau of Indian Affairs, the Department of the Interior, other Cabinet Departments, and the White House....

Greater Self-Determination
I enthusiastically endorse greater self-determination for Indian tribes and the protection of treaty rights. Like many people in Indian country and in Congress, I'm excited about the ... self-governance demonstration project. It is designed to empower tribes by allocating Federal resources and responsibilities to those tribal governments willing to assume them.... [N]ot every Indian tribe will seek self-governance compacts, and the Department must respect and honor its commitments to those tribal governments choosing different courses.

[O]ne of my highest priorities will be the publishing of the regulations implementing the 1988 [Indian Self-Determination] amendments. These regulations, now in draft form, must undergo a careful review to determine how to promote tribal self-determination in the contracting of Federal programs.

No discussion of my goals for Indian affairs would be complete without noting the critical area of Native American religious freedom. I ... endorse the process in which the Department of the Interior ... and the Native American representatives ... can jointly discuss common approaches to ... the Native American Free Exercise of Religion Act.

I look forward to forging partnerships with tribes across the country.... [W]e have a responsibility to reverse these devastating socioeconomic conditions that plague ... tribes. This task is daunting, though one we cannot afford to ignore.

Promoting Indian Values
There are many important areas ..., [such as] education, health, housing, Indian child welfare protection, natural resource protection, trust funds, gaming, and economic development, to name just a few. These are all important.... Although Indians now constitute 90 percent of the employees in the Bureau of Indian Affairs, we must remember that the Bureau was created by non-Indians. It has not been a proactive Indian institution. I want to activate and mobilize people in the Bureau, so that they can be creative and forward-looking. I want the Indian values of sharing, caring, and respect incorporated into their day-to-day work.

I want to help the Bureau to be a full partner in the effort to fulfill the Indian agenda developed in Indian country. The best way we can do this is for the tribes to decide what needs to be done, and for the tribes to do it on their own terms, with our enthusiastic and constructive support.

The constellation of history is aligned in favor of Indian people.... These times are notable, too, by the increasing number of women, and the new approach toward policy at all levels of Government.

Time to Address Injustices
So hope, healing, commitment, and change are in the skies all around us.... The time is right for a partnership to fulfill long-held promises, and to address long-overdue injustices.

We think most of all about the future of our young people. On this summer's night, tens of thousands of girls and boys across Indian country will go to sleep. Some, in my Wisconsin homeland, will hear the vibrant sounds I heard many years ago in the cabin where I grew up. Others will hear the wind in the Douglas fir trees at Warm Springs, the surging current of the great Missouri at Fort Peck, or the song of the canyon wren calling out from a redrock monument at Navajo. There is no reason why they cannot grow up to live in prosperity, in good health, with excellent educations, in clean environments, and immersed in their rich traditions.[9]

CHAPTER 59

Kevin Gover

Assistant Secretary for Indian Affairs
(November 12, 1997–January 3, 2001)

KEVIN GOVER was born on February 16, 1955, in Lawton, Oklahoma, within the former Kiowa–Comanche–Apache Reservation to a Comanche–Pawnee father and a non-Indian mother, both of whom were civil rights advocates. Gover is the great-great-great-grandson of Seal Chief of the Skidi Pawnee and the great-grandson of Hovarithka of the Yapawicka Comanche.[1] After attending local elementary schools, Gover received a scholarship to the prestigious St. Paul's School in Concord, New Hampshire, at the age of fifteen before attending Princeton University, where he studied public and international affairs, graduating in 1978. Three years later he earned a juris doctorate from the University of New Mexico School of Law.

Fresh out of law school, Gover clerked for US District Court Judge Juan G. Burciaga before joining the Washington, DC, law firm of Fried, Frank, Harris, Shriver and Kampelman. In 1986, he returned to Albuquerque where he started Gover, Stetson, Williams, and West, a private law firm representing tribal nations. His advocacy, fundraising, and campaign skills—he organized Native Americans for Clinton–Gore in 1992—caught the attention of President Clinton. While Gover remained in Albuquerque representing and lobbying on behalf of his tribal clients, with the reelection of President Clinton in 1996, the president nominated Gover as the seventh assistant secretary for Indian affairs on October 9, 1997. Despite concerns over his nomination from a *New York Times* article, the Senate unanimously confirmed Gover on November 9, and he was sworn into office three days later.

An enrolled member of the Pawnee Tribe, Gover worked with tribes to strengthen law enforcement and rebuild schools that were in disrepair. He defended tribes when the Senate proposed to waive tribal sovereign immunity after a series of high-profile tribal corruption cases. Acknowledging that there were legal challenges between states and tribes, Gover advocated resolving disputes "through the government-to-government" relationship, not through a unilateral waiving of sovereign immunity that was "reminiscent of the Termination Era."[2]

To strengthen tribal leadership, Gover encouraged tribes to restore their "warrior traditions" by redefining leadership as a "commitment and sacrifice that transcends all personal interests." Self-government was under attack, he stated—in part, not without cause—as some tribal leaders, such as Peter McDonald of the Navajo Nation, acted irresponsibly. It was important for tribes to exercise probity and guardedly exert their authority so as not to lend credence to those critical of sovereign immunity.[3] On the 175th anniversary of the Bureau of Indian Affairs, Gover issued a moving apology to American Indians and Alaska Natives for federal "ethnic cleansing and cultural annihilation" policies. Healing, Gover added, could begin only after the wrongs of the past were acknowledged and Native Americans replaced "anger with hope" and "allowed broken hearts to mend."[4]

To further self-governance, Gover signed the first government-to-government consultation policy with tribal nations on December 13, 2000. An extension of the Indian Self-Determination Act, consultation included a federal pledge to advance self-government by early involvement of tribes regarding any federal action that might affect them, including regulations.[5] The policy not only encouraged increased self-government but also reflected interest in tribal concerns. At the winter 1998 National Congress of American Indians meeting, Gover solicited a working group of tribal leaders to draft the policy. Two years later, he deployed it as a policy integral to self-government.

Gover quickly discovered that serving as head of the Bureau of Indian Affairs constituted a delicate balancing act. In 1998, he suggested that the bureau's twelve thousand employees could be reduced by as much as 85 percent within three years if Congress increased funding for tribal schools, law enforcement, and other services, and allowed tribes to operate federal programs as they saw fit. The bureau could then become "a technical" and "policy coordinating" agency with "dozens of people," rather than the hundreds then administering policy. The concept was heretical to federal employees and was met with extreme caution by tribal leaders.[6]

By late 2000, as the Clinton administration drew to a close, Gover resigned effective January 3, 2001. Upon leaving office he immediately renewed his law practice at a Washington, DC, law firm before joining the Sandra Day O'Connor School of Law at Arizona State University in 2003, where he taught federal–Indian law, as well as administrative and statutory law. In December 2007, he became director of the National Museum of the American Indian, winning acclaim for his direction. In 2008, President Barack Obama considered Gover as his secretary of the interior before selecting Colorado Senator Ken Salazar. Gover remains director of the National Museum of the American Indian and continues to serve as a judge for a number of tribal nations.

A Time for Reflection and Contemplation
In March of 1824, President James Monroe established the Office of Indian Affairs in the Department of War. Its mission was to conduct the nation's business with regard to Indian affairs. We have come together today to mark the first 175 years of the institution now known as the Bureau of Indian Affairs. It is appropriate that we do so in the first year of a new century and a new millennium, a time when our leaders are reflecting on what lies ahead and preparing for those challenges. Before looking ahead, though, this institution must first look back and reflect on what it has wrought and, by doing so, come to know that this is no occasion for celebration; rather it is time for reflection and contemplation, a time for sorrowful truths to be spoken, a time for contrition.

We must first reconcile ourselves to the fact that the works of this agency have at various times profoundly harmed the communities it was meant to serve. From the very beginning, the Office of Indian Affairs was an instrument by which the United States enforced its ambition against the Indian nations and Indian people who stood in its path. And so, the first mission of this institution was to execute the removal of the Southeastern tribal nations. By threat, deceit, and force, these great tribal nations were made to march 1,000 miles to the west, leaving thousands of their old, their young and their infirm in hasty graves along the Trail of Tears.

As the nation looked to the West for more land, this agency participated in the ethnic cleansing that befell the western tribes. War necessarily begets tragedy; the war for the West was no exception. Yet in these more enlightened times, it must be acknowledged that the deliberate spread of disease, the decimation of the mighty bison herds, the use of the poison alcohol to destroy mind and body, and the cowardly killing of women and children made for tragedy on a scale so ghastly that it cannot be dismissed as merely the inevitable consequence of the clash of competing ways of life. This agency and the good people in it failed in the mission to prevent the devastation. And so great nations of patriot warriors fell. We will never push aside the memory of unnecessary and violent death at places such as Sand Creek, the banks of the Washita River, and Wounded Knee.

Nor did the consequences of war have to include the futile and destructive efforts to annihilate Indian cultures. After the devastation of tribal economies and the deliberate creation of tribal dependence on the services provided by this agency, this agency set out to destroy all things Indian. This agency forbade the speaking of Indian languages, prohibited the conduct of traditional religious activities, outlawed traditional government, and made Indian people ashamed of who they were. Worst of all, the Bureau of Indian Affairs committed these acts against the children entrusted to its boarding schools, brutalizing them emotionally, psychologically, physically, and spiritually. Even in this era of self-determination, when the Bureau of Indian Affairs is at long last serving as an advocate for Indian people in an atmosphere of mutual respect, the legacy of these misdeeds haunts us. The trauma of shame, fear and anger has passed from one generation to the next, and manifests itself in the rampant alcoholism, drug abuse, and domestic violence that plague Indian country. Many of our people live lives of unrelenting tragedy as Indian families suffer the ruin of lives by alcoholism, suicides made of shame and despair, and violent death at the hands of one another. So many of the maladies suffered today in Indian country result from the failures of this agency. Poverty, ignorance, and disease have been the product of this agency's work.

And so today, I stand before you as the leader of an institution that in the past has committed acts so terrible that they infect, diminish, and destroy the lives of Indian people decades later, generations later. These things occurred despite the efforts of many good people with good hearts who sought to prevent them. These wrongs must be acknowledged if the healing is to begin.

I do not speak today for the United States. That is the province of the nation's elected leaders, and I would not presume to speak on their behalf. I am empowered, however, to speak on behalf of the agency, the Bureau of Indian Affairs, and I am quite certain that the words that follow reflect the hearts of its 10,000 employees.

Let us begin by expressing our profound sorrow for what this agency has done in the past. Just like you, when we think of these misdeeds and their tragic consequences, our hearts break and our grief is as pure and complete as yours. We desperately wish that we could change this history, but of course we cannot. On behalf of the Bureau of Indian Affairs I extend this formal apology to Indian people for the historical conduct of this agency. And while the BIA employees of today did not commit these wrongs, we acknowledge that the institution we serve did. We accept this inheritance, this legacy of racism and inhumanity. And by accepting this legacy, we accept also the moral responsibility of putting things right.

We therefore begin this important work anew, and make a new commitment to the people and communities that we serve, a commitment born of the dedication we share with you to the cause of renewed hope and prosperity for Indian country. Never again will this agency stand silent when hate and violence are committed against Indians. Never again will we allow policy to proceed from the assumption that Indians possess less human genius than the other races. Never again will we be complicit in the theft of Indian property. Never again will we appoint false leaders who serve purposes other than those of the tribes. Never again will we allow unflattering and stereotypical images of Indian people to deface the halls of government or lead the American people to shallow and ignorant beliefs about Indians. Never again will we attack your religions, your languages, your rituals, or any of your tribal ways. Never again will we seize your children, nor teach them to be ashamed of who they are. Never again.

We cannot yet ask your forgiveness, not while the burdens of this agency's history weigh so heavily on tribal communities. What we do ask is that, together, we allow the healing to begin: As you return to your homes, and as you talk with your people, please tell them that time of dying is at its end. Tell your children that the time of shame and fear is over. Tell your young men and women to replace their anger with hope and love for their people. Together, we must wipe the tears of seven generations. Together, we must allow our broken hearts to mend. Together, we will face a challenging world with confidence and trust. Together, let us resolve that when our future leaders gather to discuss the history of this institution, it will be time to celebrate the rebirth of joy, freedom, and progress for the Indian nations. The Bureau of Indian Affairs was born in 1824 in a time of war on Indian people. May it live in the year 2000 and beyond as an instrument of their prosperity.[7]

The Role of the Bureau of Indian Affairs in the 21st Century
[T]he best ideas in Indian affairs do not come from Washington. Instead, they come from the work of the people out there on the reservations trying to make these small and struggling governments work. They constantly are creating and innovating in order to meet the most urgent needs of their communities....

[The Bureau of Indian Affairs] ... must deliver services in over 500 communities to as many as one million Indian people. It must carry on a respectful government-to-government relation with hundreds of diverse communities in wildly different social, political, and legal contexts. It has been made to carry out profoundly contradictory policies toward tribal governments in its 160 years. It carries the baggage of every mistaken policy initiative, every naïve assistance program, and every broken promise ever directed to tribal governments.

The people of the BIA ... can do their jobs successfully if given the opportunity to apply their natural ability and creativity. This necessarily includes the right to make mistakes ... of enthusiasm rather than sloth. I want the agency to be full of optimism about its own future and that of the people it serves. I want the agency to be prepared to enter the next century with a clear vision of its place in the future Federal–tribal relations.

What will that require? First, ... we must find a consensus on what the BIA is to be in the next century. The consensus must include the tribal governments we serve, the leadership and members of this committee and its House counterpart, and the administration. There can be no other way to resolve the BIA's identity crisis than to reach such a consensus and define with specificity the mission and objectives of this agency.

Between the Snyder Act, the Self-Determination Act, and the Self-Governance Act, we have all the tools necessary to deliver services in virtually any form a tribe might desire.[8] The choice belongs to the tribe, and the tribe must accept the consequences of its choice. By the same token, Congress must provide the support, in the form of appropriations, oversight, and authorizing legislation that will allow the Bureau and the tribes to solve some of these vexing problems.

Second, the Bureau must develop and apply consistently a working model for consultation with tribal governments. From the very first days of my professional career, I have heard tribal leaders complain that the Bureau acts without letting the tribes know what is going on, and when it does consult, it presents them with a decision that has already been made. I agree with this criticism, though I do appreciate the need for a Federal agency to exercise its authority and discretion. The tribes have a right to meaningful consultation on matters that affect them as an essential element of the government-to-government relationship. We must, therefore, develop a system for meaningful consultation. ...

Third, we must constantly examine how the Bureau allocates its resources. This is not an easy undertaking. We all know the principle of doing the greatest good for the greatest number. But in Indian affairs, one must go on to examine treaty and compact commitments and the Federal trust responsibility in order to determine an appropriate allocation of Federal resources.

We are approaching a new century and a new millennium. I am not sufficiently visionary to reflect on the new millennium, but I have been thinking about what it was like 100 years ago, and how it might be 100 years from now. Just like 100 years ago, Indian people were thought to be a dying race. The assumption, and indeed the goal, of Federal policy was the disappearance of tribal communities and the absorption of Indian people into the surrounding world until their distinctiveness was gone....

And yet, somehow, 100 years later, the sun is rising again and Indian people and their communities are still here. They are recovering and growing stronger. Their profound fortitude and tenacity preserve them as distinct communities possessed of traditions and values from which all the world might learn.

The role of the BIA is going to continue to evolve and... probably shrink. I think there's always going to be a need for an agency here in Washington to serve as... a focal point and a coordinator of policy. I think it is definitely a good thing that we're seeing in this administration with every department in the Government acknowledging its responsibility to Indian tribes and allowing the tribes to participate in their programs as appropriate. But it seems to me there's always going to be a need for some focal point, some coordinating institution, and that's the role... the Bureau will play. I do think we'll see the Bureau playing a much smaller role over time, perhaps eventually no role whatsoever in the direct delivery of services in the tribal communities. The tribes will be doing that themselves.[9]

CHAPTER 60

Neil A. McCaleb

Assistant Secretary for Indian Affairs (July 4, 2001–January 6, 2003)

WITH THE ELECTION OF Republican President George W. Bush, the search for the next assistant secretary for Indian affairs began, with the president appointing James H. McDivitt as acting assistant secretary. On April 17, 2001, the president nominated Neil A. McCaleb of the Chickasaw Nation as the eighth assistant secretary for Indian affairs. The Senate confirmed McCaleb on June 29, and he was sworn into office on July 4.[1]

The youngest of four siblings, McCaleb was born in Oklahoma City on June 30, 1935, to an Arkansas-born civil engineer father and an Indian Territory-born mother. After graduating from Putnam City High School, McCaleb followed his father's footsteps and earned a degree in civil engineering from Oklahoma State University. Upon graduation in 1957, he went to work designing the interstate highway system in Oklahoma before joining the Oklahoma Engineering Department. In 1961, he launched Arrowhead Homes, Inc., an engineering and construction business. In 1974, McCaleb was elected to the Oklahoma House of Representatives, where he served eight years—four as House Minority Leader for the Republican Party—before retiring from office in 1983.

In 1986, Oklahoma Governor Henry Bellmon appointed McCaleb as the state's first secretary of transportation, while he also served as director of the Oklahoma Department of Transportation, remaining in both positions until 1991. He then became president of the Oklahoma Good Roads and Transportation Association until Governor Frank Keating reappointed him secretary of transportation and head of the Oklahoma Department of Transportation and the Oklahoma Turnpike Authority. McCaleb remained in all three positions until July 2001.

While President Bush considered three others for the assistant secretary position, he settled on McCaleb due to his long public service record that began in 1967 when he was appointed to the Oklahoma Indian Affairs Commission.

McCaleb remained with the commission until 1972, when President Nixon appointed him to the National Council on Indian Opportunity. In 1983, President Reagan appointed McCaleb to the President's Commission on Indian Reservation Economies.

Following his swearing in as assistant secretary, McCaleb announced his immediate goal of making the bureau an "Indian service" to American Indians and Alaska Natives, emphasizing economic development, education, public safety, and trust reform.[2] In an address before the National Congress of American Indians in Bismarck, North Dakota, he informed tribal leaders that they could "choose between poverty and prosperity" for their people, encouraging them to accept change and develop their economies. "If you keep doing what you've always done, then you're always going to get what you've always gotten," McCaleb exclaimed.[3]

To promote economic development, McCaleb pointed to three factors that have long limited development in Indian Country: capital, access to markets, and a skilled workforce. But he also believed it was important for tribes to create a positive climate for job growth by establishing business and legal climates that reduced risks to investors while at the same time improving economic and educational opportunities for tribal members. He endorsed a goal of creating one hundred thousand new jobs in Indian Country by 2008, notwithstanding the challenges of developing the infrastructure to support market-driven enterprises.[4] Tribal gaming, McCaleb suggested, could provide a business–government model that might be expanded to other ventures, including renewable energy.

An educated populace was essential to a sustainable, market-driven economy, with a well-educated and skilled workforce "key to . . . sustaining growth." McCaleb and Interior Secretary Gale Norton set a series of goals under the No Child Left Behind Act that every Native American child would read independently by the third grade, seven out of ten students would be proficient in reading and math, attendance in bureau and contract schools would be 90 percent or greater, and all students would demonstrate knowledge of their indigenous language and culture.[5]

McCaleb advocated for the privatization of bureau facilities to tribes, with tribes then leasing them back to the bureau to operate if they so chose, an idea that had great potential if tribes could issue tax-free bonds to expand such facilities. Public safety required trained law enforcement officers to ensure a safe and stable environment to support economic development. McCaleb called on tribes to separate their judicial from their executive functions. This, too, was an exercise of sovereignty, the assistant secretary reminded tribal leaders, one that was central to nation building.

McCaleb acknowledged there was a "trust mess" at the bureau, including administration and accounting of tribal funds and resources. When Congress established the Office of Special Trustee in 1994, the Senate considered transferring all trust responsibilities to the new agency, a proposal McCaleb opposed, believing the bureau's day-to-day functions were sufficiently broad that to transfer basic trust functions was equivalent to "the elimination of the BIA and its re-creation under another name."[6] In November 2002, Norton proposed stripping the bureau of all of its trust responsibilities, an overture McCaleb did not support, as tribes feared it was part of a larger effort to dismantle the agency.[7]

On November 21, 2002, McCaleb unexpectedly resigned, citing the weight of the *Cobell* litigation and trust reform. He left office on January 6, 2003, with Norton appointing Aurene M. Martin, a member of the Bad River Band of Chippewa, as acting assistant secretary. After leaving the bureau, McCaleb returned to the Chickasaw Nation to develop a long-term economic development plan. In 2013, the Chickasaw Nation named McCaleb its ambassador at-large, and a year later, he was selected as an honoree to the Oklahoma Hall of Fame for his fifty years of public and private service. In 2019, he was inducted into the Oklahoma State University Hall of Fame. McCaleb is retired at his home in Oklahoma City.

Sovereignty and Trusteeship

[Self-governance] and its legal foundation of tribal sovereignty have been widely and enthusiastically endorsed by tribal leaders, and have begun to produce measurable progress in the form of self-governance and economic improvement in the lives of Native Americans. This is evidenced by the fact that there are 220 self-governance tribes . . . of the total of 561 federally-recognized tribes. Second, the tribes have assumed the operation of 120 of the BIA's 185 schools, through contracting and compacting with the BIA. Third, there has been significant economic development, and outside capital investment on tribal lands. Last . . . the aggregate area of the tribal estate is expanding and not contracting. Notwithstanding these improvements, there continue to be . . . tenacious problems, poverty, under-employment, educational under-achievement, and social dysfunction experienced by Native Americans all out of proportion to the national experience. . . .

The BIA has the . . . responsibility as trustee of the tribal estate and for the individual Indian estate. The BIA has suffered an erosion of trust with its clients, recently manifested in the adjudication of the *Cobell* v. *the Department of the Interior* litigation. The Congress has anticipated and reacted to this problem . . . by the creation the Office of Special Trustee, to oversee the BIA's trust functions. This lapse of trust management . . . must be mended as rapidly as is consistent with authenticity, accuracy, and equity, in order to restore the trust with the BIA, and restore our position as trustee-in-fact of the Indian estate. . . .

Within these two broad-based goals of effectively implementing our trust responsibility and improving the quality of life in Indian country, there are . . . three primary and essential objectives.

Need for Economic Development
In order for the tribes to exercise true sovereignty of their peoples, it is necessary for the tribal governments to be able to provide the essential infrastructure and services that their constituents need for a functioning community. The financing of such infrastructure for independent governments has historically been provided from a tax base derived from a viable economy. . . .

The solution to these problems is inherent in economic development of tribal lands. To achieve lasting and self-sustaining economies on reservations, we should build upon the successes of tribal enterprises by replicating the model of government business partnerships that we have seen in the past few years, through either a partnership or a franchise with tribal government. These partnerships should be market-driven enterprises that take advantage of the unique sovereign status enjoyed by tribes. There has been abundant evidence in recent years of the financial success in gaming activities experienced by numerous tribes using this business government model. This model can be exported to a variety of other enterprises, such as generation of electrical energy. . . .

The BIA's role in this process should be one of a facilitator, providing technical assistance and capital to both tribal governments and individual Indians in private enterprise, to startup and to attract capital investment in viable market-driven enterprises. The BIA's economic development division should function as a clearing house, in concert with the Department of Commerce, to identify potential investors and businesses interested in locating on Indian lands and taking advantage of existing tax advantages attended thereto.

This cannot happen without access to markets, which is essential for economic development. This means transportation systems that are able to move personnel and product to and from the reservation and within the reservation. To overcome this significant deterrent to economic development, I suggest that the reauthorization of the Federal Highway Trust Fund . . . include a significant increase in the allocation to Indian reservation roads.

Quality Education
Education is an additional critical requirement for sustained economic expansion [which required] a well-educated and skilled work force. Indian education is both a key to economic growth and enhanced quality of life.

The BIA has the responsibility for providing access to quality education through its own schools, tribally operated schools, and the public school system. Many of the BIA schools are in disrepair and in need of additional classrooms, and the aggregate funding for these facilities is far below the demand.... [Today] 65 percent of the Indian schools are privately operated [but] lack funds for expansion, replacement, and major maintenance associated with these school facilities.

If [we] have to fund these on a pay-as-you-go basis, Indian children will be under-served for many years, and in some cases, placed in at risk marginal or unsafe facilities. To provide the tribe the ability to address this issue in a timely manner for those tribally-operated schools, as well as to address the other capital needs for their communities, I suggest that tribes be afforded the same tax-exempt status as is currently enjoyed by local governments in the issue of bonded indebtedness.

Public Safety
Public safety on the reservation is a primary responsibility of the BIA, through its officers and tribal judicial systems. There are extensive needs for improved and expanded detention facilities throughout Indian country. Privatization of these facilities by tribes and leasing [them] back to the BIA can be one avenue to address the immediate and long-term needs, especially if the tribes have the ability to issue tax free bonds to spread out the financing over an extended period of time.

The numbers of trained law enforcement officers . . . must be addressed to provide the safe and stable environment for the reservations, conducive to the protection of life, liberty, and the pursuit of happiness for America's indigenous people and their clients.[8]

CHAPTER 61

David W. Anderson

Assistant Secretary for Indian Affairs
(February 2, 2004–February 12, 2005)

PRESIDENT BUSH waited ten months after McCaleb's resignation before nominating David Wayne Anderson, founder of Famous Dave's Barbeque, to be the ninth assistant secretary for Indian affairs. While tribal leaders were puzzled by the president's delay, when Anderson's nomination was announced, others expressed concern. The National Congress of American Indians, for instance, expressed the reticence of Indian Country when its president, Tex Hall, opined that Anderson's "weakness" was his lack of experience in handling the political hot potato of the day: bureau trust fund management and *Cobell* litigation.[1]

Anderson was born in Chicago, Illinois, in 1953 to Jimmie and Iris Anderson. His father, a citizen of the Choctaw Nation, gave him his love of Southern food, while his mother, an enrolled member of the Lac Courte Oreilles Ojibwa, taught him the love of cooking. Anderson grew up in Chicago, spending summers in northern Wisconsin on the Lac Courte Oreilles Reservation. He graduated from Luther North College Prep High School in Chicago in 1971. Despite not having earned a college degree, Anderson graduated with a master's degree from the John F. Kennedy School of Government at Harvard University in 1986.[2] He started his first business at age eighteen, and within two years he owned a wholesale floral shop, contractually serving all Sears, J. C. Penny's, and retail florists in Chicago.

In 1982, the Lac Courte Oreilles Tribe hired Anderson as chief executive officer to transform tribal enterprises into profitable and stable businesses. In the 1980s, he also served on the Wisconsin Council of Tourism and the state Council on Minority Business Development. In 1983, President Reagan appointed him to the National Task Force on Reservation Gambling, and later President George W. Bush appointed him to the Presidential Advisory Council for Tribal

Colleges and Universities. By 1989, Anderson had formed a management and investment company specializing in the emerging gaming market, being recognized by *Forbes* magazine as one of the fastest growing companies in America. In 1994, Anderson opened his third publicly traded company—Famous Dave's Barbeque—in Haywood, Wisconsin, growing it into a national chain.

President Bush announced his choice for assistant secretary on September 15, 2003, with Anderson confirmed by the Senate on December 9. He was sworn into office on February 2, 2004.³ His tenure was short—less than thirteen months— and his impact minimal. To a large degree, Anderson viewed himself as a role model for Indian Country, believing that if tribes approached governance "with a positive attitude," they could overcome obstacles and achieve economic success.⁴

Anderson believed economic development was the key to the success of Indian Country, viewing gaming as simply a stepping stone to greater, sustainable development. Gaming, Anderson surmised, would enable Native Americans to learn occupations and vocations that could be permanent and that would open doors to meaningful and fulfilling lives. "If there's any future for Native America," Anderson added, "it is not going to come from the BIA—it's going to come from our own people having the drive and the determination to become economically self-sufficient." Tribes would have to take "full responsibility for their own destinies."⁵

In the spring of 2004, Anderson and Special Trustee for American Indians Ross Swimmer teamed up to reorganize the Office of the Assistant Secretary, the Bureau of Indian Affairs, and the Office of the Special Trustee to bolster their emphasis on development and self-governance. At the same time, Anderson sought to increase accountability by adding one hundred staff to improve fiduciary responsibilities at the field level. Among his other successes, Anderson increased educational funding under No Child Left Behind, and he oversaw the drafting of No Child Left Behind rules to govern bureau and contract schools.

On January 31, 2005, Anderson announced his resignation, concluding that he could have a greater impact on the future of Indian Country by focusing his time "on developing private sector economic opportunities for Indian entrepreneurs" rather than "managing the day-to-day operations" of the bureau.⁶ Before leaving office, Anderson named W. Patrick Ragsdale of the Cherokee Nation as director of the Bureau of Indian Affairs.

Once out of federal office, Anderson returned to what he does best—creating successful companies. While he served as CEO of Famous Dave's until 1994 and remained chairman of the board until his 2003 confirmation, Anderson left management of Famous Dave's in March 2014. A year later he launched Jimmie's Old

Southern Smokehouse Barbeque. Anderson was elected to the Entrepreneur's Hall of Fame in 2012 and has authored numerous business and self-help books. He remains a popular speaker. He and his wife reside in Edina, Minnesota.

A Role Model for Indian Country
I [am] a sober person even though I spent much of my younger years as a drinking person. And I am not embarrassed to admit to these things publicly because I believe that leaders like myself need to stand up, and we need to be able to say to our communities that we can overcome these debilitating things that are ravishing our people.... I am thankful for a family that believed in me. My parents, when I was younger, every night before I went to bed, would... say, son, we believe in you, we are proud of you, and no matter what happens we will support you, and throughout whatever happens in your day, we want you to know that your mom and dad are always praying for you.... [I]f young people all across America would have those things said to them, many of the heartaches that we face would be met with resolve and hope. I really believe that today it isn't that the Federal Government is non-responsive or that the BIA is inefficient. I really believe that the reasons why we have... the high alcoholism rates, the dropout rates, the high suicide rates [is because] young people [are] growing up without hope. And this is where I hope that... my story can impact the youth of tomorrow.

[T]here are two areas that I can really impact today, and that is the youth of our native lands. I also feel that I can provide some guidance in the areas of economic development. I really believe that it isn't just developing programs where we can build buildings, fill our buildings with inventory, and then hang signs and open them up for business that is going to allow us to be successful. [W]e need to address the mental health of our people so that we have young Indian people growing up with the belief that they can achieve, that they can be successful in business, because a lot of times when we are out there pressing the needs for economic development, we take people who come from disparity and from tough economic conditions, and many times these people don't believe that they can be successful.

A lot of the problems that we face today can be resolved... if we were to take a positive approach, that we start becoming solution-conscious, not problem-conscious; that all of us working together can overcome the things that we have been faced with in the past. And I believe that is what this American dream is all about, because in my own life, when I was blameful of other things, when I was blameful of my heritage, that is when I had the toughest time. But once I took responsibility for myself, then I started to realize that I was able to hold my future in my own hands, and by working hard and by believing positively things were able to turn around.

[I]f I can serve as a role model to Indian country . . . we can [learn to] approach the things that are against us with a positive attitude and we can overcome those things. I have seen tremendous success in the last few years by a number of tribes that have taken positive approaches, and they have resolved some tough things. . . .

Gaming as a Stepping Stone
I think some tribes are doing very well and some tribes are still struggling, even though gaming is part of their economic opportunity. Gaming is like any other business opportunity; you need to have positive goal-driven thinking people in there running it; you need to be in a place of good location for it to be successful. But like anything else that we are faced with in Indian country . . . we have to manage those resources appropriately [so] we don't take this gift that we have been blessed with in the last few years and let our people have an easy way. [G]aming is only an opportunity that should be used as a stepping stone, and. . . tribes . . . need to use it as a beginning, as a developing point so that we can go on and invest in other areas. . . .

[W]hen I have talked to other Indian people and I asked them about what they would like to grow up to be, they . . . tell me that . . . they would like to get out of school and then go to work in the casino. . . . I hope that we can change that around so we can get our young people to say that I would like to learn how to be an accountant and work in that casino, or I would like to learn how to be a cook and work in that casino; but that we would actually use these opportunities to learn meaningful occupations, meaningful vocations that, if gaming was no longer around, that we should learn the difference between employment and employability.

So today I think that gaming has presented an opportunity to our tribes that we have never had before. I have seen tribes that prior to gaming . . . were very dependent upon the Federal Government, had substandard school systems [and now] they have built hospitals and clinics. [T]hey have built . . . infrastructure and really have become a very meaningful part of the community. [G]aming has provided an important opportunity, but it is an opportunity that should only be used as a stepping stone.[7]

CHAPTER 62

Carl J. Artman

Assistant Secretary for Indian Affairs (March 8, 2007–May 23, 2008)

ON AUGUST 2, 2006, eighteen months after the resignation of Anderson, President Bush nominated Carl Joseph Artman III as assistant secretary, with the Senate voting 87–1 to confirm him on March 5, 2007; he was sworn into office three days later.¹ A member of the Oneida Tribe of Wisconsin, Artman was born on March 15, 1965, in Des Moines, Iowa, to Dr. Carl and Carol Artman. He earned a bachelor's degree from Columbia College in 1987, a juris doctorate from the Washington School of Law in 1991, an MBA from the University of Wisconsin–Madison, in 1999, and an LLM from the University of Denver Sturm College of Law in 2003, with an emphasis in natural resource and environmental law.

Artman served as a legislative assistant for Congressman Michael G. Oxley (Republican, Ohio) for three years before joining the Oneida Tribe as director of federal affairs in Washington, DC, in 1994. After serving in several management roles, he became chief legal counsel for the Oneida Tribe, and in 2004, he served as vice chairman of the Bush–Cheney Wisconsin Steering Committee, creating an opportunity for his February 2006 appointment as assistant solicitor—Indian affairs for the Department of the Interior. Later that year, President Bush nominated Artman as the tenth assistant secretary for Indian affairs. Serving just fourteen months, Artman had limited impact on the development of Indian policy, with the *Cobell* litigation the single greatest challenge of his administration.

While Artman pledged to address the challenges of youth suicide, drug abuse, chronic unemployment, poor health care, inadequate educational facilities and curricula, crumbling infrastructure, and crime, the brevity of his tenure precluded any substantive change. The Great Recession that began in 2006 compounded matters, although it did not change Artman's position that tribes needed to develop their natural, political, and socioeconomic infrastructure.

He believed the success of one tribe was the best incubator for the success of others.²

As did nearly all assistant secretaries before him, Artman stressed economic development. In May 2007, he convened tribal leaders to an economic summit in Phoenix to articulate policy recommendations. To his credit, the summit included tribal leaders, federal policymakers, Native American entrepreneurs, tribal economic development professionals, and private sector leaders, the first time such a diverse gathering of leaders assembled. The summit addressed key issues, including physical and legal infrastructure limitations in Indian Country, tribal access to capital and financing, and the need for developing competitive business plans for national and international markets.³ The prosperity of tribal nations was dependent not on "federal aid and guidance," Artman surmised, as much as it was on tribes making their own economic choices. More than three hundred policy recommendations emerged from the summit, including increasing tribal construction capabilities, eliminating impediments to tax-exempt bond financing, and improving the management and development of tribal lands.

Artman advanced new guidelines for federal acknowledgment in 2008 that were intended to expedite negative reviews and reduce the timeframe for tribes seeking to demonstrate federal status, while also providing policy governing splinter tribal groups seeking federal recognition. He announced new regulations regarding the Indian Gaming Regulatory Act, which prohibited land-into-trust for tribes seeking to conduct gaming activities on lands acquired after October 17, 1988. The culmination of a year-long effort to bring "predictability, stability, and accountability" to gaming, the new regulations articulated a process for the Department of the Interior to bring land into trust. The process, however, was criticized by tribal leaders who complained Artman did not consult with them on the new policy.⁴

Without reason, Artman resigned as assistant secretary on April 28, 2008, leaving office on May 23. George T. Skibone (Osage Tribe), a career bureau administrator, assumed the mantle of leadership for the Office of the Assistant Secretary, the Bureau of Indian Affairs, and the Bureau of Indian Education, remaining through the end of the Bush administration. Upon resigning, Artman joined the law firm of Godfrey and Kahn before accepting a faculty position at Arizona State University's Sandra Day O'Connor School of Law in 2009, where he also served as director of the Tribal Economic Development Program. He continues to serve on various boards, such as the Native American Venture Fund, and represent tribal clients and provide expert testimony.

Partnering with Tribes
Indian country has its unique, though historically consistent problems, like the erosion of sovereignty, expanding governance and self-determination, fighting to maintain its identity and control over its destiny and lands.... Yet, I see the determination and potential of Indians and Alaska Natives. Reservation populations are growing. Leaders are digging in to stem the spread of methamphetamines and the lawlessness that follows. Educators, parents and police are learning to identify youths at risk of committing suicide and interceding.

Teachers at tribal schools provide more with less, and inch-by-inch tribes are reclaiming their land and the inherent rights of such ownership. As Indians and Alaska Natives reclaim their rights lost through history or to societal plagues, the Department of the Interior must be their partner in these battles. [We must] expedite and streamline access to departmental goals to assist tribal and Alaska Native communities to develop their natural, political and socioeconomic infrastructure.

Trust Litigation
The trust litigation of the last decade has tested the commitment of many, especially the overarching individual Indian money account litigation. Many in the department are afraid their actions, no matter how well-meaning or beneficial to the tribes, may run afoul of the attorneys or the sitting judge, and that they may be held in contempt. This fear bogs down the department. It impedes Indian-centric goals of the department and hurts tribes and individuals across the Nation. Resolution to this matter is critical, whether it comes from Congress, the Administration or the courts.

From whatever quarter it hails... I stand ready to assist in its development and implementation. The sooner this litigation ends, the sooner we improve our relationship with tribes and the sooner we increase for Indians and Alaska Natives the impact of the benefits of that relationship.

Replicating Success
The Department of the Interior can and will be a positive force in Indian country. It is impossible to eliminate immediately that which has festered for many years. However, I will lay the foundation for an era that will provide a fresh start and new commitments through action to programmatic goals and mandated duties. This will allow tribal governments, Indians and Alaska Natives to build bulwarks against societal plagues. They can reclaim

their unique cultures, rich in tradition, spirituality and group-centric values, not one of despair or hopelessness.

I will foster an interaction of partnership and mutual goals, not just fiduciary requirements. [T]he Assistant Secretary for Indian Affairs [must] promote communications between tribes that have realized financial success through gaming or other business ventures, and those that strive for a fraction of that success, to move beyond the provision of subsistence benefits to their membership.

The success of one tribe, either in business, government administration or cultural preservation, is the best incubator for success of other tribes. Trailblazing tribes allow those that follow to go even further.

I will . . . promote more vibrant and goal-oriented communications between tribes and their neighbors, be it a local or State government or a business that seeks to partner with a tribe for their mutual benefit [and] foster the growth of tribal governments. Tribal sovereignty is inherent and this sovereignty is best exhibited in a vibrant tribal government, one that understands judicious exercise of its jurisdiction for the benefit of its members and the seventh generation.

Tribes Can Accomplish Greatness

Tribal governments embody the power of sovereignty. Tribal government cares for the present and plans for the future. It is what the outside examines to judge the health of the tribe. It is the face of the tribe and the hope of the tribe.

Tribal governments can accomplish great things. The peoples and tribes of the Haudenosaunee, the Iroquois Confederacy, comprise the oldest continuous participatory democracy on earth. Authors of our United States representative government, Ben Franklin and Thomas Jefferson, were inspired by the Iroquois Confederacy, its inner workings, and the constitution of the Iroquois known as the Great Binding Law, or in our language, *Gayanashagowa*.

Our founding fathers' inspirations rooted in the Haudenosaunee guide all of our lives today and continue to motivate people across the globe to achieve a greater freedom for themselves and their countrymen. That is the potential of tribal governments.[5]

CHAPTER 63

Larry J. Echo Hawk

Assistant Secretary for Indian Affairs (May 22, 2009–April 27, 2012)

WITH THE ELECTION OF Barack Obama as president in November 2008, the search for the next assistant secretary began, with the president nominating Larry Jack Echo Hawk as the eleventh assistant secretary on April 9, 2009. Echo Hawk was born on August 2, 1948, in Cody, Wyoming, to Ernest and Emma Jane Echo Hawk. One of six siblings—all of whom attended college, with four graduating from Brigham Young University (BYU)—Echo Hawk and two brothers (John and Tom) earned law degrees. Echo Hawk inherited the surname of his great-grandfather who, as a Pawnee scout, was given the name Hawk, which represents bravery in Pawnee culture. While his great-grandfather was a quiet man, many spoke of his accomplishments, giving rise to Echo Hawk.[1]

Echo Hawk played football at Farmington (New Mexico) High School, earning a scholarship to BYU, where he graduated with a degree in physical education in 1970. After serving a tour in the US Marine Corps—and at the encouragement of his brother John—he earned a juris doctorate from the University of Utah School of Law in 1973 and pursued postgraduate work at Stanford University's School of Business. He began his legal career with the California Indian Legal Services before opening his own law firm in Salt Lake City in 1975. Two years later, he became general counsel for the Fort Hall Shoshone–Bannock tribes, remaining there until 1986; he also served as special counsel for the Fort Hall tribes until his 2009 confirmation as assistant secretary.

In 1982, Echo Hawk entered politics by winning a House seat to the thirty-third legislative district of the state of Idaho, before winning a second two-year term representing the twenty-seventh district two years later. In 1986, he was elected Bannock County prosecuting attorney, and four years later, he became the first American Indian to be elected as state attorney general. In 1992, he served as national cochairman of Native Americans for Bill Clinton before unsuccessfully running for governor of Idaho in 1994. He then accepted a faculty position at BYU's J. Reuben Clark School of Law.²

Echo Hawk came highly recommended by scores of tribal nations and organizations when President Obama nominated him. On May 19, 2009, the Senate confirmed Echo Hawk, and he was sworn into office three days later. He advanced an ambitious agenda, stressing economic development while lamenting the 80 percent unemployment rate in some parts of Indian Country. He also praised the 670,000 jobs Indian gaming created, pledging to enforce the Indian Gaming Regulatory Act in a "reasonable manner" while working with tribes to expand gaming and take land into trust.³ He committed to amending federal acknowledgment, believing it was broken due to the length of time it took petitioning tribes to go through the process.

As assistant secretary, Echo Hawk worked with tribal leaders to reconsider the 2008 regulations governing land-into-trust under the Indian Gaming Regulatory Act, calling the Bush–era guidelines contrary to self-determination. After holding extensive consultation hearings with tribes, and after listening to their concerns, he rescinded the rules. He then revised the guidelines of the Office of Federal Acknowledgment, clarifying the review standards and definition of "reasonable likelihood" of success. He further courted improved tribal relations by committing to consult with tribes on all matters affecting them. He launched a comprehensive consultation policy developed in close cooperation with tribal nations, mandating tribal input on all statutory or administrative actions, including rule making, policy guidance, legislative proposals, grant funding formula changes, or operational activities.⁴ In line with these goals, Echo Hawk convened a conference with Salazar, tribal leaders, and tribal organizations to address a series of economic development, public safety, trust, and education reforms, beginning with organizational realignments, including elevating the line authority of the directors of the Bureau of Indian Affairs and Bureau of Indian Education to report directly to the assistant secretary.

In partial fulfillment of the Obama administration's pledge to improve public safety, Echo Hawk successfully lobbied Congress to enact the Tribal Law and Order Act (TLOA) in 2010, an act that authorized the appointment of special assistant US attorneys to prosecute tribal crimes in federal courts in an effort to address offenses that too often went unpunished due to lack of tribal resources. The TLOA empowered tribal courts to issue more stringent sentences and enabled tribal police officers to enforce federal law on tribal lands. Federal funds were available to improve drug trafficking prevention and to enhance recruitment of police officers. The law also enabled tribes to access the National Crimes Information Center database and to retrocede jurisdiction to the federal government.

The most significant achievement of the Echo Hawk era was the settlement of the trust funds mismanagement litigation in the *Cobell* lawsuit. A priority of the Obama administration, a settlement of the fifteen-year-old claim was announced on December 8, 2010, providing a "fair" settlement for the plaintiffs and a "responsible" one for the United States. The agreement led to the disbursement of $1.4 billion to more than 300,000 individual Native Americans to compensate them for their historical accounting claims. A $2 billion fund was then established to assist tribes in buying back and consolidating fractionated interests in allotted lands. That same year, Echo Hawk announced the settlement of four tribal water claims totaling $1 billion, and two years later he announced the settlement of a $1 billion trust accounting and natural resources mismanagement claim filed by forty-one tribes. Resolved in fewer than twenty-four months, the settlement ended claims that dated back more than a century.

To the chagrin of Indian Country, Echo Hawk announced his resignation on March 31, 2012, leaving office on April 27. The National Congress of American Indians summed up Echo Hawk's service, stating he had "set a new standard for generations to come" by framing a vision for Indian Country that included listening to tribal leaders and treating tribes with "dignity and respect."⁵ In his resignation letter, Echo Hawk explained his intent was to complete his term before returning to academia at BYU. Instead, he accepted a leadership position in the Mormon Church, having been appointed to the Quorum of the Seventy. In this capacity, he served several roles, becoming the first Native American to ever serve at such an elevated and respected position within the church. In February 2019, he joined the administration of Utah Governor Gary Herbert as a special assistant on Native American affairs. He continues to serve as an emeritus member of the Quorum of the Seventy, while also serving on numerous boards.

Economic Development
Many Native American communities are among the poorest segments of the ... United States. As an example, 8 out of the 10 poorest counties in the United States are within Indian reservations. The rate of unemployment of Native Americans is the highest of any ethnic group in America. People are alarmed when unemployment rates hover around 8% for the general

population, but within some areas of Indian Country the rate ... is nearly 80 percent. ...

When Indians decide to develop their mineral and energy sources on trust lands the Federal Government must act responsibly as trustee, but it must avoid unnecessary delay in giving required authorization.

Gaming has brought much needed revenue to many of the 562 federally recognized tribes. Indian gaming has created approximately 670,000 jobs and provided $11 billion to federal and state governments. Tribal revenue from gaming [continues to be] an important source of funding for education, health care, law enforcement and other tribal services. ...

Education
American Indian and Alaska Native students score significantly lower than their peers in reading and math. Native youth also experience some of the highest high school dropout rates in the country. The federally supported Indian education system has responsibility for educating 48,000 students at 183 schools. There must be an improvement in test scores and dropout rates within this educational system. Dilapidated school buildings must be repaired or replaced and housing for school teachers must be improved. Sustained economic development and prosperity cannot be achieved without a well-educated workforce. Education must be improved at all levels, including higher education.

Criminal Law Enforcement
The rate of aggravated assault against American Indians and Alaska Natives is roughly twice that of the country as a whole. Violence against Indian women and abuse of Indian children continue to be major problems. Epidemic methamphetamine use is now occurring in many Indian communities.

More criminal law enforcement officers are needed. Tribal courts need adequate funding. Tribal judges, prosecutors and defenders need better training. Jurisdictional gaps in the system of criminal law enforcement within Indian Country need to be fixed. United States Attorneys need to be more active in prosecuting crime within Indian Country.

I will fight crime and increase public safety in Native American communities. This ... includes consultation with tribal leaders and coordination with state and federal law enforcement agencies. Additional resources must be made available for police officers, judges, prosecutors, defenders, probation officers, courts, detention facilities and training.

Trust Reform

The *Cobell* litigation has focused attention on the accountability for management of trust assets. The Department of the Interior must move forward in a responsible manner in the management of trust lands, resources, and other assets....

The Bureau of Indian Affairs (BIA) and Bureau of Indian Education (BIE) provide services to 562 Indian tribes. This includes the administration and management of 55.7 million acres of land held in trust by the United States for American Indians and Alaska Natives....

The BIA and BIE have been criticized for not efficiently administering their responsibilities. Attention must be given to identifying areas of delay, mismanagement and neglect. Action must be taken to improve the administration of trust responsibilities. There must also be assurance that trust responsibilities are administered in accordance with high ethical standards.

Tribal Recognition and Land into Trust

The tribal recognition system is not working. The process of reviewing and acting upon applications for federal recognition is taking too much time. Applicants deserve a clear and timely procedure that will yield fair results.

The *Carcieri v. Kempthorne* decision by the United States Supreme Court appears to limit the Interior Secretary's authority under the 1934 Indian Reorganization Act to take lands into trust status on behalf of a tribe that was not under federal jurisdiction when the Act was adopted.[6] Many questions have arisen about the impact of this decision and about how to best resolve those questions.

Health

Forty-percent of health care needs of Native Americans are unmet. Many basic elements of good health care are lacking in Indian Country: doctors, nurses, mental health professionals, addiction counselors, and medical equipment and facilities. Native Americans suffer the highest rate of Type 2 diabetes in the world. Indian youth are twice as likely to commit suicide.

The Assistant Secretary of Indian Affairs does not have primary responsibility for addressing health care needs, but services provided by the Bureau of Indian Affairs and Bureau of Indian Education are indirectly connected to the provision of vital health care services. The Assistant

Secretary of Indian Affairs must be mindful and supportive of the need to provide quality health care services.

I pledge to work cooperatively . . . in addressing important issues that affect the lives of American Indians and Alaska Natives. I will reach out to leaders of tribal governments and listen carefully to their concerns and recommendations. Furthermore, I [will] work tirelessly and faithfully in executing my duties and responsibilities. I am confident that working together we can make significant progress in improving the quality of life for all Native Americans and honor the solemn commitments of the United States of America.[7]

CHAPTER 64

Kevin K. Washburn

*Assistant Secretary for Indian Affairs
(October 9, 2012–December 31, 2015)*

On AUGUST 2, 2012, President Obama nominated Kevin K. Washburn of the Chickasaw Nation to be the twelfth assistant secretary for Indian affairs, with the Senate unanimously confirming him on September 22. He was sworn in and took office on October 9. Washburn was born in rural southeastern Oklahoma on August 9, 1967, to the Chickasaw citizen Shirley (Wallace) Stark. His childhood was spent in small-town Oklahoma, including Purcell, Heavener, and Ada, before he graduated from Moore High School in 1985. He earned a degree in economics from the University of Oklahoma and attended law school at Washington University in St. Louis before completing his juris doctorate at Yale University in 1993.

Fresh out of law school, Washburn served as a judicial clerk for Judge William C. Canby Jr. at the US Ninth Circuit Court of Appeals in Phoenix. He then moved to Washington, DC, to work as an attorney at the US Justice Department. Three years later he returned to the West to serve as assistant US attorney for New Mexico. Washburn returned to Washington, DC, in 2000 to serve as general counsel for the National Indian Gaming Association.

A former law school professor at the universities of New Mexico (1997–2000 and 2009–2012), Minnesota (2002–2008), Arizona (2008–2009), and Harvard University (2007–2008), Washburn was a widely published Indian law scholar, having written extensively on—and drafted parts of—the Tribal Law and Order Act, and he coedited the 2012 update of Felix Cohen's 1942 *Handbook of Federal–Indian Law*. Recognizing that self-governance was not the answer for every tribal nation, Washburn worked to ensure that tribes had the ability to choose whether to contract, compact, or maintain a direct-service relationship with the bureau, believing the government-to-government relationship was strong because self-governance was at "its modern zenith."[1]

As assistant secretary, Washburn oversaw the implementation of the land buy-back program under the *Cobell* settlement. By the end of his tenure, the United States had acquired nearly 1.5 million fractionated allotted acres and restored them to tribal ownership. Working with Interior Secretary Sally Jewell, Washburn also helped restore nearly 570,800 acres of tribal homelands by bringing them into trust. In conjunction with the land buy-back program, Washburn amended the land-into-trust regulations to include a "speak now or forever hold your peace" provision.[2]

Washburn attempted to modify the federal acknowledgment process in 2013 to align the starting date for a petitioning tribal group with the 1934 Indian Reorganization Act rather than 1789. The department published proposed regulations that would allow petitioners to use the Indian Reorganization Act date to demonstrate tribal cohesion and political authority over their members and eliminate the date for being recognized as a tribe by third parties from 1900 to the present. The final rule, however, did not include the 1934 date since many tribes expressed concern that such a date might weaken the evidence for proving tribal cohesion and redefine tribes as racial, rather than political, entities.[3]

The crown jewel of Washburn's term in office was the extension of the Violence against Women Act (VAWA) to Indian Country by amending the Indian Civil Rights Act to authorize criminal jurisdiction for tribal courts over non-Indians who committed domestic violence against Native American women within Indian Country. To further tribal authority, Washburn executed a policy that intentionally reaffirmed the federal government's political relationship with tribal nations, one constructed on the foundation of the US Constitution and federal treaties, statutes, executive orders, and court rulings. The policy outlined a series of principles that included respecting tribal sovereignty and the tribal government's right to "make important decisions about their own best interests."[4] During the Washburn tenure, President Obama established the annual White House Tribal Nations Conference that focused on supporting tribes to "build a foundation for a successfully and culturally vibrant future," and for the first time established a government-to-government relationship with Native Hawaiians.

On December 10, 2015, Washburn announced his resignation, with Secretary Jewell appointing Principal Deputy Assistant Secretary Lawrence S. Roberts (Oneida Tribe) as acting assistant secretary. Washburn left office on January 1, 2016, returning to the University of New Mexico where he resumed his career as dean of the School of Law. A prolific writer, Washburn has written scores of federal Indian law articles and books, including *Gaming and Gambling: Cases and Materials*.[5] In 2017, he opined that there was a renaissance occurring with tribal self-government while at the same time cautioning tribes that self-governance has come at the expense of a diminishing federal trust responsibility.⁶ In 2020, Washburn was inducted into the Chickasaw Nation Hall of Fame. Since June 2018, he has been the dean of the University of Iowa School of Law.

A Unique Time in History
[T]his is a special time of opportunity in Indian affairs, in large part, because of the many accomplishments of Congress and this Administration.... [T]he United States has moved drastically forward in Indian affairs within the last four years.... For example, [we have] achieved settlement of the *Cobell* case, a case that was decades in the making and which cast a long dark shadow over the administration of Indian affairs.... There are some significant hurdles left for the settlement to be successful, but [our] commitment to settle the case has created strong goodwill in Indian country....

While more work needs to be done in each of these areas, [we have] shown that, with cooperation and commitment, much can be accomplished to improve the everyday lives of Indian and Native communities....

Among the principles that ... guide me ... is a strong commitment to tribal self-determination and self-governance. My commitment to these bedrock principles are borne not just from the lofty political philosophies that undergird the U.S. Constitution, but from gritty personal experience.... The government-to-government relationship between the Federal Government and tribes is strong today because tribal self-governance is at its modern zenith....

I have questioned the logic of federal agencies serving Indian people. I do not question the federal public servants who work in the Indian country... [b]ut the overall structure of having services provided by people hundreds of miles away is rarely effective. And this brings me back to the basic principle that Indian tribes can serve their citizens, in many cases, better than the Federal Government can....

Indian self-governance has improved education, health care, and most other governmental services on reservations, but we have not adopted a self-governance model for criminal justice in Indian country.... Now I realize that immediate conversion to full self-governance is not the answer for every tribe, and that an important aspect of tribal self-determination is insuring that tribes are able to choose whether they wish to contract, compact, or be a "direct-service" tribe for federal programs. I [was] educated recently by a tribal leader who helped me to understand that "direct-service" tribes wish to receive the benefits of all of the solemn treaty promises made by the Federal Government. . . . I vow to work hard to insure that those important promises are kept.⁷

A Renaissance in Indian Country
For much of American history, the federal trust responsibility was characterized by broadening federal administrative control over Indian tribes, with federal officials making most of the important decisions on Indian reservations and diminishing tribal governmental authority. More recently, however, federal control has been receding and giving way to a gradual restoration of tribal authority. More and more, the federal government defers to tribal priorities and tribal decision-making. While this development has been positive for tribes, it has come at a cost.

As tribal control has increased, courts have been less willing to hold the federal government responsible for its actions (and inactions) in Indian country. Indeed, if the most compelling way to determine the measure of a responsibility is to weigh the costs of its breach, the federal trust responsibility has been diminished. Judicial enforcement of the trust responsibility today is more rare and limited in scope.

Proclaiming the death of the trust responsibility, however, is premature. While courts have narrowed the legal enforceability of the trust responsibility to tribes, the political branches have expanded the meaning of the trust responsibility. Congress and the President have invigorated it with increased federal funding to provide the services and programs required to meet it. They have also settled dozens of breach-of-trust actions by tribes that might otherwise have been successfully defended by the federal government in the courts. In some ways, meaningful fulfillment of the federal trust responsibility has been relocated from the courts to the political branches. . . .

More importantly . . . the last fifty years have been characterized by the growth of federal contracting with tribes to perform federal trust functions. Today, billions of dollars of federal appropriations are spent not by the federal government, but by tribes that have contracted to provide federal services to Indian people through so-called "tribal self-determination contracts." In other words, tribes are being paid by the federal government to exercise federal governance powers over Indian lands and people.

In general, the new model has been very successful. As tribal governmental powers have increased and tribes have entered contracts to perform more federal functions, tribal governments have proven more institutionally competent than the federal government in serving Indian people. Consequently, while federal judicial interpretations of the trust responsibility have rendered the federal government less legally accountable to Indian people, the political branches have shifted these responsibilities to tribal governments that are much more accountable to Indian people. Today, on many reservations, the United States has been relegated to "principal underwriter" of many of the services required under the trust responsibility. As the federal trust responsibility has come to be seen in this new light, Indian people have gained greater control over their own destinies....

Tribes have been experiencing a renaissance, not just economically, but culturally and governmentally. How did this come to be...? The federal trust responsibility has evolved from a paternalistic obligation to care for Indian people to a tool protecting the boundaries of tribal governmental authority to provide that care itself. But the evolution is incomplete. Moreover, new conflicts and questions are inevitable as the power of tribal governments grows and tribes flex more governmental authority. The questions arising from tribal power will be answered in many different contexts and under different sets of rules. For some of the questions, guideposts already exist. For others, federal policymakers and judges have sometimes been left to construct answers on an ad hoc basis by muddling through specific laws and facts that fail to account for broader and more modern principles, such as norms of respect for tribal sovereignty.

As the formerly paternalistic trust responsibility gives way to a new federal policy favoring tribal self-governance, the role of the federal government on Indian reservations will continue to be debated and modified. During the coming decades, federal policymakers and courts will be forced to decide, in a range of areas, whether the federally supported tribal renaissance justifies more federal oversight of tribal decisions or, in the alternative, stronger allegiance to norms of respect for tribal sovereignty.[8]

CHAPTER 65

Tara MacLean Sweeney

Assistant Secretary for Indian Affairs (July 30, 2018–January 20, 2021)

BETWEEN THE DEPARTURE OF Washburn and newly elected President Donald Trump's nominee to head of the Bureau of Indian Affairs were three Native Americans serving in an acting capacity, including Oglala Sioux Michael S. Black (January 20 to June 11, 2017), Choctaw Gavin Clarkson (June 11 to September 3), and Kiowa John Tahsuda III (September 3 to July 30, 2018). On October 17, 2017, President Trump nominated Tara MacLean Sweeney, an Inupiat, as the first Alaska Native woman to serve as assistant secretary of the interior for Indian affairs.

An acclaimed businesswoman with the Arctic Slope Regional Corporation, Sweeney was the only daughter born to educators Dr. Bryan MacLean and Inupiaq mother and former member of the Alaska State House of Representatives, Eileen Panigeo MacLean. She attended local schools in rural Alaska before graduating from Barrow High School in 1993, the same year she became Miss National Congress of American Indians. She went on to Cornell University, graduating in 1998 with a degree in industrial and labor relations. Sweeney is a member of the Native Village of Barrow and the Inupiat community of the Arctic Slope.

Upon graduation from Cornell, Sweeney engaged in a variety of state, Alaska Native, and federal policy discussions that focused on responsible Native American energy policies and rural broadband connectivity, both of which she viewed as essential to tribal self-determination. She began her career at the Washington, DC, law firm of Van Ness Feldman as a lobbyist, before returning to Alaska where she was as a lobbyist for the Arctic Slope Regional Corporation, beginning a twenty-year career. Between 2015 and 2017 she cochaired the Arctic Economic Council while also serving on the Coast Guard Foundation board of trustees, the University of Alaska Foundation board of trustees, the Federal Communications Commission Advisory Committee, and Arctic Power. In

2003, Alaska Governor Frank Murkowski appointed her to his cabinet as a special assistant for rural affairs and education.[1] Prior to her confirmation as assistant secretary, Sweeney served as the executive vice president of External Affairs for the twelve-thousand-employee-strong Arctic Slope Regional Corporation, an Alaska Native corporation established under the Alaska Native Claims Settlement Act and in which Sweeney owned birthright shares of stock.

The president nominated Sweeney as assistant secretary on October 17, 2017, with the Senate Committee on Indian Affairs voting to move her nomination to the full Senate for a vote on June 6, 2018. On June 30, the Senate unanimously approved her nomination by voice vote; she assumed office on July 30, pledging to develop "strong relationships with tribes, Alaska Native corporations, and Hawaiian organizations to [find] innovative solutions for lifting up [tribal] communities." Her priorities included identifying efficiencies within the Bureau of Indian Affairs, providing culturally relevant curriculum to bureau schools, and creating a "more effective voice" for tribal nations within the American political system.[2] Her political philosophy includes being proactive in developing tribal resources while also gaining trust with tribal leaders through tribal consultation. In 2019, she demonstrated this philosophy by revising—with tribal consultation—the Tribal Energy Resource Agreement that expedited energy development in Indian Country.[3]

Less than four months after this policy change and amid the COVID-19 coronavirus pandemic of 2020, Sweeney found herself in a political broil that caused dozens of tribes and tribal organizations—including the National Congress of American Indians—to call for her resignation. When Congress enacted the Coronavirus Aid Relief and Economic Security (CARES) Act, it provided $8 billion to help tribal governments provide continuing governmental services to their citizens. In conjunction with the Treasury Department as the lead federal agency, Sweeney consulted with tribal leaders in early April. When she sought to disburse funds to Alaska Native corporations, tribes across the country objected since such corporations were for-profit entities.[4] While a federal court blocked the inclusion of the Alaska Native corporations from receiving stimulus funds on April 28, 2020, scores of tribes and tribal organizations stated Sweeney had "lost the confidence of Indian tribes."[5] While Alaska Native corporations did not receive such funds, they were eligible under other CARES Act provisions. As with opposition to President Trump, tribes unfairly viewed Sweeney as a lame duck. Sweeney left office on January 20, 2021, with Darryl LaCounte (Turtle Mountain Chippewa) appointed acting assistant secretary for Indian affairs by in-coming President Joe Biden.

A Proactive Approach

As Alaska Natives, like our American Indian counterparts, we are reaching for the same future with very similar tools [of] tribal governments to govern our respective social needs and traditional and cultural ways, and tribal corporations, to engage in the economic opportunities of our great Country. This reality has meant, and still means, that the Department of the Interior is very much a part of our past, our lives today, and will be in the future of the generations yet unborn. The DOI is a reality with which every Native American lives. I am honored to leave my homeland for a short time to engage in public service, but perhaps most important, to support tribal nations, tribal corporations and our tribal people across the Country.

[Our] mission . . . is "to engage in a robust government-to-government relationship with federally-recognized Indian Nations and to collaborate with Indian organizations and corporations to support socially, culturally and economically self-sufficient Indian peoples. . . ." I would like to bring the vast talent of Native leaders around the Country to help move our collective tribal and corporate interests forward. . . .

The Arctic is the most remote region in the United States. No roads connect our communities, the cost of living is extremely high, our people face significant social challenges and our region is plagued with insufficient sanitation facilities. Unfortunately, this is akin to the realities faced throughout the rest of Indian Country. To address these needs, our people have been proactive in accessing the resources of bonds markets, local taxing authority, and business investments. The work is far from done. We continue to push forward.

Tribal Consultation

I will utilize that same solutions-oriented perspective to serve all of Indian Country. I understand that the collective knowledge of our tribal leaders must be [our] top priority to serve the mission of Indian Affairs at the Department of the Interior. I [will be] listening to tribal leaders and the congressional committees of jurisdiction to hear the top priorities and establish a clear and comprehensive action plan. . . .

[F]or improved and effective service delivery, Indian Country needs a clear framework from the department, grounded in tribal consultation. . . . I expect these consultations will produce a myriad of priorities. Across this great Country, from the Southwest to the Northeast, one cannot paint Indian country with a single stroke. Indian Country is not a homogenous community. There are some stark and subtle differences that make each tribe unique.

I have great familiarity with energy development, education, housing, telecommunications, and business development issues, particularly within the context of rural and geographical isolation. . . . As I have been taught by my elders when taking on new ventures, in order to achieve success I must be guided by the principles focused on humility to hear, to be taught, to contemplate and to act. . . . I make decisions in consultation, and to act on the best ideas that move Indian Affairs and the decision-making of tribes forward.[6]

Conclusion

THE ADMINISTRATION OF INDIAN AFFAIRS has not always been dominated by the United States, and it has not always been administered by a commissioner of Indian affairs. In fact, since 1786 authority has been delegated to a superintendent of Indian affairs, a superintendent of the Indian trading houses, a superintendent of the Office of Indian Trade, a chief clerk, and a commissioner of Indian affairs, all of whom reported to the secretary of war. Since 1849, the commissioner of Indian affairs and, after 1977, the assistant secretary for Indian affairs have reported to the secretary of the interior. These administrators have been responsible for enforcing an Indian policy as directed by the president and Congress. These administrators have also executed policy based on their prevailing political and social philosophy.

Until recently the overarching goal of these administrators has been the social, economic, and political integration of Native Americans and the extinguishment of aboriginal title. This has been represented by two main policy braids. The first was exhibited in policies such as civilization, Christianization, assimilation, and termination. The second focused on gaining access to tribal land and resources as demonstrated by treaties and agreements, legislation such as the General Allotment Act, various acts authorizing the sale of original and inherited allotted land, the issuance of fee patents, and the removal of trust restrictions.

The Continental Congress was keenly aware that the success of the United Colonies was dependent on a policy of amity with tribal nations. The Congress valued the peace and friendship of the tribes so highly that it appointed men such as Benjamin Franklin and Patrick Henry as the first commissioners of Indian affairs. In fact, the Continental Congress appointed thirteen men as commissioners in 1775, underscoring the significance of the federal–Indian relationship to the fledging colonies. These commissioners included military officers, Indian traders, politicians, and men knowledgeable of tribal affairs who labored to establish an amicable relationship with the tribes during the American war for independence.

By 1786, Congress replaced these commissioners with two superintendents of Indian affairs modeled on the British style of Indian administration. Ten years later, Congress reduced the superintendents to one and assigned military men as superintendents of Indian trade. After 1806, when Congress established the Office of the Superintendent of Indian Trade, just three men held the office, including John Shee, John Mason, and Thomas McKenney. Between 1816 and 1822 McKenney served as superintendent but expanded his role to promote the civilization and agrarianism of the Indians. It was McKenney who persuaded Congress of its "duty" to adopt the civilization act that expanded federal administration of and involvement in Indian affairs.

When Congress abolished the trading houses in 1822, it created a temporary void in the administration of Indian affairs. Congress then appointed former Missouri territorial governor and Indian agent William Clark to serve as superintendent of Indian affairs. Two years later, Secretary of War John C. Calhoun administratively established an Indian Office to carry out the provisions of the civilization act and to manage the growing day-to-day administration of Indian affairs. As chief clerk of the Indian Office beginning in 1824, McKenney engaged in diplomatic and trade endeavors while promoting civilization and education, thus expanding the federal role in Indian affairs.

When Congress established the Department of the Interior in 1849 it fulfilled a goal two decades in the making. The transfer of the Indian Office into the new executive department reflected a notable change in political philosophy. Once having viewed tribal affairs as a military—and foreign—matter, Congress and the Indian Office now viewed tribal nations as domestic dependents. Commissioners such as Luke Lea and George Manypenny worked to reduce tribal landholding, helping give structure to the reservation policy. Tribes "can go no further," Manypenny explained, and with the railroads opening up the West, it would only be a matter of time before non-Indians would settle the land and build towns. Reservations, the commissioner philosophized, would provide tribes with the time to adjust to the new order.

While William Dole argued the need to recognize aboriginal title throughout the West—and then extinguish it through treaties—postbellum policy ushered in a unilateral cessation of treaty making by the United States. In conjunction with the War Department, the Indian Office confined Native Americans to reservations where Nathaniel Taylor argued the United States had a duty "to protect and care for, to elevate and civilize" the Indians. The industrialization of America encouraged settlement and the utilization of the West's natural resources. Assimilation was "inevitable," Francis Walker explained in 1872, as he advocated for a policy of submission lest Native Americans be crushed by the advancing frontier.

By the latter years of the century, land severalty became the fulcrum of assimilation, leading to a complete domination of Native Americans by the Indian Office. "The policy of the Government," Daniel Browning wrote in 1896, was to "fit" the Indians for citizenship by emphasizing land severalty. Concurrently, federal Indian schools served as the means of fostering cultural transformation while at the same time seeking to change Native Americans into yeoman farmers. For a half-century, commissioners—Republicans and Democrats—enforced policy that unshackled a continental juggernaut, which only subsided after the loss of 100 million acres of tribal land.

The single defining goal of policymakers and the Indian Office was citizenship. In theory, once Native Americans became citizens they were full-fledged Americans with all the rights and responsibilities of such. As Native Americans became citizens, the Indian Office no longer considered them tribal citizens and removed federal protections. The Indian Office transferred thousands of Indian children to local public schools. Where resistance occurred, commissioners such as William Jones enforced a mandatory policy of education, arguing no parent had "a moral or legal right to stand in the way of his child's advancement." The culmination of these efforts was the 1903 judicial pronouncement in *Lone Wolf v. Hitchcock* by which the Supreme Court affirmed federal plenary authority over tribal nations.

After the turn of the twentieth century, Francis Leupp introduced a new twist in the philosophy of integration by advancing the idea of carrying civilization to the Indians (on-reservation boarding and day schools) rather than carrying Indians to civilization (off-reservation boarding schools). In so doing, Leupp shifted the focus of integration from off-reservation to on-reservation. To foster integration, Leupp also encouraged opening such schools to "pupils of all races" as a means of breaking down cultural barriers.

Land alienation accelerated in the early twentieth century, especially under Cato Sells, who took "aggressive steps" to lease or sell Indian land. Sells used his Declaration of Policy to issue fee patents based on arbitrary competency tests and then "liberalized" the sale of such lands. By the administration of Charles Burke in the 1920s, it was apparent that federal policy had failed to transform Native Americans. Educational achievement and health care were abysmal, tribal social structures and governing bodies were in disarray, irrigation projects designed to support tribal growers instead benefited non-Indians who homesteaded or acquired land on opened reservations, and tribal law and order was in shambles. A philosophy of land ownership having a mystical power to assimilate and transform Native Americans into yeoman farmers had proven both misguided and destructive.

By the 1930s, shifting political philosophies initiated a new phase of policy and ushered in a period of cultural pluralism and self-government. Between 1929 and 1948, just three men served as commissioner of Indian affairs, including Charles Rhoads, John Collier, and William Brophy. These commissioners reflected a secular and more liberal-minded generation of progressive reformers who influenced both the development and execution of policy. Collier, for instance, sought to reverse fifty years of "individualization" by restoring tribalism and rebuilding tribal organizations. He ended land severalty and promoted self-government. Brophy, meanwhile, emphasized a tribal-specific policy rather than applying a one-size-fits-all policy that had governed Indian affairs for nearly two centuries.

But in the postwar years, Congress and the Indian Office renewed their assimilative policies by enforcing a termination policy that sought the end of the federal–Indian relationship and the release of Indian land from its trust protection. While Brophy fended off for a time the inevitable, he was powerless to stop the trajectory of policy. Dillon Myer advocated for and enforced a withdrawal of services "as rapidly as circumstances" permitted, and he actively encouraged young Native Americans to relocate to urban centers where he believed federal responsibility ended. Myer's successor Glenn Emmons undertook efforts to sever the political relationship with scores of tribes and labored to integrate Native Americans into the nation's social fabric.

Every commissioner of Indian affairs and assistant secretary for Indian affairs since the Kennedy administration influenced an evolving policy of economic development and self-determination. Philleo Nash initiated a shift in the Bureau of Indian Affairs from custodial care to technical support, emphasizing tribal tourism as a form of economic development. The appointment of Robert Bennett as commissioner in 1966 reflected a long-sought-for shift in Indian administration. Beginning with Bennett, every commissioner of Indian affairs and assistant secretary for Indian affairs was Native American, with all advancing economic development as an integral part of self-government.

To the surprise of many in Indian Country, Louis Bruce and Morris Thompson—with the support of President Nixon—advanced self-determination, encouraging tribes to contract with the federal government to assume control of federal programs and services and then adjust them to meet their needs. Indian Country in the post-1980s would not only be defined by tribal self-government but would also be influenced by tribal calls for a policy of self-determination based on a philosophy of inherent tribal sovereignty and right to self-government.

But the past forty years have also been driven by disparate political philosophies. While the federal government has been committed to a policy of self-government, each administrator of Indian affairs has reflected this national dichotomy of partisan politics. While Indian Country has enjoyed a growth in economic development as a means of improving tribal socioeconomic status, the philosophical framework of each assistant secretary for Indian affairs has reflected how the policies of economic development (i.e., land-into-trust, federal acknowledgment, resource settlements, etc.) were enforced or executed.

The political dichotomy is unlikely to change any time soon and represents the main challenge facing tribes in their quest to regain self-governance and self-determination. Policies encouraging self-government with too much federal involvement foster dependency, while policies with too little support frustrate self-governance. To ensure viability, tribes must continue to establish strategic goals unique to their cultures and resources. If they seek to develop their natural resources, the federal government "must act responsibly as trustee," as former Assistant Secretary Larry Echo Hawk stated. At the same time, if tribes "keep doing what [they've] always done, then [they're] going to always get what [they've] always gotten," as former Assistant Secretary Neil McCaleb once explained. The key is finding a balance that encourages partnership and full tribal development without federal paternalism stifling tribes.

NOTES

Introduction

1. Farrard, *The Records of the Federal Convention*, 1:316, 2:321.
2. Farrard, *The Records of the Federal Convention*, 2:367.
3. Farrard, *The Records of the Federal Convention*, 2:493, 2:495.
4. Cherokee Nation v. Georgia, 30 U.S. 1 (1831), at 18.
5. Kawashima, "Colonial Government Agencies," 245; "Daniel Gookin, 1612–1687," The Native Northeast Research Collaborative, https://nativenortheastportal.com/bio/bibliography/gookin-daniel-1612-1687.
6. Vaughn, *New England Frontier*, 176.
7. Kawashima, "Legal Origins of the Indian Reservations in Colonial Massachusetts," 42–56.
8. Vaughn, *New England Frontier*, 246.
9. Trelease, *Indian Affairs in Colonial New York*, 207–208, 309.
10. Kawashima, "Colonial Government Agencies," 247–248.
11. Kawashima, "Colonial Government Agencies," 248.
12. Kawashima, "Colonial Government Agencies," 249.
13. Prucha, *American Indian Policy in the Formative Years*, 11.
14. Jacobs, "Edmond Atkin's Plan for Imperial Indian Control," 311–320.
15. Prucha, *American Indian Policy in the Formative Years*, 22–23.
16. Graymont, *The Iroquois in the American Revolution*, 100–101.
17. Calloway, *The American Revolution in Indian Country*, 202–203.
18. *Journal of the Continental Congress, 1774–1785*, 2:174 (hereafter *Continental Congress*).
19. *Continental Congress*, 2:175–176.
20. *Continental Congress*, 2:183; Hawley resigned November 23, 1775, with Edwards taking office on November 25, 1775. *Continental Congress*, 2:367–368. See also "Silas Deane's Diary," July 13, 1775, in *Letters of Delegates to Congress*, 1:93; "John Hancock to Philip Schuyler," July 18, 1775, in *Letters of Delegates to Congress*, 1:635.
21. "Thomas Cushing to Joseph Hawley," July 24, 1775, in *Letters of Delegates to Congress*, 1:660.
22. *Continental Congress*, 5:844–845.
23. *Continental Congress*, 30:368–369.
24. *Continental Congress*, 30:426.
25. *Continental Congress*, 31:490–493.

26. *Continental Congress*, 31:516.

27. *Continental Congress*, 31:747.

28. "James White (1749–1809)," Biographical Directory of the United States Congress, 1774–Present, https://bioguideretro.congress.gov/Home/MemberDetails?memIndex=W000377.

29. *Continental Congress*, 24:72.

30. *Continental Congress*, 21:340–341.

31. DeJong, *American Indian Treaties*, 47–50, 184–194.

32. *Continental Congress*, 33:455–457.

33. *Continental Congress*, 33:457, 33:459.

34. Prucha, *The Great Father*, 61.

35. "An Act to Regulate Trade and Intercourse with the Indian Tribes, and to preserve Peace on the Frontiers," 1 Stat. 469, at 473 (May 19, 1796).

36. *The Debates and Proceedings in the Congress of the United States, with an Appendix, Containing Important State Papers and Public Documents and All the Laws of a Public Nature*, First Cong., Second Sess., April 10, 1790, 2:1575.

37. "An act making provision for the purposes of Trade with the Indians," 1 Stat. 443 (March 3, 1795).

38. "An Act to revive and continue in force, an act intituled [sic] 'An act for establishing trading houses with the Indian tribes,'" 2 Stat. 173 (April 30, 1802); "An Act making appropriations for carrying into effect certain Indian treaties, and for other purposes of Indian trade and intercourse," 2 Stat. 338 (March 3, 1805); Rockwell, *Indian Affairs*, 75–76.

39. Rockwell, *Indian Affairs*, 77.

40. Hill, *Guide to the Records in the National Archives*, 18.

41. "An Act for establishing trading houses with the Indian tribes," 2 Stat. 402 (April 21, 1806).

42. Hill, *Guide to the Records in the National Archives*, 18.

43. "An Act making provision for the civilization of the Indian tribes adjoining the frontier settlements," 3 Stat. 516 (March 3, 1819); Viola, *Thomas L. McKenney*, 26, 40–43, 48.

44. "An Act to abolish the United States' trading establishment with the Indian tribes," 3 Stat. 679 (May 6, 1822).

45. Hill, *Guide to the Records in the National Archives*, 18; Viola, *Thomas L. McKenney*, 74–75.

46. "John Calhoun to William Clark," May 28, 1822, Records of the War Department General and Special Staff, Secretary's Office, Letters Sent, Indian Affairs, RG 165, E-59, National Archives and Records Service, Washington, DC.

47. "An Act to provide for the organization of the Department of Indian affairs," 4 Stat. 735 (June 3, 1834).

48. Viola, *Thomas L. McKenney*, 93–94. Calhoun also gave McKenney two clerks: Samuel S. Hamilton and Hezekiah Miller.

49. "Letter on the Superintendency of Indian Affairs," March 20, 1826, Nineteenth Cong., First Sess., *House Document No. 146, Congressional Serial Set 138*, 69.

50. Rockwell, *Indian Affairs*, 78; Viola, *Thomas L. McKenney*, 114.

51. "Report of Thomas L. McKenney, Office of Indian Affairs, Department of War, November 1, 1828, to the Honorable P. B. Porter, Secretary of War," *Annual Report of the Commissioner of Indian Affairs* (1828), 79 (hereafter *ARCIA*).

52. "Report on Indian Affairs," February 9, 1829, Twentieth Cong., Second Sess., *House Document No. 117, Congressional Serial Set 186.*

53. "An Act making provision for the civilization of the Indian tribes adjoining the frontier settlements," 3 Stat. 516 (March 3, 1819).

54. "Report on Creating a Home Department," March 29, 1830, Twenty-First Cong., First Sess., *Senate Document No. 30, Congressional Serial Set 193.*

55. "An Act to provide for the appointment of a commissioner of Indian affairs," 4 Stat. 564 (July 9, 1832).

56. "Letter of Peter B. Porter, Secretary of War, to President John Q. Adams," November 24, 1826, *ARCIA* (1828), 22; Viola, *Thomas L. McKenney*, 22–23, 92–115.

57. *ARCIA* (1837), 90–133. President Jackson approved of the regulations on November 11, 1836, and June 18, 1837. See *Office Copy of the Laws, Regulations, etc., of the Indian Bureau, 1850*, 15–78.

58. United States v. Rogers, 45 U.S. 567 (1846), at 573.

59. *Rogers*, 45 U.S. at 572.

60. *Annual Report of the Secretary of the Treasury* (1848), 36–37.

61. "Report of Robert J. Walker," December 9, 1848, Thirtieth Cong., Second Sess., *House Executive Document 7, Congressional Serial Set 538*, 36–37.

62. *The Congressional Globe*, Thirtieth Cong., Second Sess., February 12, 1849, 33:513–514.

63. The House vote was 112 to 78. The House approved of the bill on February 16. *The Congressional Globe*, Thirtieth Cong., Second Sess., February 16, 1849, 43:543–544. The Senate debate is in *The Congressional Globe*, Thirtieth Cong., Second Sess., February 16, 1849, 43:669–680.

64. "An Act to establish the Home Department, and to provide for the Treasury Department as assistant Secretary of the Treasury, and a Commissioner of the Customs," 9 Stat. 395 (March 3, 1849). See also Prucha, *The Great Father*, 319–323.

65. *ARCIA* (1849), 17.

66. "An Act making Appropriations for the current and contingent Expenses of the Indian Department, and for fulfilling Treaty Stipulations with various Indian Tribes, for the Year ending June the thirtieth, one thousand eight hundred and fifty-two," 9 Stat. 574 (February 27, 1851).

67. *ARCIA* (1856), 20–21.

68. *ARCIA* (1906), 64; *ARCIA* (1907), 53.

69. "An Act to ratify an agreement with the Indians of the Fort Hall Indian Reservation in Idaho, and making appropriations to carry the same into effect," 31 Stat. 676 (June 6, 1900).

70. Lone Wolf v. Hitchcock, 187 U.S. 553 (1903).

71. *Public Papers of the President: Containing the Public Messages, Speeches, and Statements of the President, Richard Nixon, 1970*, 575.

72. *American Indian Policy Review Commission, Report on BIA Management*, 6; *American Indian Policy Review Commission, Final Report*, 287–289.

73. Reorganization Plan of 1950, 64 Stat. 1262. The act declared that "There shall be in the Department of the Interior one additional Assistant Secretary of the Interior, who shall be appointed by the President, by and with the advice and consent of the Senate, who shall perform such duties as the Secretary of the Interior shall prescribe, and who shall receive compensation at the rate prescribed by law for Assistant Secretaries of executive departments."

74. *Federal Register*, October 3, 1977, 42:53682.

75. "Bureau of Indian Affairs Reorganization Task Force," *Federal Register*, April 17, 1978, 43:16285 and 43:16294.

76. Prucha, *The Great Father*, 1123–1124.

77. Trahant, *The Last Great Battle of the Indian Wars*, 96.

78. *Senate Report 243*, Eightieth Cong., First Sess., *Congressional Serial Set 11115*.

79. Prucha, *The Great Father*, 1227–1229. Table 8. Indian Office Authority over Tribal Nations, 1887–1934

Chapter 1: John Harris

1. Harris, *Records of the Harris Family*, 27.

2. "Letter from Jno. Harris, Fort Washington, to Samuel Hodgdon," September 1, 1792, Post-Revolutionary War Papers, 1784–1815, RG 94, National Archives and Records Administration, Washington, DC (hereafter NARA). http://wardepartmentpapers.org/s/home/item/43209.

3. "Jno. Harris, Fort Washington, to Samuel Hodgdon," July 6, 1793, Second Congress: Reports and Communications Submitted to the Senate by the Secretary of the Treasury, RG 96, NARA, 2A–F2. http://wardepartmentpapers.org/s/home/item/43209.

4. "James McHenry to John Harris," November 11, 1796, Post-Revolutionary War Papers, 1784–1815, RG 94, NARA. http://wardepartmentpapers.org/s/home.

5. "James McHenry to John Harris," November 11, 1796, Post-Revolutionary War Papers, 1784–1815, RG 94, NARA. http://wardepartmentpapers.org/s/home.

6. "James McHenry and Samuel Hodgdon to John Harris," May 28, 1800, Consolidated Correspondence File, 1794–1890, in Papers of the War Department, 1784–1800, RG 92, NARA. http://wardepartmentpapers.org/s/home.

Chapter 2: William Irvine

1. *The Irvine–Newbold Family Papers*, 2.

2. Explore Pennsylvania History, http://explorepahistory.com/.

3. "William Irvine (1741–1804)," Biographical Directory of the United States Congress, 1774–Present, https://bioguideretro.congress.gov/Home/MemberDetails?memIndex=I000035.
4. Hill, *Guide to the Records in the National Archives of the United States*, 18.
5. *The Irvine–Newbold Family Papers*, 4.

Chapter 3: George W. Ingels

1. "Famous Early Members of the Carpenter's Company," The Carpenter's Hall, www.carpentershall.org/famous-early-members.
2. "To Thomas Jefferson from Robert Patterson and Andrew Ellicott," May 9, 1801, in Oberg, *The Papers of Thomas Jefferson*, 34:69–70.
3. "Schuylkill Arsenal to Wheeling," Discovering Lewis & Clark, www.lewis-clark.org/article/2980.
4. "George Ingels to President Jefferson," October 5, 1804, in McClure, *The Papers of Thomas Jefferson*, 44:481.

Chapter 4: William Davy

1. "Mr. Davy's Diary 1794," Part 1, 125.
2. "William Davy to George Washington," December 24, 1794, Founders Online, National Archives, https://founders.archives.gov/documents/Washington/05-17-02-0218.
3. "Mr. Davy's Diary 1794," Part 2, 276.
4. "An Act for establishing trading houses with the Indian tribes," 2 Stat. 402 (April 21, 1806).
5. "Mr. Davy's Diary 1794," Part 2, 270.

Chapter 5: John Shee

1. Klein, *Lancaster County Pennsylvania*, III:99.
2. Nichols, *Engines of Diplomacy*, 71.
3. "An act for establishing Trading Houses with the Indian Tribes," 1 Stat. 452 (April 18, 1796).
4. "An act for establishing trading houses with the Indian tribes," 2 Stat. 402 (April 21, 1806).
5. Nichols, *Engines of Diplomacy*, 71.
6. Nichols, *Engines of Diplomacy*, 2.
7. Downey, "The Illinois Indian Trade 1783–1818."

8. Illinois Company Deed of July 5, 1773, and Wabash Company Deed of October 18, 1775, in "Illinois and Wabash Land Company," in Lowrie, *American State Papers, Documents, Legislative and Executive, of the Congress of the United States, in Relation to the Public Lands* (hereafter, *American State Papers, Public Lands*), 1:21. The Senate deemed the deeds to not have vested since the lands were privately purchased.

9. "Illinois and Wabash Land Company," in Lowrie, *American State Papers, Public Lands*, 1:173.

Chapter 6: John M. Mason

1. Webb, "John Mason of Analostan Island," 21.
2. "An act additional to, and amendatory of, an act, intituled [sic] 'An act concerning the District of Columbia,'" 2 Stat. 195 (May 3, 1802).
3. Mason, *The Life and Diplomatic Correspondence of John M. Mason*, 8.
4. Webb, "John Mason of Analostan Island," 30; "An act for establishing trading houses with the Indian tribes," 1 Stat. 452 (Section 2) (April 18, 1796).
5. "An act supplemental to the act intituled [sic] 'An act for establishing trading houses with the Indian tribes,'" 2 Stat. 544 (March 3, 1809).
6. Nichols, *Engines of Diplomacy*, 72.
7. "John Mason to Secretary of War William Crawford," March 6, 1816, in Lowrie, *American State Papers, Documents, Legislative and Executive, of the Congress of the United States, from the First Session of the Fourteenth to the Second Session of the Nineteenth Congress, Inclusive* (hereafter *ASP: Congress*), 2:70.
8. The John Mason Papers are located at the Gunston Fall Library and Archives in Mason Neck, Virginia.
9. "John Mason to Secretary of War William H. Crawford," February 9, 1816, in Lowrie, *ASP: Congress*, 2:66–67.

Chapter 7: Thomas L. McKenney

1. "An Act making provision for the civilization of the Indian tribes adjoining the frontier settlements," 3 Stat. 516 (March 3, 1819).
2. Viola, *Thomas L. McKenney*, 93.
3. "An Act to abolish the United States' trading establishments with the Indian tribes," 3 Stat. 679 (May 6, 1822).
4. Viola, *Thomas L. McKenney*, 94.
5. "An act to provide for the appointment of a commissioner of Indian affairs, and for other purposes," 4 Stat. 564 (July 9, 1832).
6. See Johnson v. McIntosh, 21 U.S. 543 (1823), for a discussion of this legal question.
7. Viola, "Thomas L. McKenney, 1824–30," 1–7; Viola, *Thomas L. McKenney*, 224.
8. *ARCIA* (1828), 79–80.

9. *ARCIA* (1829), 165–166.
10. "Letter of Secretary of War Peter B. Porter to the President of the United States," *ARCIA* (1828), 20–23.

Chapter 8: William Clark

1. Foley, *Wilderness Journey*, 13–17.
2. Miller, *Native America*, 108.
3. Satz, *American Indian Policy during the Jacksonian Era*, 188.
4. "An act to provide for the organization of the Department of Indian affairs," 4 Stat. 735 (June 3, 1834).
5. "John Calhoun to William Clark," May 28, 1822, Records of the War Department General and Special Staff, Secretary's Office, Letters Sent, Indian Affairs, RG 165, E-59, National Archives and Records Service (hereafter NARS).
6. Buckley, *William Clark*, 196–197.
7. Prucha, *American Indian Treaties*, 132–136.

Chapter 9: Samuel S. Hamilton

1. Edmunds, "Samuel S. Hamilton, 1830–31," 9–11.
2. "An act to provide for an exchange of lands with the Indians residing in any of the states or territories and for their removal west of the river Mississippi," 4 Stat. 411 (May 28, 1830).
3. United States Bureau of Indian Affairs, *Indian Treaties, and Laws and Regulations Relating to Indian Affairs*.
4. "An act to regulate trade and intercourse with the Indian tribes, and to preserve peace on the Frontier," 1 Stat. 469 (May 17, 1796).
5. "An act to regulate trade and intercourse with the Indian tribes, and to preserve peace on the Frontier," 1 Stat. 743 (March 3, 1799); "An act to regulate trade and intercourse with the Indian tribes, and to preserve peace on the Frontier," 2 Stat. 139 (March 30, 1802).
6. "An act to regulate trade and intercourse with the Indian tribes, and to preserve peace on the Frontier," 2 Stat. 139 (March 30, 1802).
7. *ARCIA* (1830), 162–163.

Chapter 10: Elbert Herring

1. "An Act to regulate trade and intercourse with the Indian tribes, and to preserve peace on the frontiers," 4 Stat. 929 (June 30, 1834); "An Act to provide for the organization of the department of Indian affairs," 4 Stat. 735 (June 30, 1834).
2. Satz, "Elbert Herring, 1831–36," 13–16.

3. *ARCIA* (1831), 172.
4. *ARCIA* (1832), 160, 162.
5. *ARCIA* (1831), 163.
6. *ARCIA* (1835), 261.

Chapter 11: Carey Allen Harris

1. Satz, "Carey Allen Harris, 1836–38," 17–22.
2. "Delaware treaty with the United States," 7 Stat. 13 (September 17, 1778).
3. A House resolution on July 1, 1836, authorized the investigation, with Thomas H. Crawford and Alfred Balch appointed to conduct it. The House action occurred before Harris became commissioner. See *ARCIA* (1836), 19. See also "Message on the Creek Indians," July 3, 1838, *House Document 452*, Twenty-Fifth Cong., First Sess., *Congressional Serial Set 331*, 11:1–102.
4. *ARCIA* (1836), 30.
5. *ARCIA* (1836), 3.
6. See "Annual Message to Congress with Documents, President Jackson, December 8, 1829," *Senate Document 1*, Twenty-First Cong., First Sess., *Congressional Serial Set 192*.
7. *ARCIA* (1836), 9.
8. *ARCIA* (1836), 11–12, 24.
9. *ARCIA* (1837), 5–6.

Chapter 12: Thomas Hartley Crawford

1. "Message on Creek Indians: Report for the War Department in Relation to the Investigation of Fraud alleged to have been Committed on the Creeks in the Sale of their reservations," *House Document 452*, Twenty-Fifth Congress, Second Session, July 2, 1838, *Congressional Serial Set*, 2:331.
2. Satz, "Thomas Hartley Crawford, 1838–45," 23–27.
3. DeJong, *American Indian Treaties*, 148–149.
4. Satz, "Thomas Hartley Crawford, 1838–45," 27.
5. *ARCIA* (1840), 232–233.
6. *ARCIA* (1842), 375.
7. *ARCIA* (1840), 240–241.
8. *ARCIA* (1838), 450–451.
9. *ARCIA* (1839), 344.

Chapter 13: William Medill

1. "William Medill (1802–1865)," Biographical Directory of the United States Congress, 1774–Present, https://bioguideretro.congress.gov/Home/MemberDetails?memIndex=M000624.
2. "An Act to amend an Act entitled 'An Act to provide for the better Organization of the Department of Indian Affairs,' and an Act entitled 'An Act to regulate Trade and Intercourse with the Indian Tribes, and to preserve Peace on the Frontiers,' approved June thirtieth, eighteen hundred and thirty-four, and for other Purposes," 9 Stat. 203 (March 3, 1847).
3. Trennert, "William Medill, 1845–49," 29–39.
4. *ARCIA* (1846), 16.
5. *ARCIA* (1847), 18.
6. *ARCIA* (1848), 385.
7. *ARCIA* (1846), 6–7.
8. *ARCIA* (1848), 388–390.

Chapter 14: Orlando Brown

1. Trennert, "Orlando Brown, 1849–50," 41–47.
2. *ARCIA* (1849), 8–9.
3. *ARCIA* (1849), 11.
4. *ARCIA* (1849), 21–22.

Chapter 15: Luke Lea

1. The compromise included five separate bills, and despite opposition from John Calhoun (Democrat, South Carolina), they were all enacted into law. Senators Henry Clay (Whig, Kentucky) and Stephen Douglas (Democrat, Illinois) championed the bills through Congress. See "An Act proposing to the State of Texas the establishment of her Northern and Western Boundaries, the Relinquishment by the said State of all Territory claimed by her exterior to said Boundaries, and of all her Claims upon the United States, and to establish a territorial Government for New Mexico," 9 Stat. 446 (September 9, 1850); "Whereas the people of California have presented a constitution and asked admission into the Union, which constitution was submitted to Congress by the President of the United States, by message dated February thirteenth, eighteen hundred and fifty, and which, on due examination, is found to be republican in its form of government," 9 Stat. 452 (September 9, 1850); "An Act to establish a Territorial Government for Utah," 9 Stat. 453 (September 9, 1850); "An Act to amend, and supplementary to, the Act entitled

'An Act respecting Fugitives from Justice, and Persons escaping from the Service of their Masters,' approved February twelfth, one thousand seven hundred and ninety-three," 9 Stat. 462 (September 18, 1850); "An Act to suppress the Slave Trade in the District of Columbia," 9 Stat. 467 (September 20, 1850).

2. "An Act making Appropriations for the current and contingent Expenses of the Indian Department, and for fulfilling Treaty Stipulations with various Indian Tribes, for the Year ending June the thirtieth, one thousand eight hundred and fifty-two," 9 Stat. 586 (February 27, 1851).

3. Trennert, "Luke Lea, 1850–53," 48–55.
4. *ARCIA* (1850), 3–4.
5. *ARCIA* (1850), 7–8.
6. *ARCIA* (1850), 9–10.
7. *ARCIA* (1852), 11–12.
8. *ARCIA* (1851), 12.
9. *ARCIA* (1852), 3.

Chapter 16: George W. Manypenny

1. DeJong, *American Indian Treaties*, 151–156 (ratified treaties), 176–177 (unratified treaties).

2. Of the forty-three ratified treaties, twelve were with border tribes calling for cessions, severalty, and consolidation.

3. Kvasnicka, "George W. Manypenny, 1853–57," 57–67.

4. "An Act making appropriations for the current and contingent Expenses of the Indian Department, and for fulfilling Treaty Stipulations with various Indian tribes, for the year ending June thirtieth one thousand eight hundred and fifty-four," 10 Stat. 226, at 238–239 (March 3, 1853).

5. *ARCIA* (1853), 8–9.
6. *ARCIA* (1856), 20.
7. *ARCIA* (1854), 17.
8. *ARCIA* (1856), 23.
9. *ARCIA* (1853), 9–10.
10. *ARCIA* (1854), 10.
11. *ARCIA* (1853), 16–17.
12. *ARCIA* (1855), 18.
13. *ARCIA* (1853), 20–21.
14. *ARCIA* (1854), 20.
15. *ARCIA* (1856), 21.

Chapter 17: James W. Denver

1. "James William Denver (1817–1892)," Biographical Directory of the United States Congress, 1774–Present, https://bioguideretro.congress.gov/Home/MemberDetails?memIndex=D000261.
2. Chaput, "James W. Denver, 1857, 1858–59," 69–75.
3. *ARCIA* (1857), 4–5.
4. *ARCIA* (1857), 5.
5. *ARCIA* (1857), 6–7.

Chapter 18: Charles E. Mix

1. United States Bureau of Indian Affairs, *Office Copy of the Laws, Regulations, Etc., of the Indian Bureau, 1850*.
2. Kelsey, "Charles E. Mix, 1858," 78.
3. *ARCIA* (1858), 5–6.
4. *ARCIA* (1858), 6–7.
5. *ARCIA* (1858), 9.
6. *ARCIA* (1858), 10.

Chapter 19: Alfred B. Greenwood

1. "Alfred Burton Greenwood (1811–1889)," Biographical Directory of the United States Congress, 1774–Present, https://bioguideretro.congress.gov/Home/MemberDetails?memIndex=G000436.
2. Kansa Treaty of October 5, 1859, 12 Stat. 1111; Sac and Fox of Mississippi Treaty of October 1, 1859, 15 Stat. 467; Chippewa (Swan Creek and Black River Bands) and Munsee Treaty of July 16, 1859, 12 Stat. 1105.
3. Roberts, "Alfred Burton Greenwood, 1859–61," 81–87.
4. *ARCIA* (1859), 4–5.
5. *ARCIA* (1859), 22–23.
6. *ARCIA* (1860), 3–4.
7. *ARCIA* (1860), 25–26.

Chapter 20: William P. Dole

1. Kelsey, "William P. Dole, 1861–65," 89–98.
2. *ARCIA* (1864), 3–4.
3. *ARCIA* (1864), 5–6.

4. *ARCIA* (1861), 19–20.
5. *ARCIA* (1862), 39–40.
6. *ARCIA* (1862), 24–25.
7. *ARCIA* (1863), 5–7.

Chapter 21: Dennis N. Cooley

1. The Kansas Indians, 72 U.S. (5 Wallace) 737 (1866).
2. DeJong, *American Indian Treaties*, 42–43, 181.
3. Roberts, "Dennis Nelson Cooley, 1866–67," 99–108.
4. ARCIA (1866), 1–2.
5. ARCIA (1865), iii–iv, extract from the secretary of the interior.
6. The Kansas Indians, 72 U.S. (5 Wallace) 737 (1866).
7. *ARCIA* (1866), 15.
8. *ARCIA* (1866), 16–17.
9. *ARCIA* (1866), 21–22.

Chapter 22: Lewis V. Bogy

1. Unrau, "Lewis V. Bogy, 1866–67," 109–114.
2. Unrau, "Lewis V. Bogy, 1866–67," 112.
3. United States Congress, Condition of the Indian Tribes.
4. Unrau, "Lewis V. Bogy, 1866–67," 113.
5. "Lewis Vital Bogy (1813–1877)," Biographical Directory of the United States Congress, 1774–Present, https://bioguideretro.congress.gov/Home/MemberDetails?memIndex=B000595.

Chapter 23: Nathaniel G. Taylor

1. "Nathaniel Green Taylor (1819–1887)," Biographical Directory of the United States Congress, 1774–Present, https://bioguideretro.congress.gov/Home/MemberDetails?memIndex=T000095.
2. *ARCIA* (1868), 9–10.
3. "An Act to establish Peace with certain Hostile Indian Tribes," 15 Stat. 17 (July 20, 1867).
4. Unrau, "Nathaniel Green Taylor, 1867–69," 115–122.
5. *ARCIA* (1868), 7–14.
6. *ARCIA* (1868), 16–17.
7. *ARCIA* (1868), 19.

Chapter 24: Ely S. Parker

1. Armstrong, *Warrior in Two Camps*, 6–9.
2. Armstrong, *Warrior in Two Camps*, 66; Seneca Treaty with the United States, 11 Stat. 735 (November 5, 1859).
3. Letter on Indian Hostilities, *Senate Executive Document 13*, Fortieth Cong., First Sess., *Congressional Serial Set 1308*, July 13, 1867, 1–128.
4. "Report of Colonel Parker on Indian Affairs," *House Miscellaneous Document 37*, Thirty-Ninth Cong., Second Sess., *Congressional Serial Set 1302*, January 30, 1867, 1–11.
5. "An Act making Appropriations for the Support of the Army for the Year ending June thirty, eighteen hundred and seventy-one, and for other Purposes," 16 Stat. 315, at 319 (Section 18) (July 15, 1870).
6. "Act making Appropriations for the current and contingent expenses of the Indian Department and for fulfilling Treaty Stipulations with various Indian Tribes for the Year ending June thirty, eighteen hundred and seventy-one, and for other Purposes," 16 Stat. 335, at 360 (July 15, 1870).
7. Waltmann, "Ely Samuel Parker, 1869–71," 123–133.
8. *ARCIA* (1869), 5.
9. *ARCIA* (1869), 5–6.
10. *ARCIA* (1870), 10.
11. *Annual Report of the Secretary of the Interior, 1871*, 6–7.

Chapter 25: Francis A. Walker

1. "History," United States Census Bureau, http://www.census.gov/history/.
2. Miner, "Francis A. Walker, 1871–73," 135–140.
3. *ARCIA* (1872), 3–5.
4. *ARCIA* (1872), 5–6.
5. *ARCIA* (1872), 9–10.
6. *ARCIA* (1872), 11–12.

Chapter 26: Edward P. Smith

1. Crawford, "Edward P. Smith, 1873–75," 141–147.
2. *ARCIA* (1874), 14.
3. *ARCIA* (1873), 4, 6.
4. *ARCIA* (1873), 3–5.
5. *ARCIA* (1873), 12–14.
6. "An act making appropriations for the current and contingent expenses of the Indian Department, and for fulfilling treaty-stipulations with various Indian tribes, for the year ending June thirtieth, eighteen hundred and seventy-six, and for other

purposes," 43 Stat. 420, at 44 (Section 3) (March 3, 1875). The act required all able-bodied males to work on the reservation in exchange for annuity payments.

7. *ARCIA* (1875), 23–25.

Chapter 27: John Quincy Smith

1. "John Quincy Smith (1824–1901)," Biographical Directory of the United States Congress, 1774–Present, https://bioguideretro.congress.gov/Home/MemberDetails?memIndex=S000574.
2. Hill, "John Quincy Smith, 1875–77," 149–153.
3. *ARCIA* (1876), vii.
4. "An act making appropriations for the current and contingent expenses of the Indian Department, and for fulfilling treaty-stipulations with various Indian tribes, for the year ending June thirtieth, eighteen hundred and seventy-seven, and for other purposes," 44 Stat. 192 (August 15, 1876). The act specifically provided "That the Secretary of the Interior may use of the foregoing amounts the sum of twenty-five thousand dollars for the removal of the Poncas to the Indian Territory, and providing them a home therein, with the consent of said band."
5. *ARCIA* (1876), vi–x.

Chapter 28: Ezra A. Hayt

1. Meyer, "Ezra A. Hayt, 1877–80," 155–166.
2. Meyer, "Ezra A. Hayt, 1877–80," 156.
3. Trefousse, "Carl Schurz and the Indians," 109.
4. "Editor's Historical Record," *Harper's New Monthly Magazine*, February 1878, 476.
5. *ARCIA* (1877), 7.
6. "House Debate on Removal of Southwest Tribes," in Congressional Record, Forty-Fifth Cong., Third Sess. (December 19, 1878), 311–325. The bill prohibiting removal is "An act making appropriations for the current and contingent expenses of the Indian Department, and for fulfilling treaty stipulations with various Indian tribes, for the year ending June thirtieth, eighteen hundred and eighty, and for other purposes," 20 Stat. 295, at 313 (February 17, 1879).
7. Report of Committee to the Board of Indian Commissioners, January 31, 1880, in Records of the Board of Indian Commissioners, RG 75, NARA.
8. *ARCIA* (1877), 2–4.
9. *ARCIA* (1877), 5–6.
10. *ARCIA* (1878), iv–v.
11. *ARCIA* (1879), iii–v.

Chapter 29: Rowland E. Trowbridge

1. Goldman, "Rowland E. Trowbridge, 1880–81," 167–172.
2. "Rowland Ebenezer Trowbridge (1821–1881)," Biographical Directory of the United States Congress, 1774–Present, https://bioguideretro.congress.gov/Home/MemberDetails?memIndex=T000385.
3. Agreement with the Bannack, Sheepeater, and Shoshone (Ft. Hall) tribes, 25 Stat. 687 (May 14, 1880); Agreement with the Crow Tribe, 22 Stat. 42 (June 12, 1880).
4. *ARCIA* (1880), viii–x.
5. *ARCIA* (1880), xiii.

Chapter 30: Hiram Price

1. "Hiram Price (1814–1901)," Biographical Directory of the United States Congress, 1774–Present, https://bioguideretro.congress.gov/Home/MemberDetails?memIndex=P000525.
2. O'Neil, "Hiram Price, 1881–85," 173–179.
3. "Hiram Price (1814–1901)," Biographical Directory of the United States Congress, 1774–Present, https://bioguideretro.congress.gov/Home/MemberDetails?memIndex=P000525.
4. Indian Circulars, Records of the Bureau of Indian Affairs, RG 75, NARS.
5. Ex Parte Crow Dog, 109 U.S. 556 (1883). For the Major Crimes Act, see "An act making appropriations for the current and contingent expenses of the Indian Department, and for fulfilling treaty stipulations with various Indian tribes, for the year ending June thirtieth, eighteen hundred and eighty-six, and for other purposes," 23 Stat. 362, at 385 (Section 9) (March 3, 1885), which made the following acts federal crimes: murder, manslaughter, rape, assault with intent to kill, arson, burglary, and larceny.
6. *ARCIA* (1871), iii.
7. In 1885, Congress authorized $8 per month for privates and $10 for officers. "An act making appropriations for the current and contingent expenses of the Indian Department, and for fulfilling treaty stipulations with various Indian tribes, for the year ending June thirtieth, eighteen hundred and eighty-six, and for other purposes," 23 Stat. 362 (March 3, 1885).
8. *ARCIA* (1883), iv.
9. *ARCIA* (1880), xxii–xxiii.
10. *ARCIA* (1882), vi–vii.
11. *ARCIA* (1883), x–xi.
12. *ARCIA* (1884), xix–xxi.

Chapter 31: John DeWitt Clinton Atkins

1. "John DeWitt Clinton Atkins (1825–1908)," Biographical Directory of the United States Congress, 1774–Present, https://bioguideretro.congress.gov/Home/MemberDetails?memIndex=A000327.
2. Thompson, "John D. C. Atkins, 1885–88," 181–188.
3. *ARCIA* (1885), iii–iv.
4. *ARCIA* (1885), viii–xii.
5. *ARCIA* (1885), xvii–xix.
6. William Lewis Couch and David Lewis Payne were organizers of the "Boomer Movement," to open up the "Oklahoma District" to homesteading. In the end, Congress did open up the district on April 22, 1889.
7. *ARCIA* (1886), v–vi, xi–xii.
8. *ARCIA* (1887), vi, vii–ix.

Chapter 32: John H. Oberly

1. O'Neil, "John H. Oberly, 1888–89," 189–191.
2. John Oberly, "Report of the Superintendent of Indian Schools," in *ARCIA* (1885), 111.
3. Hagan, *The Indian Rights Association*, 82–83.
4. "An act making appropriations for the current and contingent expenses of the Indian Department, and for fulfilling treaty stipulations with various Indian tribes, for the years ending June thirtieth, eighteen hundred and eighty-nine, and for other purposes," 50 Stat. 217, at 238 (Section 8) (June 29, 1888).
5. *ARCIA* (1888), lxxxiii.
6. Hagan, *The Indian Rights Association*, 99–101.
7. *ARCIA* (1888), lxxxiii–lxxxiv.
8. *ARCIA* (1888), xviii–xix.
9. *ARCIA* (1888), lxxxix.

Chapter 33: Thomas Jefferson Morgan

1. Prucha, "Thomas Jefferson Morgan, 1889–93," 193–203.
2. *ARCIA* (1889), 3–4.
3. *ARCIA* (1890), xxxvi–xi.
4. Morgan, *Studies in Pedagogy*.
5. *ARCIA* (1892), 47.
6. *ARCIA* (1889), 3–4.
7. *ARCIA* (1891), 3–9.
8. *ARCIA* (1890), xxxix–xl.

9. Opinions of the Attorney General, 7 Opinions 746 (July 5, 1856).
10. Ex Parte Reynolds, 6 Dill. 394 (1879).
11. See de Vattal, *The Law of Nations*, 103.
12. *ARCIA* (1890), lxxiii–lxxvi.
13. *ARCIA* (1891), 25–26.
14. *ARCIA* (1892), 5–6.

Chapter 34: Daniel M. Browning

1. Moses, *Wild West Shows and Images of American Indians, 1883–1933*, 141.
2. Hagan, "Daniel M. Browning, 1893–97," 205–209.
3. *ARCIA* (1896), 7.
4. *ARCIA* (1895), 10.
5. *ARCIA* (1894), 65–66.
6. *ARCIA* (1896), 1.
7. *ARCIA* (1893), 26–27.
8. *ARCIA* (1896), 11.
9. *ARCIA* (1893), 11.
10. "An Act making appropriations for current and contingent expenses and fulfilling treaty stipulations with various Indian tribes for fiscal year 1895," 28 Stat. 313 (August 15, 1894).
11. *ARCIA* (1894), 6–7.
12. "An Act in relation to marriage between white men and Indian women," 25 Stat. 392 (August 9, 1888).
13. "An Act to secure the Right of Citizenship to Children of Citizens of the United States born out of the Limits thereof," 10 Stat. 604 (February 10, 1855).
14. *ARCIA* (1894), 65–66.

Chapter 35: William A. Jones

1. Baird, "William A. Jones, 1897–1904," 211–220.
2. *ARCIA* (1903), 3.
3. *ARCIA* (1898), 6–7.
4. *ARCIA* (1902), 9.
5. *ARCIA* (1900), 10–11.
6. *ARCIA* (1903), 84; "An Act Making appropriations for the current and contingent expenses of the Indian Department and for fulfilling treaty stipulations with various Indian tribes for the fiscal year ending June thirtieth, nineteen hundred and three, and for other purposes," 32 Stat. 245, at 275 (May 27, 1902).
7. *ARCIA* (1903), 2–3.
8. *ARCIA* (1900), 33.

9. *ARCIA* (1898), 8.
10. *ARCIA* (1899), 4–7.
11. *ARCIA* (1900), 5–6.
12. *ARCIA* (1900), 8–9.
13. *ARCIA* (1900), 11–12.
14. *ARCIA* (1900), 12–13.
15. *ARCIA* (1904), 75.
16. *ARCIA* (1901), 1–5.

Chapter 36: Francis E. Leupp

1. Parman, "Francis Ellington Leupp, 1905–09," 221–232.
2. Quick Bear v. Leupp, 210 U.S. 50 (1908).
3. *ARCIA* (1905), 1–9.
4. *ARCIA* (1907), 21–25.

Chapter 37: Robert G. Valentine

1. Putney, "Robert Grosvenor Valentine, 1909–12," 233–242.
2. Putney, "Robert Grosvenor Valentine, 1909–12," 233.
3. *ARCIA* (1909), 1.
4. *ARCIA* (1910), 28.
5. *ARCIA* (1910), 9–10.
6. *ARCIA* (1912), 39.
7. Valentine, "Is the Indian Worth Conserving?," 16.
8. *ARCIA* (1909), 1–2.
9. *ARCIA* (1910), 5.
10. *ARCIA* (1911), 6–7.
11. *ARCIA* (1910), 28.
12. *ARCIA* (1911), 20–21.
13. "An act to amend and further extend the benefits of the act approved February eighth, eighteen hundred and eighty-seven, entitled 'An act to provide for the allotment of land in severalty to Indians on the various reservations, and to extend the protection of the laws of the United States over the Indians, and for other purposes,'" 26 Stat. 794 (February 28, 1891).
14. *ARCIA* (1912), 5–6.
15. *ARCIA* (1910), 27.
16. *ARCIA* (1910), 9–10.

Chapter 38: Cato Sells

1. Kelly, "Cato Sells, 1913–21," 243–250.
2. *ARCIA* (1913), 43.
3. United States v. Nice, 241 U.S. 591 (1916).
4. *ARCIA* (1914), 50–51.
5. Debo, *And Still the Waters Run.*
6. *ARCIA* (1917), 28–29.
7. *ARCIA* (1917), 121.
8. *ARCIA* (1917), 4.
9. *ARCIA* (1919), 8.
10. *ARCIA* (1915), 60–62.
11. *ARCIA* (1916), 5–6.
12. *ARCIA* (1917), 3–4.
13. *ARCIA* (1917), 4–5.
14. *ARCIA* (1917), 13.

Chapter 39: Charles Henry Burke

1. "Charles Henry Burke (1861–1944)," Biographical Directory of the United States Congress, 1774–Present, https://bioguideretro.congress.gov/Home/MemberDetails?memIndex=B001087.
2. Kelly, "Charles Henry Burke, 1921–29," 251–261.
3. *ARCIA* (1923), 1.
4. *ARCIA* (1922), 3–5.
5. Indian Appropriation Act of 1921, 41 Stat. 408 (February 14, 1920).
6. *ARCIA* (1925), 6.
7. *ARCIA* (1927), 3.
8. *ARCIA* (1922), 8.
9. *ARCIA* (1924), 1.
10. "An Act to authorize the cancellation, under certain conditions, of patents in fee simple to Indians for allotments held in trust by the United States," 44 Stat. 1247 (February 26, 1927).
11. *ARCIA* (1921), 25–26.
12. *ARCIA* (1922), 1–3.
13. *ARCIA* (1924), 56.
14. *ARCIA* (1923), 20–21.
15. *ARCIA* (1927), 1–2.

Chapter 40: Charles James Rhoads

1. Kelly, "Charles James Rhoads, 1929–33," 263.
2. Kelly, "Charles James Rhoads, 1929–33," 263–271.
3. "An Act to authorize the Secretary of the Interior to adjust reimbursable debt of Indians and tribes of Indians," 47 Stat. 564 (July 1, 1932).
4. *ARCIA* (1930), 14.
5. *ARCIA* (1930), 1–2.
6. *ARCIA* (1930), 14.
7. *ARCIA* (1931), 7–9.
8. "An Act Making appropriations for the current and contingent expenses of the Bureau of Indian Affairs, for fulfilling treaty stipulations with various Indian tribes, and for other purposes, for the fiscal year ending June thirtieth, nineteen hundred and fifteen," 38 Stat. 582 (August 1, 1914).
9. "An Act to provide for determining the heirs of deceased Indians, for the disposition and sale of allotments of deceased Indians, for the leasing of allotments, and for other purposes," 36 Stat. 855 (June 25, 1910).
10. C. J. Rhoads to Senator Lynn Frazier, December 11, 1929, in *Congressional Record*, Part 8 (hereafter Rhoads to Frazier), 72:1051–1052.
11. Rhoads to Frazier, 72:1052.
12. Rhoads to Frazier, 72:1053.
13. Rhoads to Frazier, 72:1053.

Chapter 41: John Collier

1. Philp, "John Collier, 1933–45," 273–282.
2. Collier, *From Every Zenith*, 126.
3. See Cohen, *Handbook of Federal-Indian Law*.
4. *ARCIA* (1936), 159.
5. *ARCIA* (1934), 82.
6. *ARCIA* (1933), 68–69.
7. *ARCIA* (1933), 108–109.
8. *ARCIA* (1937), 199.
9. *ARCIA* (1935), 140–141.
10. *ARCIA* (1937), 227–229.

Chapter 42: William A. Brophy

1. Tyler, "William A. Brophy, 1945–48," 283–287.

2. United States Senate, "Nomination of William A. Brophy to be Commissioner of Indian Affairs, United States Senate, Committee on Indian Affairs," February 20, 27, 28 and March 1, 1945 (hereafter "Nomination of Brophy"), 1–6.
3. "Nomination of Brophy," 61.
4. "Nomination of Brophy," 9.
5. *ARCIA* (1945), 233.
6. *ARCIA* (1947), 345.
7. *ARCIA* (1947), 349.
8. *ARCIA* (1948), 369.
9. *ARCIA* (1946), 353–354.
10. *ARCIA* (1945), 233.
11. *ARCIA* (1946), 363–364.
12. *ARCIA* (1947), 348–349.

Chapter 43: John R. Nichols

1. Dennehy, "Roger L. Nichols, 1949–50," 289–291.
2. *Congressional Record*, Eighty-First Cong., First Sess., March 23, 1949, 95:2929–2930.
3. *Congressional Record*, Part 13 (Appendix), Eighty-First Cong., First Sess., May 5, 1949, 95:A2711–2712.
4. *ARCIA* (1949), 338.
5. *ARCIA* (1949), 366.
6. *ARCIA* (1949), 358.
7. *ARCIA* (1949), 341.
8. *ARCIA* (1949), 338.
9. *ARCIA* (1949), 340.
10. *ARCIA* (1949), 366.

Chapter 44: Dillon S. Myer

1. Ourada, "Dillon Seymour Myer, 1950–53," 293–299. Truman originally offered the position to Myer in 1947 and again in 1948, but he turned it down. See Drinnon, *Keepers of Concentration Camps*, 166.
2. Drinnon, *Keepers of Concentration Camps*, 166–167.
3. Ickes, "The Indian Loses Again," 16.
4. *ARCIA* (1951), 353.
5. *ARCIA* (1952), 393–394.
6. *ARCIA* (1950), 350.
7. *ARCIA* (1950), 364.
8. *ARCIA* (1953), 41.

9. Drinnon, *Keeper of Concentration Camps*, 240.
10. *ARCIA* (1950), 347–348.
11. *ARCIA* 1951, 375–376.
12. *ARCIA* (1953), 23.
13. "An Act to Provide for medical services to Non-Indians in Indian hospitals, and for other purposes," 66 Stat. 35 (April 3, 1952).
14. *ARCIA* (1952), 390–391.
15. *ARCIA* (1952), 393–394.

Chapter 45: Glenn L. Emmons

1. Ourada, "Glenn L. Emmons, 1953–61," 301–310.
2. United States Senate, "Nomination of Glenn L. Emmons, Hearings Before the Committee on Interior and Insular Affairs, United States Senate, 83rd Congress, 1st session on the Nomination of Glenn L. Emmons to be Commissioner of the Bureau of Indian Affairs," July 15 and 28, 1953, 7–10.
3. Indians, HCR 108, 67 Stat. B132 (August 1, 1953).
4. *ARCIA* (1954), 229.
5. "An Act to provide for a per capita distribution of Menominee tribal funds and authorize the withdrawal of the Menominee Tribe from Federal Services," 68 Stat. 250 (June 17, 1954).
6. "An Act to confer jurisdiction on the States of California, Minnesota, Nebraska, Oregon, and Wisconsin, with respect to criminal offenses and civil causes of action committed or arising on Indian reservations within such States, and for other purposes," 67 Stat. 588 (August 15, 1953).
7. "An Act to eliminate certain discriminatory legislation against Indians in the United States," 67 Stat. 586 (August 15, 1953).
8. "An Act to terminate certain Federal restrictions upon Indians," 67 Stat. 590 (August 15, 1953).
9. *ARCIA* (1955), 237.
10. *ARCIA* (1957), 249.
11. "An Act Relative to employment for certain adult Indians on or near Indian reservations," 70 Stat. 986 (August 3, 1956).
12. "Address by Glenn L. Emmons, Commissioner of Indian Affairs, Before the 66th Continental Congress, National Society, Daughters of the American Revolution, Washington, DC, April 18, 1957, Department of the Interior Information Service, https://www.bia.gov/as-ia/opa/online-press-release/address-glenn-l-emmons-commissioner-indian-affairs.
13. "An Act to transfer the maintenance and operation of hospital and health facilities for Indians to the Public Health Service, and for other purposes," 68 Stat. 674 (August 5, 1954).

14. *ARCIA* (1957), 241.

15. "Address by Glenn L. Emmons, Commissioner of Indian Affairs, Before the 66th Continental Congress, National Society, Daughters of the American Revolution, Washington, DC, April 18, 1957, Department of the Interior Information Services, https://www.bia.gov/as-ia/opa/online-press-release/address-glenn-l-emmons-commissioner-indian-affairs.

16. "Emmons Issues Policy Statement on Sale of Individually Owned Indian Lands," May 15, 1958, Bureau of Indian Affairs, Department of the Interior Information Services, https://www.bia.gov/as-ia/opa/online-press-release/emmons-issues-policy-statement-sale-individually-owned-indian-lands.

17. *ARCIA* (1959), 231.

Chapter 46: Philleo Nash

1. Szasz, "Philleo Nash, 1961–66," 311–323.

2. United States Senate, "Hearings before the Committee on Interior and Insular Affairs on the Nomination of Philleo Nash for Commissioner of Indian Affairs," Eighty-Seventh Cong., First Sess., August 14, 1961, 4.

3. "Remarks by Philleo Nash, Commissioner of Indian Affairs, before the City Club of Portland, Oregon," July 26, 1963, Department of the Interior News Release, https://www.bia.gov/as-ia/opa/online-press-release/remarks-philleo-nash-commissioner-indian-affairs (hereafter "Remarks of Philleo Nash").

4. *ARCIA* (1963), 16.

5. "The War Against Poverty—The American Indians," Address of Philleo Nash at the Abraham Lincoln Center, Chicago, Illinois, February 12, 1964, United States Department of the Interior New Release, https://www.bia.gov/as-ia/opa/online-press-release/war-against-poverty-american-indians.

6. "Secretary Udall Calls for Ten-Year Plan for Reservation Indians," July 10, 1964, Department of the Interior News Release, https://www.bia.gov/as-ia/opa/online-press-release/secretary-udall-calls-ten-year-plan-reservation-indians.

7. *ARCIA* (1965), 2.

8. "Address by Philleo Nash, Commissioner of Indian Affairs," Sunday Evening Forum, Tucson, Arizona, March 3, 1963, United States Department of the Interior News Release, https://www.bia.gov/as-ia/opa/online-press-release/address-philleo-nash-commissioner-ia.

9. "Address by Philleo Nash, Commissioner of Indian Affairs, at the 18th Annual Convention of the National Congress of American Indians, at Lewistown, Idaho, September 21, 1961," United States Department of the Interior News Release, https://www.bia.gov/as-ia/opa/online-press-release/address-nash-annual-convention-ncai.

10. "Remarks by Philleo Nash."

Chapter 47: Robert L. Bennett

1. Ellis, "Robert L. Bennett, 1966–69," 325–331.
2. United States Senate, "Nomination of Robert Lafollette Bennett to be Commissioner of Indian Affairs: Report of the Committee on Interior and Insular Affairs," *Senate Executive Report 1*, Eighty-Ninth Cong., First Sess. (hereafter "Nomination of Robert Bennett"), 1–7.
3. *ARCIA* (1966), 2.
4. "Excerpts from Remarks by Robert L. Bennett, Commissioner of Indian Affairs, Before the Indian Rights Association in Philadelphia, Pennsylvania," April 26, 1966, Department of the Interior News Release, https://www.bia.gov/as-ia/opa/online-press-release/excerpts-remarks-robert-l-bennett-commission-indian-affairs (hereafter "Bennett Indian Rights Association").
5. "Excerpts from Remarks by Robert L. Bennett, Commissioner of Indian Affairs, at the Annual Convention, National Congress of American Indians, Oklahoma City, Oklahoma," November 14, 1966, Department of the Interior News Release, https://www.bia.gov/as-ia/opa/online-press-release/excerpts-remarks-robert-l-bennett-commissioner-indian-affairs (hereafter "Bennett Oklahoma City").
6. "Nomination of Robert Bennett," 4.
7. United States House of Representatives, "Department of the Interior and Related Agencies Appropriations for Fiscal Year 1968: Hearing before a Subcommittee of the Committee on Appropriations, 90th Congress, 1st Session, part 1," 679.
8. "Remarks from Robert L. Bennett at the Governors' Interstate Indian Council, Reno, Nevada," October 19, 1967, Department of the Interior News Release, https://www.bia.gov/as-ia/opa/online-press-release/remarks-robert-l-bennett-governors-interstate-indian-council-reno-nv (hereafter "Bennett Governors' Interstate Indian Council").
9. *ARCIA* (1966), 9.
10. *ARCIA* (1966), 3.
11. *ARCIA* (1968), 4.
12. "Bennett Indian Rights Association."
13. "Bennett Oklahoma City."
14. "Bennett Governors' Interstate Indian Council."

Chapter 48: Louis Rook Bruce

1. Deloria, *Behind the Trail of Broken Treaties*, 36.
2. Cash, "Louis Rook Bruce, 1969–73," 333–340.
3. United States Senate, "Interior Nomination: Hearing before the Committee on Interior and Insular Affairs, United States Senate, on the Nomination of Louis R. Bruce, of New York, to be Commissioner of Indian Affairs," Ninety-First Cong., First Sess., August 11, 1969 (hereafter "Louis Bruce Nomination"), 1.

4. "Remarks of Commissioner of Indian Affairs Louis R. Bruce, Shiprock, New Mexico," September 6, 1969, Department of the Interior News Release, https://www.bia.gov/as-ia/opa/online-press-release/remarks-commissioner-indian-affairs-louis-r-bruce-shiprock-nm.

5. "Address by Commissioner of Indian Affairs Louis R. Bruce, at the 25th Anniversary Convention of the National Congress of American Indians, Albuquerque, New Mexico, October 9, 1969," Department of the Interior News Release, https://www.bia.gov/as-ia/opa/online-press-release/address-commissioner-indian-affairs-louis-r-bruce (hereafter "Bruce NCAI Address").

6. "Remarks by Commissioner of Indian Affairs Louis R. Bruce before the Conference on Modern American Indians, Claremont Men's College, Claremont, California," February 27, 1970, Department of the Interior News Release (hereafter "Bruce Claremont").

7. "The New BIA—The New Politics: Remarks by Commissioner of Indian Affairs Louis R. Bruce at a Dinner Meeting of Western Oklahoma Indian Leaders, Oklahoma City, Oklahoma," October 24, 1969, Department of the Interior News Release, https://www.bia.gov/as-ia/opa/online-press-release/new-bia-new-politics (hereafter "The New BIA").

8. "Nomination of Louis Bruce."

9. "Bruce NCAI Address."

10. "The New BIA."

11. "Bruce Claremont."

12. "Statement by Commissioner of Indian Affairs Louis R. Bruce before the National Archives Conference on Research in the History of Indian–White Relations," Washington, D.C., June 17, 1972, Department of the Interior News Release, https://www.bia.gov/as-ia/opa/online-press-release/statement-commissioner-indian-affairs-louis-r-bruce-national-archives.

Chapter 49: Marvin L. Franklin

1. "Marvin L. Franklin named Assistant to the Secretary for Indian Affairs," February 7, 1973, Department of the Interior News Release, https://www.indianaffairs.gov/as-ia/opa/online-press-release/marvin-l-franklin-named-assistant-secretary-indian-affairs.

2. "An Act to provide for determining the heirs of deceased Indians, for the disposition and sale of allotments of deceased Indians, for the leasing of allotments, and for other purposes," 36 Stat. 861 (Section 23) (June 25, 1910).

3. "Remarks by Marvin L. Franklin at the NCAI Convention—Tulsa, Oklahoma," October 30, 1973, Department of the Interior News Release, https://www.indianaffairs.gov/as-ia/opa/online-press-release/remarks-m-l-franklin-ncai-convention-tulsa-oklahoma.

4. "Remarks of Marvin L. Franklin, Ponca City Chamber of Commerce," August 24, 1973, Department of the Interior News Release, https://www.bia.gov/as-ia/opa/online-press-release/remarks-marvin-l-franklin-ponca-city-chamber-commerce.

5. United States Senate, "Statement of Marvin L. Franklin at the Department of the Interior and Related Agencies Appropriations for Fiscal Year 1974: Hearings before a Subcommittee of the Committee on Appropriations," Ninety-Third Cong., First Sess., on H.R. 8917, 3945–3947.

Chapter 50: Morris Thompson

1. "Morton Lauds Nomination of Morris Thompson to be Commissioner of BIA," October 30, 1973, Department of the Interior News Release, https://www.indianaffairs.gov/as-ia/opa/online-press-release/morton-lauds-nomination-morris-thompson-be-commissioner-bia.
2. Smith, "Morris Thompson, 1973–76," 341–345.
3. United States Senate, "Hearing before the Committee on Interior and Insular Affairs, United States Senate, 93rd Congress, 1st Session, on the Nomination of Morris Thompson to be Commissioner of the Bureau of Indian Affairs," November 14, 1973 (hereafter "Nomination of Morris Thompson"), 22–23.
4. "Morris Thompson, BIA Head, Addresses Indian Tribal Chairmen," December 7, 1973, Department of the Interior News Release, https://www.bia.gov/as-ia/opa/online-press-release/morris-thompson-bia-head-addresses-indian-tribal-chairmen.
5. "Nomination of Morris Thompson," 21.
6. "An Act to provide for financing the economic development of Indians and Indian organizations, and for other purposes," 88 Stat. 77 (April 12, 1974).
7. "An Act to provide maximum Indian participation in the Government and education of Indian people; to provide for the full participation of Indian tribes in programs and services conducted by the Federal Government for Indians and to encourage the development of human resources of the Indian people; to establish a program of assistance to upgrade Indian education; to support the right of Indian citizens to control their own educational activities; and for other purposes," 88 Stat. 2203 (January 4, 1975).
8. "M. Thompson—Goals and Aspirations—NTCA—Phoenix," December 6, 1973, Department of the Interior News Release, https://www.bia.gov/as-ia/opa/online-press-release/m-thompson-goals-and-aspirations-ntca-phoenix.
9. "Commissioner of Indian Affairs Morris Thompson Consults with National Tribal Chairmen's Association, National Congress of American Indians, over Current BIA Goals," January 11, 1974, Bureau of Indian Affairs News Release, https://www.indianaffairs.gov/as-ia/opa/online-press-release/commissioner-indian-affairs-morris-thompson-consults-national-tribal.

Chapter 51: Ben Reifel

1. Smith, "Benjamin Reifel, 1976–77," 347–348.

2. "Benjamin Reifel (1906–1990)," Biographical Directory of the United States Congress, 1774–Present, https://bioguideretro.congress.gov/Home/MemberDetails?memIndex=R000152.

3. "Ben Reifel Named—Commissioner of Indian Affairs," December 7, 1976, Department of the Interior News Release, https://www.bia.gov/as-ia/opa/online-press-release/ben-reifel-named-commissioner-indian-affairs#:~:text=Ben%20Reifel%2C%20a%20former%20South,Kleppe.

Chapter 52: Forrest J. Gerard

1. United States Senate, "Nomination of the Assistant Secretary of the Interior for Indian Affairs: Hearings before the United States Senate, Select Committee on Indian Affairs, 85th Congress, 1st session, on Nomination of Forrest J. Gerard to be an Assistant Secretary of the Interior for Indian Affairs, September 9 & 12, 1977" (hereafter "Nomination of Forrest Gerard"), 17.

2. United States House of Representatives, "Department of the Interior and Related Agencies Appropriations for 1979: Hearings before a Subcommittee of the Committee on Appropriations, House of Representatives, 95th Congress, 2nd session, Part 3," 574–575.

3. Trahant, *The Last Great Battle of the Indian Wars*, 10, 26.

4. "An act to implement the Federal responsibility for the care and education of the Indian people by improving the services and facilities of Federal Indian health programs and encouraging maximum participation of Indians in such programs, and for other purposes," 90 Stat. 1400 (September 30, 1976).

5. "An act to provide maximum Indian participation in the Government and education of Indian people; to provide for the full participation of Indian tribes in programs and services conducted by the Federal Government for Indians and to encourage the development of human resources of the Indian people; to establish a program of assistance to upgrade Indian education; to support the right of Indian citizens to control their own educational activities; and for other purposes," 88 Stat. 2203 (January 4, 1975).

6. *Congressional Record*, Part 8, July 23, 2013, 113th Cong., First Sess., 150:12041.

7. "Nomination of Forrest Gerard," 23.

8. Trahant, *The Last Great Battle of the Indian Wars*, 96.

9. "Top Indian Affairs Official Rates Water Policy a Plus for Reservation Development," June 9, 1978, Department of the Interior News Release, https://www.bia.gov/as-ia/opa/online-press-release/top-indian-affairs-official-rates-water-policy-plus-reservation.

10. "Gerard Tells National Indian Education Conference Educating Indian Children Is in the Hands of Tribes," December 4, 1979, Department of the Interior News Release, https://www.bia.gov/as-ia/opa/online-press-release/gerard-tells-national-indian-education-conference-educating-indian.

11. "Gerard Asks Indians for Unified Policy Statement," September 22, 1977, Department of the Interior News Release, https://www.indianaffairs.gov/as-ia/opa/online-press-release/gerard-asks-indians-unified-policy-statement.
12. "Nomination of Forrest J. Gerard," 17–23.
13. "Nomination of Forrest J. Gerard," 23–25.
14. "Nomination of Forrest J. Gerard," 25–27.

Chapter 53: William E. Hallett

1. United States Senate, "Hearing before the Select Committee on Indian Affairs, United States Senate, 96th Congress, 1st session, on Nomination of William E. Hallett to be Commissioner of Indian Affairs," October 20, 1979 (hereafter "Nomination of William Hallett"), 35–37; "Hallett to Take Oath of Office as the 42nd Commissioner of the Bureau of Indian Affairs," December 6, 1979, Department of the Interior News Release, https://www.bia.gov/as-ia/opa/online-press-release/hallett-take-oath-office-42nd-commissioner-bureau-indian-affairs.
2. "BIA Commissioner Issues Affirmative Action Policy for Indian Women," November 12, 1980, Department of the Interior News Release, https://www.bia.gov/as-ia/opa/online-press-release/bia-commissioner-issues-affirmative-action-policy-indian-women.
3. "Commissioner Hallett Initiates Plan to Benefit Minority and Indian Businesses," November 26, 1980, Department of the Interior News Release, https://www.bia.gov/as-ia/opa/online-press-release/commissioner-hallett-initiates-plan-benefit-minority-and-indian.
4. "Nomination of William Hallett," 24–32.

Chapter 54: Thomas W. Fredericks

1. Fredericks's nomination for assistant secretary was not confirmed by the Senate. President Carter then appointed him deputy assistant secretary and acting assistant secretary of the interior for Indian affairs.
2. United States Senate, "Nomination of Thomas W. Fredericks to Assistant Secretary of the Interior: Hearings before the Select Committee on Indian Affairs, United States Senate, 96th Congress, 2nd Session," July 1, 1980 (hereafter "Nomination of Thomas Fredericks"), 45.
3. "Nomination of Thomas Fredericks," 64–71.
4. "Nomination of Thomas Fredericks," 50–51.
5. "Nomination of Thomas Fredericks," 52–53.
6. Oliphant v. Suquamish, 435 U.S. 191 (1978).
7. United States v. Wheeler, 435 U.S. 313 (1978).
8. Santa Clara v. Martinez, 436 U.S. 49 (1978).

9. "Fredericks Assesses Supreme Court Decisions," A Speech Given to Area Directors, May 17, 1978, at Oklahoma City by Thomas W. Fredericks, Associate Solicitor for Indian Affairs, Department of the Interior News Release.

Chapter 55: Kenneth L. Smith

1. United States Senate, "Nomination of Kenneth L. Smith: Hearing Before the Select Committee on Indian Affairs, United States Senate, 97th Congress, 1st Session, on the Nomination of Kenneth L. Smith to be Assistant Secretary of the Interior for Indian Affairs," April 28, 1981 (hereafter "Nomination of Kenneth Smith"), 3.
2. "Nomination of Kenneth Smith," 3.
3. "Nomination of Kenneth Smith," 7.
4. "Kenneth L. Smith, Western Tribal Leader, to Be Nominated Assistant Interior Secretary," April 1, 1981, Department of the Interior News Release, https://www.bia.gov/as-ia/opa/online-press-release/kenneth-l-smith-western-tribal-leader-be-nominated-assistant-interior#:~:text=Interior%20Secretary%20James%20Watt%20said,Affairs%2C%20subject%20to%20Senate%20confirmation. Smith's nomination was sent to the Senate for consideration on April 14.
5. "Tribes Have Primary Responsibility for Reservation Programs, Assistant Secretary Says," July 23, 1981, Department of the Indian Interior News Release, https://www.bia.gov/as-ia/opa/online-press-release/tribes-have-primary-responsibility-reservation-programs-assistant.
6. Morris, "Termination by Accountants."
7. "Top Indian Official at Interior Submits Resignation," November 29, 1984, Department of the Interior News Release, https://www.bia.gov/as-ia/opa/online-press-release/top-indian-official-interior-submits-resignation.
8. "Nomination of Kenneth L. Smith," 5–6.
9. United States House of Representatives, "Bureau of Indian Affairs Budget Request for Fiscal Year 1984: Oversight Hearing Before the Committee on Interior and Insular Affairs, House of Representatives, 98th Congress, 1st Session on Bureau of Indian Affairs Budget Request for Fiscal Year 1984," February 24, 1983, 35–37.

Chapter 56: Ross O. Swimmer

1. "New Indian Affairs Nominee Experienced in Tribal Leadership and Business," September 26, 1985, Department of the Interior News Release, https://www.bia.gov/as-ia/opa/online-press-release/new-indian-affairs-nominee-experienced-tribal-leadership-and-business.
2. United States Senate, "Nomination of Ross O. Swimmer: Hearing before the Select Committee on Indian Affairs, United States Senate, 99th Congress, 1st Session, on the

Nomination of Ross O, Swimmer to be Assistant Secretary of the Interior for Indian Affairs," October 16, 1985 (hereafter "Nomination of Ross Swimmer"), 64.

3. "Ross Swimmer on Tribal Banks and the Direction of Indian Country under Trump," March 23, 2017, Citizen Potawatomie Nation, https://www.potawatomi.org/blog/2017/03/23/ross-swimmer-on-tribal-banks-and-the-direction-of-indian-country-under-trump/.

4. "Secretary Hodel Says New Assistant Secretary, Improved BIA Work to Strengthen Indian Tribes and Government-to-Government Relationship," October 7, 1985, Department of the Interior News Release, https://www.bia.gov/as-ia/opa/online-press-release/secretary-hodel-says-new-assistant-secretary-improved-bia-will-work.

5. United States House of Representatives, "Statement of the Assistant Secretary Ross Swimmer before the House of Representatives," 2.

6. United States Senate, "Nomination of Ross O. Swimmer: Hearing Before the Committee on Indian Affairs, United States Senate, 108th Congress, 1st Session, on Confirmation Hearing of the Nomination of Ross O. Swimmer to be Special Trustee for American Indians, Department of the Interior," February 12, 2003, 9.

7. "Nomination of Ross Swimmer," 10–11.

8. United States House of Representatives, "Department of the Interior and Related Agencies Appropriations for 1988: Hearings Before a Subcommittee of the Committee on Appropriations, House of Representatives, 100th Congress, 1st Session, Part 12 Bureau of Indian Affairs," 5–9.

Chapter 57: Eddie F. Brown

1. Not until August 2006 was the Office of Indian Education sequestered and renamed the Bureau of Indian Education with its own director.

2. "Assistant Secretary Eddie Brown to Keynote Conference on Economic Development of Indian Lands," March 12, 1990, Department of the Interior News Release, https://www.bia.gov/as-ia/opa/online-press-release/assistant-secretary-eddie-brown-keynote-conference-economic.

3. "An Act to specify the terms of contracts entered into by the United States and Indian tribal organizations under the Indian Self-Determination and Educational Assistance Act and to provide for Tribal Self-Governance, and for other purposes," 108 Stat. 4250 (October 25, 1994).

4. United States Senate, "Indian Trust Fund Management: Hearing before the Select Committee on Indian Affairs, United States Senate, Oversight Hearing on the Management of Indian Trust Funds by the U.S. Government," 101st Cong., Second Sess., August 12, 1992 (hereafter "Indian Trust Fund Management").

5. "Indian Trust Fund Management," 47–48.

6. United States Senate, "Confirmation of Dr. Eddie F. Brown: Hearing Before the Select Committee on Indian Affairs, United States Senate, 101st Congress, 1st Session, on Confirmation of Dr. Eddie F. Brown, the President's Nominee for Assistant

Secretary, Indian Affairs, Department of the Interior," June 20, 1989 (hereafter "Nomination of Eddie Brown"), 8–9.

7. "Nomination of Eddie Brown," 50–53.

8. "Nomination of Eddie Brown," 10, 53–57.

Chapter 58: Ada E. Deer

1. United States Senate, "Nomination of Ada Deer: Hearing Before the Committee on Indian Affairs, United States Senate, 103rd Congress, 1st Session, on the Nomination of Ada Deer to be Assistant Secretary for Indian Affairs," July 15, 1993 (hereafter "Nomination of Ada Deer"), 8.

2. The Menominee Tribe had its federal political status terminated by Congress in 1954 (effective in 1961).

3. "Nomination of Ada Deer," 8.

4. "President Clinton Names Ada Deer as Assistant Secretary for Indian Affairs," May 11, 1993, Department of the Interior News Release, https://www.indianaffairs.gov/as-ia/opa/online-press-release/president-clinton-names-ada-deer-assistant-secretary-indian-affairs#.

5. See United States Senate, H. R. Res. 3286 (Title III), "Adoption Protection and Stability Act of 1996: Hearing before the Senate Committee on Indian Affairs," 105th Cong., First Sess.

6. "Congressional Bill Threatens Indian Children," May 8, 1996, United States Department of the Interior News Release, https://www.bia.gov/as-ia/opa/online-press-release/congressional-bill-threatens-indian-children.

7. "Statement by Assistant Secretary for Indian Affairs Ada Deer," June 9, 1997, Department of the Interior News Release, https://www.indianaffairs.gov/as-ia/opa/online-press-release/statement-assistant-secretary-indian-affairs-ada-e-deer.

8. "National Native American Hall of Fame 2019 Induction Ceremony to Be Held on November 2," *Indian Country Today*, October 11, 2019.

9. "Nomination of Ada Deer," 10–12.

Chapter 59: Kevin Gover

1. United States Senate, "Nomination of Kevin Gover: Hearing Before the Committee on Indian Affairs, United States Senate, 105th Congress, 1st Session, on Kevin Gover to be Assistant Secretary for Indian Affairs," October 30, 1997 (hereafter "Nomination of Kevin Gover"), 6.

2. "Interior Department Defends Tribal Self-Determination," March 10, 1998, Department of the Interior News Release, https://www.bia.gov/as-ia/opa/online-press-release/interior-department-defends-tribal-self-determination.

3. "Assistant Secretary for Indian Affairs Delivers University of South Dakota Law School Speech on 'Indian Warriors: Then and Now'; Urges Responsible and Responsive Tribal Governments," March 19, 1998, Bureau of Indian Affairs News Release, https://www.bia.gov/as-ia/opa/online-press-release/assistant-secret-ary-indian-affairs-kevin-gover-delivers-university.

4. "Keynote Remarks of Kevin Gover, Assistant Secretary–Indian Affairs," September 8, 2000, on the 175th Anniversary of the Establishment of the Bureau of Indian Affairs, United States Department of the Interior News Release, https://www.indianaffairs.gov/sites/bia.gov/files/assets/as-ia/opa/pdf/idc1-032248.pdf (hereafter "Keynote Address of Kevin Gover").

5. "BIA and Tribes Sign an Agreement Establishing a Government-to-Government Consultation Policy," December 15, 2000, United States Department of the Interior News Release, https://www.bia.gov/as-ia/opa/online-press-release/bia-and-tribes-sign-agreement-establishing-government-government.

6. "At Indian Affairs: A Tough Act to Balance," *Washington Post*, November 17, 1998.

7. "Keynote Remarks of Kevin Gover."

8. "An act authorizing appropriations and expenditures for the administration of Indian affairs, and for other purposes," 42 Stat. 208 (November 2, 1921); "An act to provide maximum Indian participation in the Government and education of Indian people; to provide for the full participation of Indian tribes in programs and services conducted by the Federal Government for Indians and to encourage the development of human resources of the Indian people; to establish a program of assistance to upgrade Indian education; to support the right of Indian citizens to control their own educational activities; and for other purposes," 88 Stat. 2203 (January 4, 1975); "An act to specify the terms of contracts entered into by the United States and Indian tribal organizations under the Indian Self-Determination and Education Assistance Act and to provide for tribal Self-Governance, and for other purposes," 108 Stat. 4250 (October 25, 1994).

9. "Nomination of Kevin Gover," 7–9, 14.

Chapter 60: Neil A. McCaleb

1. "Neal McCaleb Sworn in as Assistant Secretary-Indian Affairs: Immediate Goals Include Meeting with Tribal Leaders," July 6, 2001, United States Department of the Interior News Release, https://www.bia.gov/as-ia/opa/online-press-release/neal-mccaleb-sworn-assistant-secretary-indian-affairs-immediate-goals (hereafter "McCaleb Sworn In").

2. "McCaleb Sworn In."

3. "Assistant Secretary McCaleb Calls on Tribal Leaders to Choose Prosperity over Poverty, Announces Tribal Economic Summit for September 16–19 in Phoenix," June 20, 2002, United States Department of the Interior News Release, https://www.indianaffairs.gov/as-ia/opa/online-press-release/assistant-secretary-mccaleb-calls-tribal-leaders-choose-prosperity.

4. "McCaleb to Develop National Strategy for Improving Tribal Economies, Summit on Emerging Tribal Economies Provides Springboard for Action," October 11, 2002, United States Department of the Interior News Release, https://www.bia.gov/as-ia/opa/online-press-release/mccaleb-develop-national-strategy-improving-tribal-economies.

5. "Remarks Prepared for Delivery by the Honorable Gale Norton, Interior Secretary, National Indian School Board Association Summer Conference," July 24, 2007, United States Department of the Interior News Release, https://www.bia.gov/as-ia/opa/online-press-release/remarks-prepared-delivery-honorable-gale-norton-interior-secretary.

6. United States Senate, "Confirmation of Neil A. McCaleb: Hearing Before the Committee on Indian Affairs, United States Senate, 107th Congress, 1st Session, on Neil A. McCaleb to be Assistant Secretary for Indian Affairs," June 13, 2001 (hereafter "Nomination of Neil McCaleb"), 18.

7. United States Senate, "Proposed Reorganization of Major Agency and Functions Related to Indian Trust Reform Matters within the Department of the Interior, 108th Congress, 1st Session," March 10, 2003.

8. "Nomination of Neil McCaleb," 11–14.

Chapter 61: David W. Anderson

1. "White House Acts to Fill Top BIA Leadership Post," *Native Sun News*, September 15, 2003.

2. United States Senate, "Nomination of David W. Anderson, Hearing before the Committee on Indian Affairs, on Confirmation Hearing of the Nomination of David W. Anderson to be Assistant Secretary for Indian Affairs," 108th Cong., First Sess., October 22, 2003 (hereafter "Nomination of David Anderson"), 9.

3. "Dave Anderson Sworn in as Assistant Secretary for Indian Affairs," February 2, 2004, United States Department of the Interior News Release, https://www.bia.gov/as-ia/opa/online-press-release/david-anderson-sworn-assistant-secretary-indian-affairs.

4. "Nomination of David Anderson," 12.

5. "Famous Dave Reflects on Career of Success," *Native Sun News*, February 17, 2012.

6. Resignation Letter from Dave Anderson to Gail Norton, Secretary of the Interior, January 27, 2004; "Assistant Secretary for Indian Affairs Dave Anderson Announces His Decision to Resign and Resume His Entrepreneur Career," January 31, 2005, Bureau of Indian Affairs News Release, https://www.bia.gov/as-ia/opa/online-press-release/assistant-secretary-indian-affairs-dave-anderson-announces-his.

7. "Nomination of David Anderson," 9, 11–13.

Chapter 62: Carl J. Artman

1. "Carl Artman Sworn in as New Assistant Secretary for Indian Affairs," March 8, 2007, United States Department of the Interior News Release, https://www.bia.gov/

as-ia/opa/online-press-release/carl-artman-sworn-new-assistant-secretary-indian-affairs. The dissenting vote was David Vitter (Republican, Louisiana).

2. United States Senate, "Nomination of Carl J. Artman: Hearing Before the Committee on Indian Affairs on the Nomination of Carl J. Artman to be Assistant Secretary for Indian Affairs, Department of the Interior," 109th Cong., Second Sess., Senate Hearing 109-665, September 14, 2006 (hereafter "Nomination of Carl Artman"), 5–6.

3. "Tribes, Native Organizations, Federal Partners to Gather in Phoenix for Groundbreaking Summit," May 8, 2007, United States Department of the Interior News Release, https://www.indianaffairs.gov/as-ia/opa/online-press-release/tribes-native-organizations-federal-partners-gather-phoenix-ground.

4. "Artman Resigns from BIA after a Year on the Job," *Native Sun News*, April 29, 2008.

5. "Nomination of Carl Artman," 5–6.

Chapter 63: Larry J. Echo Hawk

1. Echo Hawk, "With Real Intent," 76.

2. Kuersten, "Assistant Secretary for Indian Affairs: Who is Larry Echo Hawk?" AllGov, May 10, 2009, http://www.allgov.com/news/appointments-and-resignations/assistant-secretary-for-indian-affairs-who-is-larry-echohawk?news=838789.

3. United States Senate, "Nomination of Larry J. Echo Hawk to Be Assistant Secretary for Indian Affairs, United States Department of the Interior, Hearing Before the Committee on Indian Affairs," 111th Cong., First Sess., May 7, 2009 (hereafter "Nomination of Larry Echo Hawk"), 14.

4. "Tribal Consultation," *Federal Register*, November 9, 2009, 74:57,881; "Secretary Salazar, Assistant Secretary Echo Hawk Launch Comprehensive Tribal Consultation Policy," December 1, 2011, United States Department of the Interior, Office of the Secretary, News Release, https://www.doi.gov/news/pressreleases/Secretary-Salazar-Assistant-Secretary-Echo-Hawk-Launch-Comprehensive-Tribal-Consultation-Policy.

5. "NCAI Statement on Resignation of Larry Echo Hawk as Assistant Secretary-Indian Affairs," April 2, 2012, National Congress of American Indians, https://www.ncai.org/news/articles/2012/04/02/ncai-statement-on-resignation-of-larry-echo-hawk-assistant-secretary-indian-affairs-for-the-department-of-the-interior.

6. Carcieri v. Kempthorne, 554 U.S. 938 (2008).

7. "Nomination of Larry Echo Hawk," 14–16.

Chapter 64: Kevin K. Washburn

1. United States Senate, "Nomination of Kevin K. Washburn to be Assistant Secretary for Indian Affairs, United States Department of the Interior, Hearing Before the

Committee on Indian Affairs," 112th Cong., Second Sess., September 14, 2012 (hereafter "Nomination of Kevin Washburn"), 11–12.

2. "Washburn Proposes Changes to Land into Trust Procedures to Achieve Greater Transparency, Clarity, and Certainty for Tribes," May 24, 2013, Department of the Interior, Office of the Secretary, News Release, https://www.bia.gov/as-ia/opa/online-press-release/washburn-proposes-changes-land-trust-procedures-achieve-greater.

3. "Interior Proposes Reform of Federal Acknowledgment Regulations," May 22, 2014, United States Department of the Interior, Office of the Secretary, News Release, https://www.bia.gov/sites/bia_prod.opengov.ibmcloud.com/files/assets/public/press_release/pdf/idc1-026775.pdf; "Federal Acknowledgment of American Indian Tribe," *Federal Register*, July 1, 2015, 80:37,865.

4. Departmental Order 3335, "Reaffirmation of the Federal Trust Responsibility to Federally Recognized Indian Tribes and Individual Indian Beneficiaries," US Department of the Interior, August 1, 2014.

5. Washburn, *Gaming and Gambling*.

6. Washburn, "What the Future Holds," 200–232.

7. "Nomination of Kevin Washburn," 10–12.

8. Washburn, "What the Future Holds," 200–202, 231–232.

Chapter 65: Tara MacLean Sweeney

1. "History Made: Alaskan Leader Tara MacLean Sweeney Becomes First Female Alaska Native for Assistant Secretary of Indian Affairs," August 16, 2018, US Department of the Interior Indian Affairs News Release, https://www.bia.gov/as-ia/opa/online-press-release/history-made-alaskan-leader-tara-mac-lean-sweeney-becomes-first.

2. "Sweeney Sworn in for Top BIA Post," August 27, 2018, *Cordova Times*, https://www.thecordovatimes.com/2018/08/27/sweeney-sworn-in-for-top-bia-post/.

3. "Assistant Secretary Sweeney Clears the Path for Tribes to Develop Energy Resources on Tribal Lands," December 23, 2019, US Department of the Interior Indian Affairs News Release, https://www.indianaffairs.gov/as-ia/opa/online-press-release/assistant-secretary-sweeney-clears-path-tribes-develop-energy.

4. "Office of Assistant Secretary—Indian Affairs Statement on the Coronavirus Relief Fund Process," April 16, 2020, US Department of the Interior Indian Affairs News Release, https://www.bia.gov/as-ia/opa/online-press-release/office-assistant-secretary-indian-affairs-statement-coronavirus; Beitsch, "With Corporations Vying for Tribal Stimulus, Some Call for Resignation of Head of Indian Affairs," *The Hill*, April 16, 2020, https://thehill.com/policy/energy-environment/493234-with-corporations-vying-for-tribal-stimulus-some-call-for-indian.

5. Tribes and tribal organizations calling for her resignation included the Association on American Indian Affairs, the Great Plains Tribal Chairmen's Association, Midwest

Alliance of Sovereign Tribes, the National Congress of American Indians, and the United South and Eastern Tribes.

6. United States Senate, "Nomination of Tara MacLean Sweeney of Alaska to be Assistant Secretary, U.S. Department of the Interior: Hearings before the Committee of Indian Affairs, United States Senate," May 9, 2018, 115th Cong., Second Sess., 9–11.

BIBLIOGRAPHY

Published Works

Armstrong, William A. *Warrior in Two Camps: Ely S. Parker, Union General and Seneca Chief.* Syracuse, NY: Syracuse University Press, 1989.

Baird, W. David. "William A. Jones, 1897–1904." In *The Commissioners of Indian Affairs, 1824–1977*, edited by Robert M. Kvasnicka and Herman J. Viola, 211–220. Lincoln: University of Nebraska Press, 1979.

Beitsch, Rebecca. "With Corporations Vying for Tribal Stimulus, Some Call for Resignation of Head of Indian Affairs." *The Hill*, April 16, 2020. https://thehill.com/policy/energy-environment/493234-with-corporations-vying-for-tribal-stimulus-some-call-for-indian.

Biographical Directory of the United States Congress, 1774–Present. https://bioguideretro.congress.gov/.

Buckley, Jay. *William Clark: Indian Diplomat.* Norman: University of Oklahoma Press, 2008.

Calloway, Colin G. *The American Revolution in Indian Country: Crisis and Diversity in North America.* Cambridge, UK: Cambridge University Press, 1995.

The Carpenter's Hall. www.carpentershall.org/famous-early-members.

Cash, Joseph H. "Louis Rook Bruce, 1969–73." In *The Commissioners of Indian Affairs, 1824–1977*, edited by Robert M. Kvasnicka and Herman J. Viola, 333–340. Lincoln: University of Nebraska Press, 1979.

Chaput, Donald. "James W. Denver, 1857, 1858–59." In *The Commissioners of Indian Affairs, 1824–1977*, edited by Robert M. Kvasnicka and Herman J. Viola, 69–75. Lincoln: University of Nebraska Press, 1979.

Citizen Potawatomie Nation. www.potawatomie.org.

Cohen, Felix S. *Handbook of Federal–Indian Law.* Charlottesville, VA: Michie, 1982.

Collier, John. *From Every Zenith.* Denver: Sage Books, 1963.

Crawford, Richard C. "Edward P. Smith, 1873–75." In *The Commissioners of Indian Affairs, 1824–1977*, edited by Robert M. Kvasnicka and Herman J. Viola, 141–147. Lincoln: University of Nebraska Press, 1979.

"Daniel Gookin, 1612–1687." The Native Northeast Research Collaborative. https://nativenortheastportal.com/bio/bibliography/gookin-daniel-1612-1687.

Debo, Angie. *And Still the Waters Run: The Betrayal of the Five Civilized Tribes.* Norman: University of Oklahoma Press, 1984.

DeJong, David H. *American Indian Treaties: A Guide to Ratified and Unratified Colonial, United States, State, Foreign, and Intertribal Treaties and Agreements, 1607–1911*. Salt Lake City: University of Utah Press, 2015.

Deloria, Vine., Jr. *Behind the Trail of Broken Treaties: An Indian Manifesto*. New York: MacMillan and Company, 1969.

Dennehy, William J. "Roger L. Nichols, 1949–50." In *The Commissioners of Indian Affairs, 1824–1977*, edited by Robert M. Kvasnicka and Herman J. Viola, 289–291. Lincoln: University of Nebraska Press, 1979.

de Vattal, Emmerich. *The Law of Nations, or, Principles of the law of nature, applied to the conduct and affairs of nations and sovereigns, with three early essays on the origin and nature of natural law and on luxurys*. Philadelphia: T. & H. W. Johnson, 1863.

Downey, Dennis. "The Illinois Indian Trade, 1783–1818." Master's thesis, Eastern Illinois University, 1972. https://thekeep.eiu.edu/theses/3888/.

Drinnon, Richard. *Keepers of Concentration Camps: Dillon S. Myer and American Racism*. Berkeley: University of California Press, 1987.

Echo Hawk, Larry J. "With Real Intent: An Unexpected Gift." *Journal of Book of Mormon Studies* 16, no. 1 (2007).

Edmunds, R. David. "Samuel S. Hamilton, 1830–31." In *The Commissioners of Indian Affairs, 1824–1977*, edited by Robert M. Kvasnicka and Herman J. Viola, 9–11. Lincoln: University of Nebraska Press, 1979.

Ellis, Richard N. "Robert L. Bennett, 1966–69." In *The Commissioners of Indian Affairs, 1824–1977*, edited by Robert M. Kvasnicka and Herman J. Viola, 325–331. Lincoln: University of Nebraska Press, 1979.

Explore Pennsylvania History. http://explorepahistory.com.

Farrard, Max, ed. *The Records of the Federal Convention of 1787*. Vol. 1–2. New Haven: Yale University Press, 1911.

Foley, William E. *Wilderness Journey: The Life of William Clark*. Columbia: University of Missouri Press, 2004.

Goldman, Michael A. "Rowland E. Trowbridge, 1880–81." In *The Commissioners of Indian Affairs, 1824–1977*, edited by Robert M. Kvasnicka and Herman J. Viola, 162–172. Lincoln: University of Nebraska Press, 1979.

Graymont, Barbara. *The Iroquois in the American Revolution*. Syracuse, NY: Syracuse University Press, 1972.

Hagan, William T. "Daniel M. Browning, 1893–97." In *The Commissioners of Indian Affairs, 1824–1977*, edited by Robert M. Kvasnicka and Herman J. Viola, 205–209. Lincoln: University of Nebraska Press, 1979.

———. *The Indian Rights Association: The Herbert Welsh Years, 1882–1904*. Tucson: University of Arizona Press, 1985.

"Editor's Historical Record," *Harper's New Monthly Magazine* 56, no. 333 (1878).

Harris, Joseph. *Records of the Harris Family Descended from John Harris Born 1680 in Wiltshire England*. Philadelphia: Press George F. Lasher, 1903.

Hill, Edward E. *Guide to the Records in the National Archives of the United States Relating to American Indians*. Washington, DC: National Archives and Records Administration, 1981.

———. "John Quincy Smith, 1875–77." In *The Commissioners of Indian Affairs, 1824–1977*, edited by Robert M. Kvasnicka and Herman J. Viola, 149–153. Lincoln: University of Nebraska Press, 1979.

Ickes, Harold. "The Indian Loses Again." *New Republic*, September 24, 1951.

The Irvine–Newbold Family Papers. Philadelphia: The Historical Society of Pennsylvania, 2005.

Jacobs, Wilbur R. "Edmond Atkin's Plan for Imperial Indian Control." *The Journal of Southern History* 19, no. 4 (August 1953).

Kawashima, Yasuhide. "Colonial Government Agencies." In *Handbook of North American Indians*. Vol. 4, *History of Indian–White Relations*, edited by Wilcomb E. Washburn. Washington, DC: Smithsonian Institute, 1988.

———. "Legal Origins of the Indian Reservations in Colonial Massachusetts." *American Journal of Legal History* 13, no. 1 (1969).

Kelly, Lawrence C. "Cato Sells, 1913–21." In *The Commissioners of Indian Affairs, 1824–1977*, edited by Robert M. Kvasnicka and Herman J. Viola, 243–250. Lincoln: University of Nebraska Press, 1979.

———. "Charles Henry Burke, 1921–29." In *The Commissioners of Indian Affairs, 1824–1977*, edited by Robert M. Kvasnicka and Herman J. Viola, 251–261. Lincoln: University of Nebraska Press, 1979.

———. "Charles James Rhoads, 1929–33." In *The Commissioners of Indian Affairs, 1824–1977*, edited by Robert M. Kvasnicka and Herman J. Viola, 263–271. Lincoln: University of Nebraska Press, 1979.

Kelsey, Harry. "Charles E. Mix, 1858." In *The Commissioners of Indian Affairs, 1824–1977*, edited by Robert M. Kvasnicka and Herman J. Viola, 78. Lincoln: University of Nebraska Press, 1979.

———. "William P. Dole, 1861–65." In *The Commissioners of Indian Affairs, 1824–1977*, edited by Robert M. Kvasnicka and Herman J. Viola, 89–98. Lincoln: University of Nebraska Press, 1979.

Klein, H. M. J., ed. *Lancaster County Pennsylvania: A History*. Vol. III. New York: Lewis Historical Publishing Company, Inc., 1924.

Kuersten, Kyle. "Assistant Secretary for Indian Affairs: Who Is Larry Echo Hawk?" AllGov, May 10, 2009. http://www.allgov.com/news/appointments-and-resignations/assistant-secretary-for-indian-affairs-who-is-larry-echohawk?news=838789.

Kvasnicka, Robert M. "George W. Manypenny, 1853–57." In *The Commissioners of Indian Affairs, 1824–1977*, edited by Robert M. Kvasnicka and Herman J. Viola, 57–67. Lincoln: University of Nebraska Press, 1979.

Kvasnicka, Robert M., and Herman J. Viola, eds. *The Commissioners of Indian Affairs, 1824–1977*. Lincoln: University of Nebraska Press, 1979.

Mason, Virginia. *The Life and Diplomatic Correspondence of John M. Mason.* New York: Neale Publishing Company, 1906.

McClure, James P., ed. *The Papers of Thomas Jefferson.* Vol. 44, *1 July to 10 November 1804.* Princeton, NJ: Princeton University Press, 2019.

Meyer, Roy W. "Ezra A. Hayt, 1877–80." In *The Commissioners of Indian Affairs, 1824–1977*, edited by Robert M. Kvasnicka and Herman J. Viola, 155–166. Lincoln: University of Nebraska Press, 1979.

Miller, Robert J. *Native America: Discovered and Conquered: Thomas Jefferson, Lewis and Clark and Manifest Destiny.* Westport, CT: Greenwood Publishing Group, 2006.

Miner, Craig. "Francis A. Walker, 1871–73." In *The Commissioners of Indian Affairs, 1824–1977*, edited by Robert M. Kvasnicka and Herman J. Viola, 135–140. Lincoln: University of Nebraska Press, 1979.

"Mr. Davy's Diary 1794" Part 1. *Pennsylvania History* 20, no. 2 (April 1953).

"Mr. Davy's Diary 1794," Part 2. *Pennsylvania History* 20, no. 3 (July 1953).

Morgan, Thomas Jefferson. *Studies in Pedagogy.* Boston: Silver, Burdett and Company, 1892.

Morris, C. Patrick. "Termination by Accountants: The Reagan Indian Policy." *Policy Studies Journal* 16, no. 4 (Summer 1987).

Moses, L. G. *Wild West Shows and Images of American Indians, 1883–1933.* Albuquerque: University of New Mexico Press, 1996.

National Congress of American Indians (NCAI). "NCAI Statement on Resignation of Larry Echo Hawk as Assistant Secretary-Indian Affairs." https://www.ncai.org/news/articles/2012/04/02/ncai-statement-on-resignation-of-larry-echo-hawk-assistant-secretary-indian-affairs-for-the-department-of-the-interior.

Nichols, David Andre. *Engines of Diplomacy: Indian Trading Factories and the Negotiation of American Empire.* Chapel Hill: University of North Carolina Press, 2016.

Oberg, Barbara B., ed. *The Papers of Thomas Jefferson.* Vol. 34, *1 May to 31 July 1802.* Princeton, NJ: Princeton University Press, 2007.

O'Neil, Floyd A. "Hiram Price, 1881–85." In *The Commissioners of Indian Affairs, 1824–1977*, edited by Robert M. Kvasnicka and Herman J. Viola, 173–179. Lincoln: University of Nebraska Press, 1979.

———. "John H. Oberly, 1888–89." In *The Commissioners of Indian Affairs, 1824–1977*, edited by Robert M. Kvasnicka and Herman J. Viola, 189–191. Lincoln: University of Nebraska Press, 1979.

Ourada, Patricia K. "Dillon Seymour Myer, 1950–53." In *The Commissioners of Indian Affairs, 1824–1977*, edited by Robert M. Kvasnicka and Herman J. Viola, 293–299. Lincoln: University of Nebraska Press, 1979.

———. "Glenn L. Emmons, 1953–61." In *The Commissioners of Indian Affairs, 1824–1977*, edited by Robert M. Kvasnicka and Herman J. Viola, 301–310. Lincoln: University of Nebraska Press, 1979.

Parman, Donald L. "Francis Ellington Leupp, 1905–09." In *The Commissioners of Indian Affairs, 1824–1977*, edited by Robert M. Kvasnicka and Herman J. Viola, 231–232. Lincoln: University of Nebraska Press, 1979.

Philp, Kenneth R. "John Collier, 1933–45." In *The Commissioners of Indian Affairs, 1824–1977*, edited by Robert M. Kvasnicka and Herman J. Viola, 273–282. Lincoln: University of Nebraska Press, 1979.

Prucha, Francis Paul. *American Indian Policy in the Formative Years: The Indian Trade and Intercourse Acts, 1790–1834*. Lincoln: University of Nebraska Press, 1962.

———. *American Indian Treaties: A History of a Political Anomaly*. Berkeley: University of California Press, 1994.

———. *The Great Father: The United States Government and the American Indians*. Lincoln: University of Nebraska Press, 1984.

———. "Thomas Jefferson Morgan, 1889–93." In *The Commissioners of Indian Affairs, 1824–1977*, edited by Robert M. Kvasnicka and Herman J. Viola, 193–203. Lincoln: University of Nebraska Press, 1979.

Putney, Diane. "Robert Grosvenor Valentine, 1909–12." In *The Commissioners of Indian Affairs, 1824–1977*, edited by Robert M. Kvasnicka and Herman J. Viola, 233–242. Lincoln: University of Nebraska Press, 1979.

Roberts, Gary L. "Alfred Burton Greenwood, 1859–61." In *The Commissioners of Indian Affairs, 1824–1977*, edited by Robert M. Kvasnicka and Herman J. Viola, 81–87. Lincoln: University of Nebraska Press, 1979.

Roberts, Gary L. "Dennis Nelson Cooley, 1866–67." In *The Commissioners of Indian Affairs, 1824–1977*, edited by Robert M. Kvasnicka and Herman J. Viola, 99–108. Lincoln: University of Nebraska Press, 1979.

Rockwell, Stephen J. *Indian Affairs and the Administrative State in the Nineteenth Century*. Cambridge, UK: Cambridge University Press, 2010.

Satz, Ronald N. *American Indian Policy during the Jacksonian Era*. Lincoln: University of Nebraska Press, 1975.

———. "Carey Allen Harris, 1836–38." In *The Commissioners of Indian Affairs, 1824–1977*, edited by Robert M. Kvasnicka and Herman J. Viola, 17–22. Lincoln: University of Nebraska Press, 1979.

———. "Elbert Herring, 1831–36." In *The Commissioners of Indian Affairs, 1824–1977*, edited by Robert M. Kvasnicka and Herman J. Viola, 13–16. Lincoln: University of Nebraska Press, 1979.

———. "Thomas Hartley Crawford, 1838–45." In *The Commissioners of Indian Affairs, 1824–1977*, edited by Robert M. Kvasnicka and Herman J. Viola, 23–27. Lincoln: University of Nebraska Press, 1979.

Schmeckebier, Laurence F. *The Office of Indian Affairs: Its History, Activities, and Organization*. Baltimore, MD: Johns Hopkins Press, 1927.

"Schuylkill Arsenal to Wheeling." Discovering Lewis & Clark. http://www.lewis-clark.org/article/2980.

Smith, Michael T. "Benjamin Reifel, 1976–77." In *The Commissioners of Indian Affairs, 1824–1977*, edited by Robert M. Kvasnicka and Herman J. Viola, 347–348. Lincoln: University of Nebraska Press, 1979.

———. "Morris Thompson, 1973–76." In *The Commissioners of Indian Affairs, 1824–1977*, edited by Robert M. Kvasnicka and Herman J. Viola, 341–345. Lincoln: University of Nebraska Press, 1979.

Szasz, Margaret Connell. "Philleo Nash, 1961–66." In *The Commissioners of Indian Affairs, 1824–1977*, edited by Robert M. Kvasnicka and Herman J. Viola, 311–323. Lincoln: University of Nebraska Press, 1979.

Thompson, Gregory C. "John D. C. Atkins, 1885–88." In *The Commissioners of Indian Affairs, 1824–1977*, edited by Robert M. Kvasnicka and Herman J. Viola, 181–188. Lincoln: University of Nebraska Press, 1979.

Trahant, Mark N. *The Last Great Battle of the Indian Wars: Henry M. Jackson, Forrest J. Gerard, and the Campaign for the Self-Determination of American Indian Tribes*. Fort Hall, ID: The Cedars Group, 2010.

Trefousse, Hans L. "Carl Schurz and the Indians." Great Plains Quarterly (Spring 1984).

Trelease, Allen W. *Indian Affairs in Colonial New York: The Seventeenth Century*. Lincoln: University of Nebraska Press, 1997.

Trennert, Robert. "Luke Lea, 1850–53." In *The Commissioners of Indian Affairs, 1824–1977*, edited by Robert M. Kvasnicka and Herman J. Viola, 48–55. Lincoln: University of Nebraska Press, 1979.

———. "Orlando Brown, 1849–50." In *The Commissioners of Indian Affairs, 1824–1977*, edited by Robert M. Kvasnicka and Herman J. Viola, 41–47. Lincoln: University of Nebraska Press, 1979.

———. "William Medill, 1845–49." In *The Commissioners of Indian Affairs, 1824–1977*, edited by Robert M. Kvasnicka and Herman J. Viola, 29–39. Lincoln: University of Nebraska Press, 1979.

Tyler, S. Lyman. "William A. Brophy, 1945–48." In *The Commissioners of Indian Affairs, 1824–1977*, edited by Robert M. Kvasnicka and Herman J. Viola, 283–287. Lincoln: University of Nebraska Press, 1979.

Unrau, William E. "Lewis V. Bogy, 1866–67." In *The Commissioners of Indian Affairs, 1824–1977*, edited by Robert M. Kvasnicka and Herman J. Viola, 109–114. Lincoln: University of Nebraska Press, 1979.

———. "Nathaniel Green Taylor, 1867–69." In *The Commissioners of Indian Affairs, 1824–1977*, edited by Robert M. Kvasnicka and Herman J. Viola, 115–122. Lincoln: University of Nebraska Press, 1979.

Valentine, Robert G. "Is the Indian Worth Conserving?" *American Conservation*, February 1911.

Vaughn, Alden T. *New England Frontier: Puritans and Indians, 1620–1675*. Norman: University of Oklahoma Press, 1995.

Viola, Herman J. "Thomas L. McKenney, 1824–30." In *The Commissioners of Indian Affairs, 1824–1977*, edited by Robert M. Kvasnicka and Herman J. Viola, 1–7. Lincoln: University of Nebraska Press, 1979.

Waltmann, Henry G. "Ely Samuel Parker, 1869–71." In *The Commissioners of Indian Affairs, 1824–1977*, edited by Robert M. Kvasnicka and Herman J. Viola, 123–133. Lincoln: University of Nebraska Press, 1979.

Washburn, Kevin K., ed. *Handbook of North American Indians*. Vol. 4, *History of Indian–White Relations*. Washington, DC: Smithsonian Institute, 1988.

———. *Gaming and Gambling: Cases and Materials*. New York: Aspen Publishers, 2011.

———. "What the Future Holds: The Changing Landscape of Federal Indian Policy." *Harvard Law Review Forum* 130, no. 200 (2017).

Webb, Willard J. "John Mason of Analostan Island." *The Arlington History Magazine* 5, no. 4 (October 1976).

Viola, Herman J. *Thomas L. McKenney: Architect of America's Early Indian Policy, 1816–1830*. Chicago: Swallow Press, 1974.

Court Cases

Carcieri v. Kempthorne, 552 U.S. 1229 (2008)
Cherokee Nation v. Georgia, 30 U.S. 1 (1831)
Ex Parte Crow Dog, 109 U.S. 556 (1883)
Ex. Parte Reynolds, 6 Dill. 394 (1879)
Johnson v. McIntosh, 21 U.S. 543 (1821)
The Kansas Indians, 72 U.S. (5 Wallace) 737 (1866)
Lone Wolf v. Hitchcock, 187 U.S. 553 (1903)
Oliphant v. Suquamish, 435 U.S. 191 (1978)
Opinions of the Attorney General, 7 Opinions 746 (1856)
Quick Bear v. Leupp, 210 U.S. 50 (1908)
Santa Clara v. Martinez, 436 U.S. 49 (1978)
United States v. Nice, 241 U.S. 591 (1916)
United States v. Rogers, 45 U.S. 567 (1846)
United States v. Wheeler, 435 U.S. 313 (1978)

Manuscripts

American Indian Policy Review Commission. *Final Report*. Washington, DC: Government Printing Office, 1977.

———. *Report on BIA Management*. Washington, DC: Government Printing Office, 1976.

Annual Progress Report Bureau of Indian Affairs, 1965–1968. Washington, DC: Bureau of Indian Affairs.

Annual Report of the Commissioner of Indian Affairs (ARCIA), 1828–1964. Washington, DC: Government Printing Office, various years.

Annual Report of the Secretary of the Interior, 1871. Washington, DC: Government Printing Office, 1871.

Annual Report of the Secretary of the Treasury, 1848. Washington, DC: Government Printing Office, 1849.

The Congressional Globe. Washington, DC: Blair and Rives, 1849.

Congressional Record. Washington, DC: Government Printing Office, various years.

Federal Register. Washington, DC: Government Printing Office, various years.

Journal of the Continental Congress, 1774–1785. Washington, DC: Government Printing Office, various years.

Letters of Delegates to Congress. Washington, DC: Government Printing Office, 1905.

Lowrie, Walter, ed. *American State Papers, Documents, Legislative and Executive, of the Congress of the United States, from the First Session of the Fourteenth to the Second Session of the Nineteenth Congress, Inclusive,* volumes 1 and 2. Washington, DC: Gales and Seaton, 1834.

———. *American State Papers, Documents, Legislative and Executive, of the Congress of the United States, in Relation to the Public Lands, from the First Session of the First Congress to the First Session of the Twenty-Third Congress, March 4, 1789, to June 15, 1834,* volume 1. Washington, DC: Duff Green, 1834.

"Reaffirmation of the Federal Trust Responsibility to Federally Recognized Indian Tribes and Individual Indian Beneficiaries," US Department of the Interior, August 1, 2014.

Nixon, Richard M. *Public Papers of the President: Containing the Public Messages, Speeches, and Statements of the President, Richard Nixon, 1970.* Edited by Richard Milhous. Washington, DC: Government Printing Office, 1971.

United States Bureau of Indian Affairs. *Indian Treaties, and Laws and Regulations Relating to Indian Affairs: To which is added an Appendix Containing the Proceedings of the Old Congress, and other important State Papers, in Relation to Indian Affairs.* Washington, DC: Way and Gideon, 1826.

———. *Office Copy of the Laws, Regulations, etc., of the Indian Bureau, 1850.* Washington, DC: Gideon and Company, 1850.

United States Congress. "Annual Message to Congress with Documents, President Jackson, December 8, 1829." *Senate Document 1.* 21st Congress, 1st Session. *Congressional Serial Set 192.* Washington, DC: Government Printing Office.

———. Condition of the Indian Tribes. Washington, DC: Government Printing Office, 1867.

———. "Message on Creek Indians: Report for the War Department in Relation to the Investigation of Fraud alleged to have been Committed on the Creeks in the Sale of their reservations." *House Document 452.* 25th Congress, 2nd Session, July 2, 1838. *Congressional Serial Set,* 2:331. Washington, DC: Government Printing Office.

———. "Message on the Creek Indians." *House Document 452.* 25th Congress, 1st Session, July 3, 1838. *Congressional Serial Set 331,* 11:1–102. Washington, DC: Government Printing Office.

———. *The Debates and Proceedings in the Congress of the United States, with an Appendix, Containing Important State Papers and Public Documents and All the Laws of a Public Nature.* First Cong., Second Sess., April 10, 1790. Washington, DC: Gales and Seaton, 1834.

United States House of Representatives. "Bureau of Indian Affairs Budget Request for Fiscal Year 1984: Oversight Hearing Before the Committee on Interior and Insular Affairs, House of Representatives, 98th Congress, 1st Session on Bureau of Indian Affairs Budget Request for Fiscal Year 1984." February 24, 1983. Washington, DC: Government Printing Office, 1983.

———. "Department of the Interior and Related Agencies Appropriations for 1979: Hearings before a Subcommittee of the Committee on Appropriations, 95th Congress, 2nd session, Part 3." Washington: DC: Government Printing Office, 1978.

———. "Department of the Interior and Related Agencies Appropriations for 1988: Hearings Before a Subcommittee of the Committee on Appropriations, House of Representatives, 100th Congress, 1st Session, Part 12, Bureau of Indian Affairs." Washington, DC: Government Printing Office, 1988.

———. "Department of the Interior and Related Agencies Appropriations for Fiscal Year 1968: Hearing before a Subcommittee of the Committee on Appropriations, 90th Congress, 1st Session, part 1." Washington, DC: Government Printing Office, 1967.

———. "Statement of the Assistant Secretary Ross Swimmer before the House of Representatives." In "Department of the Interior and Related Agencies Appropriations for 1988: Hearings before a Subcommittee of the Committee on Appropriations, House of Representatives, 100th Congress, 1st Session, Part 12, Bureau of Indian Affairs," edited by United States Congress. October 27, 1987. Washington, DC: Government Printing Office, 1987.

United States Senate. "Confirmation of Dr. Eddie F. Brown: Hearing Before the Select Committee on Indian Affairs, United States Senate, 101st Congress, 1st Session, on Confirmation of Dr. Eddie F. Brown, the President's Nominee for Assistant Secretary, Indian Affairs, Department of the Interior." June 20, 1989. Washington, DC: Government Printing Office, 1989.

———. "Confirmation of Neil A. McCaleb: Hearing Before the Committee on Indian Affairs, United States Senate, 107th Congress, 1st Session, on Neil A. McCaleb to be Assistant Secretary for Indian Affairs." June 13, 2001. Washington, DC: Government Printing Office, 2001.

———. H.R. Res. 3286 (Title III). "Adoption Protection and Stability Act of 1996: Hearing before the Senate Committee on Indian Affairs." 105th Cong., First Sess. Washington, DC: Government Printing Office, 1996.

———. "Hearing before the Committee on Interior and Insular Affairs, 93rd Congress, 1st Session, on the Nomination of Morris Thompson to be Commissioner of the Bureau of Indian Affairs." November 14, 1973. Washington, DC: Government Printing Office, 1974.

———. "Hearings before the Committee on Interior and Insular Affairs on the Nomination of Philleo Nash for Commissioner of Indian Affairs." Eighty-Seventh Cong., First Sess., August 14, 1961. Washington, DC: Government Printing Office, 1961.

———. "Indian Trust Fund Management: Hearing before the Select Committee on Indian Affairs, Oversight Hearing on the Management of Indian Trust Funds by the U.S. Government." 101st Cong., Second Sess., August 12, 1992. Washington, DC: Government Printing Office, 1992.

———. "Interior Nomination: Hearing before the Committee on Interior and Insular Affairs, United States Senate on the Nomination of Louis R. Bruce, of New York, to be Commissioner of Indian Affairs." Ninety-First Cong., First Sess., August 11, 1969. Washington, DC: Government Printing Office, 1969.

———. "Nomination of Ada Deer: Hearing Before the Committee on Indian Affairs, United States Senate, 103rd Congress, 1st Session, on the Nomination of Ada Deer to be Assistant Secretary for Indian Affairs." July 15, 1993. Washington, DC: Government Printing Office, 1993.

———. "Nomination of the Assistant Secretary of the Interior for Indian Affairs: Hearings before the United States Senate Select Committee on Indian Affairs, 85th Congress, 1st session, on Nomination of Forrest J. Gerard to be an Assistant Secretary of the Interior for Indian Affairs." September 9 and 12, 1977. Washington, DC: Government Printing Office, 1977.

———. "Nomination of Carl J. Artman: Hearing Before the Committee on Indian Affairs on the Nomination of Carl J. Artman to be Assistant Secretary for Indian Affairs, Department of the Interior." 109th Cong., Second Sess., *Senate Hearing 109-665*, September 14, 2006. Washington, DC: Government Printing Office, 2006.

———. "Nomination of David W. Anderson, Hearing before the Committee on Indian Affairs, on Confirmation Hearing of the Nomination of David W. Anderson to be Assistant Secretary for Indian Affairs." 108th Cong., First Sess., October 22, 2003. Washington, DC: Government Printing Office, 2003.

———. "Nomination of Glenn L. Emmons, Hearings Before the Committee on Interior and Insular Affairs United States Senate, 83rd Congress, 1st session on the Nomination of Glenn L. Emmons to be Commissioner of the Bureau of Indian Affairs." July 15 and 28, 1953. Washington, DC: Government Printing Office, 1953.

———. "Nomination of Kenneth L. Smith: Hearing Before the Select Committee on Indian Affairs, United States Senate, 97th Congress, 1st Session, on the Nomination of Kenneth L. Smith to be Assistant Secretary of the Interior for Indian Affairs." April 28, 1981. Washington, DC: Government Printing Office, 1981.

———. "Nomination of Kevin Gover: Hearing Before the Committee on Indian Affairs, United States Senate, 105th Congress, 1st Session, Kevin Gover to be Assistant Secretary for Indian Affairs." October 30, 1997. Washington, DC: Government Printing Office, 1997.

———. "Nomination of Kevin K. Washburn to be Assistant Secretary for Indian Affairs, United States Department of the Interior, Hearing Before the Committee on Indian Affairs." 112th Cong., Second Sess., September 14, 2012. Washington, DC: Government Printing Office, 2013.

---. "Nomination of Larry J. Echo Hawk to be Assistant Secretary for Indian Affairs, United States Department of the Interior, Hearing Before the Committee on Indian Affairs." 111th Cong., First Sess., May 7, 2009. Washington, DC: Government Printing Office, 2009.

---. "Nomination of Robert LaFollette Bennett to be Commissioner of Indian Affairs: Report of the Committee on Interior and Insular Affairs." *Senate Executive Report 1*, Eighty-Ninth Cong., First Sess. Washington, DC: Government Printing Office, 1966.

---. "Nomination of Ross O. Swimmer: Hearing Before the Committee on Indian Affairs, 108th Congress, 1st Session, on Confirmation Hearing of the Nomination of Ross O. Swimmer to be Special Trustee for American Indians, Department of the Interior." February 12, 2003. Washington, DC: Government Printing Office, 2003.

---. "Nomination of Ross O. Swimmer: Hearing before the Select Committee on Indian Affairs, United States Senate, 99th Congress, 1st Session, on the Nomination of Ross O. Swimmer to be Assistant Secretary of the Interior for Indian Affairs." October 16, 1985. Washington, DC: Government Printing Office, 1985.

---. "Nomination of Tara MacLean Sweeney of Alaska to be Assistant Secretary, U.S. Department of the Interior: Hearings before the Committee of Indian Affairs, United States Senate." May 9, 2018, 115th Cong., Second Sess. Washington, DC: Government Printing Office, 2018.

---. "Nomination of Thomas W. Fredericks to Assistant Secretary of the Interior: Hearings before the Select Committee on Indian Affairs, United States Senate, 96th Congress, 2nd Session." July 1, 1980. Washington, DC: Government Printing Office, 1980.

---. "Nomination of William A. Brophy to be Commissioner of Indian Affairs, United States Senate, Committee on Indian Affairs." February 20, 27, 28 and March 1, 1945. Washington, DC: Government Printing Office, 1945.

---. "Nomination of William E. Hallett to be Commissioner of Indian Affairs, Hearing before the Select Committee on Indian Affairs, United States Senate, 96th Congress, 1st session, on Nomination of William E. Hallett to be Commissioner of Indian Affairs." October 20, 1979. Washington, DC: Government Printing Office, 1979.

---. "Proposed Reorganization of Major Agency and Functions Related to Indian Trust Reform Matters within the Department of the Interior." 108th Cong., First Sess., March 10, 2003. Washington, DC: Government Printing Office, 2003.

---. "Statement of Marvin L. Franklin at the Department of the Interior and Related Agencies Appropriations for Fiscal Year 1974: Hearings before a Subcommittee of the Committee on Appropriations." Ninety-Third Cong., First Sess., on H.R. 8917. Washington, DC: Government Printing Office, 1973.

United States Statutes at Large. Vols. 1, 2, 3, 4, 7, 9, 10, 11, 12, 15, 16, 19, 20, 22, 23, 25, 26, 28, 31, 32, 36, 38, 41, 42, 43, 44, 47, 50, 64, 66, 67, 68, 70, 88, 90, 108. Washington, DC: Government Printing Office, various years.

Archives

Washington, DC

National Archives and Records Service (NARS)
    Consolidated Correspondence File, 1794–1890, Papers of the War Department, 1784–1800, RG 92, http://wardepartmentpapers.org/s/home.
    Founders Online, http://founders.archives.go.
    Indian Circulars, Records of the Bureau of Indian Affairs, RG 75.
    Post-Revolutionary War Papers, 1784–1815, RG 94, http://wardepartmentpapers.org/s/home.
    Records of the War Department General and Special Staff, Secretary's Office, Letters Sent, Indian Affairs, RG 165.
    Report of Committee to the Board of Indian Commissioners, January 31, 1880, in Records of the Board of Indian Commissioners, RG 75.
    Second Congress: Reports and Communications Submitted to the Senate by the Secretary of the Treasury, RG 96, http://wardepartmentpapers.org/s/home/item/43209.

INDEX

aboriginal title, 113, 118, 423; extinguished, 427
activism, Indian, 328
Adams, John Quincy, 41
adult education, 296, 304, 379
affirmative action, 354
agriculture, 181, 191, 192–93, 209, 211, 226, 241, 242–43, 247, 265, 278, 284, 286, 287; fairs, 143
Alaska Native Claims Settlement Act, 339, 341, 342, 419
Alaska Natives, 342
Alcatraz, 328, 330
Aleuts, 285, 287
allotment, 219, 223, 228, 236, 243, 246, 256, 267, 309. *See also* General Allotment Act
All Pueblo Council, 358
American Indian Defense Fund, 274
American Indian Healthcare Improvement Act, 347
American Indian National Bank, 342, 344
American Indian Policy Review Commission, 363
American Indian Religious Freedom Act, 383
American Red Cross, 1922 health study, 265
American Revolution, 26
Anderson, David W., 399–402
annuities, 34, 64, 65–6, 70, 72–73, 81, 87, 92–93, 96, 97, 98–99, 101, 102,103, 108, 110, 155, 156–7, 160, 175, 176, 183, 227; commutation, 103, 223, 227, 241, 245; replace with farm equipment, 93
Apaches, 131, 148, 155

Arapahos, 121, 131
area offices, 337
"Arickaras" (Arikaras), 37, 148
Armstrong, Frank, 217
army officers as Indian agents, 217; opposition to, 164
Arthur, Chester, 183
Articles of Confederation, 6
Artman, Carl L., 403–6
arts and crafts, 265
assimilation, 16, 81, 101, 113, 147, 163, 183, 200, 209, 217, 254, 256, 422; process, 242; renewed efforts with termination, 297, 298
Assimilative Crimes Act, 361
assistant secretary for Indian Affairs, xxii, 18, 19, 20, 347, 348, 349, 350, 351–52, 353, 406. *See also* Indian Office
Association of American Indian Affairs, 290, 311
Athabascans, 339
Atkins, Edmund, 3
Atkins, John D. C., 190–99, 200

Babbitt, Bruce, 383
Bad River Chippewas, 396
Bannocks, 171, 176
Barbour, James, 41
Basone Resolution, 295
Beatty, Willard, 274
Bennett, Robert, 18, 320–27, 425
BIA facilities, privatization of 395, 398
Biden, Joe, 419
Black, Michael S., 20, 418
Blackfeet, 19, 37, 292, 346

475

Black Hills, 132, 147
Black River Chippewas, 88
Block Grant Program, 341
Blount, William, 7
boarding schools, 179, 203, 206, 223, 224, 259, 281, 390, 424; abolishing, 227, 266; closure of, 274, 276–77; high schools, 255, 281; as villages, 204
Board of Indian Commissioners, 141, 164, 170, 172, 178, 222, 231; abolishing, 274
Bogy, Lewis V., 127–129, 130, 131
border tribes, 70, 76, 77, 78, 80, 81, 82–83, 86, 87, 96, 97, 98, 107, 108, 114, 118–19, 122, 124, 128
Brookings Institute, 274, 285. *See also* Meriam Report
Brophy, William A., 283–289, 290, 425
Brown, Eddie F., 375–81
Brown, Orlando, 15, 71, 76–79
Browning, Daniel, 217–21, 424
Browning, Orville H., 122, 127, 128, 130
Bruce, Louis R., 328–334, 363, 425
Buchanan, James, 71, 87, 95, 100, 106
Bureau of Catholic Missions, 206, 218. *See also* Catholics
Bureau of Indian Affairs, 12, 13, 19, 21, 40, 47, 350, 351, 369; apology, 388, 389–90; budgeting, 373; as a consulting agency, 318, 321, 325–26; directors, 408; elimination, 368; newly named, 285; organization of, xvi; power struggle within, 330; reduction in staffing, 388, 393; reorganization, 329; role, 365, 388, 391–93; struggle to retain employees, 261–62; support tribes, 333–34. *See also* Indian Office
Bureau of Indian Education, 20; directors, 20–21, 408
Bureau of Reclamation, 376. *See also* Reclamation Service
Burke, Charles H., 254–62, 274, 424
Burke Act, 232, 254
Bursum Bill, 273

Bush, George H. W. 368
Bush, George W., 369, 375, 394, 399, 400, 403, 404, 408
Butler, Richard, 7
Buy Indian Act, limits of, 335

Calhoun, John, xvi, 11, 12, 15, 21, 40, 41, 47, 435n1
capital, need for, 247, 278, 312, 313, 315, 340, 342, 395, 404; private, 380
Carcieri vs. Kempthorne, 411
Carlisle Indian School, 171, 179, 180, 188, 231
Carter, Jimmy, xvi, 19, 344, 345, 348, 353, 358, 363
Cass, William, 11, 12, 13, 14, 47, 56
Catawbas, 2
Catholics, 205, 207. *See also* Bureau of Catholic Missions
Cayugas, 4
ceremonies prohibited, 256
Chapman, Oscar, 292
checker board lands, 279
Cherokees, 2, 8, 9, 13–14, 20, 41, 43, 57, 59, 60, 61, 106, 107, 123, 167, 193, 246, 367, 368, 376, 400. *See also* Five Civilized Tribes
Cheyennes, 128, 131, 132. *See also* Northern Cheyennes; Southern Cheyennes
Chickasaws, 2, 57, 58, 140, 193, 246, 394, 396, 413, 415. *See also* Five Civilized Tribes
chief clerk, xixt, 10, 12, 13, 40, 56, 100, 422, 423. *See also* Indian Office
child abuse, 378
Chiloccos, 188, 281
Chippewas, 60, 61, 72, 74, 154, 183. *See also specific Chippewa bands*
Chippewa-Crees, 291
Chippewa-Munsees, 107
Choctaws, 2, 59, 60, 123, 140, 167, 193, 246, 399, 418. *See also* Five Civilized Tribes
church-appointed Indian agents, 179
Citizen Pottawatomie, 368

citizenship, 91, 97, 140, 164, 204, 207, 210, 214, 215–16, 219, 254, 260, 266, 424; and allotment, 240, 241, 245
civil government, 90, 122, 159–60
civilization/Civilization Act, xvii, 11, 12, 40, 61, 69, 72, 76, 78, 79, 81, 84, 85, 91, 111, 112, 115, 116, 120, 124, 132, 134, 136–38, 151, 155, 156, 157, 160, 162, 163, 165, 166, 168, 172, 173–74, 176, 184–85, 186, 187, 191, 192, 203, 206, 207, 208, 209, 212, 218, 223, 224, 225, 226, 229, 233, 236, 256, 277, 293, 422, 423, 424; vs. barbarism, 85, 165, 201, 203, 210, 233, 236
civil service reform, 192, 201–3, 208, 218
Civil War, 16, 139–40, 154
Clark, William, xvi, 11, 12, 13, 14, 26, 38, 46–47, 423
Clarkson, Gavin, 418
Cleveland, Grover, 164, 190, 192, 200, 201, 207, 217, 218, 231, 246
Clinton, William J., 377, 383, 384, 387, 407
Cobell v. the Department of the Interior, 396, 397, 399, 403, 405, 409, 411, 414; settlement, 409, 415
Cohen, Felix, 274
Collier, John, 256, 263, 264, 273–82, 295, 423, 425
colonial Indian policy, 1–4; boards of trade, 3–4
Colorado River Indian Tribes, 296
Colvilles, 313
Comanches, 131, 387
Commerce Clause, 1, 8
Commission on Indian Reservation Economies, 395
commissioner of Indian Affairs, xxt, 13, 14, 15, 18, 19, 21, 88, 100, 304, 422; colonial, xviii, 5; establishment of, 41
Committee on the Organization of the Executive Branch (Hoover Report), 290, 291
Community Action Programs, 312
community schools, 206

competency (of Indians), 17, 232, 247, 248, 251–52, 256–58, 424
Constitutional Convention, 1, 4, 8
consultation, with tribes, 267, 379, 388, 392, 408
Continental Congress, xv, 30, 422; and the Crown, 2, 3, 5, 6, 7, 8
contracting (tribes) for federal services, 374, 396
Cooley, Dennis N., 121–126
Coronavirus Aid Relief and Economic Security Act, 419
Courts of Indian Offenses, 184, 207
COVID-19, 419
Cox, Jacob, 147
Crawford, Thomas H., 62–68, 69; emigration policy, 62, 63–65; options for policy, 62–63
Crawford, William H., 10, 11, 34
credit, 278, 279, 280
Creeks, 8, 9, 43, 56, 57, 59, 60, 62, 193, 246. *See also* Five Civilized Tribes
criminal jurisdiction, 155, 158, 166, 168, 183, 187–88, 295, 303, 322, 414; state assumption of, 303; and the state, 187–88, 296, 300; tribal, 360
criminal law enforcement, 410–11
Crow, John, 330
Crows, 131, 179

Davy, William, 10, 27, 28–29, 30, 31
Dawes, Henry, 201
Day schools, 179, 191, 255, 259, 281, 424; construction of, 274, 276–77, 280
Dearborn, Henry, 9, 10, 23, 25, 27, 29, 30, 31
Declaration of Policy, 247, 251–53, 255, 424
Deer, Ada E. 382–86
Delano, Columbus, 146, 154, 155
Delaware Tribe. *See* Lenni Lenape
Deloria, Vine, Jr., 357
Denver, James W., 95–99, 100
Department of the Interior, xvii, 14; creation of 15, 70–71, 423

Devil's Lake, 292
Division of Indian Health, 304
Dole, William P., 113–20, 121, 423
domestic dependent nations, 423
Doolittle, James R., 128
double jeopardy, 360
Duvall, William, 11, 47

early childhood education, 379
Echo Hawk, Larry J., 407–12, 426
economic development, 286, 291, 311, 312, 313, 315, 316–19, 321, 324–25, 329, 333, 341, 353, 364, 365, 368, 376, 378, 379–80, 383, 385, 395, 396, 397–98, 400, 401, 404, 408, 409–10, 425, 426; end exclusion in Indian Country, 326–27; factors limiting, 395; successes, 378
economic opportunity, 306, 322–23, 326
Economic Opportunity Act, 312
education, 41, 57, 60, 62, 66, 82, 97–98, 126, 171, 173–74, 200, 225, 228–29, 233, 234, 241, 250, 276–77, 312, 324, 333, 341–42, 410; co-education, 63, 66–68, 206; college attendance, 342; compulsory attendance, 206, 208, 210, 218, 223, 255, 256, 424; federal-state cooperation, 266–67; full enrollment, 255, 258–59; industrial, 179–180, 188–89, 191, 203–4, 206, 209, 219; and local control, 371, 377, 379; manual labor, 63, 66–88, 69, 71–72, 76, 79, 98, 103, 104; mechanical arts and agriculture, 56, 57, 61, 70; paradigm shift, 280–82; parents pay for, 189, 248, 252; reform of, 379; standard curriculum, 201, 206, tuition for states, 267; white vs. Indian, 229–230
Eisenhower, Dwight D., 297, 302, 328
emancipation of Indians, 243, 247, 254, 302
emigration of tribes, 41, 43–44, 47, 56, 57, 58, 62, 63–65, 70, 81, 115, 165, 167, 389; contracts for, 43–44; economy, 175–76; to Indian Territory, 119, 122, 124, 128; need to end, 89–90, 101, 102, 108; second emigration, 86, 87, 117–20, 174–75
Emmons, Glenn L., 302–10, 425
employment, off-reservation, 223, 232, 297, 298; opportunities, 266; placement agencies, 298–99. *See also* relocation
energy policy, 354, 418
English-only, 205, 206
Eskimos, 285, 287
Eustis, William, 34
Ewing, Thomas, 70, 71, 76, 80, 128
Ex Parte Crow Dog, 184
extermination, 81, 83, 92, 96, 121, 123, 209, 249

factories. *See* trading houses
Fall, Albert B., 254
federal acknowledgment/recognition, 396, 404, 408, 411, 414
federal policy, incoherent, 165–66
fee patents, 232, 241, 242, 243, 244, 247, 248, 251, 257, 258, 307; canceled, 256; opposition to, 243
Fetterman Massacre, 127, 128, 140
Fillmore, Millard, 80
fishing rights, 352
Five Civilized Tribes, 122, 158, 191, 193, 206, 213, 246; forced integration of, 197–98. *See also* Cherokees; Chickasaws; Choctaws; Creeks; Seminoles
Flatheads, 125, 196, 279, 302
Ford, Gerald, 340, 344, 347
Fort Berthold, 291, 357
Fort Hall Reservation, 179, 407. *See also* Bannocks; Shoshones
Fort Laramie Treaty of 1851, 81
Franklin, Marvin L., 335–38, 342
Fredericks, Thomas W., 357–62
fur trade, 35, 36, 37

gaming, 385, 395, 400, 406, 410; and economic development, 402, 408

Garfield, James A., 147, 148, 163, 182, 183
General Allotment Act, xvii, 192, 198–99, 205, 210, 211, 214, 215, 244, 247, 254, 267, 274, 314, 422; as cause of poverty, 314–15; end of, 274, 276, 277–78. *See also* allotment
General Crimes Act, 361
General Federation of Women's Clubs, 273
Genoa School, 188
Gerald, Forrest, 19, 346–52, 358
Gidmer, Jerald, 20
Gookin, Daniel, 2
Gover, Kevin, 377, 387–93
government-to-government relationship, 378, 388, 392, 415, 417, 420
Grant, Ulysses S., 87, 122, 132, 139, 140, 141, 154, 155, 163, 170, 263
Greenwood, Alfred B., 106–12
Gros Ventres, 37, 148
guardianship, 44, 45, 58, 135, 137–38, 198, 204, 215–16, 224, 229, 246, 247, 264, 270, 280; end of, 251, 252

Hallett, William E., 19, 353–56
Hampton Institute, 171, 179, 180, 188
Handbook of Federal-Indian Law, 274, 413
Harding, Warren G., 248, 254
Harland, James, 121, 122
Harris, Carey A., 13, 56–61, 62
Harris, John, 10, 22–23, 30
Harrison, Benjamin, 201, 205
Harrison, William Henry, 62
Hayes, Rutherford B., 87, 132, 164, 170, 178
Hayt, Ezra, 174, 170–77, 178
health contracts with states, 300
healthcare, 223, 241, 244–45, 248, 251, 255, 284, 411; health survey of 1912, 241
Herring, Albert, 13, 51–5
Hickel, Walter J., 328, 339
higher education, 379
Home Department, 12, 13, 41
Hoopa Valley Reservation, 376
Hoover, Herbert, 263

Hopis, 255, 296, 299
hospitals, 249, 300
House Concurrent Resolution, 108, 302, 309, 347
housing, substandard, 312, 313
Hualapais, 255

Ickes, Harold L., 265, 295
Illinois Tribe, 32
Indian Arts and Crafts Act, 274
Indian banking system, 336, 337
Indian Child Welfare Act, 383
Indian Citizenship Act, 256
Indian Civil Rights Act, 322, 360, 361, 414
Indian Claims Commission, 285; proposed, 264, 269–70
Indian Confederacy, 57, 59, 60
Indian Country, 13, 14, 340
Indian Departments, 4, 6, 7
Indian Financing Act, 340, 347
Indian Gaming Regulatory Act, 383, 404, 408
Indian Health Service, 346, 350, 372
Indian Health Transfer Act, 304
Indian money accounts, 251
Indian New Deal, 274
Indian Office/Service, xvii, 12, 13, 15, 16, 17, 18, 21, 42, 63, 70, 147, 179, 183, 207, 223, 240, 245; abolition of, 264; relocation to Chicago, 274; reorganization, 13, 15, 81, 277; transfer back to War Department, 114, 121, 123–24, 128, 132–36, 140, 141, 164, 171. *See also* assistant secretary for Indian Affairs; Bureau of Indian Affairs; chief clerk; superintendent of trade
Indian police, 171, 172, 180–81, 185
"Indian preference", 277, 372
"Indian problem", 184–85, 205, 208, 244, 248, 250, 252, 262, 278, 293–94, 315
Indian Removal Act, 57. *See also* emigration
Indian Reorganization Act, 184, 274, 276, 279, 287, 314, 315, 411, 414
Indian Reservation Renewal Act, 335, 337

Indian Rights Association, 200, 222, 231, 232, 240, 263, 265, 323
Indian Self-Determination and Education Assistance Act, 340, 347, 355, 383, 388, 392; 1988 amendments, 384; 1994 amendments, 376; contracting, 340. *See also* Public Law 93–638; self-governance; Tribal Self-Governance Act
Indian Territory, 59, 60, 114, 122, 124, 131, 144–45, 158–60, 164, 166, 170, 171, 172, 174, 176, 179, 180, 191; consolidation of the tribes in, 166–67, 193–96
Indian trade, 38; need to improve, 37–39
Indian Trust Council, 336
Indian Vocational Training Act, 304
Indian water rights office, 329, 376. *See also* water rights
individualization, 207–8, 234, 241, 243, 246, 277, 425; opposition to, 275
Ingels, George W., 10, 26–27, 30
intergovernmental agreements, 379
Inupiats, 418
Iowa Tribe, 74, 78, 88, 335
Iroquois, 2, 57, 406
irrigation, 264, 267, 270–72, 316; need for, 223, 227; and reimbursement of costs, 271–72
Irving, William, 9, 23, 24–25, 26, 27, 30

Jackson, Andrew, 41, 42, 47, 56, 57, 58, 62
Jackson, Helen Hunt, 182
Jackson, Henry, 19, 313, 320, 346, 347
Jamestown Clallams, 376
Jefferson, Thomas, 9, 23, 25, 26, 27, 28, 31, 33, 34, 46, 291, 294, 406
Jemez Pueblo, 256
Jicarilla Apaches, 305
Job Corps, 312
Johnson, Andrew, 114, 121, 127, 128, 130, 132
Johnson, Lyndon B., 320, 321
Johnson, William, 2, 3, 4
Johnson-O'Malley Act, 274, 296, 300
Jones, William A., 222–30, 231, 424

Kansas (Kaw) Tribe, 75, 88, 107
Kaskaskia Tribe, 32, 88
Kennedy, John F., 304, 311, 425; 1961 task force, 311, 312
Kickapoos, 74, 78
Kiowas, 131, 418
Klamaths, 109, 176, 302

Lac Courte Oreilles Chippewas, 399
LaCounte, Darryl, 20, 419
Lake Mohonk Conference, 184, 206, 222
land acquisition, 287
land base, 287
land buyback, 316, 414
land cessions/sales, 17, 58, 72, 86, 90–91, 96, 98, 101, 107, 175, 206, 241, 255, 276, 277, 288, 309, 422, 424; act of 1910, 268, 271; inherited, 244, 246, 248, 251; restrictions on, 307; and surplus lands, 211, 212, 213; tribal rights to, 308
land claims, 352
land fractionation, 279, 287, 316, 324, 409
land-into-trust, 404, 408, 411, 414
land leasing, 191, 196–97, 223, 227–28, 306; mineral, 305; opposition to, 218, 219, 244, 316
landless Indians, 276
land ownership, 265
land patents, 212–13
land purchases, 278, 279
land severalty, 16, 17, 45, 87, 96, 101, 102, 104, 107, 111, 112, 120, 125, 132, 155, 157, 158–59, 164, 166, 168, 171, 177, 183, 185–86, 191, 195, 213, 222, 232, 240, 241, 284, 424, 425; end of, 264. *See also* allotment; General Allotment Act
law and order, 59, 157–58, 159, 183
Lea, Luke, 80–85, 423
Leavitt Act, 264
Lenni Lenapes (Delaware Tribe), 24, 60, 74, 78
Leupp, Francis E., 231–39, 240, 424
Lewis, Meriwether, 26, 38, 46

Lincoln, Abraham, 107, 108, 113, 114, 121, 178
liquor, 38, 114, 167, 246, 251; laws, 185. *See also* whiskey
loans, reimbursable 247, 267–68, 271, 340
Lonewolf v. Hitchcock, 16, 424
Loudermilk, Weldon, 20
Lummi Tribe, 376

Madison, James, 1, 33, 40, 46
Major Crimes Act, xvii, 125, 184, 192
Malheur Tribe, 176
Mandans, 37, 38, 148
Manypenny, George, 16, 86–94, 423
Marble, E. M., 179
marriage, mixed, 218, 220–21
Martin, Aurene M., 391
Mason, John, 10, 31, 33–39, 40, 423; on trading houses, 34, 35–36
matrons, 228, 250
McCaleb, Neil A., 394–98, 426
McDivitt, James H., 394
McHenry, James, 10, 23
McKenney, Thomas L., 10, 11, 12, 13, 21, 40–45, 47, 200, 423; emigration policies of, 43–44; "father" of Indian Office, 42
McKinley, William, 218, 222, 231
Medill, William, 69–75, 86
Menominees, 74, 302, 387, 388; restoration of, 387; termination of, 305
Meriam, Lewis, 263
Meriam Report, 256, 263, 264, 274. *See also* Brookings Institute
Mescalero Apaches, 114
Mexican cession, 113, 116–17
Miami Tribe, 88
Mille Lac Chippewas, 376
Miller, James, 11, 47
Mills, Sidney, 348
mineral development, 317
missionaries, 57, 69, 186–87, 156, 259, 261; as Indian agents, 143–44; opposition to, 274
Mississippi Choctaws, 374

Missouria Tribe, 74, 75, 78, 87, 88
Mix, Charles, 96, 100–105, 106, 113
mixed blood people, rights of, 213–15, 220–21
Modoc Tribe, 171
Mohawks, 4, 328
Monroe, James, xvi, 11, 33, 47, 389
Morgan, Thomas J., 205–16
Morton, Rogers C. B., 330, 335
Myer, Dillon S., 295–301, 425

Nash, Philleo, 311–19, 320, 321, 425
National Congress of American Indians, 18, 320, 321, 325, 328–30, 340, 342, 388, 395, 399, 409, 419
National Council on Indian Opportunity, 395
National Indian Conference on Housing, 328
National Indian Gaming Association, 413
National Tribal Chairman's Association, 18, 322, 330, 340, 353, 364
Native American Rights Fund, 357, 358, 383
Native American Youth Conference, 328
natural resources, 369, 378, 379
Navajos, 114, 255, 256, 260, 280–81, 285, 296, 299, 300, 305, 314, 374, 388; lack of schools, 260; relocation, 302
Navajo-Hopi Rehabilitation Act, 285, 291
new federalism, 376
Nez Perces, 171
Nichols, John R., 290–94
Nixon, Richard M., 18, 328, 329, 330, 335, 339, 346, 347, 395, 425; address to Congress, 329
No Child Left Behind Act, 395, 400
non-federally recognized tribes, 314, 322, 336
Non-Intercourse Act. *See* Trade and Intercourse Acts
Northern Cheyennes, 131, 155, 171, 174
Northwest Ordinance, 8, 13, 292
Norton, Gale, 395, 396
nurses, 262, 264

Obama, Barack, 389, 407–9, 413, 414
Oberly, John, 192, 200–204
occupation of the Bureau of Indian Affairs (1972), 340
Office of Federal Acknowledgment, 20, 408
Office of Indian Affairs, 21, 389
Office of Indian Education, 375
Office of Indian Gaming, 20
Office of Indian Trade, xv, 10, 11, 22, 27, 28, 29, 31, 34; reorganized, xvi
Office of Indian Trust Transition, 369
Office of the Special Trustee, 20, 396, 397, 400
Office of the Superintendent of Indian Trade, 10
Oliphant vs. Suquamish, 360, 361
Omaha Tribe (Mahas), 37, 74, 75, 88
Oneidas, 4, 18
Oneida WI, 320, 403, 414
Onondagas, 4, 328
Osages, 75, 88, 122, 301, 404
Ottawa Tribe, 60, 61, 72, 74, 75, 88, 90
Ottoe Tribe, 78, 87, 88
outing system, 188

Papagos, 148, 155, 281, 291, 305. *See also* Tohono O'odhams
Parker, Eli, 18, 139–43, 147, 320
partnerships, federal and tribal, 405–6
Pasqua Yaquis, 375
paternalism, 44, 45, 276, 321, 322, 329, 368, 417, 426
Pawnees, 74, 78, 88, 167, 174, 387, 407
Peace Commission of 1867, 131, 132, 135
peace policy, 132, 150
Pembina Chippewas, 167
Peoria Tribe, 88
Philadelphia, 2, 10, 22, 25, 26, 27, 28, 29, 30, 31, 32, 33, 34
physician, 262, 264
Piankeshaw Tribe, 88
Pierce, Franklin, 81, 86
Pimas, 281

plenary power, 8, 14, 16, 284, 288, 424
pluralism, 18, 273, 275, 425; opposition to, 296
Pogue, Brian, 20
policy, hostile tribes vs. friendly tribes, 148–49; tribal involvement, 359–60; tribe-by-tribe, 284, 358–59, 425
political patronage, 202, 217
Polk, James K., 15, 62, 63, 69, 139
Poncas, 37, 74, 78, 148, 164, 167, 171, 174
Pope, John, 114, 121, 122
Porter, Peter, 12, 41
Pottawatomies, 61, 72, 74, 183, 241, 286, 302
poverty, 284, 287, 305, 312, 313–16, 321, 325, 332, 350, 396; War on Poverty, 312, 323
Pratt, Richard H., 171, 179, 180, 231
prejudice, 84–85, 116
Prentice, Thomas, 2
Presidential Commission on Indian Economies, 367
Preston-Engel irrigation report, 264
preventive medicine, 264, 300
Price, Bryan, 20
Price, Hiram, 182–89
public health, 255, 300
Public Health Service, 241
Public Housing Administration, 312
Public Law 81–291, 300
Public Law 83–277, 303
Public Law 83–280, 300, 303, 322, 361
Public Law 83–281, 303
Public Law 93–638, 369; contracting, 369, 370. *See also* Indian Self-Determination Act
public safety, 398, 408, 410
public schools, 258, 259, 260, 264, 280, 295, 298, 300, 321, 324; and merging Indian schools into, 300
Pueblo Relief Act, 274

Quakers, 139, 140, 143, 263; as Indian agents, 141–42
Quapaw Tribe, 88

Quick Bear vs. Leupp, 232
Quinaults, 376

Ragsdale, William P., 20, 368, 400
Reagan, Ronald, 354, 358, 363, 366, 367, 368, 395, 399
Reclamation Service, 264, 272. *See also* Bureau of Reclamation
Red Lake Chippewas, 19, 196, 303, 353, 354
reformers, 17
Reifel, Benjamin, 101, 344–45
religious freedom, 340, 385
religious schools, 114
relocation, 297, 304, 306, 307, 425; opposition to, 313. *See also* employment; U.S. Employment Service
reservation policy, 16, 70, 77–79, 80, 81, 82–83, 90–92, 96–97, 100–101, 103–5, 107, 108–9, 111, 113, 122, 131, 132, 148–53, 316–18, 423; California, 109–11, 118; colonizing policy, 74–5; move to abolish, 206, 207, 211–12, 223, 229, 238
Reservation Acceleration Program, 330
resources, management of, 312
restoration, 387–88
Revolutionary War, 24, 30
Rhoads, Charles J., 263–72, 425
Roberts, Lawrence S., 414
Rocky Bois reservation, 291
role models for Indian Country, 401–2
Roosevelt, Franklin D., 265, 274
Roosevelt, Theodore, 231, 240

Sac and Fox Indians, 74, 78, 88, 107, 241
San Carlos Apaches, 172, 180
San Creek Massacre, 114, 121
Santa Clara Pueblo v. Martinez, 360, 361
Sault St. Marie Chippewas, 20
Scattergood, Joseph H., 263
schools, 239, 370; day vs. boarding, 23, 237–38; federal control of, 201; lack of, 254, 255, 293; local control of, 322; new, 312; role of BIA, 318–19

Schurz, Carl, 170, 171, 172, 178, 179
Second Continental Congress, 25
sectarian schools, 186, 218, 232
sectional differences, 77, 81, 106
self-determination, 323, 328, 329, 332–34, 335, 336–38, 340, 341, 343, 347, 348, 354, 355, 356, 359, 364, 368, 373, 374, 380, 384, 390, 415, 418, 425; and tribal autonomy, 373. *See also* Indian Self-Determination Act; Self-Governance Act; self-government
Self-Governance Act, 376, 392; pilot agreements, 376, 384
self-government, 59, 111–12, 274, 276, 283, 303, 321, 340, 347, 354, 365, 370, 373–74, 376, 396, 400, 425, 426; under attack, 388. *See also* Indian Self-Determination Act; self-determination
self-support, 226, 230, 258, 265
Sells, Cato, 246–53, 255, 424
Seminole Tribe, 57, 140, 193, 246. *See also* Five Civilized Tribes
Seneca, Martin E., 19
Seneca and Shawnees, 88
Senecas, 4, 18, 88, 139, 140
Shawnees, 46, 286
Shee, John, 29, 30–32, 34, 423
Sherman, William T., 130, 132
Sioux, 37, 74, 75, 78, 122, 128, 131, 141, 148, 155, 164, 167, 171, 174, 184, 196; at Fort Peck, 20; Oglala, 20, 328, 348, 418; Pine Ridge, 305; Rosebud, 232, 344; Sisseton-Wahpeton, 183, 291; Standing Rock, 291, 357
Skibone, George T., 404
Smith, Caleb, 113
Smith, Edward P., 154–62, 163
Smith, Hoke, 217, 231
Smith, John Q., 163–69, 170
Smith, Kenneth L., 363–66, 367
social engineering, 114, 201, 241
social scientists, 274
Southern Cheyennes, 114, 121, 131, 155

sovereignty, tribal, 18, 57, 303, 383, 383, 396, 397, 406, 414, 425
Special Trustee for American Indians, 369, 400. *See also* Office of the Special Trustee
St. Louis, 37, 46
Stanton, Edwin, 121, 122
states' rights, 5, 6, 76
stealing children, 218
Stuart, Alexander H., 80
Stuart, John, 3, 4
student bill of rights, 340
submission of the Indians, 151–53
superintendent of Indian Affairs, xv, xvi, xviiit, 7, 9, 11, 44, 46, 47, 60, 81, 422
superintendent of Indian trade, xixt, 10, 22, 23, 24, 30, 31, 33, 34, 40, 47, 422, 423. *See also* Indian Office
superintendent of Indian trading houses, xixt, 22, 25, 26–27, 28, 422. *See also* Office of Indian Trade
superintendent of military stores, 9, 22, 25, 27
surplus lands, 256. *See also* land loss
Swan Creek Chippewas, 88
Sweeney, Tara MacLane, 418–21
Swimmer, Ross O., 367–74, 400

Taft, William H., 232, 240, 241
Tahsuda, John, III, 418
Taos Pueblos, 256, 342; restored Blue Lake, 342, 347
Taylor, Nathaniel G., 128, 130–38, 423
Taylor, Zachary, 71, 76, 80
taxation: exemption from, 212, 257, 398, 494; of tribes, 383;
tax-free bonds, 395
Teller, Henry, 183, 184
termination policy, 18, 283, 284, 285, 290, 295, 296, 299, 302, 303, 304, 309–10, 320, 329, 422, 425; bills for, 302, 303; economic, 364; end of, 331, 336, 337, 339; factors for readiness, 288–89; opposition to, 329; Senate Concurrent Resolution, 26, 347; withdrawal of services, 284, 288–89, 299–301, 303
Thompson, Jacob, 108
Thompson, Morris, 336, 339–43, 344, 425
Three Affiliated tribes. *See also* Fort Berthold
timber policy, 154, 287
Tohono O'odhams, 375, 377. *See also* Papagos
tourism/recreation, 317, 321, 425
Trachoma, 241, 245
Trade and Intercourse Acts; xvii, 12, 14, 15, 70, 87, 93–94; 1790, 9; 1796, 9; 1802, 9, 11; 1834, 106, 125–26, 183
trade/traders, 63, 65, 69, 70, 71, 77, 87, 97, 128; licensing of, 6
trading houses, xv-xvi, 9, 10, 11, 22–23, 30, 31, 34, 35, 40, 65, 423; British competition, 36; closure of, 11, 36–37, 40, 47; colonial 2
treaties (federal), 9, 32, 47, 57, 60, 61, 62, 78, 81, 83–84, 86, 87–89, 100, 101–2, 103, 107, 108, 110–11, 114, 115–16, 117, 122, 124–25, 131, 132, 183, 197, 241, 270; abrogation of, 291; broken, 210; end of, 141, 142–3, 155–7, 423; need for uniformity in, 83–84; rights, 358; termination of, 301; treaty tribes v. non-treaty, 107
treaties (state), 6, 8
Treaty of Medicine Lodge Creek, 131
tribal consultation, 369, 419, 420–22
Tribal Energy Resources Agreement, 419
tribal governments, 341, 364, 365–66; authority of, 360–62
tribal incorporation, 278
Tribal Law and Order Act, 408, 413
tribal relations, abolishing, 224
Tribal Self-Governance Act, 376
tribal trust funds, 369; Mismanagement of tribal funds, 377
Trowbridge, Roland, 132, 178–81
Truman, Harry, 290, 295, 311

Trump, Donald, 418, 418
trust, 314, 318, 324; end of, 321, 324; extensions, 296; free of encumbrances, 271; management of trust assets, 372–73, 411; management of trust resources, 372, 409; patents, 247, 257, 267, 271. *See also* trusteeship
trusteeship, 283, 284, 288, 291, 336, 353–54, 359, 364, 365, 368, 376, 378, 380–81, 383, 393, 410, 416, 417, 425; end of, 301, 303; reaffirmed, 329, 331 332, 341, 348–50; reform, 411; role of federal government, 292–93; stripping BIA of, 396. *See also* trust
trust funds/moneys, 101–2, 252, 371–72, 377, 380, 385
tuberculosis, 241, 245, 300
Turtle Mountain Chippewas, 20, 302, 419
Tuscaroras, 4
Tyler, John, 62

Udall, Stewart, 313, 323
Uintah-Ouray Utes, 303
Uintah Utes, 232
U.S. Army, 9, 44, 59, 104–5, 122, 131, 150–51, 164; as Indian agents, 140–41, 142, 143
U.S. Employment Service, 298. *See also* relocation
United States vs. Wheeler, 360
usufruct right, 102, 103, 117
Ute Tribe, 87, 171, 305

Valentine, Robert G., 232, 240–45
Van Buren, Martin, 56, 57, 62, 69
vanishing Indian myth, 249, 275, 393
Violence Against Woman Act, 410, 414
Virden, Terrance, 20
vocational training, 251, 317–18, 324, 379

Walker, Francis, 146–53, 155, 423

wards of the government, 124, 143, 155, 156, 198, 204, 223, 224–26, 244
Warm Springs Reservation, 303, 363, 364. *See also* Wasco Tribe
War Relocation Authority, 295, 297
Wasco Tribe, 363. *See also* Warm Springs Reservation
Washburn, Kevin, 413–17, 418
Washington DC, delegations to, 147
Washington, George, 9, 24, 28
water rights/policy, 316, 348, 409. *See also* Indian Water Rights Office
Wea Tribe, 46, 88
Welsh, Herbert, 141, 170, 200, 201
Whipple, Henry B., 114
whiskey, 63, 66, 73, 99, 124, 181. *See also* liquor
White Earth Chippewas, 20, 164, 166, 191
White River Utes, 172
Wilbur, Ray L., 274
Wild West shows, 201, 218, 223
Wilson, Woodrow, 246
Winn, Richard, 7
Winnebagos, 74, 96
Worcester, Samuel, 41
Work, Hubert, 274
work as educational, 240, 242; and well-educated workforce, 395, 398
workforce, competition for 372
World War One, 247, 255, 263
World War Two, 295, 344, 346; veterans returning home, 285–86, 288
Wounded Knee Occupation, 340
Wyandotte Tribe, 88, 90

Yakimas, 164, 166, 167, 176, 196, 342
Youth Corps, 312
youths involved in policy, 330–31

Zia Pueblos, 256
Zimmerman, William, 284, 285
Zimmerman Plan, 297

ALSO BY DAVID H. DEJONG

American Indian Treaties: A Guide to American Indian Treaties and Treaty-Making: 1607–1911. Salt Lake City: University of Utah Press, 2015.

The Commissioners of Indian Affairs: The United States Indian Service and the Making of Federal Indian Policy, 1824–2017. Salt Lake City: University of Utah Press, 2020.

Diverting the Gila: The Pima Indians and the Florence–Casa Grande Project, 1916–1928. Tucson: University of Arizona Press, 2021.

Forced to Abandon Our Fields: The 1914 Clay Southworth Gila River Pima Interviews. Salt Lake City: University of Utah Press, 2011.

The Indian Medical Service: A Chronicle of Indian Health Care, 1908–1955. Lanham, MD: Lexington Books, 2008.

Plagues, Politics and Policy: A Chronicle of the Indian Health Service, 1955–2008. Lanham, MD: Lexington Books, 2010.

Promises of the Past: A History of Indian Education in the United States. Boulder, CO: North American Press, 1993.

Stealing the Gila: The Pima Agricultural Economy and Water Deprivation, 1848–1921. Tucson: University of Arizona Press, 2009.

CPSIA information can be obtained
at www.ICGtesting.com
Printed in the USA
LVHW110746180822
726159LV00028B/47